Pre-Raphaelite Drawing

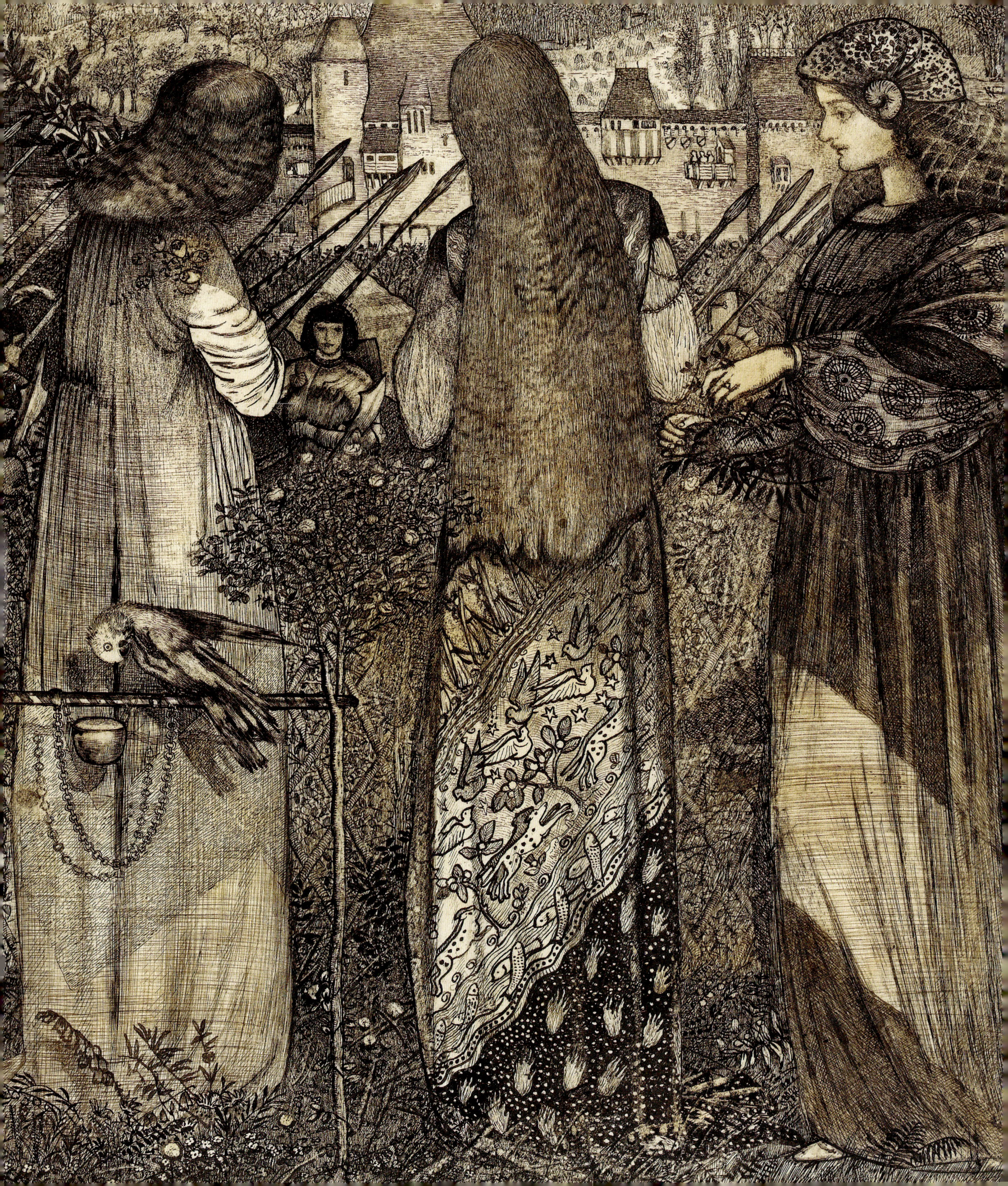

Colin Cruise

Pre-Raphaelite Drawing

With 313 illustrations

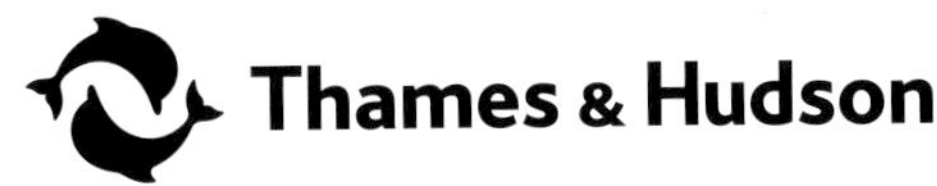
Thames & Hudson

Published on the occasion of the exhibition
The Poetry of Drawing: Pre-Raphaelite Designs, Studies and Watercolours
organized by Birmingham Museums & Art Gallery, and shown at
Birmingham Museum & Art Gallery (29 January–15 May 2011) and
The Art Gallery of New South Wales, Sydney (17 June–4 September 2011)

First published in the United Kingdom in 2011 by Thames & Hudson Ltd,
181A High Holborn, London WC1V 7QX

First paperback edition published in 2012
Reprinted 2019

Pre-Raphaelite Drawing © 2011 Birmingham Museums & Art Gallery
Text © 2011 Colin Cruise
Edited, designed and produced by Thames & Hudson Ltd, London

British Library Cataloguing-in-Publication Data
A catalogue record for this book is available from the British Library

ISBN 978-0-500-29029-3

Printed and bound in China by Toppan Leefung Printing Limited

To find out about all our publications, please visit **www.thamesandhudson.com**.
There you can subscribe to our e-newsletter, browse or download our current
catalogue, and buy any titles that are in print.

Frontispiece Edward Burne-Jones, *Going to the Battle*, 1858,
Fitzwilliam Museum, Cambridge (detail)

p. 6 John Everett Millais, *Study of the Head of Elizabeth Siddal for
'Ophelia'*, 1852, Birmingham Museums & Art Gallery (detail)

p. 9 Frederick Sandys, *A Nightmare*, 1857, Birmingham Museums & Art
Gallery (detail)

Contents

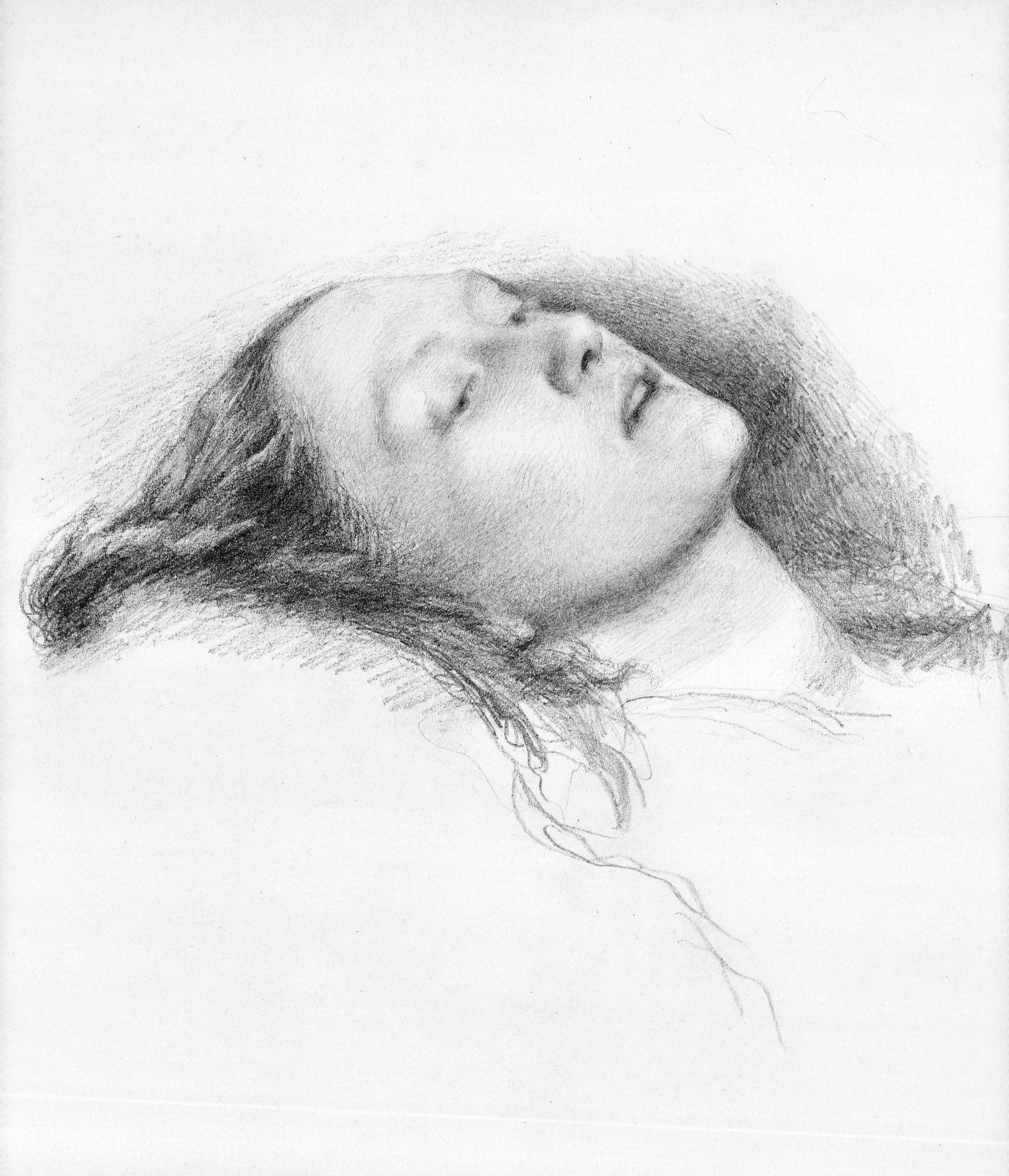

Director's Foreword

Pre-Raphaelite Drawing examines the central importance of drawing and design in the works of the Pre-Raphaelites, their associates and followers, from the earliest days of the Brotherhood to the development of Symbolism and Art Nouveau. While drawing is often regarded as being secondary to painting, this book argues that it was vital for the creation of new ideas and images in Pre-Raphaelite art, and that the activity of drawing remained primary to Pre-Raphaelitism and the realization of its artistic vision.

The book accompanies a major loan exhibition, *The Poetry of Drawing*, which is the most comprehensive survey of Pre-Raphaelite works on paper to date. It showcases the collections of Pre-Raphaelite and later nineteenth-century fine and applied art held at Birmingham Museum & Art Gallery alongside key works from public and private collections, including significant drawings and watercolours that have not previously been published or exhibited.

Birmingham Museum & Art Gallery has long been recognized as an important centre for the collection and study of Pre-Raphaelite art. The Museum's first Pre-Raphaelite acquisitions, Dante Gabriel Rossetti's unfinished oils *La Donna della Finestra* and *The Boat of Love*, were purchased by the Corporation of Birmingham from the artist's studio sale in 1883 and predated the building of the Museum itself by two years. The Museum & Art Gallery continued to acquire important Pre-Raphaelite paintings throughout the 1890s, but it was the purchase by subscription in 1903 and 1906 of Charles Fairfax Murray's collection of over a thousand Pre-Raphaelite works on paper that established the Museum's reputation for its collection of works by the Brotherhood and their circle, and particularly its importance as a centre for the study of Pre-Raphaelite drawing. The addition over the succeeding century of a series of gifts, bequests and purchases, among them the bequest by James Richardson Holliday of a major collection of drawings by Birmingham-born Edward Burne-Jones, sealed the Museum's pre-eminence as the greatest single repository of Pre-Raphaelite works on paper in the world. The recent digitization of these collections and creation of an online resource, funded by JISC, has helped to bring the Pre-Raphaelite paintings, drawings, books and applied art held at the Museum to a wider audience than ever before.

This book and the exhibition it accompanies would not have been possible without the help and support of many organizations and individuals. The City of Birmingham Museums & Art Gallery Development Trust provided a generous grant to support the project, for which we extend warm thanks. We are also grateful to The Limoges Trust, The Paul Mellon Centre for Studies in British Art, and The William A. Cadbury Trust, whose support contributed to the publication of this book. We are most grateful to all our funders for their support.

We are indebted to the many public and private lenders who have so generously agreed to make their works available for the exhibition and for publication in this book. To all those named, and to those who wish to remain anonymous, we extend our grateful thanks.

We are delighted that following its showing in Birmingham the exhibition travels to the Art Gallery of New South Wales in Sydney, itself the home of an important collection of nineteenth-century art, which includes significant Pre-Raphaelite and High Victorian paintings. It is especially exciting that the exhibition provides an opportunity for five of the drawings by Ford Madox Brown relating to *Chaucer at the Court of Edward III*, held at Birmingham, to travel to Australia and be shown alongside the finished painting

for the first time. It has been a pleasure to work with our colleagues in Sydney, and we are grateful to Edmund Capon, Director and Chief Curator; Peter Raissis, Curator of European Prints and Drawings; Erica Drew, Project Officer Exhibitions; and the staff at the Art Gallery of New South Wales for making the tour possible.

Colin Cruise is both the author of this book and the guest curator of the exhibition. The project makes available the results of new research into Pre-Raphaelite drawing and its contexts carried out over a number of years, during which he has traced missing works, explored the application of drawing in nineteenth-century art training, studio practice and design, and examined the range of critical responses that Pre-Raphaelite drawing provoked. The resulting book makes a significant contribution to the understanding of both Pre-Raphaelitism and the wider context of British drawing, and we are grateful to Colin for his scholarship, as well as for the enthusiasm and good humour he has brought to the project.

The exhibition has represented a major undertaking for Birmingham Museums & Art Gallery, and I should like to thank the organizing curator, Victoria Osborne, and the many other staff involved for their dedication in bringing it to fruition.

Finally I should like to thank the staff at Thames & Hudson who have produced this publication, which both stands alone as a contribution to the study of Pre-Raphaelitism and nineteenth-century British art, and provides a lasting legacy of the exhibition.

Rita McLean
Head of Birmingham Museums

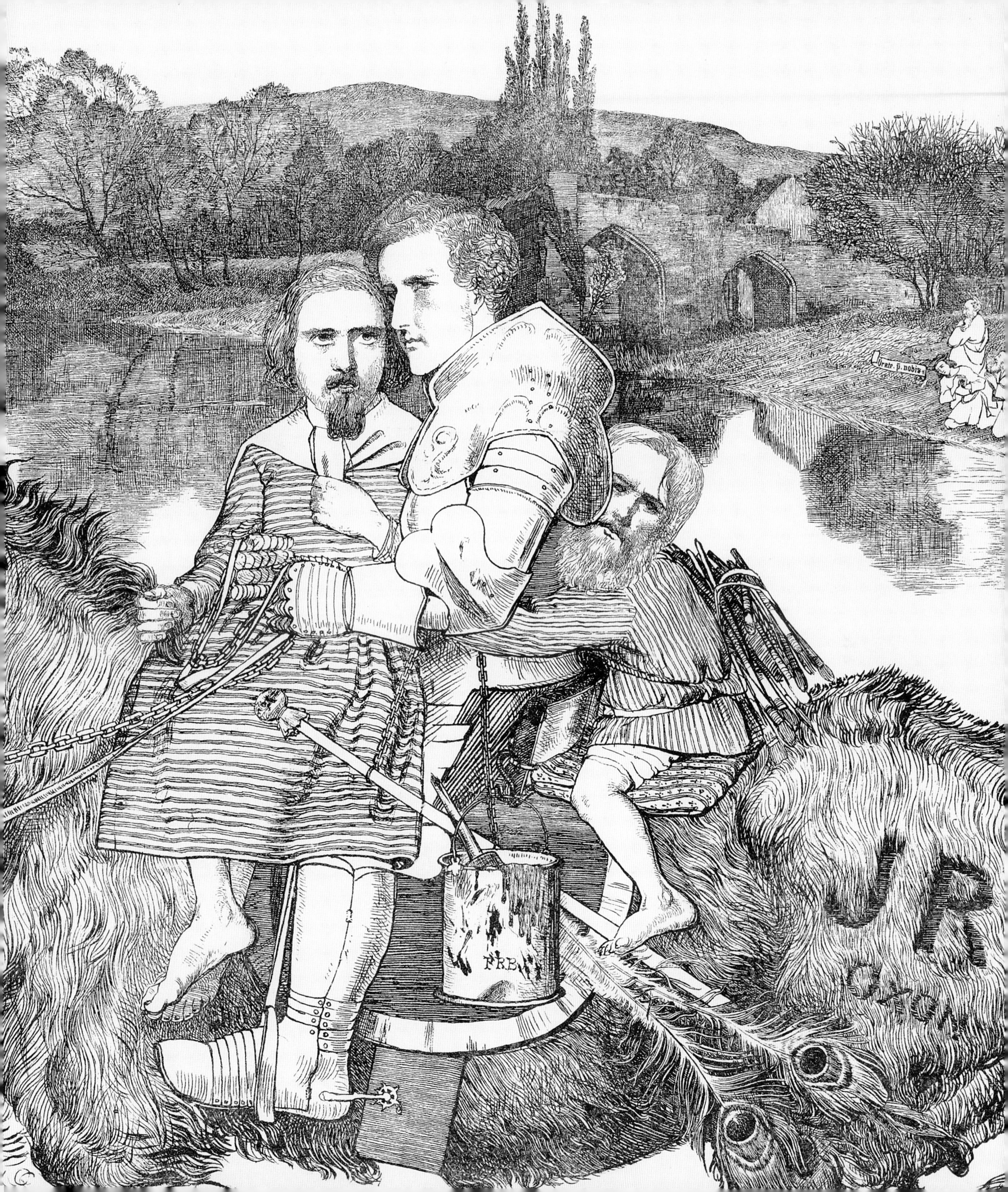
Orate p. nobis
F.R.B.

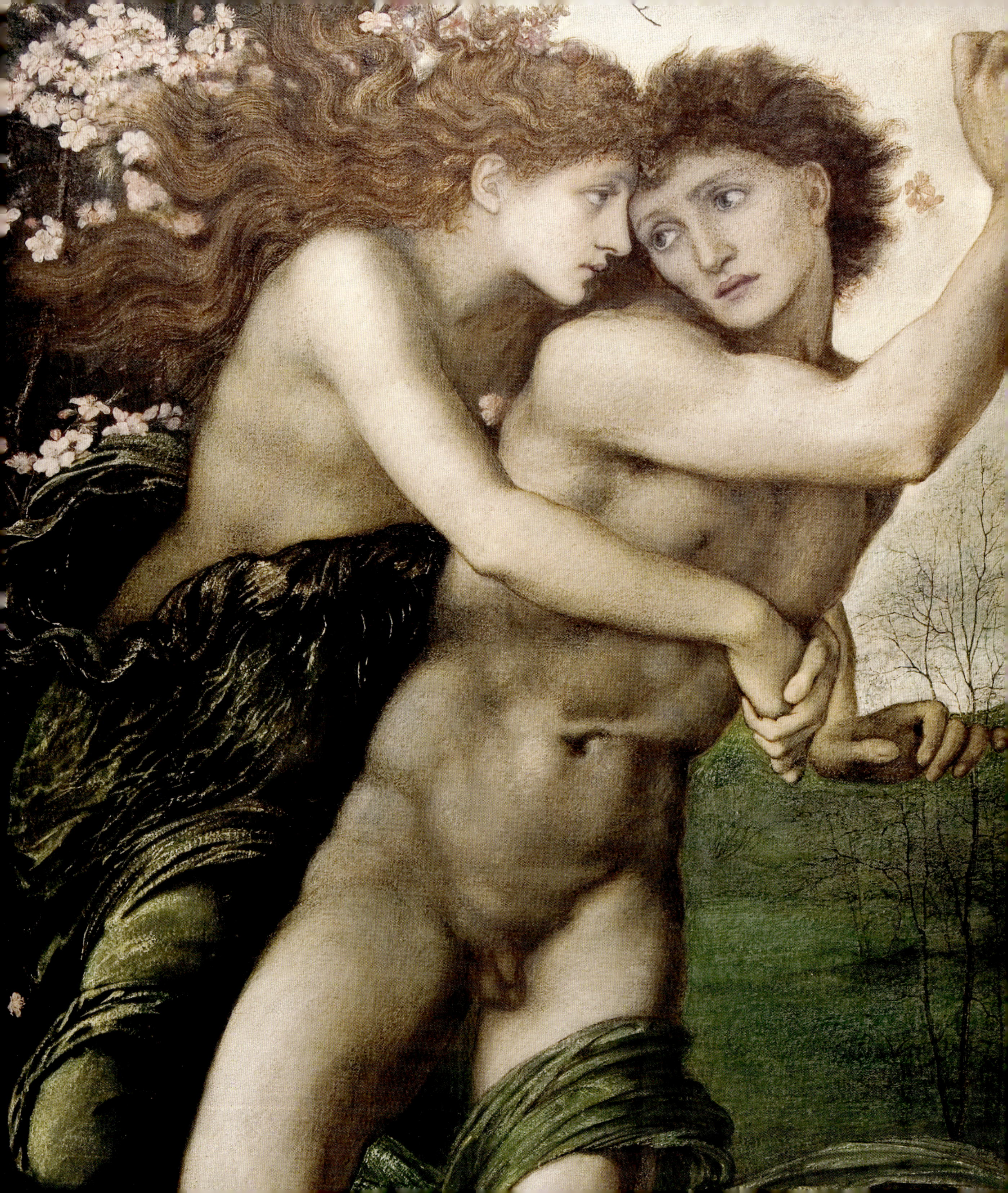

Drawings and Drawing:
A Pre-Raphaelite Introduction

The work of the Pre-Raphaelite Brotherhood has been
the subject of much reappraisal in the years following the
major exhibition at the Tate Gallery in 1984. The subsequent
process of writing new histories of the period has done
much to uncover the genesis of Pre-Raphaelitism and
its development into a force that changed the nature of
British painting in the nineteenth century. In the first half
of the twentieth century there was a critical silence about
the Brotherhood's work, its importance and influence.
Its members' formative role in producing a new and
original narrative painting and their challenge to the
art establishment of their time were misunderstood or
misinterpreted. They were grouped with the generality
of academic art and regarded as much the enemy of a
free and expressive painting as their more conservative
contemporaries. Moreover, they were written out of a history
of modern art that extended to their near-contemporaries
in France, the Impressionists. In fact, the Pre-Raphaelites
were part of a pan-European revolt against academic
conventions that had suppressed originality, creativity and
experimentation, particularly in the branches of art that
dealt with the representation of the human figure.

It should not surprise us that the critical hostility and
general opposition that greeted the early works of the Pre-
Raphaelites were extreme. Many of the paintings at the Royal
Academy in the first half of the nineteenth century were
constructed using rules laid down at the foundation of the
institution in 1768 and taught in its schools. They were seen
as representative of the best practices of the art of ancient
Greece and Rome as well as of the Renaissance. Convention
– against which the Pre-Raphaelites reacted so vehemently
– was a product of the ways in which academic rules had
been interpreted for generations. The seemingly authoritative
nature of these pictorial conventions made them difficult to
challenge. In the art of drawing the human figure, ideals of
proportion, the range of facial and body types, poses and

1   Edward Burne-Jones, *Phyllis and Demophöon*, 1870,
Birmingham Museums & Art Gallery (detail)

gestures were reproduced year after year in the drawings of students. In addition, the features of landscape and the range of natural phenomena from rainbows to oceans and hedgerows to forests were also restricted in the marks used to represent them pictorially. It would be true to say that conventionality affected not just the final work and all the stages of its creation but its very conception – the ways in which the artist looked at, and thought about, nature rather than simply how they represented it.

When it was founded in 1848, the Pre-Raphaelite Brotherhood marked a significant departure in British art. Its key personalities – the poet and painter Dante Gabriel Rossetti (1828–82), William Holman Hunt (1827–1910) and John Everett Millais (1829–96) – were among the most talented and imaginative artists of the century, yet they chose to turn away from the British art establishment in order to free themselves from academic conventions of representation. They were initially joined by James Collinson (1825–81), whose career as a religious and genre painter faltered after he left the Brotherhood in 1850, and by two men whose fame was attained through their critical and art historical writings: William Michael Rossetti (1829–1919), brother of Dante Gabriel, and F. G. Stephens (1828–1907). Following the hostile reception of the work of Millais and Hunt when it was shown at the Royal Academy in 1850, their reputations were defended by John Ruskin (1819–1900), the towering figure of critical and historical writing on art and architecture of the century. Ford Madox Brown (1821–93), who briefly gave private lessons in painting to Dante Gabriel Rossetti in 1848, was closely associated with the Pre-Raphaelite Brotherhood but had already begun his work as a history painter and continued his highly individual and productive career independently. Brown, Edward Burne-Jones (1833–98) and William Morris (1834–96) were the most significant of the artists whose names were linked to the Brotherhood. Burne-Jones and Morris owed their involvement in art to their contact with the Brotherhood when they were undergraduates at Oxford. Rossetti's friendship was particularly important to them. In the writings of Ruskin and, later, Morris, the wider concerns of the 'political economy of art' had two of the most eloquent voices who continued the debate about Pre-Raphaelitism, society and the function of art into the twentieth century.

The importance of drawing

This book argues for the central importance of drawing in the history of Pre-Raphaelitism, both in the foundation of the Brotherhood and in the development of its members' art. Criticism of their paintings often took issue with their perceived lack of ability to draw. In his *Aphorisms on Drawing*, published in 1856, the Rev. S. C. Malan slipped in a typically anti-Pre-Raphaelite observation. While voicing an antagonism to their painterly practices ('their glaring colours', for example), Malan's chief criticism was of their abilities as draughtsmen. Writing of the importance both of 'Nature' as a model for art and of the necessity for the artist to have a 'cultivated mind', Malan observed:

> since we have in Nature a perfect model to follow, our imitation of it must be either right or wrong. And in proportion as we depart from Nature to follow a design of our own, do we also degenerate from real to relative art. That is clearly proved by the style, as it is called, of Medieval (or even of Pre-Raphaelite) artists. They did, and do, draw regardless of TRUTH, after a fashion of their own, and not after Nature. Their wry-headed figures in buckram, their glaring colours, their utter carelessness about light and shade, their trees like brooms or cabbage-tops, their hills like sugar-loaves, their houses out of perspective, may, possibly, in their opinion, suit the kind of illustration to which they are often consecrated, but that is not DRAWING.[1]

Malan's objections to Pre-Raphaelite draughtsmanship were

to one aspect only, the high degree of stylization in figure drawing, which was inspired by medieval illumination and early Renaissance art. A contrary feature of their work was an excessive 'truth to nature'. The Pre-Raphaelites advocated drawing from nature to an extent almost unprecedented in British art. The unconventional combination of stylization and truthfulness was one of the more provocative and certainly most confusing characteristics of their work.

Accounts of the formation of the Pre-Raphaelite Brotherhood stress the importance of the Royal Academy Schools and their method of instruction in drawing at the time. John Guille Millais, the artist's son, reconstructed the first conversation between Hunt, at the time an independent student not attached to the Royal Academy Schools, and John Everett Millais. Hunt had witnessed Millais being presented with a medal for 'drawing from the Antique' in 1843. This conversation about drawing between the young men indicates its importance for those aspiring to be professional artists. Hunt was drawing in the East Room of the British Museum, also known as the 'Sculpture Gallery', a haunt for students of the Royal Academy Schools keen to supplement their instruction, such as it was. J. G. Millais quotes Hunt:

> the doors opened, and a curly-headed lad came in and began skipping about the room; by-and-by he danced round until he was behind me, looked at my drawing for a minute, and then skipped off again. About a week later I found the same boy drawing from a cast in another room, and returned the compliment by staring at his drawing. Millais, who of course it was, turned round suddenly and said, 'Oh, I say, you're the chap that was working in No. 12 the other day. You ought to be in the Academy.'[2]

Despite their youth, the pair had a long conversation about drawing, its methods and materials that was serious and considered. J. G. Millais records part of the conversation that deals with Hunt's desire to know the best way of doing the drawings to be admitted to the Academy. The young Millais's reply seems airily confident and experienced, acknowledging the current practice but claiming his own independence from it: 'Oh, I always do mine in line and stump, although it isn't conventional.' The 'stump' referred to was a tool for producing tone or shade by rubbing the marks made by soft drawing media, such as chalk or charcoal, on the surface of the paper. The more acceptable contemporary academic method would have been to draw hatched lines of varying degrees of thickness, which produced a harder effect. As if to confirm the later consequences of this conversation about drawing, J. G. Millais's account stresses the early rejection of 'conventionality' as foreshadowing the founding of the Pre-Raphaelite Brotherhood:

> the two boys fell into a discussion on the conventionality and pedantry of art as displayed in the paintings of the day, and it was evident that in both their minds had sprung up a sense of dissatisfaction and the idea of rejecting what they considered to be false and stunted.[3]

When we write about painting – despite the advent of dense theory on the subject – we often think of it in terms of subject and theme and the historical and social contexts of the work's production. Most often the technique, method and materials concern only specialized writers. The subject of drawing has been quite different: there, matters of technique, method and material have predominated and the artist's training in drawing has been of central interest. Both approaches have their drawbacks and reflect, perhaps, the comparative status of the two arts: painting – the 'finished thought' of the artist – being regarded highly; drawing – often both provisional and private, preparatory and unfinished – is the province of the enthusiastic amateur, the collector or the museum specialist. The materials and techniques have been given too

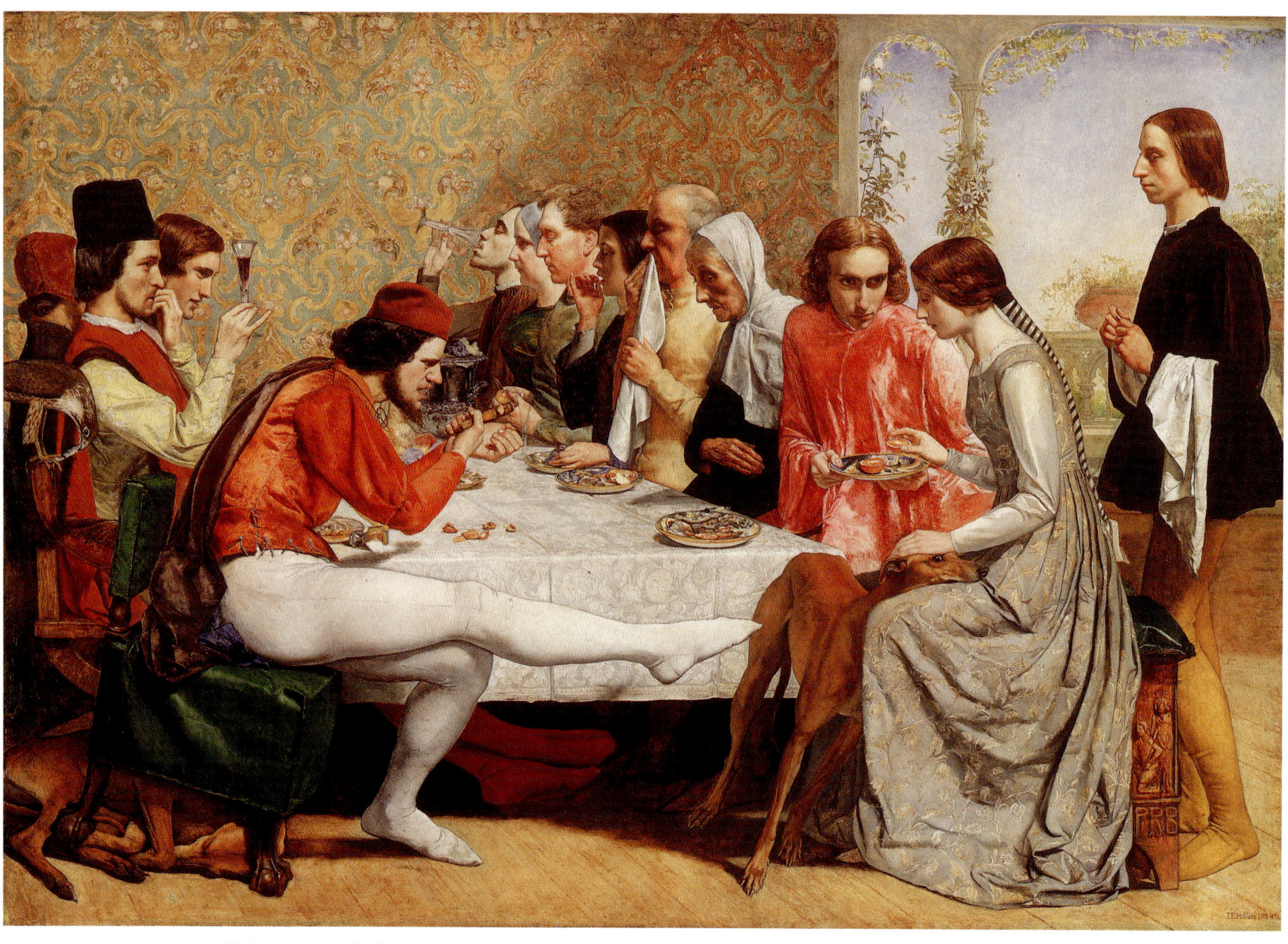

2   John Everett Millais, *Isabella*, 1848–49, National Museums Liverpool (Walker Art Gallery)

great an importance because the drawing is regarded as in some way unfinished and too unstable for more considered discussion. This approach was challenged by Surrealism and other modernist art movements, following the popular reception of psychoanalytic theory. The Surrealists promoted automatism, which held that unconscious and unguarded drawing could be more revelatory than more finished and considered works.[4]

While painting was – perhaps still is – the art that had the highest status and the most complex structures of professionalism, it was drawing that provided the key to the profession. Entry into the Royal Academy Schools was gained by demonstrating proficiency in drawing, and the attainment of suitable standards of draughtsmanship was significant for young artists. In training, drawing was a vehicle for the acquisition of important elements of art such as dexterity and steadiness of hand, as well as knowledge of anatomy, proportion, perspective, chiaroscuro and

composition; it also helped develop taste. Yet it is drawing, both as a branch of art and as a creative act, that is obliterated in the painting process. It often disappears, too, from accounts of artists' careers and is neglected in histories of art. Drawing is fascinating because often – although not always – it offers us the most immediate contact with the artist's imagination. Out of the handling of simple materials, from the most fundamental processes, come marks, signs, figures and, ultimately, narratives. We find meaning in the most casual of marks. If there is a difficulty, it is with deciphering the artist's intention in the mass of marks – some of them hesitant, some over-bold, others nearly invisible. The marks offer points of communication between the imaginations of both artist and viewer. They appear to form on the paper beneath our gaze. We need to take time to look closely at these marks to enjoy them for their own sake, for their own beauty as well as for the narratives they struggle to formulate.

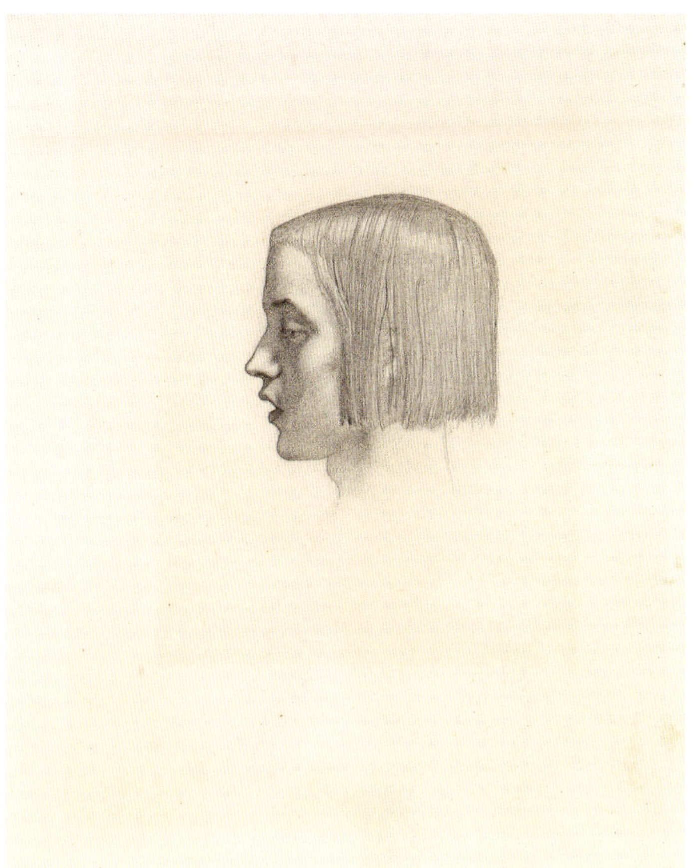

Rather than being simply a matter of materials and techniques, or even functions, one can see drawing as key to an understanding of Pre-Raphaelitism, its development and extended influence. The members of the Pre-Raphaelite Brotherhood became notorious for the linear 'stiffness' and archaism in their representation of the human figure. Although these are qualities usually associated with drawing, they are found equally in paintings such as Millais's *Isabella* (1848–49) [2], the first work he exhibited as a Pre-Raphaelite. Millais's drawings for this work [3, 4] show him using a clear, hard line and yet, conversely, striving to imbue the models with a sense of their individuality. The strange 'stiffness' of the figures that struck contemporary viewers so strongly when they first saw the painting is located primarily in the spiky clarity of line and the harshly defined shadows of the drawings.

In 1857, in its review of the 'Manchester Art Treasures Exhibition', the *Quarterly Review* grudgingly acknowledged the growing fame of the Pre-Raphaelite Brotherhood but felt it necessary to admonish them on their shortcomings in the drawing of the human figure:

> Whilst endeavouring to labour in the spirit of the old masters, the Pre-Raphaelites appear to have fallen into the grave error of believing that the correct drawing of the human frame is not essential, because it is not to be found in the works of the painters of the fourteenth century. Indeed they seem to think, and would lead the public to think, that its absence forms one of the claims of the old masters to our admiration, as if the fame of Chaucer was to be attributed to the quaintness of his spelling. It is a proof of the genius of those great men, that we almost forget their technical defects, arising

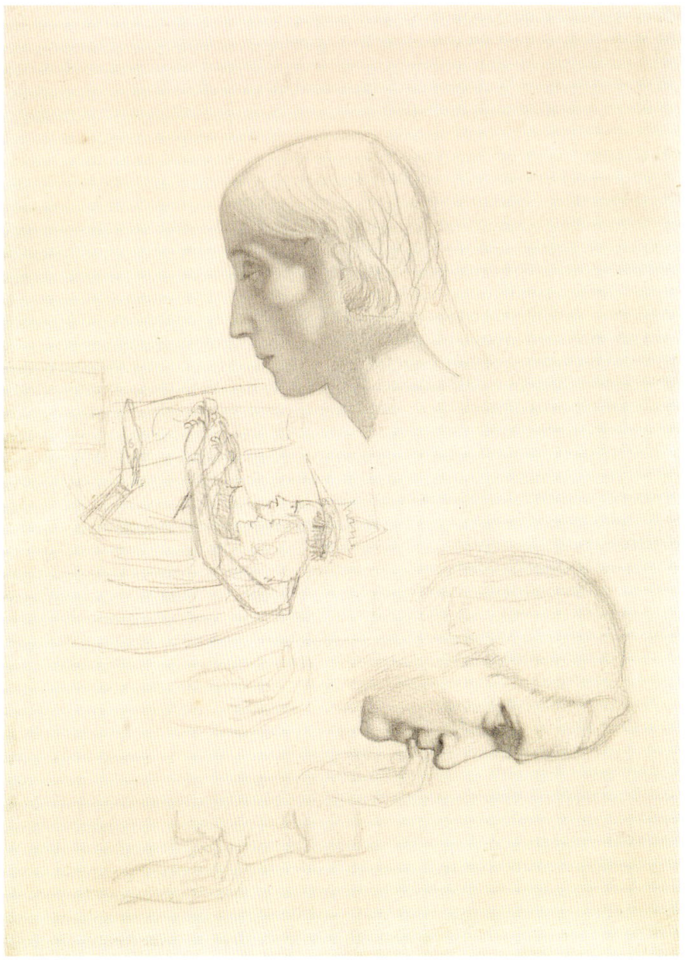

3   John Everett Millais, *Study for 'Isabella': Head of a Boy*, 1848, Birmingham Museums & Art Gallery

4   John Everett Millais, *Study for 'Isabella': Two Heads*, 1848, Birmingham Museums & Art Gallery

from imperfect knowledge, in our sympathy for their earnest endeavours to embody the true and beautiful.[5]

'The vehicle of a disquieting private passion'

The key artists considered in this book – Hunt, Millais, Rossetti and Burne-Jones – each had individual gifts as draughtsmen, different approaches to drawing and separate visions of the role of drawing in their art. Only at the very outset of the Pre-Raphaelite enterprise was there a strong similarity in style or shared approach to drawing. It will be helpful to survey some of the tendencies in individual drawing practices and the development of personal styles before moving to the wider survey of themes, issues and characteristics covered in the chapters of this book.

An account of Pre-Raphaelite drawing practices can usefully commence with Millais. His training was thoroughly conventional, if somewhat pressurized. No amount of training, however, could have provided him with the acuity of vision that belonged to his earliest professional drawing. J. G. Millais paraphrased a contemporary view of his father's talents as a draughtsman which deftly combined the diverse, and sometimes contradictory, influences on him:

> Millais was gifted with a sense of sight of crystalline clearness to which Nature made a perpetual and brilliant appeal; but he had a hand that, even in childhood, was singularly skilful to record the impressions of the eye. And his hand had been severely trained, first by the prescribed academic methods, and later by the minutely elaborate labour of his Pre-Raphaelite work, until it set down facts almost with the facility with which the eye perceived them.[6]

Millais took pains to distance himself from academic convention in his earliest drawings as a Pre-Raphaelite 'Brother'; arguably the drawings for his controversial painting *Christ in the House of his Parents* (*c.* 1849) [6] are more outrageously anti-academic than the exhibited work [5]. *Blackwood's Magazine* argued bitterly that the Pre-Raphaelites had set out to imitate the

> early masters, not only in their earnestness of purpose visible in their productions, but in their errors, crudities, and imperfections – renouncing, in fact, the progress that since then has been made; rejecting the experience of centuries, to revert for models, not to art in its prime, but to art in its uncultivated infancy.

Turning his attention to Millais, the reviewer noted the bad figure drawing in particular:

> We can hardly imagine anything more ugly, graceless, and unpleasant than Mr. Millais' picture of Christ in the carpenter's shop. Such a collection of splay feet, puffed joints, and misshapen limbs was assuredly never before made within so small a compass.[7]

More than a century and a half after Millais's first Pre-Raphaelite paintings were exhibited, we tend to take for granted his experimental draughtsmanship. Following the various movements of early twentieth-century Modernism, such as Cubism and Expressionism, we have grown to expect the abandonment of the rules of perspective and look for expression rather than correctness in figure drawing. In 1953, the curator John Commander, introducing the first major exhibition to survey Pre-Raphaelite drawing, argued that:

> the stilted angular style of drawing [in] *Christ in the House of His Parents* – characterized by Dickens as 'odious, repulsive and revolting' – has now a certain validity in the way in which it arrests the spectator's eye and prevents too easy an acceptance of the painting; and that very *gaucherie* may be regarded as an effective expressionistic statement of inner disturbance, the vehicle of a disquieting private passion.[8]

Rossetti is perhaps the most controversial of the major subjects of this study. Some commentators on Pre-Raphaelitism, even recent ones, have regarded his drawings as inept, while others see him as the most important

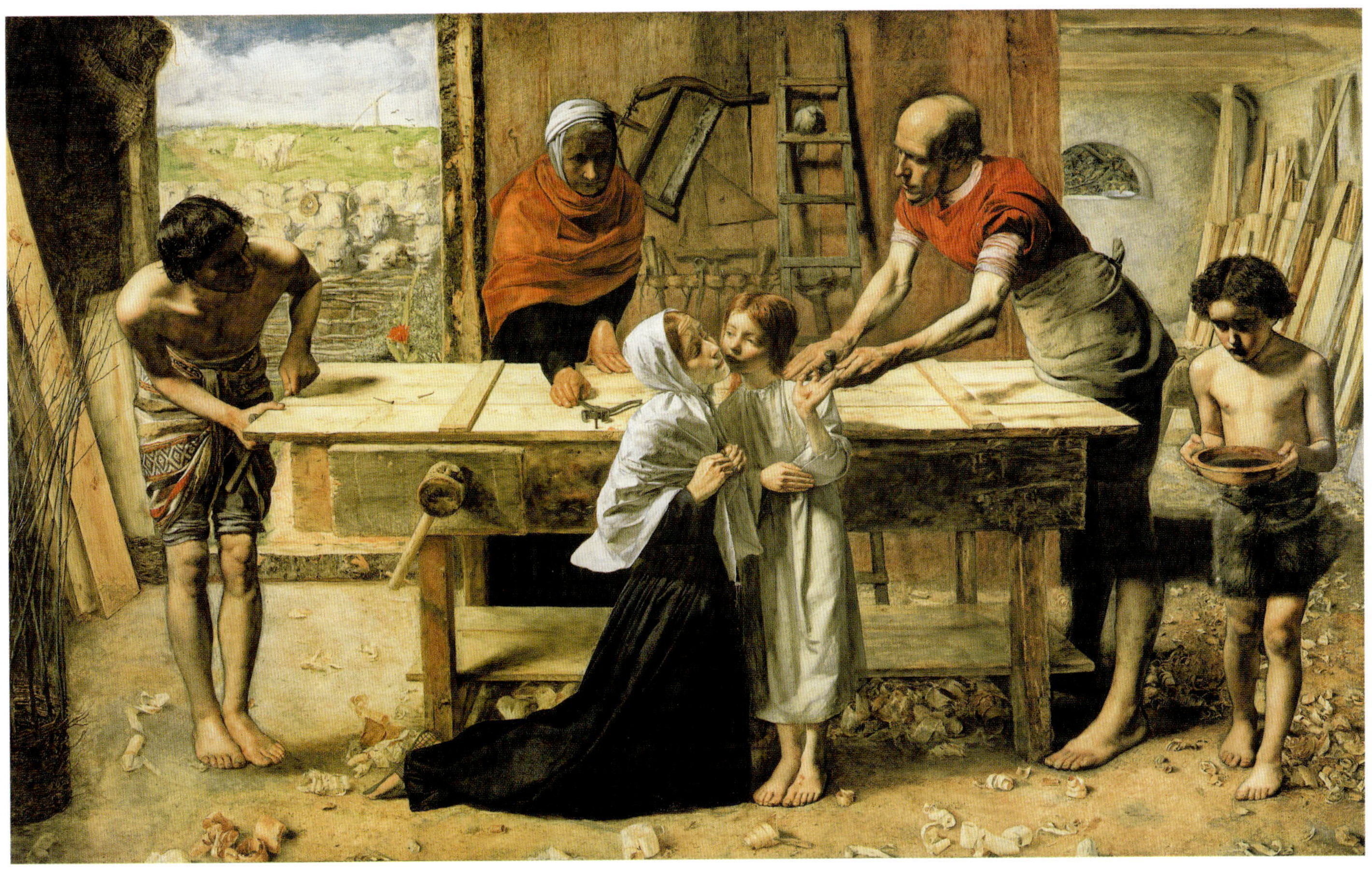

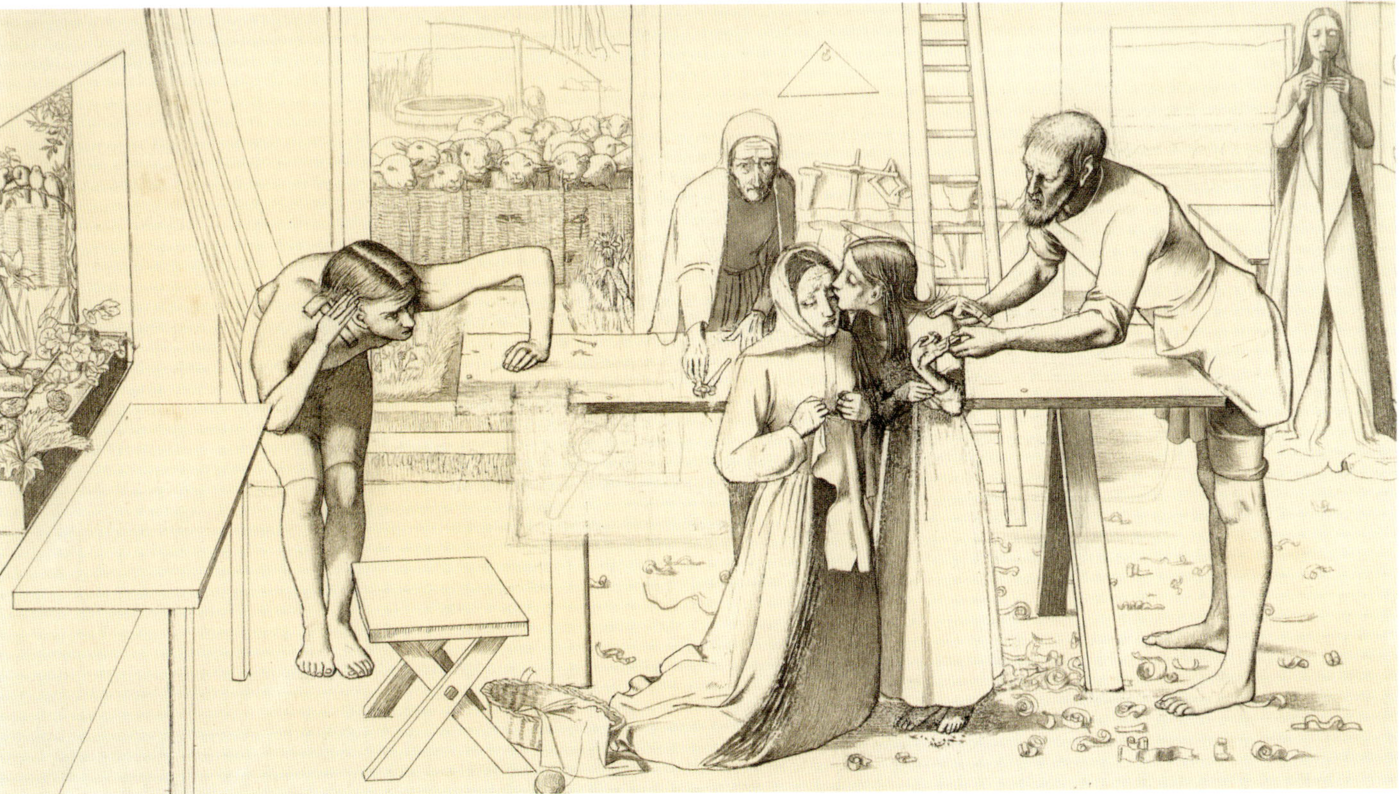

5 John Everett Millais, *Christ in the House of his Parents* ('*The Carpenter's Shop*'), 1849–50, Tate
6 John Everett Millais, *Study for 'Christ in the House of his Parents'* ('*The Carpenter's Shop*'), c. 1849, Tate

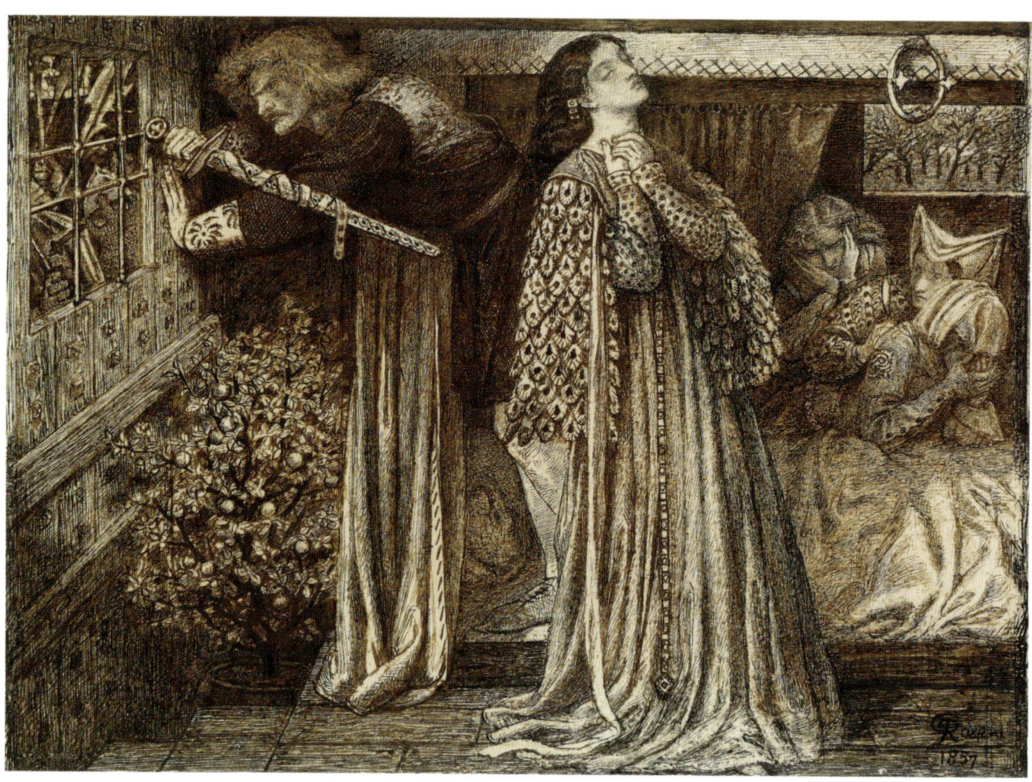

7   Dante Gabriel Rossetti, *Sir Launcelot in the Queen's Chamber*, 1857, Birmingham Museums & Art Gallery

draughtsman of his generation. In the first full-length study of Rossetti, published in 1894, Esther Wood put forward an idea of the artist's 'imperfect technique' which was to have an impact on other scholars of the Pre-Raphaelite Brotherhood:

> with all his ardour, his real though very fitful diligence, and his sincere delight in his chosen profession, Rossetti never fully conquered that imperfection of technique in draughtsmanship which has been the stronghold of hostile criticism throughout the Pre-Raphaelite movement, but which in fact arose from the inevitable deficiency of a mind too impatient for ideas, too eager for subject-matter, to be steadfastly concerned with the science of expression.[9]

Wood was responding to a particular objection to Rossetti that was current during his lifetime and which had at least one surprising advocate. In 1883, the year following Rossetti's death, Beatrix Potter recorded in her journal that her father had come back from a meeting with Millais in which the artist had voiced the opinion that Rossetti's paintings were 'rubbish' and that he had 'never learnt drawing and could not draw'.[10] Nonetheless, many of Rossetti's major works are drawings or watercolours. His

drawings found their most admiring audience in a group of younger contemporaries, the most notable of whom were Burne-Jones and Simeon Solomon (1840–1905).

Burne-Jones, whose work most readily characterizes the later stages of Pre-Raphaelitism and whose drawings show a strong Rossettian influence, had a visual imagination which contrasts with Millais's in almost every way. Where Millais had a lively curiosity about people and things that displayed itself in an extraordinary pictorial variety, Burne-Jones's visual repertoire was narrow. He displayed no interest in contemporary life but was inventive about decorating the surface of the work, adapting motifs endlessly, sometimes on an ambitious scale. His drawing style changed throughout his long career from the detailed, cramped style of the works of the late 1850s to the elegant Symbolism of his final manner. Indeed, we might say that drawing, as his primary expressive form, changed the way in which he thought about all aspects of art: form, colour, media and even subject. We ask ourselves questions of each of Burne-Jones's works: Is it a work of fine art or design? Is it a painting or a drawing? Is this preparatory for some more complete expression of the idea or is it self-sufficient?

William Holman Hunt is the major Pre-Raphaelite who suffered the least adverse criticism of his drawing ability.

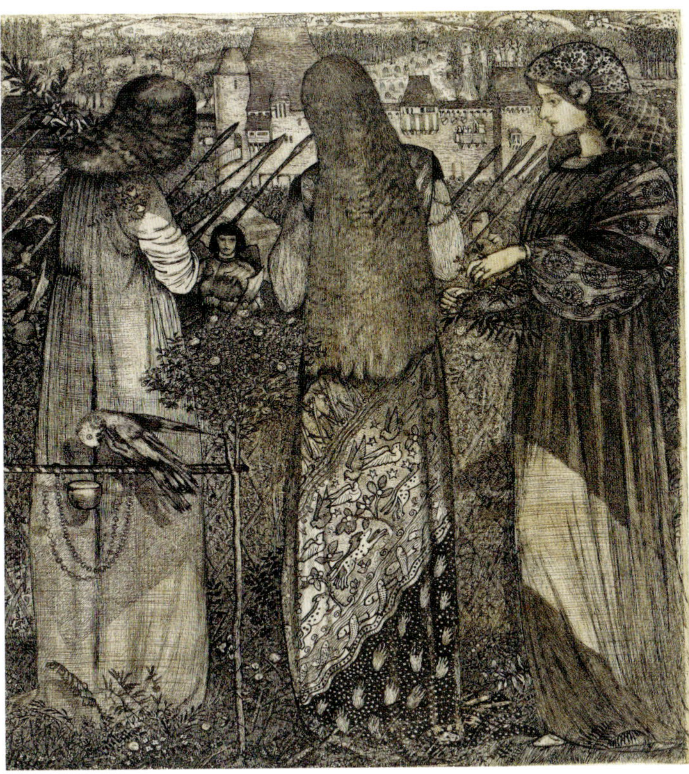

8 Edward Burne-Jones, *Going to the Battle*, 1858,
Fitzwilliam Museum, Cambridge

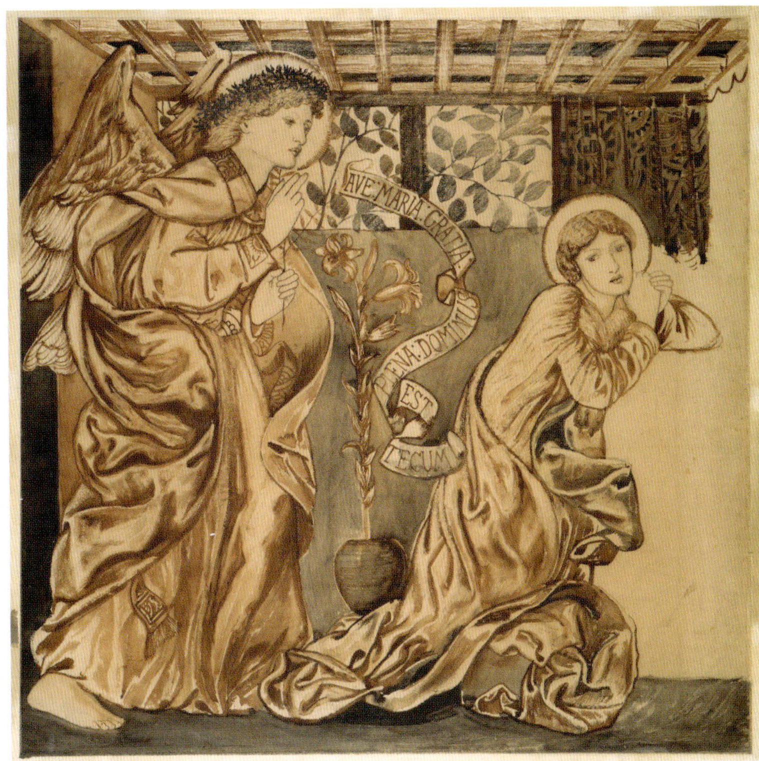

9 Edward Burne-Jones, *Design for Stained Glass: 'The Annunciation'*,
1862, Birmingham Museums & Art Gallery

Certainly he was the artist who used drawing in the least
experimental way and was always anxious to express his
pictorial ideas in the more permanent record of paint
– in this respect he could not be more different from
Rossetti. Hunt left comparatively few drawings other than
compositional sketches (such as those revealing the various
workings-out of compositions for extraordinary paintings
such as *The Light of the World* and *The Finding of the
Saviour in the Temple*) and his illustrations, which show his
particular sensitivity to narrative nuance, a matter in which
he was deeply influenced by Millais. His later drawings
reveal neither an adherence to the poetic impulse of Rossetti
nor, despite his constant adherence to Pre-Raphaelite core
belief, unflinching 'truth to nature'. They consist chiefly
of studies of fragments of the body, the head or face, or
accessories, traditional in the history of drawing practices,
which helped build up the symbolic realism of the highly
finished, brightly coloured paintings. It was painting rather
than drawing that was of supreme importance to him, and
drawing, having been a fundamental tool in compositional
experiment, became increasingly a notational form. A

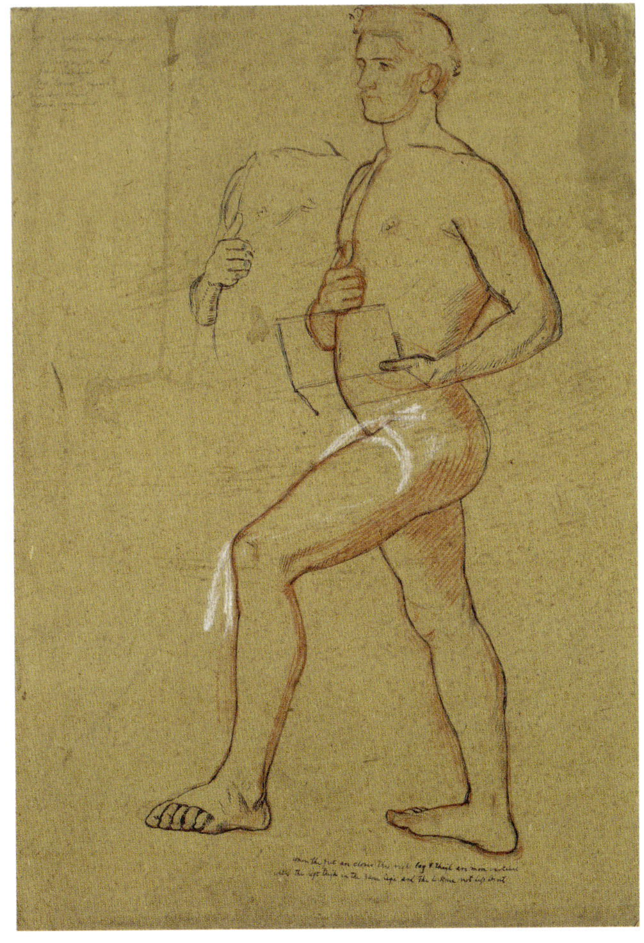

10 William Holman Hunt, *Study of a Male Nude for 'May Morning on
Magdalen Tower'*, 1888–89, Birmingham Museums & Art Gallery

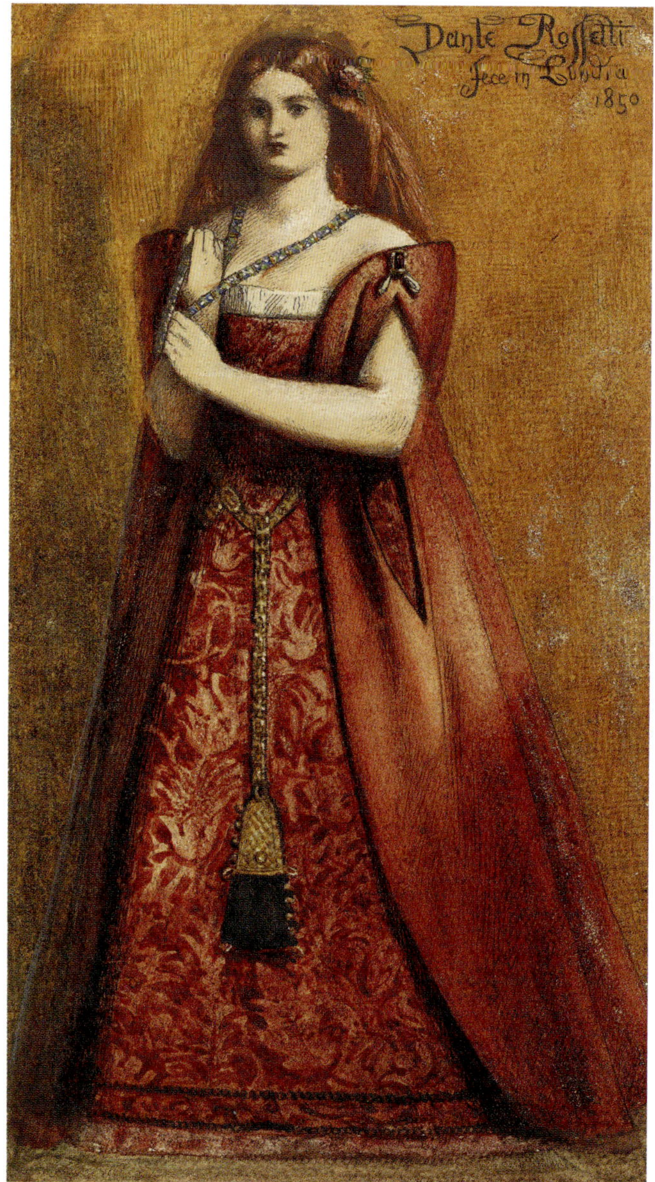

11   Dante Gabriel Rossetti, *Rossovestita*, 1850,
Birmingham Museums & Art Gallery

drawing for *May Morning on Magdalen Tower* (1888–90)
[**10**], for example, is typical of Hunt's method of working.
It is a full-length study of a male nude, with other sketches
from the figure on the same sheet, and handwritten notes
reminding the artist of details that he had not been able to
record in the drawing: 'When the feet are closer the right leg
and thigh are more vertical.'

These opening observations should indicate that the Pre-
Raphaelites did not produce one single type of drawing, but
rather developed a set of attitudes to drawing that helped
challenge accepted rules of representation and encouraged
individuality and variety. Drawing could be intimate and
personal, an exact record of an event recorded in a diary or

letter and an expression of a shared sense of friendship: the
many inscribed and dedicated portraits and presentation
drawings they made attest to that purpose. It had other
professional and public functions, too, and it is in the
public sphere that the Pre-Raphaelites had their greatest
impact on the history of drawing. It was in the setting up
of a new way of drawing that they built the foundations of
a new movement in painting. It was in drawing that the
Pre-Raphaelite Brotherhood first explored unfamiliar or
extreme compositional ploys that assisted in the creation
of new narrative works that were poetic, dramatic and
visionary, and that rethought religious and historical
subjects. Sometimes their experiments began and ended
in drawing. In these cases – and all of the Pre-Raphaelites
share this – drawing was not a stage in the development of
an idea but an end in itself.

In order to stress the variety of nineteenth-century
commentaries on drawing, this study quotes from a variety
of sources: letters, diaries, pamphlets, books, newspapers
and journals – from general literature as well as from the
relatively new and expanding art press. Exhibition reviews,
novel features of the mid-Victorian press, were particularly
useful in revealing the important part drawing played in
debates about the function of art in society and the role it
had in the training of artists.

This survey of Pre-Raphaelite drawing includes not
only works produced in pencil and other drawing media
– such as pen-and-ink, silverpoint and chalk – but also,
on occasion, prints that were produced by direct drawing,
such as etchings and lithographs. The survey also discusses
watercolour as a type of coloured drawing rather than
as painting. In experimenting with coloured drawing,
Rossetti was not only making connections between
drawing and painting and, to some extent, between visual
art and literature, but also breaking down barriers between
painting and drawing.

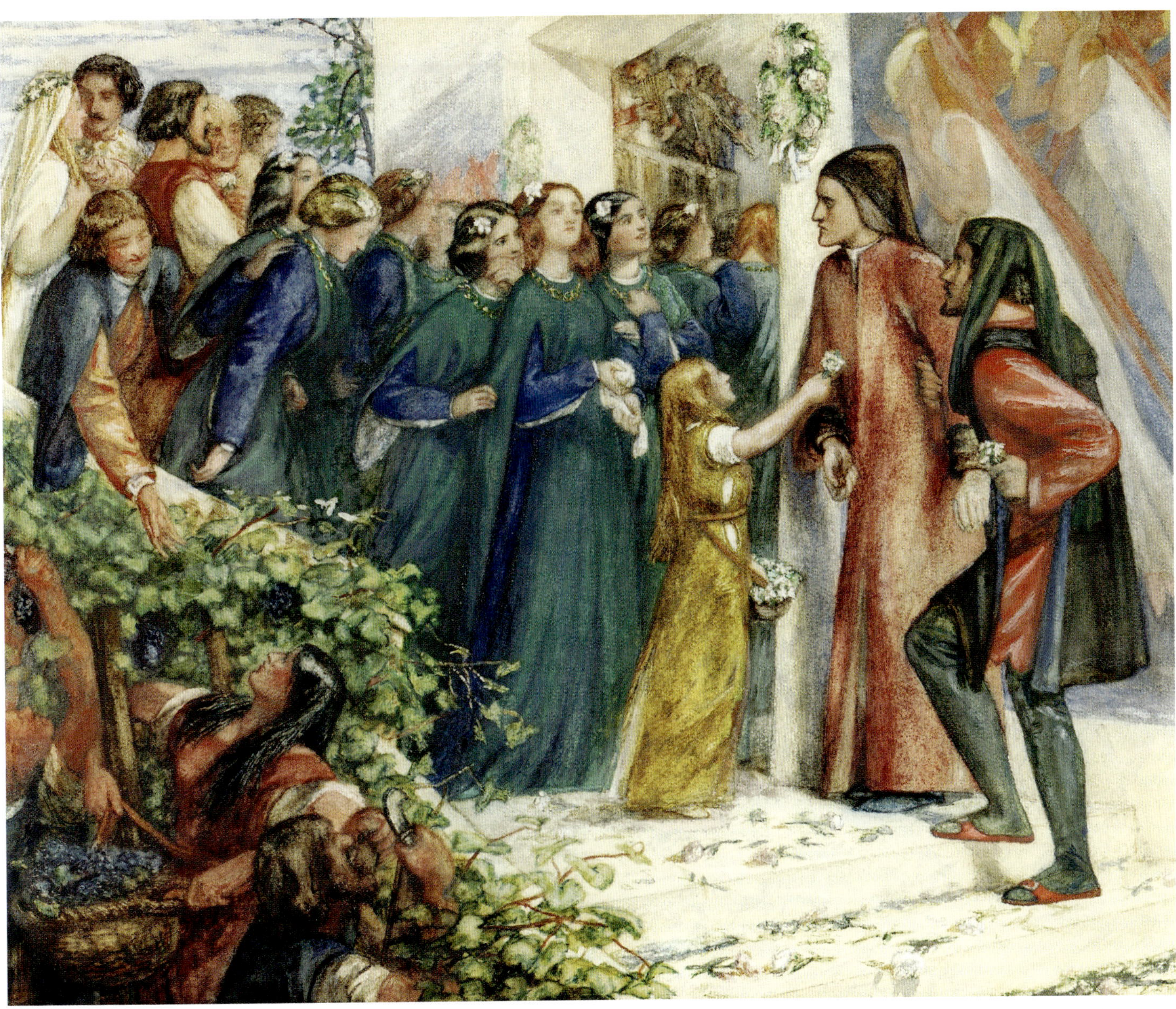

In order to organize these observations on drawing and assess its importance for the Pre-Raphaelite Brotherhood, this book adopts an approach that is both chronological and thematic. Starting with a discussion of the training of artists in England in the first decades of the nineteenth century, the narrative moves on to the ways in which the members of the Pre-Raphaelite Brotherhood sought alternative drawing modes in the earliest stages of their careers. The thematic chapters consider portraiture and caricature (Chapter 4), drawing for illustration (Chapter 6) and drawing for design (Chapter 7). Chapter 6 also examines commercial wood engraving where original drawings are not available – some lost in the engraving process when drawn on to the block, others untraced, perhaps destroyed – in order to show the new and powerful compositional designs introduced by Pre-Raphaelite artists. The book ends by tracing the reception of Pre-Raphaelite drawing in the last decades of the nineteenth century when there was an early reassessment of their achievement that was to extend further the influence of their work and ideas.

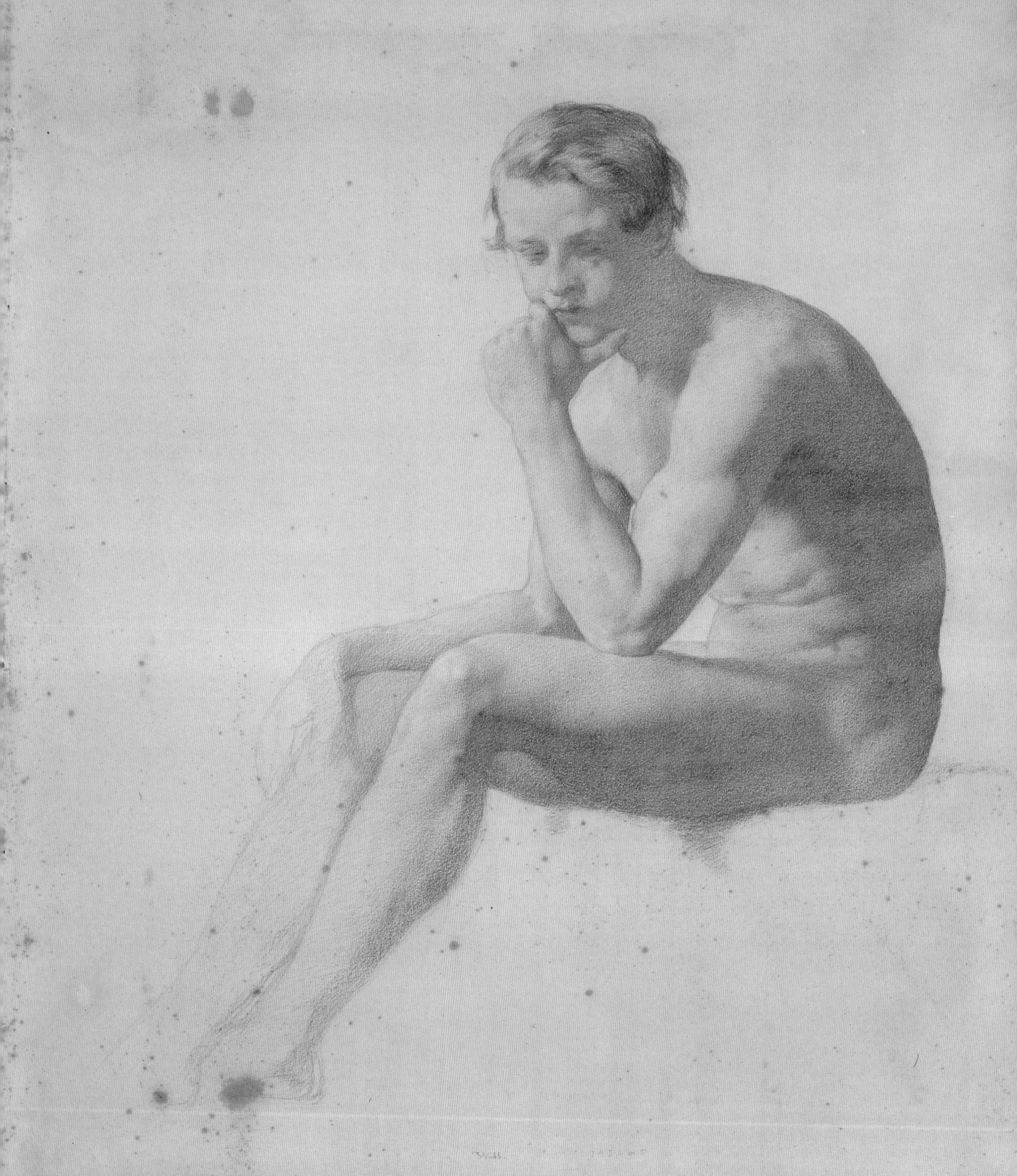

Chapter 1

The Flat, the Antique and the Life: Academic Drawing and the Pre-Raphaelites

In December 1843 the young John Everett Millais, then aged fourteen, was given a copy of the *Lectures* of the portrait painter John Opie (1761–1807) as a prize, along with a silver medal for the best drawing 'from the Antique'. Millais had commenced his studies at the Academy as a probationer in 1840, aged eleven, the youngest pupil ever to enrol at the Royal Academy Schools.[1] 'From the Antique' was one of the academic stages of instruction, between 'from the flat' and 'the life room'. Drawing 'from the Antique', a process entailing copying from the casts of ancient sculptures such as the *Pancrastinae* [14] provided a link between the practices of the Renaissance workshop and the training of artists in the contemporary European academies. The cast became symbolic of the enterprise of representing the human figure as well as of the canon. Drawing from ancient sculpture and casts became the primary test of ability and developed taste and discrimination in the artist.

Opie's *Lectures* re-presented for a new audience many of the principal ideas of Sir Joshua Reynolds (1723–92), the first President of the Royal Academy. Reynolds acknowledged that facility in drawing was only the first stage in becoming a painter and that the young artist should paint rather than draw; nevertheless, he believed that drawing was 'very properly called the Language of Art'. Comparing drawing to the learning of a musical instrument, Reynolds advised that 'continual application' was essential: 'the port-crayon ought to be for ever in your hands'.[2] Opie went much further than Reynolds in defining the role of drawing, both in the academic syllabus and in the entire understanding of the pictorial arts. He insisted on the efficacy of anatomical study, which must not be allowed to take over the study of art and must always be accompanied by an understanding of proportion nurtured by a study of the antique. Nature was observed chiefly as a kind of verifying agent to achieve an acceptable, if generalized, concept, rather than one that sought to record the idiosyncrasies of the original.

13 William Mulready, *Study of a Male Nude*, mid-1850s, Royal Academy of Arts, London

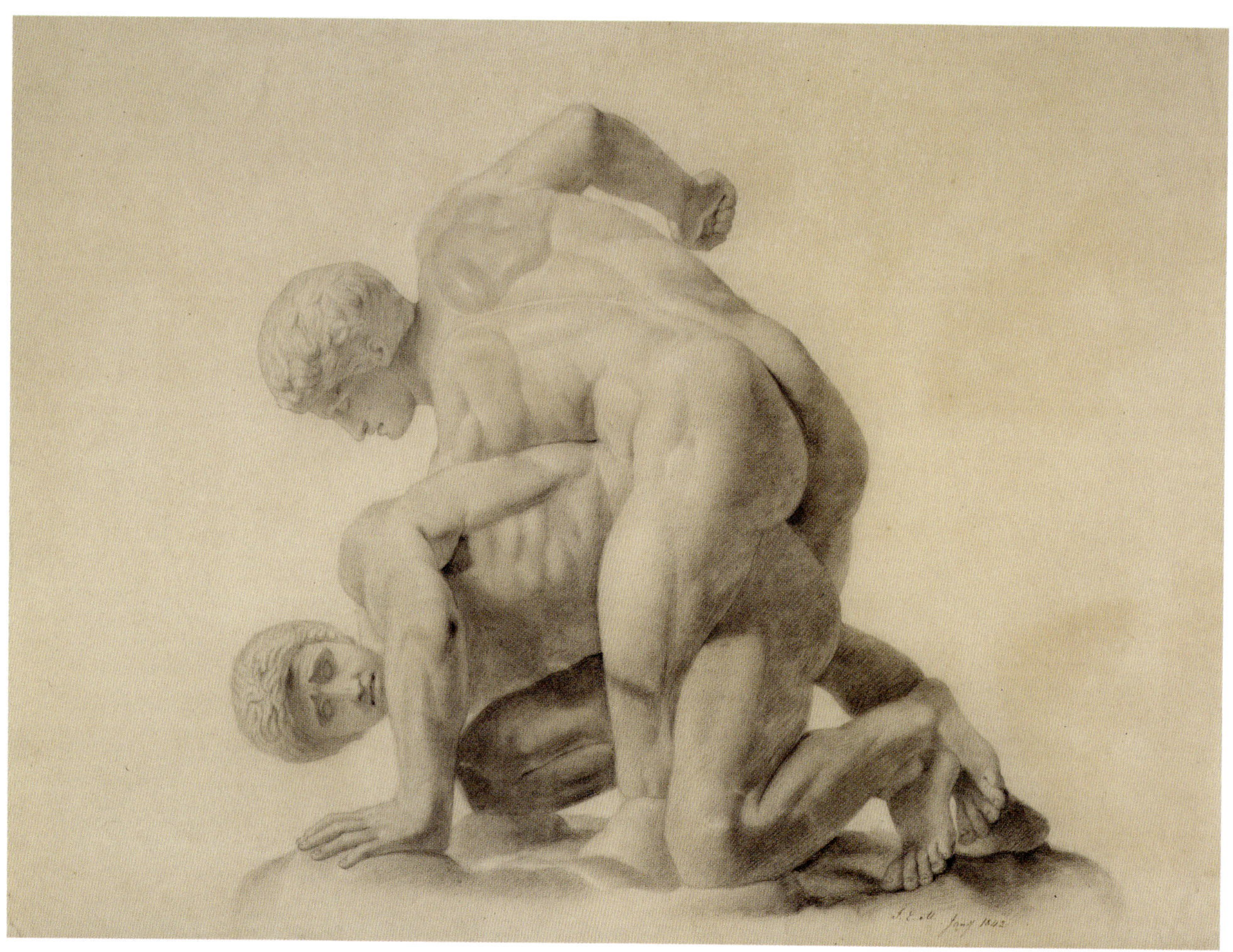

14 John Everett Millais, *The Pancrastinae*, 1842, Royal Academy of Arts, London

15 John Everett Millais, *Sheet of Studies Caricaturing the Post-Raphaelesque Style*, 1853, Birmingham Museums & Art Gallery

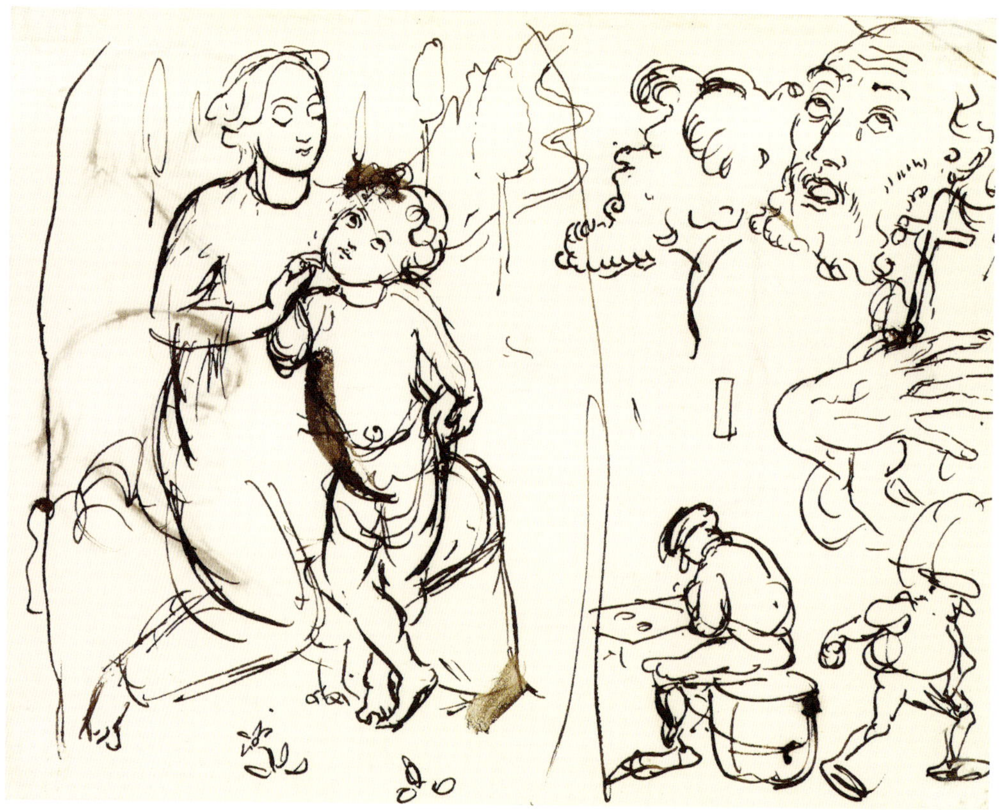

   The Flat, the Antique and the Life: Academic Drawing and the Pre-Raphaelites

Opie posed his readers a question:

If you ask them [the academies], 'What is the first requisite in a painter,' will they not say, Drawing? 'What the second?' Drawing. 'What the third?' Drawing. They tell you, indeed, to acquire colouring, chiaroscuro, and composition, *if you can*; but they *insist* on your becoming draughtsmen.[3]

Opie stresses that drawing is the primary activity in art and central to the academic ideal. The Academy School had been set up as a 'School of Academy of Design' rather than as a painting school, and Opie's approach to teaching reinforces that fact.[4]

Although Opie's volume of lectures was still being awarded as a prize at the Academy in the mid-nineteenth century, his tenets were largely neglected in practice and were already atrophying. Throughout the nineteenth century there was a disparity between what was expected from an artist in training and the paintings that gained accolades when exhibited at the annual Academy exhibition. Opie's opinions more or less reflect core academic concepts, for example those of 'the Grand Style' and the 'Ideal' in form and proportion, against which the Pre-Raphaelite Brotherhood revolted. A decade later Opie was still seen as a force of academic correctitude when Simeon Solomon was a student at the Academy Schools. He depicted an imagined family row taking place in the young artist's studio over old and new authorities in art [**16**]. A comically angry father, seeing his son converted from an academic artist to a Pre-Raphaelite, brandishes a copy of Opie's *Lectures* (here sharing a volume with lectures by fellow Academicians James Barry and Henry Fuseli). The beguiled son clutches Ruskin to his bosom; the initials of the names of his heroes radiate from his eyes.

The Pre-Raphaelite Brotherhood was formed at a time when association with the Royal Academy was the chief way

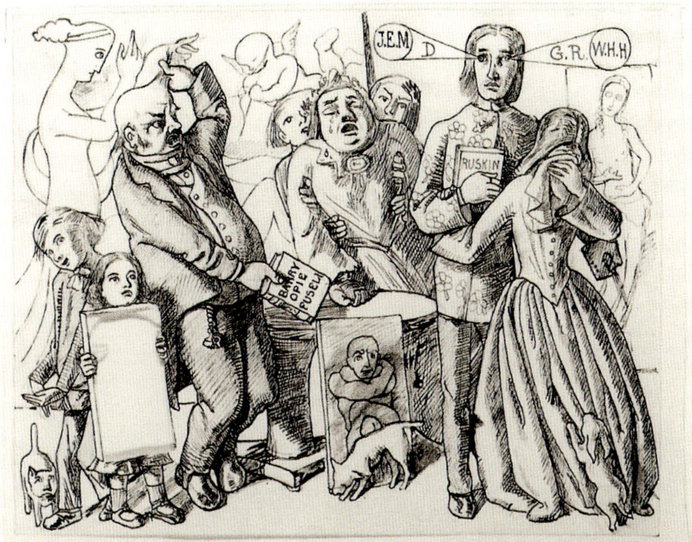

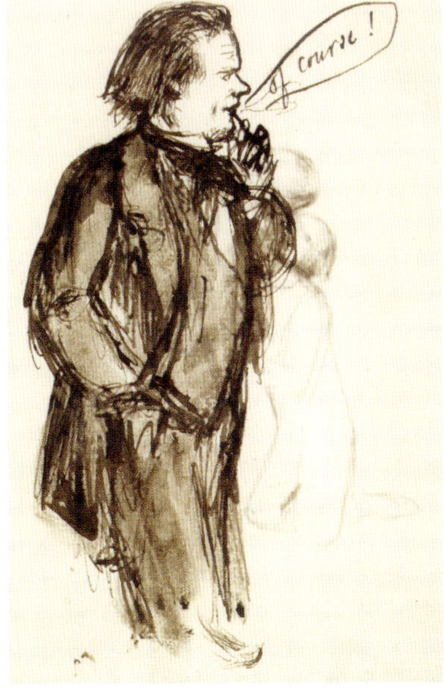

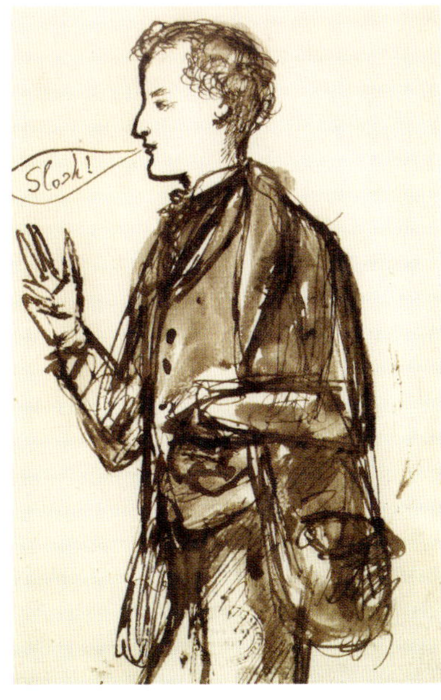

16 Simeon Solomon, *A Pre-Raphaelite Studio Fantasy*, undated, private collection

17 Dante Gabriel Rossetti, *'Of Course!': Caricature of William Holman Hunt*, early 1850s, Birmingham Museums & Art Gallery

18 Dante Gabriel Rossetti, *'Slosh!': Caricature of John Everett Millais*, early 1850s, Birmingham Museums & Art Gallery

in which the professional careers of artists could
be advanced. Attendance at the Royal Academy Schools
was the primary step in the career of an artist, and entrance
was delayed until the correct standard of accomplishment
in drawing had been obtained. Rather than studying
the individual form of the life model in detail and with
its distinctive and personal characteristics, students were
encouraged to use the processes of drawing to erase such
features through a system of selection and idealization.
For the study of the human figure, students were first
introduced to casts of ancient sculptures found in the
Antique Room of the Academy Schools. The academic
system dictated the ways in which prospective students
were trained to prepare for the observance of the Academy's
entry requirements. All of the available forms of tuition
had a concern with the conventional: to study the rudiments
of art by learning rules, even tricks, of representation
that were practised or sanctioned by academic tradition.
These conventions were caricatured by Millais, who satirized
the tired subject matter and stylistic mannerisms of
Old Master drawings. In portrait sketches of Hunt and
Millais, Rossetti inscribed the word 'Slosh' in a speech
bubble coming out of Millais's mouth [18]. 'Slosh' was
a favourite Pre-Raphaelite Brotherhood term, derived
from the name of the first President of the Royal Academy,
Sir Joshua Reynolds, used by the Brotherhood to describe
bad art or bad ideas. Hunt, obviously in full agreement
with his friend, replies, 'Of course' [17]. The drawings
memorialize what must have been a familiar exchange
among the Brotherhood, disparaging the sterility of
academic practices at all times.

Like all prospective students at the Academy Schools,
the members of the Pre-Raphaelite Brotherhood had had
to prepare for entrance in the prescribed manner, by the
submission of a drawing to be inspected by the entrance
committee. Candidates often received specialized tuition in

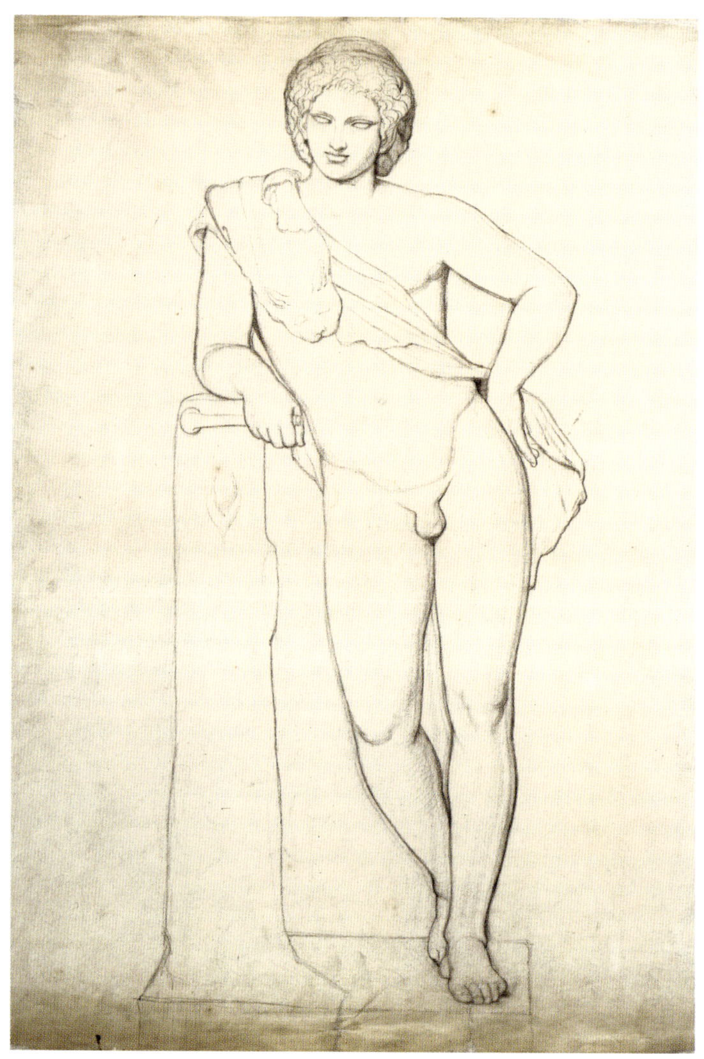

19 John Everett Millais, *The Marble Faun*, c. 1844,
    Royal Academy of Arts, London

order to achieve this standard either from a private drawing
master or at a drawing school. Millais's early training in art
is a good example of the educational opportunities of the
time. At the age of eight he began his studies with a drawing
master, Mr Bettall. Moving to London from Jersey, Millais

enrolled at Henry Sass's Drawing Academy where one of his contemporaries was William Powell Frith (1819–1909), who, in his autobiography, recalled the course of study at Sass's:

> The master had prepared with his own hand a great number of outlines from the antique, beginning with Juno's eye and ending with the Apollo – hands, feet, mouths, faces, in various positions, all in severely correct outline. …This course, called 'drawing from the flat', was persisted in till the pupil was considered advanced enough to be allowed to study the mysteries of light and shade. A huge white plaster ball, standing on a pedestal, was the next object of attention; by the representation of which in Italian chalk and on white paper the student was to be initiated into the first principles of light, shadow and rotundity.[5]

Before studying at the Royal Academy Schools, Hunt had taken lessons from a portrait painter, Henry Rogers, but had little experience of drawing and failed on his first two attempts to become a probationer at the Academy Schools. In his memoirs he reflected that he had not 'developed the habit of mechanical neatness' needed for gaining access to the 'lowest stages of strict training'.[6] He noted too that other candidates, especially those from Sass's, had been schooled in the formulae of success – techniques of 'shading and blocking', for example – that would appeal to members of the acceptance committee.

Rossetti, on the other hand, had no formal teaching before attending King's College School in 1837, aged nine. He developed his talent through copying from engravings and periodical illustrations, some of them French. The drawing master at King's College School was the celebrated landscapist John Cotman (1782–1842), whose teaching method was to provide his own drawings in the classroom for copying.[7] In 1841 Rossetti enrolled at Sass's, where he was distinguished chiefly by unruly behaviour, perhaps in revolt against the repetitive exercises in drawing. However, writing to his mother in a letter of 1843, Rossetti, aged fifteen, seemed fully engrossed in his studies. He outlined his progress:

> I have finished the outline of the Hercules, and drawn upon the anatomy figure. I am now engaged on a finished drawing of the Antinous, which, supposing it to prove good enough, I may perhaps send in to the Academy.… Every successful candidate is required to execute a second drawing, in order to prove that the merit of the first is entirely his own. Added to which he must make drawings of the anatomy-figure and of the skeleton, in any of which if he fails he ceases to be student; and very few have the courage to venture on a second trial after the disgrace of a rejection.… I intend to commence drawing at home from those casts which I possess, and thus endeavour to get into the habit of working without assistance of any kind.[8]

Rossetti developed his skill in imaginative drawing outside the institutions in which he studied; it was one of the ways in which he established his anti-academic stance because he neither adopted the academic convention for the representation of the human figure nor graduated immediately into painting as his central practice. Instead, he concentrated on drawing and watercolour for many years, following his first experiments in the Pre-Raphaelite oil-painting technique. Drawing was not only a relatively immediate method of producing an image but also provided Rossetti with a way of uniting the act of writing poetry with another graphic activity in which he visualized pictorial symbols. His manuscripts and drawings encode the same poetic inspiration. It is little wonder that Rossetti was to take William Blake as a model. The graphic impulse that one can detect in Rossetti's work has as much to do with Blake's poetic and visionary graphics as it has with Giotto, Gozzoli or the early Italian or Northern European artists he discovered with Hunt and Millais. Both Blake and early Renaissance art provided strong, alternative, anti-academic models.

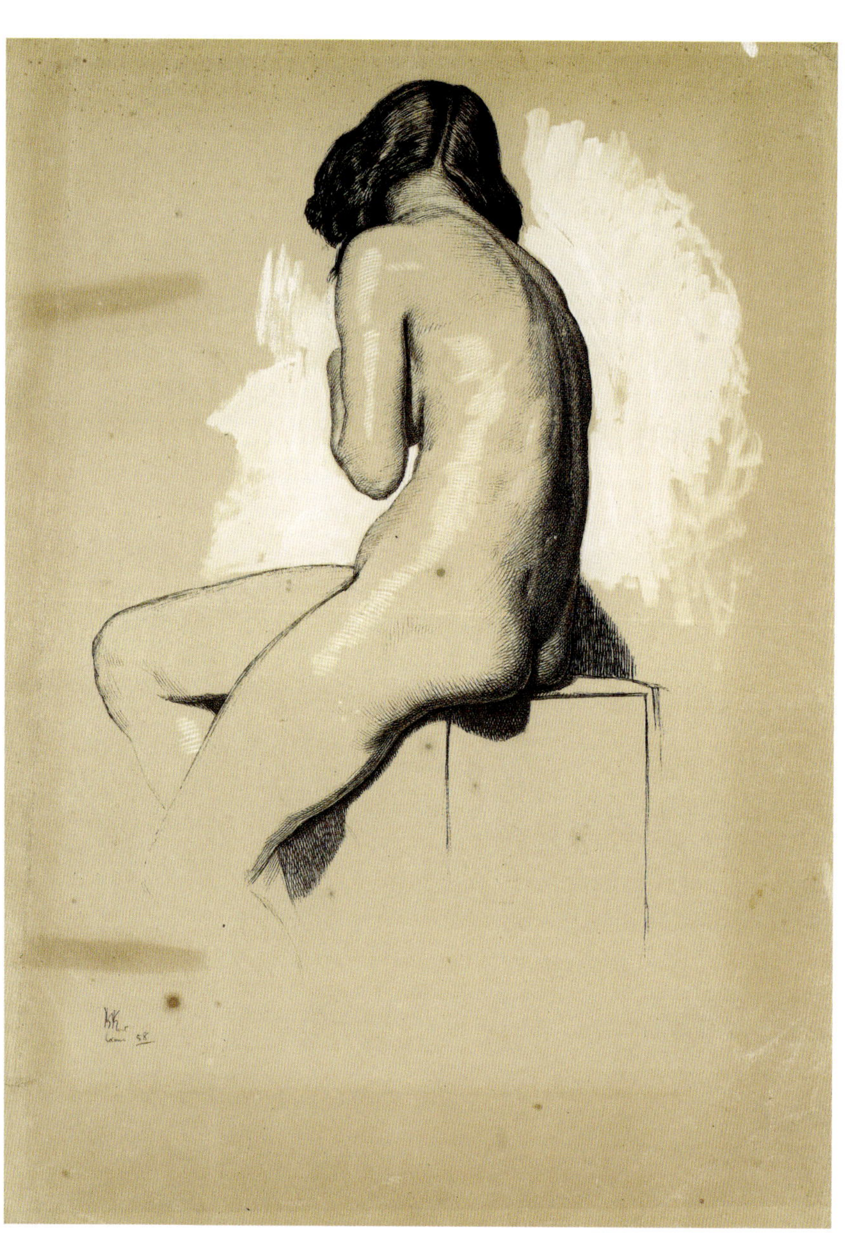

20 William Holman Hunt, *Life Study of a Seated Female Nude, Seen from Behind*, 1858, Birmingham Museums & Art Gallery

The life room

Millais's earliest student drawings are in the perfect academic manner, demonstrating the skill in chiaroscuro and accuracy of proportion that were valued at the Royal Academy Schools. Although teaching at the Academy might be perceived to be run-of-the-mill, there was the example of William Mulready (1786–1863), one of the most distinguished yet popular of the Academicians. Mulready was still attending life classes at the end of his long career, and he continued to offer instruction. His drawings show not only the perfection of the academic technique but its development into a more personally inflected manner.

The year 1848 marked not only the founding of the Pre-Raphaelite Brotherhood but also the Mulready exhibition that opened at the Society of Arts in early June. It was the first retrospective of a living artist to be mounted in Britain and was formative in the setting up of a permanent gallery of British art, following the success of the National Gallery. *The Times* found it a 'striking instance of the importance which the British public is beginning to assign to British art'.[9] The notice continued:

> It is a collection of this sort that really teaches a spectator to know an artist, and the 'Mulready exhibition' is rendered still more complete by the addition of his academical studies in chalk – wonderful specimens of industry and talent, in which red and white chalk has been able to produce effects almost equal to those of the brush.[10]

In addition to life studies, Mulready included compositional sketches and informal drawings, an important, if unusual, instance of drawings being exhibited in their own right.

In her catalogue of Mulready's drawings, Anne Rorimer discusses Mulready and the close study of nature that she relates to his interest in detail and accuracy.

The Pre-Raphaelite call to 'study nature' and reject reliance on formulas derived from previous art was

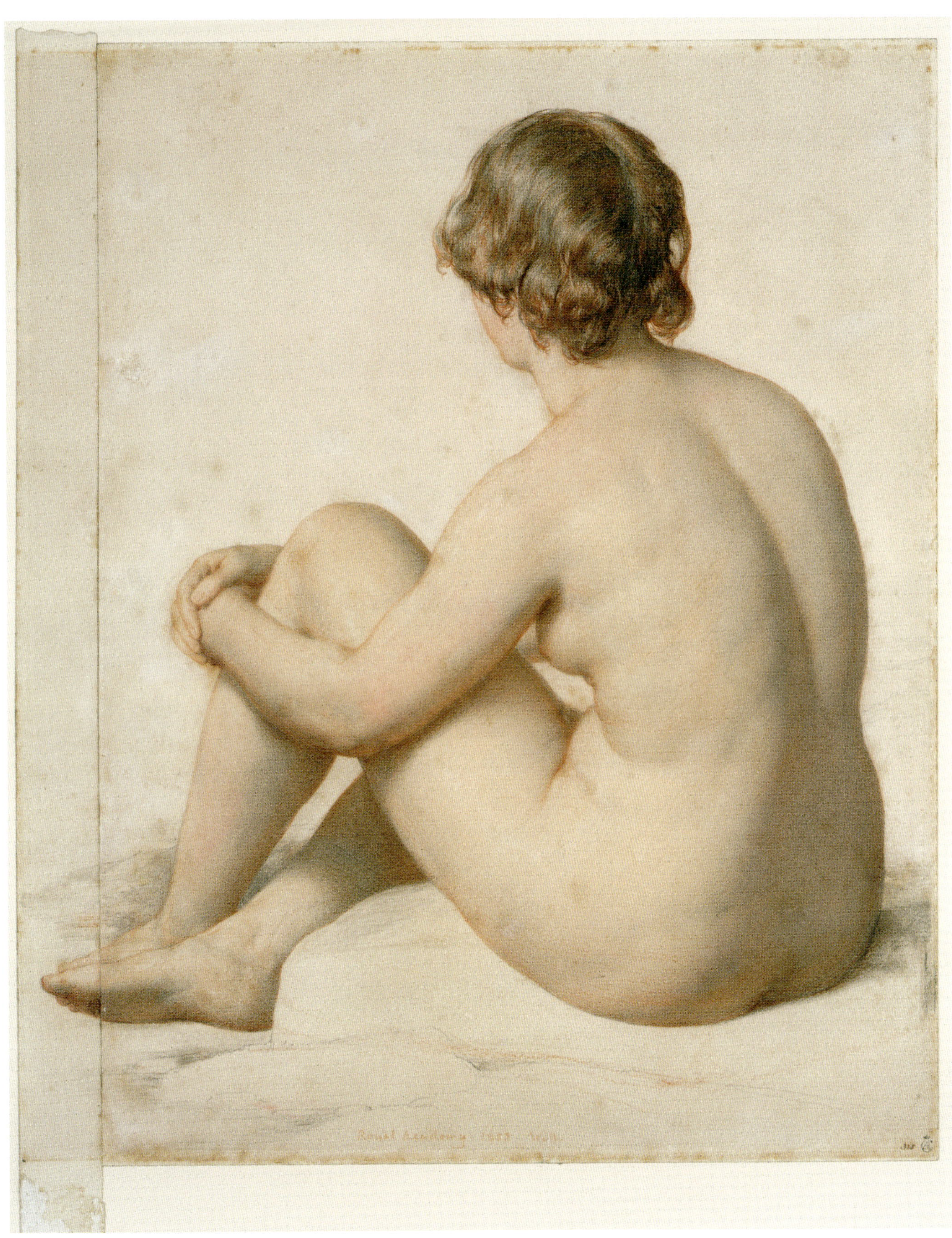

21　William Mulready, *Study of a Seated Female Nude, Seen from Behind*, 1853, Victoria and Albert Museum, London

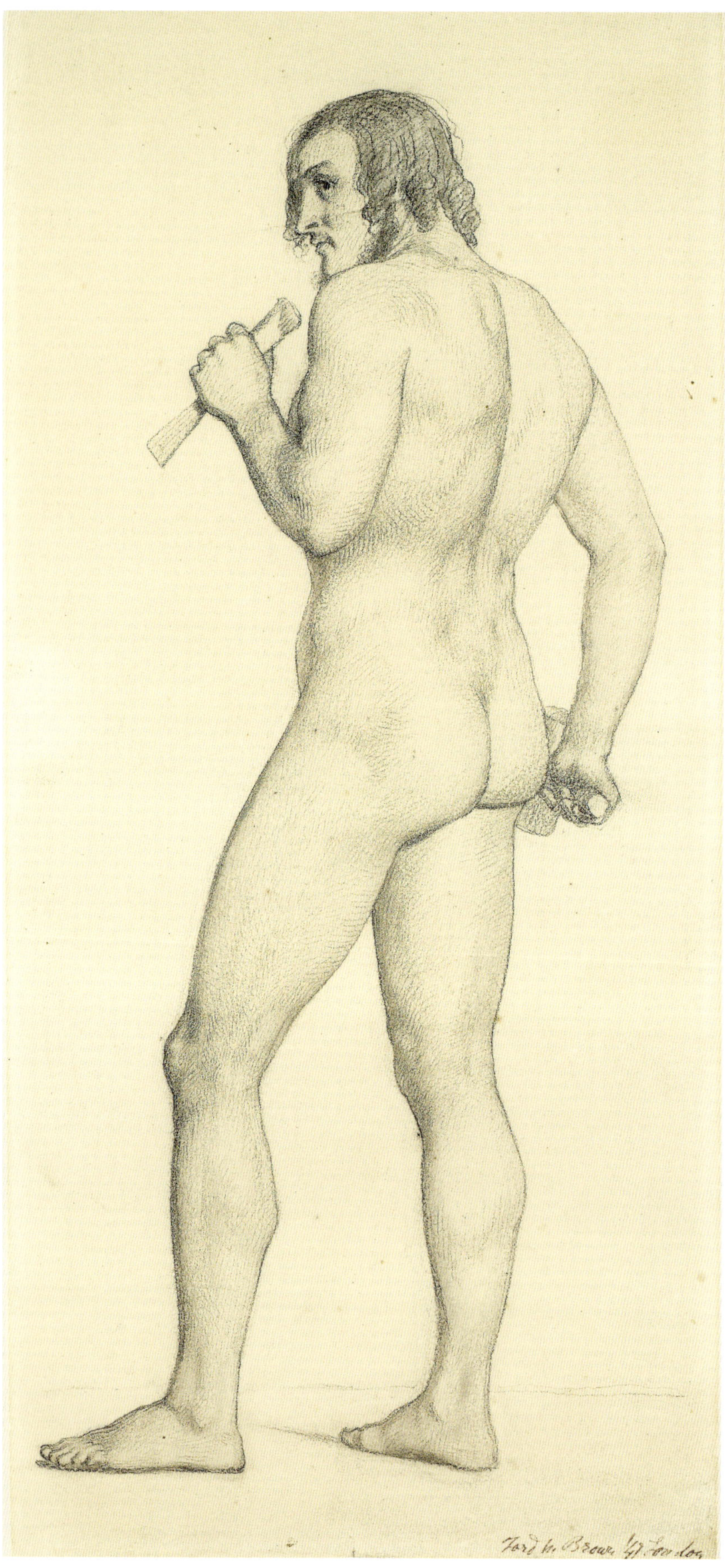

22 Ford Madox Brown, *Study of a Male Nude Posed as a Sculptor*, 1847,
Birmingham Museums & Art Gallery

not in itself new, but had already been resounding among artists of the older generation. Mulready's own statement about this can be found in his sketch-book, where he insists, 'Never dispute about principles of art & the laws of nature – *try them* in your works – watch them in art and nature. The things most praised "that have stood the test of ages" are overrated, and a sound code of laws cannot, in a direct manner, be deduced from them.'[11]

Mulready's achieved a high degree of 'finish' in his drawings by working on the surface of the paper until there was a harmony in the various illusions of light, shadow and texture. His life studies are virtuoso pieces of exhibition standard, not simply intended as preparatory works. Not only was his example of some importance to the Pre-Raphaelites but he was to have closer professional connections with Hunt in the late 1850s. For several years, from 1856 onwards, Hunt joined a group of established Academicians that included Mulready, Frederic Leighton (1830–96) and the genre painter Augustus Leopold Egg (1816–63). The Kensington Academy, as it became known, was set up by artists solely for drawing from the figure. We can see the influence of Mulready's 'finished' style in Hunt's drawing of this time, not a conventional idealized academic style but one with an emphasis on representing the surface of the body rather than anatomy or pose [20].

The adoption of Mulready's drawing style enabled Hunt to construct figures that could be both symbolic and realistic. Other Pre-Raphaelite artists sought a different concept of the body as the representation of an idea or as a symbol. It is significant that the two greatest exponents of this Symbolist tendency in Pre-Raphaelite art, Rossetti and Burne-Jones, never learned the tricks of the academic life room nor adopted the Mulready style of drawing the nude figure. Some of their associates, such as Simeon Solomon, who had been a student at the Royal Academy Schools, had

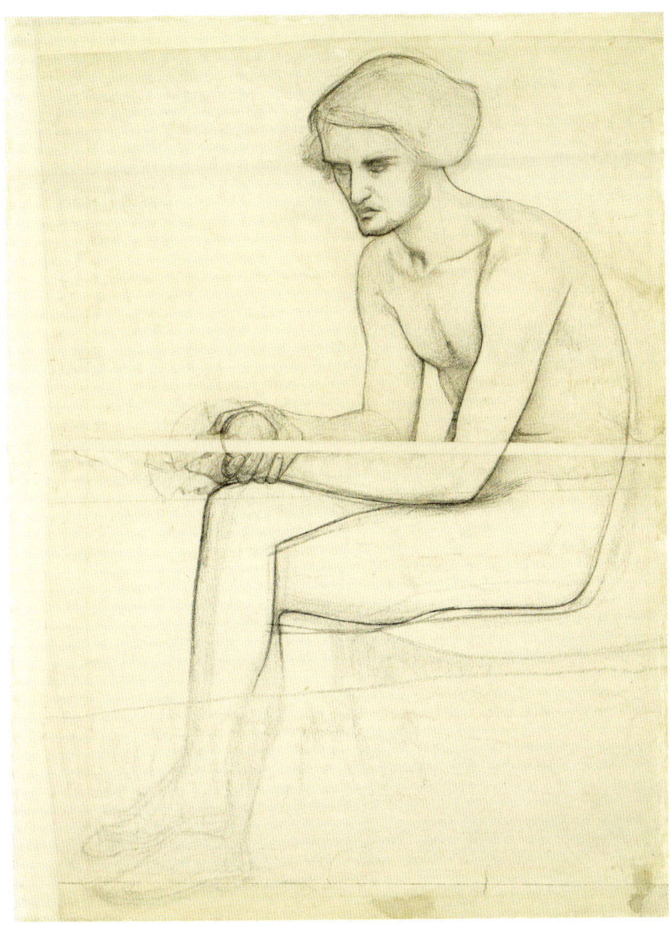

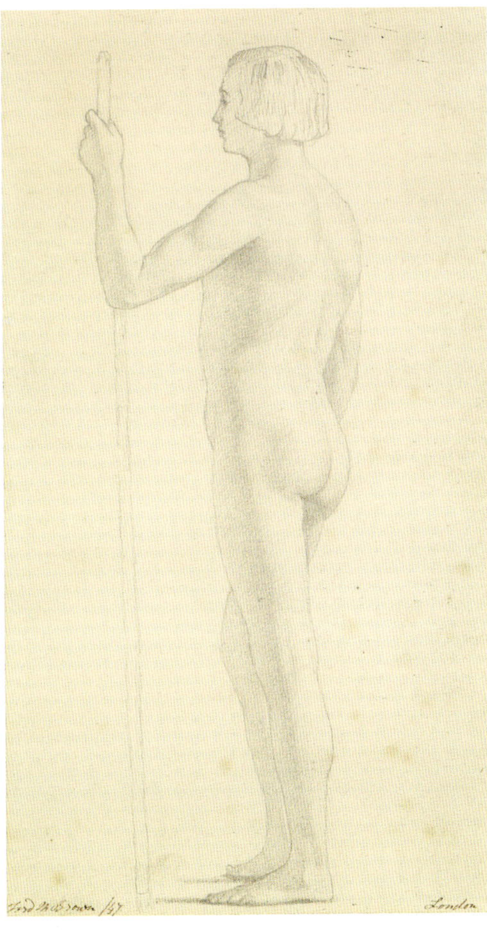

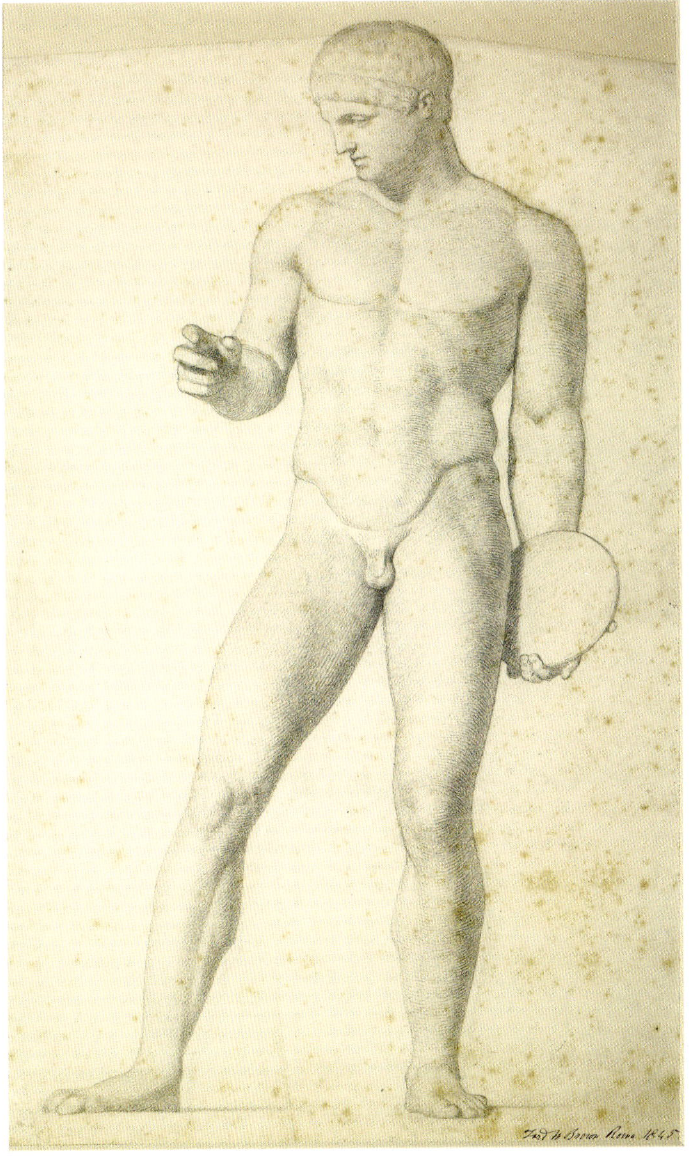

23 Dante Gabriel Rossetti, *Study of a Male Nude for 'Giotto Painting the Portrait of Dante'*, c. 1852, Birmingham Museums & Art Gallery
24 Ford Madox Brown, *Study of a Male Nude Holding a Staff*, 1847, Birmingham Museums & Art Gallery
25 Ford Madox Brown, *Discobolus*, 1845, Birmingham Museums & Art Gallery

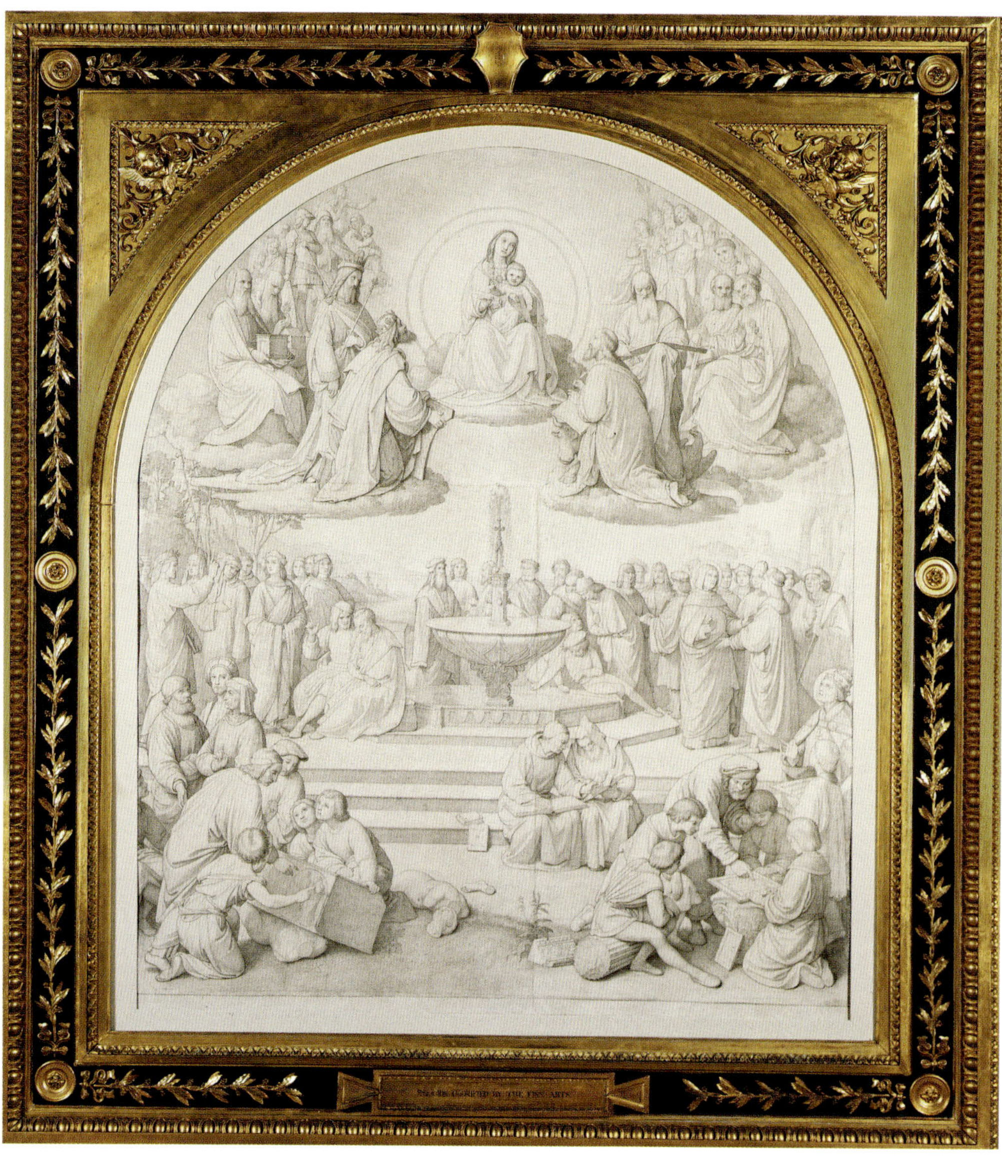

26 Johann Friedrich Overbeck, *Cartoon for 'Religion Glorified by the Fine Arts'*, *c.* 1840,
The Royal Collection

only limited contact with the life room. Rossetti's choice of
models was anti-academic, as demonstrated in his life study
for the figure of Giotto (*c.* 1852) [**23**]. He chose a model with
a slimmer build than the professional academic models
whose bodies were used to mimic the heroes of classical
mythology depicted in ancient sculpture. In Rossetti's
early drawings the male figures – Dante, Faust, Hamlet,
Poe – are poets or philosophers first: their heads and faces
have greater significance than their bodies. In much the
same way Rossetti reimagined the beauty of the female face,
eschewing the types of facial beauty offered by classical
statues or the paintings of Raphael.

Ford Madox Brown's training in life drawing was
more thorough than that of his younger Pre-Raphaelite
friends. His first biographer, the novelist Ford Madox
Hueffer, claimed that 'drawing was with him a passion that
continued, and grew as he grew, and was not merely the
malady of paint and pencil incidental to most childhood'.[12]
He studied under an Italian drawing master and then in
Bruges under Albert Gregorius (1774–1853) and Pieter van
Hanselaere (1786–1862), which, according to Hueffer, 'seems
to have done little more than temporarily extirpate any
individuality that he may have possessed'.[13] He completed
his grounding in the continental academic system by
two years' study in Antwerp under Baron Wappers, the
celebrated Belgian history painter, then at the height of his
fame. The experience of the continental system was to serve
him well and it did not, in fact, impair his imagination.
Indeed, the thoroughness of the system at the Antwerp
Academy provided him with a basic knowledge of human
anatomy that allowed him a freedom in the representation
of the body in complex figure compositions. By the time

he settled in London in 1844, Brown was exceptionally well equipped to be a history painter.[14]

Alternatives to the Academy

The Pre-Raphaelites were not alone in expressing disaffection with the Academy. The training of artists was under scrutiny in the early 1840s, in part as a challenge to the autocracy of the Royal Academy in part as a response to the awareness that industry had need of different methods of training designers. Ralph Wornum (1812–77), the art historian and curator, observed coolly that academies generally failed to elevate standards of taste or attainment but that they 'multiply the number of artists'. He argued that

> the advocates of academies are not agreed as to the objects of their establishment, many asserting that they are intended for the *promotion*, while others maintain, on the contrary, that their establishment was imperative for the *preservation* of the arts; by affording an adequate elementary instruction, and by offering as an inducement to exertion, honours and distinction to those deserving of them.[15]

Wornum expressed the belief – as Millais did nearly thirty years later – that the result of 'preserving the arts' had been to formulate a uniform style throughout Europe. This led to a further danger – the suppression of originality – and to what he described as a 'levelling of all capacities to one standard', which was the result of copying the same models and 'constantly aiming at the same ends'.[16] The supposed virtue of the British academic system – exposing students to identical methods of instruction through close study of the same canonical works – was the cause of its failure.

In a barbed review of financial and other arrangements at the Academy, *The Guardian* criticized its schools, and exhibitions that consisted of 'hundreds of square yards of painted canvas which fatigue the spectator's eye'. However,

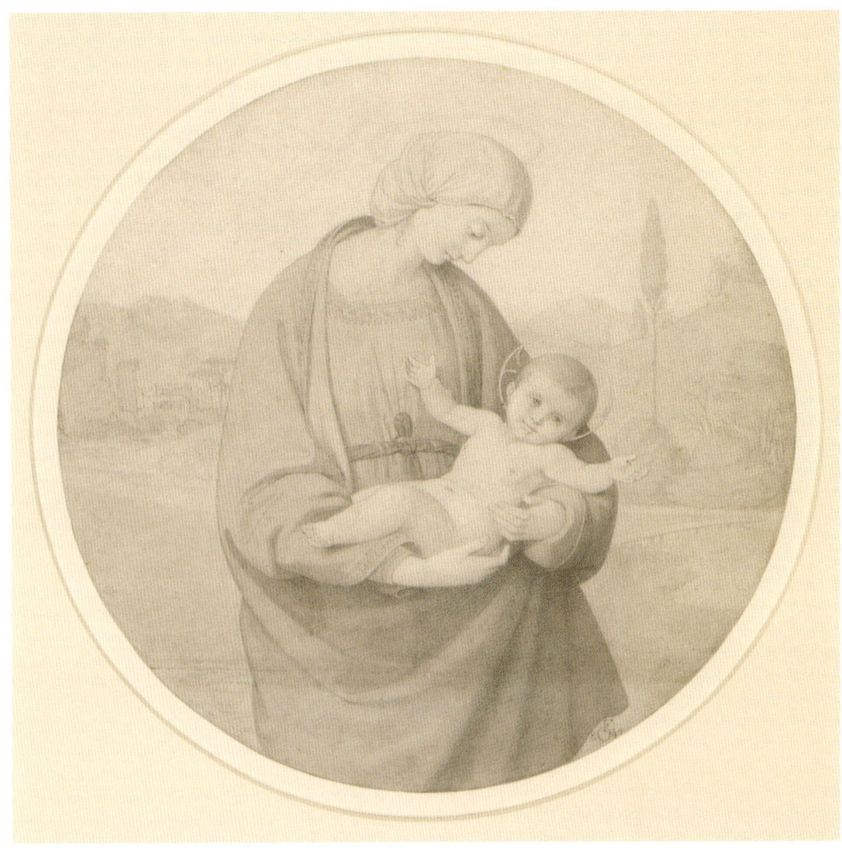

27 Johann Friedrich Overbeck, *Madonna and Child*, 1842, The British Museum, London

in the Westminster Hall Cartoons competitions for the decoration of the new Houses of Parliament *The Guardian* found proof

> that artistic talent is not confined within the narrow limits of an Academy, and the crowded condition of the immense Hall may teach us that the faculty of relishing the highest style of historic painting is not to be tested by the capacity of paying a shilling at the door.[17]

The 'Westminster Cartoons' exhibitions can be seen as a challenge to the annual Royal Academy exhibition. They raised issues about appropriate styles and subjects for contemporary art and the training of artists. In the process they also drew attention to the art of drawing and its communicative potential as well as to the perception that drawing was undervalued in Britain despite its centrality in the curriculum at the Academy Schools.

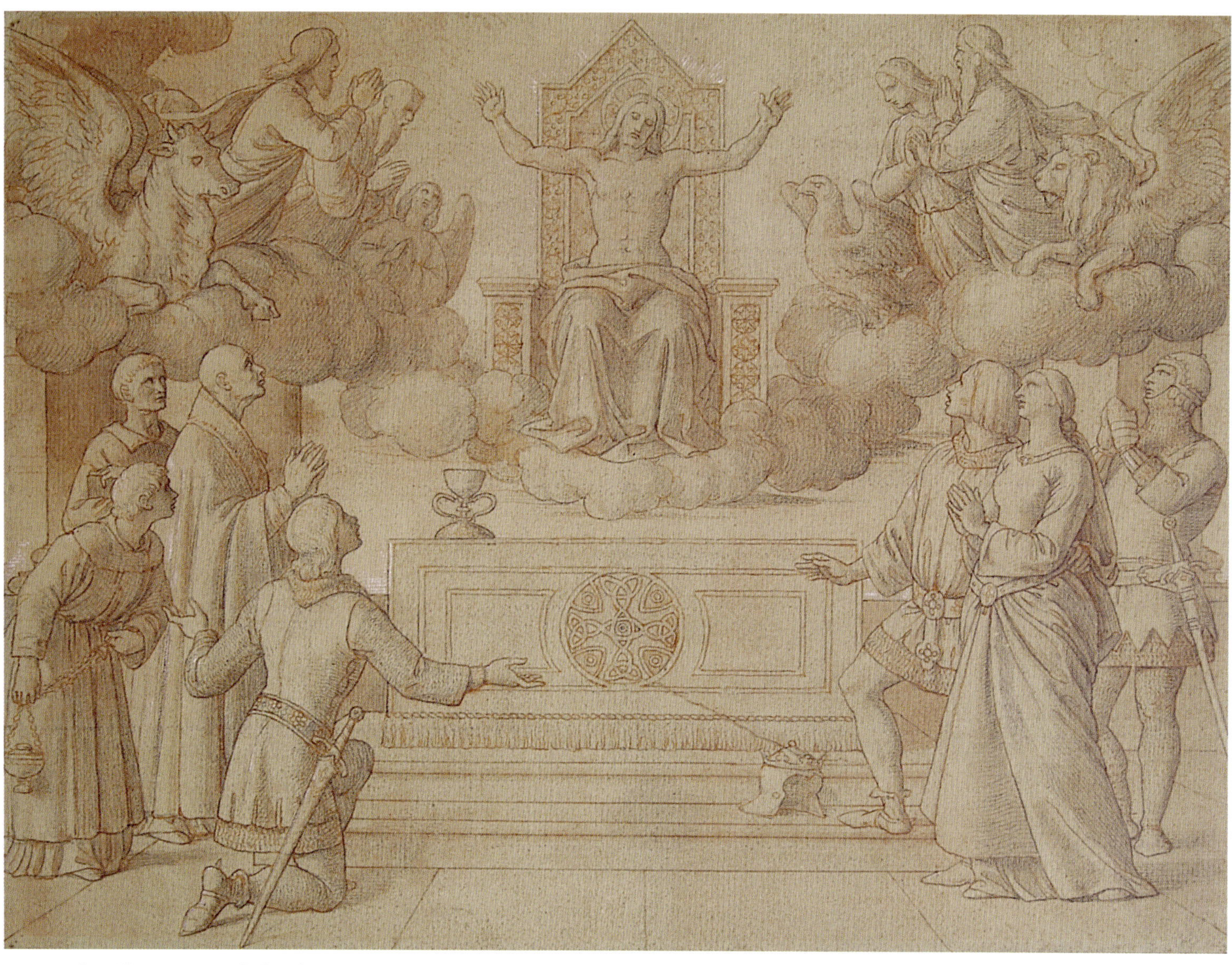

28 William Dyce, *Study for 'The Vision of Sir Galahad and his Company'*, *c.* 1847, Aberdeen Art Gallery & Museums Collections

The competitions held for the decoration of the Houses of Parliament were for cartoons rather than paintings, although the winning designs were to be executed in fresco. Britain could look to Germany for contemporary models of how such a scheme might be implemented. German artists had revived the art of mural painting and developed a suitable drawing style for conveying large historical, religious or allegorical cartoons. Ford Madox Brown's personal contact with the Nazarene artists in Rome had given him first-hand knowledge of their methods, although his approach to depicting physical action and facial expression was more distinctive and certainly livelier than theirs.

The differences between Brown's work and that of Johann Friedrich Overbeck (1789–1869), the German fresco painter,

are telling. Overbeck was a revivalist who eschewed modern art. In his earnest pursuit of the manner of the Renaissance masters his pictures exclude representations of costumes, furniture and architectural settings dating after the sixteenth century [26, 27]. The American art journal *The Crayon* observed:

> Had Overbeck lived in a cloister four centuries ago and painted as he does now, his pictures would be very precious as representations of the feeling and the power of an artist of that early time – but being painted to-day, they are only exhibitions of a talent that finds itself in the world too late, and seeks its inspiration in the works of long past men, instead of ever-living Nature, fresh and full of beauty, as on

   The Flat, the Antique and the Life: Academic Drawing and the Pre-Raphaelites

that day when God first looked upon his works and saw it was good.

However, the same writer noted the beauty of Overbeck's drawings, which set a standard for clarity and precision:

[His drawings are] beautiful from their delicacy and finish. They are superior to his larger works, in so far as the larger are often only magnified copies of the former, without any increase of power, variety, or fullness and when colored become hard and cold.[18]

The influence of Overbeck's figure drawing is evident in the compositional studies by William Dyce (1806–64) [28] and Daniel Maclise (1806–70) [29] in the winning schemes for the Houses of Parliament as well as in Brown's unsuccessful cartoons. Maclise's proposal for the set subject 'The Spirit of Justice' was more coherent than Brown's, whose composition was arranged to show many of the characters staring out of the picture space, as if confronting the viewer, while the main drama is enacted in the foreground [32]. The figure of the Baron, accused of murder by a widow clutching a child to her breast, was particularly effective [30, 31].

Although Brown's entries for the cartoon competitions were not successful, the idea of giving a contemporary significance to history paintings using accurate historical details was to have a lasting effect on his subsequent work. Not only does *The Spirit of Justice* have the general compositional groupings of large simple forms important for fresco painting, but Brown also introduces a wealth of incident that depends upon individual life drawings and drapery studies, some of them finely detailed. The three works that developed out of the Westminster competition – *The Seeds and Fruits of English Poetry* [33], *Chaucer at the Court of Edward III* [34, 35] and *Wycliffe Reading his Translation of the Bible* (1848, Cartwright Hall, Bradford), are stages in an increasingly inflected realism that anticipates and runs parallel to Pre-Raphaelitism. When Rossetti approached Brown asking for lessons, he did so

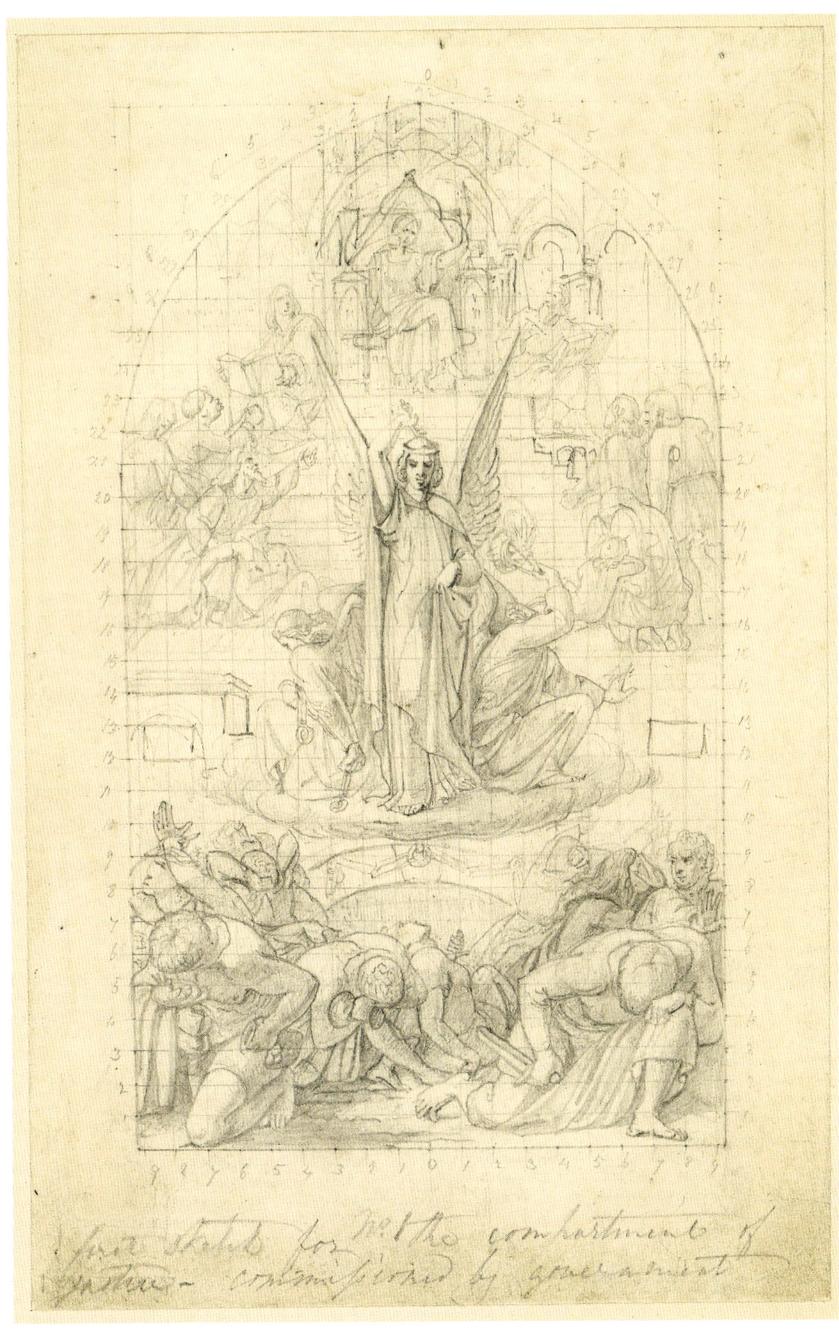

29 Daniel Maclise, *Study for 'The Spirit of Justice'*, c. 1848, The British Museum, London

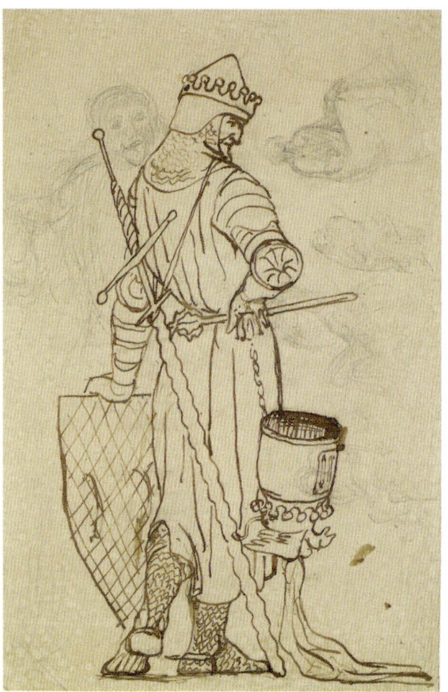
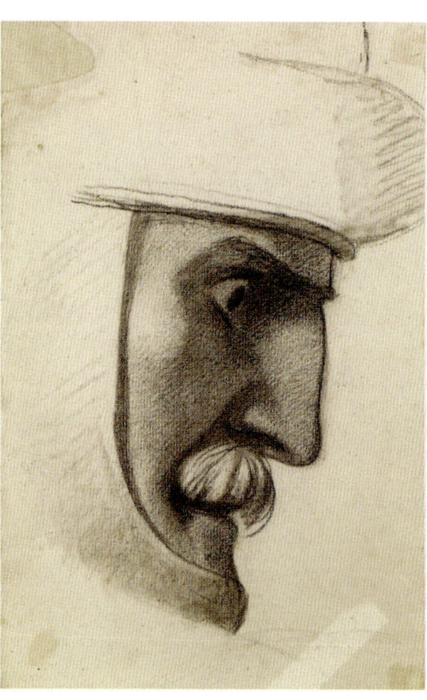

30 Ford Madox Brown, *Study for 'The Spirit of Justice': A Baron and his Advisor*, 1845, Birmingham Museums & Art Gallery

31 Ford Madox Brown, *Study for 'The Spirit of Justice': Head of a Baron*, 1845, Birmingham Museums & Art Gallery

because he found qualities in his work not present in other contemporary paintings or in the instruction offered at the Royal Academy Schools.

Brown's interest in representing the inner motivation of his characters, and the historical accuracy of their surroundings and costumes, places these works beyond the usual practices or abilities of his contemporaries. Both elements imbue his works with a kind of transgressive authenticity that cuts through the conventions of high art. On the other hand, his drawings for scenes from Shakespeare's *King Lear* [36], for example, have a large element of the theatricality that one would expect from James Barry (1741–1806) or even Henry Fuseli (1741–1825), history painters of an earlier generation; the central action is seemingly bound by a proscenium arch. In this way

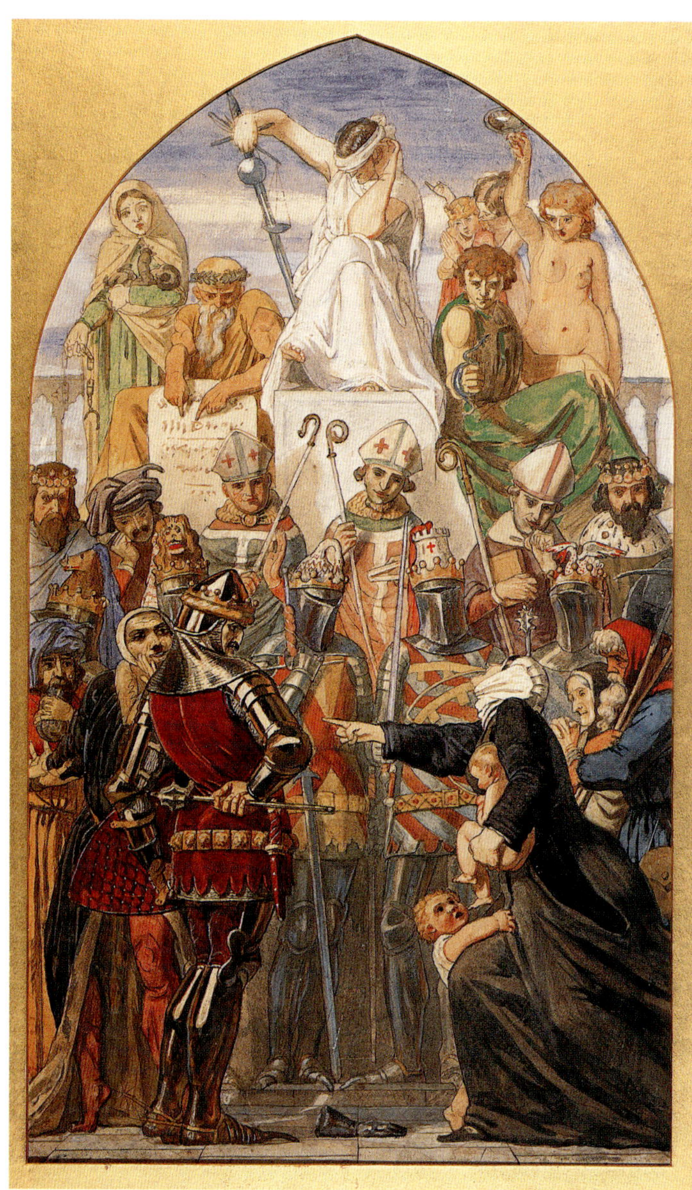

32 Ford Madox Brown, *Study for 'The Spirit of Justice'*, 1845, Manchester City Galleries

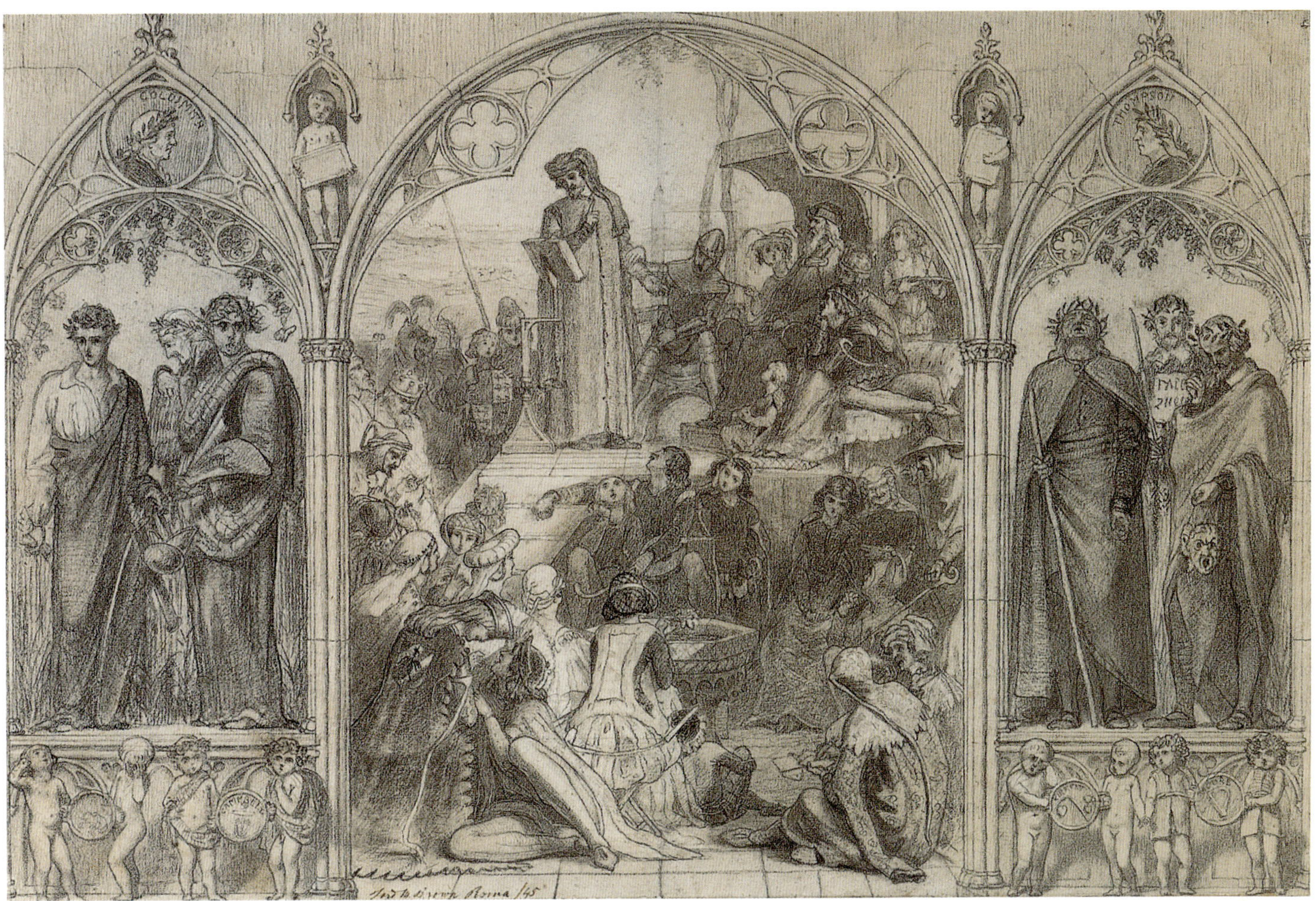

33 Ford Madox Brown, *Study for 'The Seeds and Fruits of English Poetry'*, 1845, Cecil Higgins Art Gallery, Bedford

Brown's compositions differ from the intimacy of the emotional confrontations that we encounter in Shakespearean compositions by Millais, Hunt and Rossetti. Even at an early stage of its compositional evolution, however, Brown's work has a truth of gesture and relationship that leads the viewer away from the stage and acting and towards life and observed behaviour.

Brown outlined his methods for history painting in his essay 'On the Mechanism of a Historical Picture', published in *The Germ* in 1850. Having selected the 'fit subject', the initial stages were research, deep consideration of 'every means that may assist the clear development of the story' and the grouping of the figures, 'disposing of them in such agreeable clusters or situations…as may be compatible with the dramatic truth of the whole'.[19] Then came the sketching stage. Brown recommended that it should include observing oneself in the mirror or drawing from friends, but not –

at this point – using 'ordinary paid models' who would be 'stiff and feelingless…and curb the vivacity of a first conception'.[20] The process was intended to make the artist feel each gesture and to understand his 'actors':

> studying them one after the other, limb for limb, hand for hand, finger for finger, noting each inflection of joint, or tension of sinew, searching for dramatic truth internally in himself, and in all external nature, shunning affectation and exaggeration, and striving after pathos and purity of feeling, with patient endeavour and utter simplicity of heart.[21]

This is strikingly close to Ruskin's advocacy of fidelity to nature but is here applied to the study of the human figure rather than landscape. Brown's emphasis on internality, feeling and simplicity is similarly concerned with the practicalities of finding 'truth' in pictorial representation. This aim is also present in Pre-Raphaelite subjects that deal

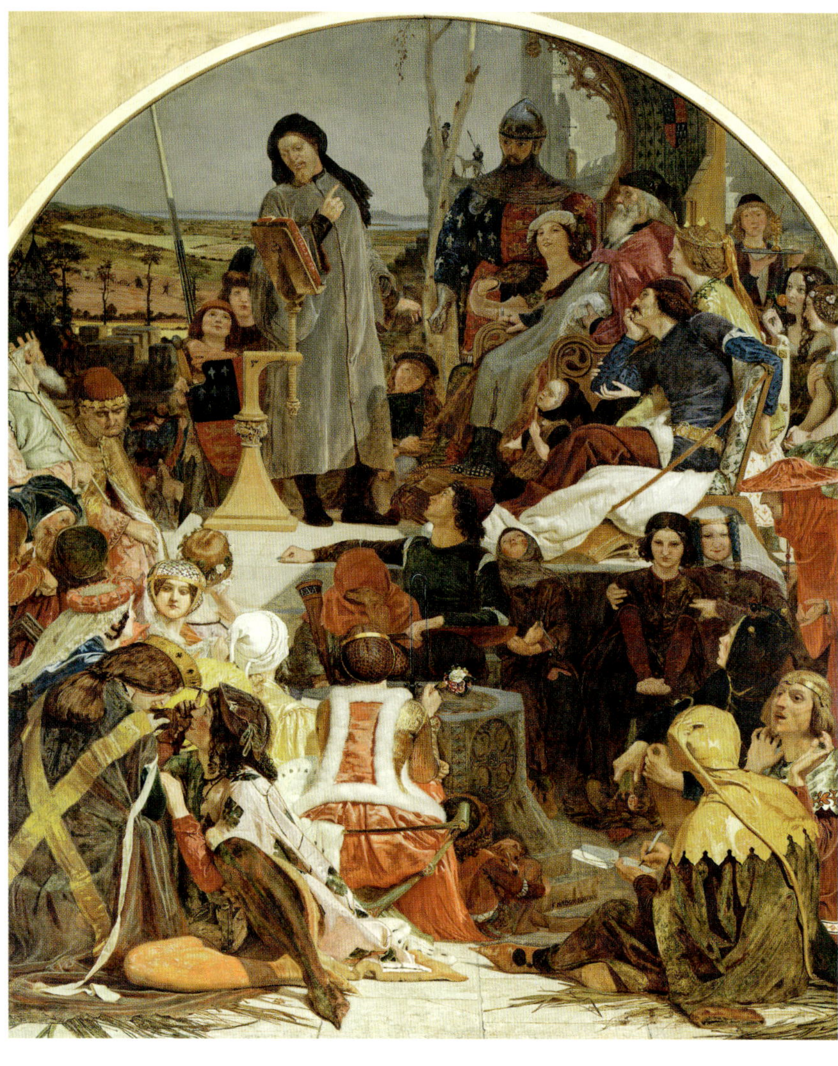

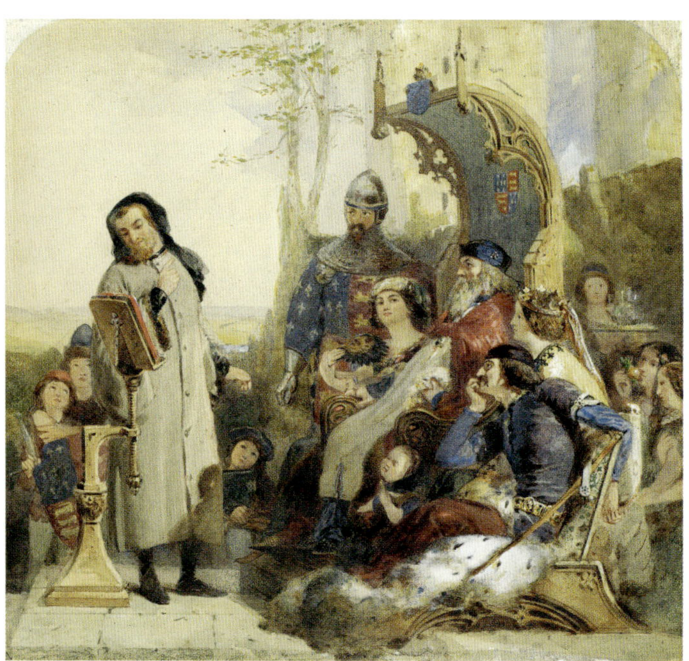

34 Ford Madox Brown, *Chaucer at the Court of Edward III*, 1847–51,
Art Gallery of New South Wales, Sydney

35 Ford Madox Brown, *Chaucer at the Court of Edward III*, *c.* 1854,
Birmingham Museums & Art Gallery

with dialogue and silence, internal struggle and mixed emotion, which were to be a strong feature of the drawings and paintings by Millais and Hunt.

A good example of how such narratives were explored pictorially can be found in Hunt's working out of the dramatic possibilities of internality in his drawings for *Claudio and Isabella* (1850) [37]. The subject, derived from Shakespeare's *Measure for Measure*, depicts an emotionally charged exchange between brother and sister. Hunt chose a moment from Act 3 in which their conversation is just about to turn to denunciation on the one hand and pleading on the other. Claudio, condemned to die after being found guilty of fornication, declares, 'Death is a fearful thing.' Isabella, whose virginity might have to be sacrificed to his captor to save his life, contradicts him, arguing, 'And shamed life a hateful.' In the studies for the picture, Hunt works out how much of the moral argument can be expressed through physical awkwardness. One aspect of the drawing threatens to undercut another: Hunt's attention to the details of clothing, even in a preparatory drawing, threatens the emotional truth of Isabella's gesture of affection and Claudio's mixed guilt, uncertainty and reluctance. The loving attention given to Claudio's pointed shoes is, perhaps, rather ludicrous in a painting striving for pathos and subtlety of feeling. Yet this uncomfortable relationship between various categories of truth and accuracy is characteristic of the early work of the Pre-Raphaelite Brotherhood. It is clearly at odds with the Old Master harmoniousness of pictorial elements that was the goal of academic history painting.

A general Pre-Raphaelite ambition for illustrating similar literary themes can be traced to the subjects set at the Cyclographic Society, a student society set up in 1848 for the encouragement of drawing. Several of the Pre-Raphaelites were members of the Cyclographic, which is often regarded as a preliminary stage in the formation of the Brotherhood. It was founded by Walter Howell Deverell

    The Flat, the Antique and the Life: Academic Drawing and the Pre-Raphaelites

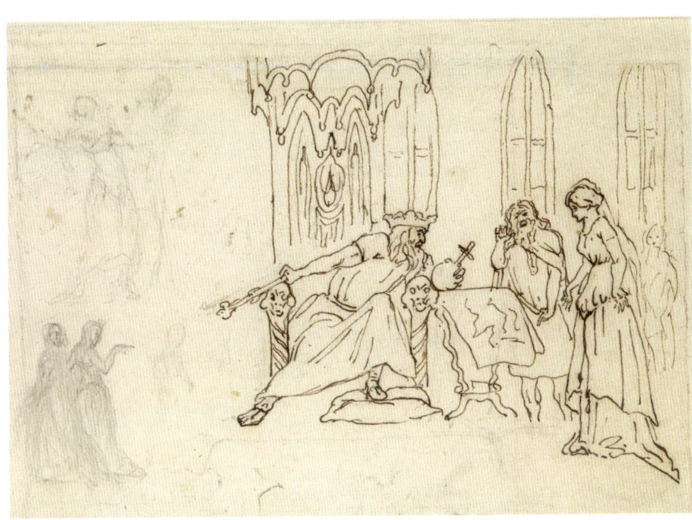

36 Ford Madox Brown, *Study for 'Lear and Cordelia'*, 1843–44, Birmingham Museums & Art Gallery

(1827–54) with N. E. Green and Richard Burchett, none of them destined to become full members of the Brotherhood, although Deverell was particularly close to the original group and his pictures share many characteristics with theirs. The historian of Pre-Raphaelitism William E. Fredeman has suggested that the Cyclographic was 'in some sense an exercise in Self-Help designed to supplement the instruction available in the various art schools and in the several training divisions of the Academy'.[22] Certainly there is a degree of truth in this assertion, although the Cyclographic was only one of several such societies that were formed by Royal Academy students in the first half of the nineteenth century, some of which foreshadowed Pre-Raphaelitism in their calls to reject convention. In these anti-academic aims we can find parallels between the Pre-Raphaelites and the group called 'The Ancients', whose key members were Samuel Palmer, Edward Calvert and George Richmond, who had met at the Academy Schools a generation before.[23] The rejection of academic rules by Palmer and his colleagues, their interest

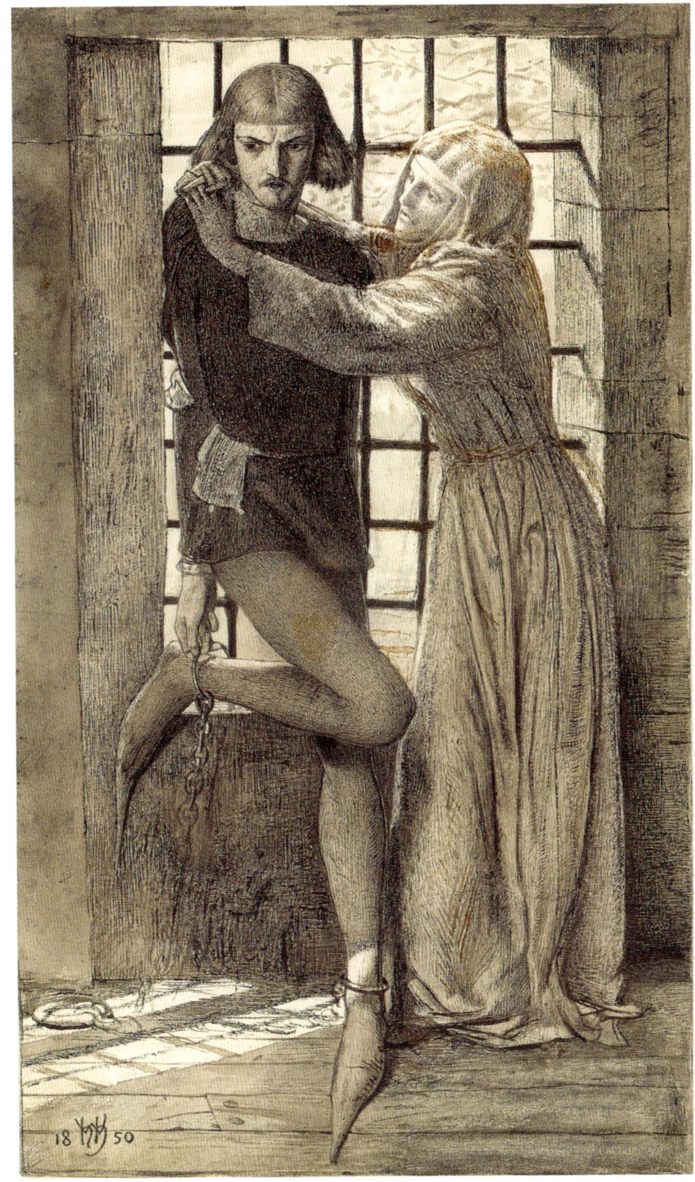

37 William Holman Hunt, *Study for 'Claudio and Isabella'*, 1850, Fitzwilliam Museum, Cambridge

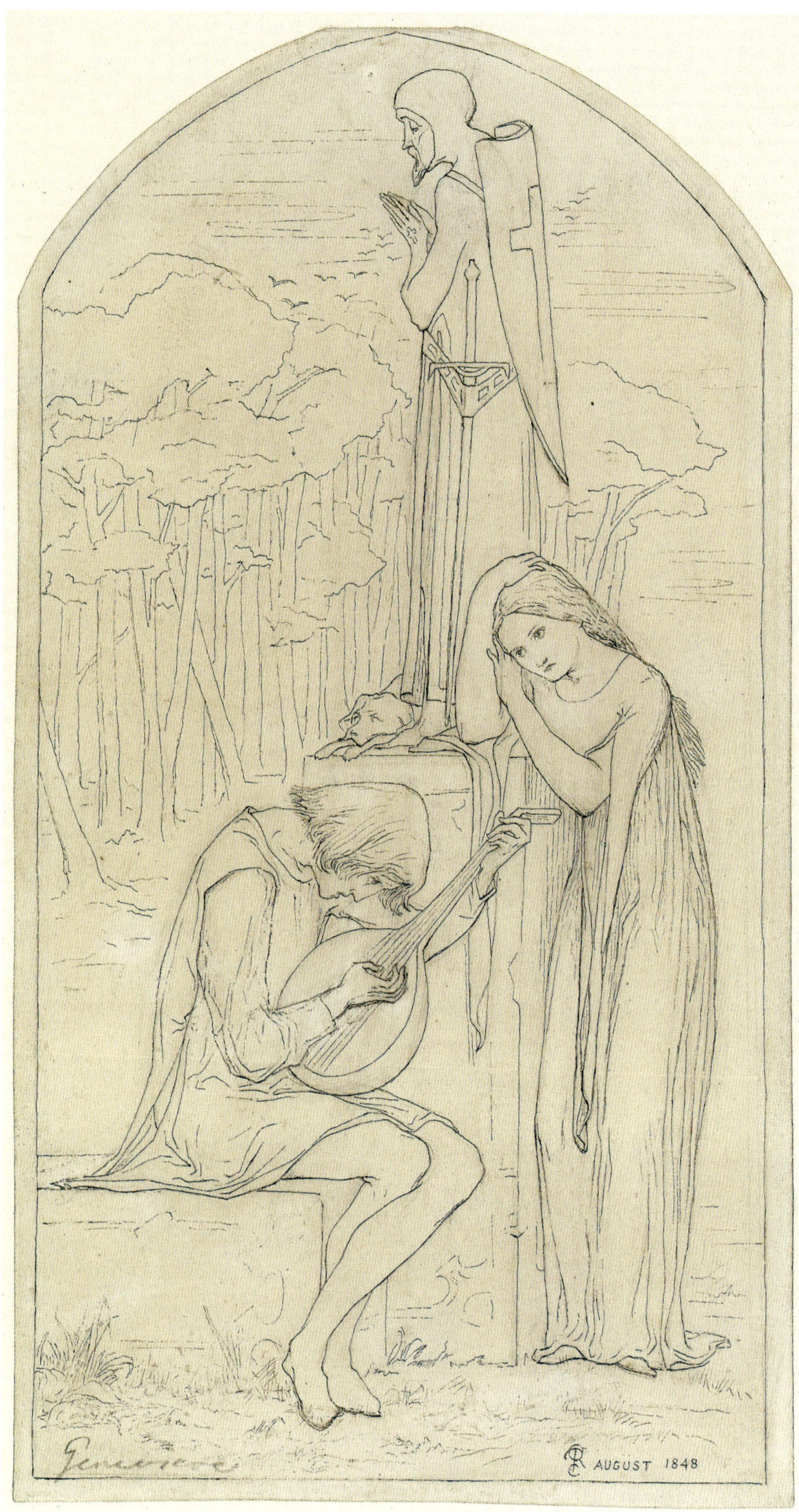

38 Dante Gabriel Rossetti, *Genevieve*, 1848, Fitzwilliam Museum, Cambridge

included Anna Mary Howitt (1824–84). In the history of the Pre-Raphaelite Brotherhood, the formation of the Folio Sketching Club in 1854 and the Hogarth Club in 1858 is further evidence of this tendency to form into groups and clubs, often centred around the activity of drawing. The Hogarth Club combined some of the social aims of these informal groups with professional concerns such as the exhibiting of works by its members.[24]

Groups such as the Cyclographic had a practical purpose rather than a radical or reforming one: they offered professional support and friendly advice or criticism from within the artist's peer group, and helped in sharing the costs of hiring models, even providing models from within the group. They augmented rather than challenged the Royal Academy and its schools, and asserted their difference from the prevailing orthodoxies in a variety of ways, often more startling than substantial, such as smoking pipes and drinking quantities of ale, growing their hair long and wearing unusual clothes. Their existence is part of a lively history of bohemianism in Britain in the mid-nineteenth century. The significance of the Cyclographic, however, was in bringing together the three artists who would become the most active members of the Pre-Raphaelite Brotherhood: Rossetti, Hunt and Millais. It offered them the opportunity to challenge the picture-making formulae of the Academy Schools by stimulating the revival and modification of the outline style in their drawings (see Chapter 2), and encouraging experimentation in new compositional strategies for the production of subject paintings. Members nominated subjects for compositions; the drawings were then circulated at meetings and critical notices were written in response. They were requested

> to write their remarks in ink, concisely and legibly, avoiding SATIRE or RIDICULE, which ever defeat the true end of criticism, and are more likely to produce unkindly feeling and dissension.[25]

in early Italian painting and their sincerity of purpose have an echo in the later movement.

Rossetti had joined a sketching club in 1843 and later was, with Barbara Bodichon (1827–91), instrumental in the formation of the Portfolio Club, whose members

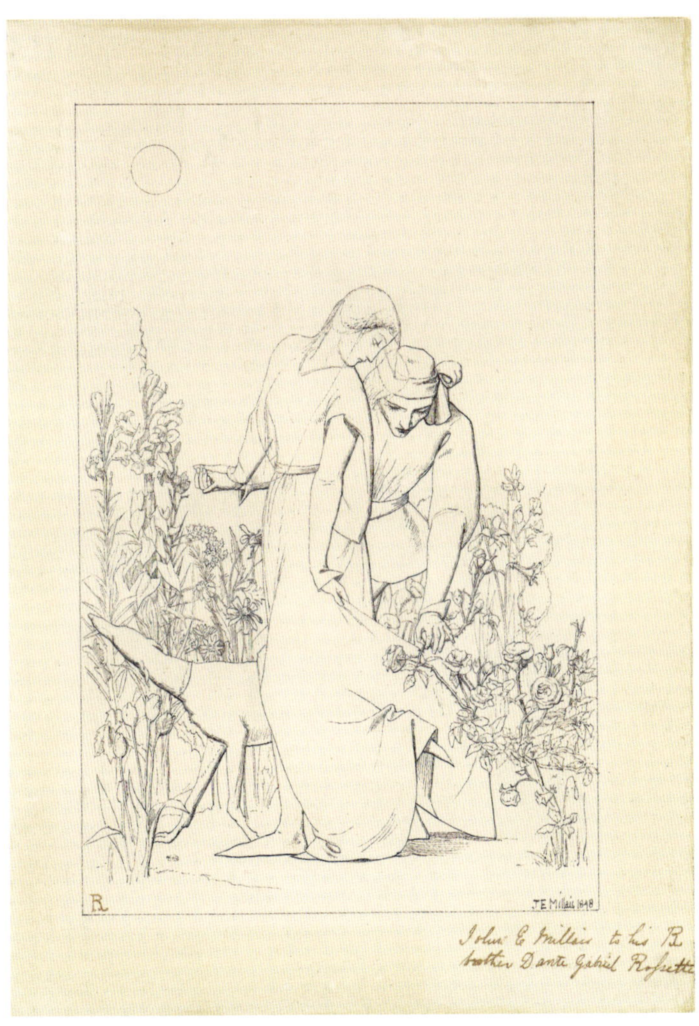

39 John Everett Millais, *Lovers by a Rosebush ('My Beautiful Lady')*, 1848, Birmingham Museums & Art Gallery

It is seen also in Hunt's *Claudio and Isabella* (1850, Tate) and Millais's *Lovers by a Rosebush* (1848) [**39**] and was a significant narrative device for all three artists throughout their careers. The criticisms of the rest of the members of the Cyclographic reveal a close reading of the delicate emotions portrayed in the drawing. Millais commented on the way in which

> the love of St. Genevieve growing simultaneously with the strains of the minstrel's touch is well expressed; but the latter is apparently too deeply absorbed in his occupation and thus seems heedless of her sympathy.[27]

This theme anticipates the motifs of music in Rossetti's later works, and the issue of self-absorption was to emerge in one of his first Pre-Raphaelite drawings, *Dante Drawing an Angel on the First Anniversary of the Death of Beatrice* [**56**].[28] In *Genevieve*, as in other early compositional studies by members of the Pre-Raphaelite Brotherhood, we catch a glimpse of narrative approaches and stylistic innovations that promised much for later developments.

The Cyclographic encouraged imagination over academic skill. It was important in setting its members subjects derived from literature that invited small-scale compositions where the emphasis was on individual interpretation. These were key factors in the more ambitious works just about to be undertaken by the Pre-Raphaelite Brotherhood, which were to distance them further from the Royal Academy, its training methods and the expectations of its annual exhibitions.

Rossetti's surviving Cyclographic work, *Genevieve* (1848) [**38**], which he described as 'certainly the best thing I have done',[26] was derived from a subject by Samuel Taylor Coleridge. It introduced an important compositional device that was to become a trademark of his later work: a drama concentrated on a dialogue between a man and a woman.

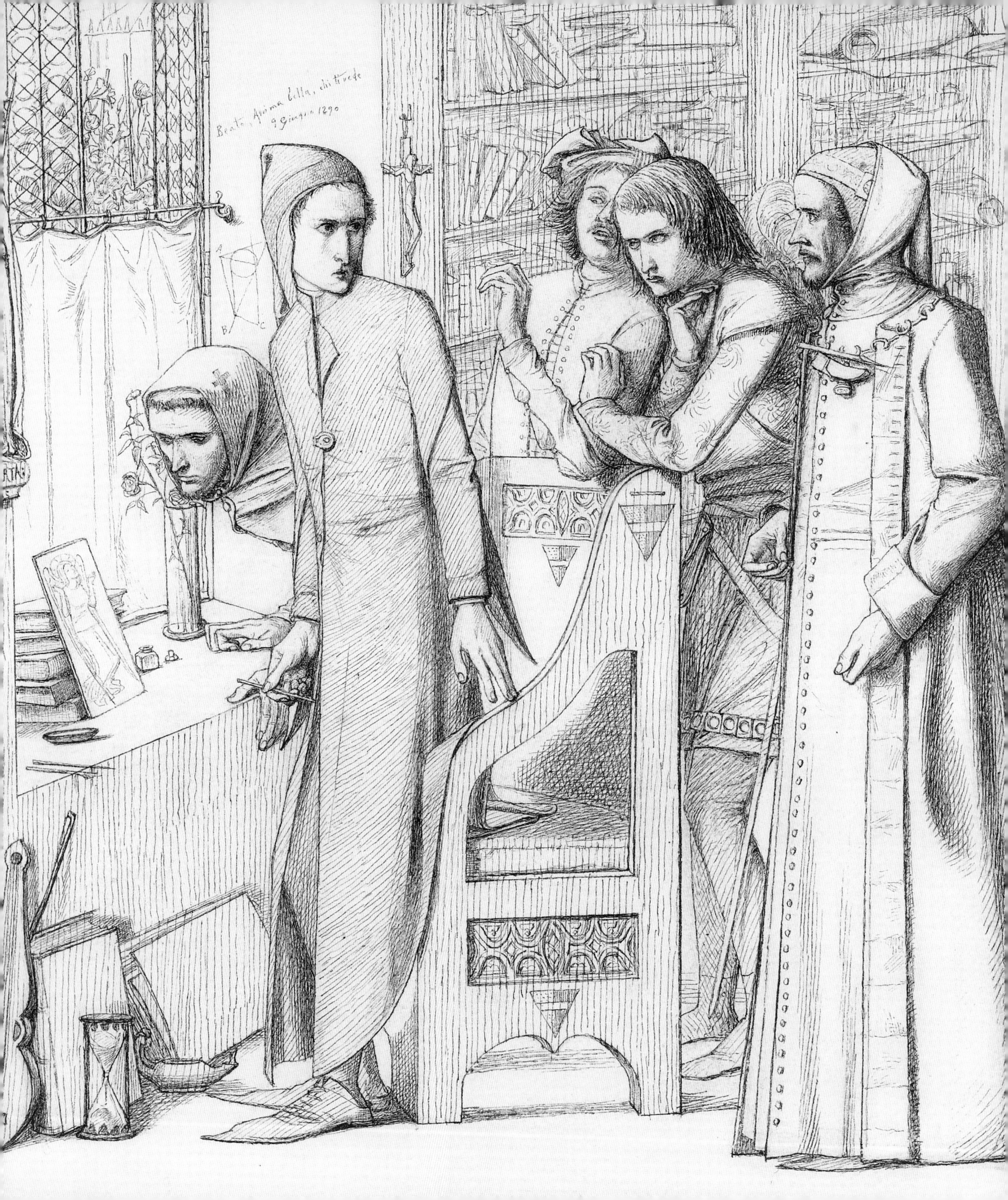

Beata Anima bella, chi ti vede
9 Giugno 1290

Chapter 2 *Direct and Heartfelt: Early Influences on Pre-Raphaelite Drawing*

The concept of 'correct drawing' haunted writings on art and the training of artists in the nineteenth century. It was challenged not by artists alone, but by writers on art, too. In his hugely influential study of early Italian art, *Sketches of the History of Christian Art* (1847), Lord Lindsay offered a revision of the subject of art training and its goal that was suggestive for artists and historians alike:

> It is not by studying art in its perfection – by worshipping Raphael and Michel Angelo exclusively of all other excellence – that we can expect to rival them, but reascending to the fountain-head – by placing ourselves as acorns in the ground those oaks are rooted in, and growing up to their level.[1]

Lindsay advised starting at the beginning – with artists such as Giotto – in order to arrive at the qualities of Raphael and Michelangelo. In many ways the Pre-Raphaelites adopted a similar attitude. Their belief in the sincerity of the artist was to lead them to seek alternatives to the canon of Old Master art and to strive to reinvigorate the practice of making pictures.

Lasinio and a version of Christian art

To illustrate several of his points on wall-painting, Lord Lindsay noted with approval the engravings of Carlo Lasinio (1759–1838) published in his *Pitture a fresco del Campo Santo di Pisa* (1828). Lasinio had been appointed conservator and curator at the Campo Santo in 1807. His appointment coincided with the first wave of British antiquarian scholarship in early Italian painting, which included Lindsay's work.[2] John Ruskin noted Lasinio's book disparagingly when reviewing Lindsay's *Christian Art* for the *Quarterly Review* in June 1847, criticizing the 'inaccuracy' of the engravings:

> No work of Lasinio's can be trusted for *anything* except the number and relative position of the figures. All masters are by him translated into one monotony

40 Dante Gabriel Rossetti, *Dante Drawing an Angel on the First Anniversary of the Death of Beatrice*, 1849, Birmingham Museums & Art Gallery (detail)

of commonplace: he dilutes eloquences, educates naïveté, prompts ignorance, stultifies intelligence, and paralyses power; takes the chill off horror, the edge off wit, and the bloom off beauty. In all artistical points he is utterly valueless, neither drawing nor expression being ever preserved by him. Giotto, Benozzo, or Ghirlandajo are all alike to him; and we hardly know whether he injures most when he robs or when he redresses.[3]

Nevertheless, Lasinio's engravings (and those of his son, G. P. Lasinio) were to be of immense importance for the understanding of how Quattrocento art looked.

In the first volume of his recollections of the Pre-Raphaelite Brotherhood, published in 1905, Hunt described the impact of Lasinio's volume, admitting its appeal while rejecting its influence. He conflated the frescoes by Benozzo Gozzoli (*c.* 1421–97) with their representation in the engravings, a confusion apparent in his comments:

> We had recognized as we turned from one print to another that the Campo Santo designs were remarkable for incident derived from attentive observation of inexhaustible Nature, and dwelt on all their quaint charms of invention….Yet we did not curb our amusement at the immature perspective, the undeveloped power of drawing, the feebleness of light and shade, the ignorance of any but mere black and white differences of racial types of men, the stinted varieties of flora, and their geometrical forms in the landscape; these simplicities, already out of date in the painter's day, we noted as belonging altogether to the past and to the dead revivalists, with whom we had determined to have neither part nor lot.[4]

By the time of writing his memories of the formation of the Brotherhood in 1904, Hunt might have confused his earlier, more positive memories of Lasinio's work. In recalling collective amusement at the 'immature perspective' and the 'undeveloped power of drawing', he forgot that these were the very qualities imitated by his Pre-Raphaelite Brothers in their own drawings at the time. Despite Hunt's disavowal it is clear that Lasinio's volume of engravings represented an alternative pictorial expression to that presented by the Old Masters as translated by the instructors at the Royal Academy Schools. In turning the attention of his audience towards works that were so clearly 'primitive' and unorthodox, Lasinio's work had an impact far in excess of the many contemporary volumes of engravings after works of art.

Despite Hunt's mixed reception, it is clear that Lasinio's book was important for the young artists in allowing a proximity, even if at one remove, with non-canonical works that had a freshness of vision based on observation of 'inexhaustible Nature'. A significant factor in the importance of the book for the Pre-Raphaelites was that they had limited access to early Renaissance art at this time, when the National Gallery was only just beginning to amass its holdings in early Renaissance paintings. The appreciation of the works of artists such as Gozzoli was otherwise confined chiefly to curators and connoisseurs. Lasinio's book of engravings – itself restricted to relatively wealthy print collectors, even by 1848 – was to permit close scrutiny of works otherwise almost completely inaccessible. Confining wall-sized frescoes to the limits of the printed page allowed the easy assimilation of compositional structures and narrative details. However crowded and varied compositions such as Gozzoli's *The Drunkenness of Noah* (1832) [41] were in fresco, in print form they could be taken in at a glance as if they were single-sheet compositional studies.

In his summary of the aims of the Pre-Raphaelite Brotherhood, William Michael Rossetti recalled that they wanted to 'sympathize with what is direct and heartfelt in previous art to the exclusion of what is conventional and

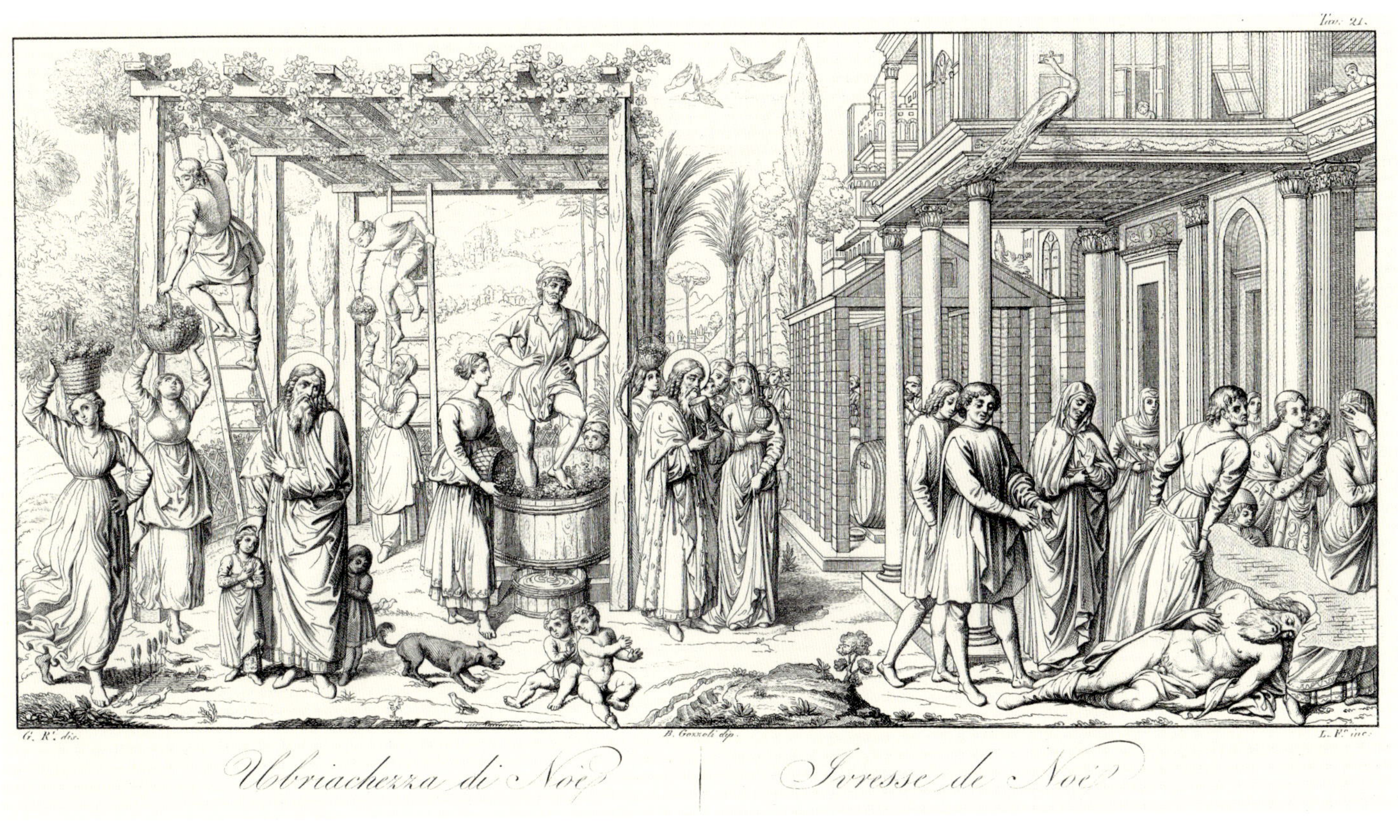

41 G. P. Lasinio after Benozzo Gozzoli, *The Drunkenness of Noah*, 1832, Birmingham Libraries & Archives

self-parading, and learned by rote'.[5] Many of those qualities of directness and heartfeltness were gained by looking at early Italian and Northern European art. Yet the emulation of these qualities by the Pre-Raphaelites was suggested by examination of engravings rather than easel paintings or frescoes. There is an implicit conflict in advocating the practices of working directly from nature while working from sources in which nature has already been selected and stylized. This is further complicated when, as Ruskin held, the source material is 'translated' by an engraver of suspect skill. G. F. Waagen (1794–1868), the German art historian, saw emulation of early Italian and Northern European art as arising from an 'erroneous principle'. He believed that contemporary German and British artists produced a retrogressive art, which had

> not only the beauties, but the defects of their great models; unmindful of the fact, which a general survey of the history of art does not fail to teach, that those early masters attract us not on account of their meagre drawing, hard outlines, erroneous perspective, conventional glories, &c., but, on the contrary, in spite of these defects and peculiarities.[6]

For Waagen, striving for 'feeling' through emulation of technical defects was retrogressive and produced 'faults'

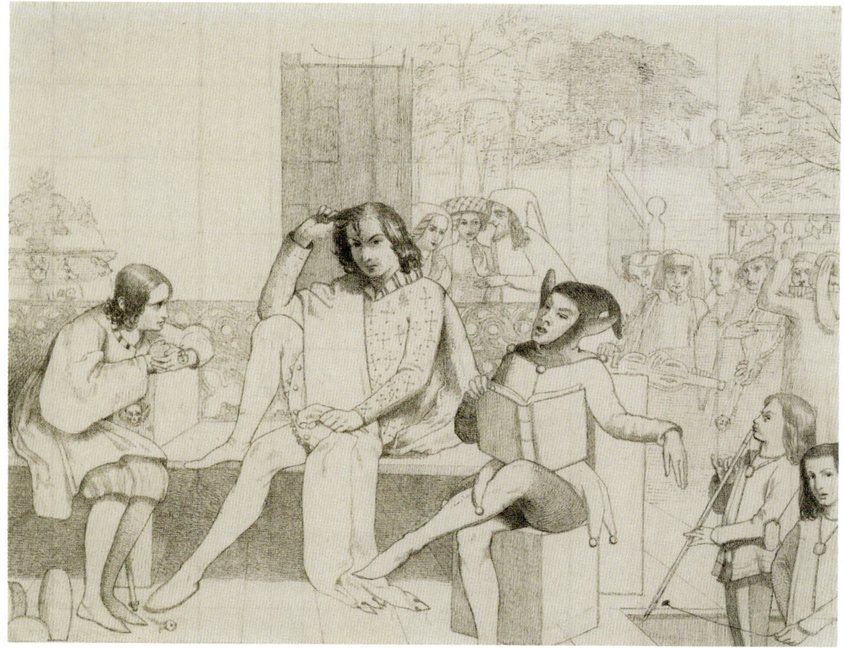

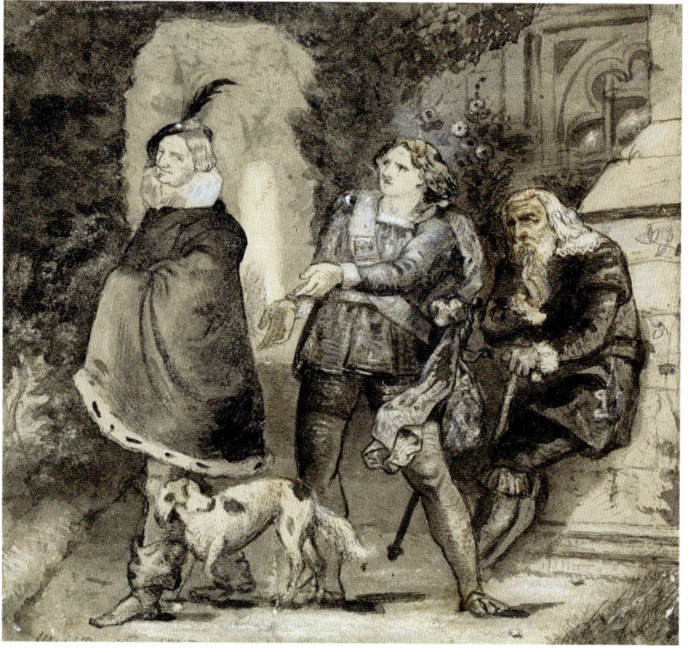

42 Walter Howell Deverell, *Study for 'Twelfth Night'*, c. 1850, Tate
43 Walter Howell Deverell, *Study for 'The Banishment of Hamlet'*, 1847, Ashmolean Museum, University of Oxford

directly relating to issues traditionally ascribed to drawing rather than to painting, such as perspective, distortions of proportion and a faulty understanding of anatomy.

Lasinio's engravings, being both linear and monochromatic, demonstrated the strength of composition and structure over colour and texture. Such was the case,

too, with the outline engravings after designs by Moritz Retzsch (1779–1857), the German illustrator and painter. His work was extraordinarily successful in engraved form throughout the first half of the nineteenth century. Although already a little old-fashioned by the late 1840s, Retzsch's style provided a distinct alternative to the tonal drawing method taught at the Royal Academy. The 'stiffness' of the figures of Lasinio's engravings and the austere outlines found in Retzsch's, became the twin signs of a graphic modernity, an abandonment of the tyranny of academic drawing. Both represented the power of graphic communication through simple – even stark – linearity, the result of which was that early Pre-Raphaelite drawings were often so restricted in their range of marks that they seemed like engravings.

Two compositional studies by Walter Howell Deverell, both of them Shakespearean subjects, are good examples of this tendency [42, 43]. The significance of the choice of Shakespeare was itself, no doubt, stimulated by the example of Retzsch, whose outline illustrations to Shakespeare's plays were among his most influential publications. The studied awkwardness of Deverell's figures and the use of disrupted background spaces to make compositional groupings that help in narrating a story could be seen as derivative of the Campo Santo volume. On the other hand, the focus on the figures rather than the setting, the individual reactions of the figures, their groupings and interrelationships, are derived from Retzsch.

F. G. Stephens's *Dethe and the Riotours* (1852) [50] also bears distinct signs of acquaintance with Lasinio's engravings. The artist's attention to the hard folds of drapery, the deliberate masking of the reactions of one figure by another, the inclusion of a little dog to add anecdote to the narrative, as well as the spiky awkwardness of the poses, are clearly derived from the Campo Santo plates, such as *The Drunkenness of Noah* [41]. It is striking, however, that Stephens arranged his figures in an English landscape of open fields seen from the edge of a wood – a landscape in keeping with the subject's Chaucerian source – rather than the architectural settings favoured by Gozzoli. This variation suggests that the two impulses – of copying from the early Italian artists and working directly from nature (discussed in Chapter 3) – were operating together to produce the unique combination of drawing styles in Pre-Raphaelitism.

The Pre-Raphaelites and the outline style

The 'outline style', as it became known, reduced the description of the world to line; it withdrew from the sophisticated, highly elaborated form of expression that had been the role of painting, reducing the repertoire of visual experience to the sparsest language. Everything in the resulting picture was delineated, nothing shaded or, except in the most rudimentary way, patterned. Yet conversely, this reduction of pictorial means stimulated the viewer's imagination. Outline encouraged the viewer to develop a new and heightened imaginative relationship with the engraved illustration. The viewer's role in both deciphering spatial relationships and reading nuances of feeling was acute. A review of *Retzsch's Outlines to Shakespeare* (1828) emphasized the suggestive nature of this drawing style:

> As in the instance of the first slight sketch of the
> painter, our imagination fills up the imperfect outline
> with the colours and effects of nature, and embodies
> the faint indication with the animated realities of life.[7]

Outline raised issues about the relationship of the illustration to the text, too. It challenged the primacy of literature to communicate complex situations or heightened emotions. Outline engravings were often published separately from the text, yet invited comparison with the poetic or dramatic source. As the Pre-Raphaelite scholar Alastair Grieve notes, the outline style 'was particularly suitable for illustrating plays and narrative poems',[8]

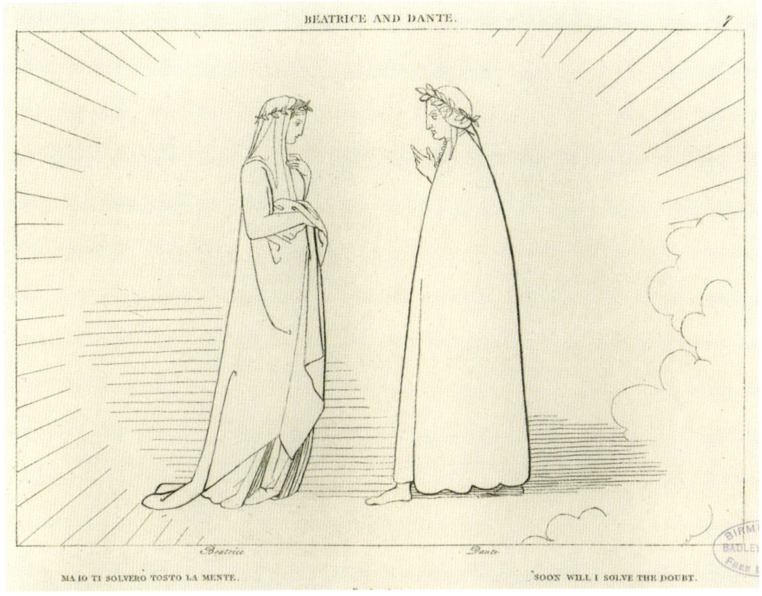

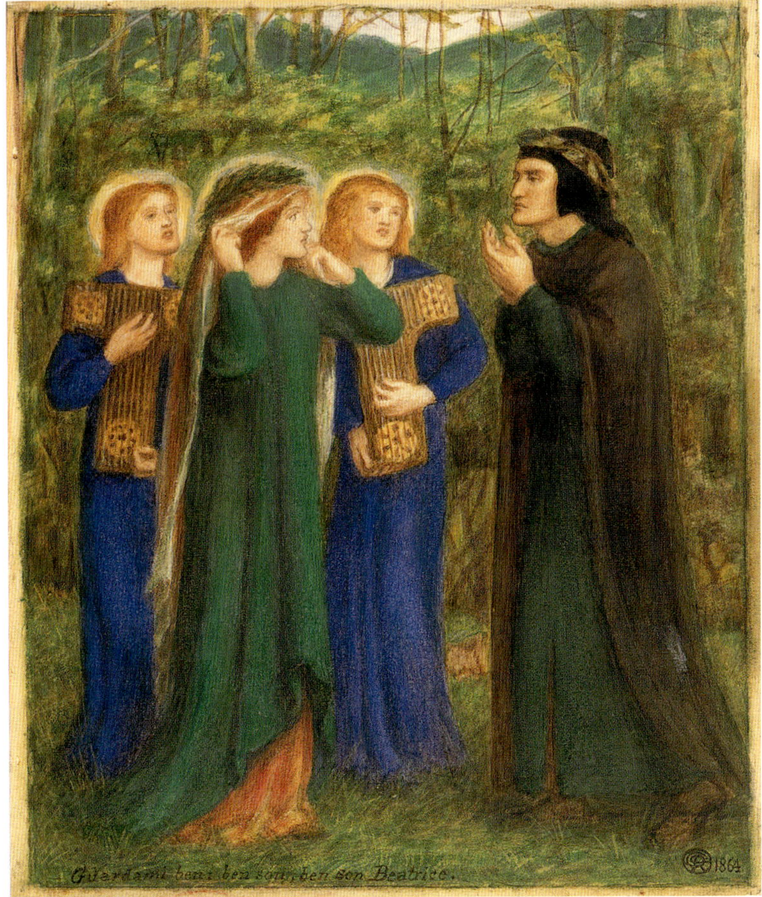

44 John Flaxman, *Paradise: Beatrice and Dante*, 1807, Birmingham Libraries & Archives

45 Dante Gabriel Rossetti, *The Meeting of Beatrice and Dante in Paradise*, 1864, Manchester City Galleries

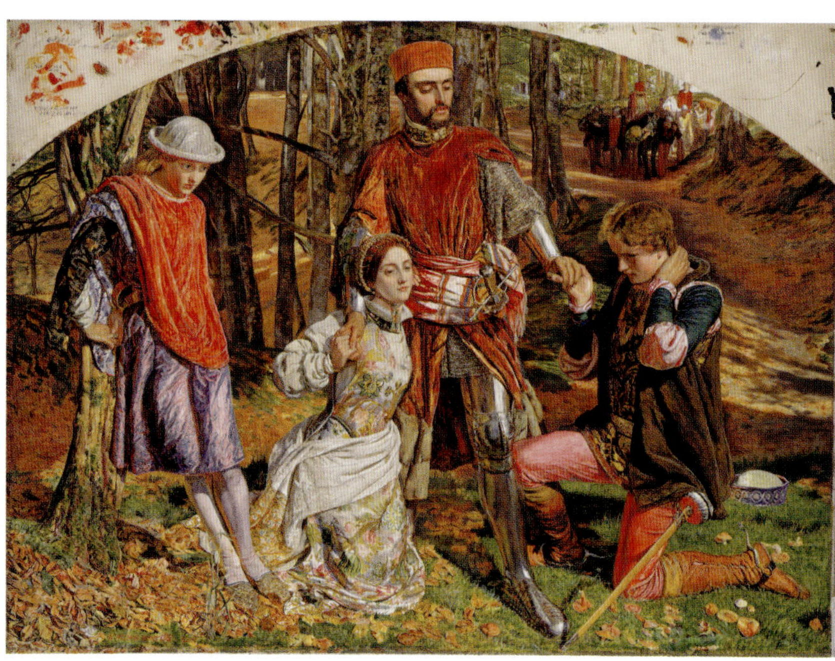

46 William Holman Hunt, *Valentine Rescuing Sylvia from Proteus*, 1850–51, Birmingham Museums & Art Gallery

a tradition that had grown up in the 1820s and 1830s but which had its origins in the suites of engravings after drawings by John Flaxman (1755–1826), the neoclassical sculptor and draughtsman. Flaxman's designs had a huge impact on early nineteenth-century illustration and even some lingering influence on the Pre-Raphaelites in the mid-century. In a notable example, Rossetti directly borrowed a composition from one of Flaxman's illustrations to Dante's *Paradiso* [44] to depict the meeting of Beatrice and Dante [45].

Flaxman's outlines to Dante were not approved of by Ruskin, who cited them as

> examples of almost every kind of falsehood and feebleness which it is possible for a trained artist, not base in thought, to commit or admit, both in design and execution…you cannot have a more finished

example of a learned error, amiable want of meaning, and bad drawing with a steady hand.

He added that

> Retzsch's outlines have more real material in them than Flaxman's, occasionally showing true fancy and power; in artistic principle they are nearly as bad, and in taste, worse.[9]

While Flaxman's greatest successes were with illustrations to the epic poems of Homer and Dante's *Divina Commedia*, in the hands of Retzsch the outline style became associated with a more modern literature of Northern Europe, of Shakespeare and Goethe. As a consequence, the outline style migrated from its association with neoclassicism to become the preferred illustration mode of early Romanticism. The further utilization of outline in Pre-Raphaelitism speaks of its ability to represent dramatic and poetic themes often from Romantic and medieval sources.

Often there were direct quotations from Retzsch's illustrations to Goethe (first published in 1816) [57] and Shakespeare (published from 1828 onwards) [52] in both Cyclographic and early Pre-Raphaelite drawings in the outline style. For example, Hunt's drawing for Shakespeare's *The Two Gentlemen of Verona*, *Valentine Rescuing Sylvia from Proteus* [46, 47], shown at the Royal Academy in 1850, bears the signs of a close acquaintance with Retzsch's *King Lear* (Act 2, Scene 4) in its method of assembling a varied group of figures. Hunt did not always approve of Retzsch. In his critical response to Rossetti's outline for *Faust, Gretchen and Mephistopheles in Church* (1848), presented for the appraisal of the members of the Cyclographic Society, Hunt commented:

> This design is in such perfect feeling as to give me a far higher idea of Goethe than I have before obtained either from a translation, or the artificial illustrations of Retsch [sic].[10]

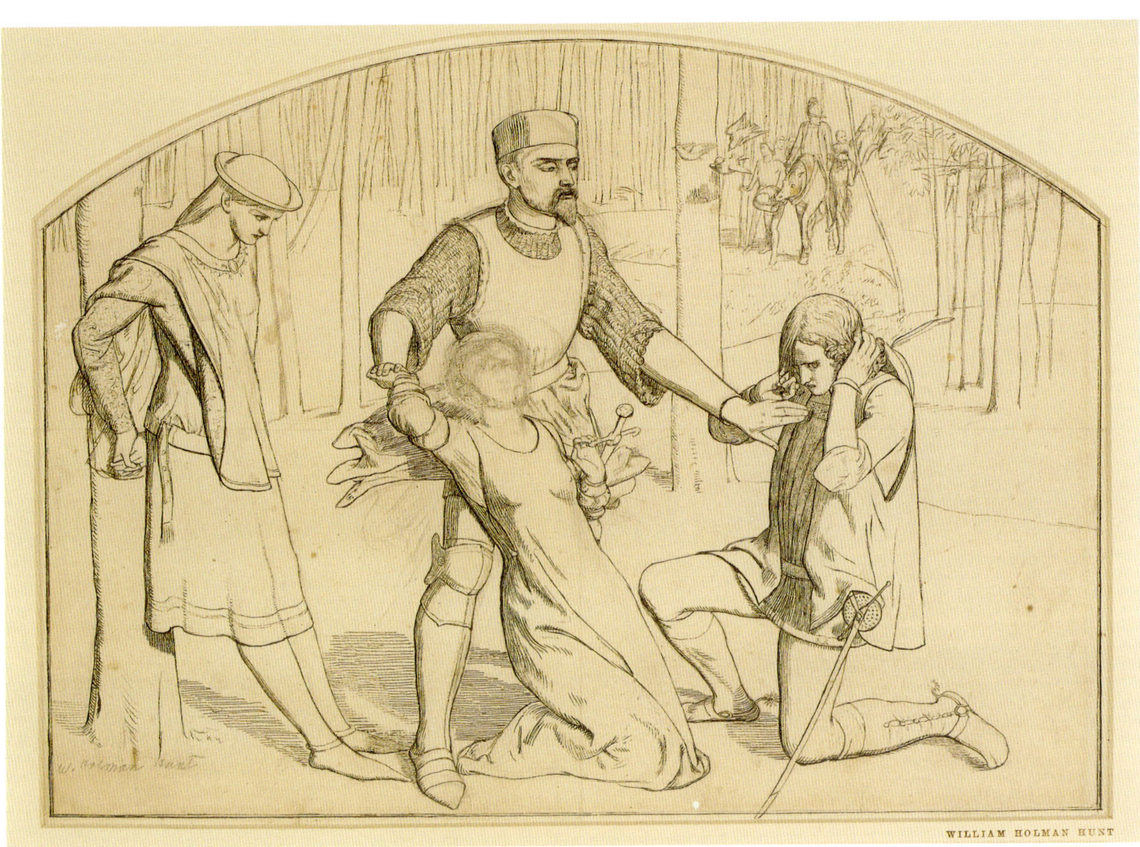

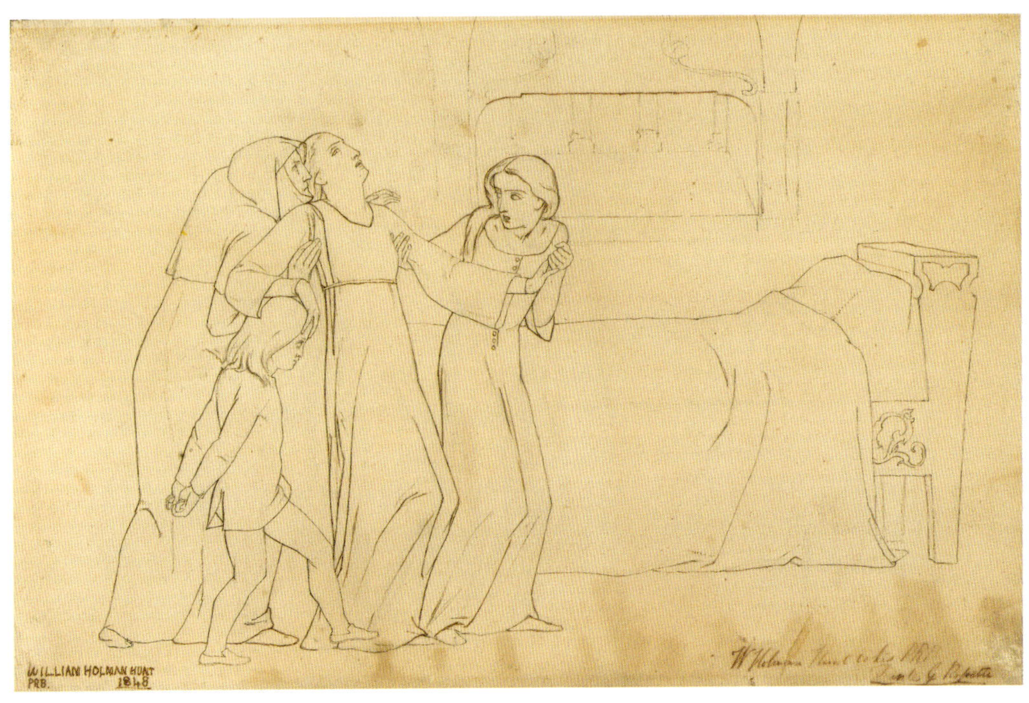

47 William Holman Hunt,
    Study for 'Valentine Rescuing
    Sylvia from Proteus', 1850,
    The British Museum, London

48 William Holman Hunt,
    One Step to the Death Bed, 1848,
    Yale Center for British Art

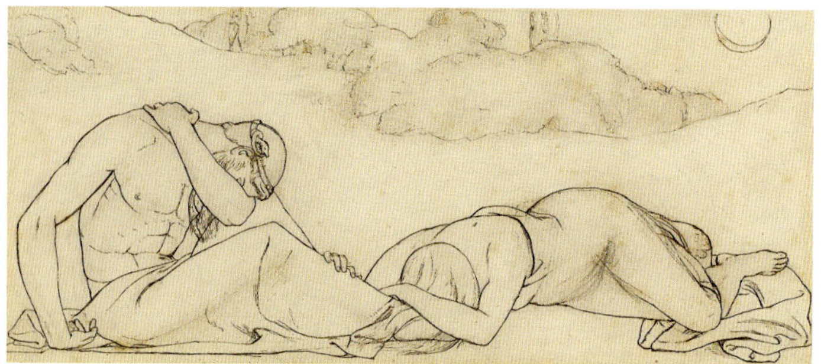

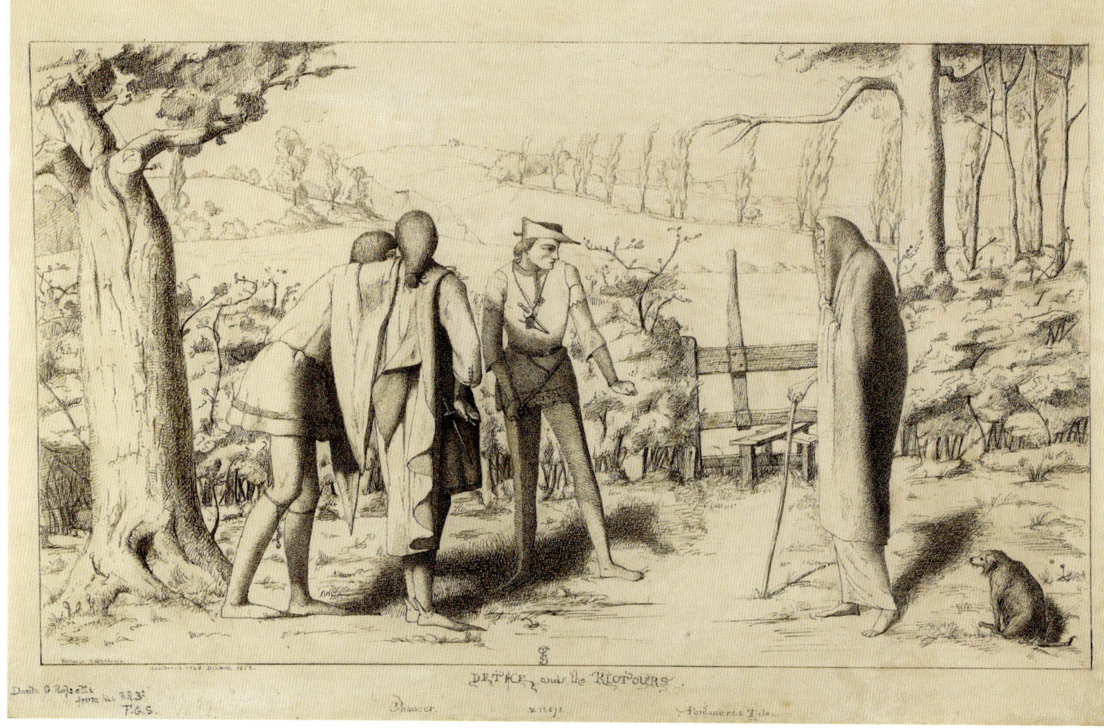

50 Frederic George Stephens, *Dethe and the Riotours*, 1852, Ashmolean Museum, University of Oxford

Nevertheless, Hunt himself was to use outline effectively several times, eliciting deep emotion from it – for example, in his designs for Keats's *Hyperion* (1847) [49] and *One Step to the Death Bed* (1848) [48], an illustration for Shelley's 'Ginevra', both of which were most probably designed for the Cyclographic. The figure of Saturn in the Keats drawing is based on the Dionysos of the Parthenon frieze, indicating that Hunt's studies at the British Museum earlier in the decade had an impact on the way in which he imagined the human figure. It shows, too, the influence of Flaxman's outlines in dealing with weighty themes such as those contained in *Hyperion*. There is a tantalizing mixture of old neoclassical influences in Hunt's drawing as well as a feeling for Romantic poetry, just at the point when the Pre-Raphaelite Brotherhood was to formulate its radical aesthetic programme.

Millais's drawing for *The Tempest, Ferdinand Lured by Ariel* (1848) [53], predating his painting of the same subject exhibited at the Royal Academy in 1850 [54], is a good example of his early attempts to imagine the fantastic within the strict conventions of outline. It retains some of the elegant but tired linearity of Retzsch, which is noticeably absent in the painted version.[11] Millais used outline for a variety of youthful productions of varying ambitions. One example is particularly potent because it anticipates Millais's most controversial early painting. Like the compositional studies for *Christ in the House of his Parents* [6], the drawing *Andrea Ferara: The Armoury* (1844) [51] arranges figures in a workshop space, replete with fanciful tools and work implements, a cage of birds and two openings into varied exterior spaces. *Andrea Ferrara*, a subject reflecting the young artist's interest in armour, betrays the influence of Retzsch's outlines to Schiller's *Song of the Bell* of 1834, particularly Plate 2, *The Prologue – The Interior of the Foundry*, in which the complex interior space is handled with a particular crispness of line.

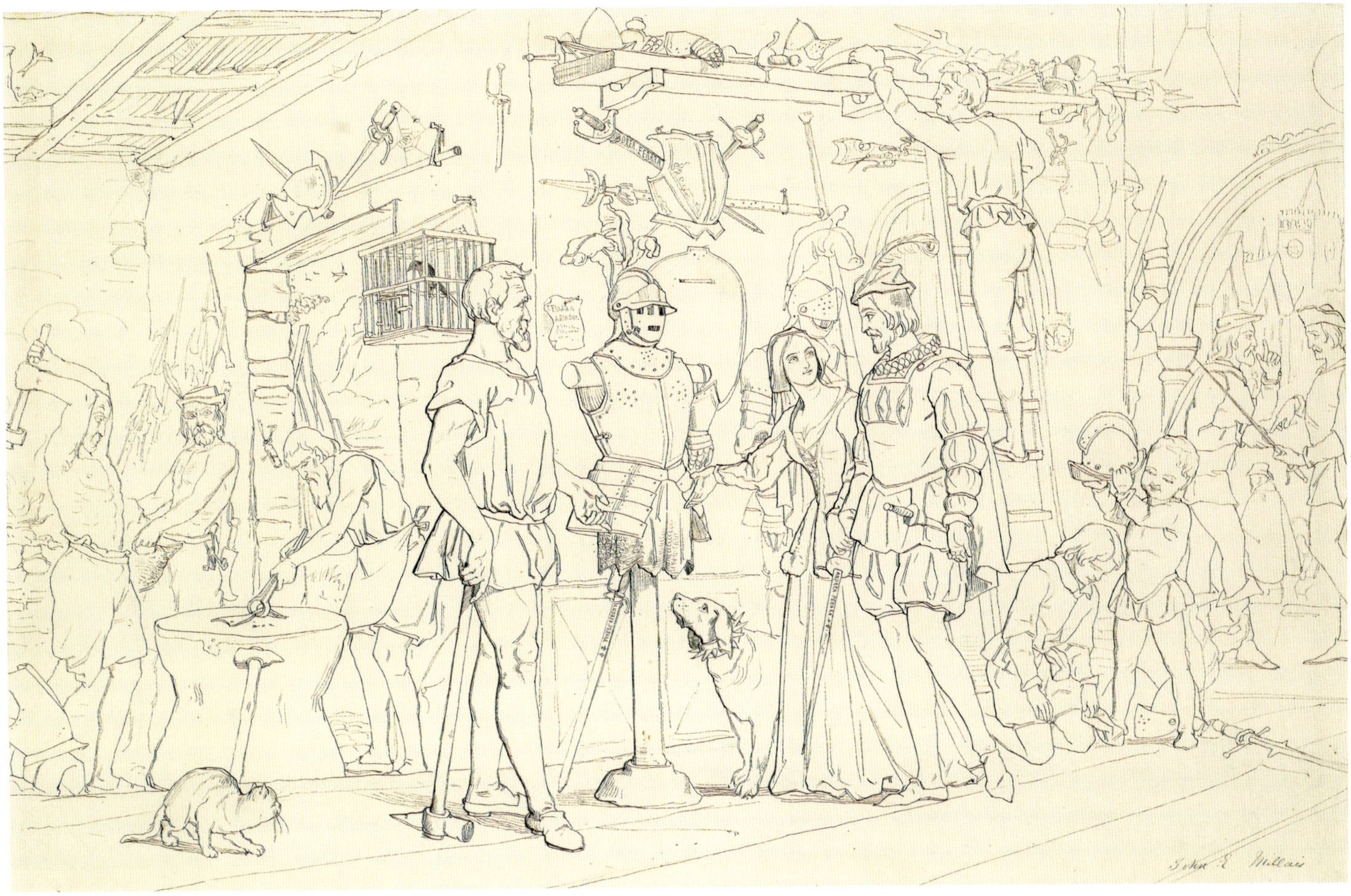

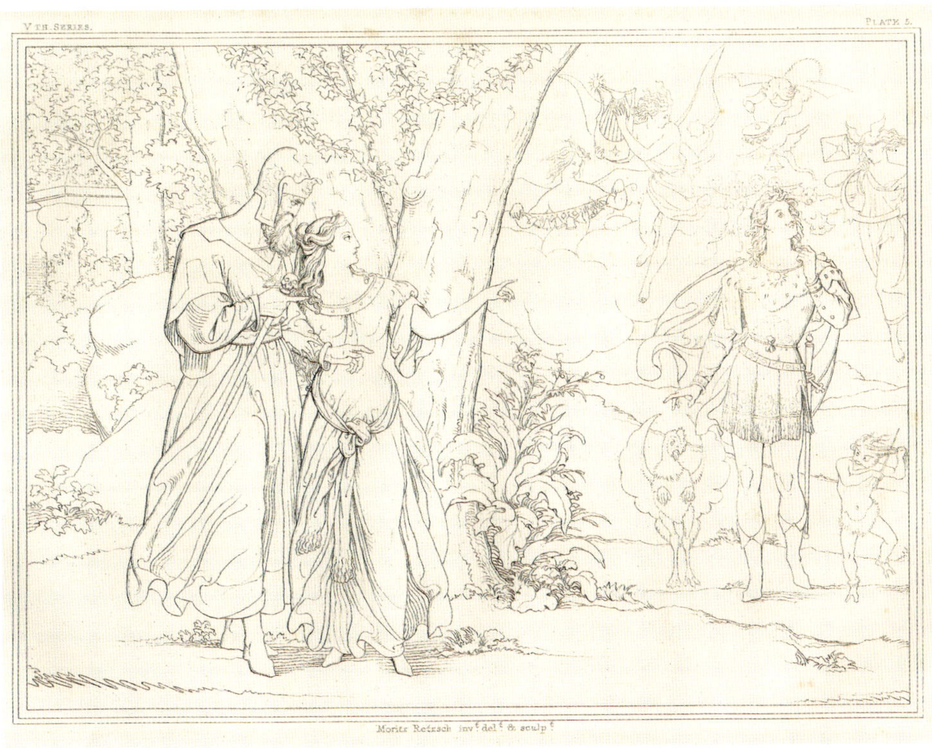

51 John Everett Millais, *Andrea Ferara: The Armoury*, 1844, Birmingham Museums & Art Gallery

52 Moritz Retzsch, *The Tempest, Act I, Scene II: Prospero and Miranda Watching Ferdinand*, 1841, from Outlines to Shakespeare, 4th series (1841), Birmingham Libraries & Archives

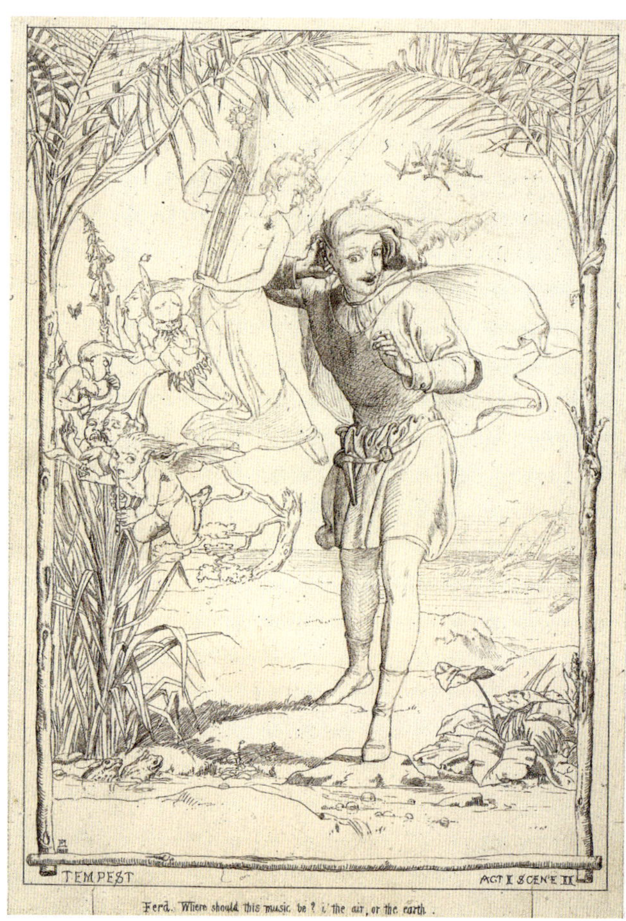

53 John Everett Millais, *Study for 'Ferdinand Lured by Ariel'*, 1848, National Museums Liverpool (Walker Art Gallery)

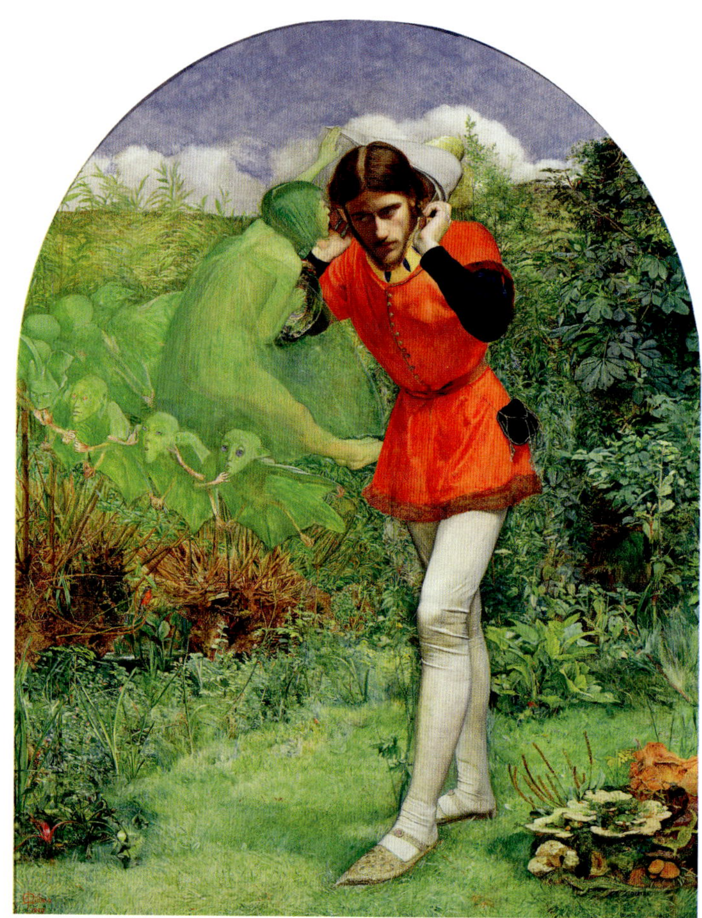

54 John Everett Millais, *Ferdinand Lured by Ariel*, 1848, The Makins Collection

Millais represents the swordmaker's workshop and its variety of implements with a virtuosic clarity.

Outline could be adapted from its use to illustrate the type of historical subject that had been nominated for the Westminster Hall Cartoons competitions in the early 1840s. For example, the influential art magazine *The Art-Union*, set up some six years previously for the improvement of taste and the promotion of high art in Britain, announced a prize competition in 1842 for a series of ten outline designs, 12 inches by 8 inches, illustrative of some epoch in British history, or of some English author. The qualities aimed at are simplicity of composition and expression, and correct drawing. In the event of obtaining a series of fine designs…it is proposed to engrave them, and present a copy, bound as a book, to each subscriber…in lieu of the annual engraving.[12]

Millais entered the competition, unsuccessfully, with

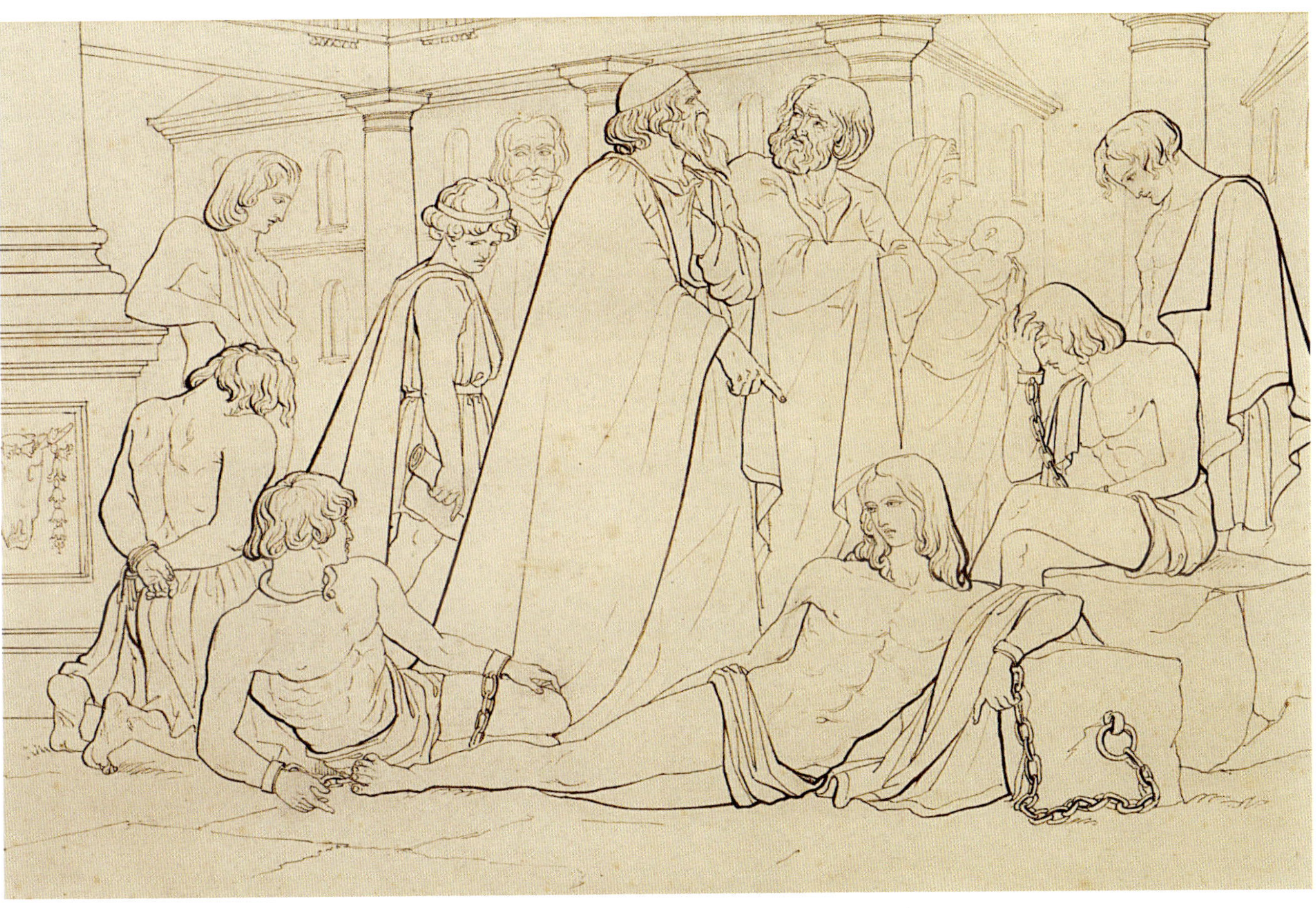

55 John Everett Millais, *Pope Gregory and the Slaves from Britannia*, 1843, Courtauld Gallery, London

a drawing illustrating the suggestive, if apocryphal, story in which Pope Gregory encounters the English slaves in the marketplace in Rome [55]. Despite Millais's extreme youth, the drawing is confident and accomplished. He chose to illustrate the incident when Pope Gregory, seeing the captives from Anglia for sale in the Roman Forum and impressed by their beauty, remarked: 'Non Angli, sed angeli' (Not Angles, but angels). Millais took the opportunity to represent the angelic young men, stripped in the manner of life-room models, in poses that mimic several of the figures of the Parthenon frieze. Millais's monumental treatment of the pope is particularly impressive, its solidity contrasting with the languishing naked figures at his feet.

Rossetti and the modified outline style

While Millais can be seen as being the most accomplished draughtsman of the Pre-Raphaelites, the full potential of compositional drawing was explored by Rossetti in several

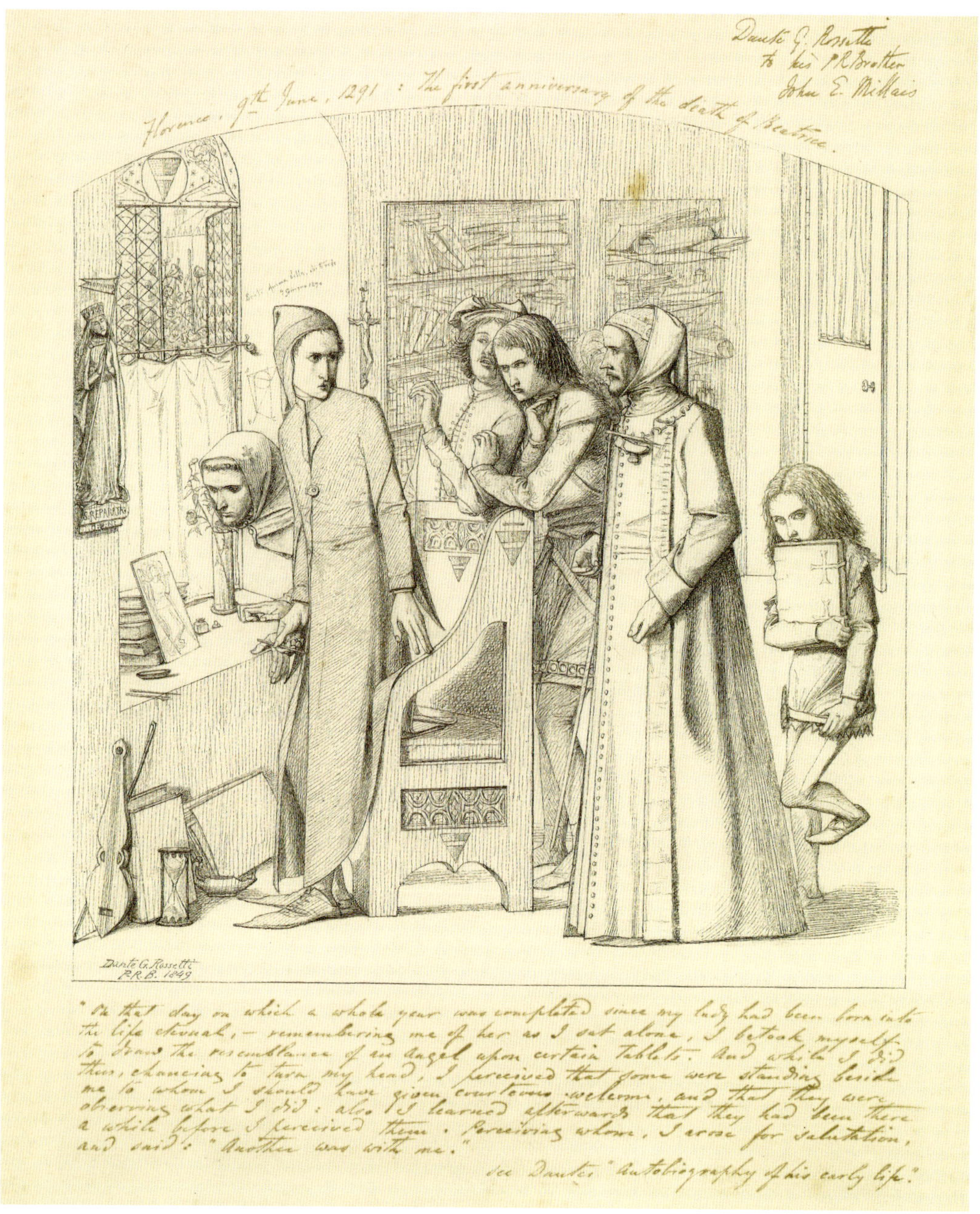

56 Dante Gabriel Rossetti, *Dante Drawing an Angel on the First Anniversary of the Death of Beatrice*, 1849, Birmingham Museums & Art Gallery

designs made in the late 1840s. *Dante Drawing an Angel on the First Anniversary of the Death of Beatrice* (1849) [56] is a key example of how outline could be modified to enable a more personal expression of ideas. Virginia Surtees, the author of *Dante Gabriel Rossetti: A Catalogue Raisonné*, describes it as having 'the peculiarities characteristic of the Brotherhood, notably in the stiffness and angularity of the figures'. She notes that this graphic direction was 'stimulated by the work Millais was doing at the time' and adds that Rossetti's drawing 'should be regarded as a true expression of the early movement'.[13] She remarks on the 'care for detail' that anticipates Rossetti's concerns in his watercolours of the late 1850s. All the varied and curious objects in the room are represented in outline alone, only the use of short parallel lines being admitted to represent spatial recession or shadow. It immediately calls to mind Retzsch's depiction of Faust sitting in his study surrounded by the objects of his profession [57], although Rossetti's line

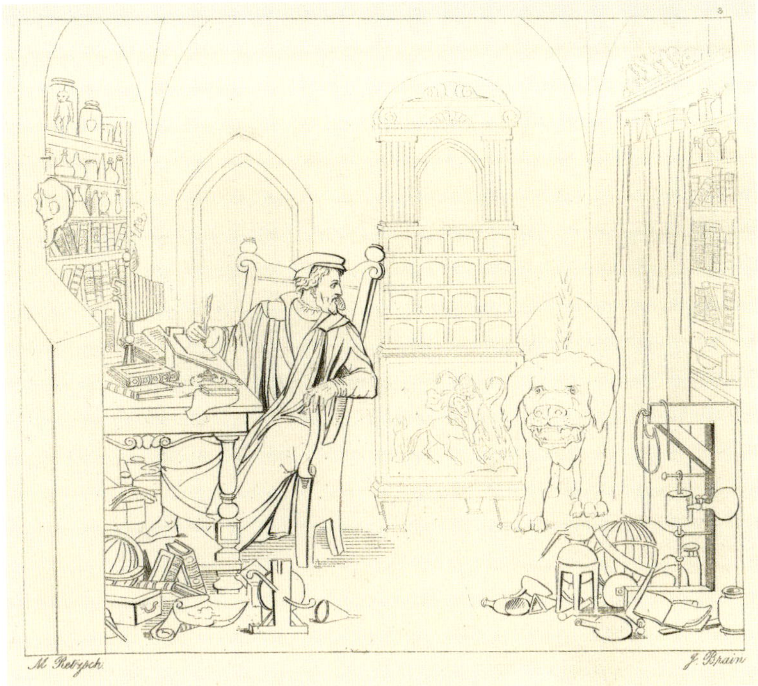

57 Moritz Retzsch, *Faust in his Study*, 1816, reproduced in *Goethe's Faust in Two Parts* (1879), Birmingham Libraries & Archives

is much more angular, spiky and awkward than Retzsch would ever have permitted his to be.

Rossetti had absorbed influences as diverse as Albrecht Dürer (1471–1528) and A. W. N. Pugin (1812–52), as well as Flaxman and Retzsch. In particular, there are striking similarities between Rossetti's *Dante Drawing an Angel* and Pugin's frontispiece – drawn in 1834 – for the second volume of *Examples of Gothic Architecture* (1836) [**58**], especially in the use of objects, furniture and detail to evoke the medieval setting. Yet more strikingly, the use of religious sculpture, its placing in the room and the scale in relation to the figures suggest that Pugin's drawing might have been used directly as a template by the younger artist. However, the drawn sculpture demonstrates the way in which Rossetti refines Pugin's example. Pugin imagines himself as a kind of St Jerome in his study, and the presence of a statue of the Virgin Mary is a reminder not only of the role of the Virgin in Pugin's devotions but also the significance of Mary as 'England's dowry' in the reconversion of the nation to Catholicism, an issue of much interest in the 1840s. It is not a statue of the Virgin, however, that occupies the wall in Rossetti's imagining of Dante's chamber but St Reparata, the second-century virgin and martyr who was regarded as protectress of Florence, Dante's home city.[14]

At the same time that Rossetti was portraying Dante in his study, Hunt was also depicting the meditations of a figure, the prophet Daniel, in a private space. *Daniel Praying* (1849) [**59**], Hunt's earliest biblical subject, makes a compelling comparison with Rossetti's *Dante Drawing an Angel*, suggesting a shared – or perhaps even competitive –

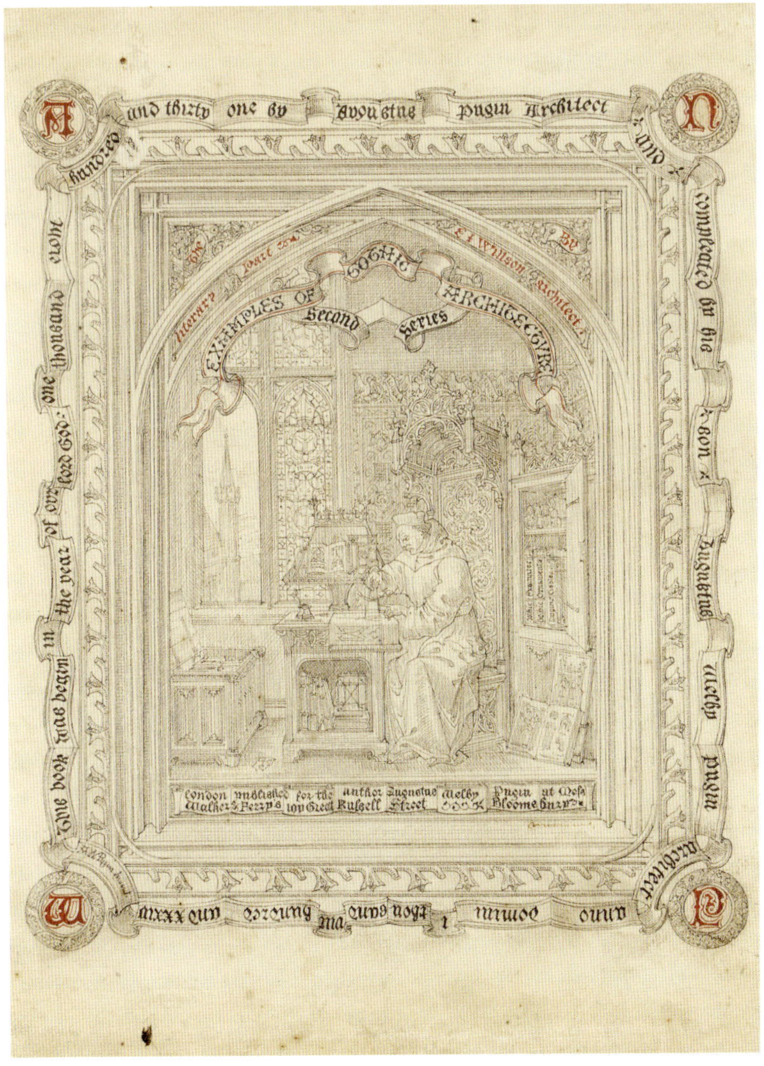

58 Augustus Welby Northmore Pugin, *Design for the Frontispiece to Volume II of 'Examples of Gothic Architecture' (1836)*, 1834, Victoria and Albert Museum, London

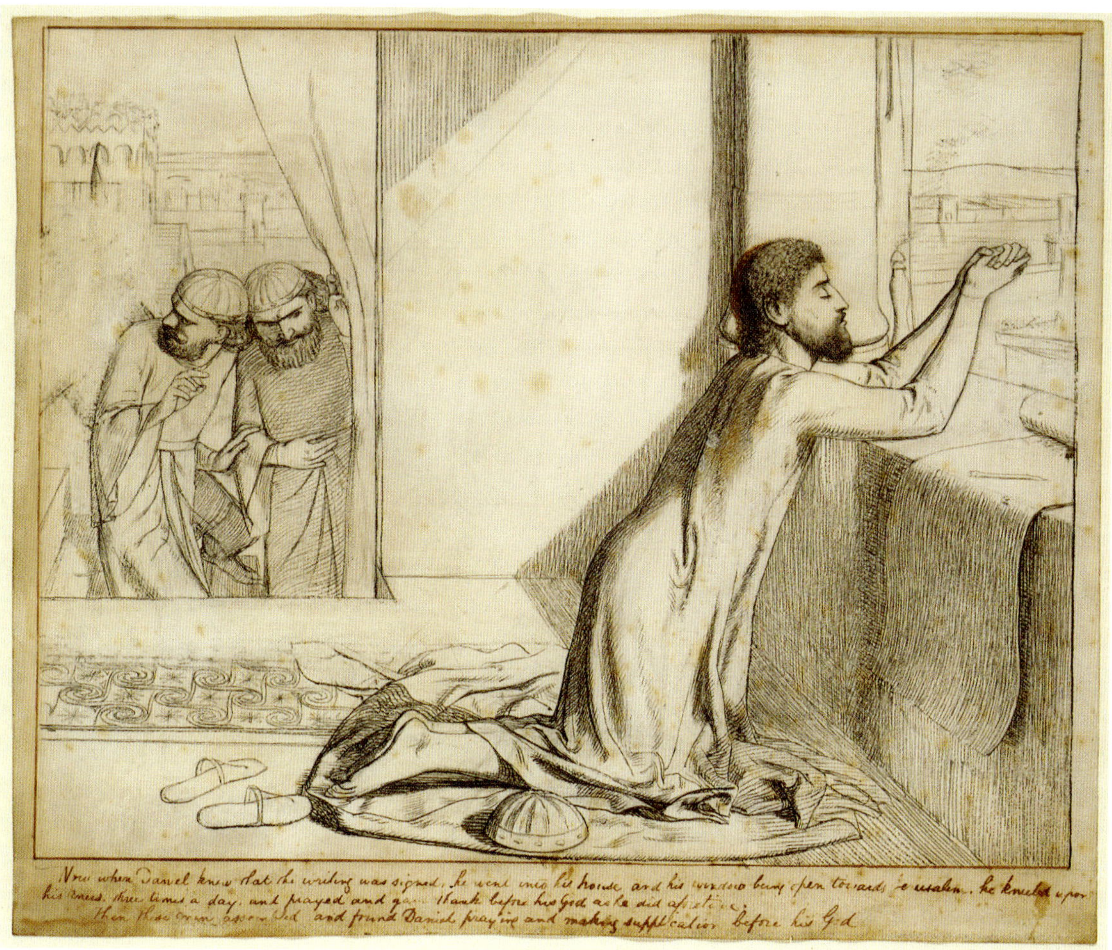

59 William Holman Hunt, *Daniel Praying*, 1849, private collection

project. It is tempting to see the two drawings as part of a now-lost dialogue about historicism, although it is striking that both works depict meditation and trance. Hunt might have begun his composition for *Daniel Praying* for the consideration of his fellow members of the Cyclographic Society.[15] He abandoned strict outline for a slightly more complex handling of the pen and ink, particularly in his rendering of the folds of Daniel's garment. Rossetti's medieval revivalism is matched by Hunt's Assyrian one. The pattern of the rug, the architecture and the details of dress and accessory in *Daniel Praying* all speak of a new kind of antiquarian interest following the display of objects from the excavations at Nineveh at the British Museum in 1847 and the publication of A. H. Layard's *Nineveh and its Remains* in 1849, the year of Hunt's drawing.

The subject of a poet drawing would have had great appeal to Rossetti, who struggled himself to choose between both art forms. In *Dante Drawing an Angel* he expressed a desire for artistic duality and depicted it as being achieved in a solitary trance-like state. The work anticipates the vogue for trance-drawing, which moved from the inner circles of Spiritualism later in the century and which would later reappear in the psychoanalytically driven 'automatic drawing' of early twentieth-century modernism, in works by André Masson and other Surrealist artists. It is significant that the work never became a painting, although there is a watercolour version, with a substantially changed composition, begun in 1853, now in the Ashmolean Museum, Oxford. Rossetti's transcription of the relevant passage from Dante's *Vita Nuova* (The New Life) underneath the 1849 drawing (which he presented to Millais) brought together the activities of drawing and writing and the importance of the artist engaging with his innermost desires. In his edition of the *Vita Nuova* Rossetti described

the work as 'the Autobiography or Autopsychology of
Dante's youth'.[16]

Rossetti's drawings for Edgar Allan Poe's 'The Raven'
(1847) [60] also depict a poet preoccupied with the loss of
a lover through death. The poet's study in the drawings for
'The Raven' is a meditative space, similar to that in *Dante
Drawing an Angel*, in which the earthly and unearthly can
intersect. It is a space that appears in some of Rossetti's
most important pictorial inventions, such as *Beata Beatrix*
(in multiple versions from 1864 onwards, including the
example held by the Tate), where glimpses of the afterlife
interrupt the ordinary diurnal spaces of the street or
the house. Stylistically, this move to the personal and
supernatural space of Poe's poem is marked by the use of a
mixed technique of fine pen marks that suggest the outline
style combined with atmospheric hatching and tonal
marks, the residue of Rossetti's copying of French
illustrators such as Paul Gavarni (1804–66). These
techniques seem opposed and irreconcilable, yet their
synthesis here is highly sophisticated, more so than the
relatively straightforward borrowing of the outline style,
which had marked Rossetti's earlier drawings.

Between 1845 and 1848 Rossetti drew a sequence of
illustrations for Goethe's *Faust*. They have something of the
same description of space as his illustrations to Poe's 'The
Raven', and there is a looseness of handling of the pen and
ink in both sets of drawings that allows the representation
of shadowy spaces. In the *Faust* drawings, these shadows,
sometimes heavy and expressive, describe the diabolic
atmosphere of Goethe's text, in which the drama is seen
through the eyes of Gretchen, tortured by visions of the
devil Mephistopheles. Sometimes the two subjects overlap,
and Rossetti's ghost-haunted Poe illustrations and *Faust*
drawings give way to the works that mark the transition
to his own version of 'Christian art'. This synthesis of
sources is most striking when we compare the drawing

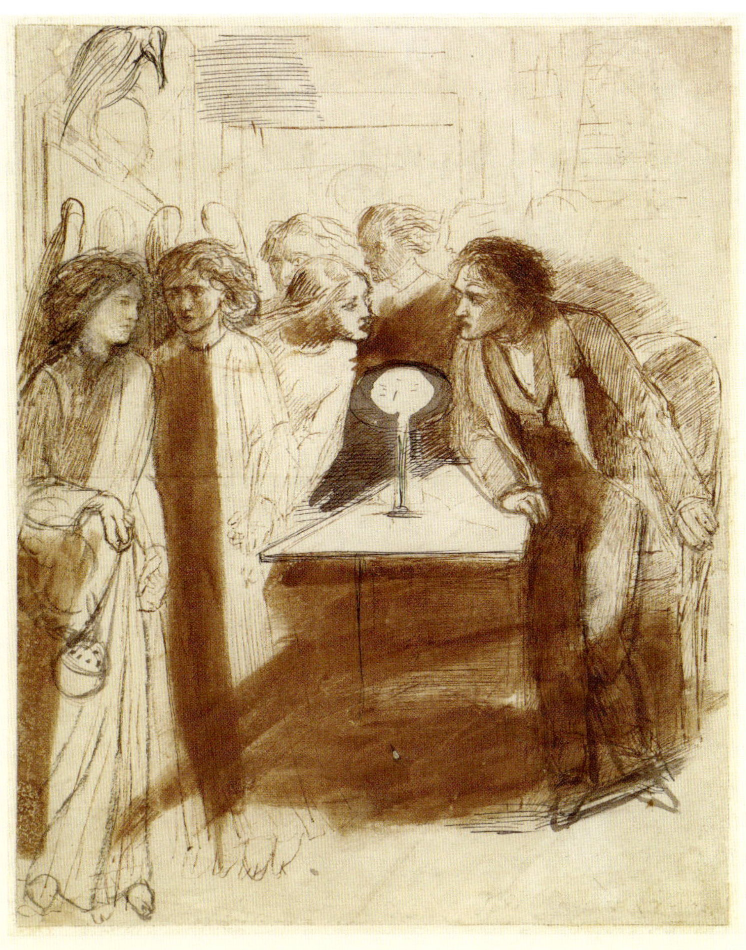

60 Dante Gabriel Rossetti, *'The Raven': Angel Footfalls*, 1847,
Birmingham Museums & Art Gallery

Faust: Margaret in the Church (1848) [61] with Rossetti's
depiction of the Annunciation [62]. A curious feature of the
drawings is the use of curtaining as a method of dividing
the interior space. Its origins might be in the curtained
door that features in Pugin's self-portrait reproduced as
the frontispiece to *Examples of Gothic Architecture* [58].
Rossetti used the curtaining device again in his depiction
of *Margaret in the Church*, as well as in both of his earliest
exhibited paintings of episodes in the life of the Virgin. The
panel that represents the front of the prayer desk in the *Faust*
drawings reappears as the embroidery panel and frame in
the paintings *The Girlhood of Mary Virgin* (1848–49) [73] and
Ecce Ancilla Domini! (The Annunciation) (1849–50, Tate).
All three works represent a female character in the grip of
an otherworldly vision, an overwhelming encounter with a
spiritual being. The female figures in both the *Faust* subject
and the Annunciation crouch in fear, hemmed into a corner.

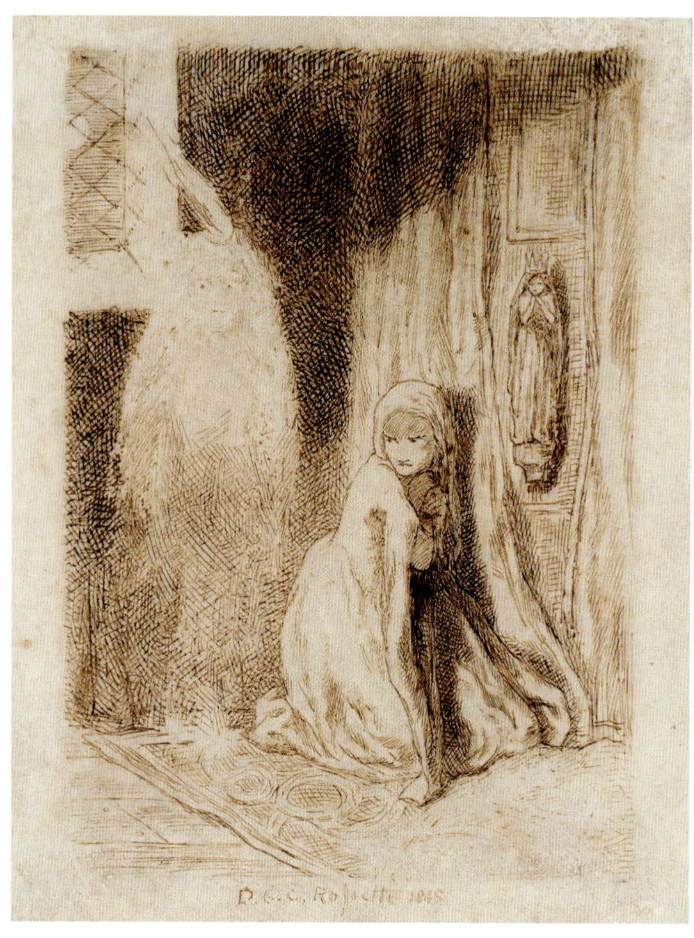

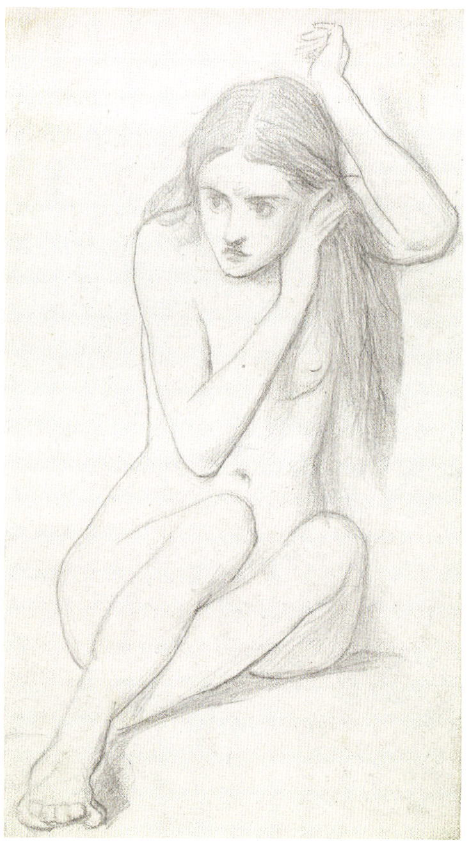

After outline

We need no clearer example of the changes that were taking place in the drawing practices of each member of the Pre-Raphaelite Brotherhood than to look at Millais's modification of the outline style into a more personal and complex mode of graphic expression. The two drawings for his Pre-Raphaelite tour-de-force, *Ophelia* (1852), show how much he had moved away from his earlier use of pure outline. In the full compositional study [64], the figure of Ophelia struggling in the pool is a little more agitated than in the final painted version of the subject, and the wealth of natural detail is much reduced (although the bird is still there, an important motif of the continuance of nature and something of a 'poetic fallacy', the birdsong a kind of funeral song over the body of the young woman). The study for the head of Ophelia [63] is perhaps one of the most extraordinary drawings of its time: intimate and probing, yet sensitive, it acts as both an imaginary and a real portrait. Elizabeth Siddal (1829–62), the model for Ophelia, made one of her earliest appearances here, posing as Shakespeare's ill-fated heroine. Yet, rather than idealizing Siddal's features, it is her idiosyncrasies that the artist concentrates on: her pale eyelashes, for example, which the painter has rendered both here and in the painting.

We can glimpse the genesis of Millais's invention of the head of Ophelia in a drawing of his earliest juvenilia [66], a copy after a picture by Correggio, *Christ Presented to the People (Ecce Homo)* [65], which had been acquired by the National Gallery in the 1830s. The painting shows the Virgin Mary swooning at the sight of her suffering son,

61 Dante Gabriel Rossetti, *Faust: Margaret in the Church*, 1848, Tate
62 Dante Gabriel Rossetti, *Study for 'Ecce Ancilla Domini!'*, 1849, Birmingham Museums & Art Gallery
63 John Everett Millais, *Study of the Head of Elizabeth Siddal for 'Ophelia'*, 1852, Birmingham Museums & Art Gallery
64 John Everett Millais, *Study for 'Ophelia': Finished Compositional Study*, 1852, Plymouth City Museum & Art Gallery

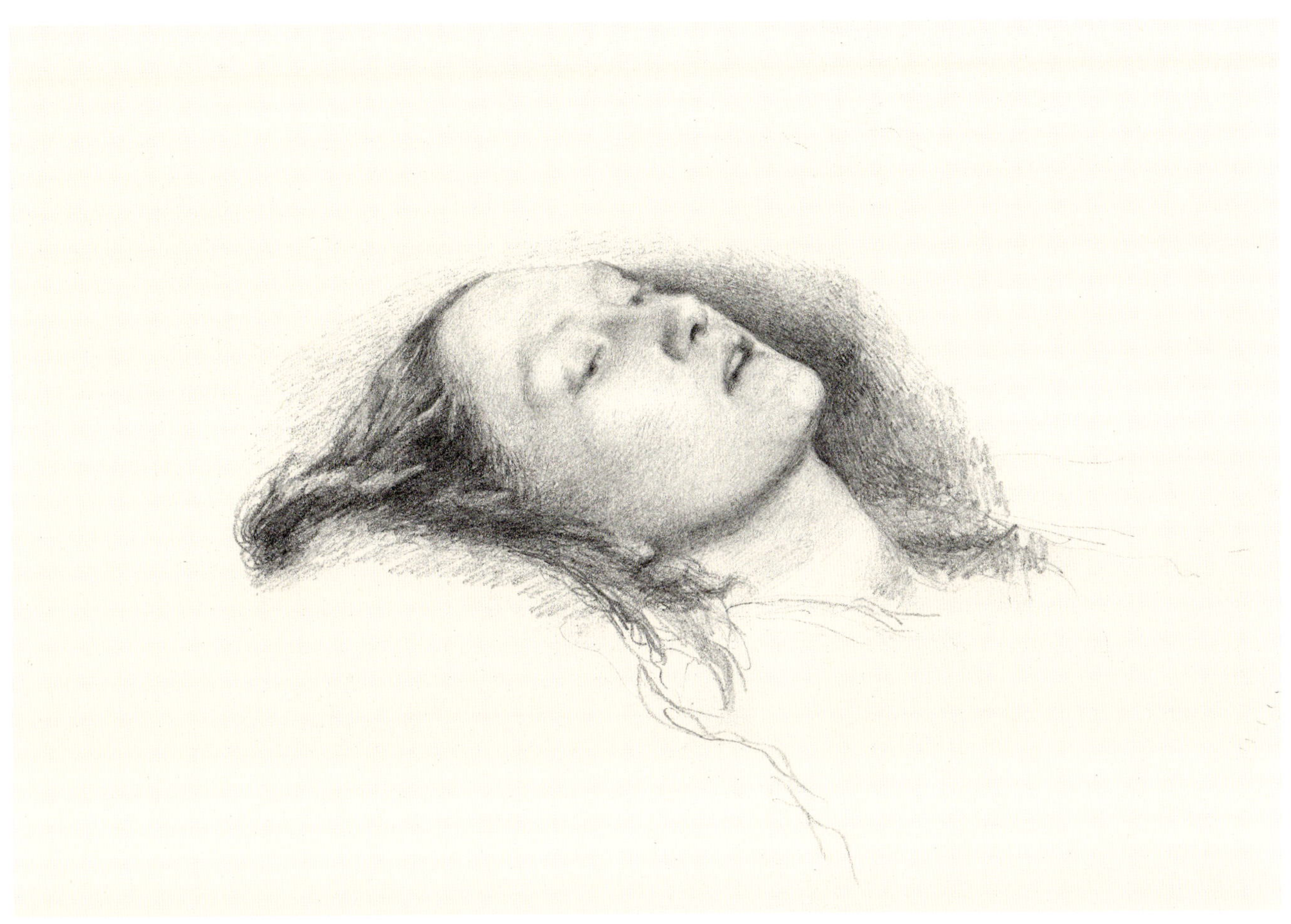

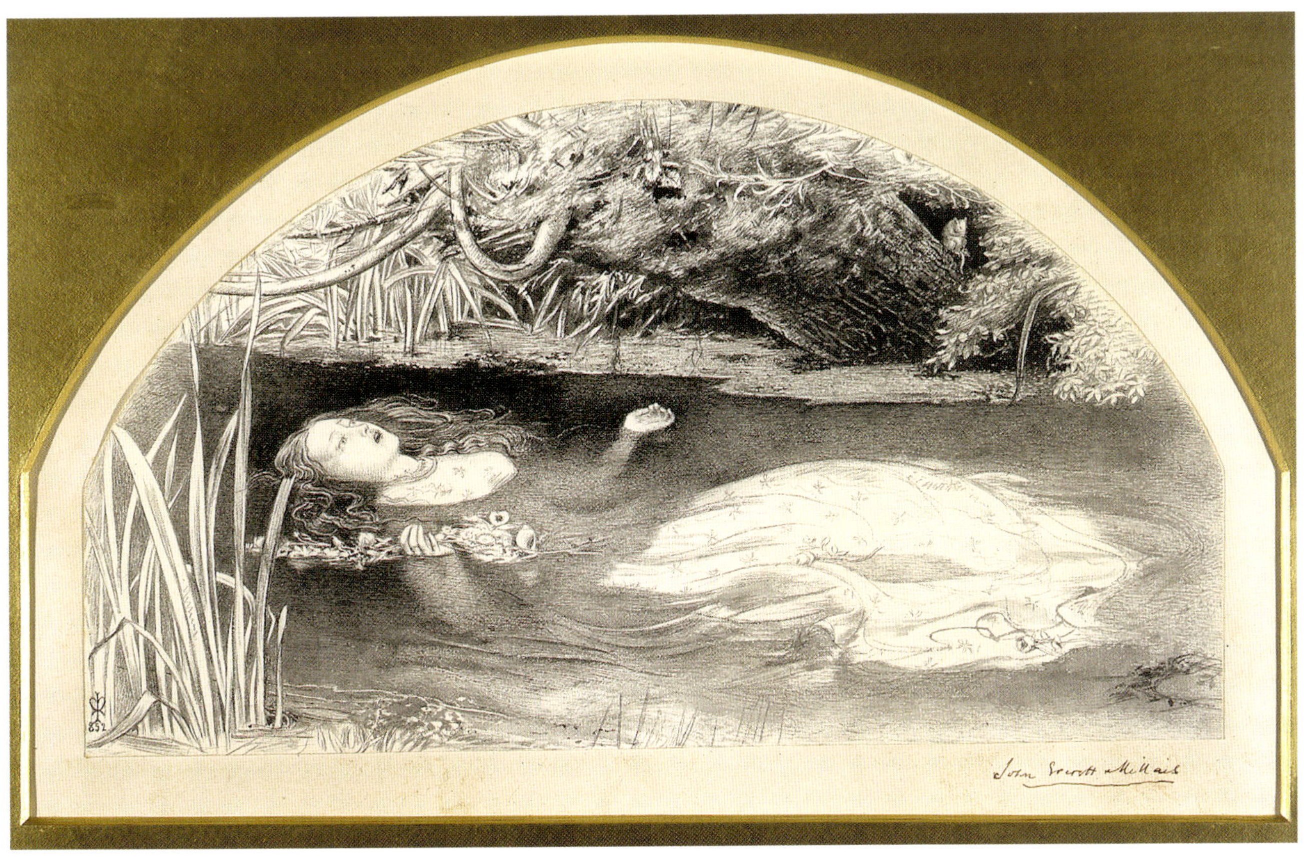

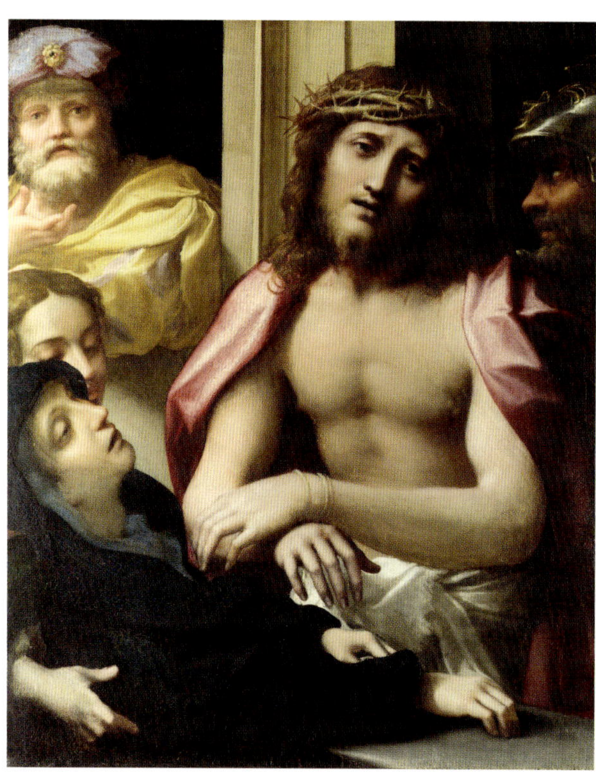

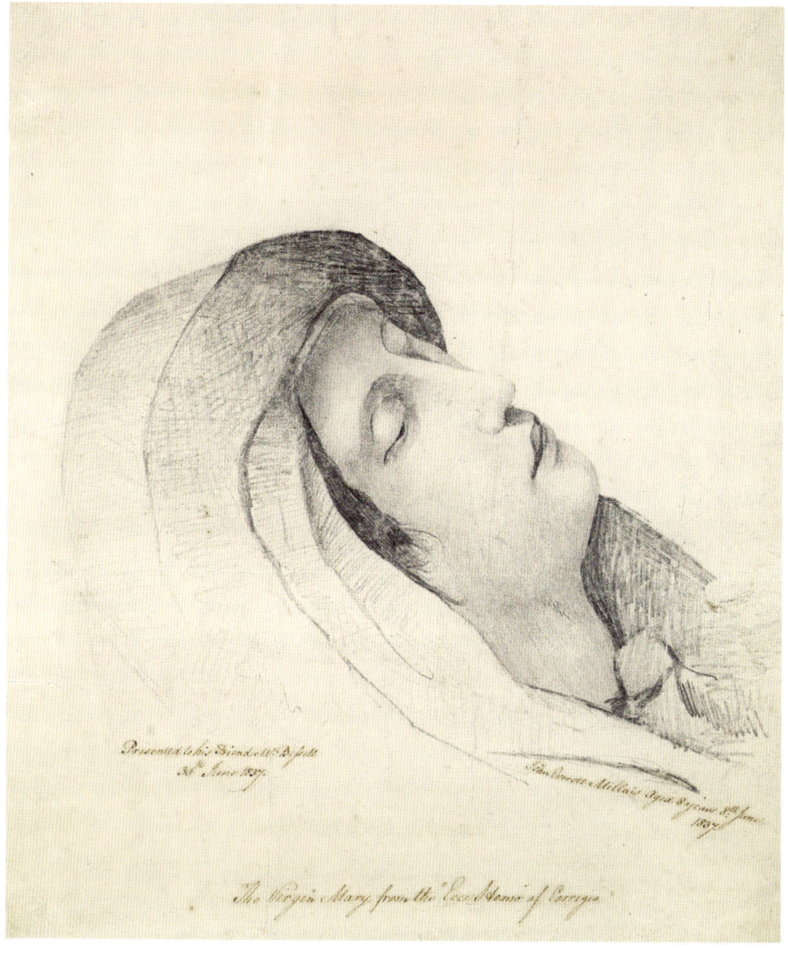

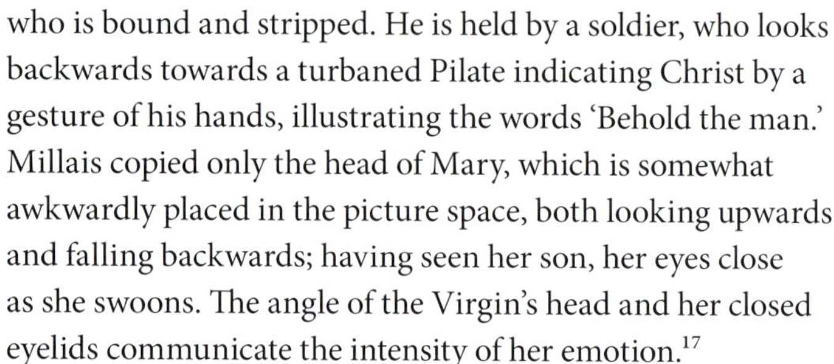

65 Antonio Allegri di Correggio, *Christ Presented to the People (Ecce Homo)*, probably *c.* 1525–30, The National Gallery, London

66 John Everett Millais after Correggio, *Study of the Head of the Virgin Mary*, 1837, Birmingham Museums & Art Gallery

who is bound and stripped. He is held by a soldier, who looks backwards towards a turbaned Pilate indicating Christ by a gesture of his hands, illustrating the words 'Behold the man.' Millais copied only the head of Mary, which is somewhat awkwardly placed in the picture space, both looking upwards and falling backwards; having seen her son, her eyes close as she swoons. The angle of the Virgin's head and her closed eyelids communicate the intensity of her emotion.[17]

Correggio's image of female suffering seems to have left a strong impression on the young artist, since he returned to it for a key compositional device more than a decade later in picturing the head of Ophelia. The drawing of Ophelia has had a life of its own, moreover, as an independent work rather than as a study for a finished painting. It is suggestive of a development in Rossetti's work that began around the same time that Millais was planning *Ophelia* – those studies of female heads such as Proserpine [**286**] – and, later, in the works of Simeon Solomon in which heads stand in for a variety of qualities and emotions, often painful or tragic. As in Millais's *Ophelia*, the drawings Rossetti made in 1851 for

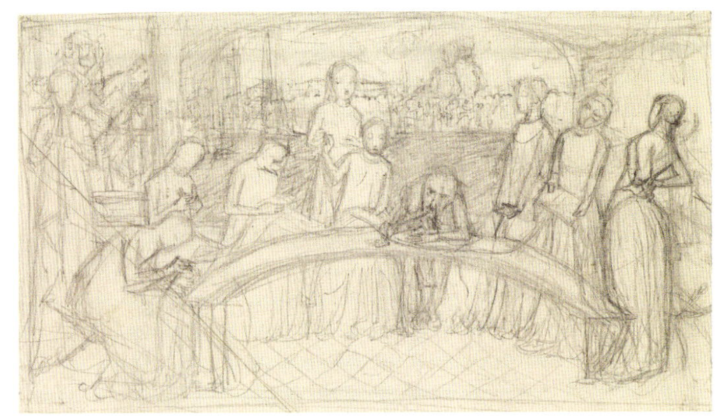

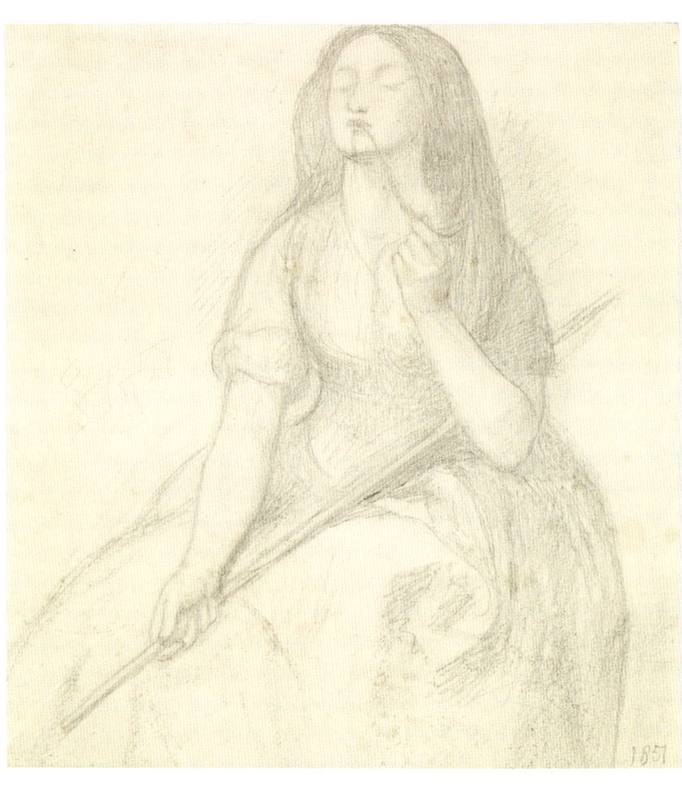

67 Dante Gabriel Rossetti, *Study of Elizabeth Siddal for 'The Return of Tibullus to Delia'*, 1851, Birmingham Museums & Art Gallery

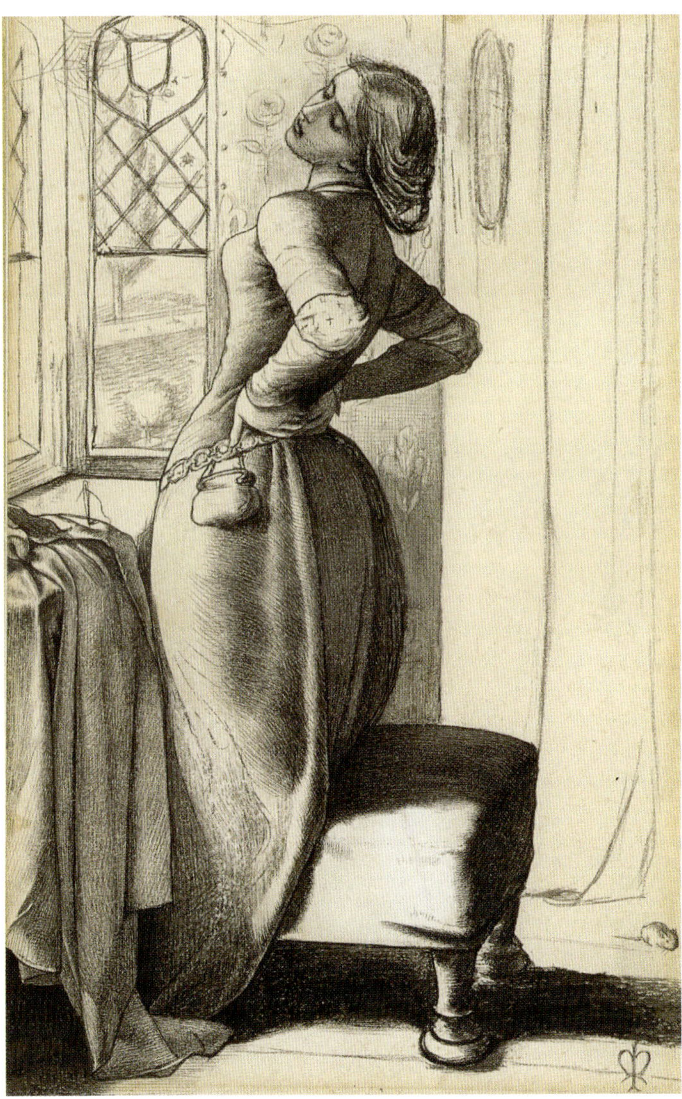

68 John Everett Millais, *Compositional Study, Possibly Related to 'The Eve of the Deluge'*, 1850, Birmingham Museums & Art Gallery
69 John Everett Millais, *Study for 'Mariana'*, 1850, Victoria and Albert Museum, London

the watercolour *The Return of Tibullus to Delia* (1853, private collection) depict Siddal with her eyes closed, as if she is sleeping or meditating [67]. Although made as studies for narrative subject paintings, the absence of an engaging glance in both these early drawings of Siddal distinguishes them from the tradition of portraiture. The figures appear like decapitations or representations of corpses, yet we read in them so much of the fate of the characters they portray – not their personalities alone, but their emotional histories, too.

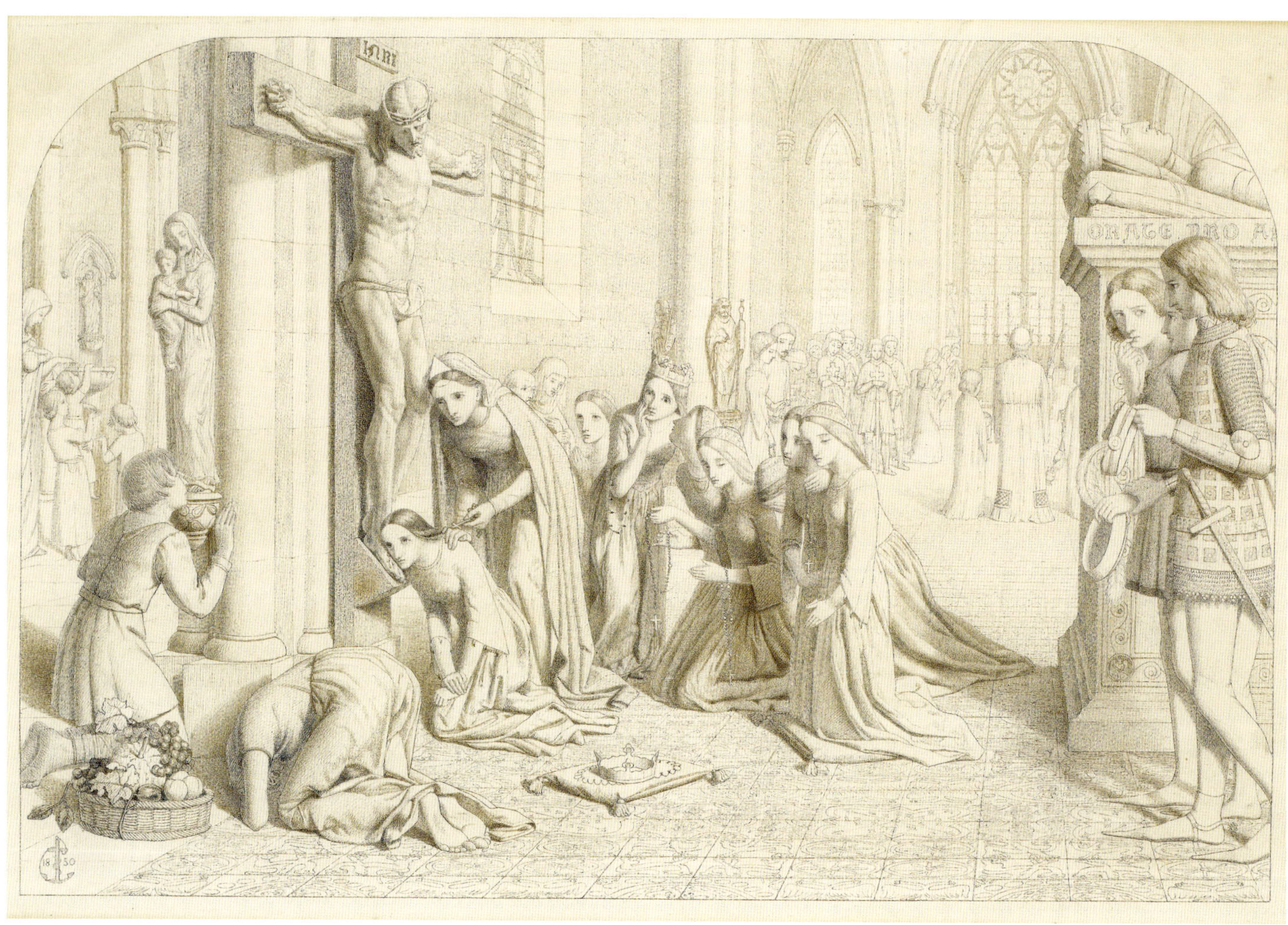

70 James Collinson, *An Incident in the Life of St Elizabeth of Hungary*, 1850, Birmingham Museums & Art Gallery

Millais was both prolific and inventive at this early stage of his career. He produced so many sketches for ideas for pictures that it was impossible for them all to have been worked out in finished paintings. Occasionally he would return to these sketches and plans, sometimes elaborating them, sometimes paring them down. As we have seen, the germ of the composition of *Christ in the House of His Parents* can be found in the outline drawing *Andrea Ferara; or The Armoury*. The little boy in Millais's drawing *Childhood* (*c*. 1848, Royal Academy) reappears much later as *Bubbles* (1885–86, Unilever, on loan to National Museums Liverpool, Lady Lever Art Gallery), one of his most famous works in his later manner. The complicated interrelationships drafted in numerous unidentified sketches, some of which might relate to his plans for depicting the eve of the Deluge [68], gave rise to

the awkward stance of the figure of Mariana [69] as she stretches in boredom and frustration in her moated grange in the painting that bears her name (1851, Tate). *Mariana* is one of the most emotionally charged of Millais's Pre-Raphaelite works because the editing and selection processes have condensed it to a single, highly charged gesture; the intensity of a whole fresco by Gozzoli – at least as engraved by Lasinio – has been concentrated on a single figure.

These examples explain something of the significance of compositional drawing and its enduring importance in the realization of figure compositions, complex in emotional range as well as pose and gesture. At a point when the appeal of the outline style would seem to have been all but exhausted as a force in European art, it was revived by the Pre-Raphaelites. Outline offered quick ways of exploring significant literary and biblical subject matter. However, the outline style and associated graphic strategies could only do so much to challenge the status quo of academic art. While Hunt, Millais and Rossetti could manipulate line to communicate new and exciting narratives, the modified outline of the Pre-Raphaelites could easily fall into conventions and posturings of its own: stiffness, stereotyped gesture and second-hand emotion, characteristics of lesser artists associated with the Brotherhood.

We can detect these tendencies in drawings by James Collinson, one of the original Pre-Raphaelite Brothers, and Charles Allston Collins (1828–73), who was closely associated with the group in the 1850s. Collinson's extraordinarily spiky compositional drawing [70] for his painting *The Renunciation of Queen Elizabeth of Hungary* (1851, Johannesburg Art Gallery) and Collins's *The Devout Childhood of St Elizabeth of Hungary* (1852) [71] demonstrate the interconnections of Pre-Raphaelite art with religious debates, the study of the lives of the saints and their representation in art. Through artistic sincerity the artist might approach a sincerity of religious feeling. Both works owe their enthusiasm for St Elizabeth to the poet and novelist Charles Kingsley (1819–75), whose first book, *The Saint's Tragedy*, had been published in 1848. The linear style adopted by both artists is similar to that used for the outline illustrations to Anna Jameson's *Sacred and Legendary Art* (1848) as well as Lasinio's Campo Santo engravings and Retzsch's outline designs for texts by Shakespeare and Goethe.

Although it provided a starting point for a revolt against the academic drawing system, the outline style had to be modified or abandoned altogether to develop its potential for new and unhackneyed narrative forms. To get closer to the kind of truth that was needed to produce new and relevant narratives for a modern subject painting, the Pre-Raphaelites had to further experiment with drawing and composition. To the formal beauty and suavity of the outline style they needed to add something less familiar

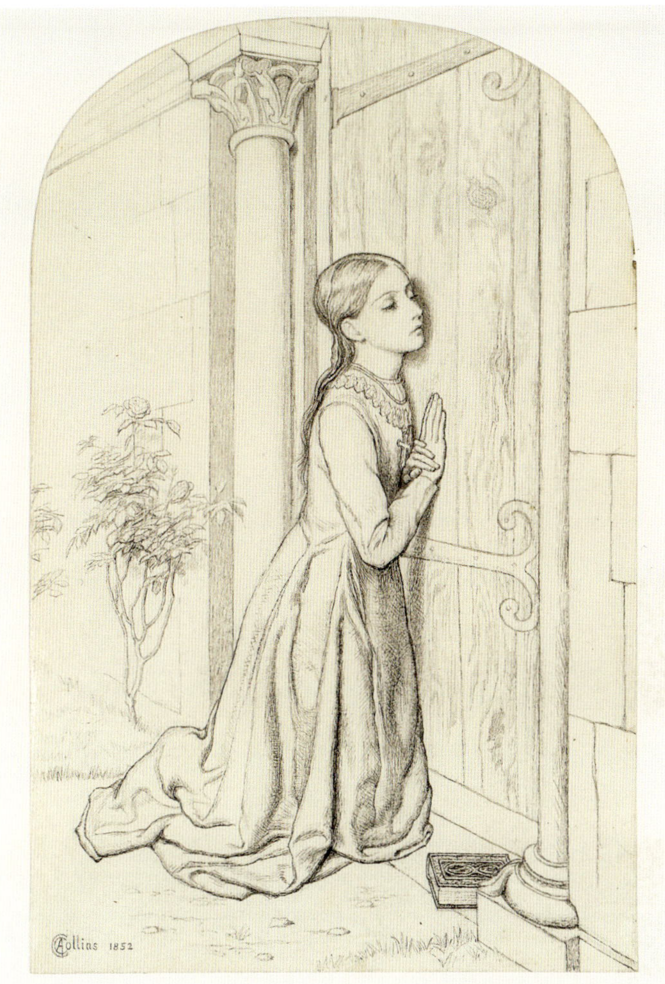

71 Charles Allston Collins, *The Devout Childhood of St Elizabeth of Hungary*, 1852, Tate

and more challenging: the close observation of nature. In his account of the development of Pre-Raphaelitism, Hunt revealed that he was uneasy about both what he called 'classicalism' and 'medievalism'. These two impulses were connected with the rise of the outline style, and with revivalism generally, the product of 'seeking after dry bones', as Hunt described it to Millais. Rather than stylistic revival, Hunt thought that the Pre-Raphaelites wanted 'simply fuller Nature'.[18] In this quest they were assisted by the writings and drawing practices of Ruskin, whose own rejection of convention in art and architecture was to dominate British art criticism throughout the rest of the century.

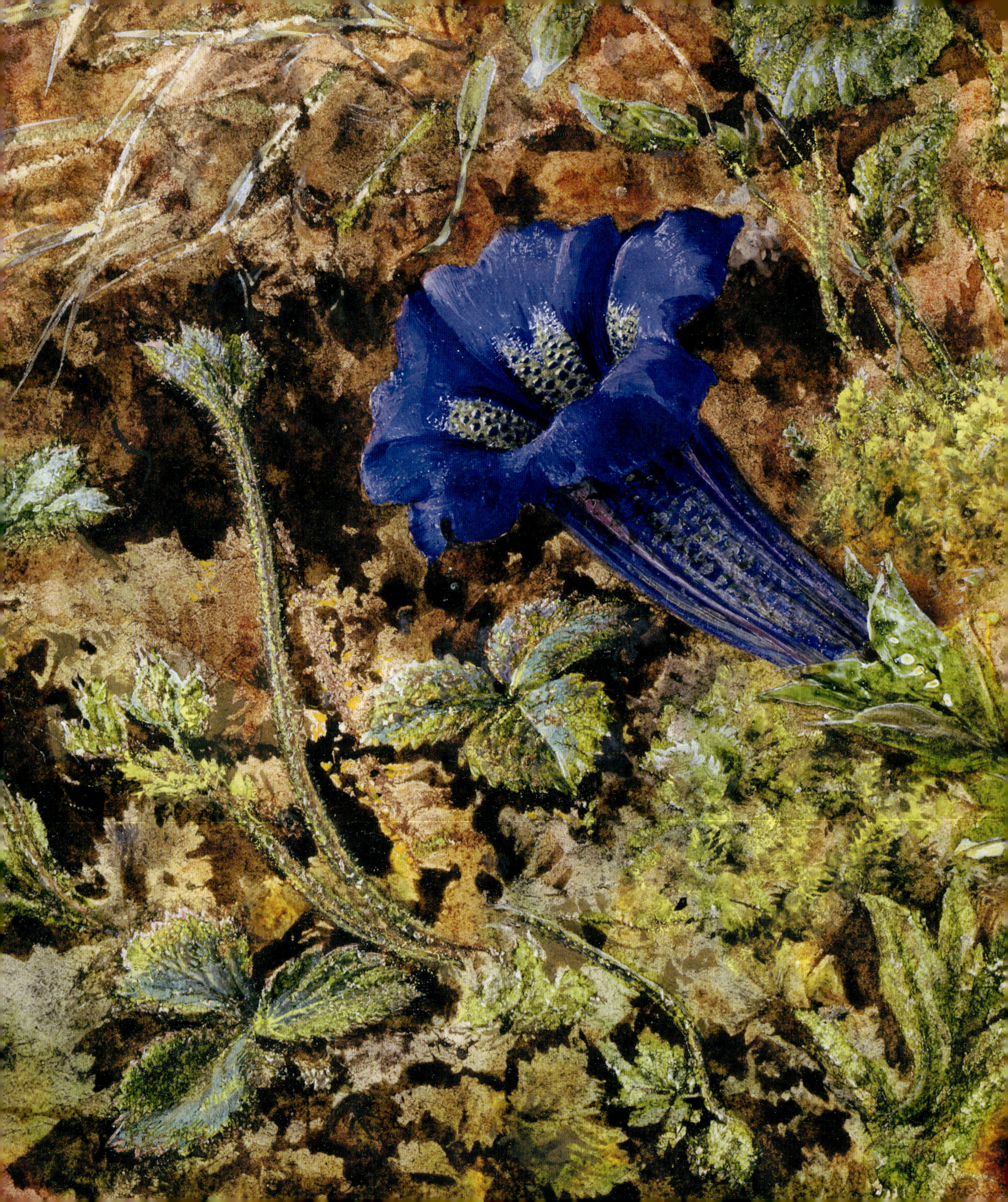

Chapter 3 *Studying Nature Attentively: Ruskin and Pre-Raphaelitism*

Summarizing the aims of the Pre-Raphaelite Brotherhood, William Michael Rossetti linked two fundamental aspects of their programme: 'to have genuine ideas to express' was combined with the desire to 'study Nature attentively' in order to 'know how to express' these ideas.[1] The direct study of nature appeared as a type of allegory in Millais's *Garden Scene* (1849) [74] in which a young woman is represented in the act of drawing alongside companions who attend to other activities; she regards her model, a lily, with earnest attention. The subject is, perhaps, allegorical in intention. The lily appears to stand in for all of nature, the young woman for all artists and the activity of drawing for all art – or all Pre-Raphaelite art, at least. The young artist's pose has strong similarities to that of the Virgin Mary in Dante Gabriel Rossetti's first exhibited work of 1849 [73], in which Mary is depicted embroidering from a lily held in place by an angel. There, art and religion are concentrated in one image, and two types of discipline – artistic and spiritual – are represented together.

In presenting the practice of working directly from nature as a method of engaging with the natural world, Millais would have been conscious that flower painting had become identified as one of the lowest of artistic achievements in the academic hierarchy. Flower and plant drawing was, in modern and contemporary art, a skill associated with amateur artists, chiefly women. This status was an inheritance from the 'polite' drawing taught by drawing masters to the daughters of wealthy families. It was related to the bourgeois taste for 'the language of flowers', as it had become known, in which flowers could be interpreted as having particular meanings in certain contexts. However, the accurate representation of plants and flowers was a feature of the art of the Northern European Renaissance, for example, in Dürer's watercolours or in printed herbals such as Leonhart Fuchs's *De historia stirpium comentarii insignes* (1542). Earlier, in medieval Books of Hours, accurate

72 John Brett, *Gentian*, 1862, The Williamson Art Gallery and Museum, Birkenhead, Wirral (detail)

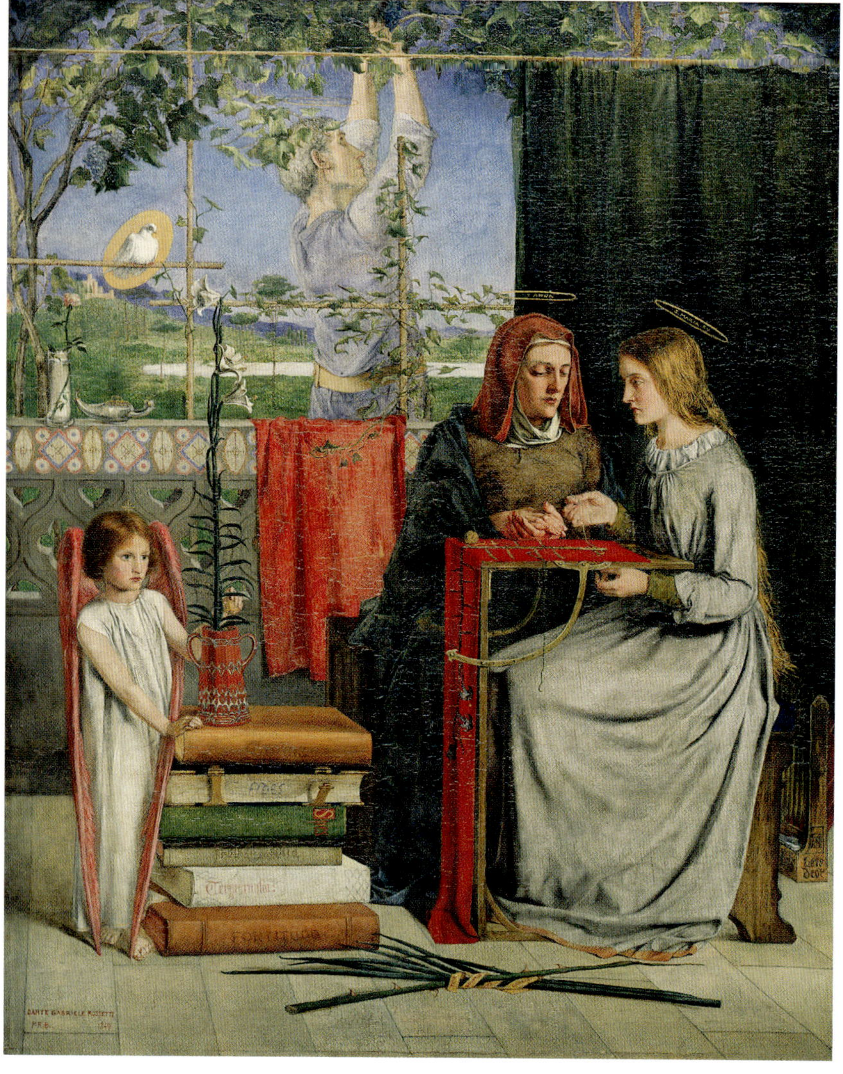

73 Dante Gabriel Rossetti, *The Girlhood of Mary Virgin*, 1848–49, Tate

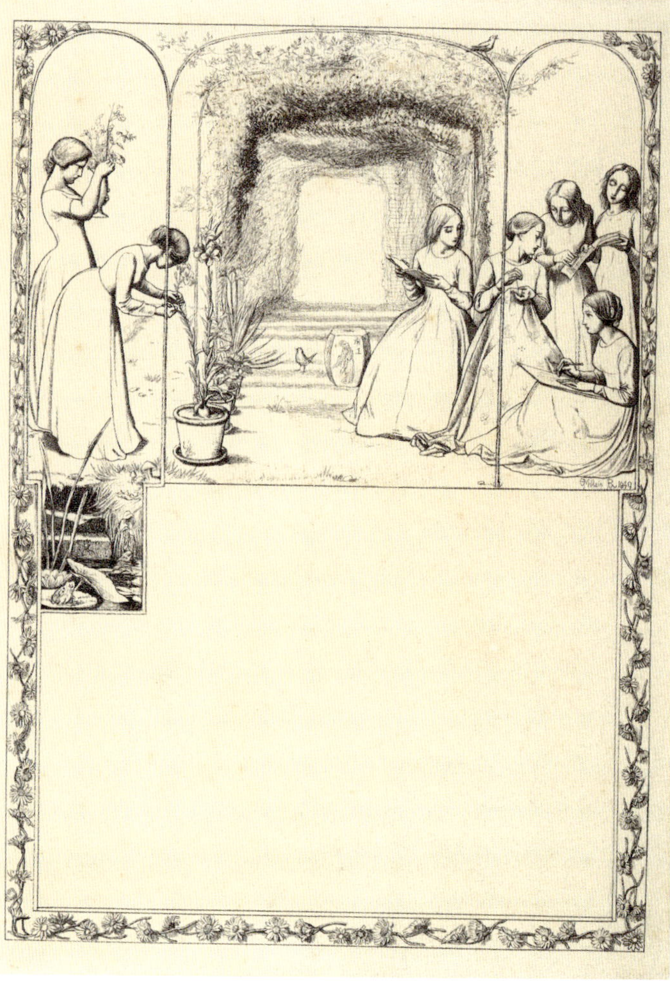

74 John Everett Millais, *Garden Scene*, 1849, private collection

depictions of plants graced the margins of religious texts. From the earnestness of the young woman drawing flowers, as represented by Millais in *Garden Scene*, to the exercises advocated by Ruskin in *Elements of Drawing*, it is clear that in the Pre-Raphaelite circle flower drawing was neither a pursuit for 'idle young ladies' nor a recreation, but that its aim was more disciplined and purposeful.[2]

Ruskin's most famous statement on the principle of 'truth to nature' is often quoted as a direct inspiration for the Pre-Raphaelites:

> Go to Nature in all singleness of heart and walk with her laboriously and trustingly, having no other thought but how best to penetrate her meaning, rejecting nothing, selecting nothing, and scorning nothing.[3]

As we have seen in previous chapters, the Pre-Raphaelites were experimenting with various modes of representation that were broadly to do with 'truth' and with a rejection of convention but which were less concerned with a literal 'truth to nature'. In coming to the defence of the Pre-Raphaelites in 1851 during the time they were suffering their most abusive criticism, Ruskin more publicly united his cause to theirs. In a letter to *The Times* he wrote of claims that they were revivalists:

> they intend to return to early days in this one point only – that, as far as in them lies, they will draw either what they see, or what they suppose might have been the actual facts of the scene they desire to represent, irrespective of any conventional rules of picture making.[4]

In his pamphlet *Pre-Raphaelitism* (1851), Ruskin brought together his enthusiasm for J. M. W. Turner (1775–1851), whose reputation he defended in *Modern Painters*, with that for the young and misunderstood Pre-Raphaelites. He used the example of the education of a young poet in the writing of poetry and asked a rhetorical question: what is our way of setting to work to produce a poet on canvas?

> We begin, in all probability, by telling the youth of fifteen or sixteen, that Nature is full of faults, and that he is to improve her; but that Raphael is perfection, and that the more he copies Raphael the better; that after much copying of Raphael, he is to try what he can do himself in a Raphaelesque, but yet highly original manner: that is to say, he is to try to do something very clever, all out of his own head, but yet this clever something is to be properly subjected to Raphaelesque rules….This I say is the kind of teaching which through various channels, Royal Academy lecturing, press criticisms, public enthusiasm, and not least by solid weight of gold, we give to our young men. And we wonder we have no painters![5]

It was not painting, however, but drawing that was the focus of Ruskin's own teaching and the chief object of his passion for collecting. His writings on drawing concern themselves with the close observation of nature and the recording of natural phenomena.

Having mastered what he called the 'Proutesque' and then the 'Turneresque' styles of drawing, Ruskin had a revelation when his attention was captured by 'a bit of ivy round a thorn stem'. He proceeded 'to make a light and shade pencil study of it…carefully, as if it had been a bit of sculpture, liking it more and more as I drew'. In his autobiography, *Praeterita*, Ruskin confessed that, for all his training in drawing, he 'had never seen the beauty of anything, not even of a stone – how much less of a leaf!'[6] In the 'bit of ivy' Ruskin found a model, one entirely natural and outside academic drawing conventions. Ruskin's memory of the moment is that it marked a change from the mastering of techniques of drawing to the vital encounter with nature that characterizes his mature work, as, for

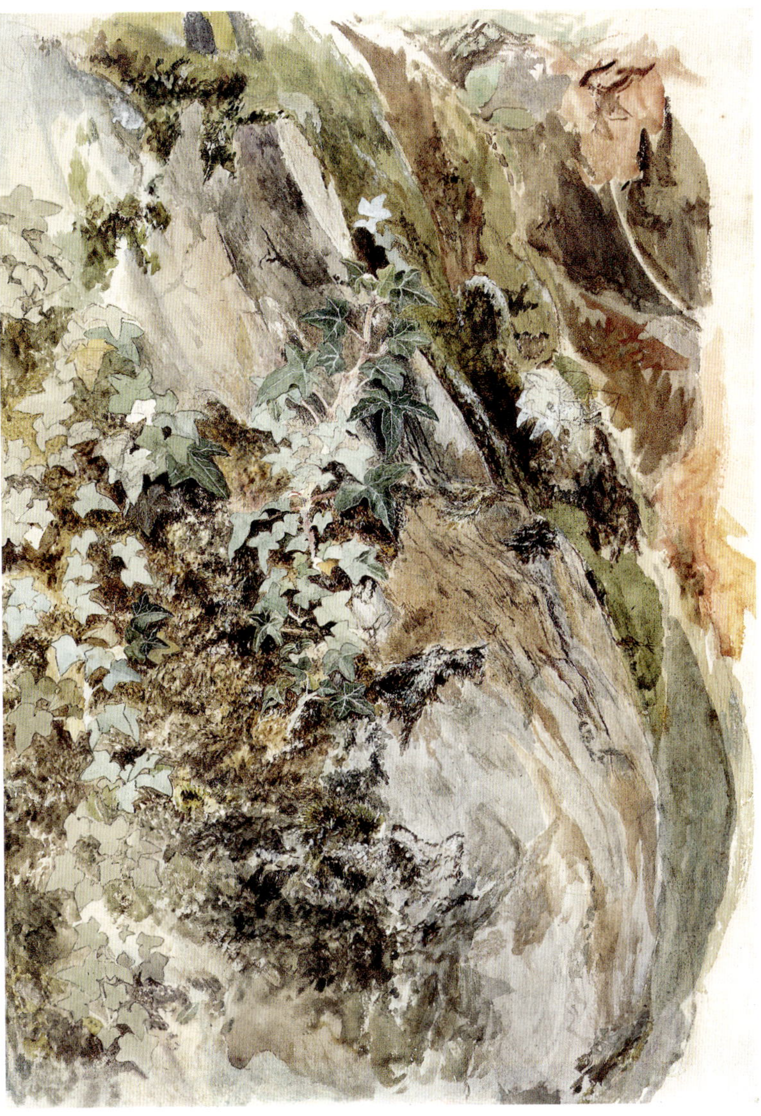

75   John Ruskin, *Study of Ivy*, 1872 or later, The British Museum, London

example, in the study of ivy made in the 1870s [75].

Ruskin particularly appreciated the works of William Henry Hunt (1790–1864), who exhibited at the Royal Academy and the Society of Painters in Watercolours throughout his long career. Ruskin took occasional lessons from him during 1854 and 1861. 'I am aware of no other pieces of art, in modern days, at once so sincere and so accomplished' he wrote of Hunt, adding that by 'sincere' he implied 'the unbiased directness of aim at the realization of very simple facts'.[7] The words 'sincere', 'unbiased' and 'simple' make clear a new kind of relationship between the artist and nature.

Ruskin among the drawing masters

Ruskin found models for his own ideas of what great landscape drawing might be in two books. The first, given

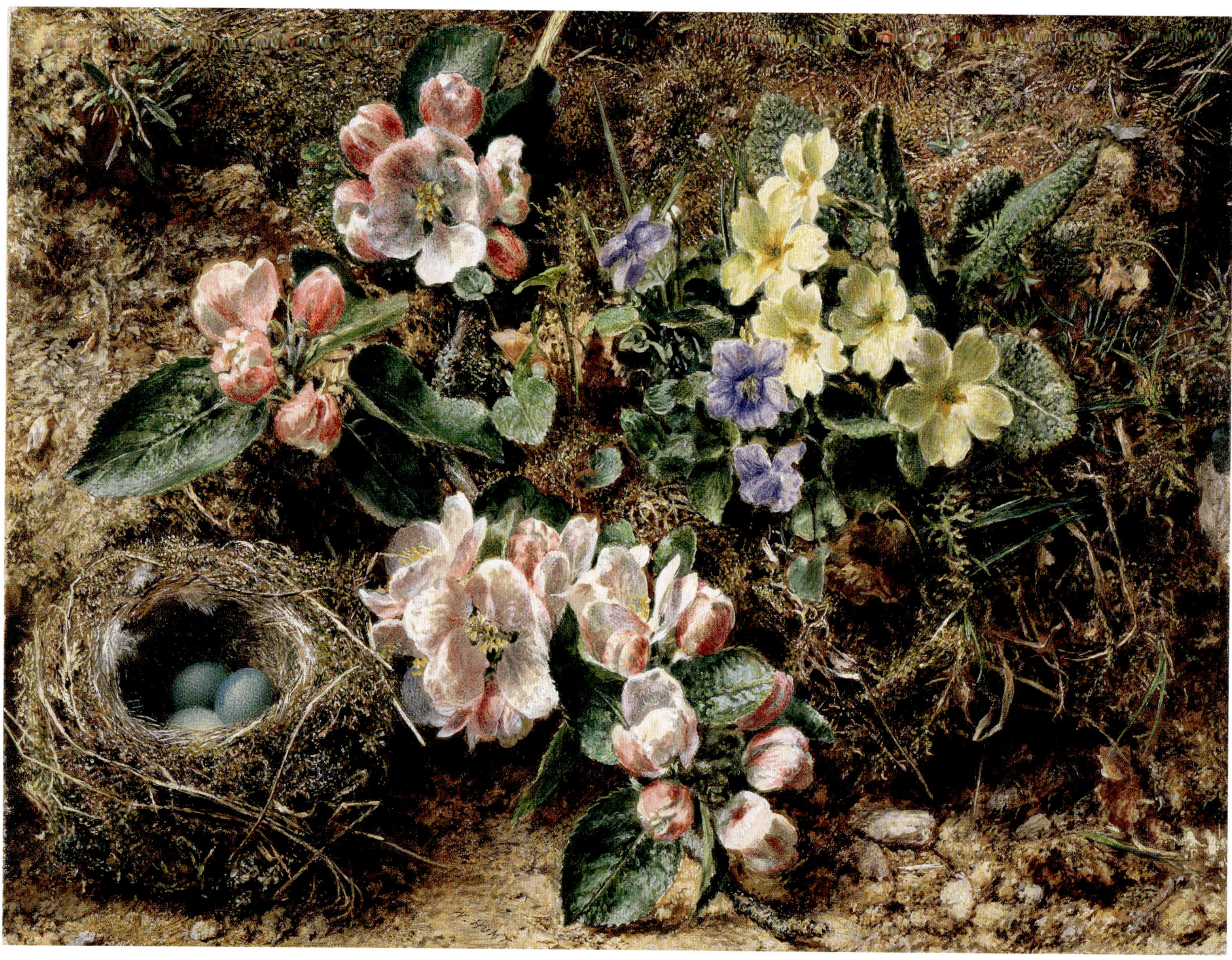

76 William Henry Hunt, *Bird's Nest, Apple Blossom and Primroses*, c. 1845–50, Birmingham Museums & Art Gallery

to him on his thirteenth birthday, was Samuel Rogers's *Italy* (1830), with vignettes by Turner. A year later Ruskin acquired a copy of Samuel Prout's *Facsimiles of Sketches Made in Flanders and Germany* (1833):

> We got the book home to Herne Hill before the time of our usual annual tour; and as my mother watched my father's pleasure and mine in looking at the wonderful places, she said, why should we not go and see some of them in reality?[8]

The connection between art, landscape and travel was firmly established for Ruskin at this point and was to remain important for the rest of his life. Topography and cartography lie at the heart of his graphic sensibility and he advocated the study of these branches of learning to students.

Ruskin studied drawing under three distinguished teachers: Charles Runciman (1825–67), A. V. Copley Fielding (1787–1855), President of the Society of Painters in Watercolours, and James Duffield Harding (1798–1863), who enjoyed fame as an author of handbooks on drawing and as a landscapist. From them Ruskin learned the conventions of picturesque landscape and techniques of handling a variety of drawing media.[9] Ruskin's early drawings show all the signs of instruction by drawing masters. Perhaps because they are landscape studies their conventions are not quite as obvious as they would be if their subject was the human figure, the representation of which, as we have seen, was bound by an observance of the rules of idealization. *An Italian Village* (c. 1845) [78] demonstrates one of Ruskin's earliest accomplishments: the soft pencil technique that aided the

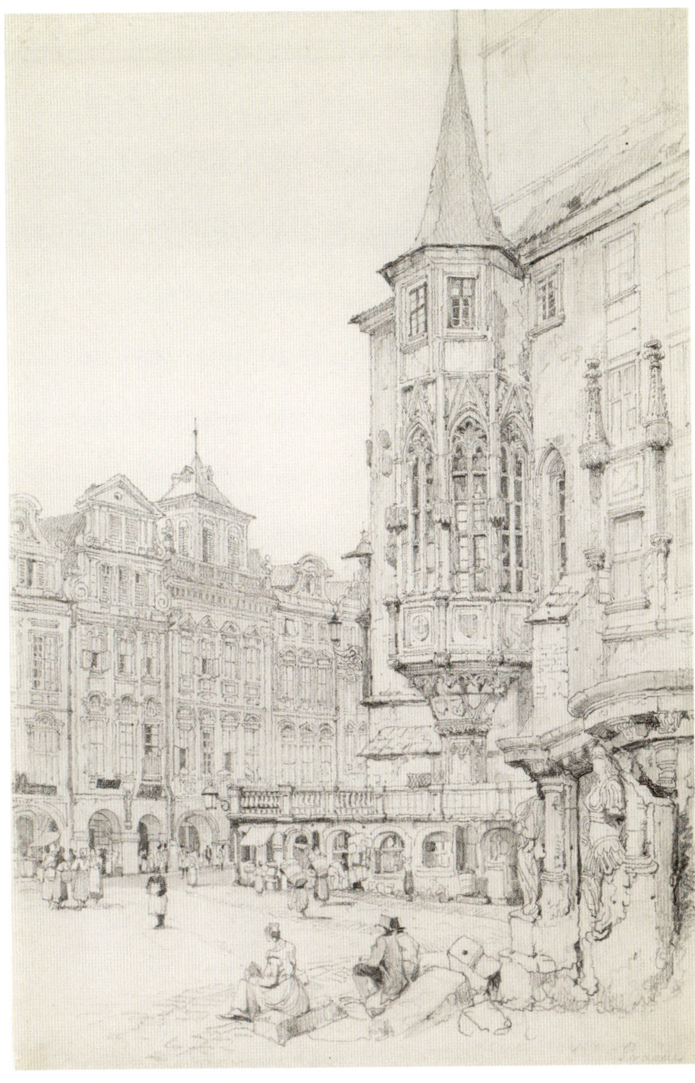

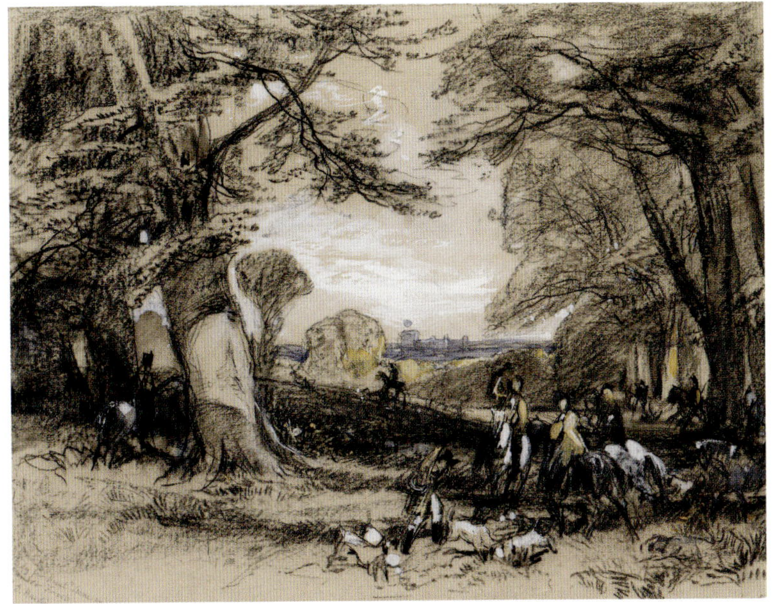

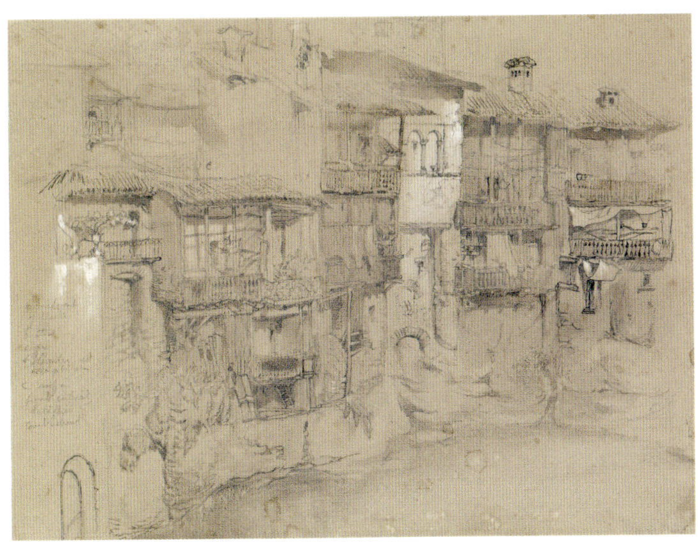

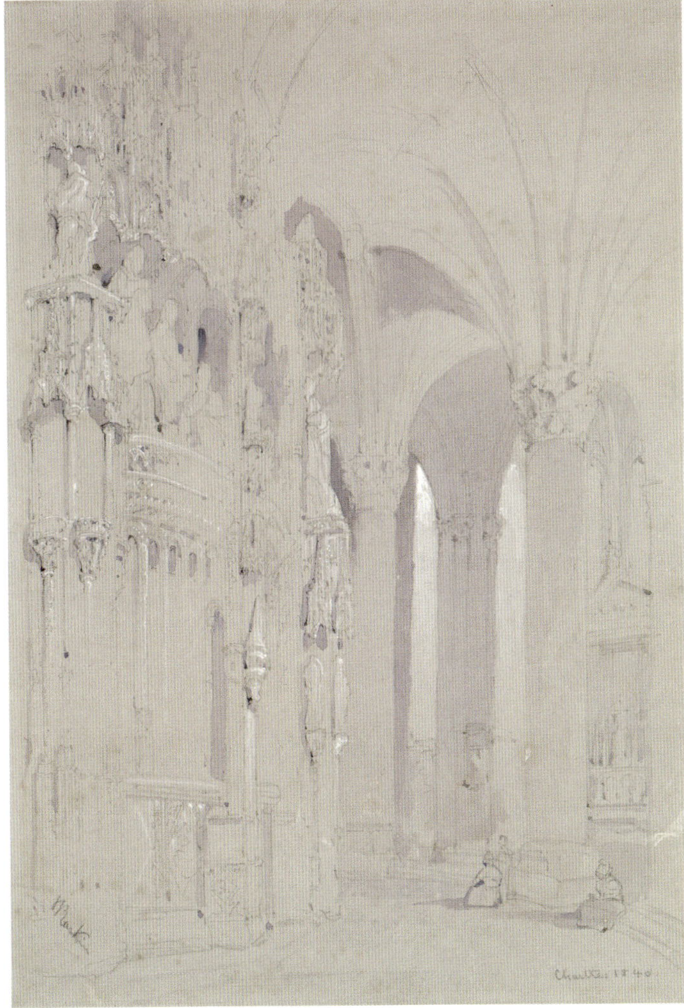

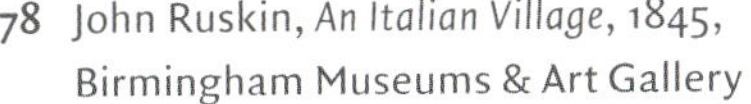

77 Samuel Prout, *The Altstadt, Prague*, undated,
Birmingham Museums & Art Gallery

78 John Ruskin, *An Italian Village*, 1845,
Birmingham Museums & Art Gallery

79 James Duffield Harding, *A Hunt Scene in Windsor Forest*, undated,
Birmingham Museums & Art Gallery

80 John Ruskin, *The Ambulatory, Chartres Cathedral*, 1840,
Birmingham Museums & Art Gallery

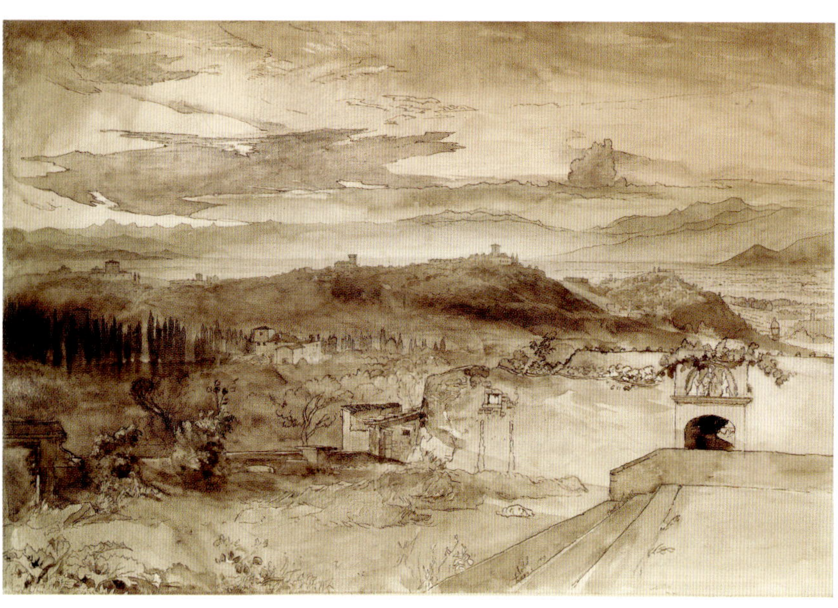

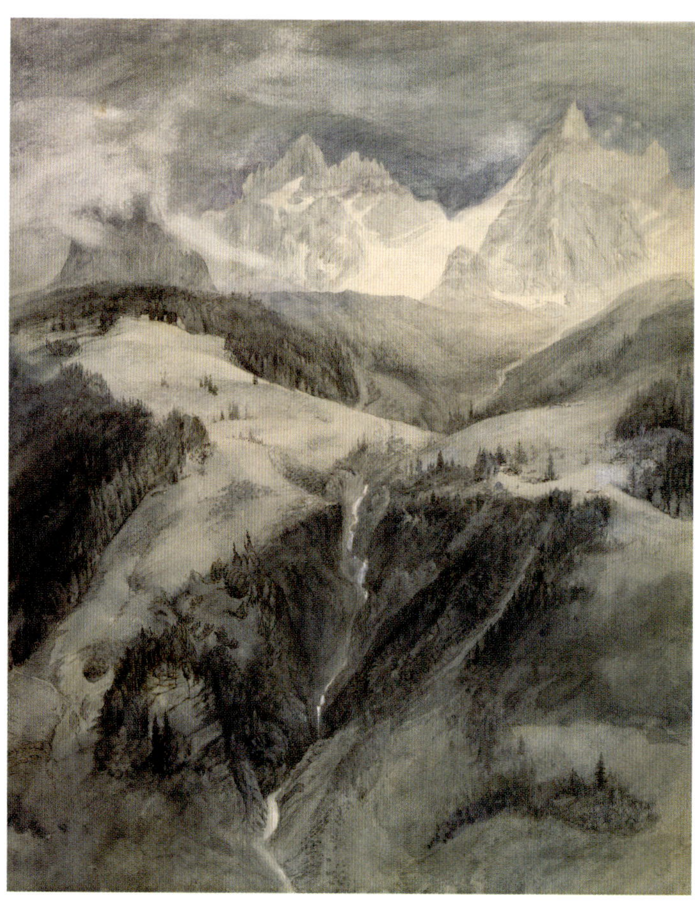

81 John Ruskin, *View from San Miniato al Monte, Florence*, 1845, Birmingham Museums & Art Gallery

82 John Ruskin, *Cascade de la Folie, Chamonix*, 1849, Birmingham Museums & Art Gallery

production of a wide range of tones and delicate modelling. His instruction was entirely in landscape drawing, which led to a deep understanding of that branch of art but did not encourage contact with history, genre and other types of subject painting that depended on the representation of the body. In landscape, Ruskin was to find a range of ideas that could be as significant in explaining historical events and spiritual experiences as any history painting. Likewise, he found drawing and printmaking as significant as the loftier art of painting.

Under Charles Runciman's instruction Ruskin's accomplishments were not distinguished, but under Harding's he became more discriminating. He perceived his teacher's 'shortcomings' but recalled that his 'knowledge of tree form was true, and entirely won for himself, with an honest original perception'.[10] Harding was himself the son of a professional teacher of drawing who was also an

engraver; he studied under both his father and Samuel Prout, among others. Like Prout, he was a successful author of handbooks for amateur artists. *Sketches at Home and Abroad* (1844), which sold for 6 guineas, was described by the publisher as having been

> entirely drawn on Stone by Mr. Harding himself, and printed under his immediate inspection. The resemblance to the Original Sketches is complete, and each Subject may be considered as a *bona fide* and first rate Drawing.

There was a lucrative market for drawing manuals throughout the nineteenth century, a feature of Victorian public self-improvement and self-education.

Harding was appreciative of Turner's landscapes and found in his *Liber Studiorum* (1807–19) an almost total absence of errors in composing landscape subjects, evidence that 'they have been studiously avoided'. Harding's

opinions chimed with Ruskin's and probably helped in their
formulation. While he regretted that his pupil's admiration
for Turner

> should partake so much of the nature of adoration;
> nevertheless, no work of modern times has made its
> appearance better calculated to be of use to students
> and amateurs of Art, or effectually to counterpoise,
> or clear away, the rubbish of antiquated prejudice,
> and make a fair field for the exercise and appreciation
> of talent.[11]

If this strikes us now as a little high-handed a judgment, we
must remember that Turner's reputation was not secure in
the decades leading up to his death and that Harding was
an admired, commercially successful artist and an authority
on the techniques of landscape drawing. Nevertheless it was
Turner who had the greatest impact on Ruskin, who copied,
collected and analysed his works in all media: painting,
watercolour, pencil and print of all kinds. The first volume
of *Modern Painters* (1843), which sets out to vindicate
Turner's talents, contains some adverse criticisms of his
works but makes huge claims for his skills, too, comparing
him favourably with the greatest painters of history. 'I
believe myself that these works are at the time of their first
appearing as perfect as those of Phidias or Leonardo' and
that Turner was 'the only painter who ever drew the stem of
a tree, Titian having come the nearest before him'.[12]

It was Turner's clarity of vision and his technical skill
in recording the totality of what he saw that impressed
Ruskin, who believed that the education of the eye was the
beginning of the education of the whole person. Ruskin's
ambitions were not professional in the narrowest sense but
profoundly concerned with achieving the truest response
from his eye and hand in response to nature. In fact, one
might say that he strove to create a new standard in the
production of art that had, at its centre, a moral quality
rather than an entirely, or even chiefly, aesthetic one.

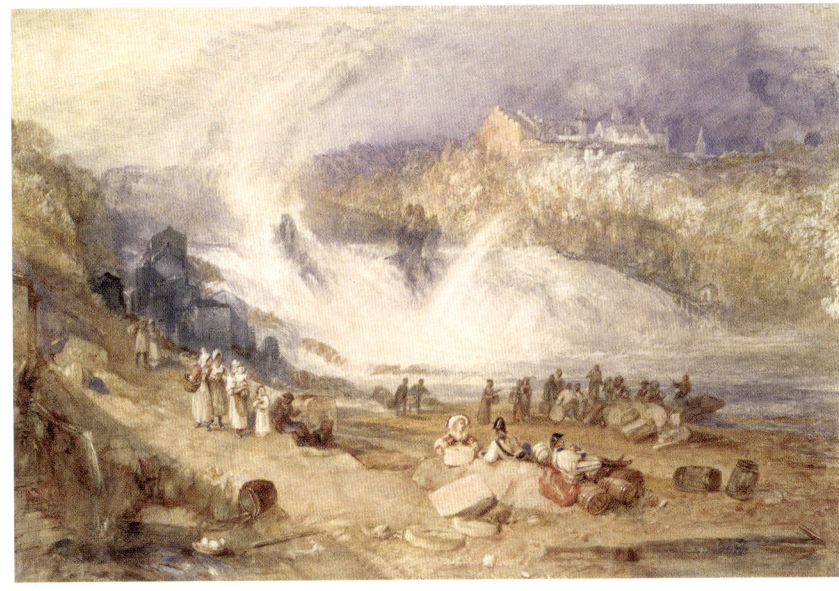

83 Joseph Mallord William Turner, *The Falls of the Rhine at Schaffhausen*,
1831–32, Birmingham Museums & Art Gallery

Ruskin separated the practice of teaching drawing from
its older, more polite meanings for the amateur, middle-
class enthusiast acquiring a genteel accomplishment.

Writing, drawing, reforming

Ruskin wrote three books directly concerned with the
practice of drawing: *Elements of Drawing* (1857), *The
Elements of Perspective* (1858) and *The Laws of Fésole*
(1877). Unsurprisingly – given his evolving views on
industrialization and labour – Ruskin's opinions were
radical, although his writings on drawing can be seen as
continuing rather than initiating a debate on art training
that had begun in the 1840s and had questioned the role
of both the Royal Academy and the recently formed
Schools of Design. Ruskin's instruction in drawing was
slow, demanding and sometimes dull. He advocated basic
drawing exercises before direct drawing from nature,

and selective copying from the works of reputable artists (such as Dürer or Turner, whose *Liber Studiorum* was of particular value). It was a process that led the participant to encounter nature, its structures and beauty, rather than design a conventional surface decoration or paint a picture. It was different to the 'kind of drawing which is taught, or supposed to be taught in our schools' which Ruskin found 'profitless alike to performer and beholder'.[13]

Ruskin became actively involved in the Working Men's College in Red Lion Square where, from 1854, he taught evening classes in 'Elementary Drawing'. Thomas Woolner (1825–92), Rossetti and Burne-Jones joined him as instructors. When Ruskin's *Elements of Drawing* was published, several reviewers noted his work as a teacher but traced the book's origins to his own somewhat conventional education as an amateur artist. *The Athenaeum*, for example, remarked that the

> enthusiasm that led Mr. Ruskin to turn drawing-master at the Working Men's College has now led him to publish the result of that self-instruction which honest teaching always brings to the honest teacher. Like Mr. Ruskin's other books, eloquent and acute as it is, it conveys a deep, but restricted, view of Art. It is, in fact, the book of an amateur of water-colour landscape, who knows little of even the technicalities of oil, and thinks figure-drawing out of all reach, – of a clever thinker, who has the word 'delicate' too much on his lips, with respect to Art – who prefers filmy gradation to robust contrast – who learned landscape from Harding and perspective from Runciman.[14]

Ruskin's other educational work was aided by the investment of the inheritance he received in 1864 following the death of his father. His investment in the Company of Saint George (which became the Guild of Saint George in 1878) brought together many of his concerns with industrialization and work, the political economy of art – as he was to describe it – as well as nature and beauty. Central to this project was the establishment of a museum, which in many ways resembled the teaching collections assembled by drawing masters in previous generations – drawings and watercolours, geological specimens, architectural fragments, illuminated manuscripts and printed books – brought together to educate the whole person: eye, hand and spirit. Ruskin was created Slade Professor of Fine Art at Oxford and inaugurated his own school of drawing there.[15]

Despite Ruskin's philanthropy, the far-sighted nature of his educational activities was not always respected by other teachers. His ideas were conceived in opposition not only to the traditions of the Royal Academy but also to the newly formulated system of instruction at the Government Schools of Design recently introduced throughout Britain. William Bell Scott (1811–90), who taught at the design school in Newcastle-upon-Tyne, was particularly exercised by Ruskin's ideas on art education. On a visit to the class at Red Lion Square he was shocked:

> I found drawing from copies as preliminary practice, drawing from beautiful ornamental objects or human figures – everything indeed to be seen in academic or Government schools of art practice – ignored....Instead of these, here everyone was trying to put on small pieces of paper imitations by pen and ink of pieces of rough stick crusted with dry lichens...[Ruskin] drew my attention to the beauty of these as giving the pupils a love of 'nature'!...I came away feeling that such pretence of education was in a high degree criminal; it was intellectual murder; not one of the young men who attended at the Working Man's College ever acquired any power of drawing.[16]

Scott's judgment is unfair. Ruskin was not attempting to create professional artists but to inspire amateurs to learn to look closely and accurately. This is true of all his

educational work – teaching classes, writing books
of instruction and setting up educational foundations.
In other critical writings Ruskin's agenda was a broader
one, going to the heart of the moral issues of making art
in a society where the chief aim was making wealth.
Despite Scott's opinion to the contrary, Ruskin had some
success in creating professional artists and teachers.
T. C. Farrer (1839–91) studied under Ruskin at the Working
Men's College and then migrated to the USA. He was
described by the *New York Times* as 'leader of the group
known as the Pre-Raphaelites in our city' and characterized
his work as 'faithful drawing'.[17] Farrer specialized in figure
compositions, portraits and still life subjects in pencil,
drawings of great elaboration typical of an American
Ruskinism that fed into contemporary American concerns
with landscape, nature and transcendentalism.[18]

Indeed, Ruskin's writings found a receptive audience in
the USA, where 'truth to nature' laid the foundation for an
art movement where microscopic treatment of fragments
of nature, landscape and even the human face was the
aim. His own drawings were shown in Boston in October
1879 following a showing the year before in London. In his
introduction to the catalogue, Charles Eliot Norton (1827–
1908) wrote that the exhibition was

> of peculiar interest to the numerous students of Mr.
> Ruskin's writings, and especially to that large body of
> readers who recognize their obligation to him as the
> teacher by whose lessons in the study of nature and of
> art their faculties of observation and of perception have
> been chiefly cultivated, their powers of appreciation
> best directed and developed, and their capacities of
> enjoyment indefinitely increased and enlarged.[19]

Ruskin's intentions as an artist and teacher appeared to
have found their ideal audience in the USA.

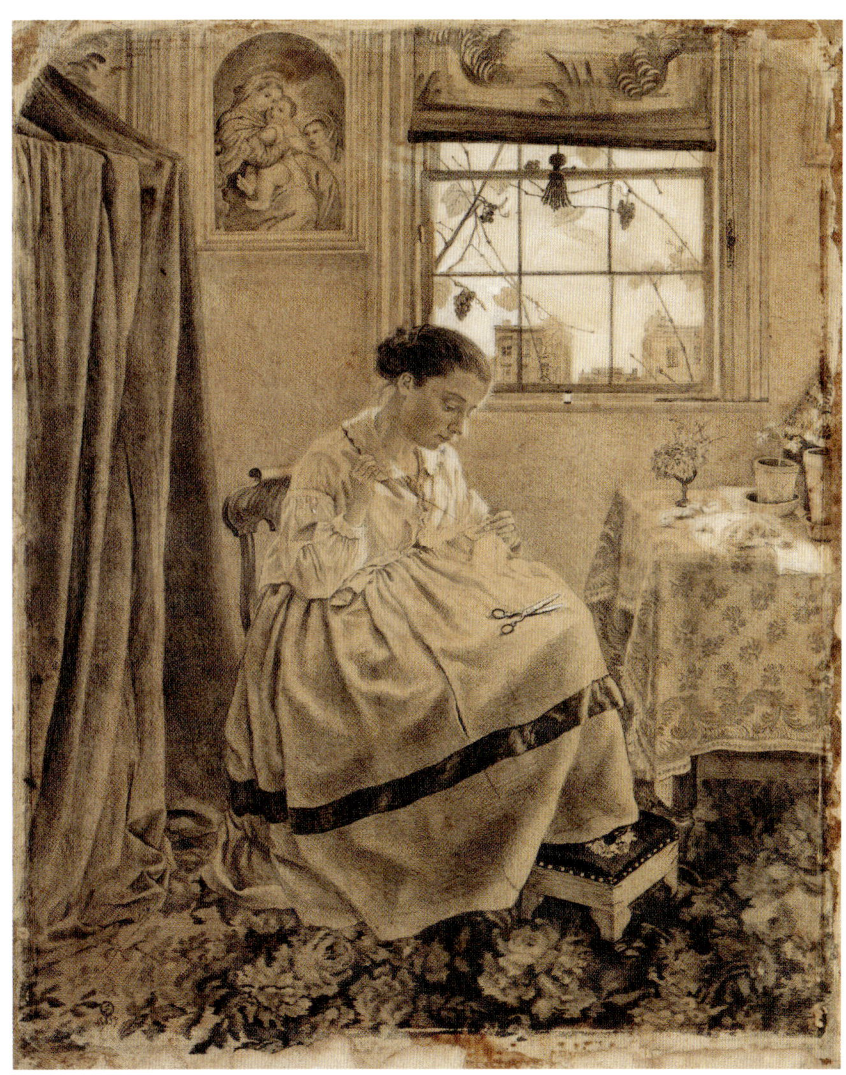

84 Thomas Charles Farrer, *Woman Sewing*, 1854,
Princeton University Art Museum

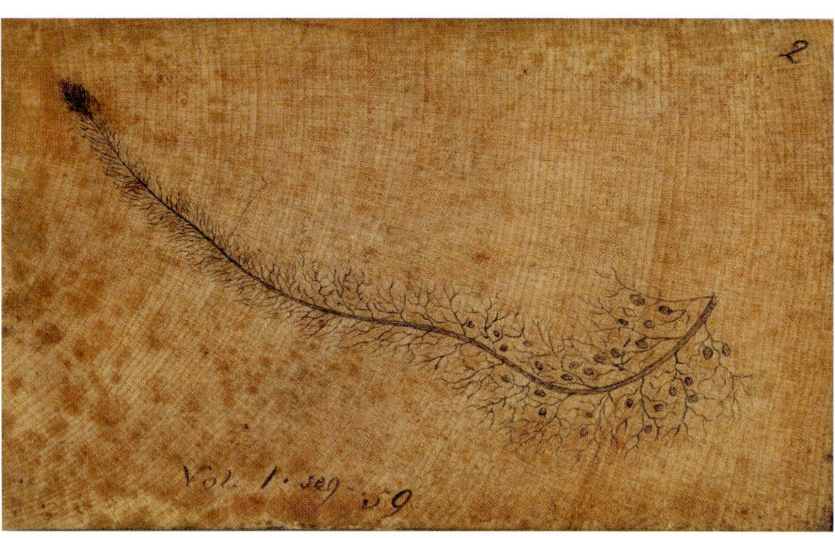

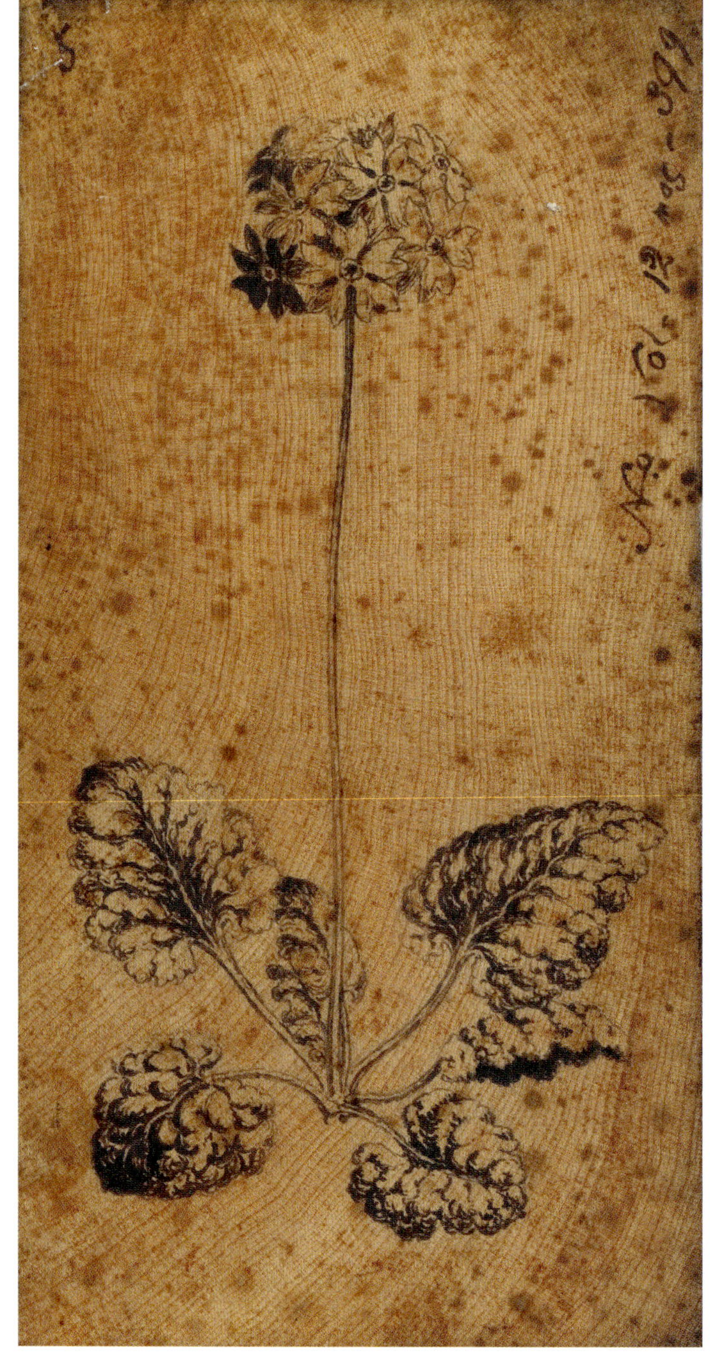

85, 86 Arthur Burgess after John Ruskin, *Two Unused Designs for 'Proserpina: Studies of Wayside Flowers'*, uncut woodblocks, c. 1875, Birmingham Museums & Art Gallery

Bits of nature

In 1863, in a skit on the Royal Academy exhibition of that summer, the satirical magazine *Fun* invented a work called *Docks and Marsh Mallows*, which it described as a Pre-Raphaelite bit of nature.[20] The title was a poke at the proliferation of those many 'bits of nature' that were produced by young artists during the 1860s, inspired as much by Ruskin's critical writings as by works exhibited by the Pre-Raphaelites. Ruskin's enthusiasm for drawing botanical specimens accurately is communicated in *Elements of Drawing* and *The Laws of Fésole*, both illustrated with line engravings after his drawings [88, 89, 90].

Ruskin's teaching in *Elements of Drawing* is directed towards encouraging steadiness of hand and precision of observation as well as inculcating habits of accuracy in his students rather than an abstract concept of 'truth' in itself. What is set out in the chapters is a series of

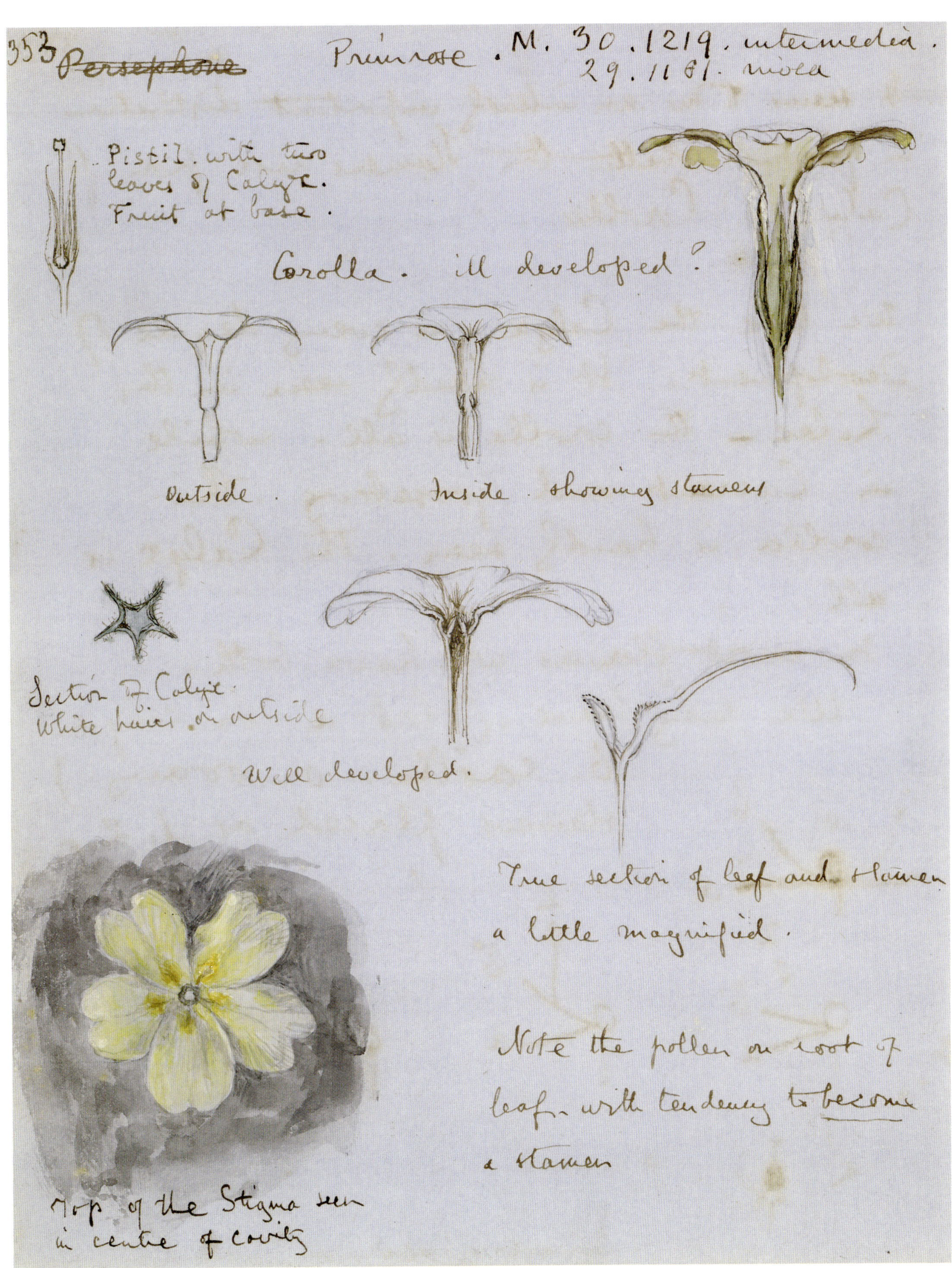

87 John Ruskin, *Eight Studies of a Primrose*, probably 1870s, Birmingham Museums & Art Gallery

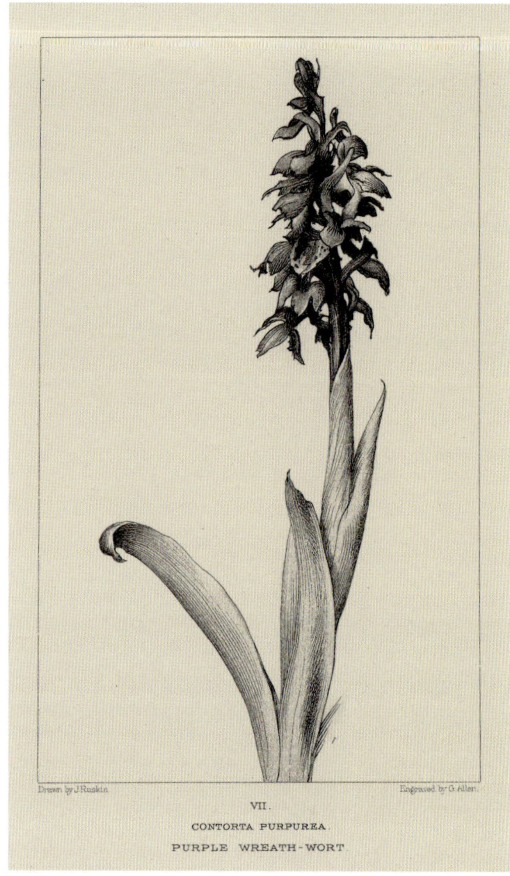

Drawn by J.Ruskin.   Engraved by G.Allen.

VII.

CONTORTA PURPUREA.

PURPLE WREATH-WORT.

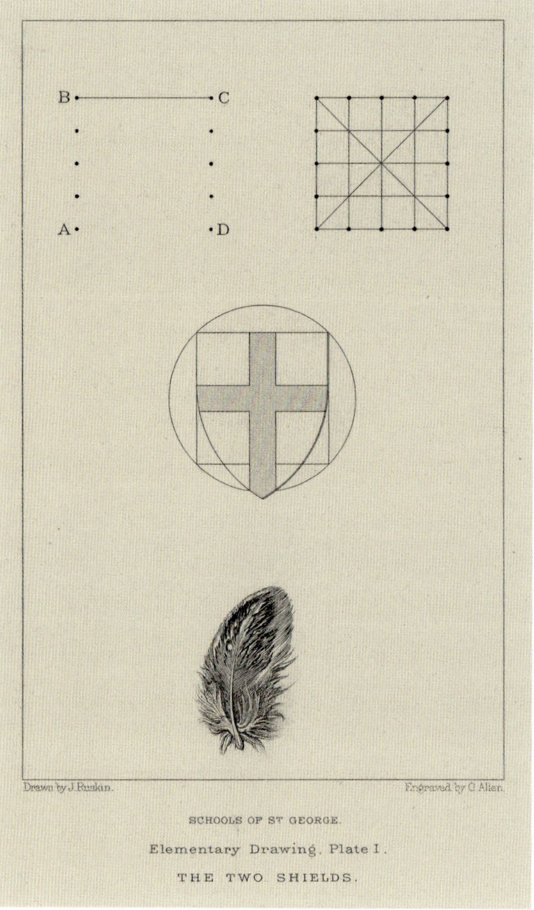

Drawn by J.Ruskin.   Engraved by G.Allen.

SCHOOLS OF ST GEORGE.

Elementary Drawing. Plate I.

THE TWO SHIELDS.

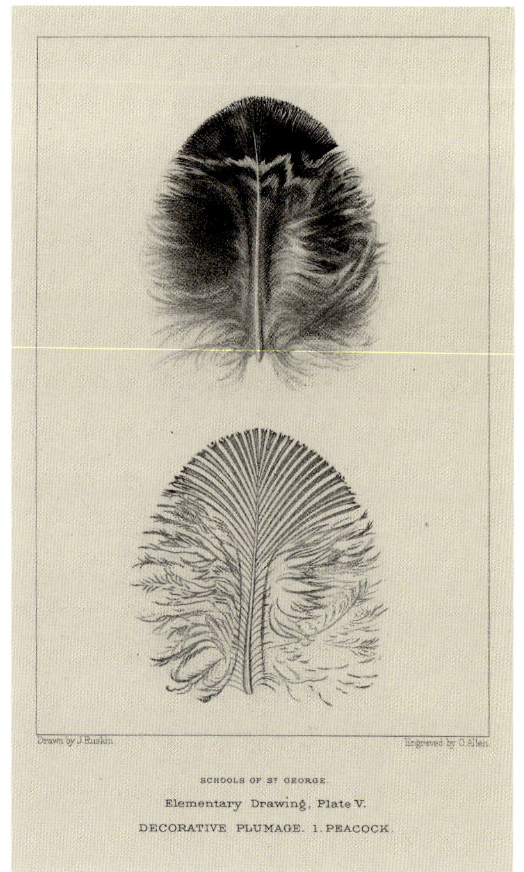

Drawn by J.Ruskin.   Engraved by G.Allen.

SCHOOLS OF ST GEORGE.

Elementary Drawing. Plate V.

DECORATIVE PLUMAGE. 1. PEACOCK.

88 George Allen after John Ruskin, *Plate from
    'Proserpina: Studies of Wayside Flowers'*:
    Contorta Purpurea (Purple Wreath-wort), c. 1877,
    Birmingham Museums & Art Gallery

89 George Allen after John Ruskin, *Plate from
    'The Laws of Fésole': Decorative Plumage I: Peacock*,
    c. 1877, Birmingham Museums & Art Gallery

90 George Allen after John Ruskin, *Plate from
    'The Laws of Fésole': The Two Shields*, c. 1877,
    Birmingham Museums & Art Gallery

exercises in line, the drawing of curves and the use of colour, among others. The hen's feather recommended for study in Chapter 6 of *The Laws of Fésole* is the subject of a long disquisition on the various classes of birds and the different structures of their feathers [89, 90]. Ruskin draws the reader's attention to radiating lines in nature but, before the drawing is attempted, he directs the student to consider the idea of function and design in nature as a whole. Nature, multi-layered and complex, is thus understandable to the draughtsman if correct principles are applied to its study. Part scientific, part poetic, Ruskin's

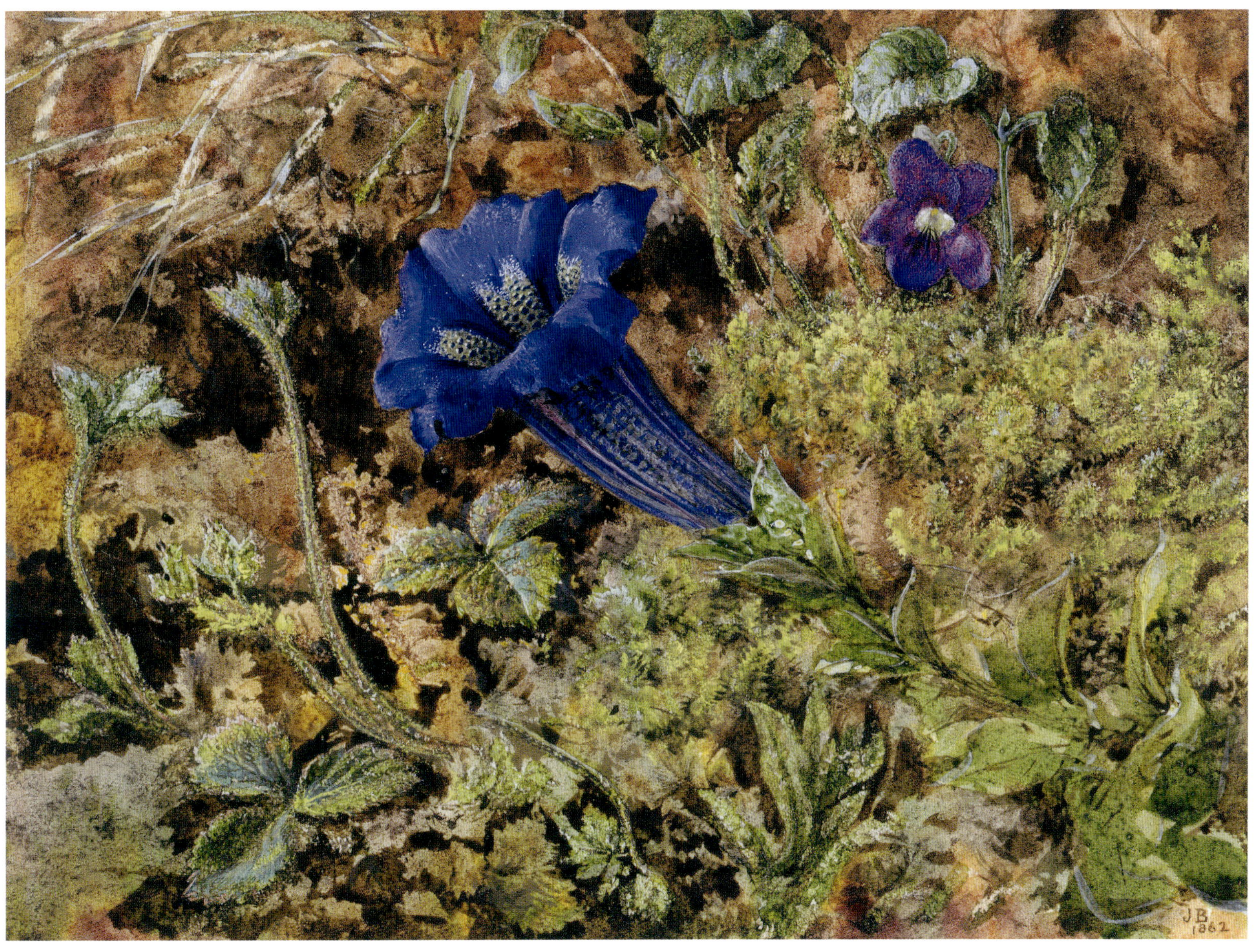

91   John Brett, *Gentian*, 1862, The Williamson Art Gallery and Museum, Birkenhead, Wirral

observations force us to consider the function of each part of nature, demanding that the artist take all of these various functions into consideration at all points in the creation of works of art. Ruskin's educational system attempts to encapsulate a variety of natural phenomena: meteorological, geological, botanical and atmospheric. In a telling passage in *Elements of Drawing*, Ruskin hints at the most daunting characteristic of landscape representation, 'mystery'. Ruskin goes further:

> how much of all that is round us, in men's actions or spirits, which we at first think we understand, a closer

and more loving watchfulness would show to be full of mystery, never to be either fathomed or withdrawn.[21] According to Ruskin, Turner was the only artist to achieve an expression of the 'mystery' of landscape.

Ruskin's writings directly influenced the early career of John Brett (1831–1902) who read *Modern Painters* and the pamphlet *Pre-Raphaelitism* before alighting on what he described as 'Ruskin's Letters', *Elements of Drawing*.[22] Brett showed several works at the Pre-Raphaelite exhibition at the Hogarth Club, London, in 1857, where the poet Coventry Patmore noted that

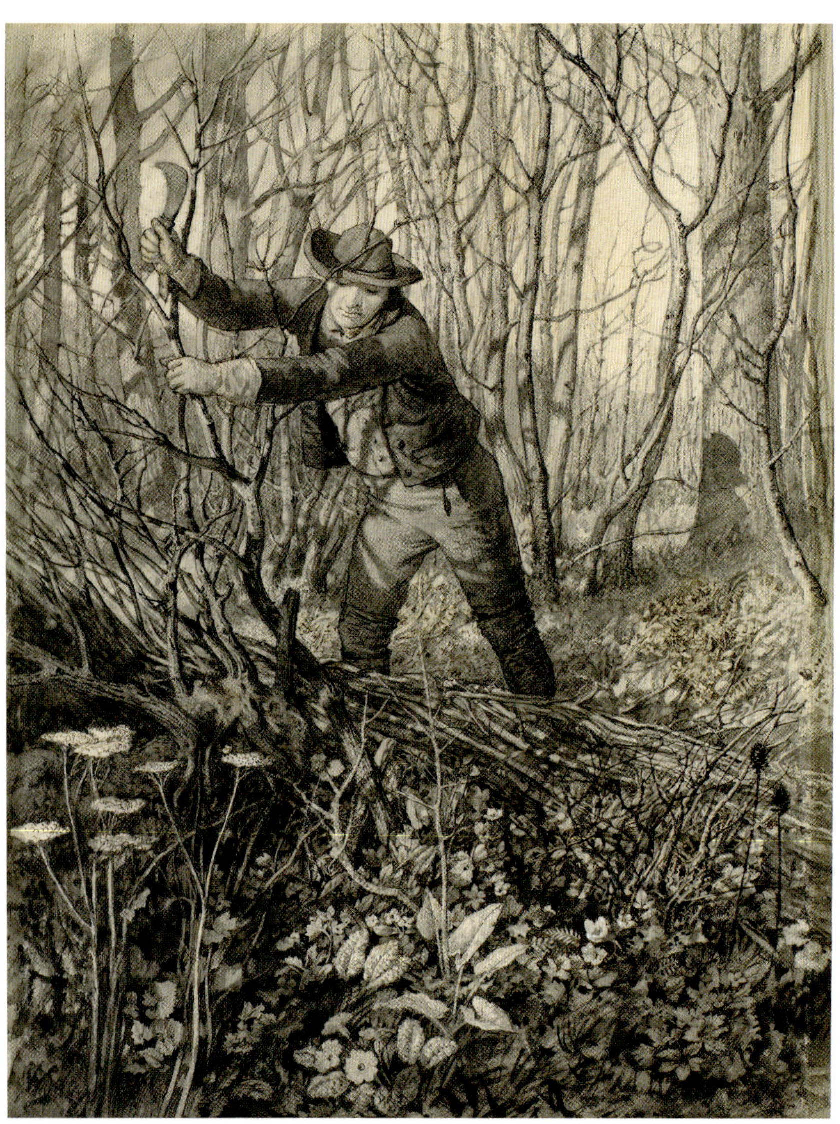

92 John Brett, *The Hedger*, c. 1859, private collection

Brett and Thomas Seddon (1821–56) had eyes that were 'simple photographic lenses', remarking further that

Mr Brett's drawing of 'The Engel's Hörner and Glacier from Rosenlaui', and 'Moss and Gentians from the Engel's Hörner', are wonders of laborious and effective finish.[23]

A version of the same subject, gentians growing through moss, was completed in 1862 [91].

Brett's major works of the late 1850s and early 1860s were truly Ruskinian: they moved beyond description of landscape to include social, scientific and spiritual ideas, and were distinguished by their attention to natural phenomena of all kinds. Ruskin encouraged Brett to tackle Alpine landscape in the Pre-Raphaelite manner. The foreground studies in his major works *The Val D'Aosta* (1858, Collection of Lord Lloyd Webber) and *The Glacier at Rosenlaui* (1856, Tate) outdo other Pre-Raphaelite works in virtuosity, even when compared to paintings like Millais's *Ophelia*, which shocked its original audience in its detailed treatment of the flora of an English riverbank.[24]

John Brett's landscapes of the 1850s and early 1860s are characterized by extraordinary botanical, geological and meteorological observation. *The Hedger* (c. 1859) [92] records everything from undergrowth to sky with a steady and consistent uniformity of handling, and contains, like several of Brett's other landscapes of this early period, an implicit social narrative. Ruskin's *Academy Notes* of 1858 contained a very specific exhortation – a development of his original appeal to artists to go to nature – to examine various subjects, seasons and flowers:

How strange that among all this painting of delicate detail there is not a true one of English spring!…
that no Pre-Raphaelite has painted a cherry-tree in blossom.

He listed specific flowers and their habitats, ending, 'Everything has to be done yet.'[25] Several fine drawings

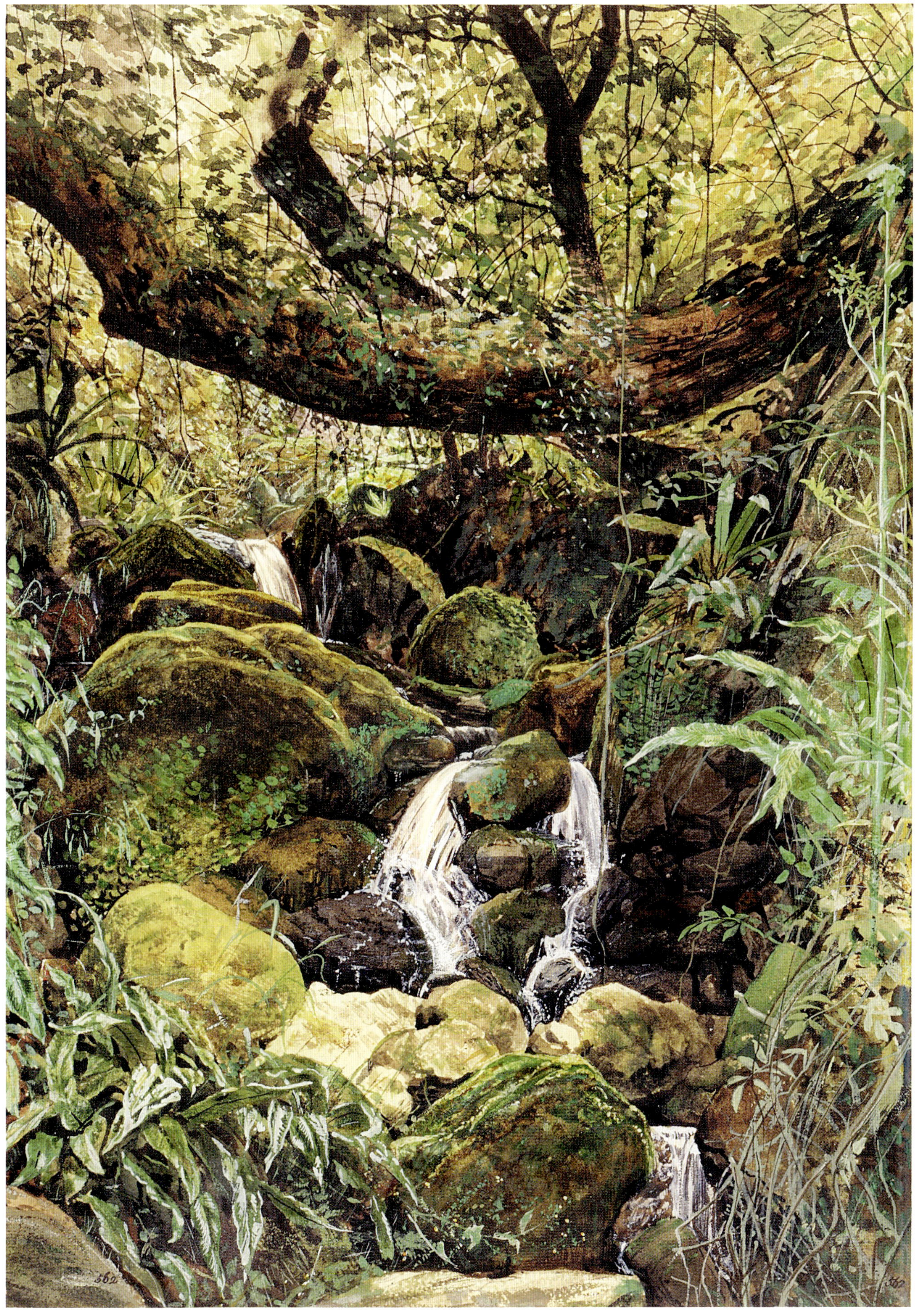

93 Henry Bowler, *Luccombe Chine, Isle of Wight*, 1860, Victoria and Albert Museum, London

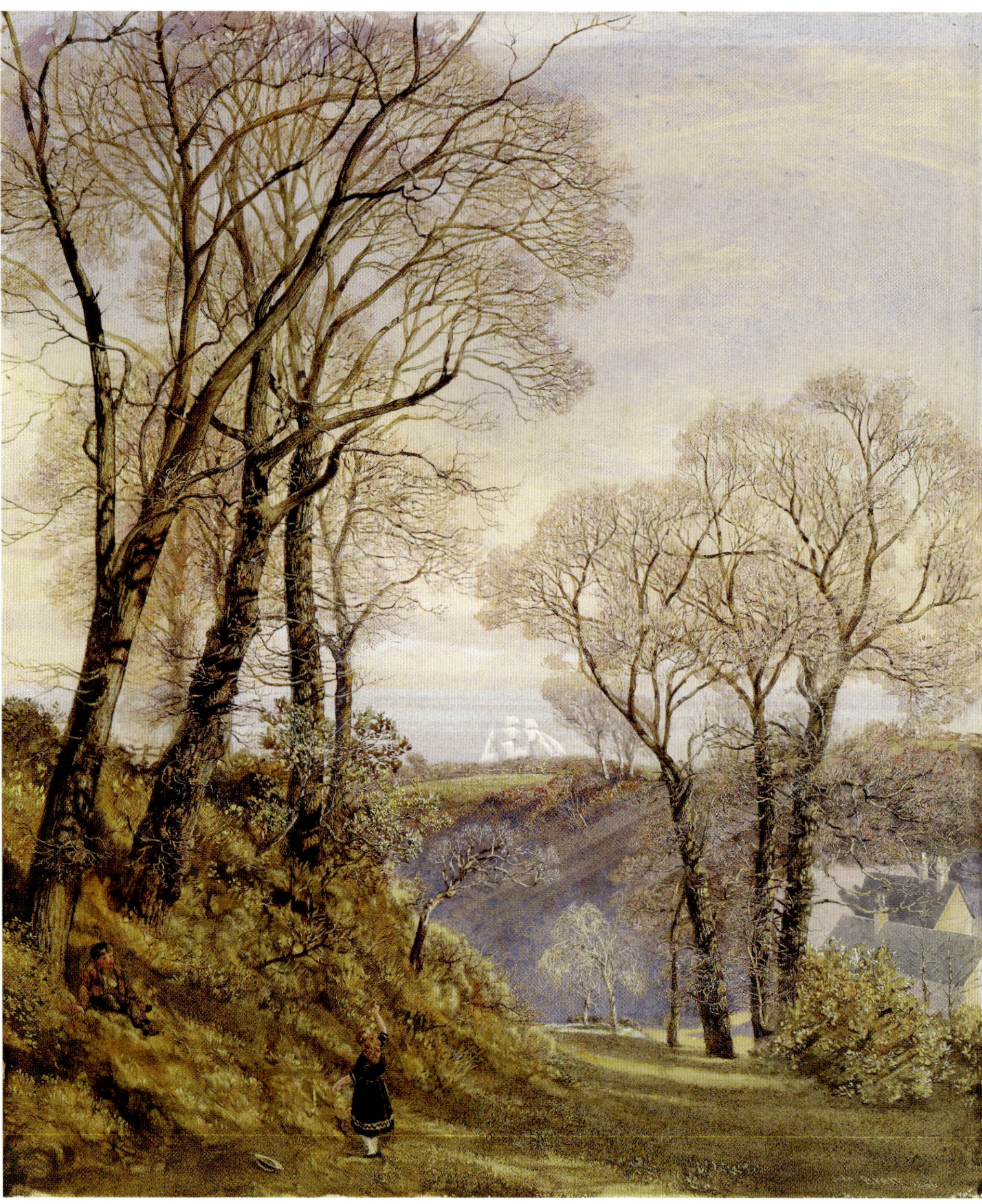

94 John Brett, *February on the Isle of Wight*, 1866, Birmingham Museums & Art Gallery

and paintings by Brett, such as *The Hedger*, appear to respond directly to this challenge. However, despite Brett's faithful response to Ruskin's advice, some of Ruskin's published references to Brett were highly critical and almost dismissive. In the *Academy Notes* of 1859, Ruskin, reviewing Brett's *The Val D'Aosta*, suggested that the artist had succeeded in producing 'historical landscape', only to find a strange fault in it and to declare the result 'wholly emotionless'. His most damning observation on the picture, pithily expressed, was: 'I never saw the mirror

so held up to Nature; but it is Mirror's work, not Man's.'[26] Ruskin demanded a kind of landscape painting that moved seamlessly from the depiction of nature as a series of accurately observed and drawn fragments – the leaf and the flower – to the reproduction of the atmospheric effects and profound impressions of nature in its entirety. Hence – and confusingly – he found Brett's depiction of the Swiss valley 'notable' yet not 'noble'.[27]

The historian of Pre-Raphaelite landscape painters Allen Staley concluded that after Brett's *The Val D'Aosta*

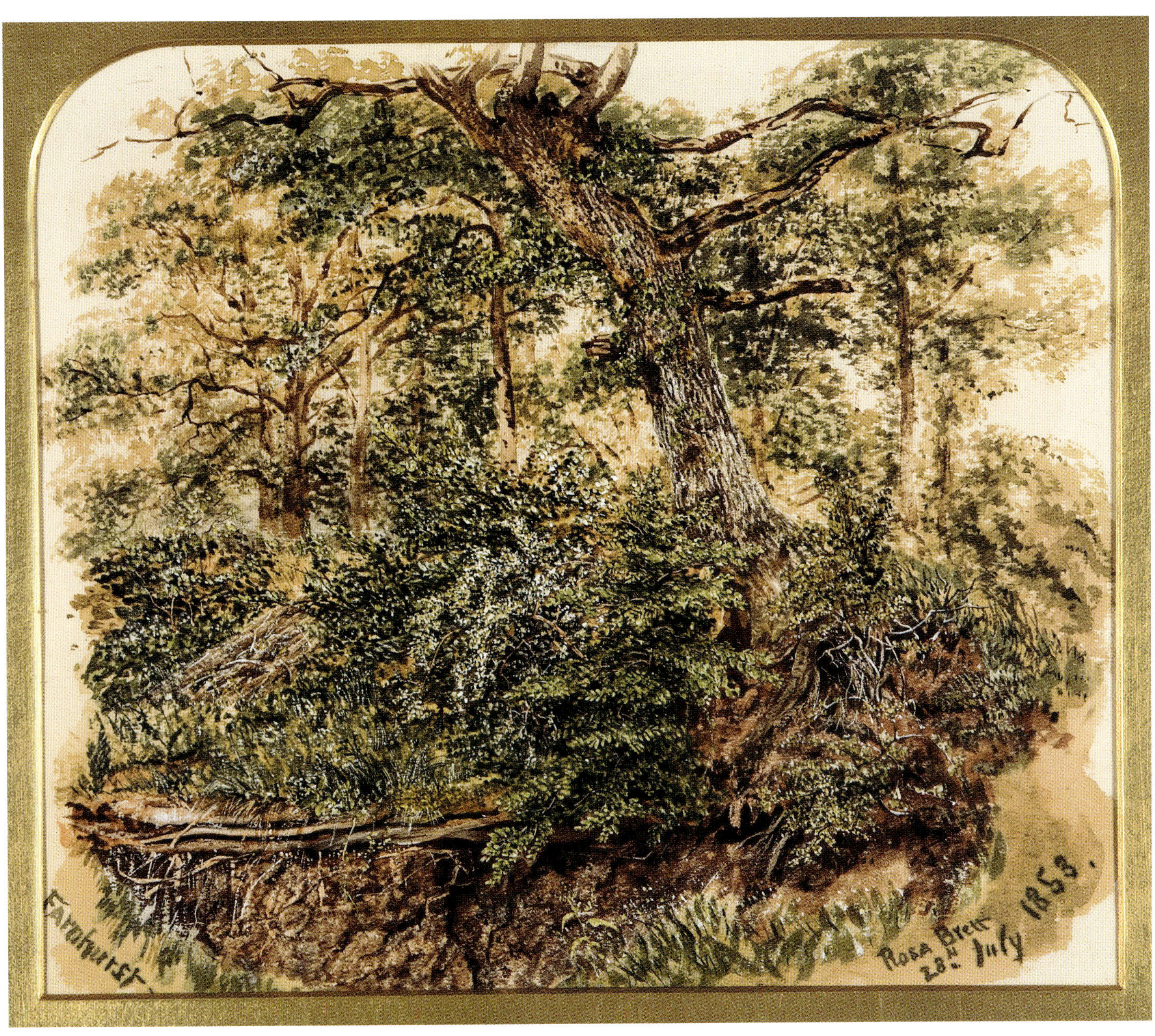

95 Rosa Brett, *Farnhurst*, 1853, private collection

Ruskin 'largely abandoned his active encouragement of contemporary artists'.[28] However, the movement in landscape painting that he encouraged continued to grow throughout the 1860s in works by professional and amateur artists. A view of Luccombe Chine on the Isle of Wight by Henry Bowler (1824–1903) [93], known chiefly for his painting *The Doubt: 'Can these Dry Bones Live?'* (1855, Tate), anticipates Brett's *February on the Isle of Wight* (1866) [94] in attempting to communicate the total experience of being in a landscape. Bowler could scarcely have attempted a more complex view of undergrowth; indeed, this is a landscape composed almost entirely of undergrowth details. In looking downwards Bowler avoids the more traditional landscape viewpoint of looking outwards towards a panoramic or picturesque view. In *Luccombe Chine* Bowler featured several elements already tackled by Millais in paintings such as *Ophelia* and *Portrait of John Ruskin* (1853–54, private collection): a cascading stream, mossy rocks, ferns and a fallen tree. In *February on the Isle of Wight* Brett attempts something

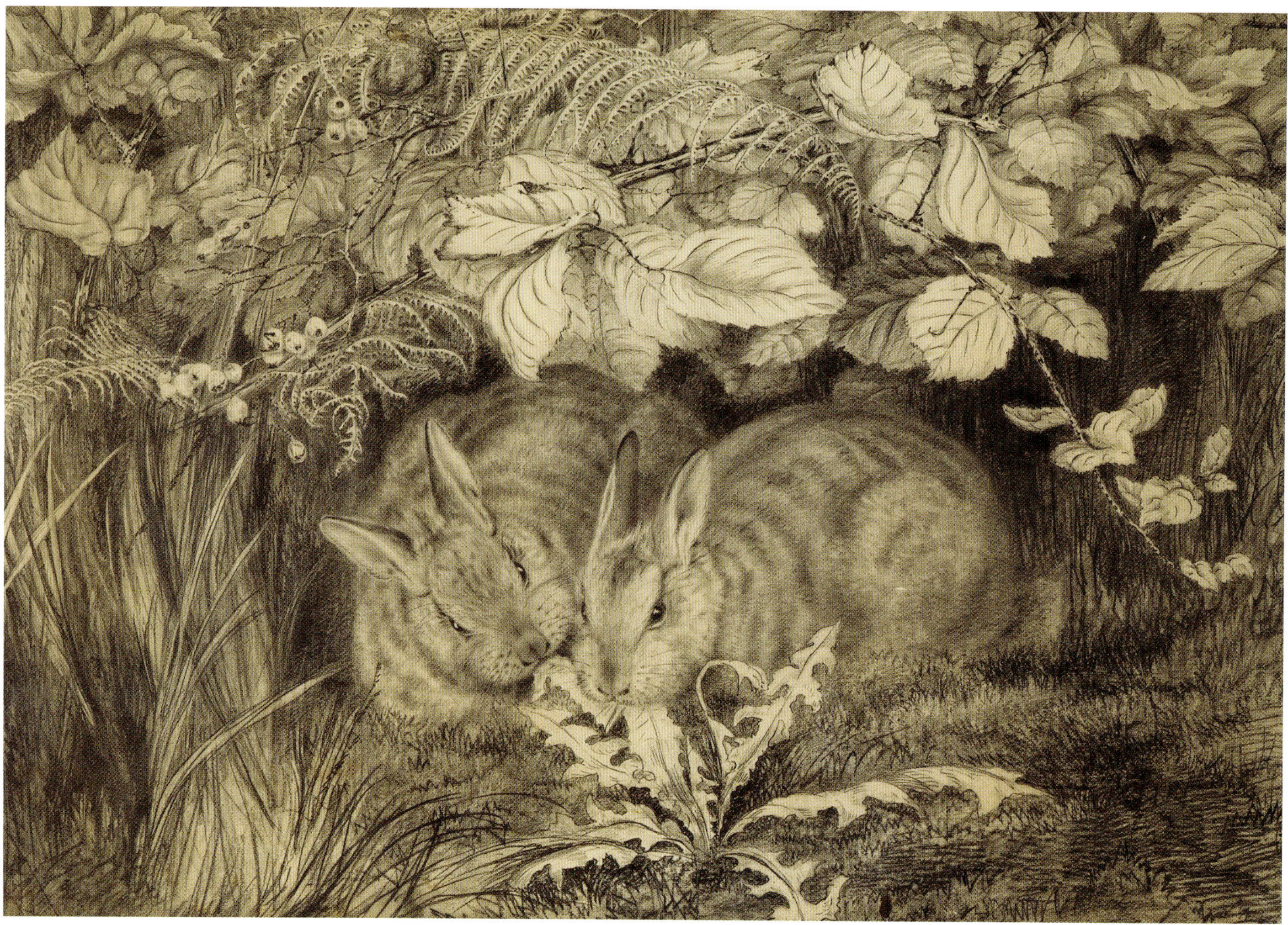

96 Rosa Brett, *Study of Two Rabbits*, undated, private collection

more ambitious, if less detailed. The trees seem just about to bud in the chill sunlight of late winter, and the land disappears in an evanescence of light, mist and smoke in the middle distance, which is an almost Turneresque effect. The gracefulness of the trees shows the influence of J. D. Harding, with whom both John Brett and his sister Rosa (1829–82) had studied at Ruskin's recommendation.

Brett modified his early Ruskinian mode in favour of a somewhat broader one. He passed his enthusiasm for Ruskin on to Rosa, whose acuity of vision sometimes surpassed her brother's. Her landscape watercolour showing the edge of a wood in Farnhurst [95], a favourite sketching place, demonstrates a love of the detail of nature.[29] Her depictions of corners of gardens and haylofts often describe a meeting point between the domestic or cultivated world and an untamed nature. Indeed, we might see in many of these drawings and watercolours glimpses of nature as almost suburban – the ivy-clad bole of a tree, the bird's nest, the corner of a garden flecked with sunlight – fragments of a lost wilderness. Such is the case with Rosa Brett's drawing of rabbits [96], which follows on the tradition of William Henry Hunt. Nature is uprooted and brought into the studio as a reminiscence of a wilder, more forbidding force. It is tempting to see the drawing as mirroring two of Dürer's most famous exercises in drawing from nature, *The Large Piece of Turf* (1503, Albertina, Vienna) and *The Hare* (1502, Albertina, Vienna).

Following Ruskin's advocacy, many artists – among them Frederick Sandys (1829–1904) [98, 99, 100, 101], Albert Moore (1841–93) [97] and Arthur Hughes (1832–1915) [170, 171, 172] – used undergrowth or small foreground details such as the ivy-clad stump or tree as a central subject,

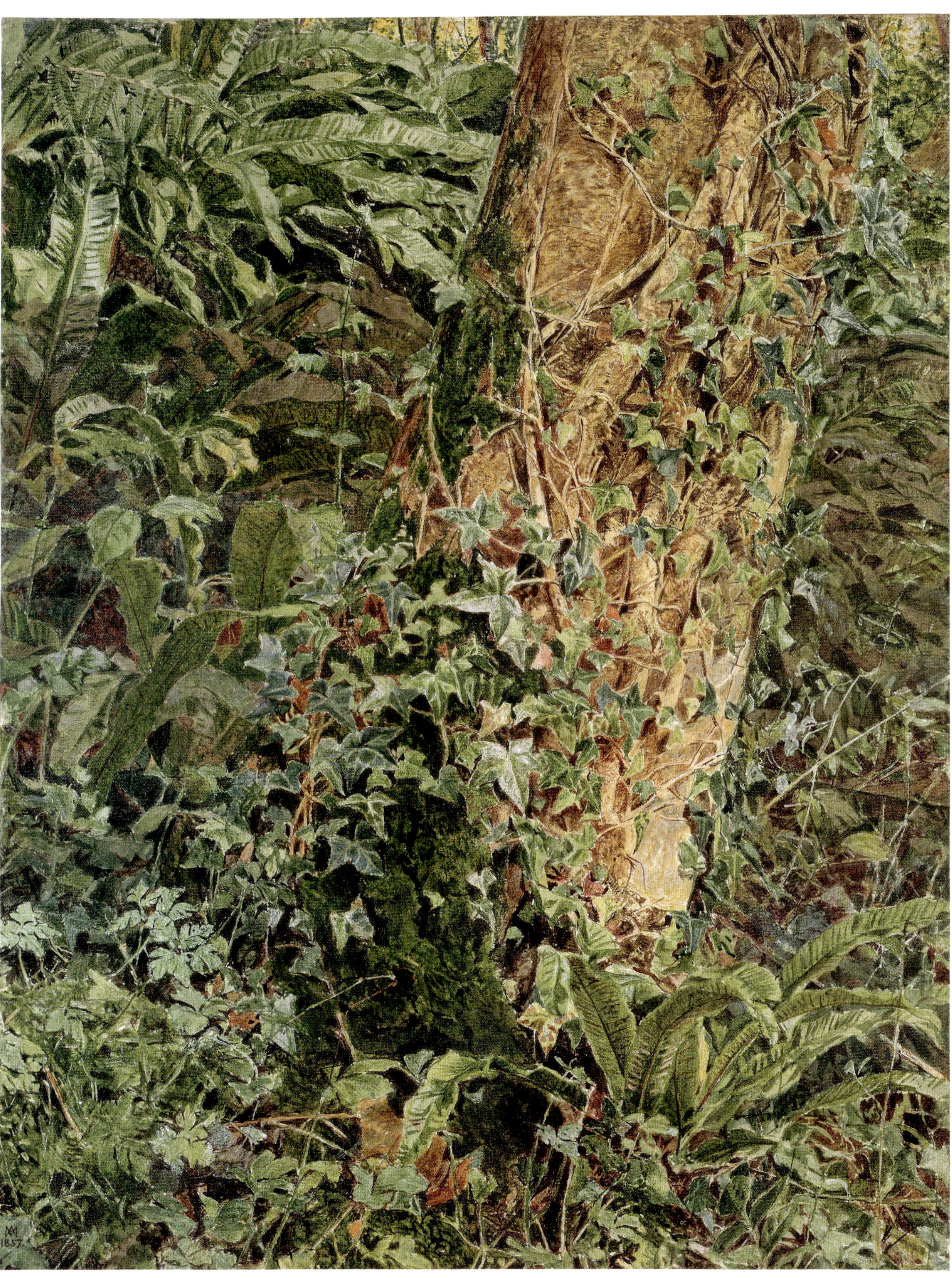

97 Albert Moore, *Study of an Ash Trunk*, 1857, Ashmolean Museum, University of Oxford

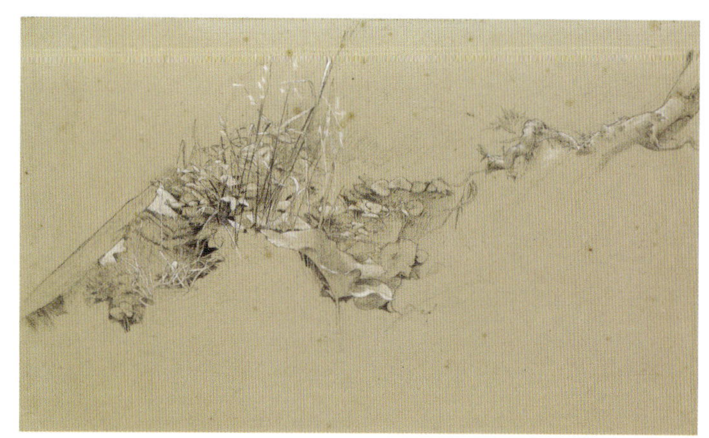

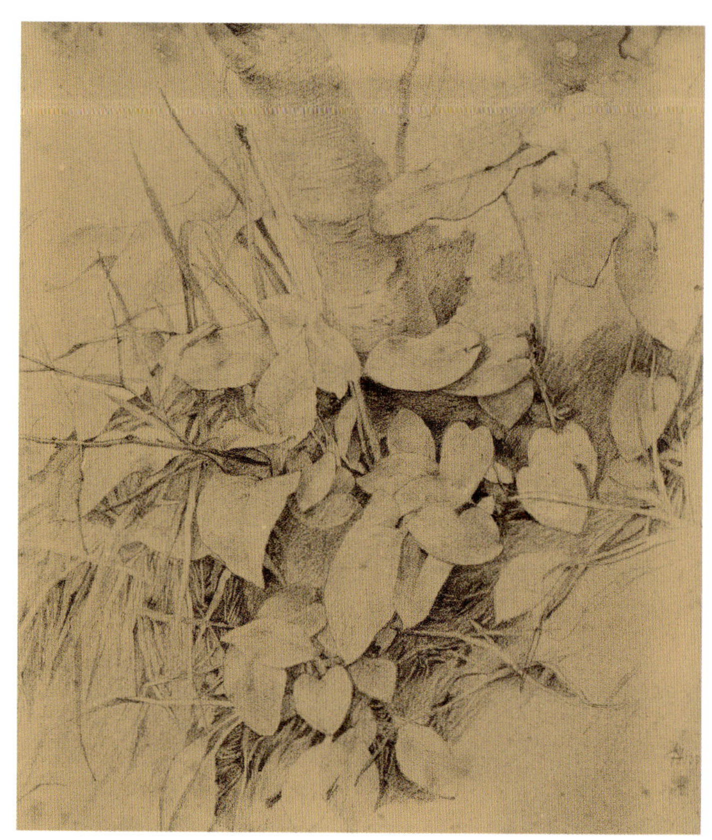

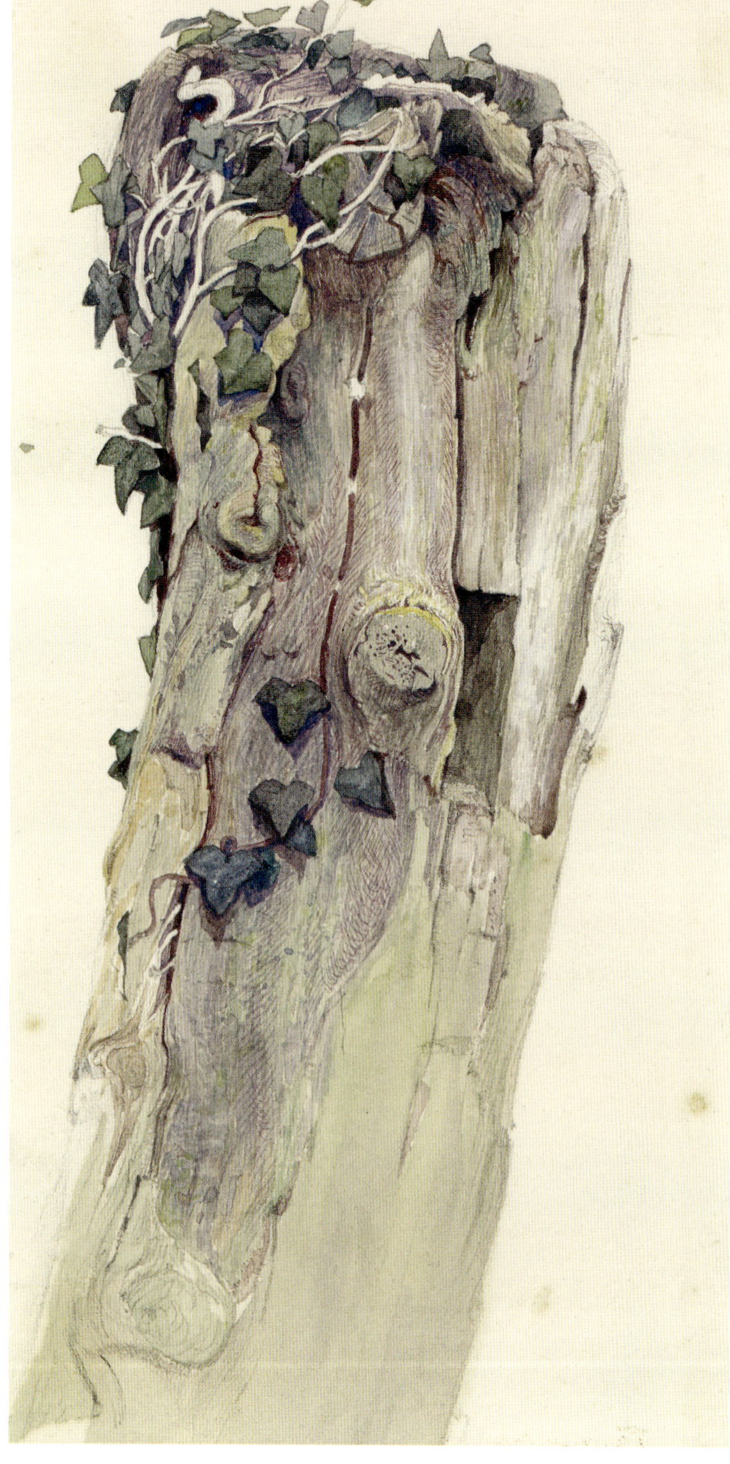

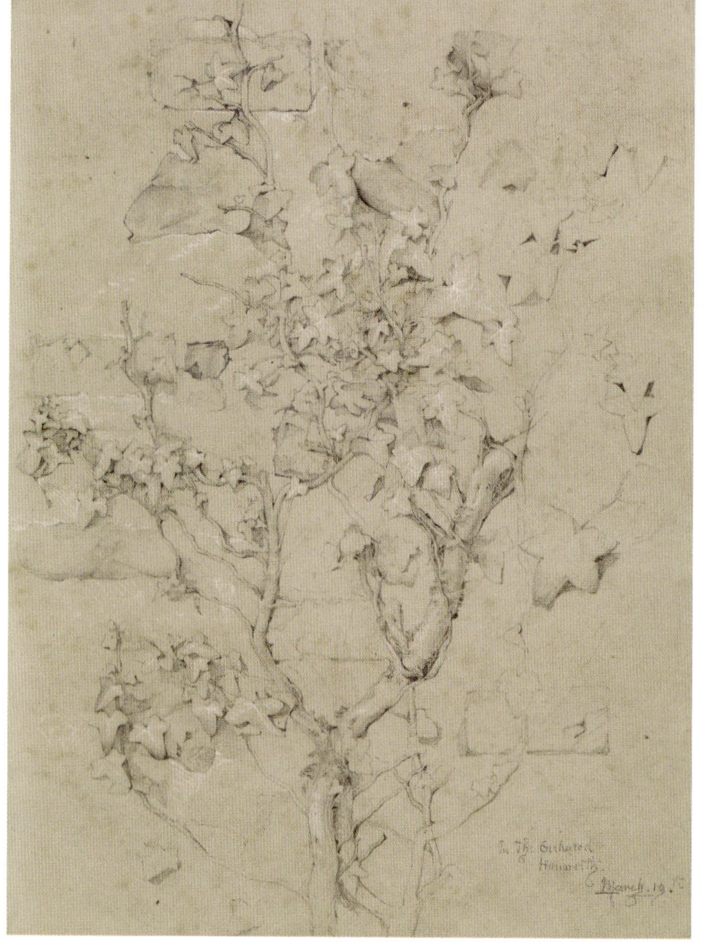

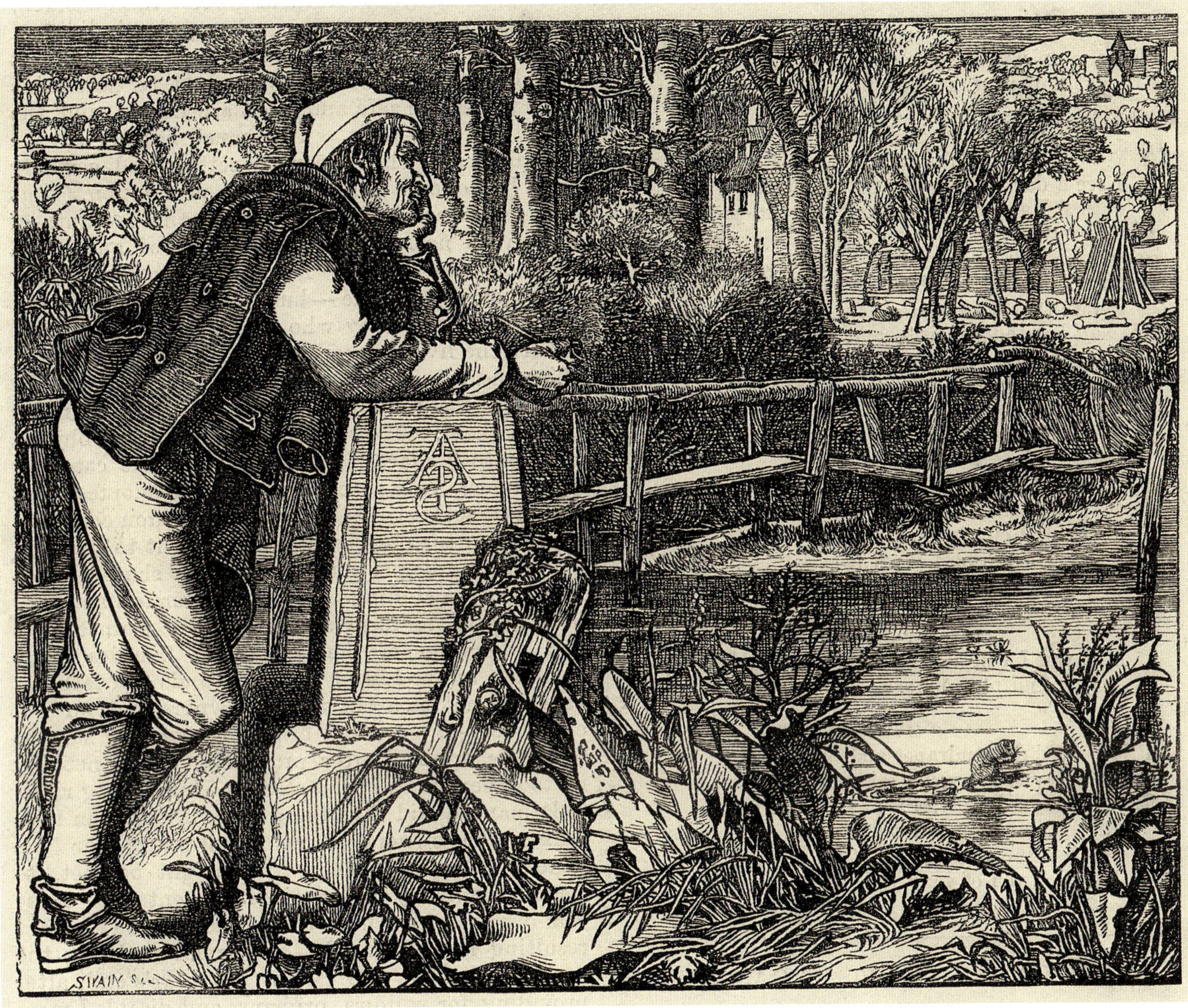

98 Frederick Sandys, *Study of Wild Arum, Grass and a Tree Stump*, 1858, Birmingham Museums & Art Gallery

99 Frederick Sandys, *Study of Wild Arum and Grass at the Foot of a Tree*, 1858, Birmingham Museums & Art Gallery

100 Frederick Sandys, *Study of Ivy on a Tree Stump*, 1858, Birmingham Museums & Art Gallery

101 Frederick Sandys *Study of Ivy on an Old Wall*, 1858, Birmingham Museums & Art Gallery

102 Joseph Swain after Frederick Sandys, *The Old Chartist*, 1862, Aberystwyth University, School of Art Gallery and Museum

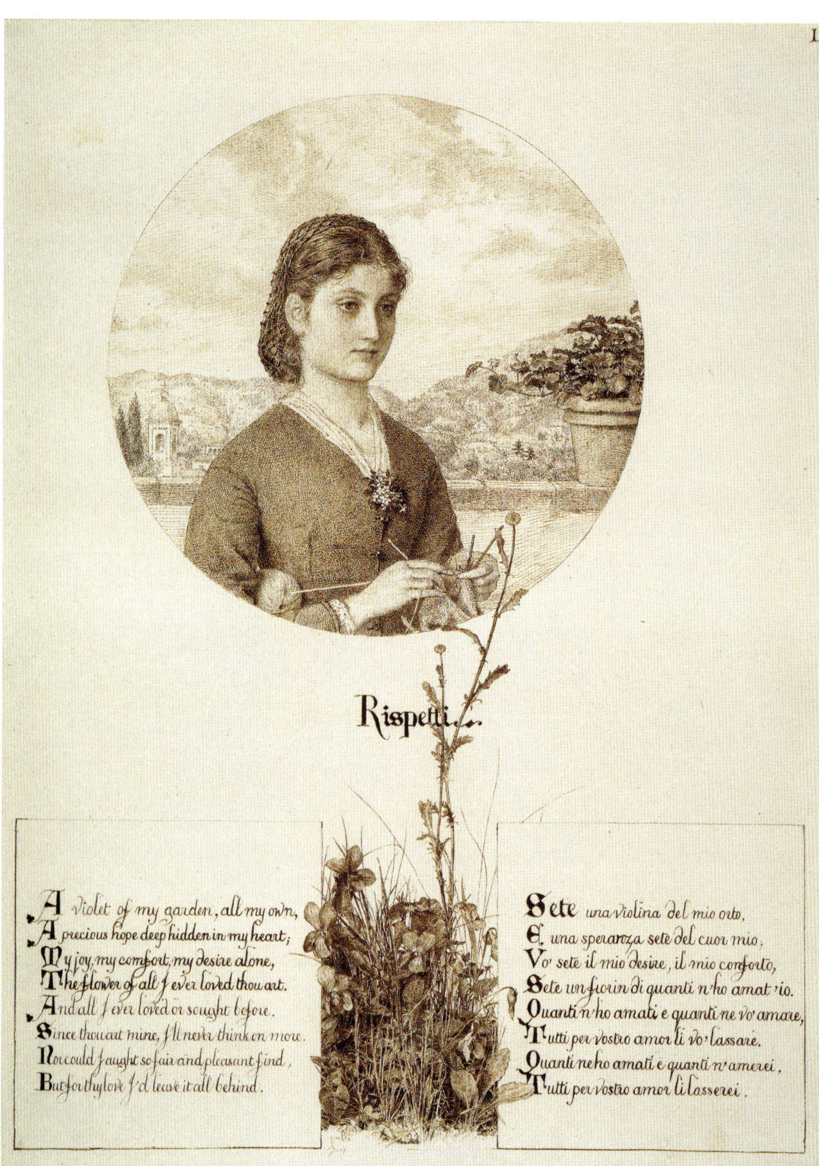

103 Francesca Alexander, *Rispetti*, c. 1868–82,
Birmingham Museums & Art Gallery

allegorical in the way in which the lily was for Millais in his *Garden Scene* [74]. Ivy became a kind of symbol of their practice, combining a quality of the plant's growth pattern with a suggestion of the passing of time. Several of these works appear to be direct responses to Ruskin's advice on subjects and locations for the practice of drawing from landscape in *Elements of Drawing*:

> Banks are beautiful things, and will reward work better than large landscapes.…In woods, one or two trunks, with the flowery ground below, are at once the richest and easiest kind of study: A not very thick trunk, say nine inches or a foot in diameter, with ivy running up it sparingly, is an easy, and always a rewarding subject.[30]

Several commentators pointed out the similarity between Frederick Sandys's illustrations and the engravings of Dürer. Percy Bate noted

> that unerring touch, that resolute draughtsmanship, which is so notable a feature of his work; the masterly handling to equal which we must go back to the drawings of Dürer and the panels of Van Eyck.[31]

The comparison with Dürer invokes a kind of nostalgia that arises from Sandys's drawings, as if the viewer is thrown back to a world that they could not possibly know except through the graphic records of earlier artists.

Sandys incorporated 'bits of nature', the result of close study of hedgerows and undergrowth [100, 101], into several of his most memorable illustrations. *The Old Chartist* [102], an illustration for a poem by George Meredith, published in *Once a Week* in 1862, demonstrates Sandys's ability to use such source material. Drawings of an ivy-covered stump, and arum and grass, are introduced into a subject composition, and simplified into outlines that were highly legible in an engraving. The clearly articulated forms are a wonder of observational drawing, both modern and revivalist at the same time.

In his correspondence with the watercolourist Louisa, Marchioness of Waterford (1818–91), Ruskin advocated not only direct copying from nature but also the close study of artists such as William Henry Hunt, sending her Hunt's drawings of filberts and peach blossom and one watercolour, a 'study from nature by a working carpenter'.[32] The instruction in this instance is not only about nature and art but about class and gender relationships, too, exposing a female aristocratic pupil to the work of a male working-class contemporary.

Although Ruskin corresponded with several female artists who were interested in flower and nature painting, it was his late championing of the American artist Francesca Alexander (1837–1917), who lived in rural Tuscany, that was to be one of his greatest successes. Alexander's work is almost completely based on the direct drawing of nature. She painted little but concentrated instead on drawing in pen and ink, the medium she used for her *Rispetti* ('Songs'). Ruskin edited her illustrated translations of traditional songs of Tuscan peasants for the press under the title *Roadside Songs of Tuscany* (1885–88).[33] One of the plates, bearing the generic title 'Rispetti', illustrates the song 'Sete una violina del mio orto' ('A Violet of my Garden') [**103**].

The song, transcribed in Alexander's beautiful script, is part of the design of the entire page, a harmony of word and image. The page is dominated by a circular portrait of a young woman (possibly Alexander's favourite model, Ida). At the foot of the page is a piece of turf, an entanglement of wild violets and other plants; it thrusts upwards in a flourish of growth that cuts across the circular drawing and makes a connection between the woman's activity – crocheting – and the entanglement of nature. The work is rendered in detail painstaking enough to satisfy even Ruskin at his most critical.[34] Alexander's drawing implies a narrative connection between the needlework of her peasant model, the artist's work and the complexity

of nature itself. It suggests, too, a direct link between her work and the young woman's work represented in Millais's *Garden Scene*, associating drawing, femininity and nature.

Ruskin's writings helped to offer a rationale for a new and separate 'school', one in which all academic conventions were abandoned and the eye and hand were retrained. While his work was supportive of the aims of the Pre-Raphaelites, it ran on a parallel path, concerned less with subject painting and narrative and more with landscape and still life painting. From within the Pre-Raphaelite Brotherhood, William Michael Rossetti also attacked conventionality in his critical writings and advocated the use of the 'faculties of observation and analysis'. His method of argument was to set out from the start of his essay 'two classes' of rules for art: the positive and the conventional, and although he stressed that the latter was not used in the 'invidious' sense but implied simply 'the presence of general consent', he noted that such conventions were matters of opinion rather than fact. The positive rules were factors such as perspective or those governing the representation of anatomy. Nature, as he observed, 'is always in perspective'.[35] Nonetheless, the truth-to-nature agenda was only part of Pre-Raphaelitism and was extended to more than the production of landscape representation. It influenced the recording of the human face and figure, concepts of authenticity and to ways of thinking about the activity of making art, which could not be confined to a series of exercises in training the eye to observe or the hand to trace. At its most vital, Pre-Raphaelitism was about the body, the face and the human figure in relation to others. A concept of 'truth' had its part to play there, too, and drawing had a key role to play in uncovering it.

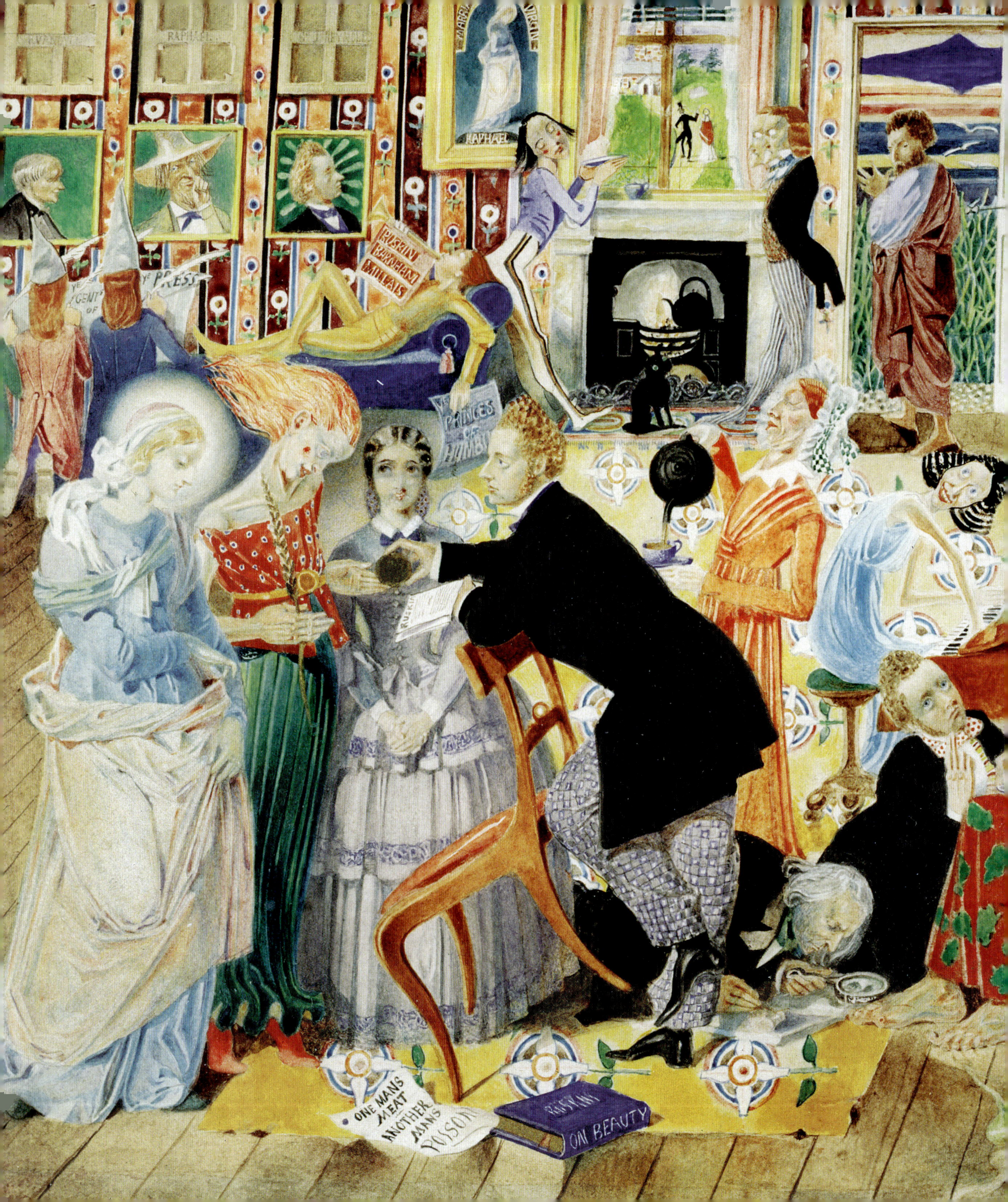

RUSKIN
BAROTHAN
MILLAIS
PRINCES OF HUMBUG
RAPHAEL
Ye GENT'S OF Ye PRESS
ONE MANS MEAT ANOTHER MANS POISON
RUSKIN ON BEAUTY

<h1>Chapter 4   *Drawing the Circle: Portraits, Self-Portraits and Caricatures*</h1>

When the painter and illustrator Florence Claxton (fl. 1840–79) sought a central motif for her pictorial satire on the Pre-Raphaelites, *The Choice of Paris: An Idyll* (1860) [105], she found it in their perverse sense of female beauty. In choosing to satirize the Brotherhood, Claxton may have been prompted by the hostile reception of two of Millais's paintings, *The Vale of Rest* and *Spring*, shown at the Royal Academy in 1859. *Blackwood's Magazine* described *Spring* as depicting 'a sisterhood deliberately dedicated to the ungraceful'.[1]

Claxton published her caricature of the Brotherhood and their works in the *Illustrated London News* in June 1860. The central joke is a good one: that Millais – recognizable by his classical profile – is awarding a golden apple to the 'fairest' of his models. She stands before him, awkward and stiff, her hair wild, her face grotesque; she is flanked by a Raphaelite saint and a modern young lady in a crinoline. Millais holds a volume of Ruskin in his left hand while at his feet lies another volume *On Beauty*, also labelled 'Ruskin'. A long-haired artist (a generalized embodiment of Pre-Raphaelitism, perhaps) studies the toenails of a female model. The figure of Michelangelo stands in the open doorway, aghast at the ugliness around him, while a male figure labelled 'Middle Ages', clearly based on William Holman Hunt's depiction of Claudio, hides behind the door.

The drawing contains parodies of Millais's *Spring, Sir Isumbras at the Ford* and *The Vale of Rest*, as well as of Brett's *The Stonebreaker*, and *Burd Helen*, the most famous of the Pre-Raphaelite-inspired works of the Liverpool painter W. L. Windus (1822–1907). The ivy on the wall that acts as a separation between the two halves of the picture might stand in for the predominance of ivy in works by Millais and Brown, as well as being a comment on the Ruskinian 'bits of nature' discussed in Chapter 3. It is clear that what is being commented on is a general lack of grace as well as a specific ugliness of face and feature in the models chosen by Pre-

104 Florence Claxton, *The Choice of Paris: An Idyll*, 1860, Victoria and Albert Museum, London (detail)

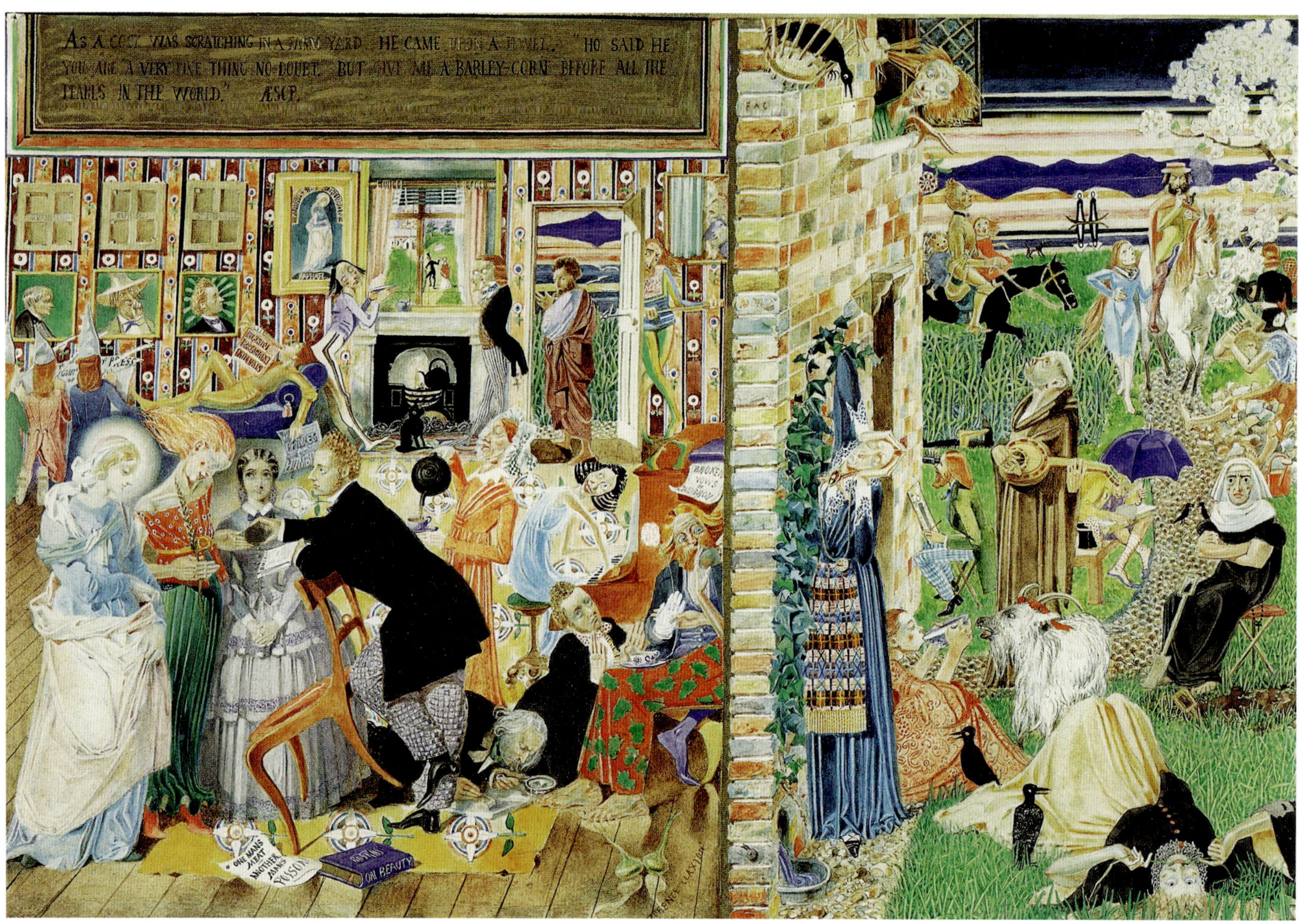

105 Florence Claxton, *The Choice of Paris: An Idyll*, 1860, Victoria and Albert Museum, London

Raphaelite artists. A depiction of an artist drawing a wall, close-up yet wearing binoculars, neatly caricatures the whole 'truth to nature' belief of the Brotherhood and their followers.

Female faces

Since the 1970s, when the process of the reassessment of the Pre-Raphaelites coincided with the rise of a feminist art history and a more general re-evaluation of nineteenth-century painting, the study of the female model has been given a new emphasis. In addition, much has been made in recent accounts of the history of the Pre-Raphaelite Brotherhood of the relationships between the artists and their female models, although they were not exceptional in having emotional and sexual entanglements with women who were paid to pose for pictures. There is often a palpable imbalance of power between the male artist and the subject of his gaze, but to overstress this as a feature of the work of the Pre-Raphaelite Brotherhood would be to ignore the continued presence of such power relations in contemporary society. Nonetheless, there was a degree of urgency to the position of women in an industrialized and urbanized Victorian Britain that intensified the representation of gender relationships. In some cases the undoubted intimacy between a male artist and his model permitted a frankness that helped to break down the pictorial conventions present in other branches of art.

The physicality of the representations of these women must have been disturbing to audiences used to the less confrontational, highly conventionalized and idealized portraits at the annual exhibition at the Royal Academy. Undoubtedly, too, there was a class dimension to Pre-Raphaelite depictions of their models, and an element of work in the act of posing, but familiarity and intimacy must have had some further effect on that class relationship. It was not just mistresses but – eventually – wives, as well as female relatives and family friends, who were represented in drawings and paintings by the Pre-Raphaelites; different kinds of familiarity, in other words, are apparent in the act of representation.

Paintings featuring Elizabeth Siddal, the most important of the early Pre-Raphaelite models, were derided because her features did not conform to ideals of feminine beauty.

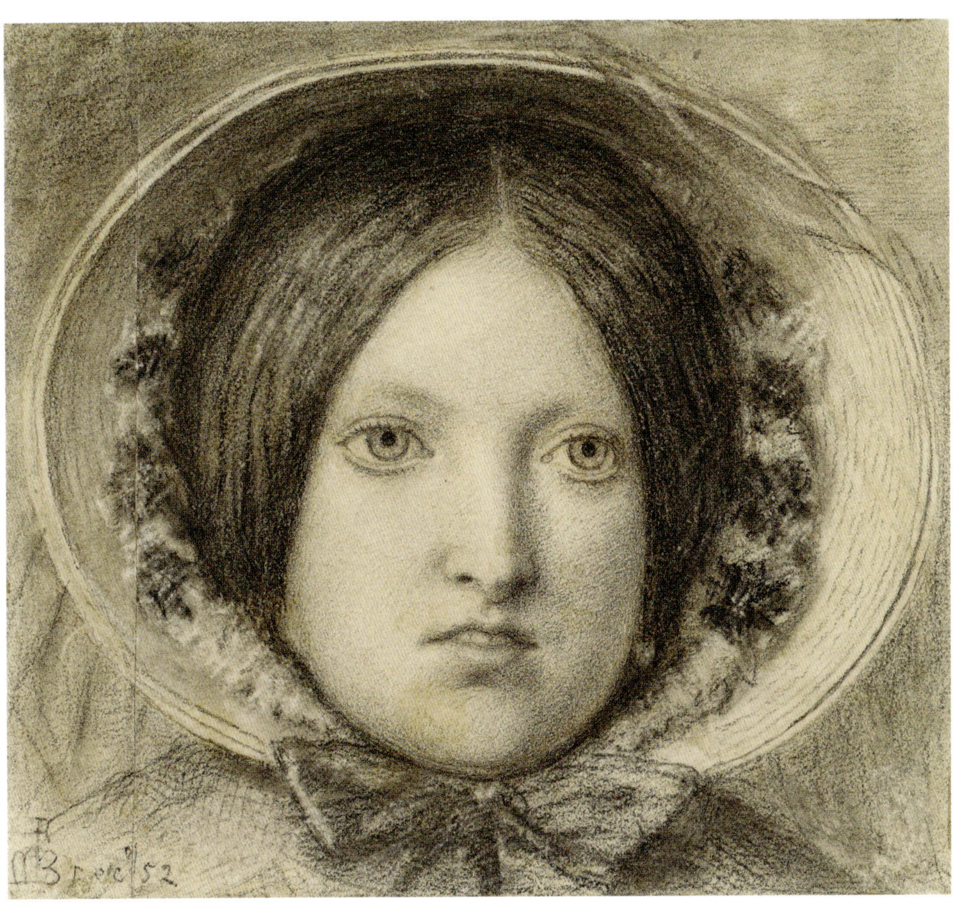

106 Ford Madox Brown, *Study of Emma Hill for 'The Last of England'*, 1852, Birmingham Museums & Art Gallery

Some paintings were altered to accommodate the tastes of their purchasers. Conversely, at other times it was in representations of the female face that the conventions of academic facial proportion lingered; Brown continued the tradition of constructing the head as an oval – the 'Ideal' head of academic theory – and subdividing it in a Raphaelite rather than a Pre-Raphaelite manner. The proportions achieved by utilizing this academic formula produced a stereotyped facial beauty. It was both so conventionalized and ubiquitous that it proved hard to challenge. Both 'High Art' and populist representations of the female face were subject to the formula, and audiences had grown used to its effect.

We can see this tendency to conform to it in Ford Madox Brown's drawing for *The Last of England* (1852) [153] of the working-class woman who was to become his second wife, Emma Hill (1829–90) [106]. Brown depicted a large forehead, long, straight nose, short upper lip, rounded chin and over-large dewy eyes. She is reduced to a pattern of female loveliness without character or individuality. It is a face capable only of communicating the most

sentimental of messages, and its conventionality vies with the psychological depth Brown otherwise demands for the subject. He modified the features for the finished picture, making it capable of communicating deeper and more complex feelings. In the representation of the faces and bodies of men particularly, Brown, along with members of the Pre-Raphaelite Brotherhood, proclaimed an independence from representational convention. Oddly, given Brown's search for authenticity in historical painting, the female face accords with those in the illustrated annuals such as *The Keepsake*, which enjoyed much commercial success between 1828 and the 1850s and which became a byword for a cloying and unreal kind of feminine beauty. The stylization of Emma Hill's features sat uneasily with the unconventional features of Brown's other works: brightly illuminated landscapes, accuracy of historical detail, vigorous gestures and emphatic facial expressions.

Millais was the focus of much of the public's disquiet at the disruption of these conventions of female beauty, both academic and populist. In his study for the head of Ophelia, for example, Siddal's pale eyelashes and heavy eyelids are

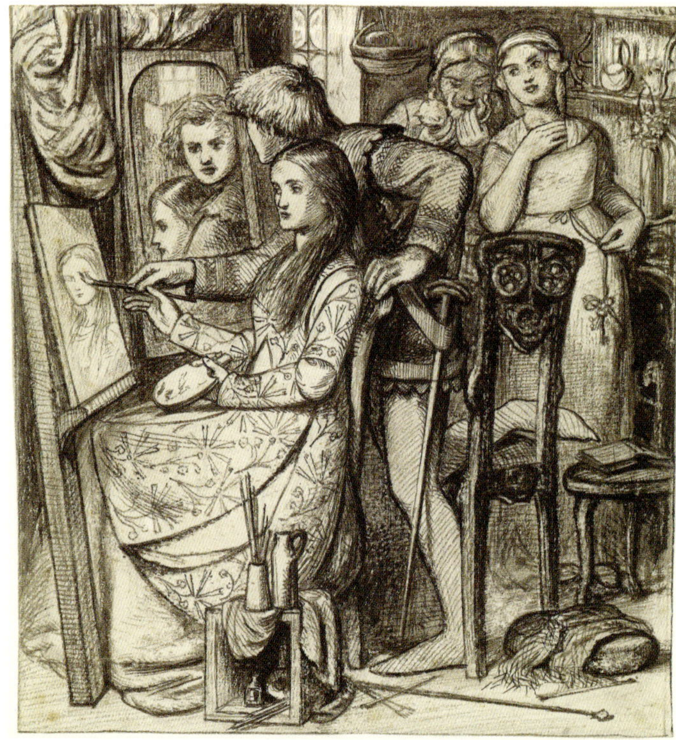

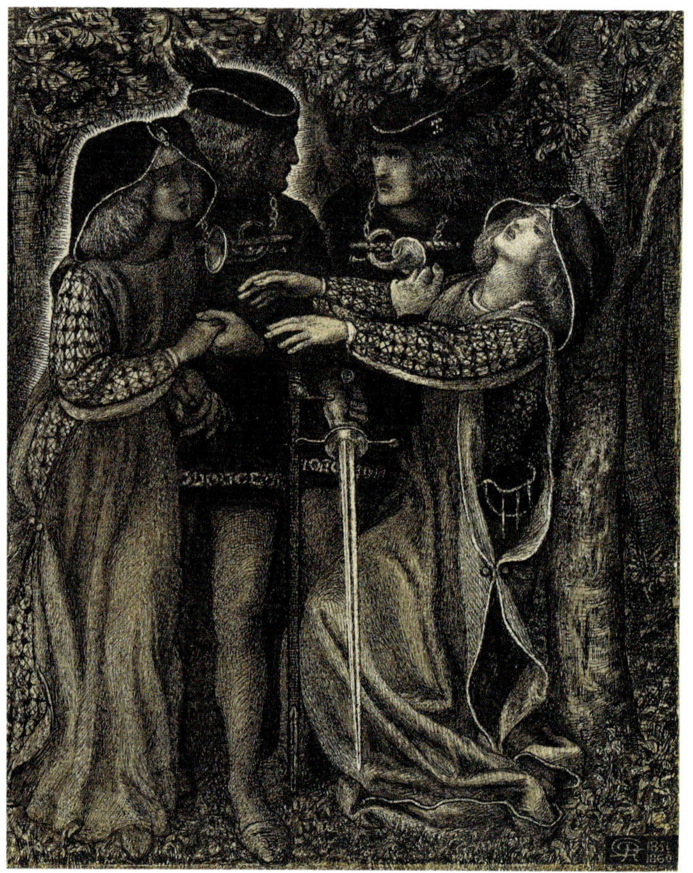

107 Dante Gabriel Rossetti, *A Parable of Love (Love's Mirror)*, *c.* 1849–50, Birmingham Museums & Art Gallery
108 Dante Gabriel Rossetti, *How They Met Themselves*, 1860, Fitzwilliam Museum, Cambridge

evidence of how 'truth to nature' translated into portraiture [63]. In this matter the Pre-Raphaelites became subject to many of the pressures placed on women themselves – to conform and to be conventional. This is perhaps less true of Rossetti, who might be said to have invented a kind of feminine beauty so unorthodox as to be deemed a special kind of plainness. Indeed, the term 'Rossetti woman' was one of the most familiar in the later reception of Pre-Raphaelitism; acceptance of it as a pattern of beauty was to become a sign of a more discerning taste in art, although not without controversy. A patron of Ford Madox Brown, Thomas Dixon, most famous as the working man to whom Ruskin addressed the letters contained in *Time and Tide* (1867), wrote to the painter warning him that he had to distance himself from the tendency of other Pre-Raphaelite artists to paint ugly women:

> Our pictures seem to come out badly in the Reviews this year and is owing to nothing but the ugly female faces in the bulk of the Pre-Raphaelite work. Rossetti has much to answer for this, for he has constantly red hair and the same type of face in his models. I feel sure that this is a great obstacle to the popularity of the Pre-Raphaelite work. I consider you are not liable to this charge, but those who follow Rossetti are.[2]

Dixon particularly requested that, in the picture that he had commissioned, Brown did not paint women with red hair.

Rossetti was drawn to portraiture as a subject for prose and poetry, as evidenced in his earliest published story *Hand and Soul* and his poem 'A Portrait', as well as drawings such as *A Parable of Love (Love's Mirror)* (1850–52) [107]. The literary historian Elizabeth Helsinger has traced the origin of Rossetti's fascination with portraiture to gothic novels of the late eighteenth and early nineteenth centuries such as Wilhelm Meinhold's *Sidonia the Sorceress* (1848). Many of these novels feature portraits with supernatural properties. Helsinger sees this 'gothic centre to Rossetti's imagination' as

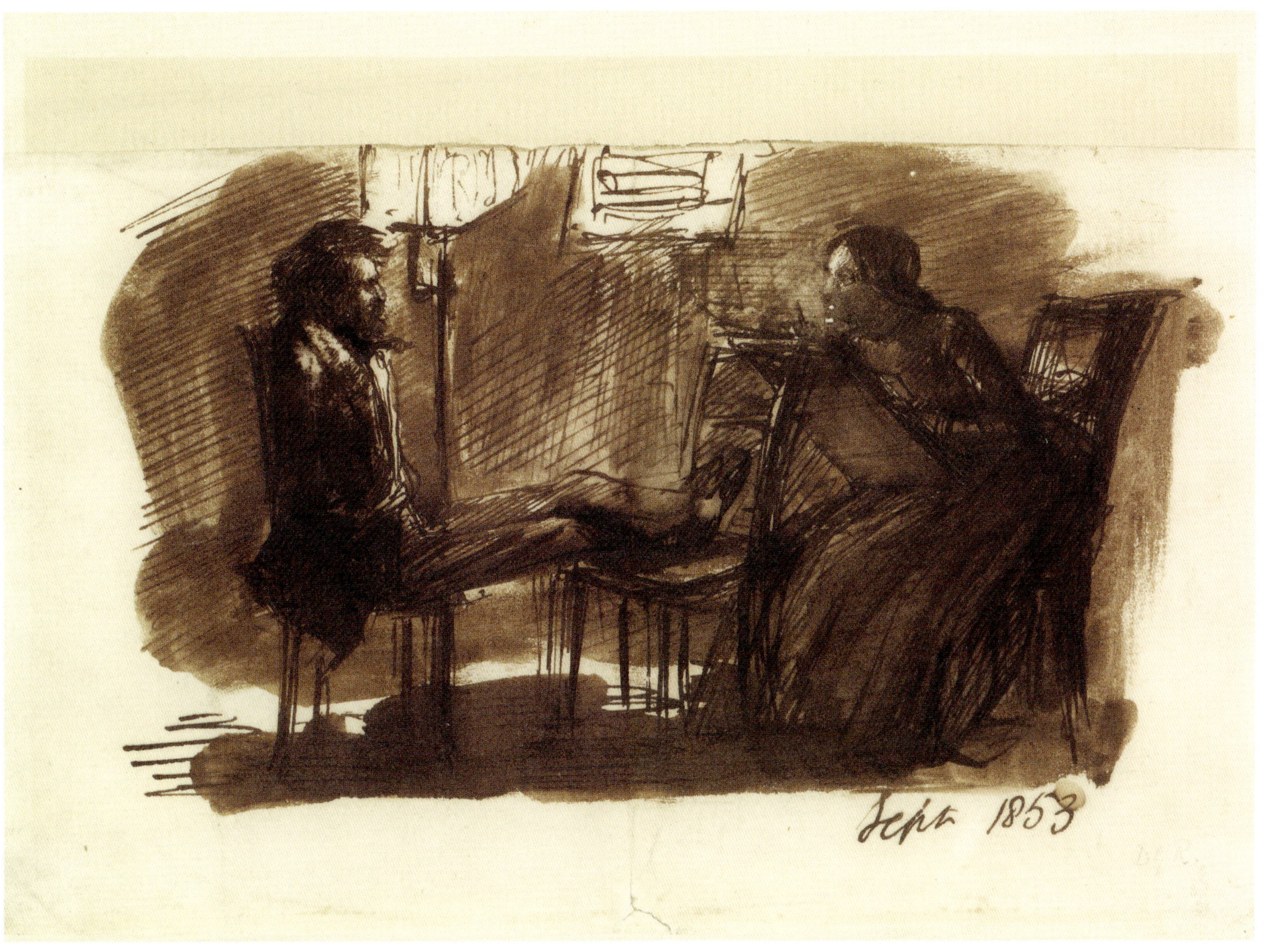

109 Dante Gabriel Rossetti, *Rossetti Sitting to Elizabeth Siddal*, 1853, Birmingham Museums & Art Gallery

feeding into his painting *Beata Beatrix* (*c.* 1864–70, Tate), with its pictorial parallels between Rossetti and Dante, Siddal and Beatrix.[3] Certainly these gothic sources provided Rossetti with inspiration but they also seem to have created a sense of unease that haunted him throughout his life. One of his most sensational drawings, for example, *How They Met Themselves* (versions 1851 and 1860) [108], is a dramatized double portrait of Siddal and himself made into a haunting narrative with a *doppelgänger* theme. Clearly his personal relationships were imagined in terms of gothic romance, even in its darkest and most haunted expression.

In Rossetti's works, meetings between lovers are often momentous and highly charged with emotion, although they could have a more matter-of-fact representation, too. For instance, in the drawing *Rossetti Sitting to Elizabeth Siddal* (1853 [109]), which is a combination of self-portraiture, reportage and caricature, he depicts his lover, pupil and muse peering at him as she draws his likeness. Siddal's gesture of looking closely – her head cranes forward – echoes that of the angelic spirits who scrutinize the poet's face in Rossetti's '*The Raven*': *Angel Footfalls* [60]. It is a gesture of familiarity yet unfamiliarity at the same time – of searching a well-known face for signs of change yet seeming to see it as if for the first time. This ambiguity of recognition is a constant feature of Rossetti's interest in the face as a subject for art. He returned to the face repeatedly both as the central image of his symbolic and allegorical works and for more straightforward portrait drawings. Sometimes the two activities – drawing the face of a sitter to record a likeness and drawing a model as a character for a dramatic and literary subject painting – overlap and become indistinguishable.

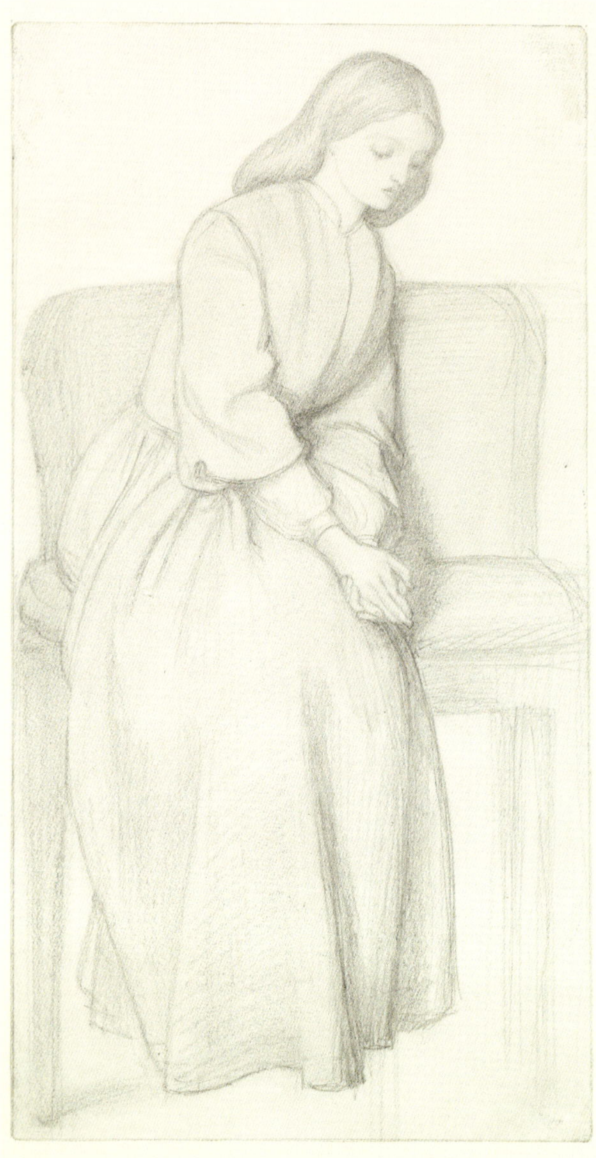

110 Dante Gabriel Rossetti, *Study of Elizabeth Siddal*, 1855, Birmingham Museums & Art Gallery

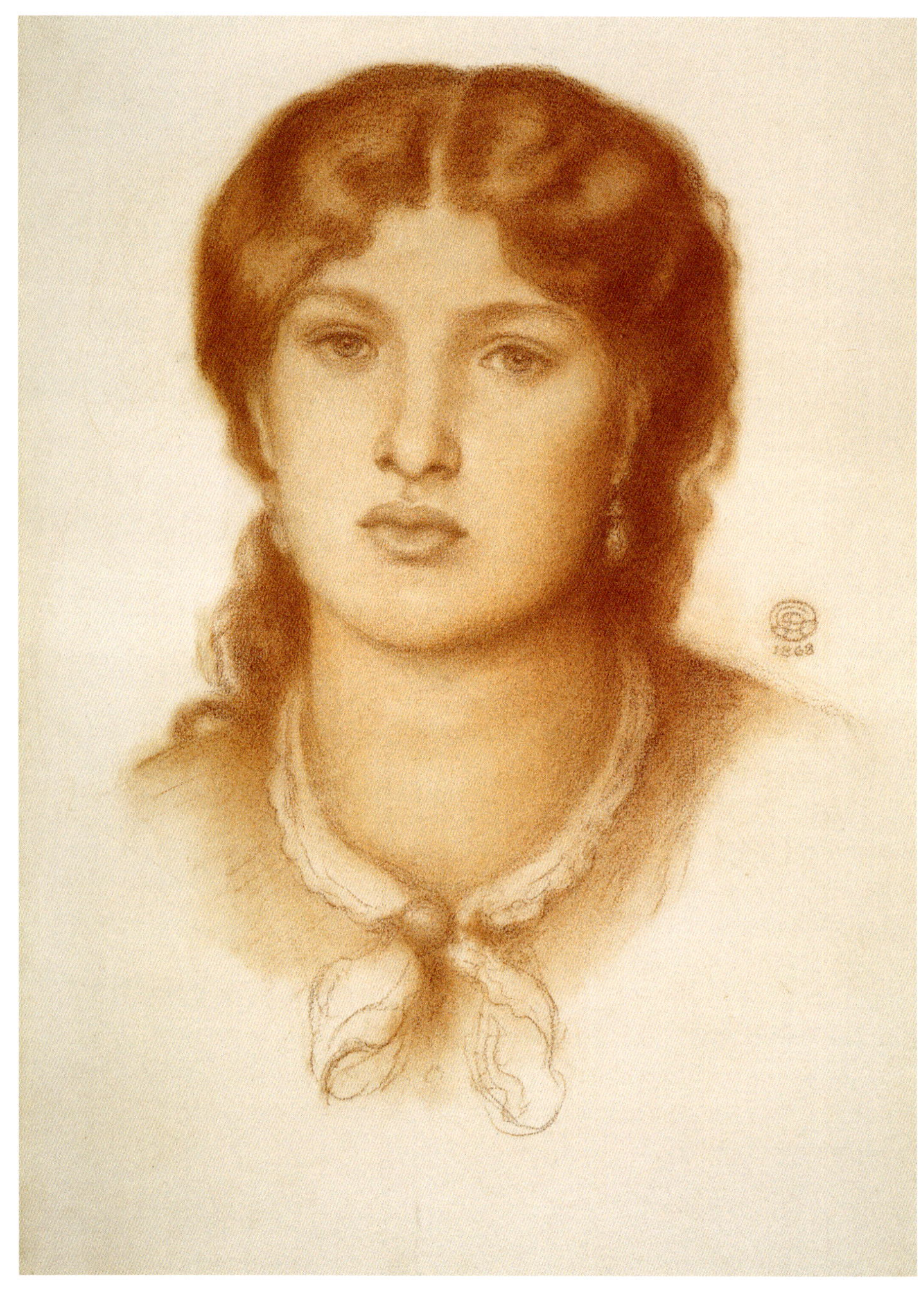

111 Dante Gabriel Rossetti, *Fanny Cornforth*, 1868, Birmingham Museums & Art Gallery

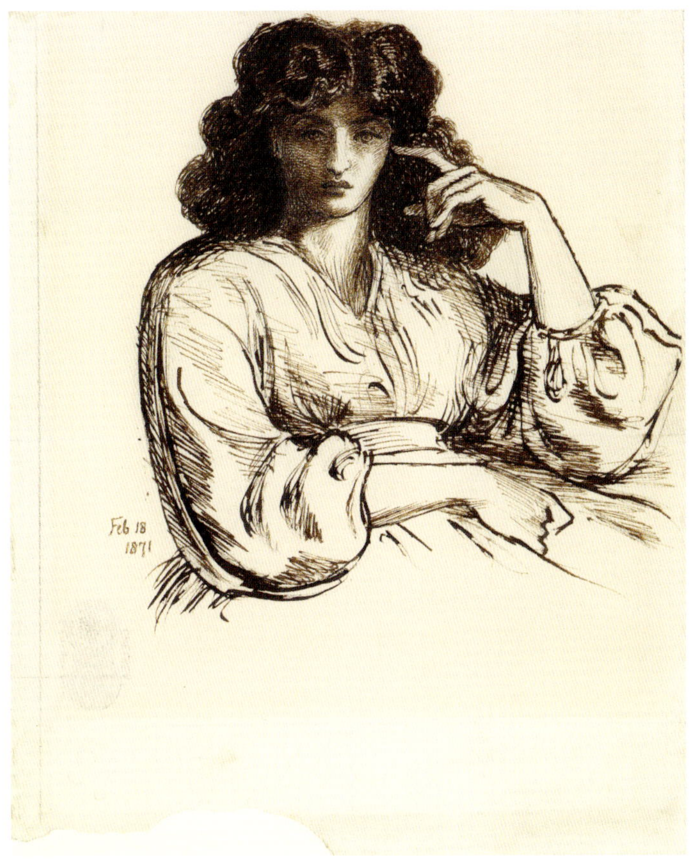

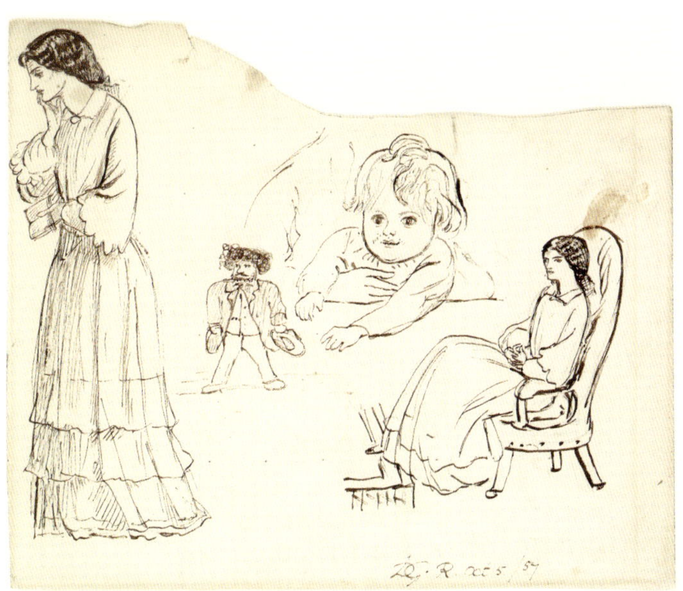

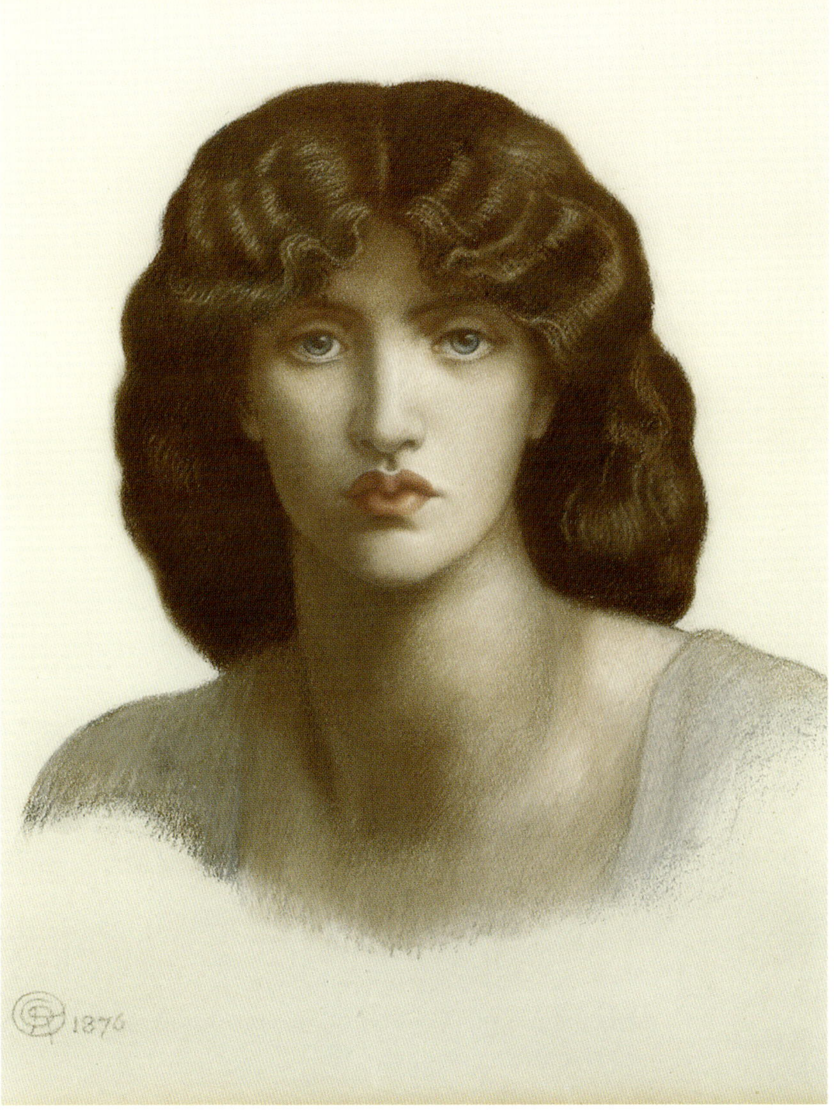

112 Dante Gabriel Rossetti, *Jane Morris*, 1871,
Birmingham Museums & Art Gallery

113 Dante Gabriel Rossetti, *Sheet of Studies of Jane and William Morris
and a Child*, 1857, Birmingham Museums & Art Gallery

114 Dante Gabriel Rossetti, *Study of Jane Morris for 'Mnemosyne'*, 1876,
private collection

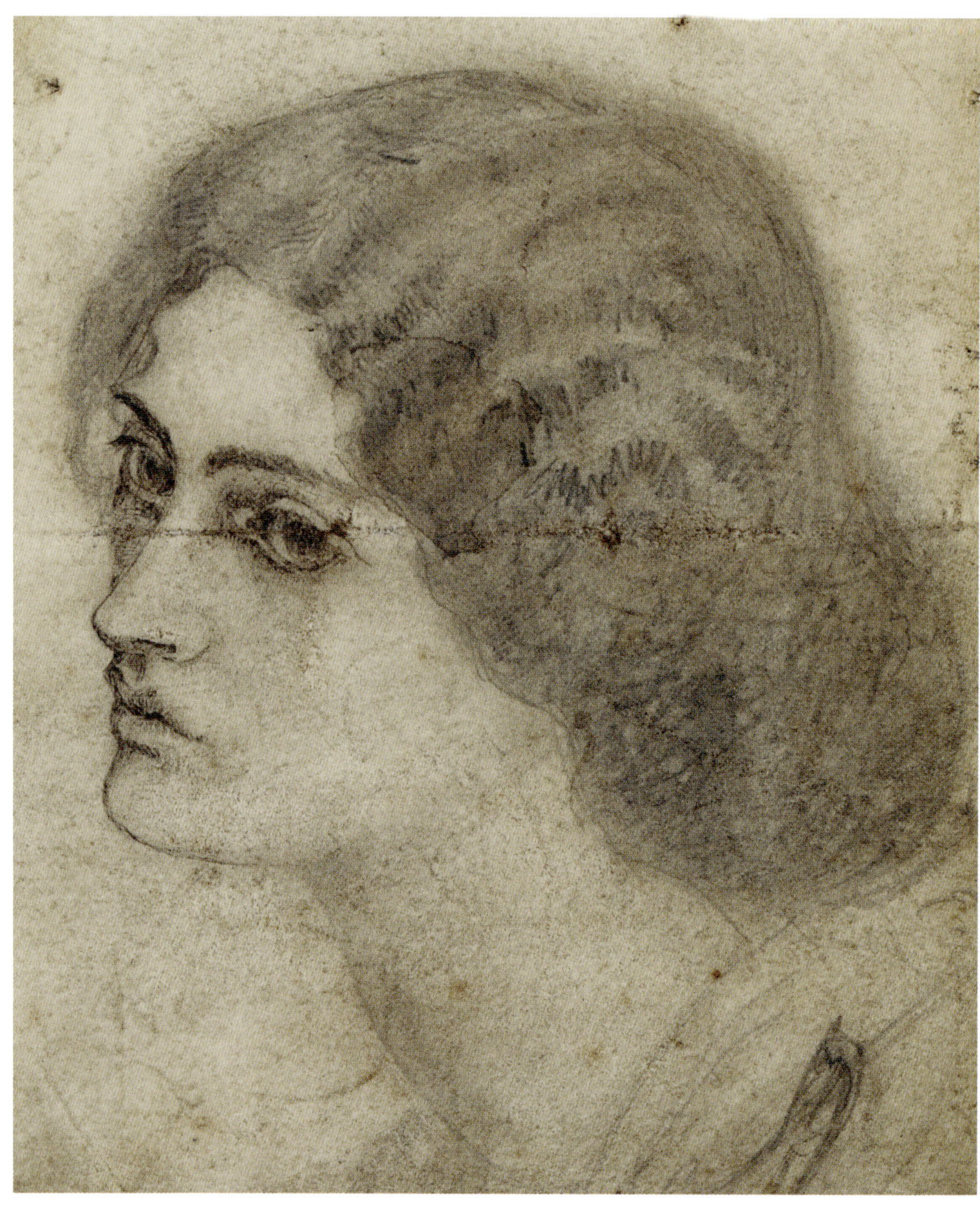

115 William Morris, *Jane Burden*, 1857, The British Museum, London

This repetition is most strikingly the case in representations of Elizabeth Siddal. Rossetti drew her obsessively during the 1850s both as herself and as a character – Beatrice, Marguerite, Delia – the distinction between the functions of each sitting often being blurred. In the series of drawings of Siddal that Rossetti showed to Ruskin and Brown in 1855 – the 'drawerful of "Guggums"' as Brown called it, referring to Rossetti's pet name for Siddal – she appears 'as herself'.[4] In one [110], however, the pose was modified for the watercolour

Dante's *Vision of Rachel and Leah* (1855, Tate) in which Siddal was transformed into the introspective Rachel regarding herself in the waters of the well. In others of the series she became, eventually, Beatrice or some other literary character.

Rossetti drew other highly individual models, such as Fanny Cornforth (*c.* 1835–*c.* 1906) [111] and Ruth Herbert (*c.* 1832–1921). The most often repeated face, however, was that of Jane Morris (1839–1914) [112, 113], who was depicted variously 'as herself' in informal portraits, or exaggerated

   Drawing the Circle: Portraits, Self-Portraits and Caricatures

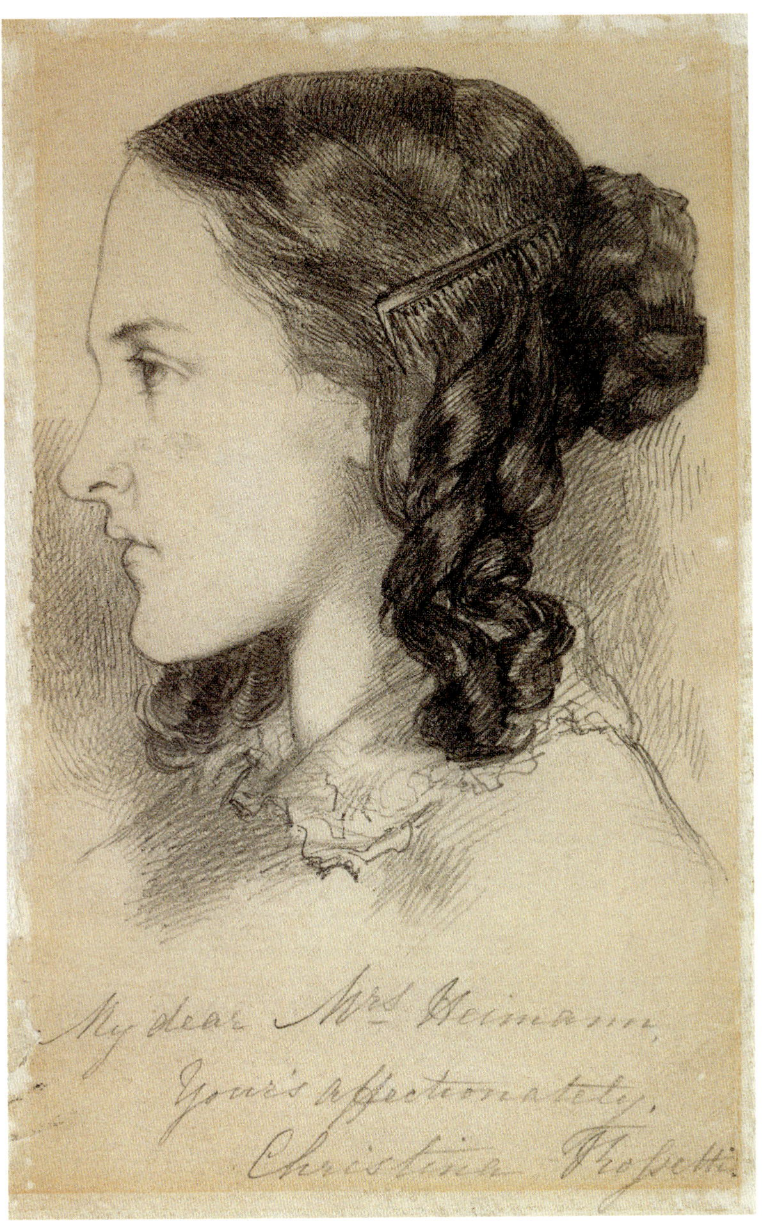

116 Dante Gabriel Rossetti, *Christina Rossetti*, 1847,
Victoria and Albert Museum, London

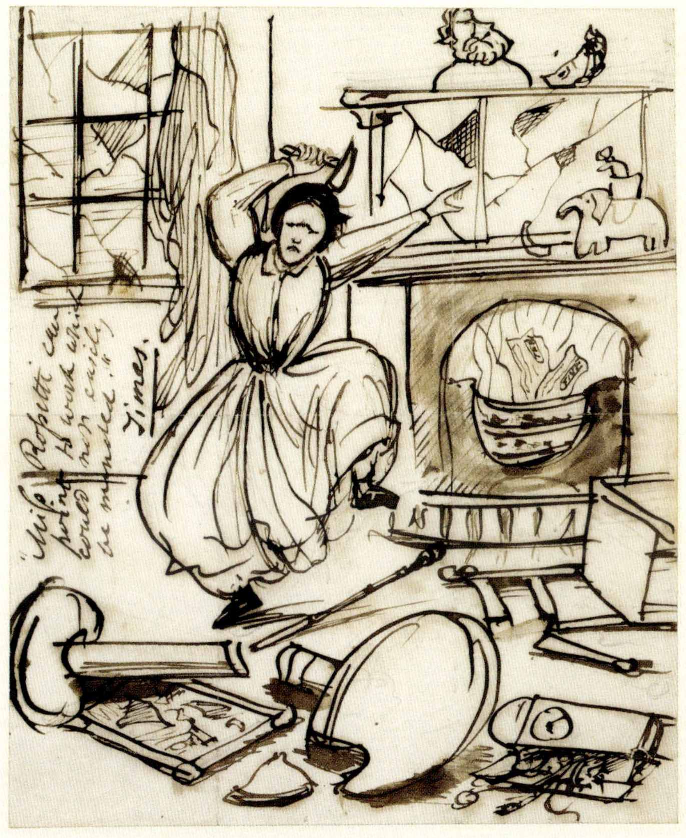

117 Dante Gabriel Rossetti, *Christina Rossetti in a Tantrum*, 1862,
National Trust, Wightwick Manor and Gardens

in caricatures, and who was a kind of blank tablet on which various allegorical or historical figures could be inscribed. Her handsome, impressive features are consistent in all these different manifestations, perhaps becoming more brooding when allegorical attributes or mythological personae were adopted [114]. Significantly, William Morris's portrait of Jane at the time of their meeting in Oxford [115] – when she was Jane Burden – has no indication of the multiple identities that were to emerge for Rossetti or that were to be imposed on her by him.

Rossetti also used female friends and relatives as models for his early paintings, notably his mother and his sister, Christina (1830–94), for his first Pre-Raphaelite painting, *The Girlhood of Mary Virgin* [73]. As a consequence, the picture has an intimate atmosphere, a little at odds with the supernatural character of the subject, absent in the work of history paintings of his contemporaries. In a portrait of Christina in 1847 [116], Rossetti shows her looking apprehensive and hopeful at the same time. The profile might have suggested that used by the painter

for the head of Mary two years later. The drawing has
a signed dedication from the sitter to 'My dear Mrs
Heimann', indicating the use of such intimate portraits
as affectionate mementoes before the exchange of
photographic portraits became a vogue later in the century.
The artist's treatment of her hair, her ringlets caught
back by a comb, is striking, anticipating the use of such
ornaments in several paintings, such as *Monna Vanna*
(1866, Tate), in which the model's hair is held in place with
a spiral of pearls.

However, in a later caricature [117], the artist's depiction
of his sister's temper, while amusing as an exaggeration,
fits uneasily with the depiction of her as a quiet, sedate
and reflective Victorian poetess. And the professional
ambition that the drawing records – her rage at bad
reviews of her poetry – is anomalous, perhaps the very
nub of the joke that such a gentle soul should ever
express anger, let alone break up the furniture in a fit.
These instabilities of representation of character are only
unsettling, however, if we fail to realize that portraits
can only ever be partial, no matter how fixed they appear
at first. In the case of portraits of Christina, the artist
could use the art of portraiture to observe changes in her
appearance over a long period, and his representations
of her features in several images bear the traces of his
deep knowledge and understanding of her. One of the
last, drawn in 1877 [118], following the breakdown of his
own mental and physical health, records the effect of
Christina's search for fulfilment in her face, which is sad
and resigned in expression. F. G. Stephens thought that
'It attests that time had not effaced from the lady's face
the likeness of the Virgin in *Ecce Ancilla Domini!* of 1849'.[5]
The experience of disappointment and loss shown there
mirrors Rossetti's own fragility. The drawing confirms
the reflectivity and ambiguity that the art of portraiture
had for him.

Brothers and friends

One of the characteristics of drawn portraits by members of
the Pre-Raphaelite circle is that, for the most part, they were
private and unavailable for public scrutiny. The chief way
in which likenesses of members of the Brotherhood were
encountered by the public was in the form of masquerades
as historical personages, poets, saints or kings. Thus
Rossetti's poetic identity was invoked by his fellow artists
and he was 'seen' by the public that viewed Brown's *Chaucer*
[34] or Deverell's *Twelfth Night* [42]. However, one of the
problems of regarding such works as portraits is that the
intention complicates the recording of the likeness. They
are portraits in fancy dress. The identity of the sitter has
changed and the model, whether friend or lover, is made to
impersonate a character.

Self-portraiture raises yet other questions about likeness,
wish fulfilment and the adoption of other identities for a
variety of reasons. Rossetti's self-portrait of 1847 [119] recalls
the account by his fellow member of the Brotherhood,
F. G. Stephens, of his first impression of Rossetti with
his long hair and second-hand clothes, bearing 'the
outward and visible signs of a mood which cared even
less for appearances than the art-student of those days
was accustomed to care'.[6] Yet other representations reveal
a different Rossetti. His self-portrait of 1861 [120], for
example, is a less idealized depiction than Hunt's oval
portrait of him drawn in 1853 with its exaggerated mystical
expression [121].

Likewise, an examination of portraits of Brown suggest
variations in the reading of his character. These are not
simply due to differences of age and appearance: the
adoption of a beard, the abandonment of a hat or advancing
stoutness. In Rossetti's 1867 drawing of Brown [123] there
is more humour in the eyes than in Brown's cooler 1850
self-portrait [122] or or Rossetti's 1852 portrait, now in the
National Portrait Gallery, in which the sitter looks decidedly

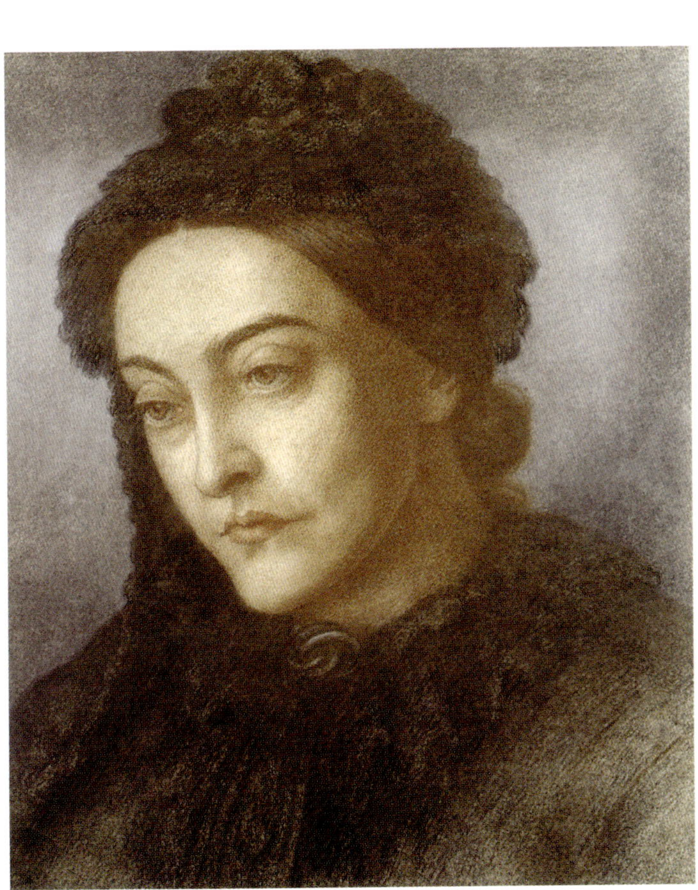

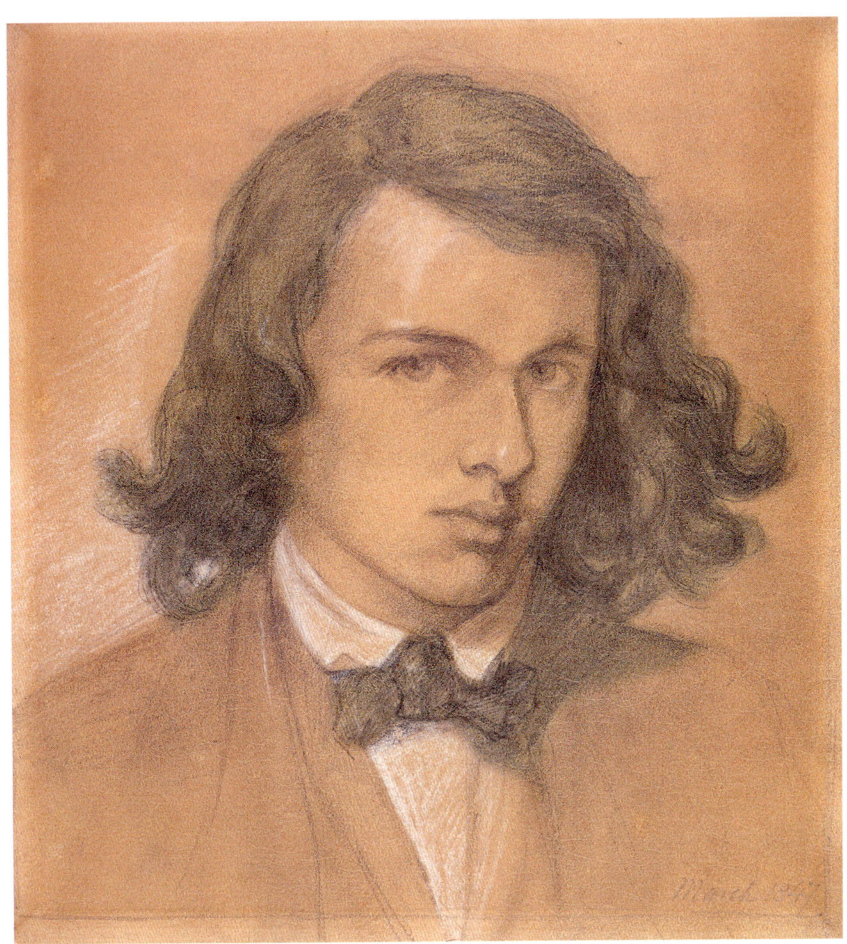

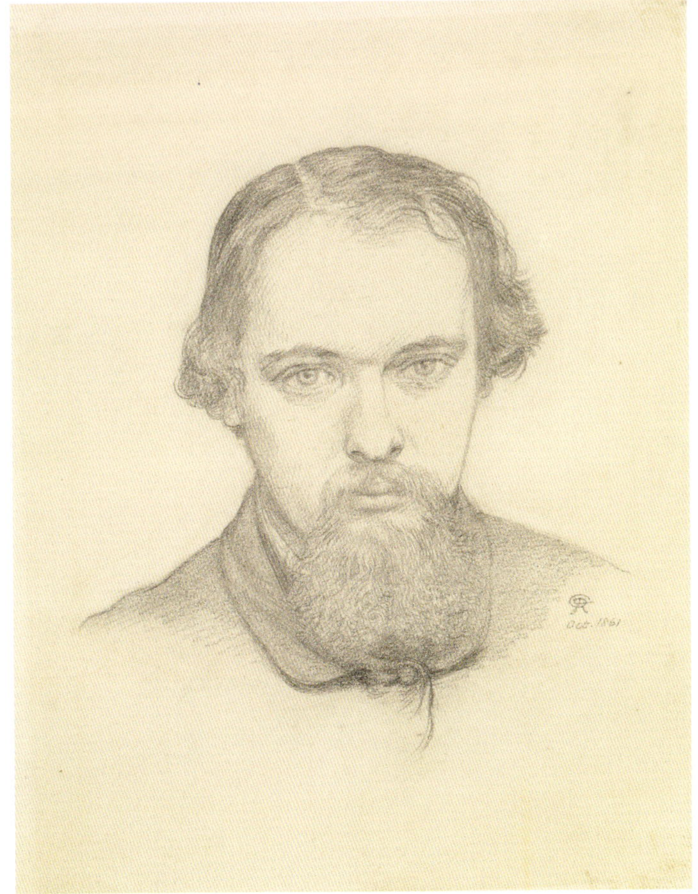

118 Dante Gabriel Rossetti, *Christina Rossetti*, 1877, present whereabouts unknown

119 Dante Gabriel Rossetti, *Self Portrait*, 1847, National Portrait Gallery, London

120 Dante Gabriel Rossetti, *Self Portrait*, 1861, Birmingham Museums & Art Gallery

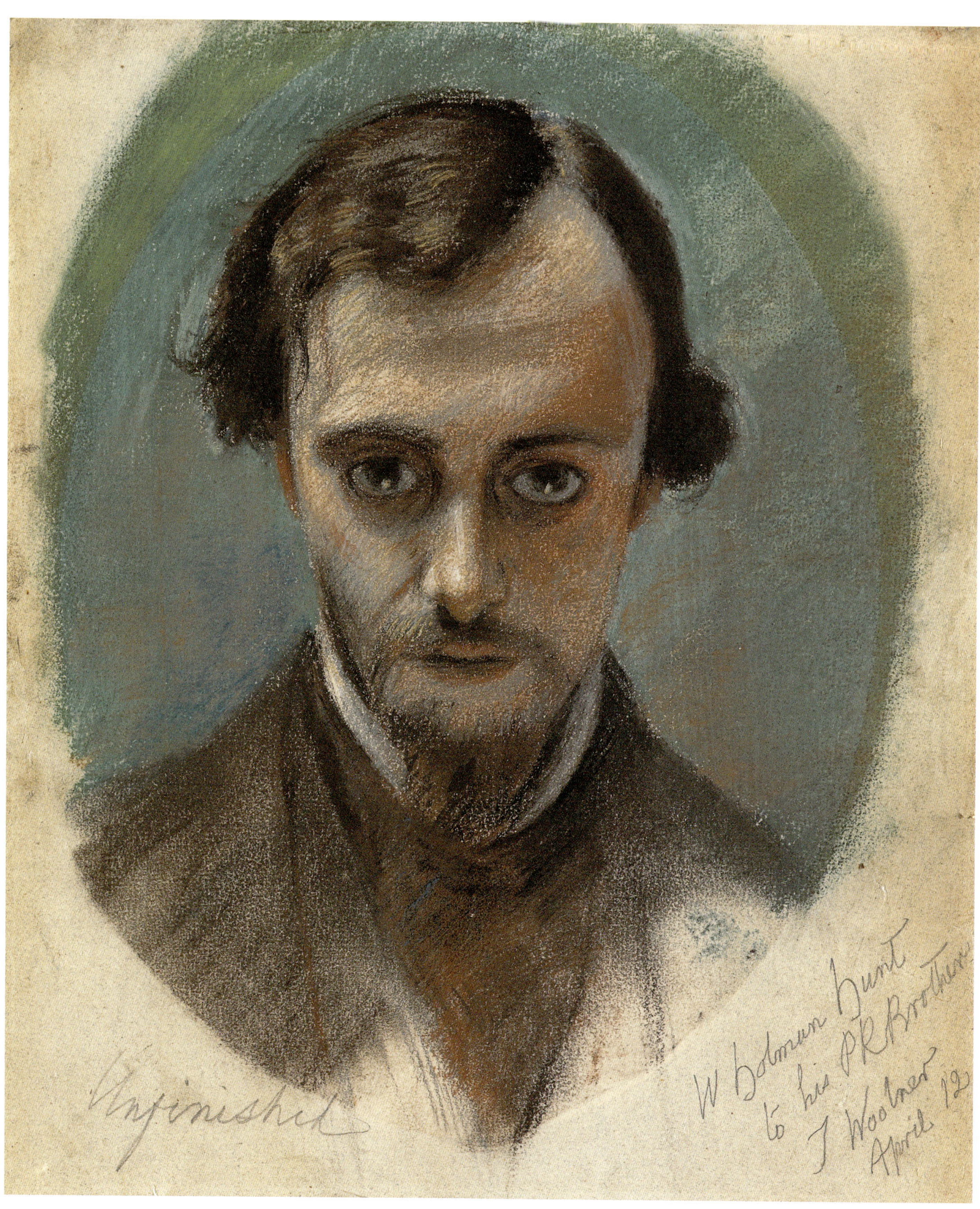

Unfinished
W Holman Hunt
to his PR Brother
T Woolner
April '92

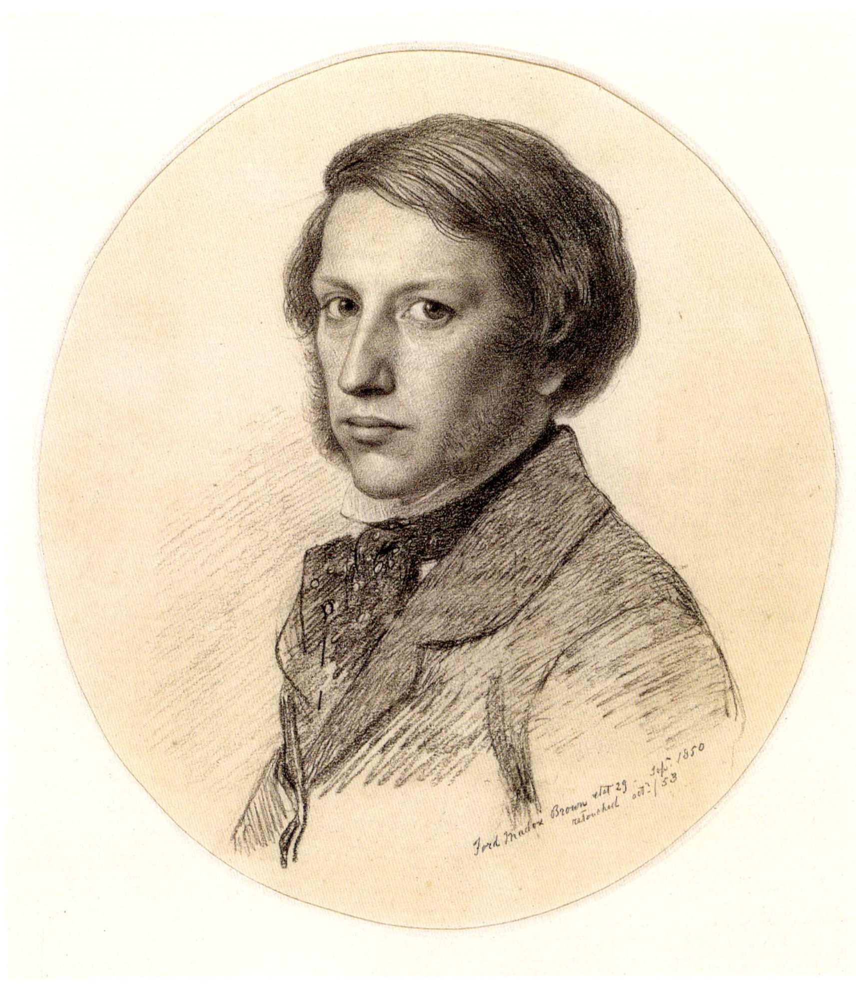

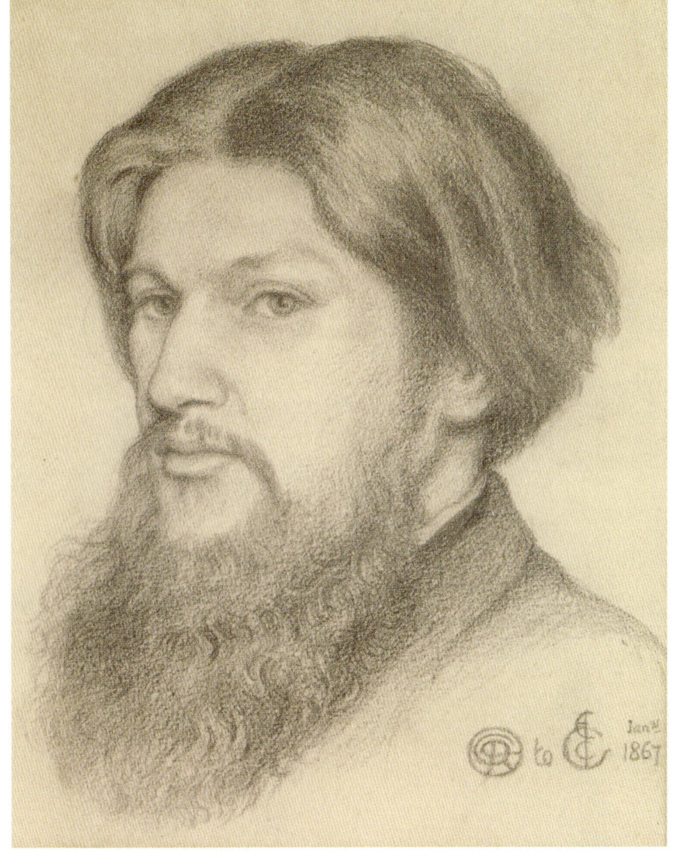

121 William Holman Hunt,
Dante Gabriel Rossetti, 1853,
Manchester City Galleries

122 Ford Madox Brown, *Self
Portrait*, 1850–53, National
Museums Liverpool (Walker
Art Gallery)

123 Dante Gabriel Rossetti, *Ford
Madox Brown*, 1867, private
collection

124 Dante Gabriel Rossetti,
Ford Madox Brown in Profile,
c. 1856–57, Birmingham
Museums & Art Gallery

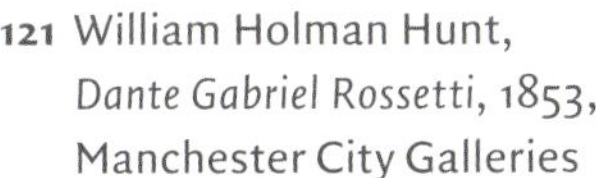

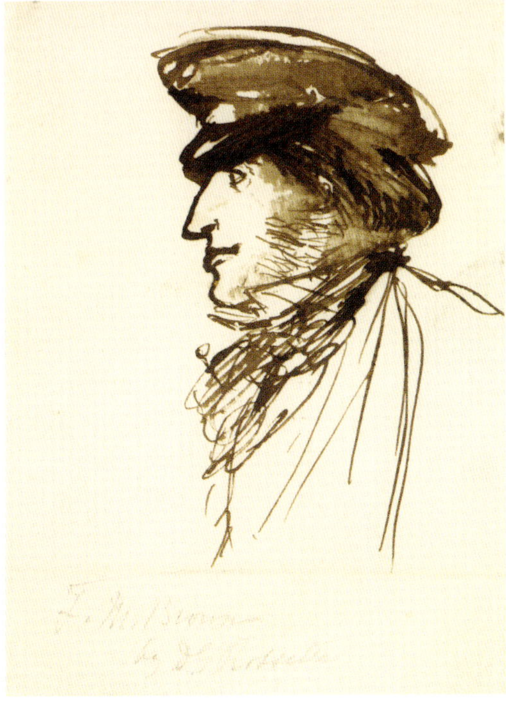

suspicious. Perhaps, as William Michael Rossetti implied, Brown got better looking as his circumstances became more secure. Rossetti's semi-caricature [123] of Brown sporting a peaked cap (of the sort worn by students in Germany at the time) also shows a warmer and more expressive personality than that represented by Brown himself.

It is significant that many of the likenesses recorded by the members of the Brotherhood and their followers are found in drawing media rather than in paint. Millais was to be made wealthy, as well as famous, by his skill as a portraitist, but

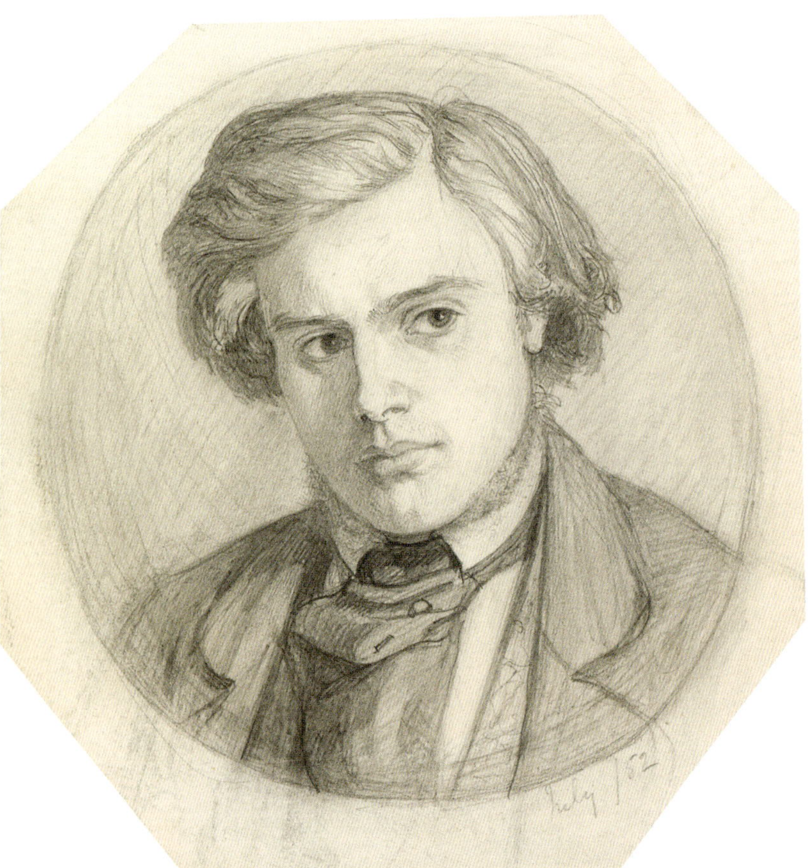

125 Dante Gabriel Rossetti, *Thomas Woolner*, 1852, National Portrait Gallery, London

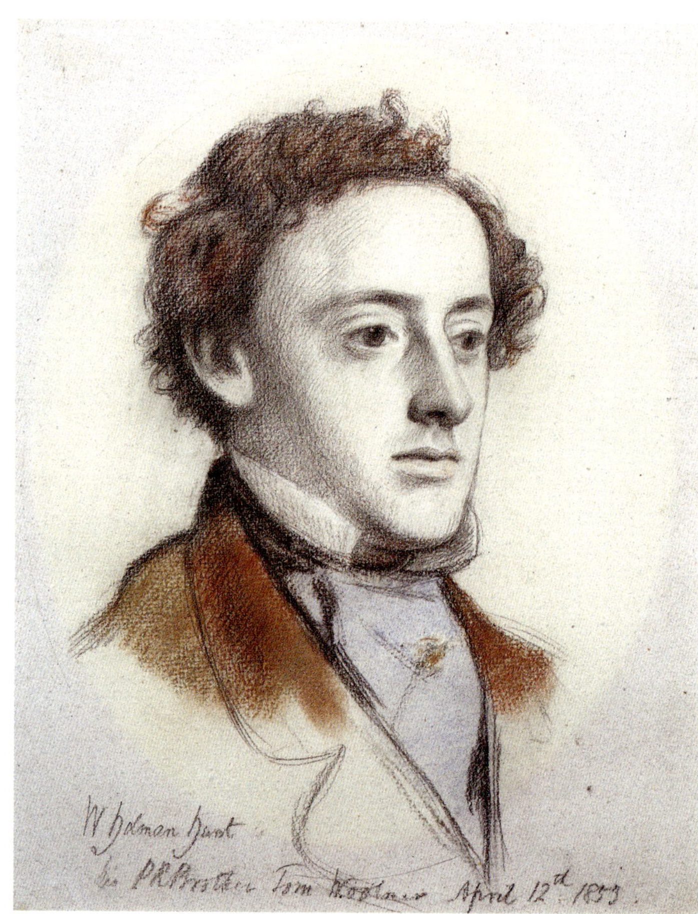

126 William Holman Hunt, *John Everett Millais*, 1853, National Portrait Gallery, London

chiefly those sitters who commissioned likenesses preferred their features to be immortalized in oils. The drawn portrait, while more modest in its methods and materials, was frequently more intimate and revealing. The sitters, with few exceptions, were most often friends or family members.

A set of drawings [126, 127, 128, 129] was sent to Australia in the spring of 1853 to Thomas Woolner, the only sculptor to be a member of the Brotherhood, who had emigrated the previous year. In this set of drawings the completeness of the facial

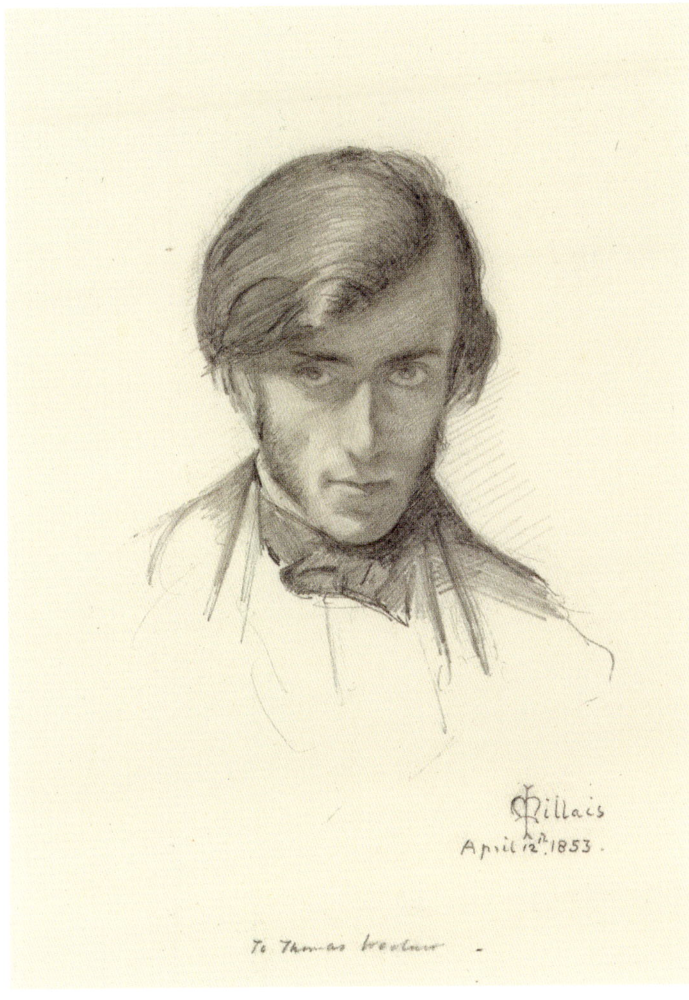

127 John Everett Millais, *Frederic George Stephens*, 1853, National Portrait Gallery, London

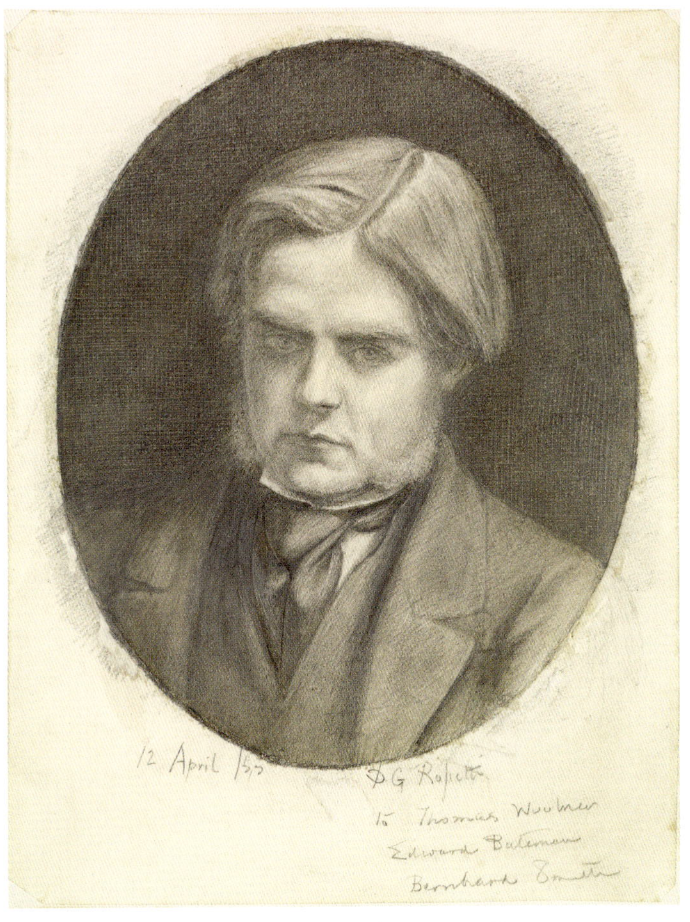

128 Dante Gabriel Rossetti, *William Holman Hunt*, 1853, Birmingham Museums & Art Gallery

image seems at odds with the impulse to record the likeness with the kind of spontaneity that characterized the informal portraits of the eighteenth and early nineteenth centuries. If anything, these Pre-Raphaelite portraits seem a little stilted, notable for their accuracy and painstaking detail but not for their depth of feeling. In their realistic rendering of the flesh they are somewhat akin in technique to Mulready's life drawings. There are none of those exuberant signs of just-suspended animation that are found in the best British portraiture of an earlier age. Those graphic highlights – dashes of chalk that mimic the light dancing off lips and hair and the gleams in the eyes, the half smiles or playfully engaging glances of Ramsay and Raeburn and their kind – are not present here.

Instead these drawings present us with serious, somewhat sober presences where we might have expected – from a group dedicated to artistic revolt – more fire and attitude, and a greater sense of rebellion shown in pose or accessory.

There are scarcely any indications of the artistic occupation of the sitters, no tools of the trade such as we find in the portraits of – say – Roubiliac, in which the artist might be depicted finishing a work with a flourish. These Pre-Raphaelite drawings of their fellow artists and comrades are unlike portrait drawings of the Nazarene circle, done in Rome earlier in the century, in which earnest young sitters were depicted with the utmost delicacy of line, sometimes in pairs, as a celebration of a shared enterprise.[7] As in

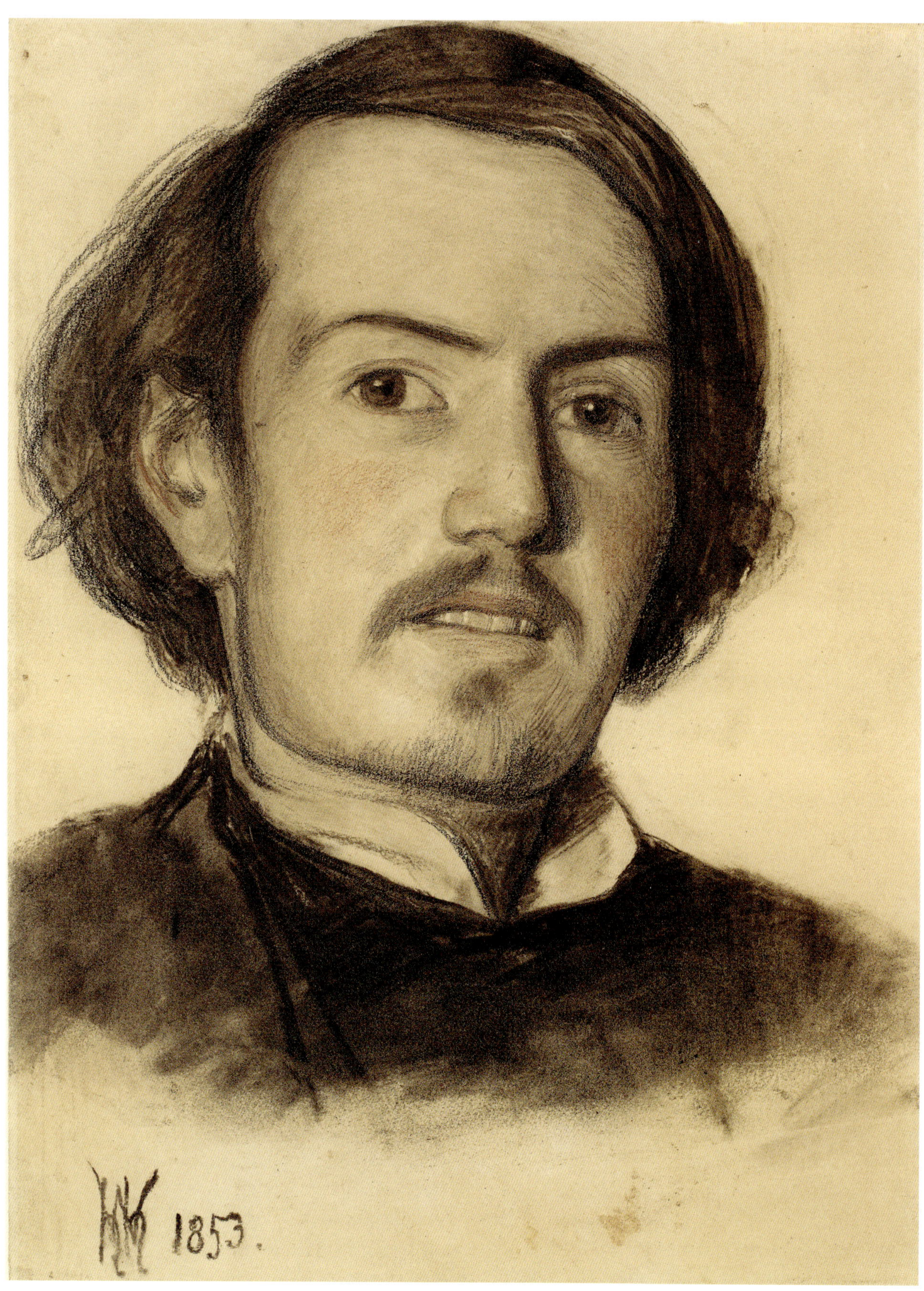

129 William Holman
Hunt, *Walter
Howell Deverell*,
1853, Birmingham
Museums & Art
Gallery

 Drawing the Circle: Portraits, Self-Portraits and Caricatures

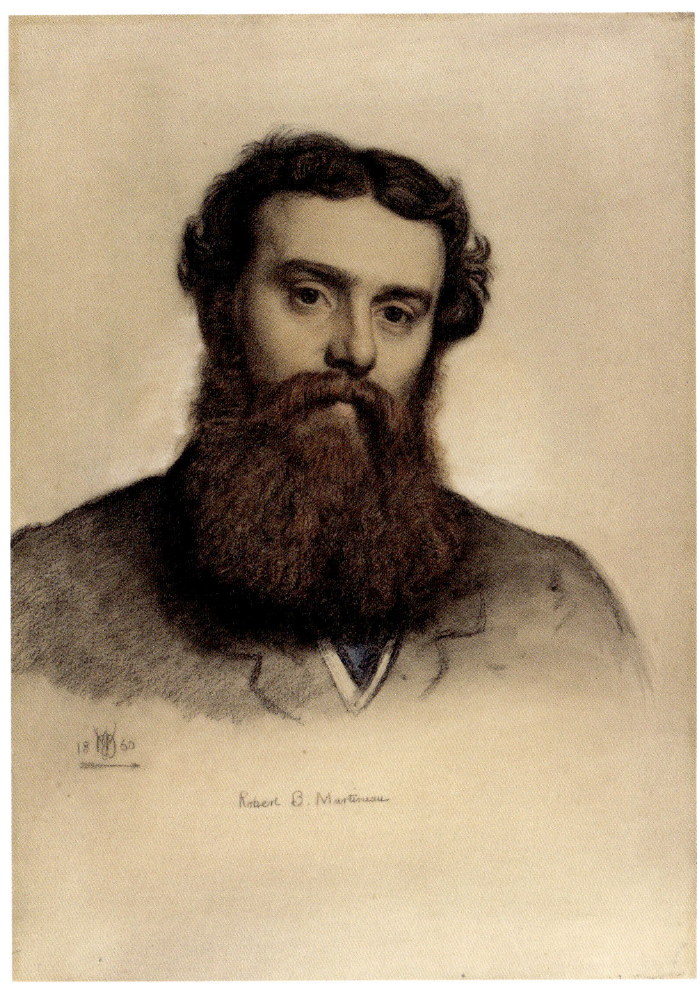

130 William Holman Hunt, *Robert Braithwaite Martineau*, 1860,
National Museums Liverpool (Walker Art Gallery)

Nazarener portraits, however, there is a scrupulous lack
of pretence or show. The lack of virtuosity might itself be
the sign of a shared seriousness of purpose, and the
Pre-Raphaelites might be deliberately eschewing the tricks
of portraiture perfected by earlier generations of portraitists.

These are drawings of heads, rarely of hands, and the
rest of the body is indicated as a coated shoulder, a collar,
a neck-tie. Does this withholding of bodily details indicate
anything? It speaks to us not just of an emotional proximity
but of a physical one too. The portraitists are never far away
from their subjects. The field of vision is small and the subject
fills the space. F. G. Stephens recalled the circumstances of
the making of these likenesses when the artists were paired
to draw each other. The occasion was one of the last in which
the Brothers met as a group, and the growing strangeness
between them – at odds with the act of recording the

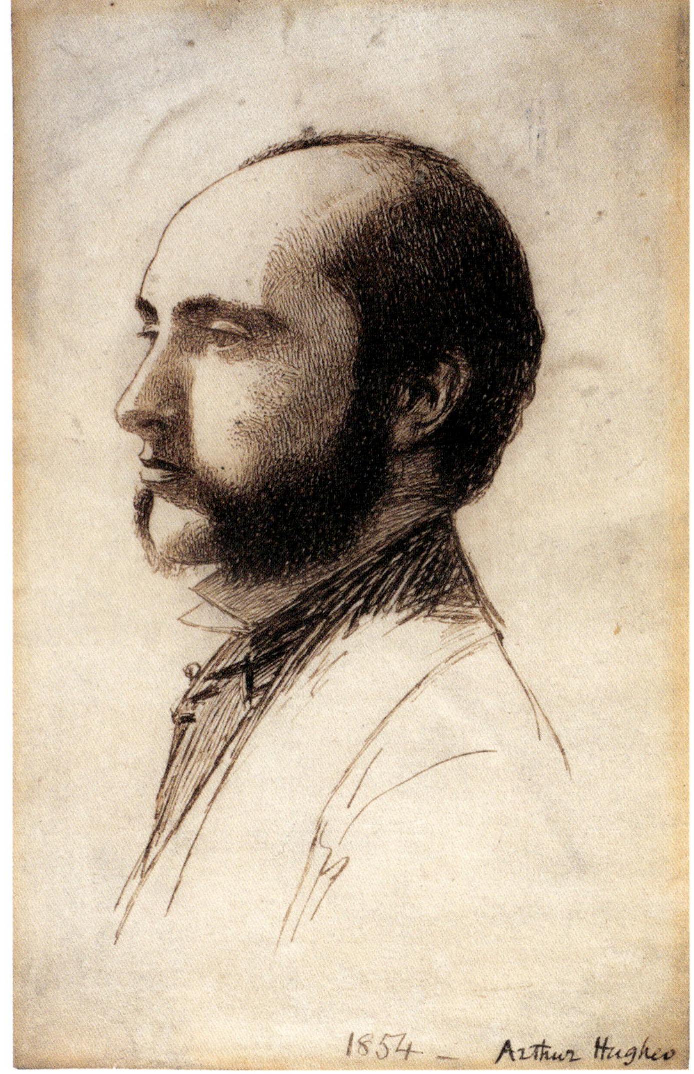

131 Arthur Hughes, *William Michael Rossetti*, 1854, private collection

appearance of each other for a friend – may also account for
the formality of the works which, nevertheless, have a certain
fascination mixed from the physical proximity of artist to
sitter and an emotional distance between them.

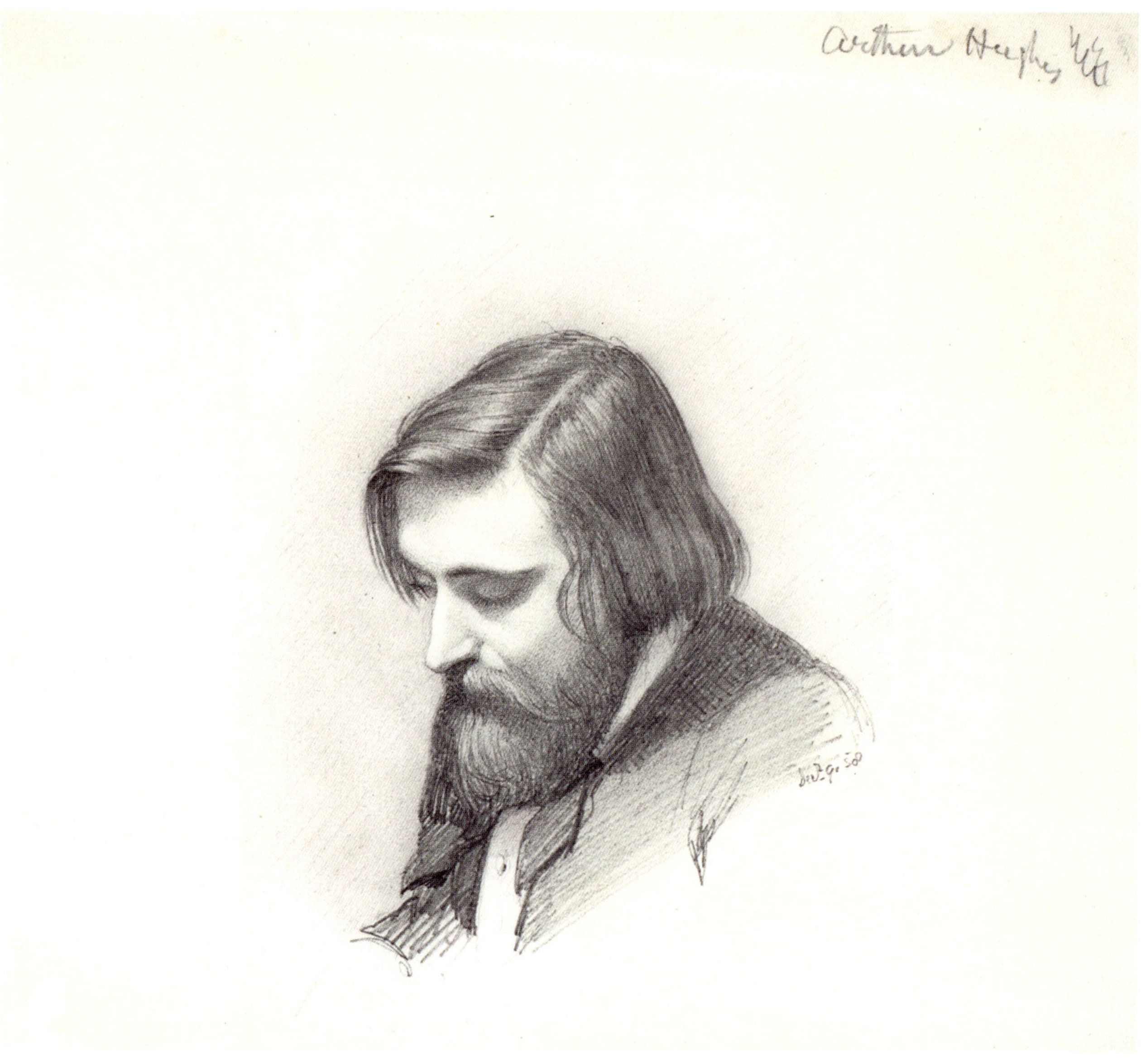

132 John Brett, *Arthur Hughes*, 1858,
National Portrait Gallery, London

Although this was a mutual drawing activity, Stephens abandoned his portrait of Millais and it was decided that Hunt make a portrait of Millais to send to Woolner instead [126]. Despite the circumstances there remains a curiosity about faces that the artists knew well, but it lends a stilted quality to all of these pictures drawn by young men of other young men. Hunt is consistently strenuous in his efforts to record large amounts of information; the textures of things (including beards) are important for him to put on record. In his portrait of Deverell [129] there is a penetration not apparent in portrait drawings of others of the group. The same is true of his portrait of Robert Braithwaite Martineau (1826–69) [130], drawn in 1860, in which

some of the humour and liveliness of their connection is communicated.

Yet again, an examination of drawings of the portraits of other men in the Pre-Raphaelite circle shows a different kind of register, more exploratory and less descriptive. Arthur Hughes's pen and ink study of William Michael Rossetti [131] and John Brett's detailed pencil drawing of Hughes [132] are good examples of this more sensitive approach to the sitter. Both Hughes and Brett have taken pains to present less formal portraits that offer a glimpse into the creativity of their subjects. In these drawings William Michael Rossetti looks dreamy and inspired, Hughes studious and diligent. In this quality of completeness of personality they are strikingly different to the set of portraits sent to Woolner in Australia.

In other drawings of friends, such as Rossetti's semi-caricatures of Hunt [17], Millais [18], Brown [124] and Woolner [133], there is a more generalized depiction of

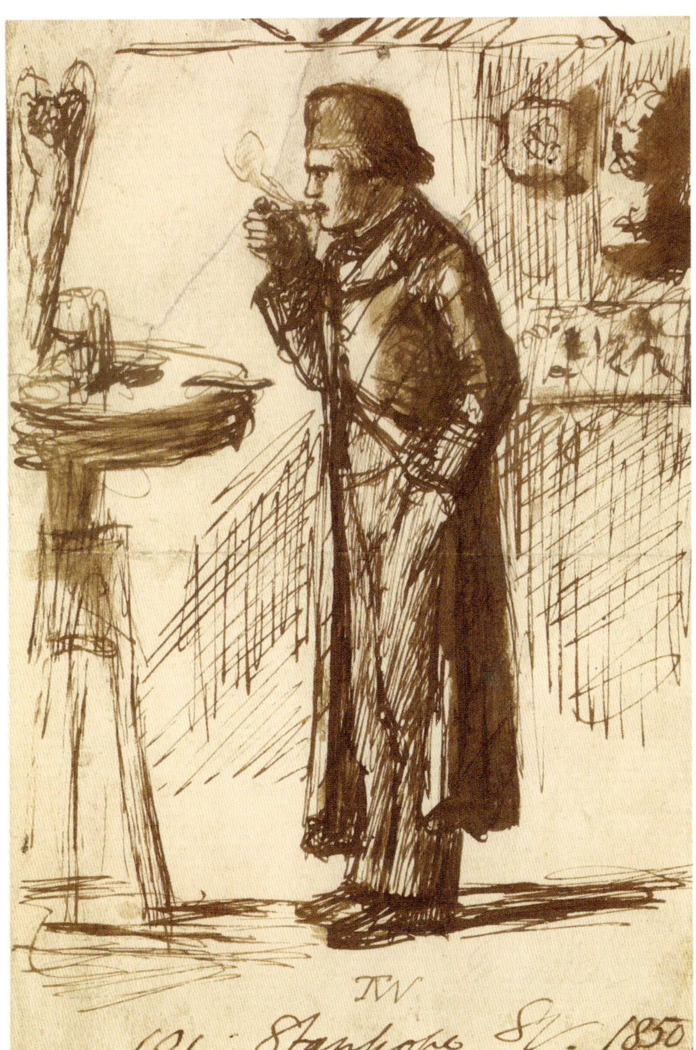

133 Dante Gabriel Rossetti, *Thomas Woolner*, 1850, Birmingham Museums & Art Gallery

appearance and a greater emphasis on differences of personality. These drawings were done from memory and are less bound up in striving for accuracy or fidelity to the model and the precise moment of depiction. In these semi-caricatures the act of recording the likeness of the subject is, however, more urgent and more comprehensive. The portrait of Woolner, in particular, is revealing as a complete picture of the man – showing not only his facial features but also giving a sense of his personal style,. This is the nearest we get to seeing a picture of a Pre-Raphaelite artist in the act of creation. As the sculptor regards the work at hand, he smokes a pipe to aid his contemplation.

Portrait drawings of the Pre-Raphaelite circle

One of the most significant of the artists working in portraiture in the Pre-Raphaelite circle was Charles Fairfax Murray (1849–1919), part of whose collection of Pre-Raphaelite drawings was bought by Birmingham Museum and Art Gallery when it was dispersed between the years 1903 and 1906. Murray's self-portrait, aged seventeen [134], is reminiscent of the celebrated self-portrait of 1824–25 by Samuel Palmer (1805–81), now in the Ashmolean Museum, Oxford. It is remarkable for its frankness, showing an expression of youthful surprise at the artist's own appearance and is evidence of the talent that so impressed Ruskin.[8] This self-portrait was completed in the year that Murray asked Ruskin for advice on becoming an artist, an encounter which led to his introduction to the Pre-Raphaelite circle. He was subsequently employed by Burne-Jones as a studio assistant, by Morris as a designer and painter for 'the Firm', as Morris's design company was known in its many manifestations, and by Ruskin and Rossetti as a copyist – all of these jobs requiring exemplary precision and skill. His sharpness of vision is demonstrated in his portraits of Morris [135] and Burne-Jones [136] which are remarkably cool and objective.

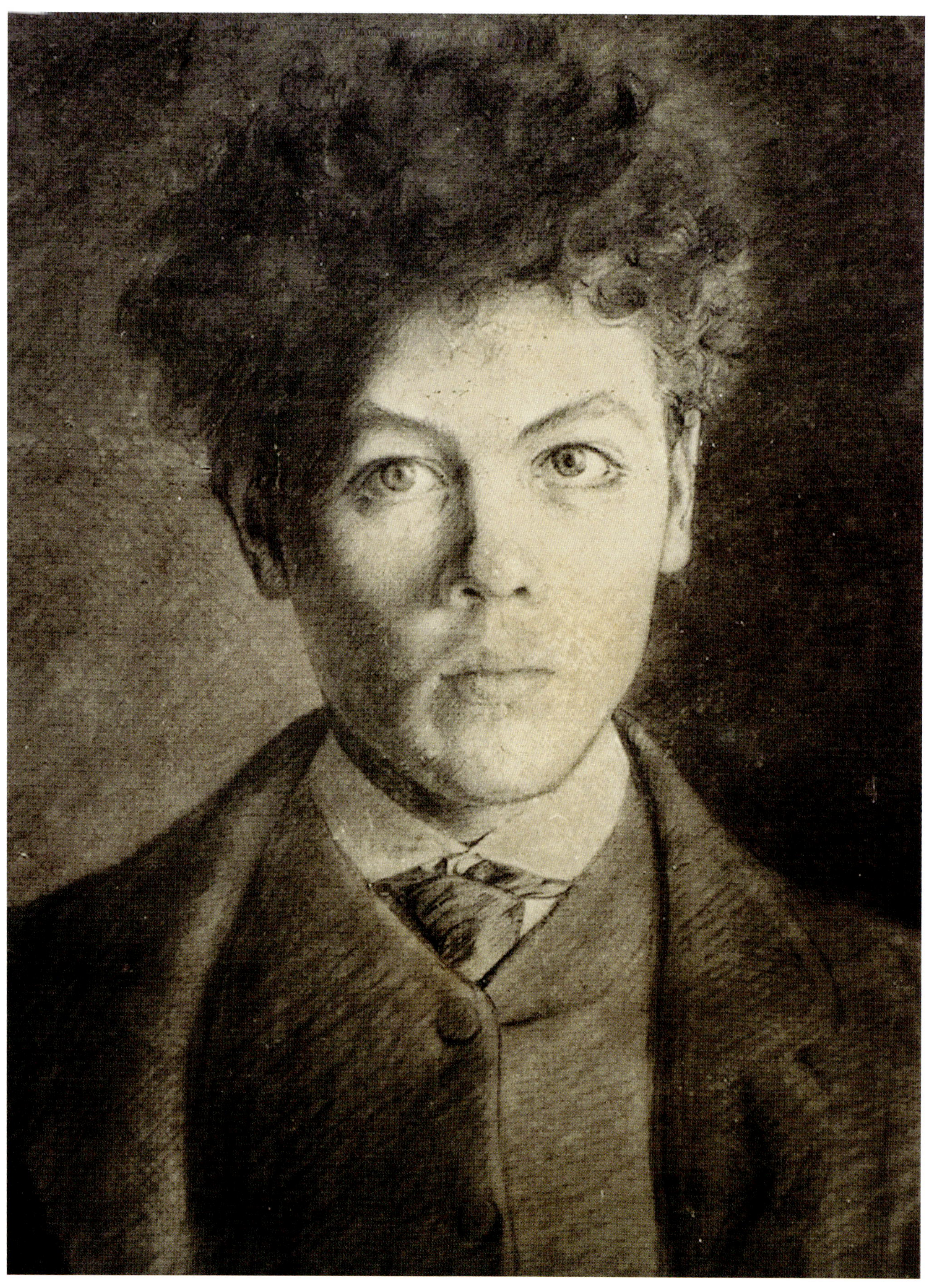

134 Charles Fairfax
Murray, *Self
Portrait Aged
Seventeen*, 1866,
private collection

 Drawing the Circle: Portraits, Self-Portraits and Caricatures

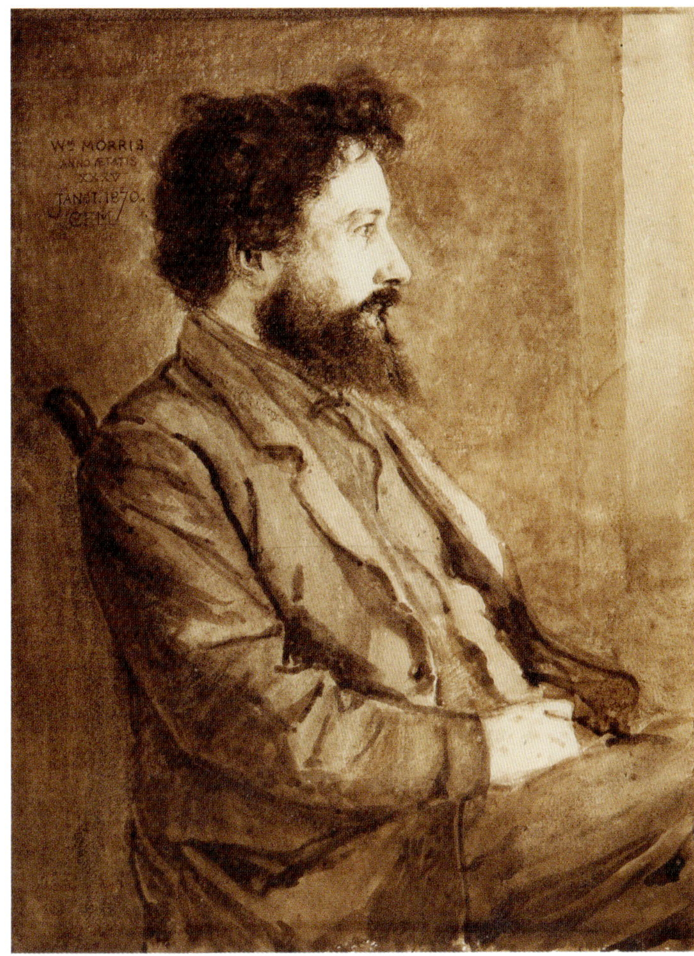

135 Charles Fairfax Murray, *William Morris*, 1870,
The Whitworth Art Gallery, The University of Manchester

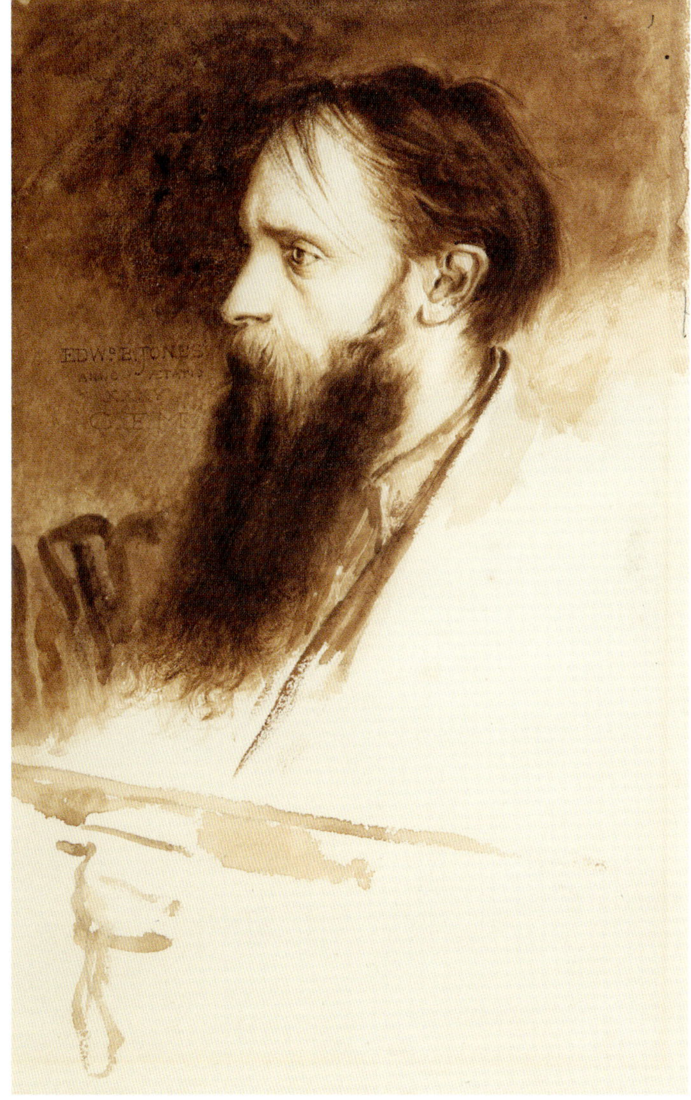

136 Charles Fairfax Murray, *Edward Burne-Jones*, c. 1869,
The Whitworth Art Gallery, The University of Manchester

The watercolour portrait of Ruskin from 1875 [137]
– when Murray had become a successful picture dealer – is
as searching as a self-portrait, being both confrontational
and penetrating.[9] The proliferation of likenesses of Ruskin
during his lifetime rivals that of statesmen such as William
Ewart Gladstone and literary celebrities such as Alfred,
Lord Tennyson and Sir Walter Scott. The poet Algernon
Charles Swinburne, likewise, was widely depicted, although
frequently in caricature and rarely in straightforward
portraits. He was one of the most notorious figures of
his generation – superseded in notoriety only later in the
century by Oscar Wilde.

Rossetti's two drawings of Swinburne [138, 139]
demonstrate different representational choices – one
recording and the other idealizing the features of his sitter.
In the watercolour of 1862 the artist presents the viewer
with a handsome young man with clearly defined, regular
features, a square jaw, straight nose and purposeful mouth.
The head is turned slightly, giving the impression of action
and energy. However, in the pencil drawing of 1860, not
only is the hair tamed from its exuberance but the chin
is weak, the mouth soft, the glance mild, the face almost
boyish, even placid. Neither drawing presents the most

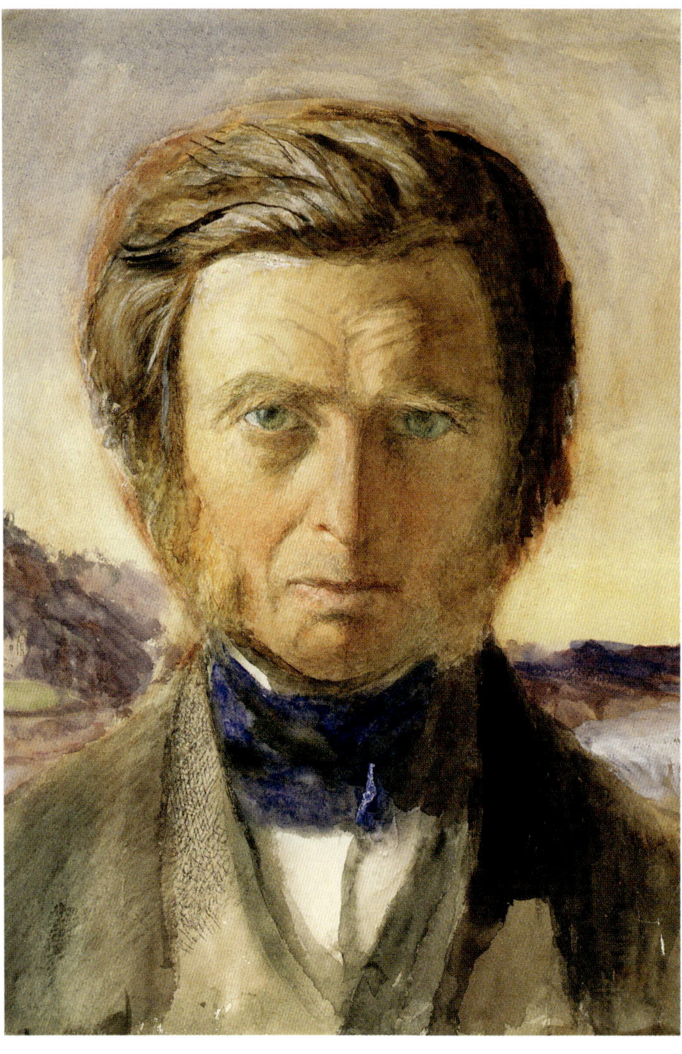

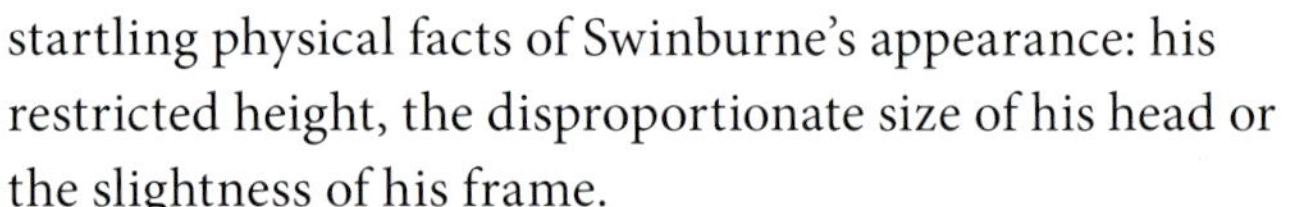

137 Charles Fairfax Murray, *John Ruskin*, 1875, Tate

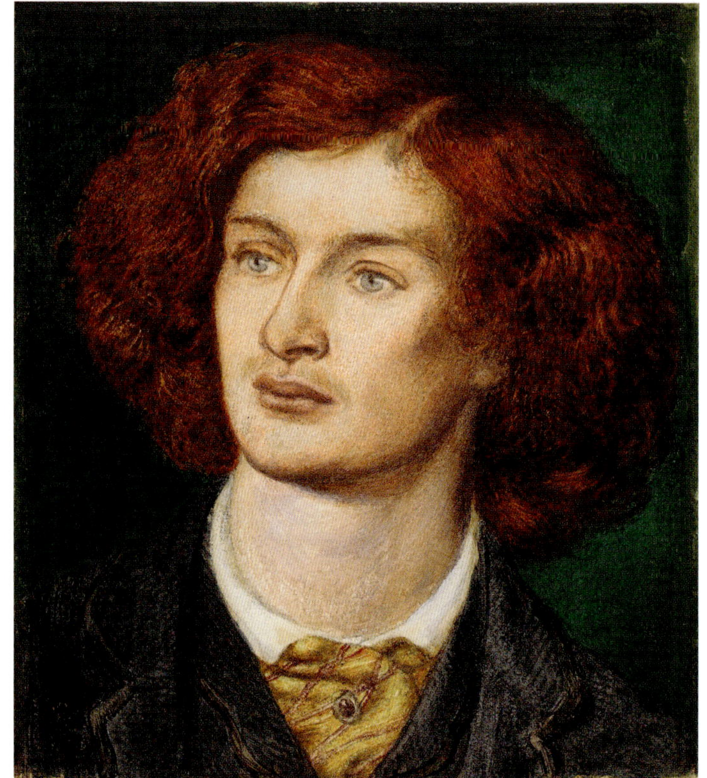

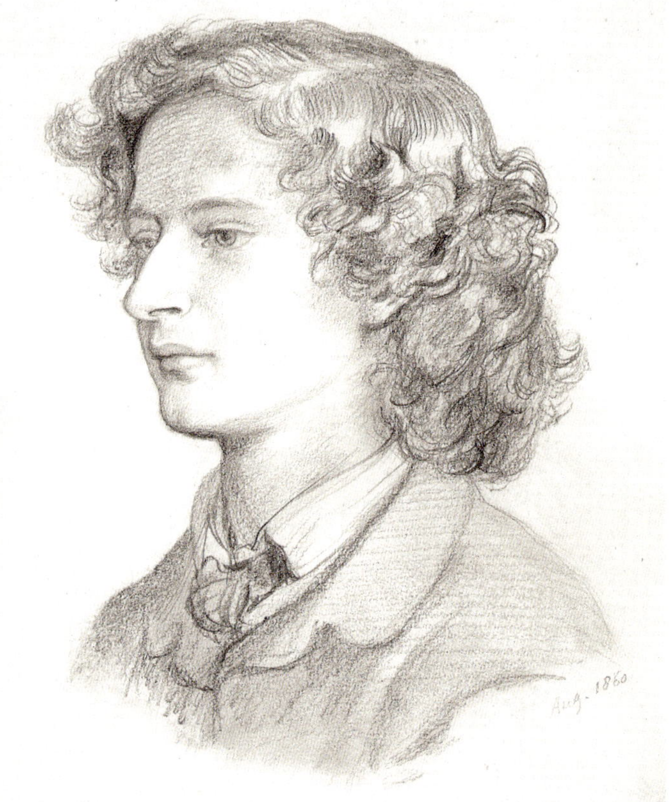

startling physical facts of Swinburne's appearance: his restricted height, the disproportionate size of his head or the slightness of his frame.

These were unsparingly satirized in caricatures, however, including that which features in the group caricature of the Rossetti 'circle' by Max Beerbohm (1872–1956) [140]

138 Dante Gabriel Rossetti, *Algernon Charles Swinburne*, 1861, Fitzwilliam Museum, Cambridge

139 Dante Gabriel Rossetti, *Algernon Charles Swinburne*, 1860, Mark Samuels Lasner Collection, on loan to the University of Delaware Library

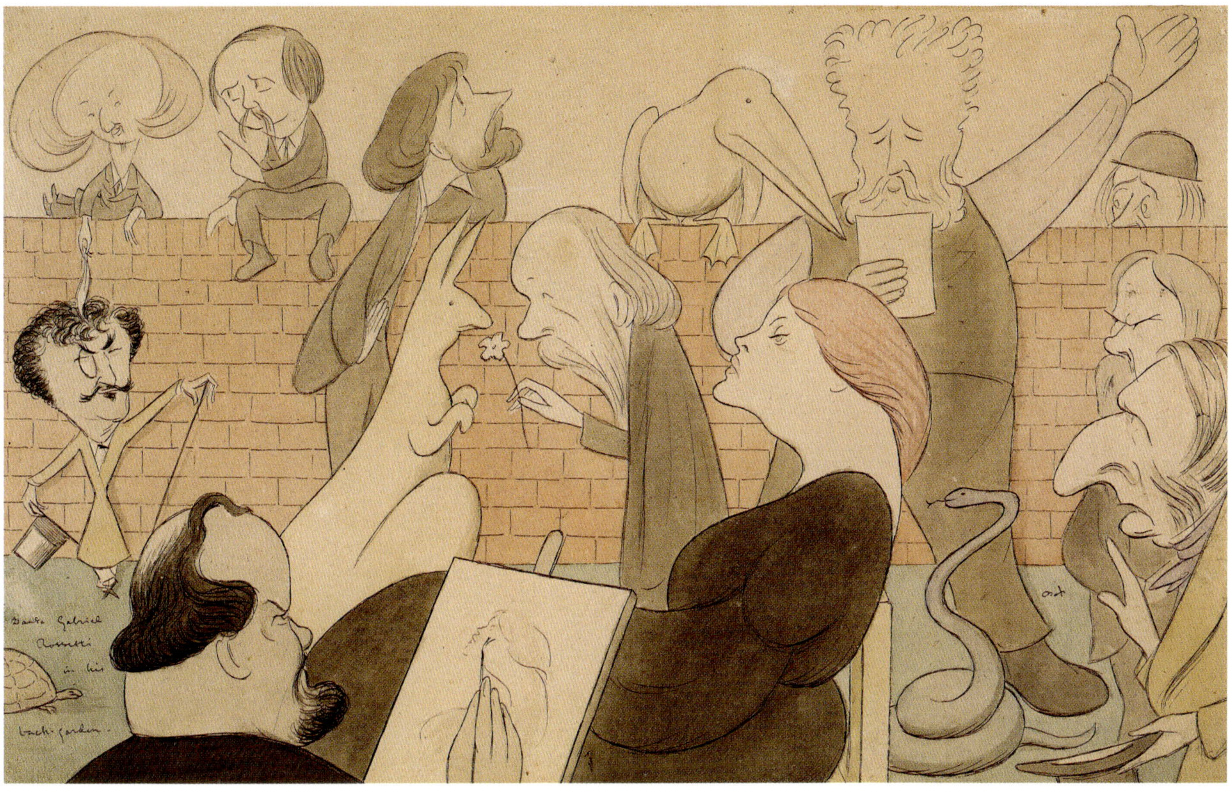

140 Max Beerbohm, *Dante Gabriel Rossetti in his Back Garden*, c. 1904, Birmingham Museums & Art Gallery

published in *The Poet's Corner* (1904). *Dante Gabriel Rossetti in his Back Garden* satirizes the bohemian culture of the Queen's House, Cheyne Row, where Rossetti lived for the last twenty years of his life. He maintained a menagerie there and Beerbohm depicted some of the animals in the garden mixing with the humans. Burne-Jones, for example, is shown handing a flower to a wallaby; he bows towards it slightly as if he is paying court. The Swinburne depicted here is so small he has to sit on a wall, his enormous head forcing a resemblance to Humpty Dumpty; the lower half of his body is residual and ineffective. On the other hand, Morris is so tall and broad that he dominates half the picture. The caricature of Ruskin emphasizes his nose and characteristic pendulous lip. His pointing finger suggests a ponderous pedagogue, as if he were always lecturing his audience (even when, as in this case, they are not paying him any attention). The model from whom Rossetti draws sits in the centre of the caricature. With her goitrous throat, red hair and half-closed eyes she stands in for various Rossettian 'stunners', an amalgam of their idiosyncrasies. All of the characters are so grotesque that the entire notion of a Pre-Raphaelite

sense of beauty is thrown into question or, more decidedly, dismissed as nonsense.

Beerbohm was working from memory, aided by photographs, but he made his figures more grotesque – fatter, smaller, madder – than they were in life. Half a century earlier Sandys's *A Nightmare* [141], published as a broadsheet in 1857, had parodied one of Millais's paintings, the badly received *Sir Isumbras at the Ford*. Sandys swapped the painting's rescued children for three members of the Brotherhood – Millais, Rossetti and Hunt – and branded the braying ass on which they cling to each other with the initials 'J. R.': John Ruskin. The portrait caricatures were drawn from memory. The image of Ruskin as an ass was, of course, constructed without reference to his physiognomy at all, although his critical method was savagely satirized in the use of the beast. The braying Ruskin clearly caused offence: there is not a single reference to Sandys's subsequent works, however detailed and truthful to nature, in any of Ruskin's writings.

After Millais, Sandys is the most singular of the Pre-Raphaelite circle who worked extensively as a portraitist. From the very beginnings of his career Sandys was dependent

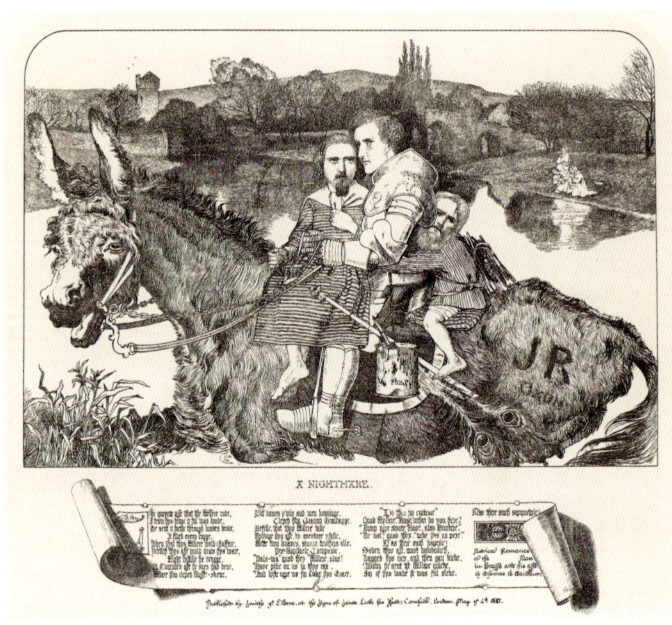

141 Frederick Sandys, *A Nightmare*, 1857,
Birmingham Museums & Art Gallery

on drawing likenesses of fashionable folk for a living.
Executed in a combination of media – pencil, coloured chalk
and pastel – often with inscribed dates and titles in scrolls,
his portraits were monogrammed in the manner of Albrecht
Dürer. Indeed, he invented a new kind of drawn portrait,
elaborately mounted and framed, which became a sign of
an advanced aesthetic taste for those who commissioned
them. Although Sandys was influenced by Dürer, the nearest
equivalent to these works was Holbein's group of drawn
portraits of the Tudor court, mainly done in the 1530s.

Like the works of Burne-Jones and Simeon Solomon,
Sandys's drawings graced the interior-decoration schemes
of Aesthetic movement collectors. His drawings could
sit easily alongside the photographs of works by the
Old Masters as well as original works of art by the
Pre-Raphaelites and the quaint objects of decorative art
that such taste demanded. As Betty Elzea, Sandys's

biographer and author of his *Catalogue Raisonné*, has
written, his

> ravishing coloured-chalk portraits, cheaper than
> oils and faster to produce, now became an end in
> themselves…taking the long British tradition of chalk
> portraiture into the Aesthetic '70s with exquisite
> floral backgrounds inspired by Japanese art. With
> their handsome Foord and Dickinson frames of the
> Rossetti–Madox Brown type they must have graced
> many an Aesthetic interior.[10]

These were drawings of extraordinarily glossy individuals
– their skin and eyes shining, their clothes picturesque and
pristine. Often the gloss gets in the way of character study
but they are nonetheless revealing portraits of fashionable
self-presentation as an aid to social position.

In Sandys's portrait of Charles Augustus Howell (1840–90
[**142**]), Rossetti's business agent for a while, the sitter looks
outward directly but does not confront; rather he appears
bored by the very idea of being the subject of the gaze of the
artist or anyone else. In her portrait, his wife Kitty, on the
contrary, seems keen to invite anyone into the world she
inhabits [**144**]. She leans out towards the viewer, yet her gaze
is more wary than one might expect from such a welcoming
stance. Her dress is more revealing than might have been
usual for a society hostess. It is, on second glance, a portrait
full of conflicting information, and the sitter remains
something of a cipher, her gaze remaining as polished as the
Chinese vase at her side. We are struck not only by the social
pretensions of the couple but also by the gender differences
that Sandys enshrines in their portraits, reflecting, no doubt,
society's expectations, even those of a racy bohemian circle.
Both sitters are perfectly turned out, as is often the way with
Sandys's subjects. Charles's crisp cuffs, his jewelled tie pin and
cufflinks and Kitty's turquoise necklace are props in a game
of identities. The necklace reappears in Sandys's portrait
of Mary Emma Jones [**143**], his mistress and model for

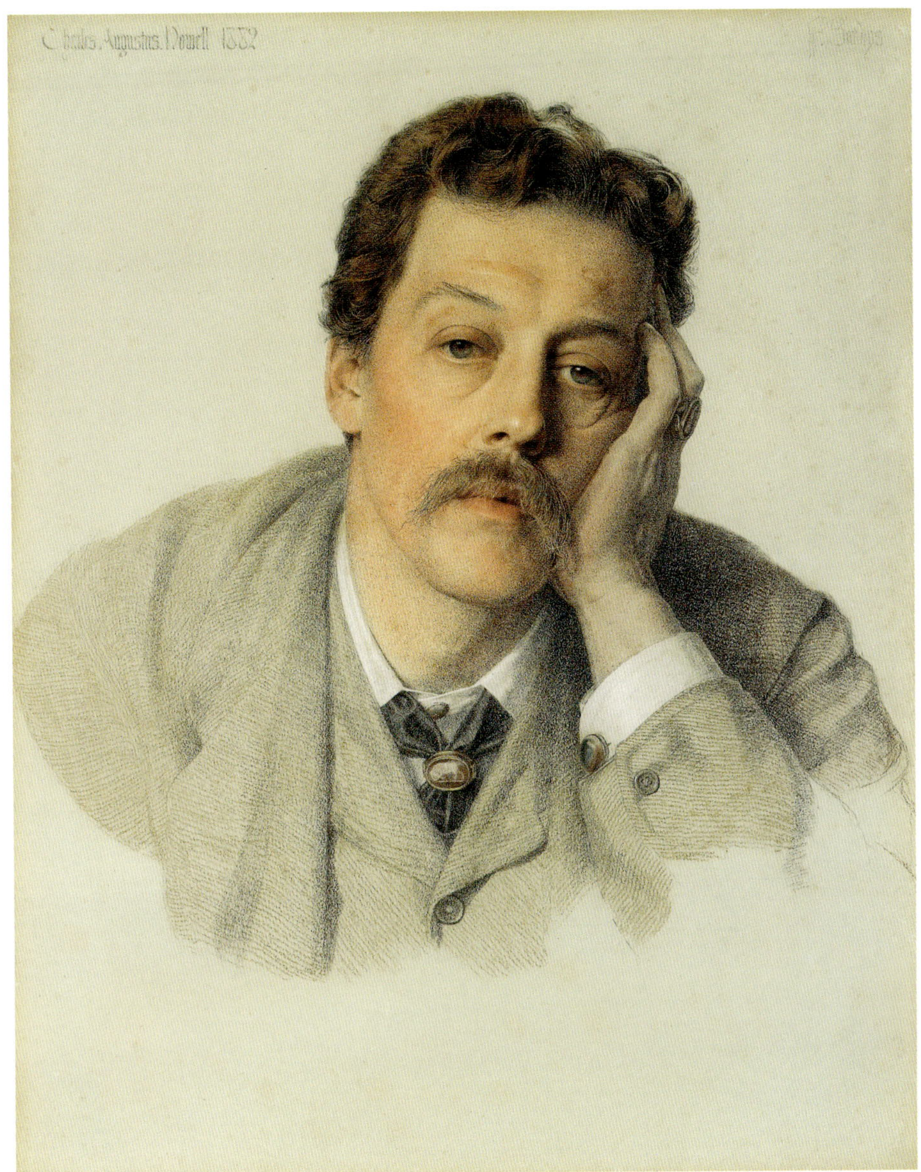

142 Frederick Sandys, *Charles Augustus Howell*, 1882, Ashmolean Museum, University of Oxford

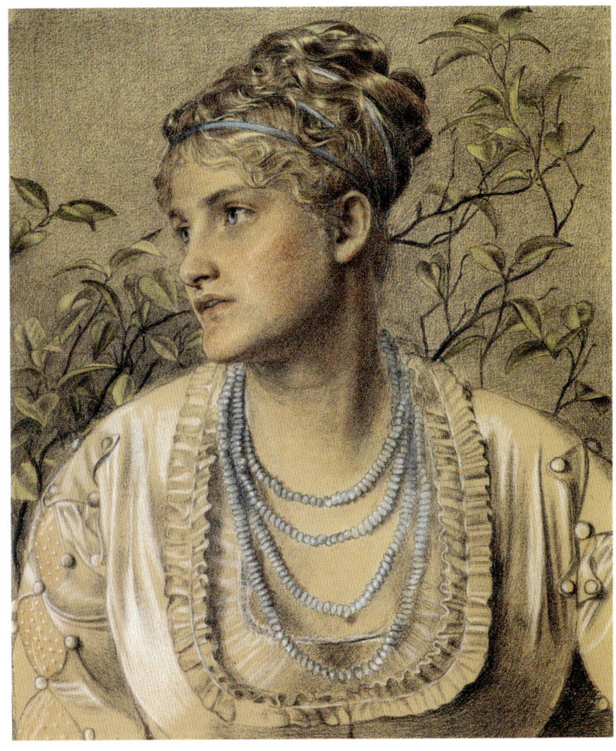

143 Frederick Sandys, *Portrait of a Lady (Mary Emma Jones)*, c. 1873, Birmingham Museums & Art Gallery

several subject paintings and drawings; it would seem to be, therefore, something of a studio prop rather than a treasured personal item. It signalled the sitter's supposed taste: Kitty appears to reject the cut precious stones of high society in favour of something more unusual and individual if only for the act of sitting for her portrait.[11]

Unpainted masterpieces: caricatures and portraits from memory

The action of memory on likeness is a particularly interesting issue in drawings of the human face. All of the Pre-Raphaelites, with perhaps the exception of Ford Madox Brown, seem to have drawn from memory a great deal,

producing works of reportage as well as of caricature. Hunt, Millais and Rossetti decorated their letters with marginal drawings, additional sketches and illustrations, often comic. Hunt's letters from the Holy Land, Millais's from the Highlands and Rossetti's to his family from various jaunts, abound in these private graphic notations.

The Pre-Raphaelite Brotherhood were working during a period when caricature was enjoying huge popularity in periodicals such as *Punch* and *Tomahawk*. The existence of so much black-and-white illustration encouraged a general ambition to succeed in the graphic arts, and to experiment with imagery and techniques. Through a wider circle of connections with journalists, editors and illustrators, the

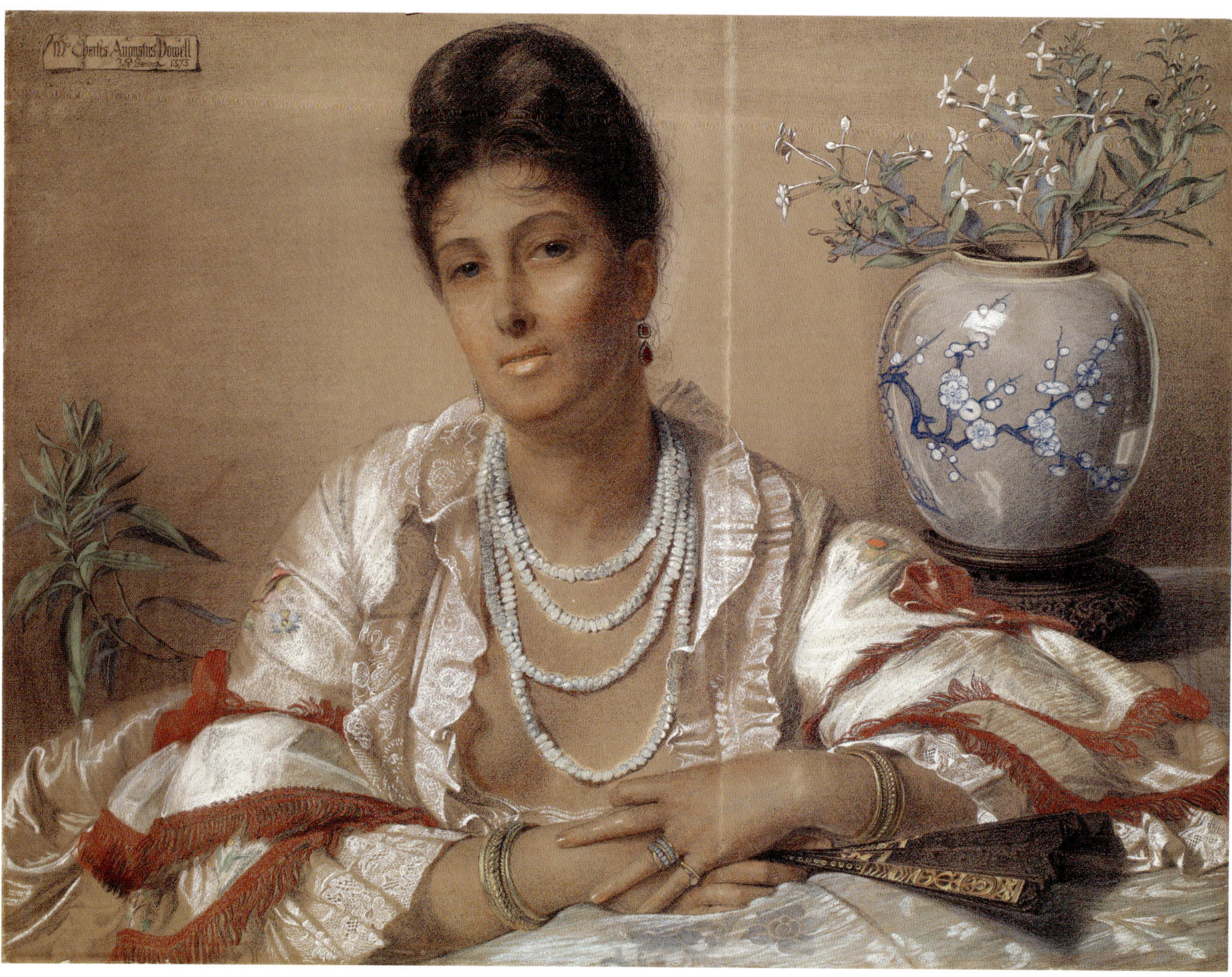

144 Frederick Sandys, *Mrs Charles Augustus Howell*, c. 1873–74, Birmingham Museums & Art Gallery

Pre-Raphaelites had social connections with caricaturists and humorists such as Kenny Meadows (1790–1874) and Millais became close friends with one of the most distinguished caricaturists, John Leech (1817–64), famous for his many drawings for *Punch*.[12]

In his biography of William De Morgan (1839–1917), Martin Geenwood refers to the grotesque and humorous elements of De Morgan's design. He cites both Edward Lear (1812–88) and Lewis Carroll (1832–98) as influences in devising a game of 'cartoons' that involved making fantastic drawings to illustrate well-known poems.[13] De Morgan's work in applied design is at its most imaginative when it introduces grotesque creatures, which, although often based on Renaissance prototypes, have all the strength of original inventions [267].

Often the grotesque element in caricature emerges as a strong feature of Pre-Raphaelite drawings. Millais's earliest drawings contain several humorous figures, and his letters and journals have a joy and light-heartedness in recording day-to-day events while demonstrating his extraordinary memory and facility as a draughtsman. It is hardly a surprise that such was his interest in everyday life and the situations he observed that he considered becoming a caricaturist. Many of Millais's drawings are reflexive: they respond to an incident or a memory of an incident and the intention is not to caricature but simply to record. Others, such as the strange drawings of Effie wearing 'natural ornament' consisting of squirrels, dormice and lizards, were flights of fancy showing the artist's more bizarre imagination [145]. In the early 1860s the Pre-Raphaelites produced curious drawings that suggest a game of consequences similar to the 'exquisite corpses' produced by the Surrealists in the twentieth century. The images were the product of collaboration but the process was 'assisted' by not knowing what one's fellow artists previously had drawn. The results were grotesque figures with disparities between head and body, costume and gender.

Even more surprising were the humorous designs made
by Burne-Jones, who frequently depicted himself in letters
to his family and friends. He revealed an ability to stand
back from himself and treat himself as a subject, even
sometimes as the object of derision. We might conjecture
what this says about his relationship with himself and
others. In addition, there are caricatures of children,
domestic animals and little monsters, all of which suggest
his undeveloped abilities as an illustrator of children's
books. This tendency to illustrate revealed itself early in
Burne-Jones's life. Not only did he constantly draw as
a schoolboy, but his satirical tendencies continued and
increased as an adult. The critic and curator Sidney Colvin
(1845–1927), recalled that Burne-Jones was

> very capable of original Dickens-like observations and
> inventions of his own. No one had a quicker or more
> healthy amused sense, without sting or ill-nature, of
> the grotesque and the absurd in everyday life. No one
> loved better to make or had a better gift for making,
> by speech or pencil, happy fun and laughter with his
> children and grandchildren.[14]

However child-like and playful, caricature brings us nearest
to some of the darker edges of the Pre-Raphaelite circle, its
infidelities and rivalries. Some were clearly too strong to
survive, such as the scurrilous doodlings of Burne-Jones
and Solomon sent to titillate Swinburne's taste.[15] Burne-
Jones sends up his more serious classically based subjects
in a caricature such as *The Sirens* [**146**], with its shapeless
female nudes awkwardly mounted on phallic rocks and
vulgarly importuning the ship that sails into view. The
joke is that the drawing, in its very coarseness, represents
something closer to the way of the world and the matter of
sexual allure than is usual in the slightly more attenuated
pictorial world of Burne-Jones.

The conventions of portraiture, like those of landscape,
had to be broken before they could yield a new art;

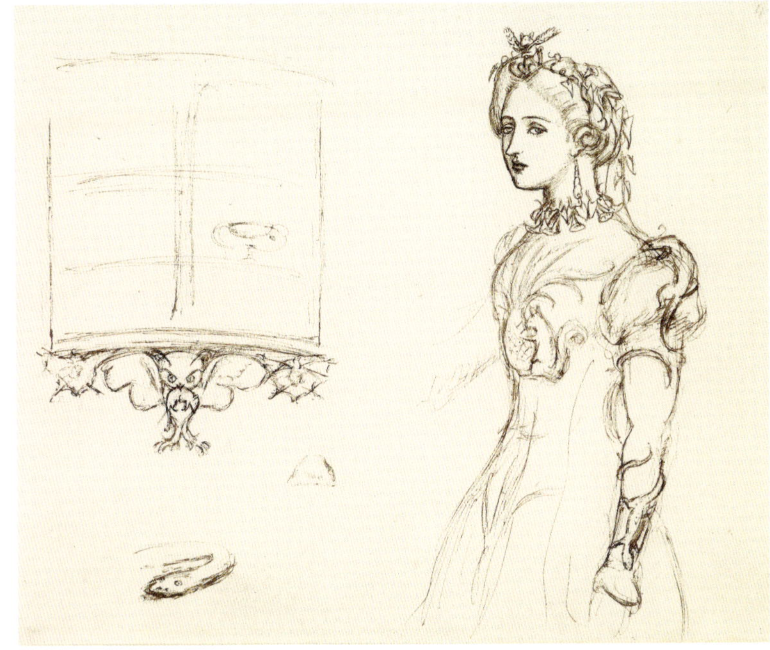

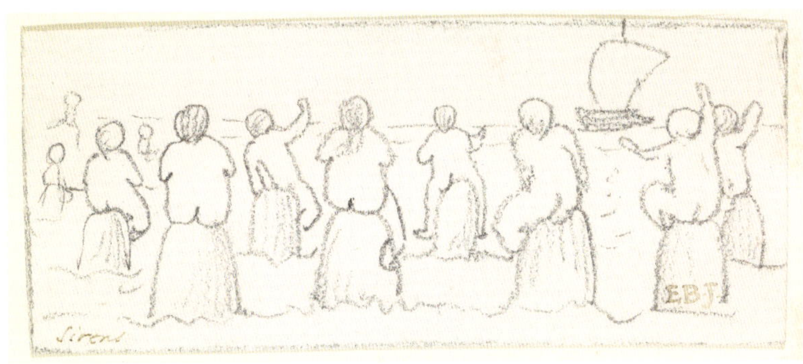

145 John Everett Millais, *Natural Ornament (Effie Gray Ruskin)*,
1853, Birmingham Museums & Art Gallery
146 Edward Burne-Jones, *The Sirens*, c. 1878–80,
Birmingham Museums & Art Gallery

arguably, caricature helped in its expression. While they
could be full of 'jolly mirth', as Colvin observed of Burne-
Jones's caricatures, they could also be revelatory and
personal. The great number of caricatures done by the
circle of the Pre-Raphaelites and their followers shows
the affection that they had for each other, but sometimes
reveals puzzling aspects of their relationships as well. The
one striking difference between the likenesses drawn from
life and the caricatures drawn from memory is that one
was known to the sitter, the other not. Thus caricature,
however affectionate – although most often not quite
– is done without the subject's knowledge. The result is
somewhat clandestine and is bound to represent a feature
in the subject's physique or character that is not usually
represented. The persistent satirizing of Morris as a fat,
trouser-splitting character (an anticipation of the fall
guys in early silent-cinema comedies) contrasts with the
somewhat exaggerated glamour of his wife, Jane, and with

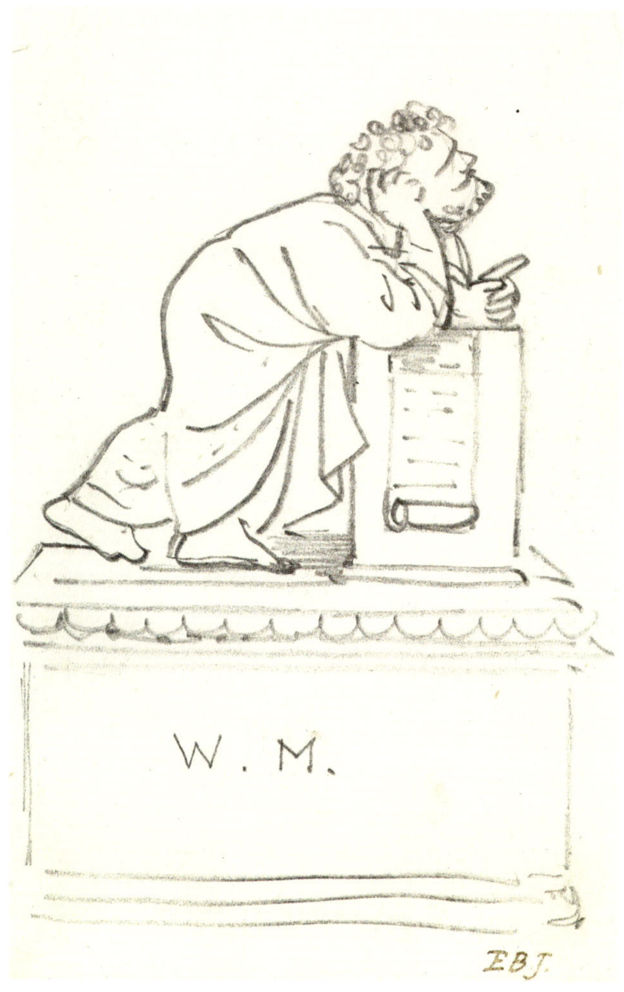

147 Edward Burne-Jones, *William Morris as an Ancient Poet*, c. 1870–73, Birmingham Museums & Art Gallery

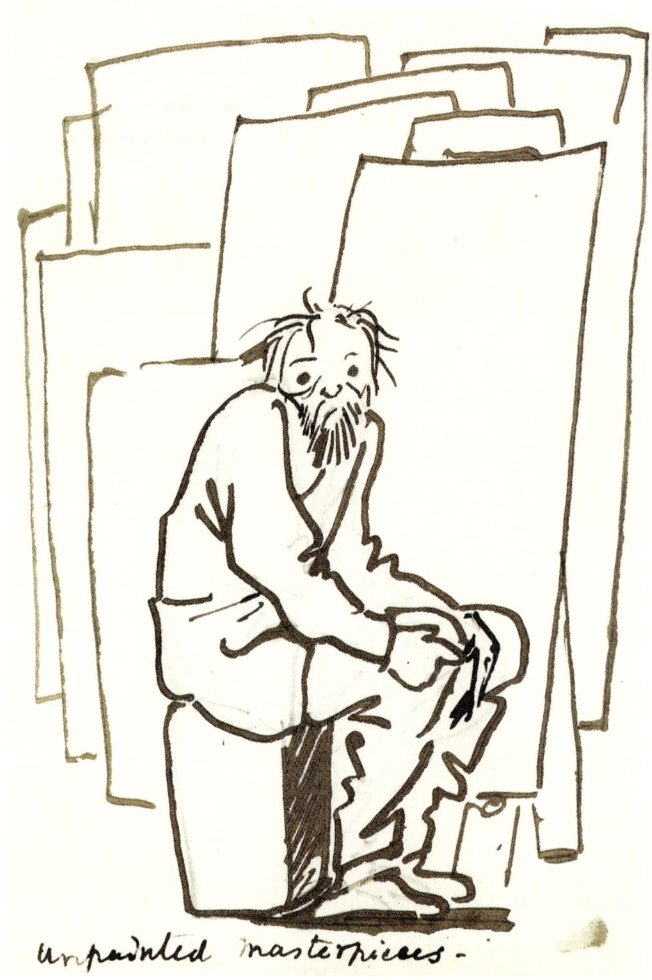

148 Edward Burne-Jones, *Self Portrait Caricature: 'Unpainted Masterpieces'*, early 1890s, Birmingham Museums & Art Gallery

Burne-Jones's self-represented elegant dishevelment [48]. In Rossetti's drawings the contrast might point us to the underlying sexual rivalry between the two men.

In caricatures drawn by Philip Burne-Jones (1861–1926) and sent to his family from Marlborough College in the 1870s he recorded his memories of scenes from home and school-life and from his father's studio [149, 150]. The drawings imitate his father's caricatural style closely but are also clearly influenced by Edward Lear's *Book of Nonsense* (1846), particularly in representations of himself as an innocent, even oafish, observer. Caricature, even when it was meant affectionately, undercut the importance or self-importance of those artists who filled his domestic world, one of the most distinguished yet bohemian of late Victorian England. The boys and masters at school were not spared either. Caricature was a weapon that could be used

to defend oneself against the greater powers of other people, and more straightforward portraiture – the recording of likenesses faithfully or flatteringly – was more a servant of the Establishment.

In individual caricatures Philip depicted his father painting his elegant *Annunciation* (1876–79, National Museums Liverpool, Lady Lever Art Gallery) and designing cartoons for stained-glass windows. In one Burne-Jones's studio assistant T. M. Rooke (1842–1942) appears to be working on a version of *Danaë and the Brazen Tower* (c. 1879, Fogg Art Museum, Harvard) [150]. The caricatures reveal a highly developed visual memory that aided the reconstruction of complicated poses and gestures as well as the features of family members and friends. These skills of recollection and representation, which were encouraged in the young throughout the nineteenth century, were

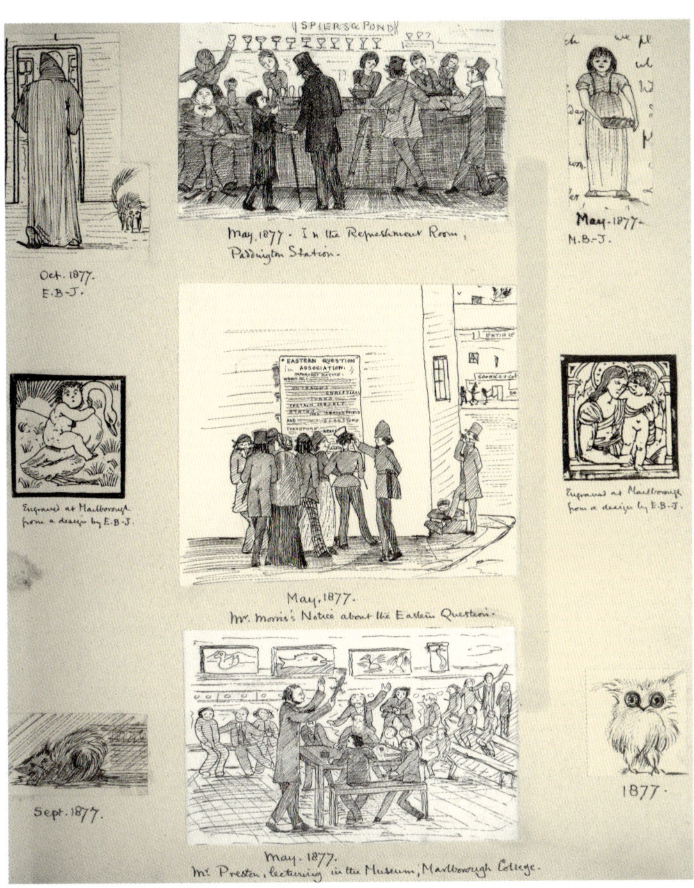

149 Philip Burne-Jones, *Page from an Album of Caricatures*, late 1870s, private collection

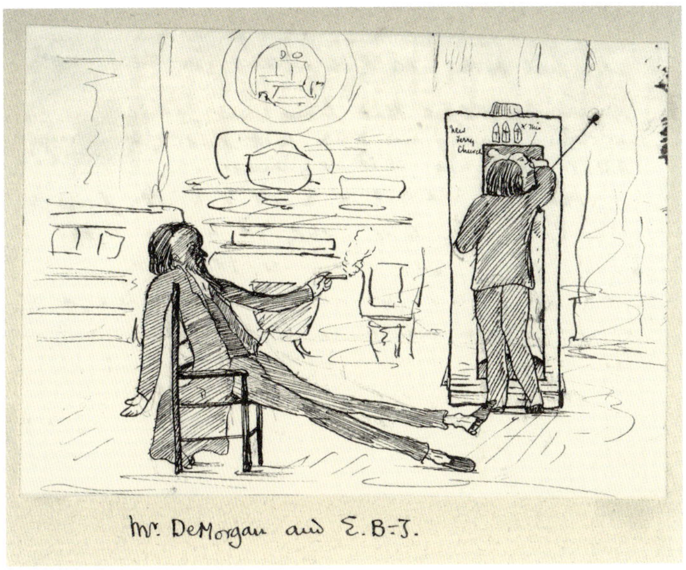

150 Philip Burne-Jones, *Page from an Album of Caricatures: Mr De Morgan and E.B-J*, late 1870s, private collection

challenged and eventually displaced by the ubiquity of popular photography in the decades that followed.

One of the moments that signalled the end of Pre-Raphaelitism as a revolutionary movement was when the informal pencil drawings that represent the group identity of relatively young and relatively poor men were abandoned in favour of the commissions to paint elder statesmen, society beauties and people of the more privileged classes. No matter how lifelike or penetrating Millais's painted portraits are, they belong in a gallery devoted to privilege and wealth. Millais's popularity might be said to date from the point that this shift became apparent, and his formal portraits in oils belong to a different register than his earlier drawn portraits. In society portraits Millais represented people already well enough known to be the subject of other portraits or, indeed, caricatures. The historian and biographer Colin Matthew noted in the exhibition catalogue *Millais: Portraits*, that in his paintings of Victorian statesmen, the artist was

> to a considerable extent commentating on a face that was already well known, rather than introducing it to the viewer….This was a new situation for a public artist….It meant that the picture could hardly avoid relating to the grammar of depiction established by others, mostly photographers.[16]

It was in making more personal records that the portraits of the Pre-Raphaelites work best. Despite their hesitant and sometimes gauche handling, drawn likenesses and caricatures became the unpainted masterpieces of the group and remain a valuable record of their relationships.[17]

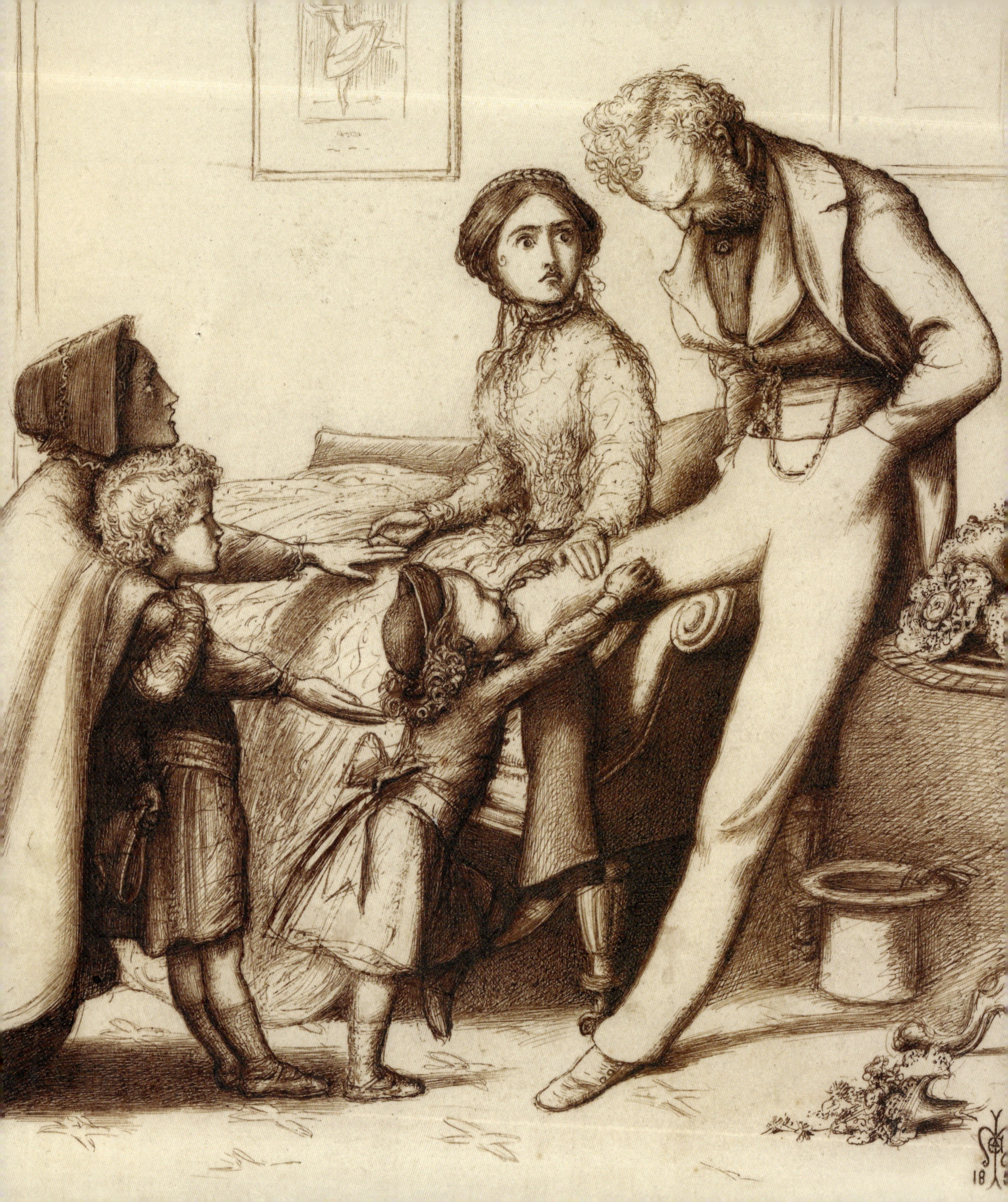

Chapter 5 *Pre-Raphaelite Compositions: Drawing History, Drawing Modernity*

In the 1850s, Ford Madox Brown turned his attention from history to contemporary life to paint two works of social commentary, *The Last of England* (1852–55) [**153**] and *Work* (1852–65, Manchester City Galleries). Both required the artist to make large numbers of drawings for the constituent parts as he had for history paintings such as *Chaucer at the Court of Edward III*. This was particularly the case for *Work*, a panoramic survey of English social class divisions. The result was a kind of 'modern-life drawing' with an emphasis on grouping figures, evoking their attitudes and psychological motivation. Social and emotional interconnections between figures were conveyed through relative proximity as much as touch and expression. It is evident from Brown's drawings that these groupings and interrelationships are present at the earliest stages of invention, implying that the relationships are absolutely key to the pictorial exploration of the subject. It is a quality shared with Millais's modern-life subjects, such as *The Blind Girl* (1854–56, Birmingham Museums & Art Gallery). Brown wrote that his picture *The Last of England* was, 'in the strictest sense, historical'.[1] He viewed the present as he would a historical period, requiring the same processes of research and analysis.

One of the striking things about Pre-Raphaelite modern-life subjects is a broadly religious quality suggesting some eternal meaning that enriches the modern subject. This is not a matter of textual material appended to the works, either as labels or as catalogue entries, but to the combination of symbolic and realistic motifs within the same picture space. A clue to the power of Brown's *The Last of England* can be found in his explanation of the couple who look out at us:

> The husband broods bitterly over blighted hopes, and severance from all he has been striving for. The young wife's grief is of a less cantankerous sort, probably confined to the sorrow of parting with a few friends of early years. The circle of her love moves with her.[2]

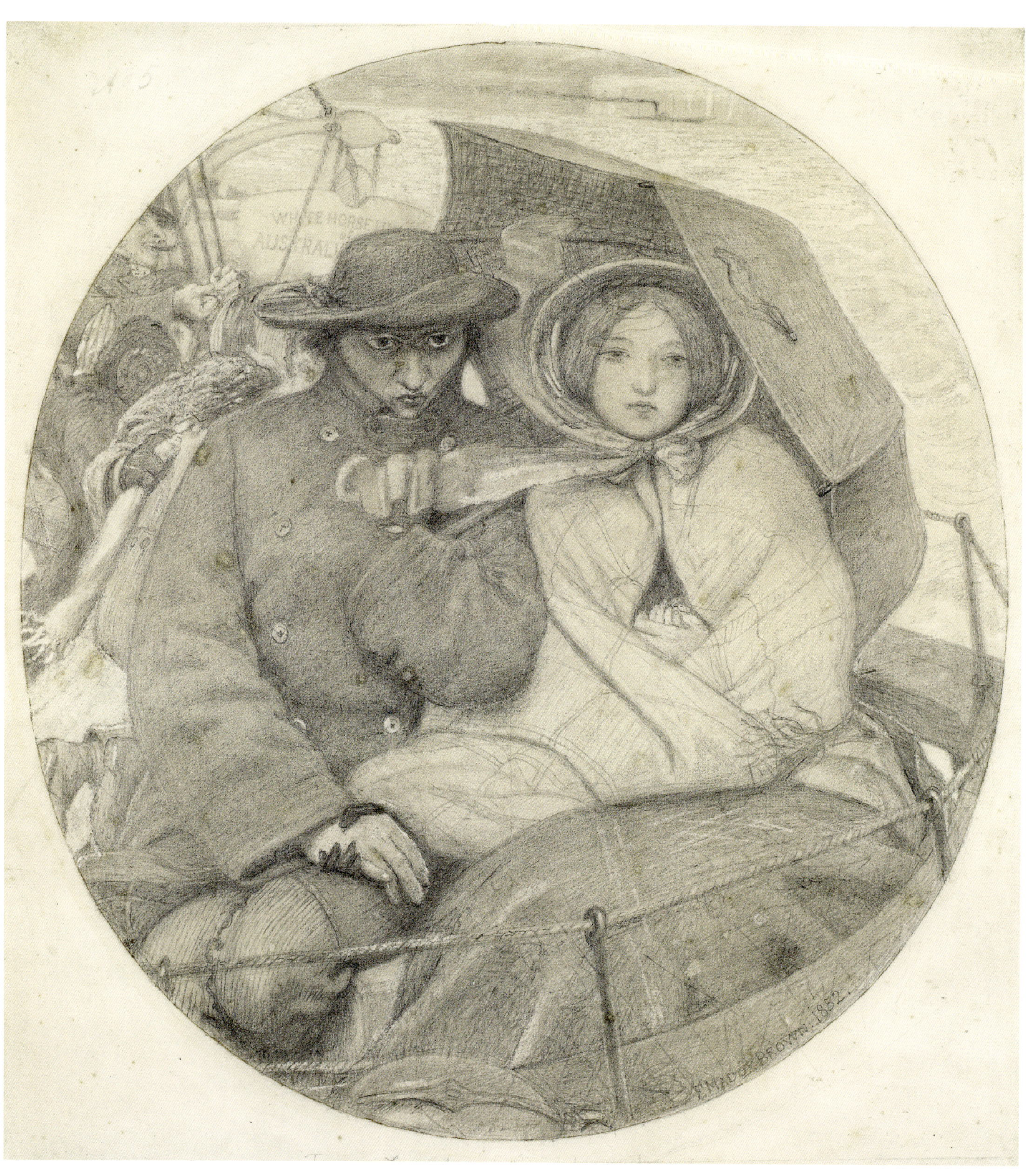

152 Ford Madox Brown, *Study for 'The Last of England'*, 1852, Birmingham Museums & Art Gallery

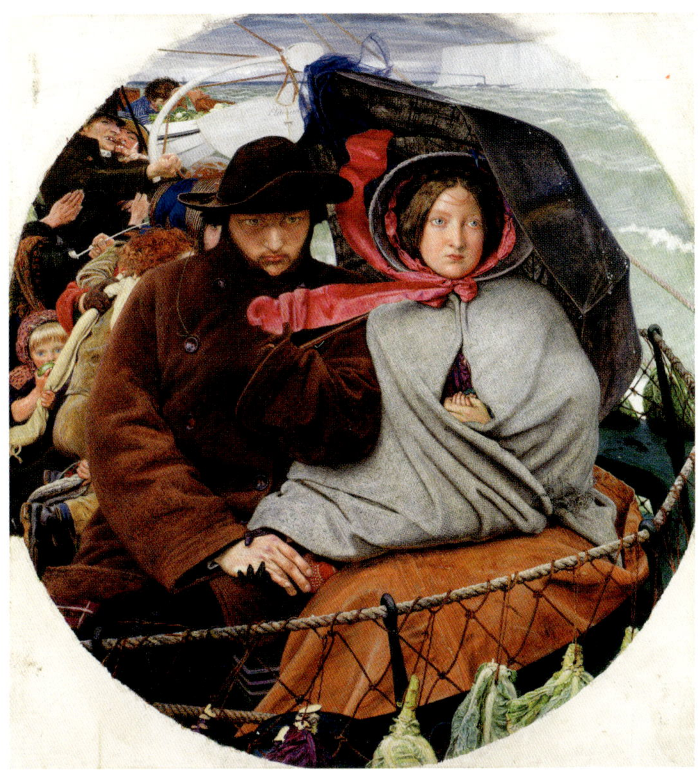

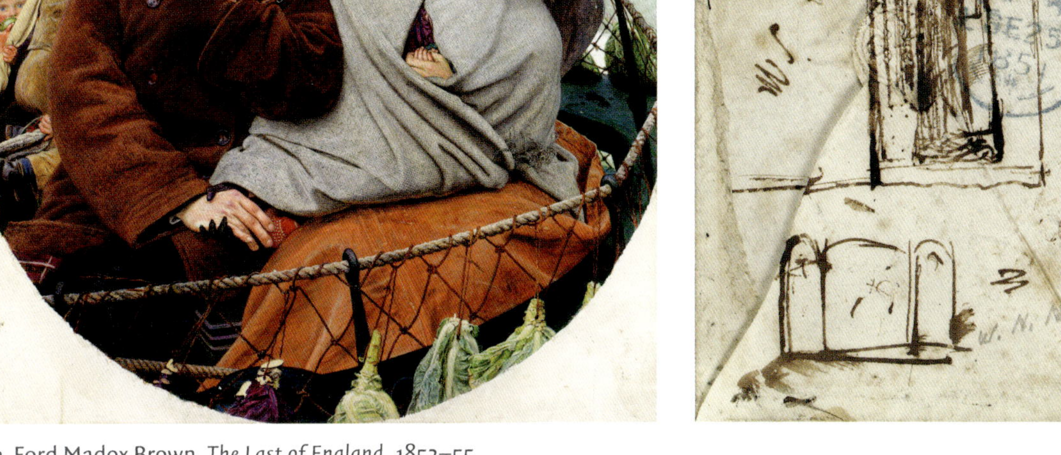

153 Ford Madox Brown, *The Last of England*, 1852–55, Birmingham Museums & Art Gallery

This idea of the 'circle of love' is articulated by a pictorial conceit: the circles that dominate the composition. The 'circle-as-bonnet', for example, can be read as a halo as much as a fashionable hat. Although the woman's destination is Australia, the painting suggests the New Testament story of the Flight into Egypt. The couple, therefore, 'double' as Joseph and Mary, and the baby, hidden in the mother's shawl, as Christ. Homelessness, restlessness and alienation were narrative features of Brown's modern-life subjects, reflecting the concerns of a society acutely aware of change. Here they are given a more resonant meaning. The composition must convey both ideas – the modern and the biblical – at the same time.

Composing new narratives

Throughout the 1850s Millais and Hunt exhibited paintings of linked contemporary and historical themes. Hunt's complex moral dramas, *The Light of the World* (1851–53, Kebel College, Oxford) and *The Awakening Conscience* (1853, Tate), began as rudimentary compositional sketches that contain the elements of the finished works represented in the roughest shorthand dashes [**154, 155**].

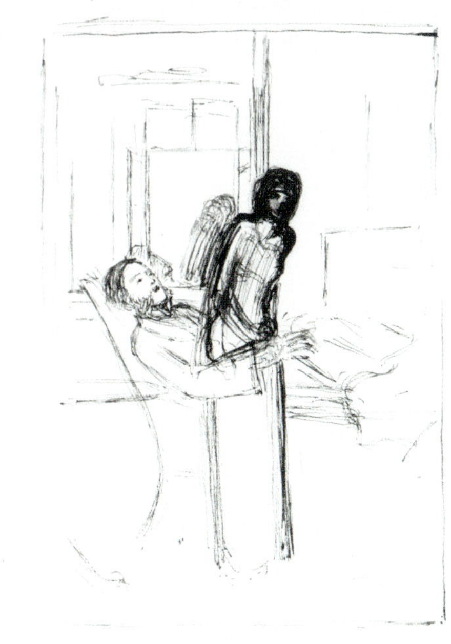

154 William Holman Hunt, *Study for 'The Light of the World'*, undated, Ashmolean Museum, University of Oxford
155 William Holman Hunt, *Study for 'The Awakening Conscience'*, 1853, The Pollitt Collection

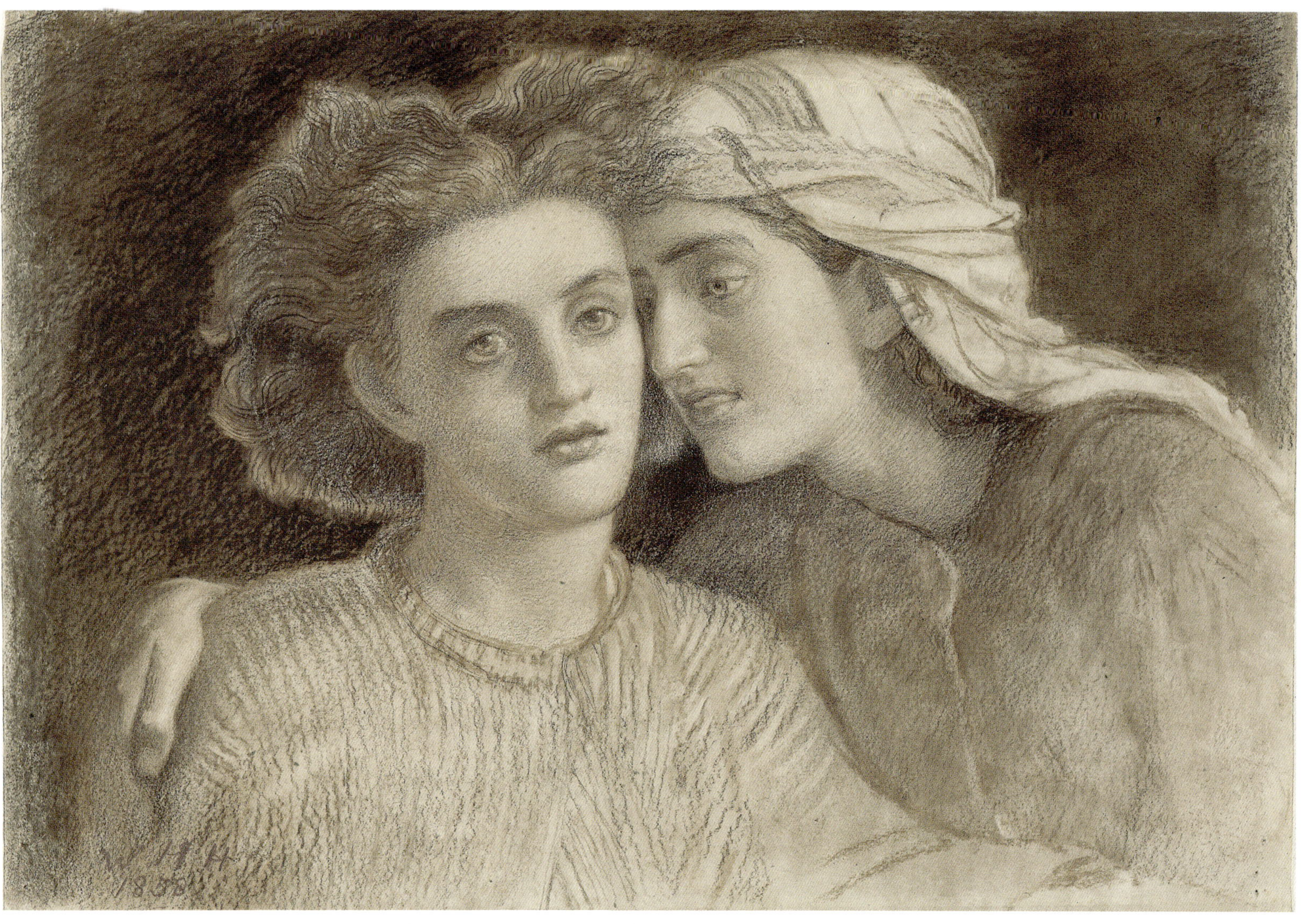

156 William Holman Hunt, *Study of the Heads of Mary and Jesus for 'The Finding of the Saviour in the Temple'*, c. 1858, National Museums Liverpool (Walker Art Gallery)

A concern with meaningful groupings of figures was part of the religious work of Hunt, neither 'modern' nor 'historical' but timeless. Hunt's religious convictions, located in the idea of the living relevance of the Bible and the teachings of Jesus, led him to envisage the biblical subject in a new way. Hunt's paintings began and ended with religious belief, even when they were concerned with the restless 'now' of the 1850s. At the centre of these narratives was a timelessness, an eternal relevance, that Hunt wanted to communicate. In his lecture 'The Art of England', Ruskin described the differences in the art of Hunt and Rossetti perceptively:

> To Rossetti, the Old and New Testaments were only the greatest poems he knew; and he painted scenes from them with no more actual belief in their relation to the present life and business of men than he gave

also to the Morte d'Arthur and the Vita Nuova. On the other hand, such biblical texts revealed to Hunt 'not merely a Reality, not merely the greatest of Realities, but the only Reality'.[3]

The studies for *The Finding of the Saviour in the Temple* [156, 157] are more tentative than those by Millais for works such as *The Proscribed Royalist, 1651* (1853). Hunt struggles for nuances of meaning that seem to come easily to Millais and he attempts to imply several layers of meaning in one gesture. As a result, his works have a tendency to become 'tableaux', more stilted than the animated emotional encounters depicted by Millais. Both artists bring characters together in embraces, although Hunt seems keen to make his key figures turn to the viewer as if conscious that a picture is being made.

    Pre-Raphaelite Compositions: Drawing History, Drawing Modernity

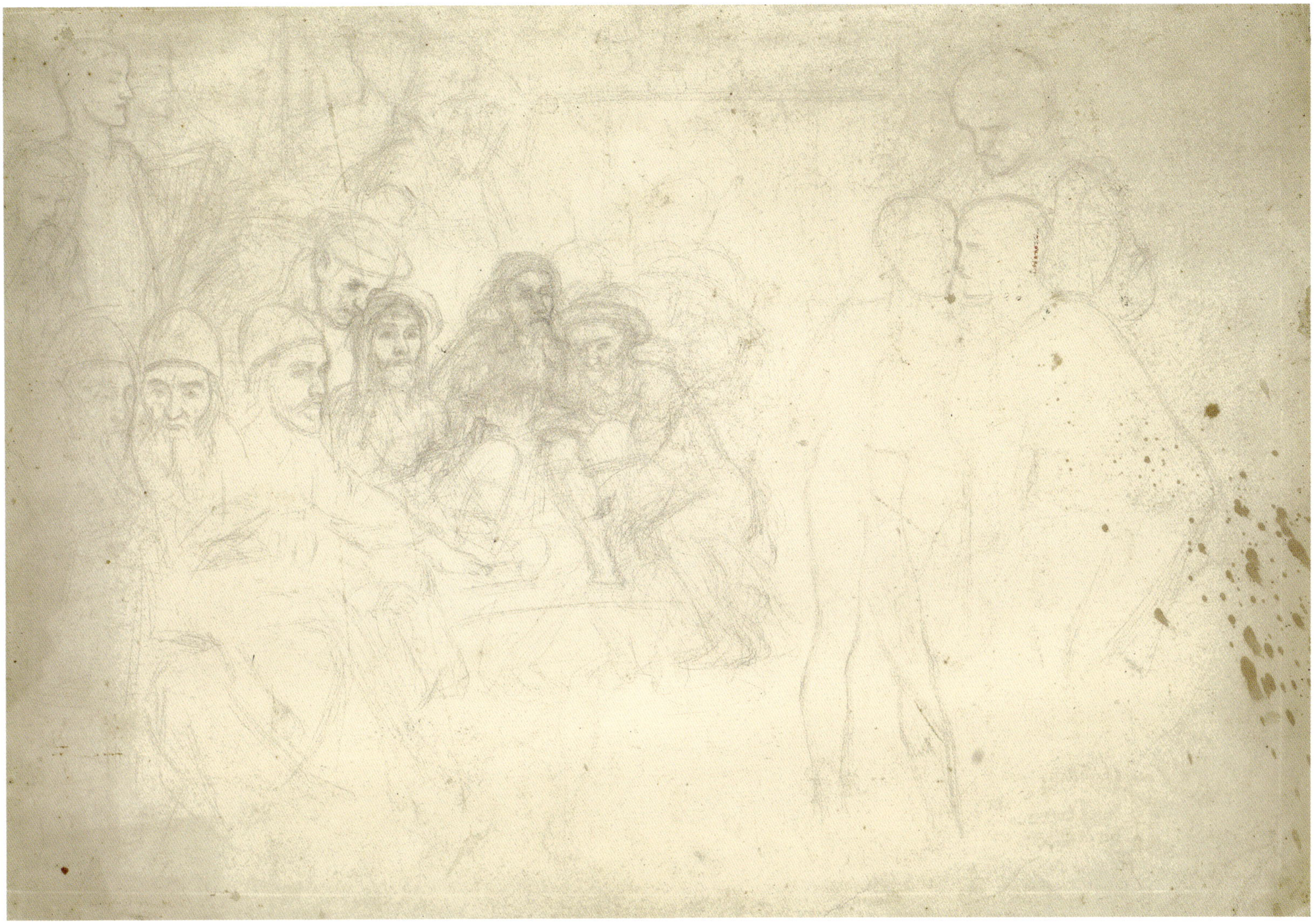

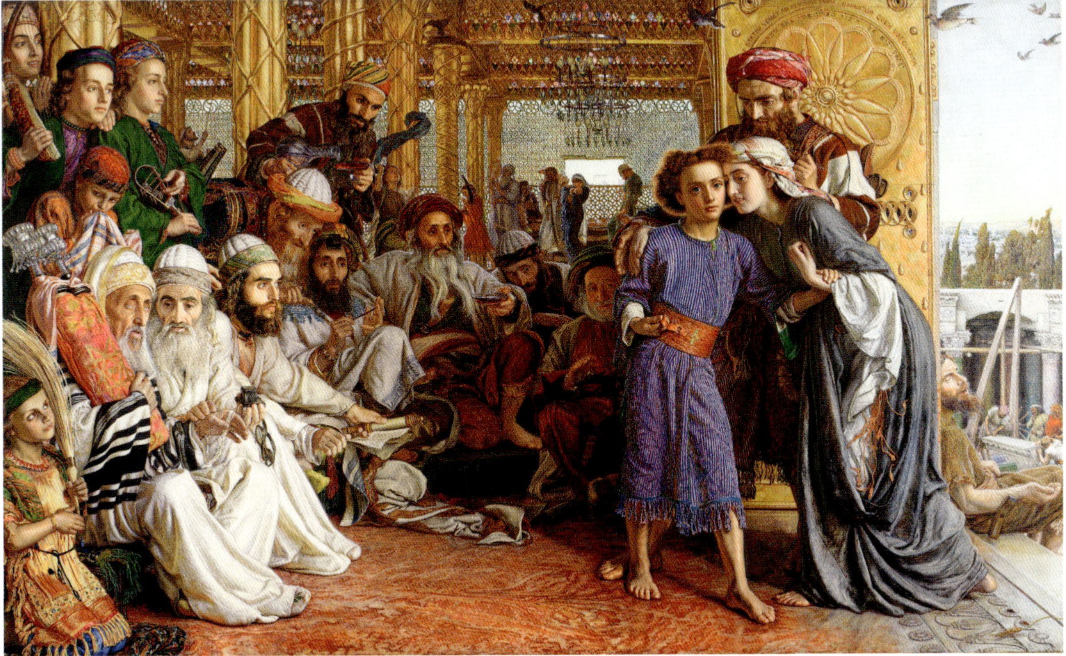

157 William Holman Hunt,
Compositional Study for
'The Finding of the Saviour in
the Temple', *c.* 1854, Birmingham
Museums & Art Gallery

158 William Holman Hunt,
The Finding of the Saviour in
the Temple, 1854–55, 1856–60,
Birmingham Museums
& Art Gallery

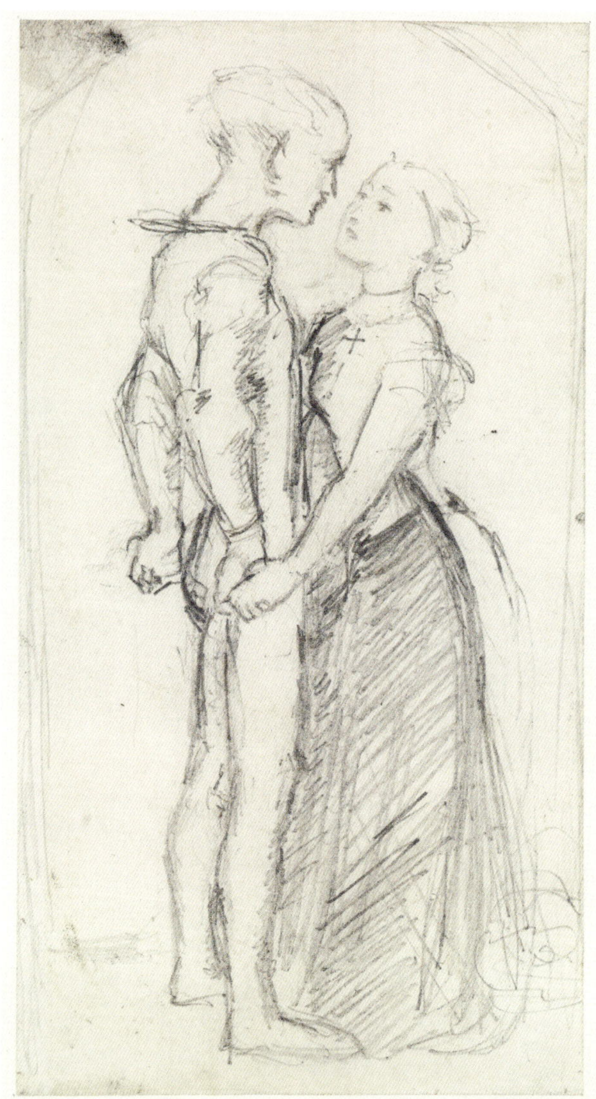

159 John Everett Millais, *Study for 'A Huguenot'*, c. 1851, Birmingham Museums & Art Gallery

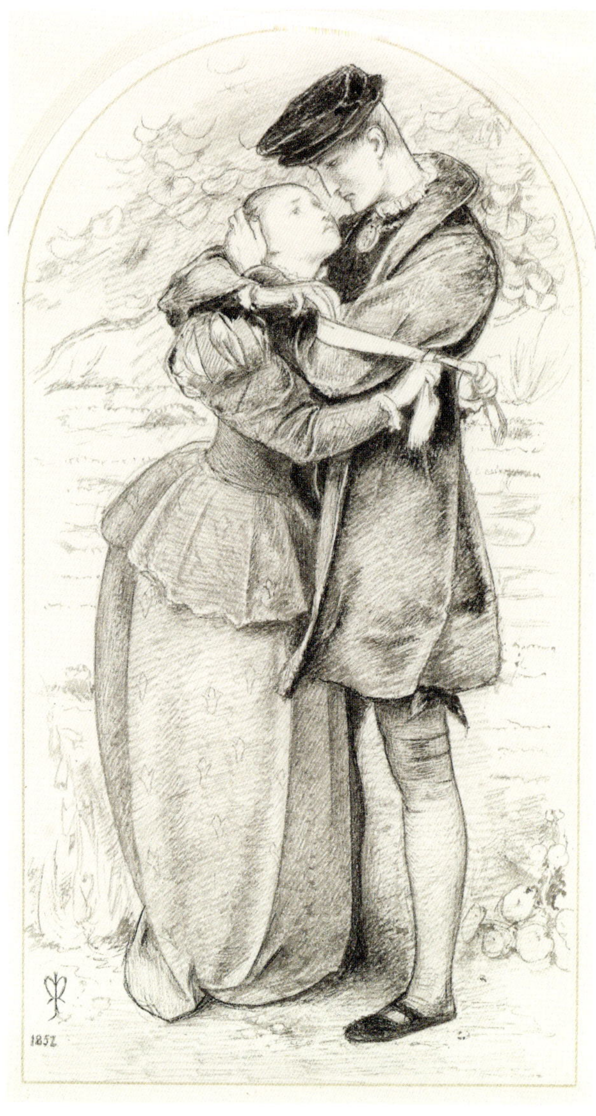

160 John Everett Millais, *Finished Compositional Study for 'A Huguenot'*, 1852, Birmingham Museums & Art Gallery

The art historian Paul Barlow has described Millais's *A Huguenot* as 'a delicate struggle' in which the play 'on restraint, conflict and intimacy is remarkably subtle'.[4] The genre painters David Wilkie (1785–1841) and William Mulready were the forerunners of this development in narrative subtlety. For its success it must be convincing in all its parts, most particularly in the ways in which the figures engage with each other. In drawings for *A Huguenot* [**159, 160**] we can see Millais working out the problem of opposing feelings of intimacy and resistance. In the earliest of the sketches the discussion between the lovers is clearly lively yet ambiguous. The man holds his lover's hands with such firmness that they are forced to his hips. When

resolved, this 'mixed' gesture has been replaced by a more tender one, closer to the finished work. The struggle of religious and political ideas represented in the subject was concentrated in gesture and expression: the contradictory hand gestures, the searching gaze. The poet and artist Laurence Housman (1865–1959) described the effect of such compositional devices:

> In Pre-Raphaelite pictures, closely grouped faces
> and hands have a new and curious significance;
> and the figures are generally arrested figures, brought
> to a standstill by some appeal to the emotions,
> often as though they were trying deeply to read each
> other's thoughts.[5]

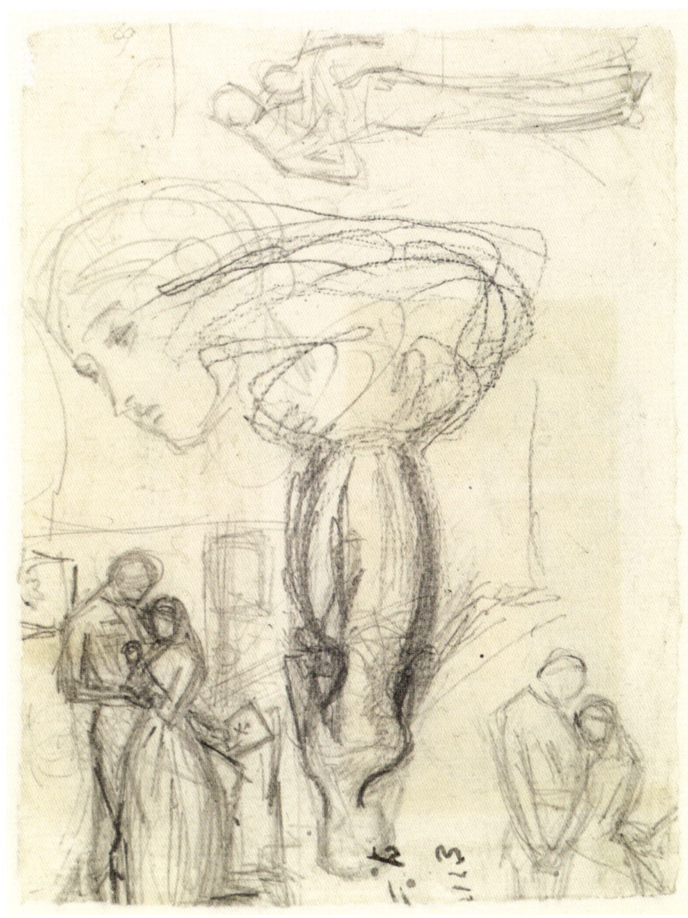

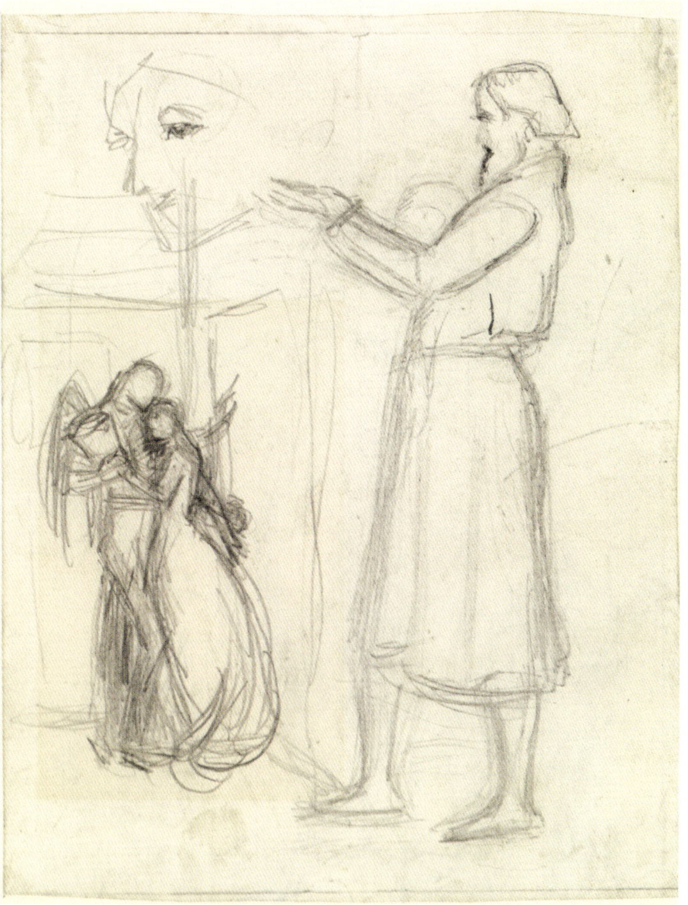

161–62 John Everett Millais, *Recto and Verso of a Sheet of Studies Including Studies for 'The Black Brunswicker'*, c. 1859–60, Birmingham Museums & Art Gallery

The result of Millais's compositional method was to combine the modern with the historical, to historicize modern experience. Millais achieved this complexity through gesture and expression, and through the spatial relationship of one figure to another. The core of the subject – in all its emotional power – was present early in the compositional stages. Drawings for *The Proscribed Royalist, 1651* (1852–53) [**166**] demonstrate how early the woman's pose was to the final painting and how repetition changed it subtly [**164, 165**].

Unhampered by the need to produce historically based narratives, Millais produced a series of modern-life drawings which, to a greater or lesser extent, abandon the outline style. In his pioneering study of Millais's drawings, the curator Malcolm Warner observed that

> The portrayal of modern life, with which he was increasingly concerned in the 1850s, is a quite separate strain in Millais's work as a draftsman and is associated with broken line, hatching and cross-hatching.[6]

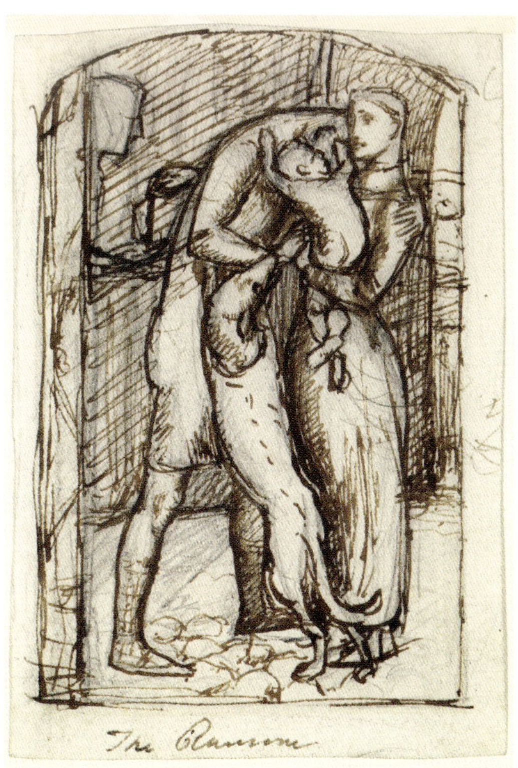

163 John Everett Millais, *Study for 'The Order of Release, 1746'*, 1852, Birmingham Museums & Art Gallery

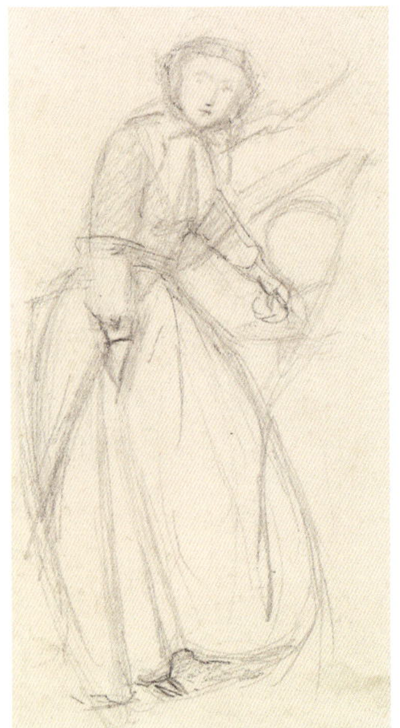
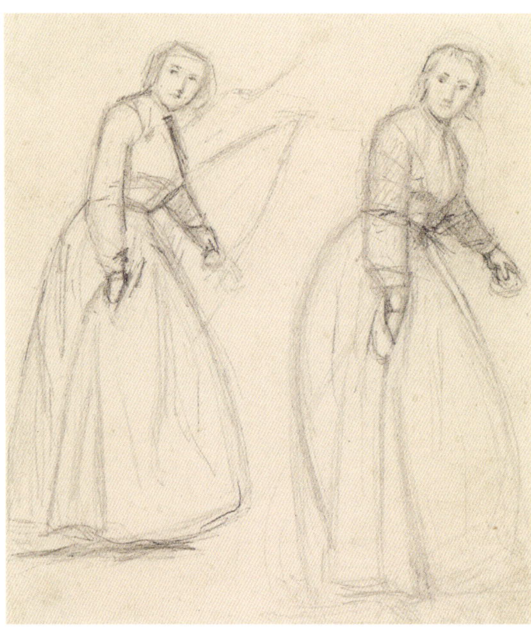
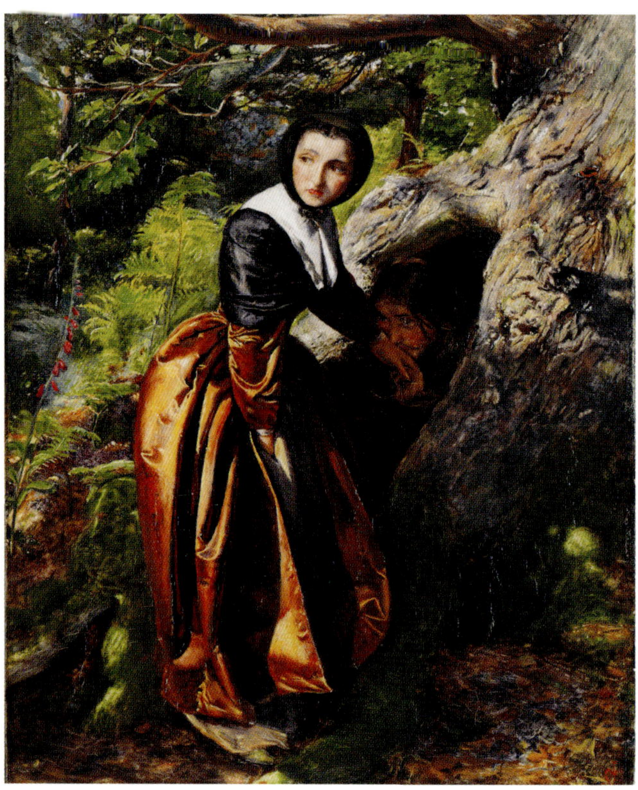

164–65 John Everett Millais, *Two Sets of Studies for 'The Proscribed Royalist, 1651'*, 1852, Birmingham Museums & Art Gallery
166 John Everett Millais, *The Proscribed Royalist, 1651*, c. 1852–53, Birmingham Museums & Art Gallery

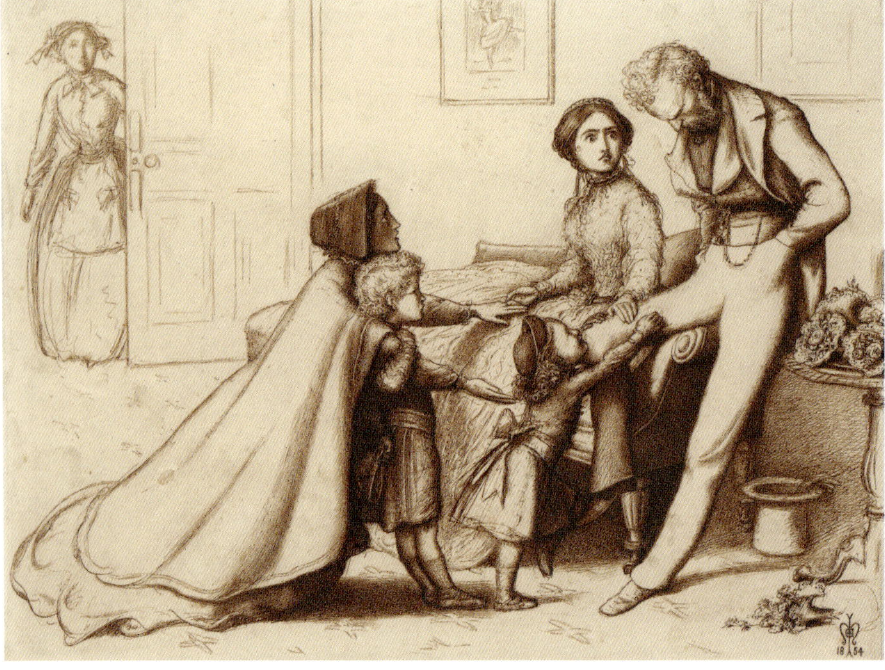
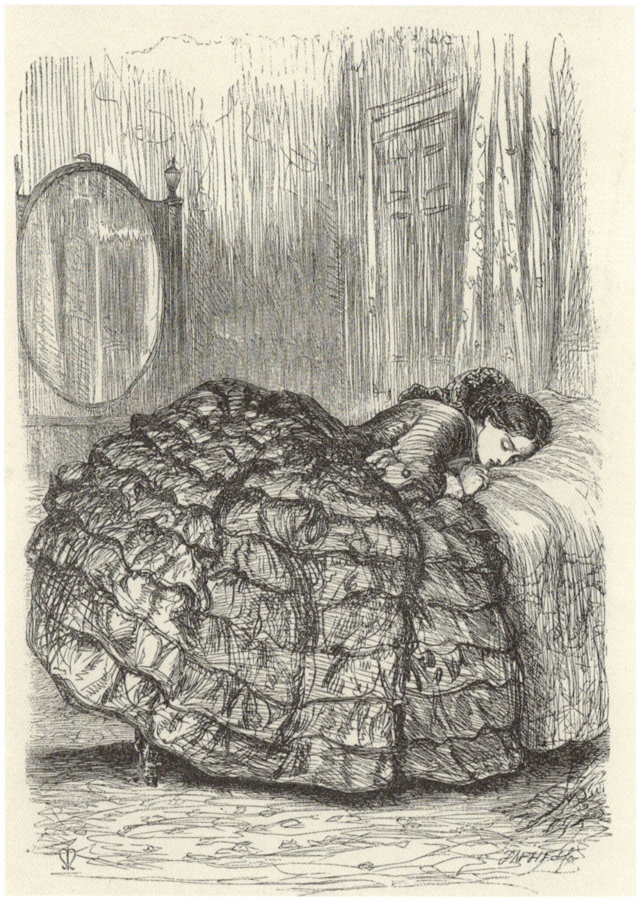

167 John Everett Millais, *Retribution*, 1854, The British Museum, London
168 Dalziel Brothers after John Everett Millais, *'Was it Not a Lie?'*, 1860, Birmingham Museums & Art Gallery)

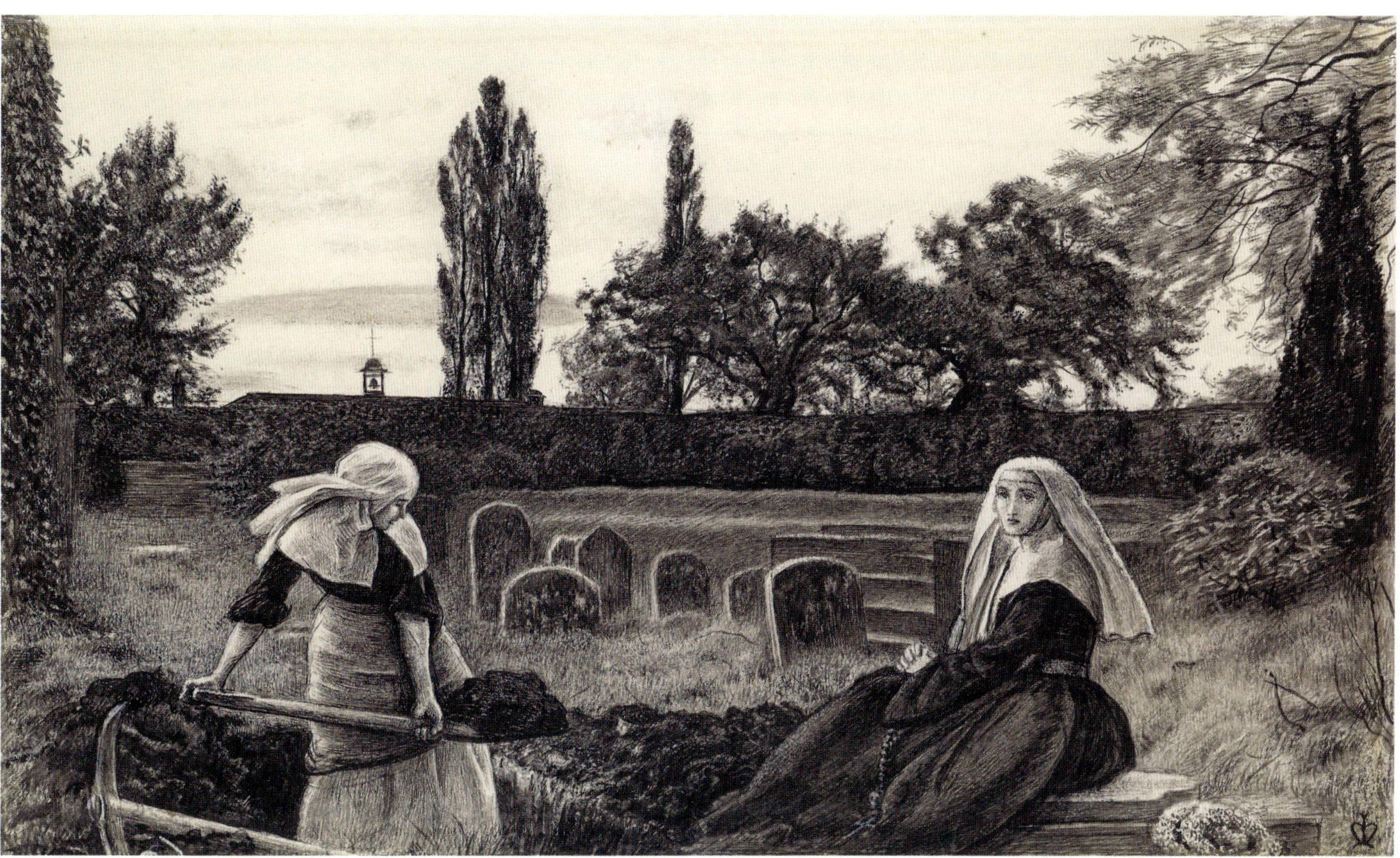

169 John Everett Millais, *Finished Compositional Study for 'The Vale of Rest'*, 1858, Birmingham Museums & Art Gallery

These works are committed to representing modern people in modern settings and are strongly graphic rather than painterly. However, in these drawings Millais's graphic style changed from that of the compositional and preparatory drawings made for his subject paintings. It is basically outline but enhanced with fine pen marks to produce dark shadows that both model the figures and place them in relief against a much more indistinct background. The result of Millais's changes to the outline technique was to add emotional subtlety to drama. The purity of the neoclassical line was subjected to modification, perhaps we could say modernization, to respond to the changes in subject.

In some of these drawings Millais appears almost Hogarthian in his observations on the social mores of his time, although a more important contemporary influence was the caricaturist Charles Keene (1823–91). In 1853, Millais made a sequence of drawings on the theme of marriage, as a kind of Pre-Raphaelite 'Marriage à-la-Mode'. *Married for Money* (private collection), *Married for Love* (The British Museum) and *Married for Rank* (private collection) prefigure Millais's illustration work, suggesting in particular

the genesis of his designs for novels by Anthony Trollope made in the 1860s. In *Retribution* (1854) [167] the subject is bigamy and the confrontation represented is remarkably easy to read. All the figures in the drawing, male or female, child or adult, have clearly expressed reactions to the situation, although the narrative is tantalizingly withdrawn. There is no doubt that these private works had an impact on Millais's more public paintings and illustrations. The finished composition for *The Vale of Rest* (1858) [169], for example, is as legible in its final stage as a drawing as it is as a painting. The viewer is struck by the sense of dramatic confrontation avoided yet still imminent, and the physical proximity but emotional distance of the two figures. Here – as in the *Marriage* series – there is the uncanny impression that an unwritten text is being acted out.

One of Millais's most successful followers was Arthur Hughes. The compositional studies [170, 171] for his most famous painting, *The Long Engagement* (1859) [172] introduced motifs of the passing of time. The work shows two lovers in discussion on the edge of a wood; their conversation, both intimate and painful, seems to have

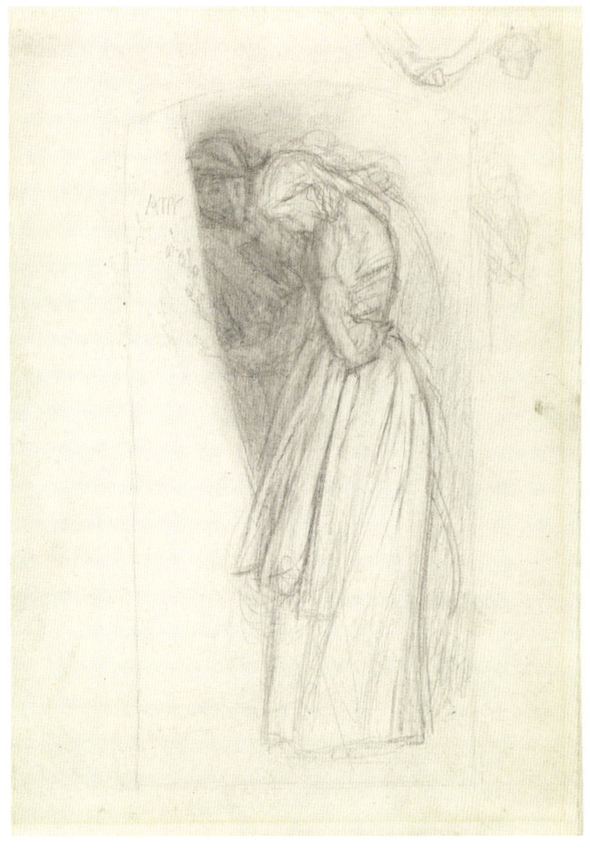

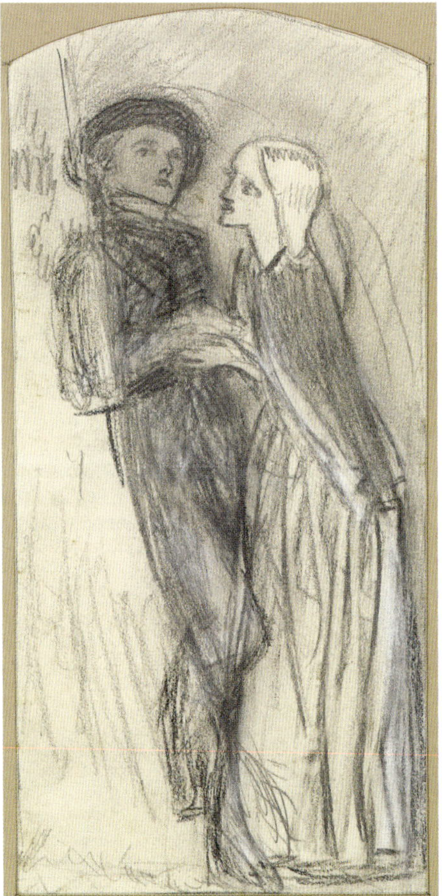

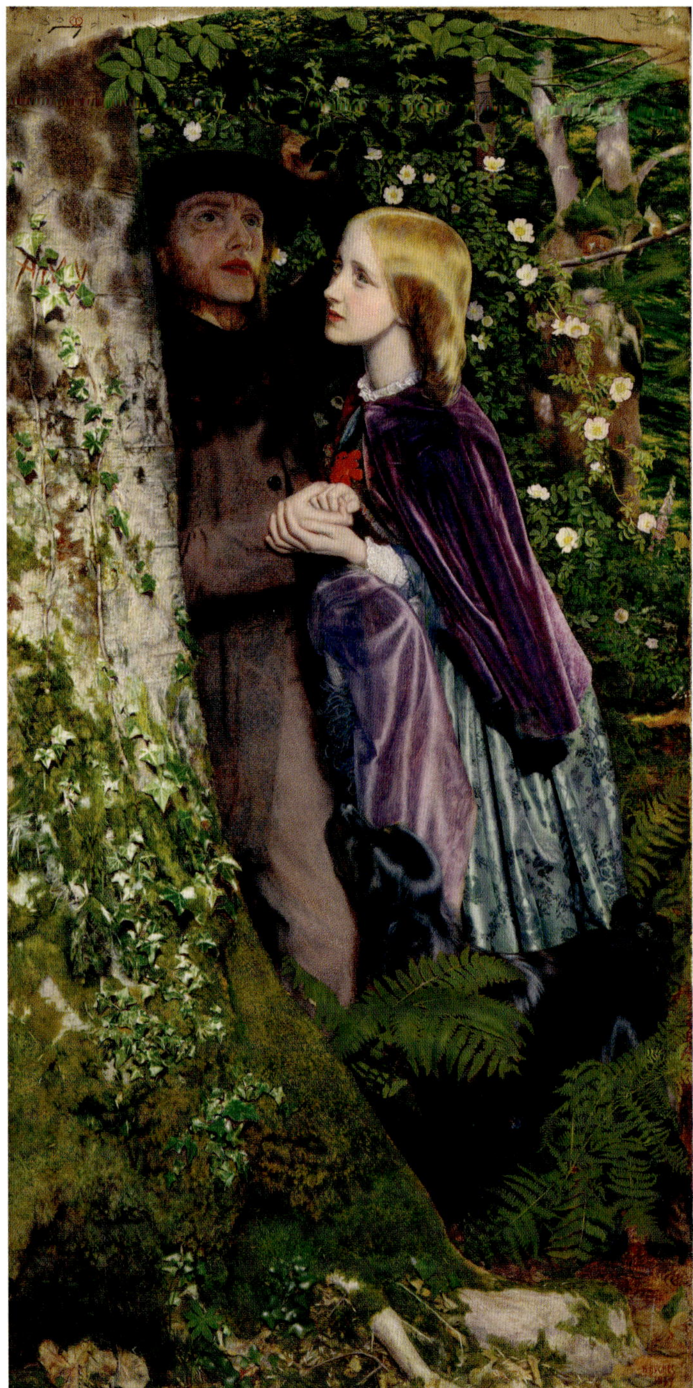

170–71 Arthur Hughes, *Two Studies for 'The Long Engagement'*,
  c. 1858, Birmingham Museums & Art Gallery
172 Arthur Hughes, *The Long Engagement*, 1859,
  Birmingham Museums & Art Gallery

come to an end; they stand silently contemplating their
emotions, their separate positions. What appears to be
straightforwardly a 'modern-life' subject dealing with
sexual relations in Victorian Britain started life as a scene
from Shakespeare's comedy *As You Like It*, with the figures
of Rosalind and Orlando depicted in a suitably sylvan
setting. Following Millais's compositional experiments

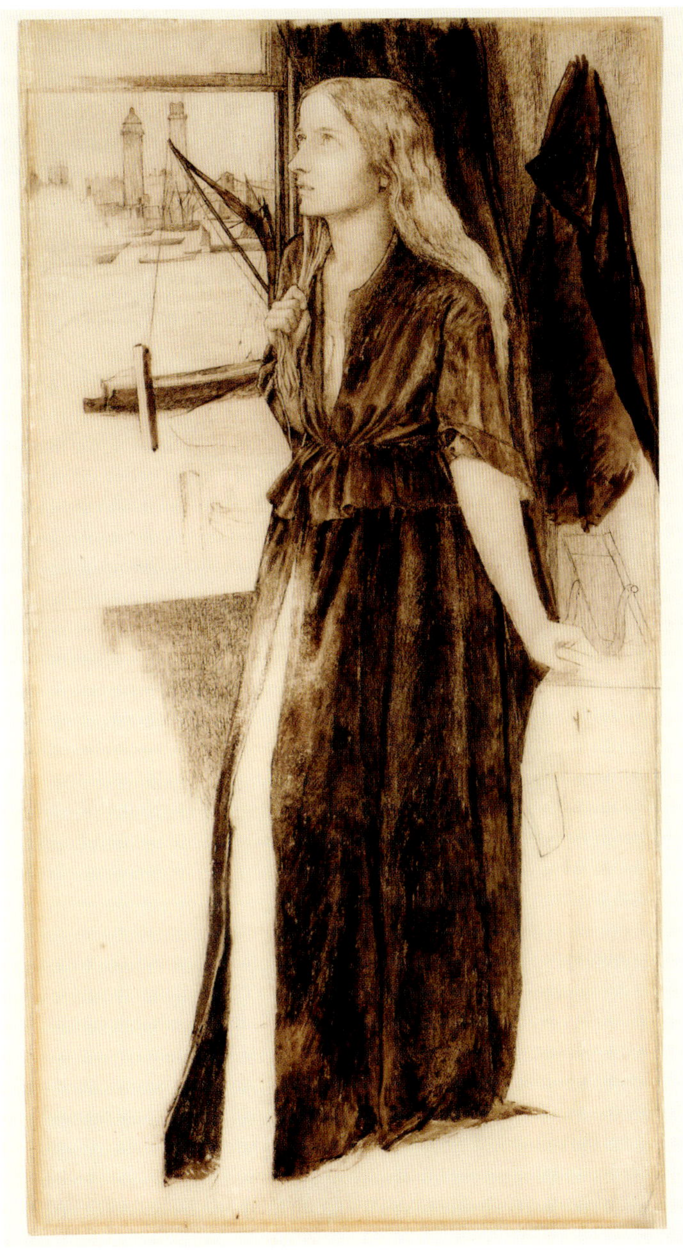

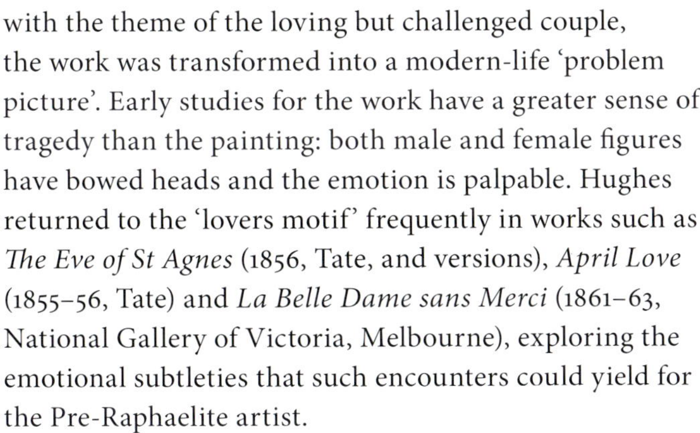

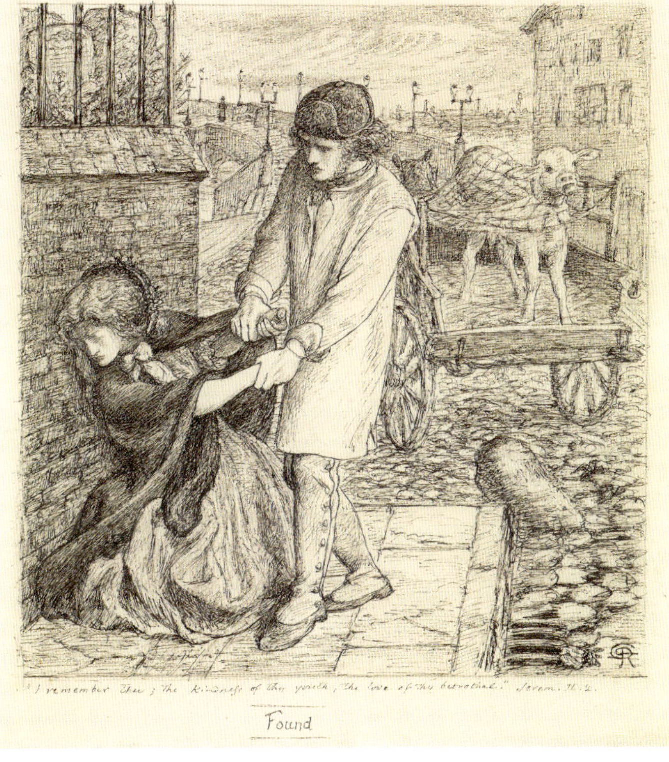

173 John Roddam Spencer Stanhope, *Study for 'Thoughts of the Past'*, c. 1859, Tate
174 Dante Gabriel Rossetti, *Study for 'Found'*, c. 1853, Birmingham Museums & Art Gallery

with the theme of the loving but challenged couple, the work was transformed into a modern-life 'problem picture'. Early studies for the work have a greater sense of tragedy than the painting: both male and female figures have bowed heads and the emotion is palpable. Hughes returned to the 'lovers motif' frequently in works such as *The Eve of St Agnes* (1856, Tate, and versions), *April Love* (1855–56, Tate) and *La Belle Dame sans Merci* (1861–63, National Gallery of Victoria, Melbourne), exploring the emotional subtleties that such encounters could yield for the Pre-Raphaelite artist.

Less romantic ideas of love could also be depicted and might have had a more urgent need for presentation in contemporary subject painting. Hunt's *The Awakening Conscience* (1853, Tate), Rossetti's *Found* (begun 1853, Delaware Art Museum) and J. R. Spencer Stanhope's (1829–1908) *Thoughts of the Past* (1857–59, Tate) all found a motif of modern life in the figure of the prostitute. Stanhope's isolated female figure standing at a window [173] forces a comparison with Millais's *Mariana* [69]. Leslie Parris suggests that the woman's eyes (in the drawing rather than the painting) are 'raised as if in supplication'.[7] Certainly,

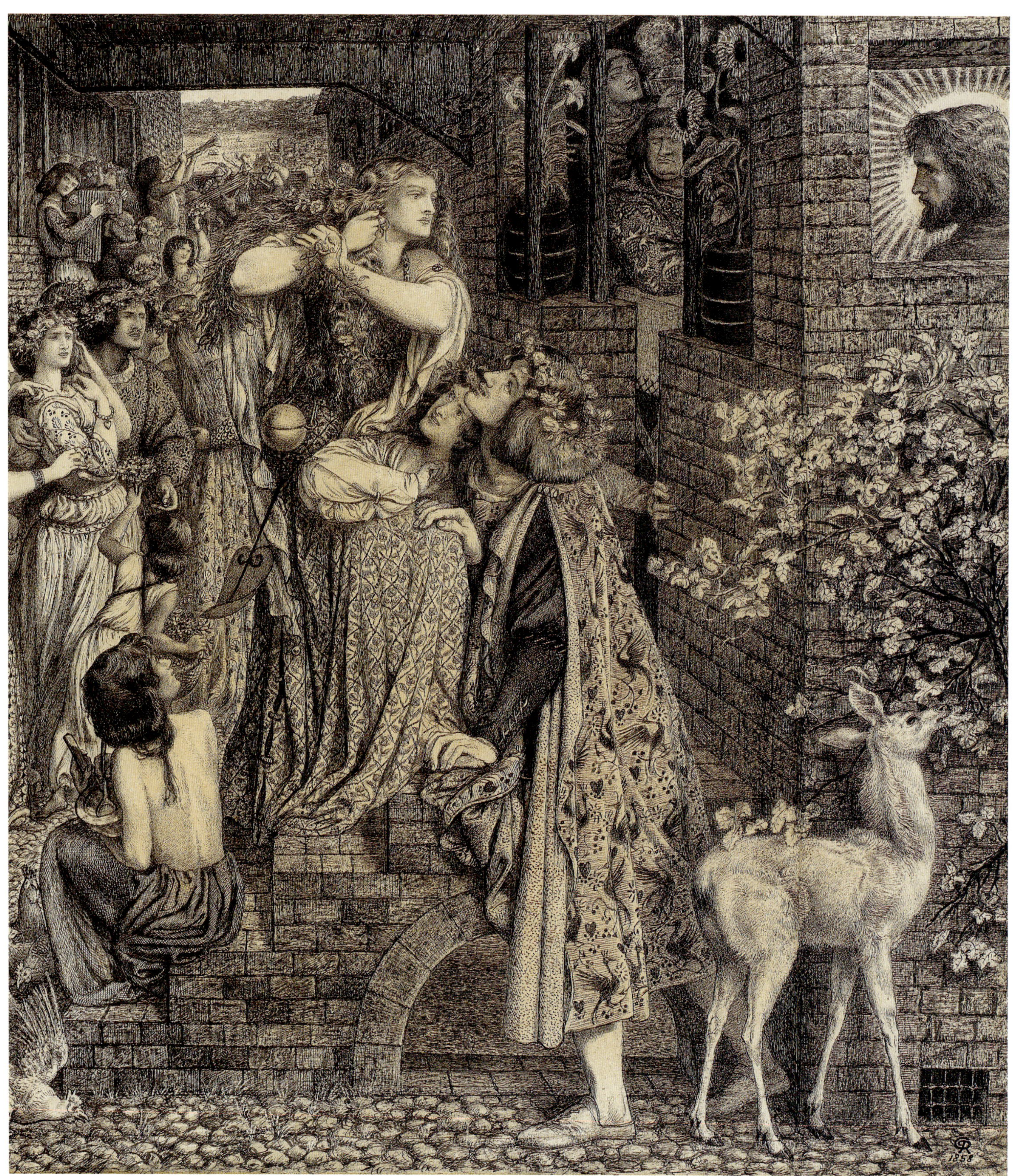

175 Dante Gabriel Rossetti, *Mary Magdalene at the Door of Simon the Pharisee*, 1858–59, Fitzwilliam Museum, Cambridge

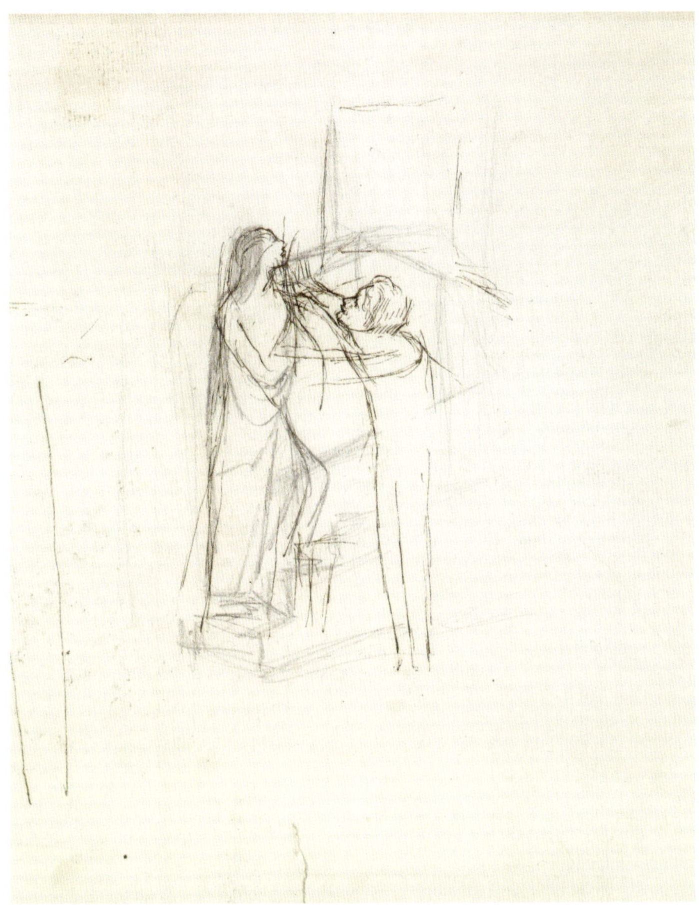

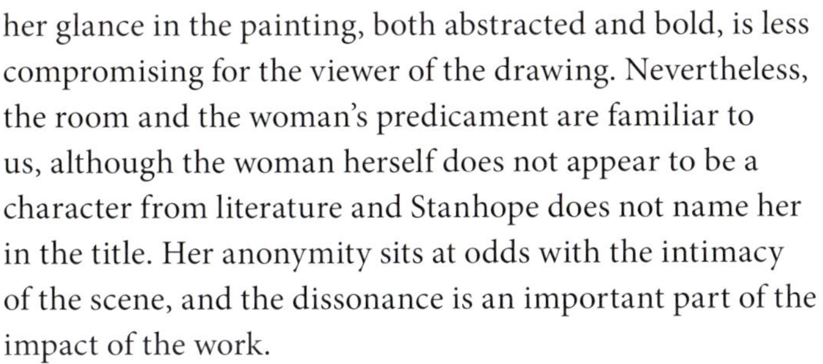

176 Dante Gabriel Rossetti, *Study for 'Mary Magdalene at the Door of Simon the Pharisee': Female and Male Figure*, c. 1858, Birmingham Museums & Art Gallery

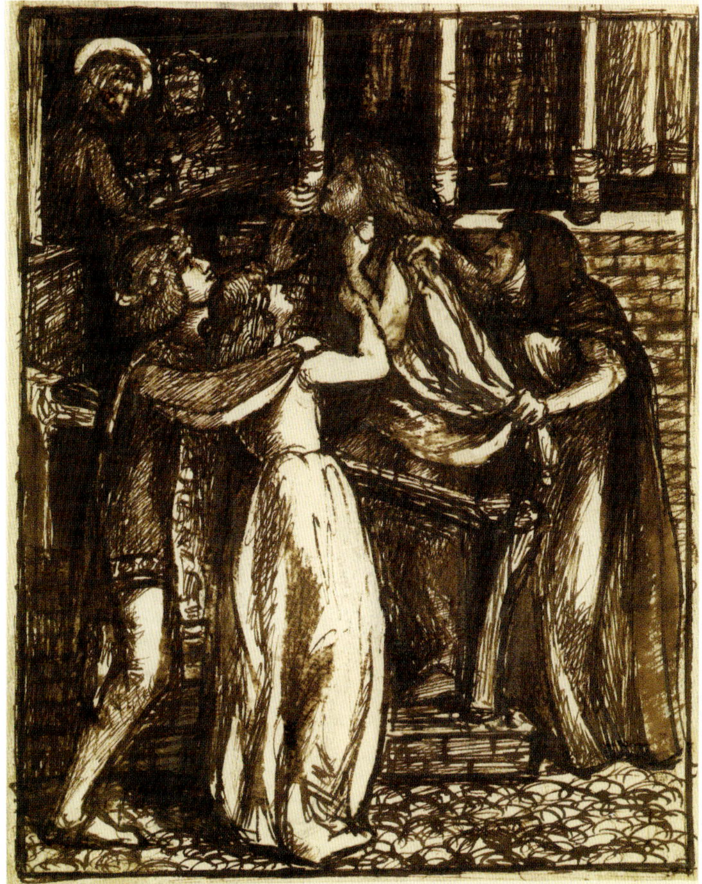

177 Dante Gabriel Rossetti, *Study for 'Mary Magdalene at the Door of Simon the Pharisee': Study for the Composition*, c. 1858, Birmingham Museums & Art Gallery

her glance in the painting, both abstracted and bold, is less compromising for the viewer of the drawing. Nevertheless, the room and the woman's predicament are familiar to us, although the woman herself does not appear to be a character from literature and Stanhope does not name her in the title. Her anonymity sits at odds with the intimacy of the scene, and the dissonance is an important part of the impact of the work.

Although Rossetti's *Found* was eventually abandoned as a painting project, the compositional drawings made for it [174] communicate the prostitute's story clearly. Perhaps it did not need anything beyond what would be conveyed in the clear graphic outlines of its preparatory studies, while Hunt's *The Awakening Conscience* could be realized only when its full panoply of painted accessories were in place. Rossetti's portrayal of the biblical story of the reformed prostitute Mary Magdalene also remained as a drawing project [175, 176, 177]. Mary's resoluteness in the face of the anxious pulling and pleading of her friends is tellingly in place in all versions of the subject, from the diagrammatic first sketch to the fully detailed final version.

As Mary Magdalene mounts the steps she draws her headdress of roses from her hair while simultaneously detaching an earring with her other hand. Her determination to reach Jesus is clearly communicated: she strides forward possessed with love. The rendering of the surface in ink is impressive, mimicking Dürer's engraving technique at its most elaborated. Indeed, the composition bears a strong resemblance to an allegorical print by Dürer, *The Dream of the Doctor* (c. 1498, The British Museum), in which a nude female figure with flowing hair admonishes a sleeping man, although Rossetti's acquaintance with this rare image is impossible to prove.

'Sketching is deceptive and dangerous'

In the mid-1850s Rossetti began a sequence of works on medieval themes, many of them based on Arthurian stories. In these works he invented a technique of watercolour, rejecting the thin glazes of subtle colour

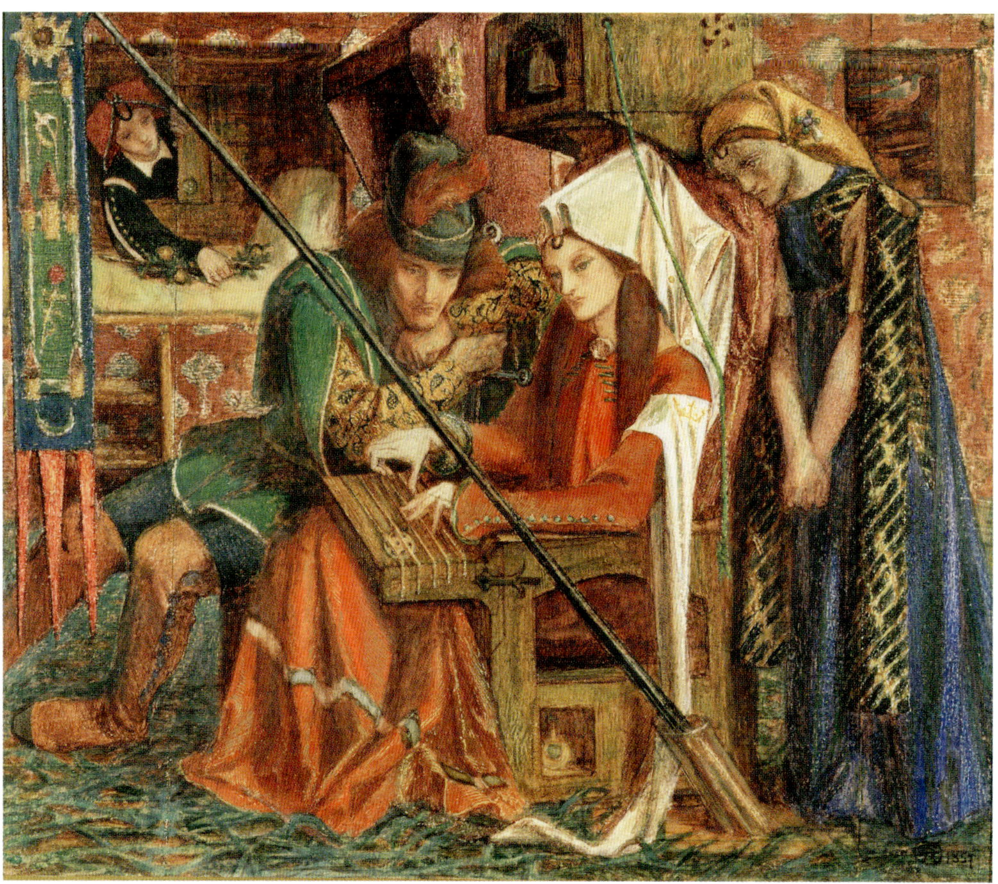

178 Dante Gabriel Rossetti, *The Tune of the Seven Towers*, 1857, Tate

and delicate gradation of tone as well as the airy spatial effects that had made watercolour the preferred medium for rapid descriptions of landscape. Watercolour had been developed as a means of tinting drawings in lead point and other drawing media. In Britain in the eighteenth century it had become a highly sophisticated medium used chiefly to represent landscape because, having the virtues of flexibility, delicacy and purity of pigment, it could reproduce a wide range of effects such as the varied textures of the land. It was also light and portable, enabling it to be used easily *en plein air*. Turner developed his skill as a landscape watercolourist, challenging the aesthetic expectations of watercolour and extending the effects of which it was capable with his daring technique. His practices followed a diverse range of predecessors and contemporaries such as Francis Towne (1739–1816), Thomas Girtin (1775–1802) and John Sell Cotman (1782–1842).

Rossetti's watercolours developed a different aesthetic closer to illuminated manuscripts, with an emphasis on human figures rather than landscape or still life subjects. The scale of Rossetti's works is important, too; they are much smaller than exhibited oil paintings and require a different kind of viewing, closer and more contemplative. The lack of perspective and the liberties taken with the drawing of the figures are further amplifications of the primitive quality that many critics had perceived in the first paintings exhibited by the Pre-Raphaelite Brotherhood. These works are striking for their dense, ambiguous and suggestive narratives and their technical experimentation. The atmosphere of love, passion and underlying menace they contain is articulated by the artist's knowledge of medieval poetry and art. Rossetti rejected Pre-Raphaelite moral narratives – both historical and modern – and invented a new kind of Pre-Raphaelitism, an art of suggestion rather than narration. If there is a literary analogy in these differing approaches it is that Millais and Hunt record incident, Rossetti feeling; one is derived from the narratives of biblical stories or modern novels, the other from poetry.

Rossetti's project to illustrate stories from the *Morte D'Arthur* for the newly built Oxford Union in 1857 adapted the design elements of these medievalist drawings and

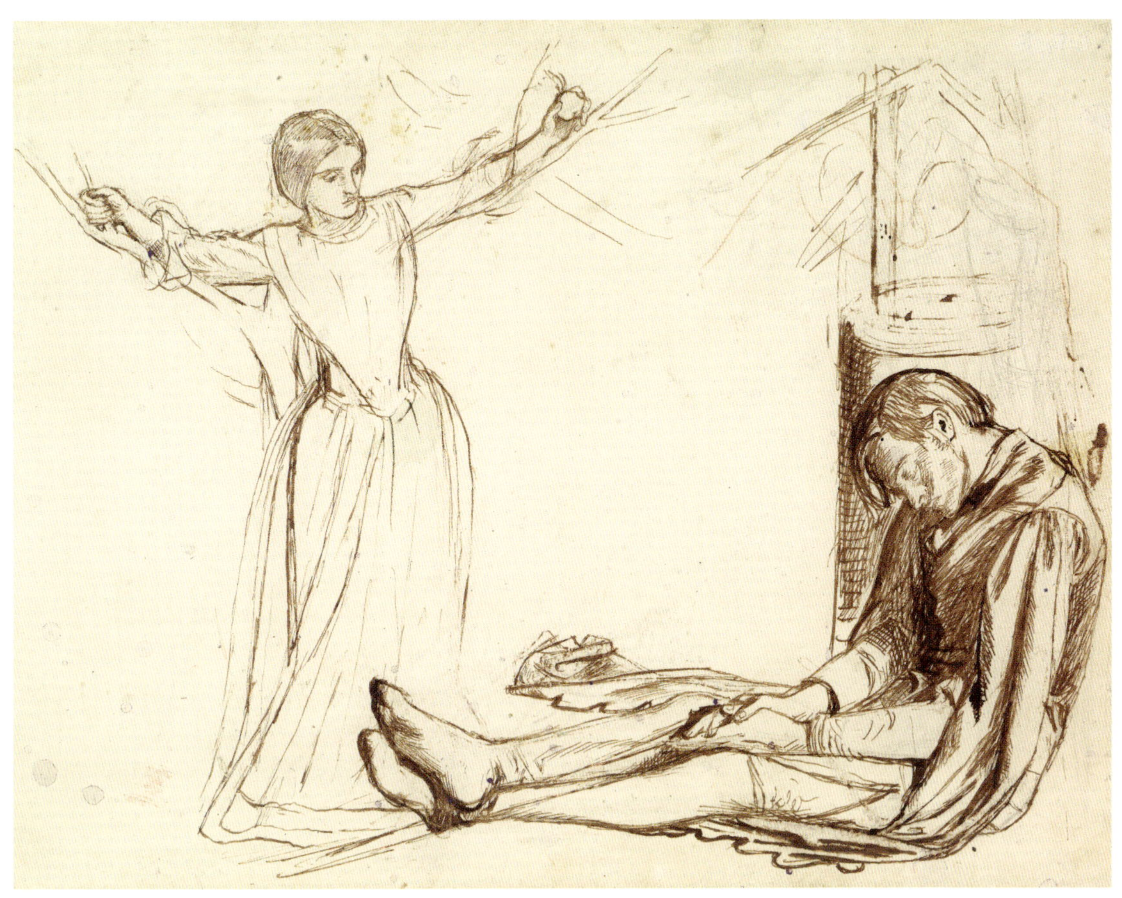

179 Dante Gabriel Rossetti, *Study for the Oxford Union Murals: The Sleeping Launcelot*, c. 1857, Birmingham Museums & Art Gallery

180 Dante Gabriel Rossetti, *Study for the Oxford Union Murals: Guenevere in the Apple Tree*, c. 1857, Birmingham Museums & Art Gallery

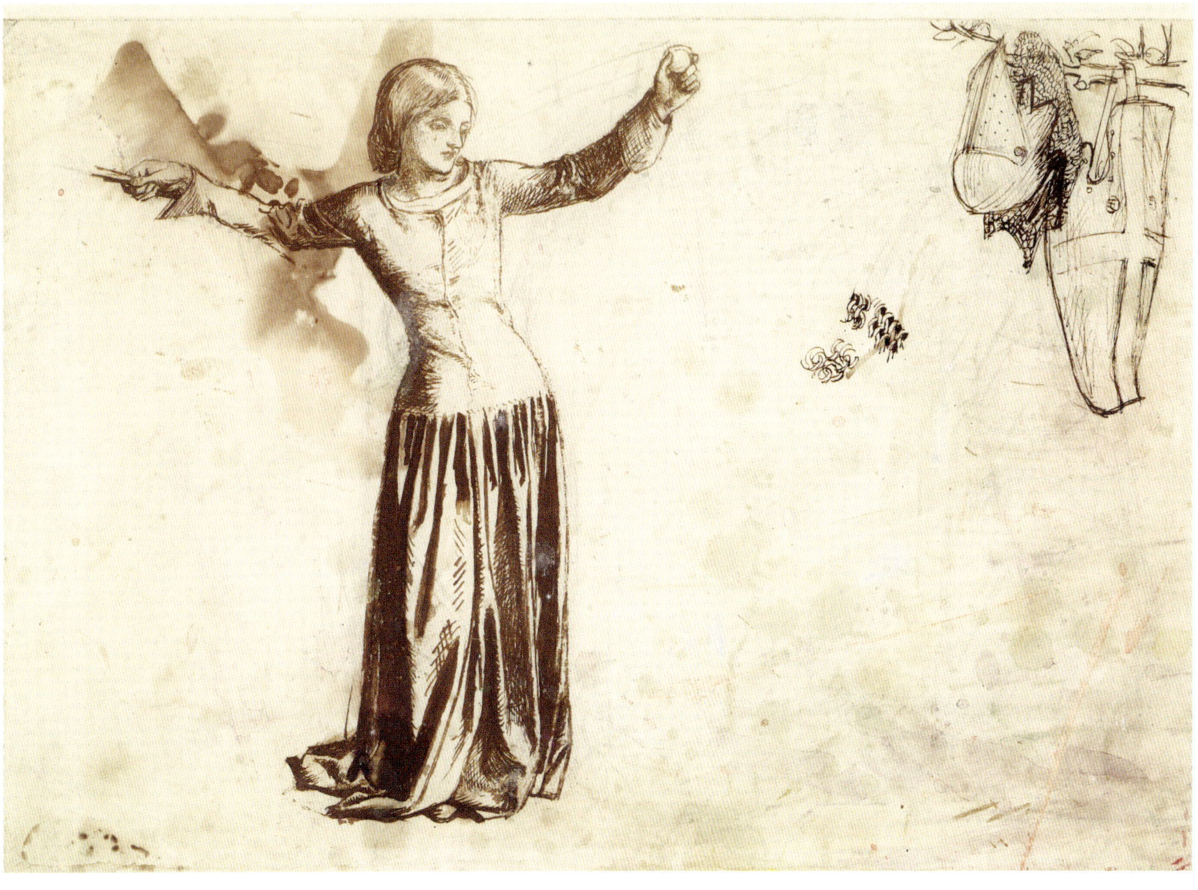

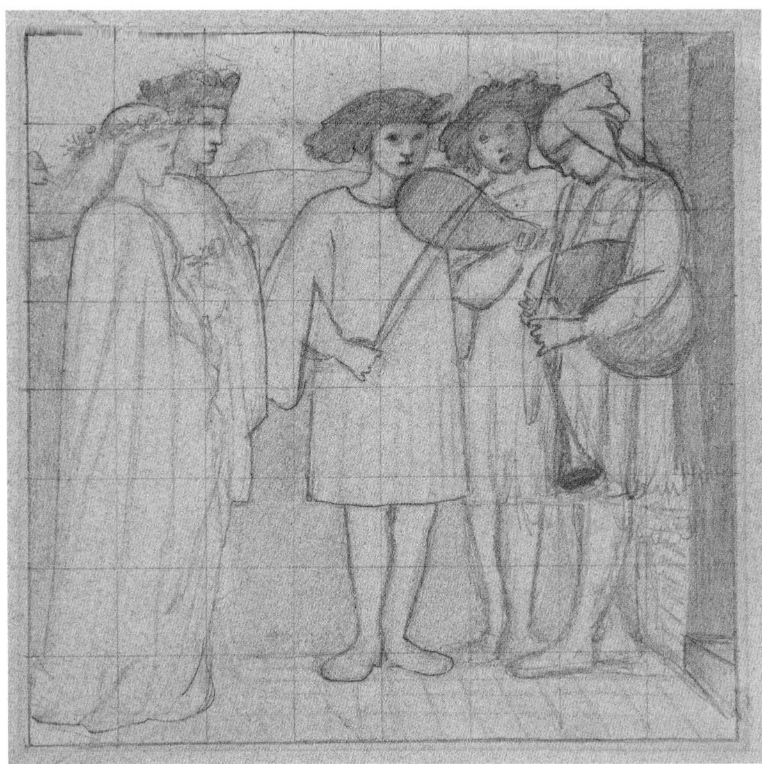

181 Edward Burne-Jones, *Study for a Mural: 'The Wedding of Sir Degrevaunt'*, 1860, Birmingham Museums & Art Gallery

attempted to reproduce their intensity on a larger scale [**179, 180**]. The leap into a cycle of murals was, however, ultimately defeated by inexperience. In the realization of this scheme, the 'jovial campaign', as the participants called it, he was joined by Burne-Jones, Morris, Arthur Hughes, J. Hungerford Pollen (1820–1902), Spencer Stanhope and Val Prinsep (1838–1904).[8] Rossetti's feeling for, and identification with, the Middle Ages is apparent in the Oxford Union designs, and his understanding of the stories is original – *Sir Launcelot's Vision of the Sanc Greal*, for example, is poignant rather than heroic [**179, 180**]. The design represents the knight asleep in front of the Chapel of the Sanc Greal, prevented from entering by his sin, symbolized by a vision of Guenevere, who stands with her arms spread out before the apple trees, as a kind of fallen Eve. The angel of the Grail is diagonally opposite, her ethereality a contrast to the sensuality of Guenevere. Rossetti used Burne-Jones as a model for Launcelot and Jane Burden as Guenevere.

As with the modern-life project *Found*, the Oxford Union murals were not completed and were abandoned by Rossetti in 1858. For all the ambition of their scale, the murals were really illustrations struggling to be paintings. Nonetheless, the undertaking marked the pivotal point in the history of Pre-Raphaelitism from a small and relatively exclusive group of artists engaged in easel painting to a wider group with interests in applied and decorative arts as well as painting.

The Pre-Raphaelite exhibition at the Hogarth Club in the summer of 1857 was the first opportunity the public had to see Rossetti's works on paper, which had been previously shown only to friends and prospective buyers. Reviewing the exhibition for the *Saturday Review*, the poet Coventry Patmore noted the inclusion of Rossetti's drawings and, using a particularly considered critical language, commented on their qualities:

The drawings displayed by Mr. Rossetti…are by no means his best works, but they are sufficient to convey to those who have seen no others, a very high opinion of his capacity, and perhaps to afford a clue of his unwillingness to exhibit his works upon the walls of the Academy. Profound thoughtfulness, and the peculiar tenderness which comes of profound thoughtfulness when directed to humanity, are the leading characteristics of Mr. Rossetti's performances. These qualities seem to have rendered him impatient of long labours and technical finish. He finds himself able to note down his ideas in a pen-and-ink sketch or a watercolour drawing; and having so noted them down with sufficient clearance for the comprehension of a congenial mind, he prefers noting down sources of fresh ones in the same approximate and suggestive manner, to a full elaboration of a few.[9]

Patmore confessed that it was difficult to criticize Rossetti's drawings: 'The greatest charm of them is in the inspired and untraceable mode by which he obtains his effects.'[10] Not all the critics were so approving. The reviewer for *The Athenaeum*, for example, although impressed by Rossetti, remarked on his tendency to draw rather than paint: 'That he is a poet and a thinker, we are the last to doubt, – but sketching is deceptive and dangerous. It is the day-dream of painting.'[11] In these two criticisms we get opposing ideas of

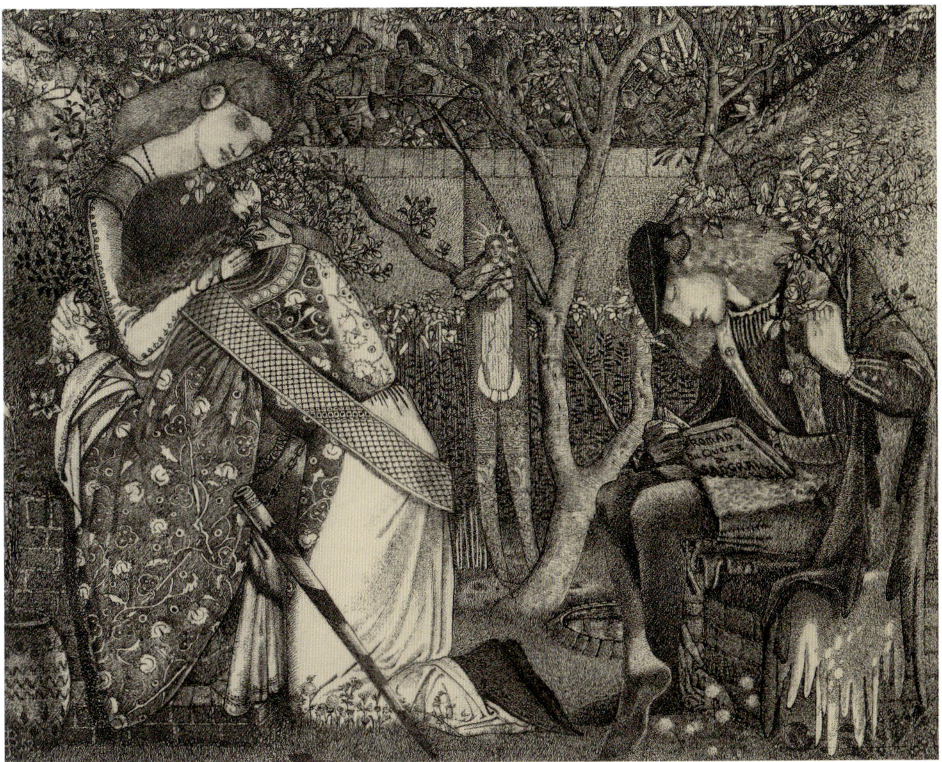

182 Edward Burne-Jones, *The Knight's Farewell*, 1858, Ashmolean Museum, University of Oxford

the role of drawing in Rossetti's work. Is it 'approximate and suggestive' or 'dangerous…the day-dream of painting'? The controversy was to haunt criticisms of the work of younger artists inspired by Rossetti. Certainly, Rossetti's own work was not conventional either in technique or in imagery. Throughout his career his personal preoccupations remained with medieval Italian and English literature – Dante, Arthurian legends – and with drawing rather than painting.

Marvels of finish: Burne-Jones's early drawings

The Oxford Union was to be Burne-Jones's first public venture as a painter. Although reckless, the decision to join Rossetti's mural scheme seemed innocent enough, but the critic Harry Quilter (1851–1907), looking back to the Oxford Union project in the 1890s, regarded it as fatal to Burne-Jones's development as an artist. His criticism was just one of many expressions of distrust of both Rossetti's techniques and his imagery:

> Having begun as a method of work, pre-Raphaelitism now became a method of feeling, a question of sentiment.…it was medievalism with a difference; with the modern spirit added to the ancient form, and with a bias overwhelming and unfortunate towards a view of life which was neither wholesome nor manly. I have

tried for many years to explain the effect of the spirit of this later pre-Raphaelitism, especially as shown in the work of its chief master, Edward Burne-Jones, and I shall only repeat here that, in my opinion, this very beautiful art is not of a kind which will do the world much good, or upon which any true school can be founded.

Quilter took pains to link this development back to Rossetti:

> I remember [Burne-Jones] telling me some years ago that art was to him an enchanted world, to which Rossetti had given him the key, and in which he had lived ever since. And this is, I think only a slightly exaggerated expression of his point of view. He does rather pride himself on living apart, in this enchanted country, and on refusing to consider himself as belonging to England and the nineteenth century.[12]

In his choice of a subject for the decoration of the Red House, William Morris's home designed by Philip Webb (1831–1915), Burne-Jones's theme was taken from a medieval Arthurian-related poem, *Sir Degrevant*, published in an edition edited by James Orchard Halliwell for the Camden Society in 1844.[13] Other designs [**182, 183**, for example] also reflect the influence of illuminated manuscripts, which can

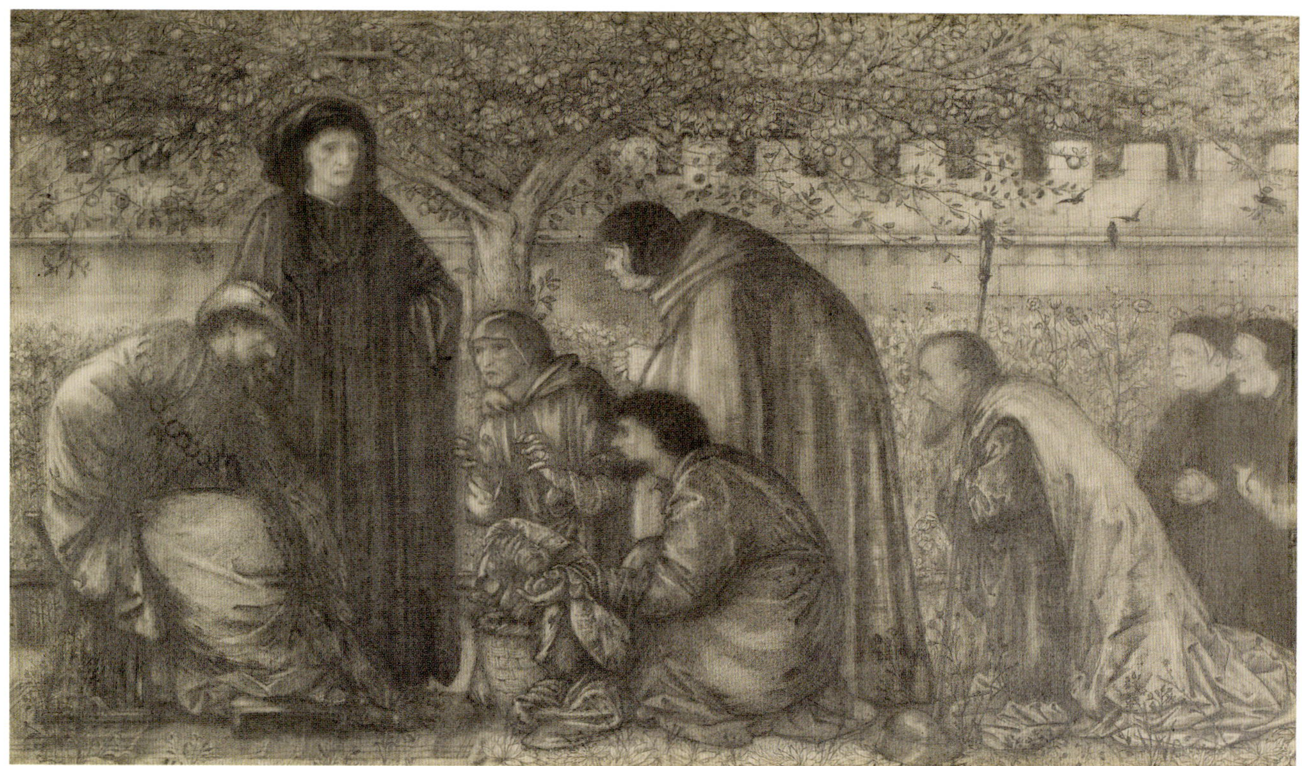

183 Edward Burne-Jones, *The Petition to the King*, 1865–67, The British Museum, London

be seen, ambiguously, as either paintings or drawings or, in their relationship with text, as illustrations. Dürer's prints were an influence, too. When Rossetti met Burne-Jones at Oxford he wrote to William Bell Scott that 'Jones's designs are marvels of finish & imaginative detail, unequalled by anything except perhaps Albert Dürer.'[14] Indeed, Burne-Jones's early drawings appear to revel in that nexus of image and text that is shared by both illuminated manuscripts and Dürer's graphic work.

Burne-Jones was an obsessive draughtsman, constantly drawing and designing, devising pictorial schemes and sketching.[15] The constant repetition of motifs, faces, attitudes and ideas is a compelling feature of his vast output. What is clear is that the morbidity and sadness of the figures that populate his imagination are themselves representative of an extraordinary pictorial impassivity that is one of the chief characteristics of English art of the period. If this is a part of a nostalgia for a Golden Age, with medieval Northern Europe standing in for Arcadia, then it is a very sad Golden Age, an age on the brink of tears or even neurosis. Sitting in a pasture, an orchard or some desacralized 'hortus conclusus', Burne-Jones's characters

are no happier – indeed somehow much unhappier – than their nineteenth-century audience in their stuffy drawing rooms. The lack of expression on the faces of the three figures in *Le Chant d'Amour* (1868–77, Metropolitan Museum of Art, New York) is typical of the artist [184, 185, 186]. Yet these are finely modulated degrees of expressionlessness and they invite close scrutiny. The female figure, for example, has a subtly frantic expression that moderates her impassivity and draws the viewer in.

'Startling peculiarities': Siddal and Solomon

It is striking that Rossetti's immediate followers, such as Burne-Jones, Solomon and Elizabeth Siddal, were all untrained or partially trained artists whose ambitions were not for amateur achievement but for the highest genre in modern art – imaginative subject painting. All three made their most individual contributions in the field of drawing rather than painting. They also share a tendency to repeat subjects, seemingly obsessively, returning to the same themes and motifs many times.

Until her meeting with the Pre-Raphaelites, who employed her as a model, Siddal had no association with

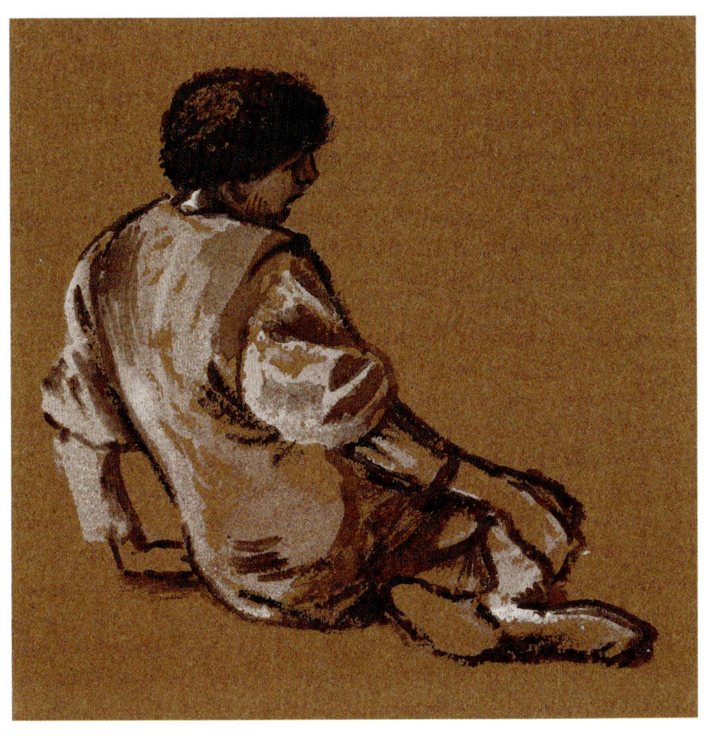

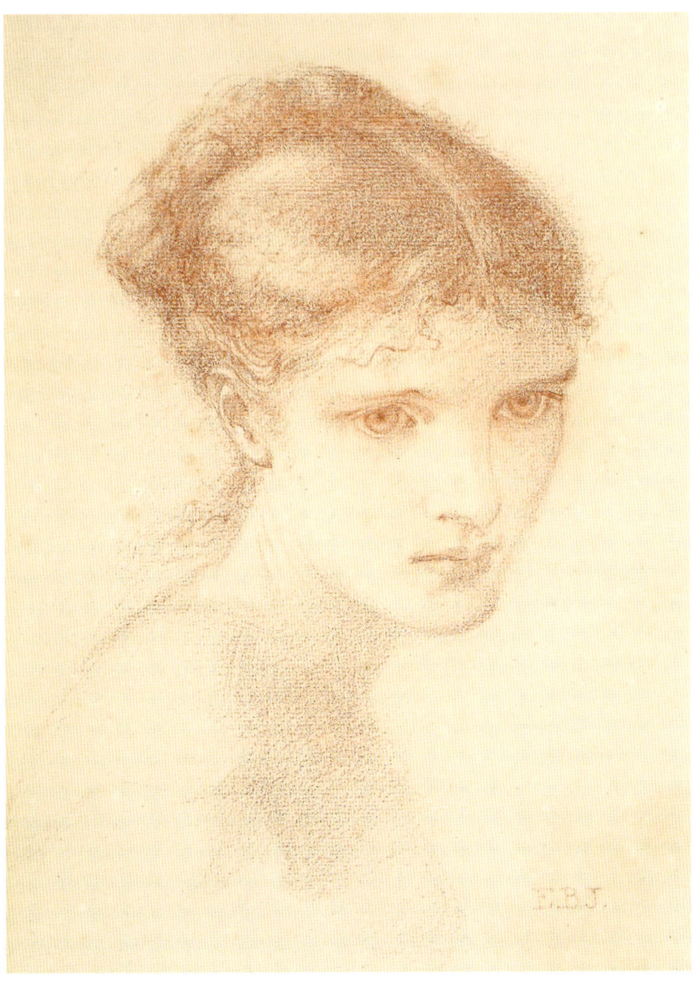

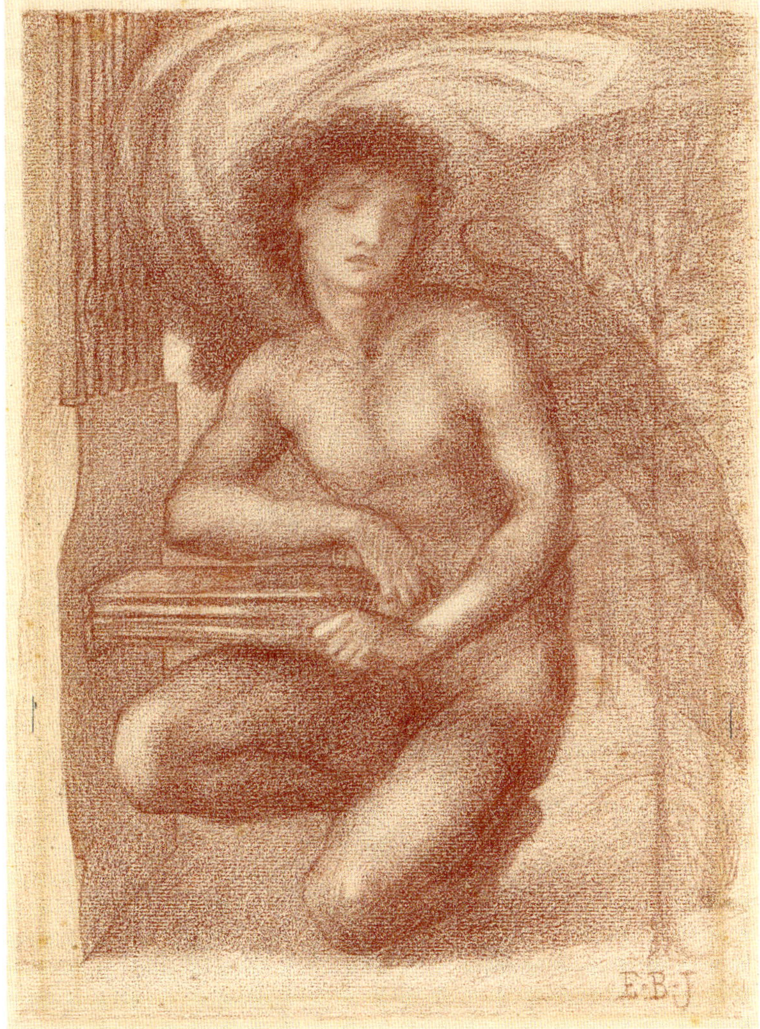

184 Edward Burne-Jones, *Study for 'Le Chant d'Amour': Lover*, c. 1865, Birmingham Museums & Art Gallery
185 Edward Burne-Jones, *Study for 'Le Chant d'Amour': Woman's Head*, 1868, Aberystwyth University, School of Art Gallery and Museum
186 Edward Burne-Jones, *Study for 'Le Chant d'Amour': Seraph*, 1868, Aberystwyth University, School of Art Gallery and Museum

art. The extent of her amateur attempts at drawing and
painting, if there were any, are unknown. She became both
Rossetti's mistress – later his wife – and his pupil at a time
when he showed an interest in instructing and encouraging
untrained artists. At the Working Men's College, Rossetti
permitted freedom of expression and in this he was different
from Ruskin. His approach accorded with his earlier Pre-
Raphaelite interest in the 'primitive' quality of early Italian
art; he detected it in Siddal's early attempts at composition.
As William Michael Rossetti recalled:

> As to the quality of [Siddal's] work, it may be admitted
> at once that she never attained to anything like
> masterliness…[In] those early 'Praeraphaelite' days,
> and in the Praeraphaelite environment, which was
> small, and ringed round by hostile forces, things were
> estimated differently.

The subtext here is that she was overrated at a time when
her talents represented, for her friends, an alternative to
conventional art. Although his assessment of Siddal was not
always generous, William Michael Rossetti granted that she
could invent and compose images with 'much facility' and
that she had

> eminent purity of feeling, dignified simplicity,
> and grace; little mastery of form, whether in the
> human figure or drapery and other materials; a right
> intention in colouring, though neither rich nor deep.
> Her designs represented those of Dante Rossetti at
> the same date: he had his defects, and she had the
> deficiencies of those defects. He guided her with the
> utmost attention, but I doubt whether he ever required
> her to study drawing with rigorous patience and apply
> herself to the realizing of realities.[16]

In his estimation of Siddal, William Michael Rossetti did
not take into consideration her almost complete lack of
training, let alone her poverty and inability to buy drawing
materials or, indeed, her restricted working space. These are

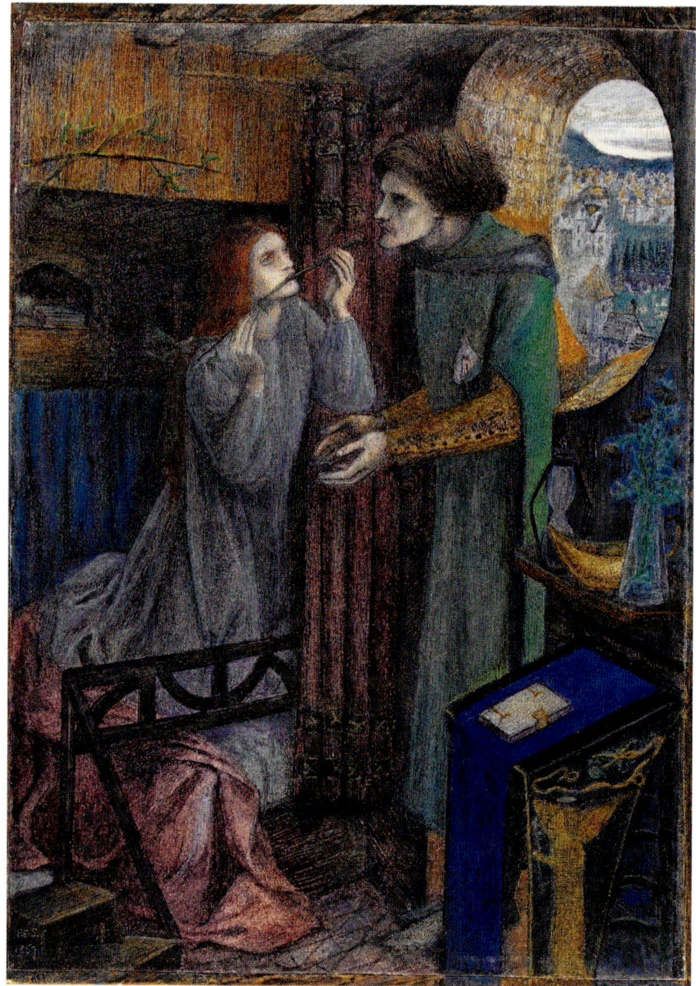

187 Elizabeth Siddal, *Clerk Saunders*, 1857,
Fitzwilliam Museum, Cambridge

all factors that Jan Marsh has pointed out in her reappraisal
of Siddal's career.[17]

Ambitious plans for Siddal to illustrate a volume of
Scottish ballads, edited by the poet William Allingham, fell
through but stimulated independent works such as *Clerk
Saunders* (1857) [187]. This and other works inspired by
poetry demonstrated 'an attractive earnestness and naivety',
that prompted Rossetti to insist to Brown that his pupil's
'fecundity of invention and facility are quite wonderful,
much greater than mine'.[18] *Clerk Saunders* was exhibited at
the Hogarth Club in 1857. Coventry Patmore, writing in the
Saturday Review, observed:

> There was one lady contributor, Miss E. E. Siddal,
> whose name was new to us. Her drawings display
> an admiring adoption of all the more startling
> peculiarities of Mr Rossetti's style, but they have
> nevertheless qualities which entitle them to high
> praise. Her 'study of a head' is a very promising
> attempt, showing great care, considerable technical
> power, and a high, pure, and independent feeling for

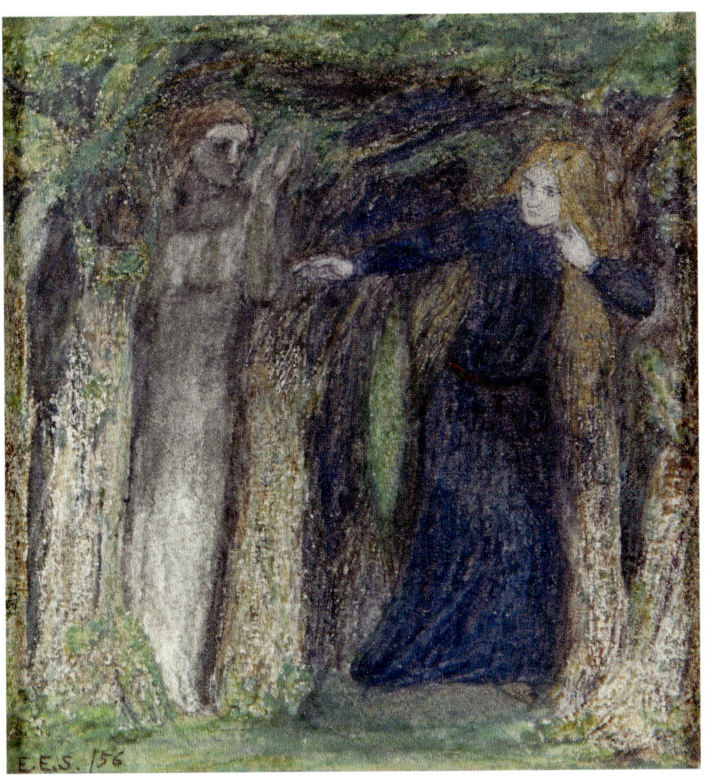

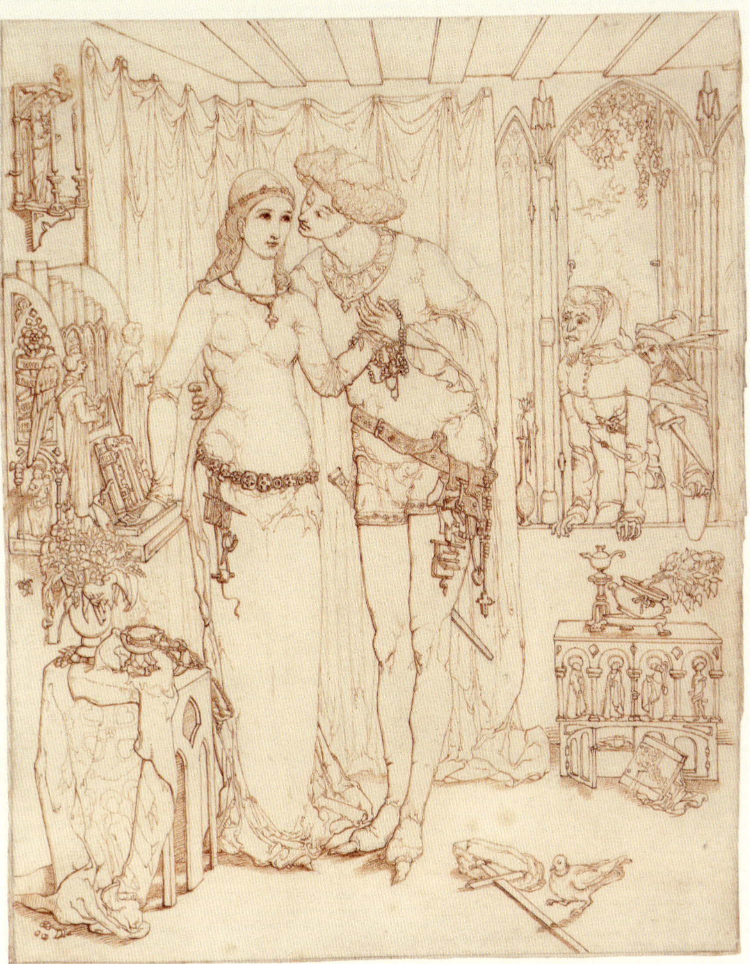

188 Elizabeth Siddal, *The Haunted Wood*, c. 1856, National Trust, Wightwick Manor and Gardens

189 Simeon Solomon, *Faust and Marguerite*, c. 1856, Tate

that much misunderstood object, the human face divine. 'We are Seven' and 'Pippa Passes', by the same lady, deserve more notice than we can stop to give them. Her 'Clerk Saunders', although we have heard it highly praised by high authorities, did not please us so much.[19]

Nevertheless, Charles Eliot Norton bought *Clerk Saunders* for a good sum, 40 guineas, and it was included in an exhibition that travelled to New York in 1857. Rossetti reacquired it two years later. 'It even surprised me', Rossetti wrote to Professor Norton, 'by its great merit of feeling and execution.'[20]

At her best, Siddal had a unique quality that expressed itself well in subjects such as *Clerk Saunders* and *The Haunted Wood* (1856) [**188**]. Despite the flaws in technique – or because of them, perhaps – they communicate their eerie subject matter effectively. The awkwardness of her depiction of the human figure, shared with Simeon Solomon at the first stage of his career, revived the drawing style of the earliest phase of the Pre-Raphaelite Brotherhood in

1848–49 before its members moved on to more individual expressions of their talents and beliefs.

Solomon's early drawings were passed around at a Pre-Raphaelite evening party in 1857 when he was sixteen years old. The watercolourist George Price Boyce (1826–97) recorded in his diary that he 'saw some remarkable designs' of Solomon's, 'showing much Rossetti-like feeling'.[21] His Faust subject, the product of his earliest phase, is a fascinating record of how both the outline style and Pre-Raphaelitism were absorbed by younger artists [**189**]. Altogether more cluttered than Rossetti's, and wildly more fanciful, Solomon's drawing further extends the idea of the reimagined medieval interior as an essential part of the drama. The young artist exhibited his drawings publicly from 1858 onwards. At this early stage of his career, Solomon joined in on the craze for Arthurian and other medieval subjects, looking back to early Pre-Raphaelite drawing in all its stiffness and angularity, and to a time when it was at its most Ritualistic in religious imagery. In *The Death of Sir Galahad* (c. 1857–59) [**191**] the extreme

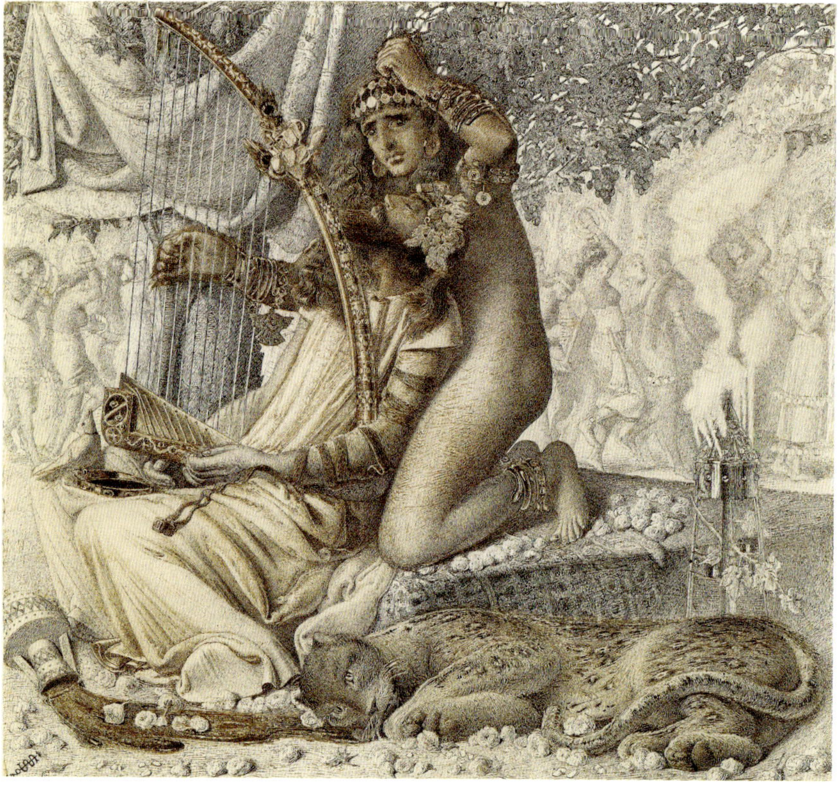

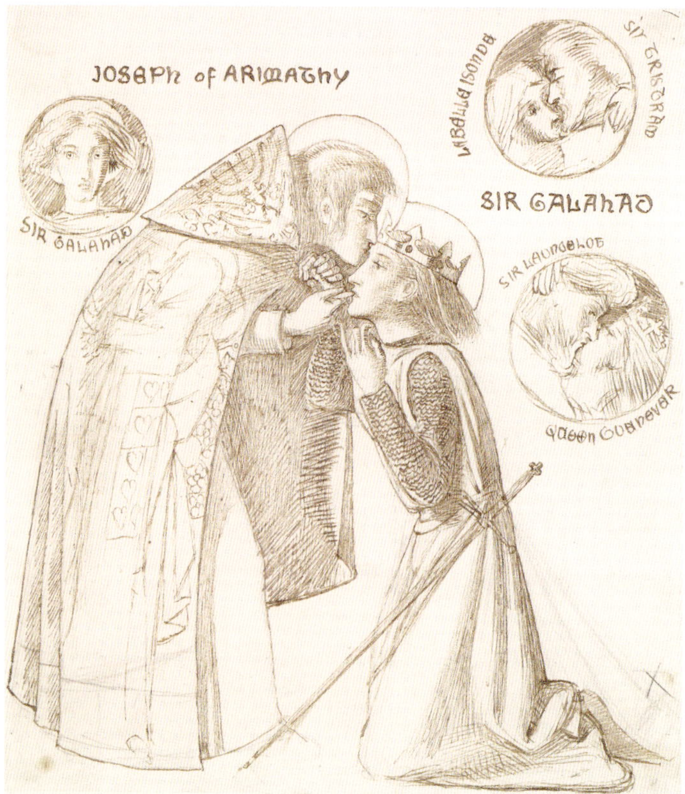

boyishness of the knight reflects the artist's own youth. The composition is strikingly like Rossetti's designs for the Oxford Union murals [**179, 180**], and the sharpness of the facial features with their long noses and thin lips recalls a shared taste of Millais and Rossetti for a certain pinched and attenuated physical type. The closeness of this drawing and similar ones to Pre-Raphaelite prototypes suggests that Solomon had access to the artists' studios and saw their drawings privately rather than experiencing their finished paintings at public exhibitions.

Although Solomon's paintings were displayed from 1859 onwards at the Royal Academy annual exhibitions, where they generally enjoyed good critical reception, he remained essentially a draughtsman, producing major works in pencil and coloured inks. Much time was expended on these graphic extravaganzas – in contrast to his later, much looser, chalk drawings of the 1880s and 1890s – and it seems generally acknowledged among his contemporaries that Solomon was more of a draughtsman than a painter. Many of his drawings of the 1850s and 1860s were produced laboriously in pen and ink, with form and surface texture added by the application of hatchings, broken lines and dots. It was a kind of colouring-in process but without very much colour added. The results were often remarkably effective. The powerful and mysterious design *Babylon Hath Been a Golden Cup* [**190**], which was exhibited at the French Gallery in 1859, with its ambiguous sexual overtones and fantastic historical details, owes its visual impact to its very beautiful and subtle colouring. The shimmering greys and browns produced by tiny flecks of ink are particularly beguiling.[22]

'Offshoots from almost forgotten pre-Raphaelitism': drawing at the Dudley

The Dudley Gallery, set up in 1865 as a free exhibition, became the most important venue for young artists to exhibit their drawings. William De Morgan, Walter Crane

190 Simeon Solomon, *Babylon Hath Been a Golden Cup*, 1859, Birmingham Museums & Art Gallery
191 Simeon Solomon, *The Death of Sir Galahad While Taking a Portion of the Holy Grail Administered by Joseph of Arimathea*, 1857–59, Birmingham Museums & Art Gallery

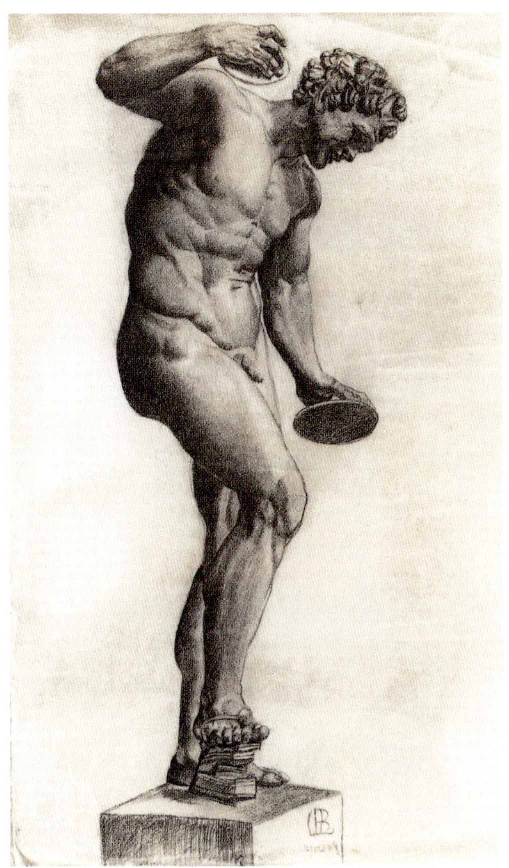

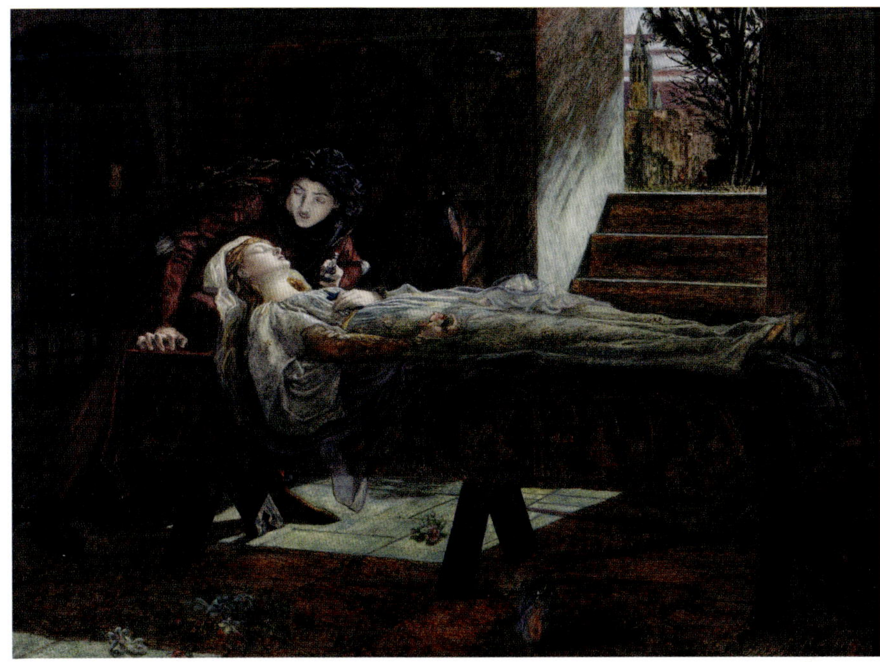

192 Lucy Madox Brown, *The Dancing Faun*, 1869, private collection
193 Lucy Madox Brown, *The Tomb Scene from Romeo and Juliet*, 1870,
National Trust, Wightwick Manor and Gardens

(1845–1915), Robert Bateman (1842–1922) and Edward Poynter (1836–1919) all showed their work there, many of them making their public debuts as artists. Well-established painters, such as Hunt, also took advantage of a new opportunity to exhibit and sell watercolours and drawings.[23] The opening of the new gallery was seen as an important asset in the rapidly expanding London art world, and the Dudley acted as a lively alternative to the Royal Academy, the exhibitions of the 'Old' and 'New' Watercolour Societies and the fading British Institution. The bulk of the exhibits, as might be expected, were landscape watercolours, but the Dudley was to become more notable as the home of a new school of British subject watercolour, often based on historical and literary themes such as those favoured by Millais and Rossetti. In this new type of watercolour, the underlying pencil or chalk drawing was entirely obliterated; gum and bodycolour added to the pigment changed its transparency, rendering it opaque. These figure studies were rarely of modern-life subjects; neither were they of genre scenes, the staple of watercolourists such as William Henry Hunt, who, when he was not painting birds' nests or still life arrangements, was keen to display his skill at figure painting.

A number of women artists chose to show their work at the Dudley as an adjunct to the exhibitions of the Society of Female Artists, which had been inaugurated in 1857

(the Society had been formed two years earlier). Simeon Solomon's sister, Rebecca Solomon (1832–86), Marie Spartali (1844–1927), Evelyn De Morgan (1855–1919) and Lucy Madox Brown (1843–94), all of them with strong Pre-Raphaelite affiliations, showed literary-themed works at the Dudley. As a pupil of her father, Ford Madox Brown, Lucy had been encouraged to study the human figure as much as possible; this is attested by her dashing study of antique sculpture *The Dancing Faun* (1869) [**192**].

Lucy Madox Brown had some success with watercolours shown at both the 1870 and 1871 Winter Exhibitions. In 1870 one of her works, *Après le Bal*, unusually a modern-life subject, was moderately well received. In the following year, her *Romeo and Juliet* [**193**] was approved of by *The Times*. Despite adversely criticizing the drawing of Romeo's hands and hair, the reviewer commented on 'all its very obvious faults' but found it 'a drawing of rare sentiment'.[24] It depicts Romeo leaning over the figure of Juliet as she lies, seemingly dead, in the tomb. It is the moment before Romeo drinks from the phial of poison that he clutches in his left hand. He leans across the seemingly dead body of Juliet who, posed somewhat in the manner of Millais's Ophelia, is dressed in a white wedding dress, her figure illuminated by the sun streaming through the window. The work heralds a new relationship with Pre-Raphaelitism that was to grow

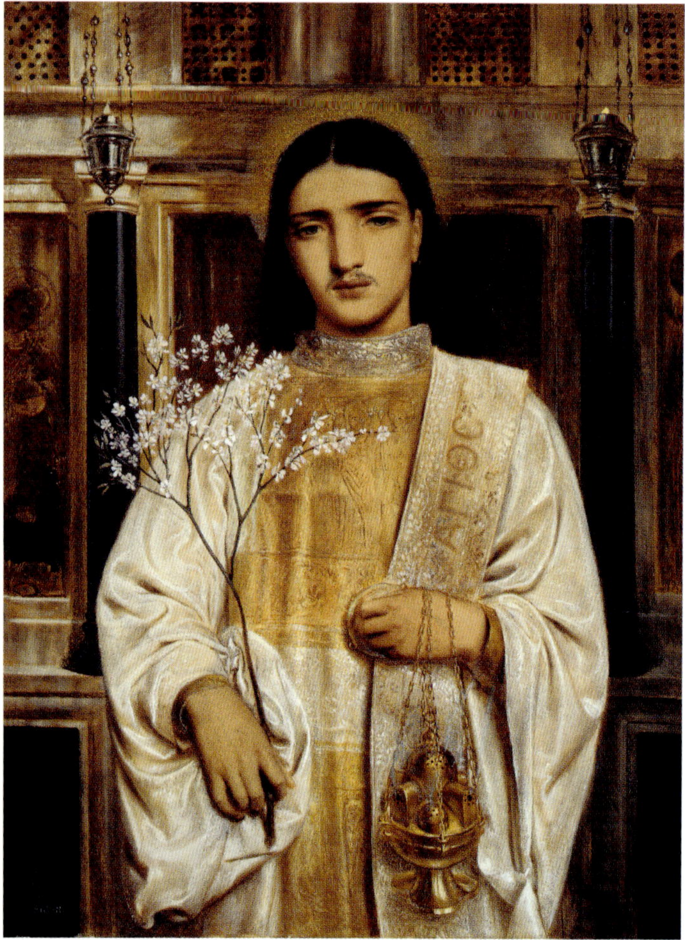

194 Simeon Solomon, *A Saint of the Eastern Church*, 1867–68, Birmingham, Museums & Art Gallery

throughout the next three decades, the formation of a dialogue with the works of an older generation of artists who pioneered new and original approaches to dramatic and poetic subjects and who often found personal viewpoints on familiar texts. In this case it is tempting to see Lucy Madox Brown in dialogue with her father, Ford Madox Brown, whose *Romeo and Juliet* was painted in the same year, 1870, and whose experiments with Shakespearean narrative subjects had begun in the mid-1840s.[25]

The Dudley was perceived as having an important role to play in promoting a change in British drawing. The Ruskinian critic Richard St John Tyrwhitt (1827–95), writing in the *Contemporary Review*, thought that at the 1868 Winter Exhibition at the Dudley, 'Messrs. Solomon and Stanhope's [works] give watercolour a new importance'.[26] It became clear, however, that the presence of a new school of Pre-Raphaelite-inspired watercolourists was challenging and even disruptive. Simeon Solomon became the focus of much of the attendant criticism. All five of his contributions to the 1872 Dudley Watercolour Exhibition were adversely criticized. *The Times*, for example, found that a difficult act

of discrimination had to be made about Solomon's work: 'It seems to us hard to say whether a certain effeminacy and morbid mysticism, affectation, or insipidity, is uppermost.'[27] The vehemence of much of the criticism recalls the original reception of works by the Pre-Raphaelite Brotherhood. The old hostility had not died out but, rather, had become more suspicious and abusive in tone.

The *Times* review of the Dudley Gallery Watercolour Exhibition in 1869 opened with some general thoughts on what this new school of watercolour drawing was and what it meant. It went to the heart of the issue by characterizing the faults of these new tendencies and their origin:

> In the Dudley Gallery we look out for and find unhackneyed talents and unfamiliar styles.…as in other watercolour exhibitions, landscape has the predominance. Such figure drawings as there are belong most of them to the school which, for want a better term, is often called 'Preraphaelite'; a more descriptive title would be 'Archaic', or 'Mediaeval'. It is a school that affects the past in subject, sentiment, and style, down to such minor matters as labelling and framing; its forms are stiff and angular, its colour tending to the funereal or sickly; its ideal of loveliness seems ugliness to the uninitiated, and the last thing it suggests is relish of healthy life, outdoor nature, or cheerful sunlight.[28]

Despite all the fuss about archaisms and revivals it is clear that the real challenge to contemporary critics was the strangeness and unfamilarity of the exhibited works of Solomon and his associates. The *Illustrated London News* was historically reflective in pointing out the origin of these 'eccentric or peculiar' images:

> Many of the peculiarities are offshoots from almost forgotten pre-Raphaelitism; but instead of uniting (which was the professed object of that schism) primitive simplicity of feeling to modern scientific truth, the former is often regarded as all in all, or one particular quality of art is exalted at the expense of all others.[29]

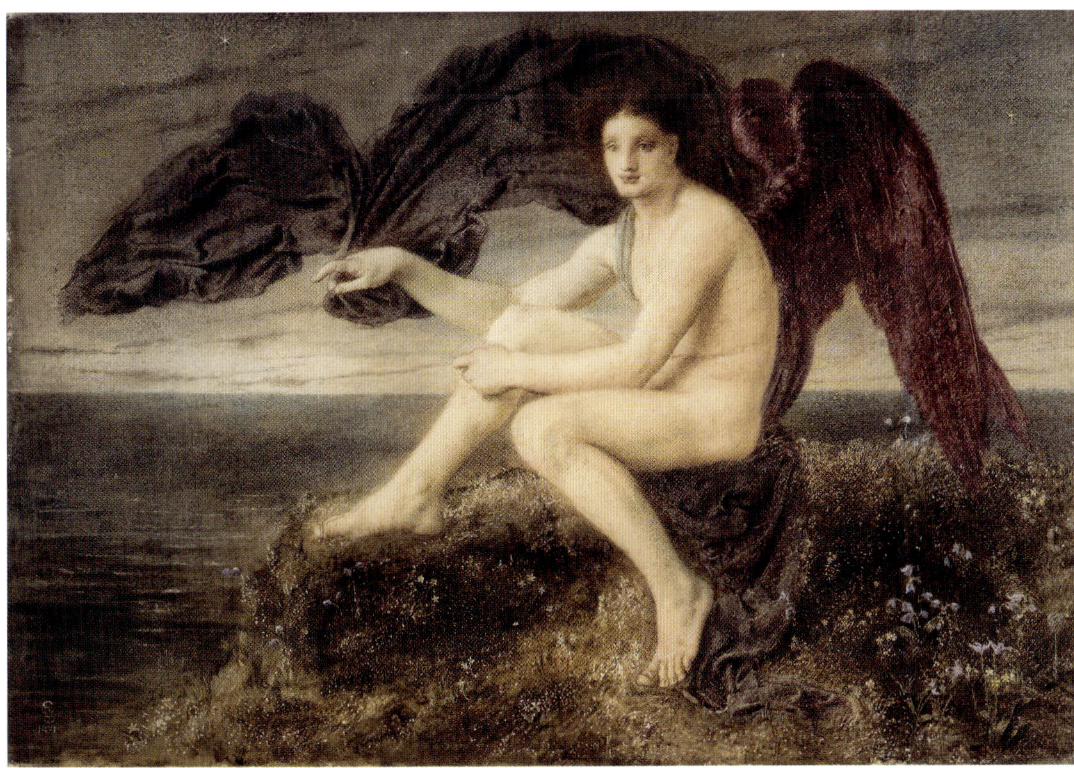

195 Simeon Solomon, *Dawn*, 1871, Birmingham Museums & Art Gallery

The singular quality of the work Solomon exhibited at the Dudley seemed to be its 'eccentricity', a term that seems to have covered several characteristics: the artist's drawing technique, the types of figure (most of them male nude or draped figure) or the subjects, many of which were of his own devising or loosely based on classical or other literary sources. Depictions of Bacchus and Heliogabalus, as well as several varieties of the allegorical figure of Love, made up a good proportion of the subjects that he exhibited there throughout the 1860s and early 1870s. Another sequence of watercolours depicted Jewish rabbis, Roman Catholic, Anglican and Greek Orthodox priests in their religious vestments, most often holding ritual objects [194]. Solomon's *Dawn* [195], which was shown at the Dudley in 1872, had a fairly anodyne allegorical conceit at its centre: an angelic male figure pulls away the dark sky of night to reveal the first light breaking on the horizon. The face of the young man, with its half-smile and heavily lidded eyes, its languid sexual ambiguity, is Leonardesque, and could hardly be mistaken for an 'offshoot' of Pre-Raphaelitism. Clearly what was detected by critics of the Dudley Gallery was an extended Pre-Raphaelitism, a much looser cultural term than that devised by the original Brotherhood. This 'Pre-Raphaelitism' reflects the movement towards Aestheticism as a theory and practice in advanced art circles. With this change came a sense that works being publicly exhibited at the Dudley might have amoral or even immoral subjects and messages. In Solomon's subjects, the appeals made to beauty rather than morality, to love rather

than duty, to the externals of religious ritual rather than to religious ideals, were highly suspect; that their articulation was through the medium regarded as being quintessentially British and morally neutral – watercolour – was itself strangely threatening.

The new Pre-Raphaelite-inspired practice of watercolour permitted younger artists to experiment with one of the most striking features of Pre-Raphaelite painting: colour. It encouraged, too, new approaches to composition as well as to figural and spatial arrangements. The deliberate formal awkwardness that resulted was deemed a sign of a revival or survival of Pre-Raphaelitism but in a form so changed that it threatened to destroy the distinctive features and reputation of the original movement. Nearly two decades after the first appearance of the Pre-Raphaelite Brotherhood, the term 'Pre-Raphaelite' was attached to the most advanced and contentious drawings being exhibited in London. In this climate of change, the modern-life subject was all but abandoned. The graphic record of modernity did not sit easily with drawing or watercolour but it did with illustration and, with artists such as Millais, it was to emerge as a new force in British art. It transmuted seamlessly into the kinds of periodical illustration produced by Millais and his followers in which the dramatic encounters between historical characters were re-expressed in pen and ink and reproduced thousands of times.

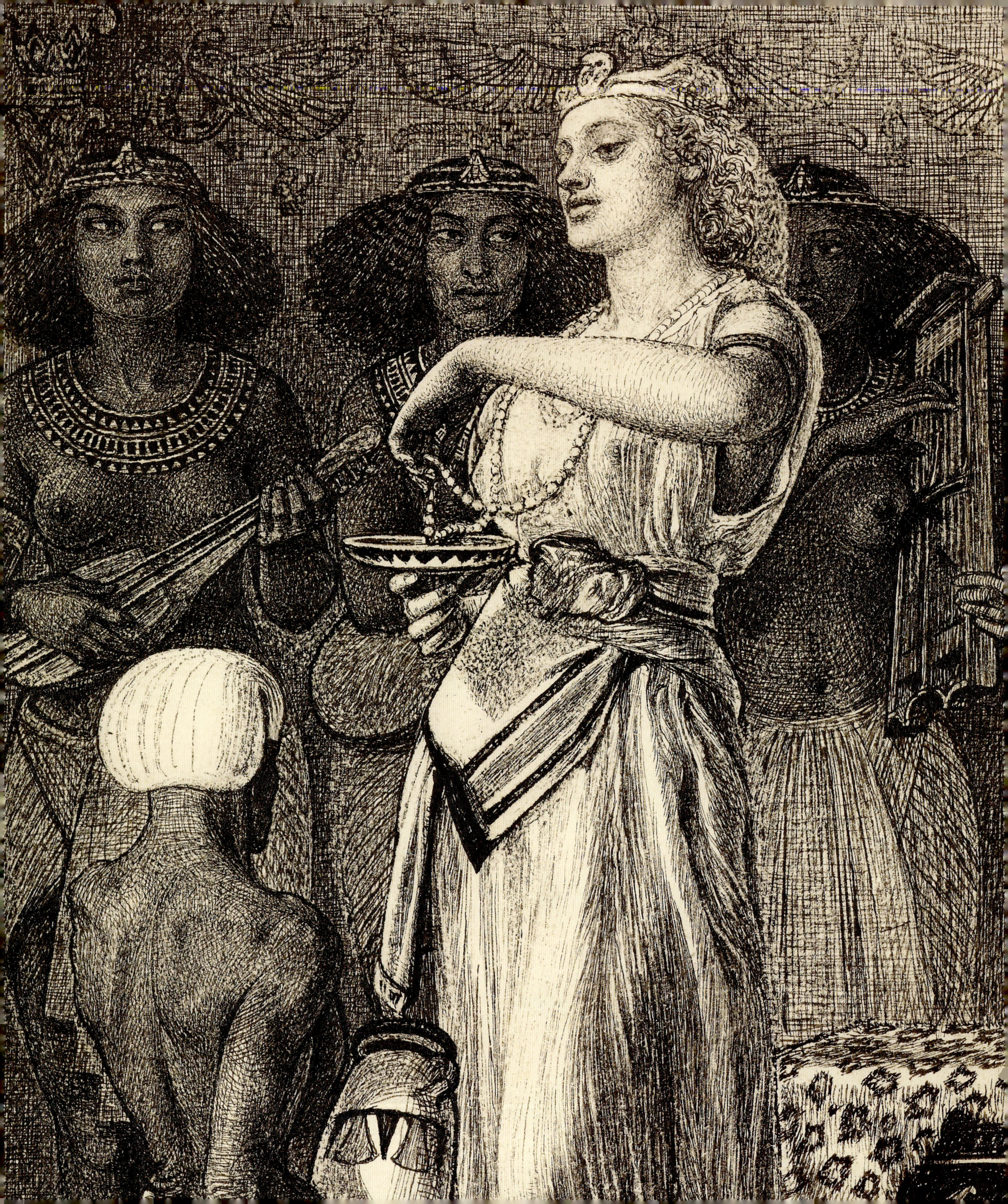

Chapter 6 *The Poetry of Illustration: Disseminating Pre-Raphaelite Drawing in the 1850s and 1860s*

The proliferation of illustrated literature is a striking feature of Victorian visual culture. The appreciation and collection of these multiplied images extended the tradition of connoisseurship formerly accorded to limited edition prints, such as etchings, into a new area. Most commercial book illustration in Britain was engraved (rather than lithographed) and in black and white, a choice dictated by the economics of printing and speed of production rather than aesthetic choice. However, for collectors the monochromatic quality of the work was not a limitation; rather, it stimulated an interest in the individual nuances that each illustrator could bring to the medium. Rossetti had been much influenced by French periodical illustration and was particularly proud of his collection of prints by Gavarni and his contemporaries.[1] In much the same way, a later generation of British collectors was to enthuse about the illustrations of the Pre-Raphaelites and their contemporaries such as George Pinwell (1842–75) and Arthur Boyd Houghton (1836–75).[2]

Ruskin was deeply interested in the subject of print. He had been captivated by prints of drawings and paintings, such as Turner's, before experiencing them as originals. He exhorted engravers to copy the works of great artists almost as a religious ideal, the multiplication of print seemingly an evangelical imperative. In this sense, Ruskin acknowledged the power of print, preferring it to painting:

> It is not like a single picture or a single wall painting; this multipliable work will pass through thousand thousand hands, strengthen and inform innumerable souls, if it be worthy; vivify the folly of thousands if unworthy. Remember, also, that it will mix in the very closest manner in domestic life. This engraving will not be gossiped over and fluttered past at private views of academies; listlessly sauntered by in corners of great galleries. Ah, no! This will hang over parlour chimney-

196 Fredrick Sandys, *Design for 'Cleopatra Dissolving the Pearl'*, 1862, Birmingham Museums & Art Gallery (detail)

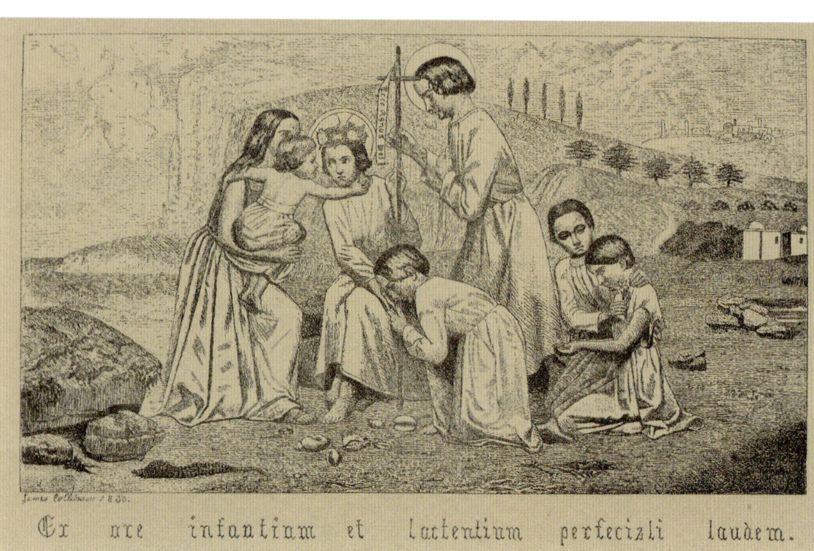

197 James Collinson, *Christ Blessing the Children ('Ex ore infantium et lactantium perfecisti laudem')*, 1850, published in *The Germ*, Birmingham Museums & Art Gallery

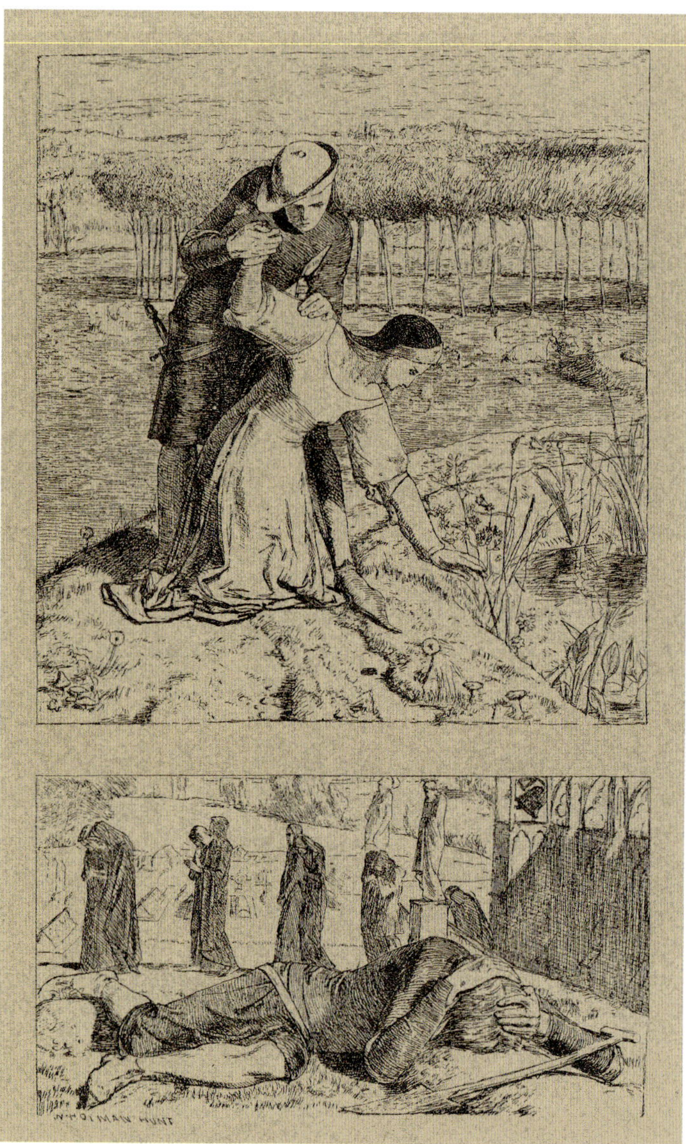

198 William Holman Hunt, *My Beautiful Lady*, 1850, published in *The Germ*, Birmingham Museums & Art Gallery

pieces – shed down its hourly influence on children's forenoon work.[3]

Periodical and book illustration invited a slightly different engagement than did the single-sheet print. The viewer of the book or periodical illustration was presented with a picture in a page otherwise filled with printed words while engaged in the solitary activity of reading.

Reinventing illustration

The Pre-Raphaelites first experimented with printed illustrations in their own periodical *The Germ* by including an etching, bound as a frontispiece, with each issue. The inexperience of the artists in the craft of etching lent a kind of primitive quality to their prints that is absent from Lasinio's engravings after Gozzoli, which had a coldness to their linear clarity. The 'awkwardness' of the etched line in the illustrations of *The Germ* communicates the 'sincerity' at the heart of the earliest Pre-Raphaelite work, akin to the

abandonment of academic convention. Such is the case for both James Collinson's *Christ Blessing the Children ('Ex ore infantium et lactantium perfecisti laudem')* (1850) [**197**] and William Holman Hunt's illustration for Thomas Woolner's poem 'My Beautiful Lady' (1850) [**198**].

The Collinson print is tentative, almost painfully so, yet it clearly reveals an enthusiasm for the Italian primitives in both iconography and style. The religious sentiment of the etching is of the most characteristically 'early' and 'Italian' in the context of religious debates of the 1840s and 1850s. It would fit easily as the frontispiece of a work by a Tractarian writing on the Church Fathers. The accompanying motto is part of the opening sentence of Psalm 8, translated as 'Out of the mouths of babes and sucklings you have perfected praise.' There was significance, no doubt, in both Collinson's choice of the Latin Vulgate version rather than the King James translation, and in his use of thin gothic lettering for the plate's inscription. The reviewer in *The Ecclesiologist*, who found other etchings in *The Germ* 'far too angular', singled it out for praise: 'We like Mr. Collinson's "*Ex ore infantium et lactantium perfecisti laudem*" very much; – it is simple and devotional.'[4] There is something of the same feeling in Hunt's illustration for 'My Beautiful Lady', in which the etching is presented in two parts, the smaller – *Of My Lady in Death* – acting as a kind of *predella* (the pendant to an altarpiece) to the larger. The implication is that the love represented in both images is somehow sacred and that the two parts deal with separate, if related, episodes.

Neither Rossetti nor Millais published drawings in *The Germ*, although Millais worked on a least two designs, the more striking of which was for Rossetti's story 'St Agnes of Intercession' (1850) [**200**]. It depicts the moment when an artist draws the portrait of his lover, urgently attempting to achieve a likeness of her before she dies. In its groupings and details, the sensitivity of the etched line and the vividness of the subject this design looked forward to the equally harrowing 'modern-life' drawings that Millais undertook later in the 1850s, which were also concerned with death and loss.

Although Millais, Arthur Hughes and Rossetti were involved in an illustration project for William Allingham's collection of poems *The Music Master* (1855), it was Rossetti's single contribution, a design for Allingham's poem 'The Maids of Elfen-mere' (1854–55) [**201, 202**], that was to have the greatest impact. The female figures are closely modelled on the angelic figures in Flaxman's Dante illustrations, such as that illustrating the Salutation (*Purgatorio* 10) [**203**]. Their heads with flowing hair surmounting a straight body defined by a kind of nightdress, and the absence of wings, suggest that, though they might be otherworldly, they are not angelic.

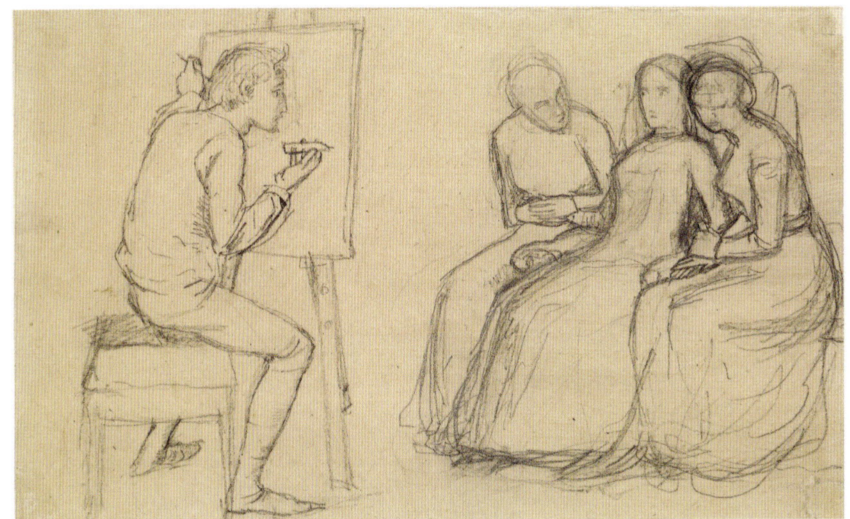

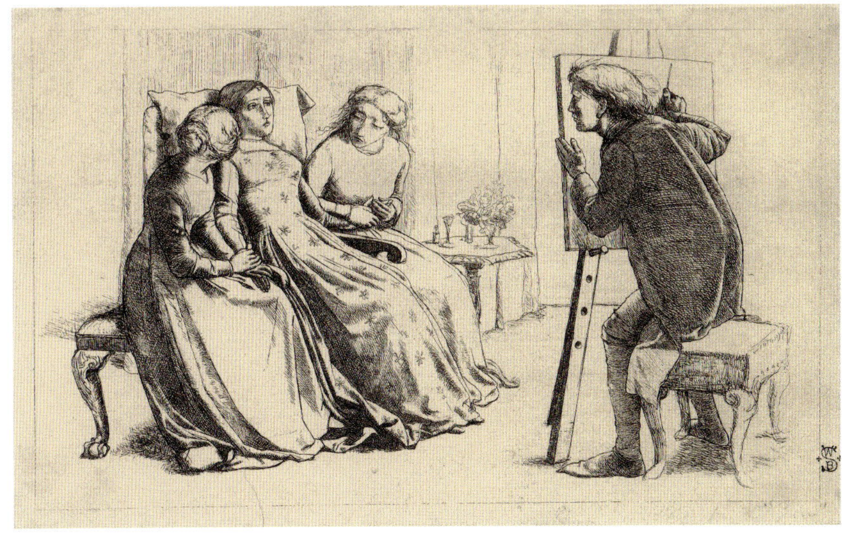

199 John Everett Millais, *Study for 'St Agnes of Intercession'*, 1850, Birmingham Museums & Art Gallery
200 John Everett Millais, *St Agnes of Intercession*, 1850, Birmingham Museums & Art Gallery

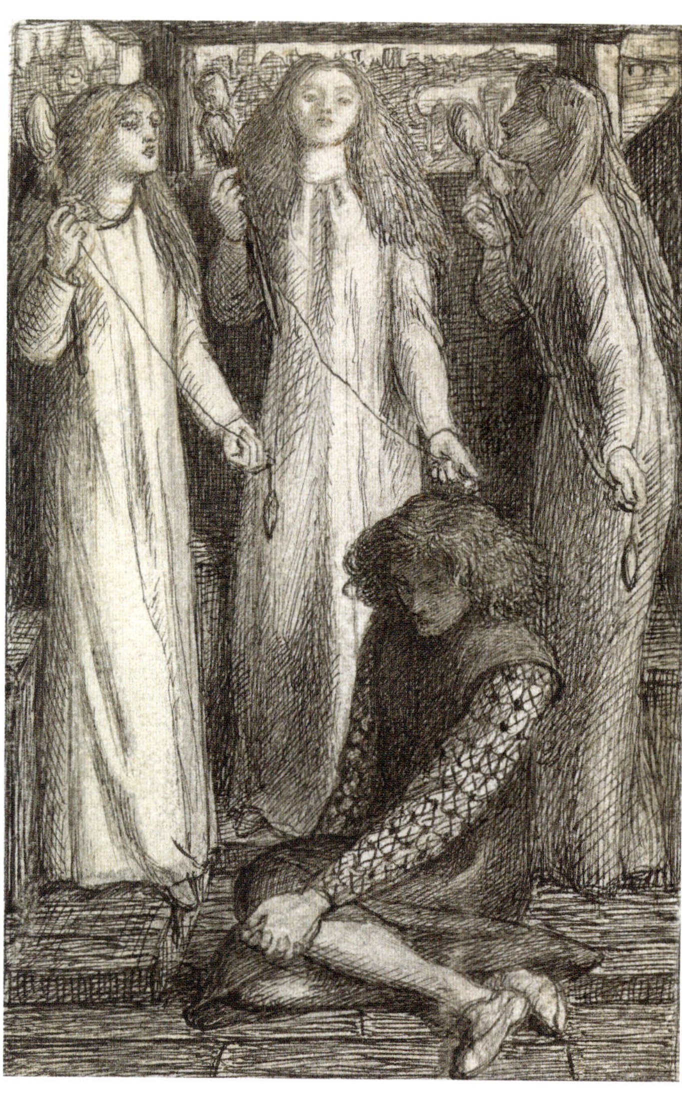

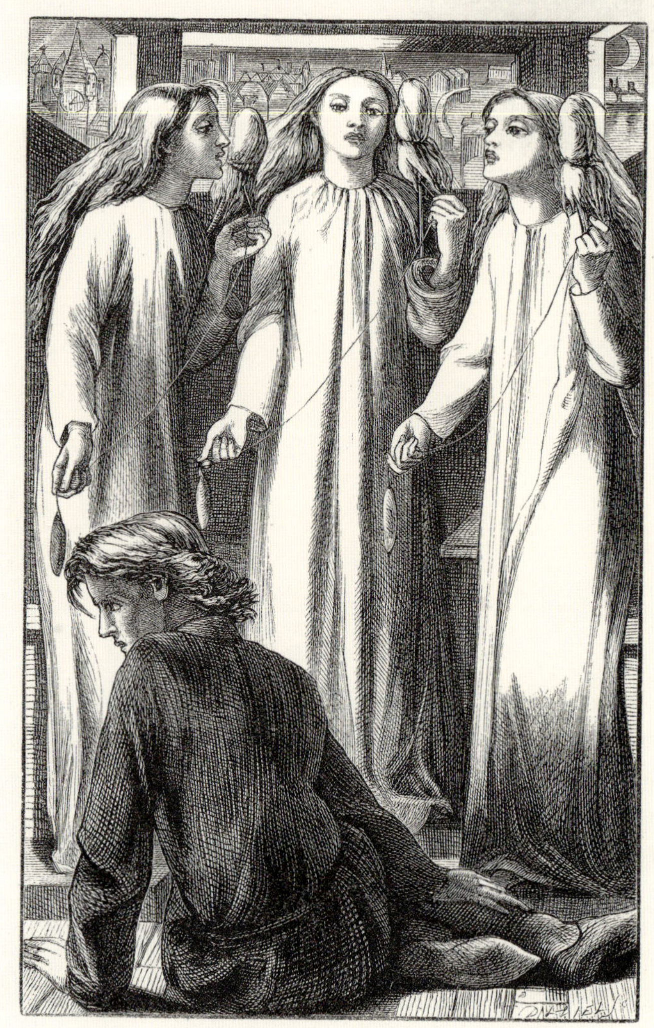

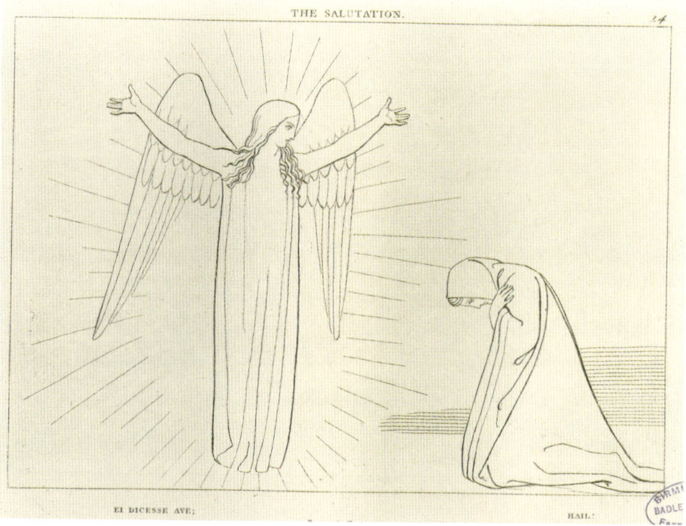

The uncanniness is further enhanced by the repetition of the female figure across the composition, a device that had previously been explored in his drawings for Poe's 'The Raven' [60] and for the Oxford Union mural *How Sir Galahad, Sir Bors and Sir Percival Received the Sanc Greal* (1857, British Museum). It is a powerful motif that suggests otherworldliness. The novelist Forrest Reid (1875–1947), who

201 Dante Gabriel Rossetti, *The Maids of Elfen-mere*, 1854, Yale Center for British Art

202 Dalziel Brothers after Dante Gabriel Rossetti, *The Maids of Elfen-mere*, 1855, Birmingham Museums & Art Gallery

203 John Flaxman, *Purgatory: The Salutation*, 1807, Birmingham Libraries & Archives

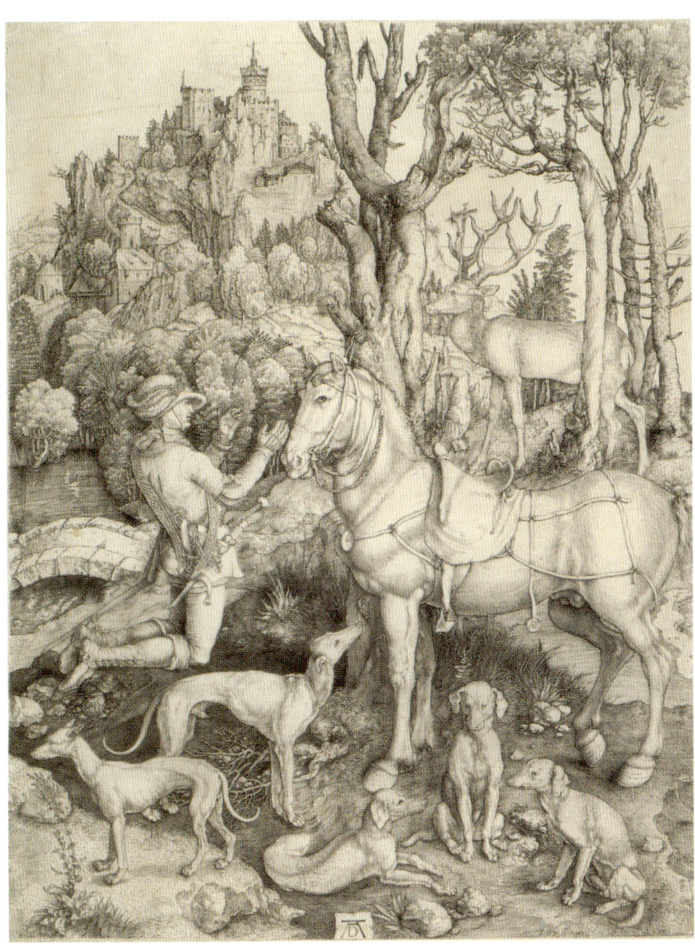

204 Albrecht Dürer, *St Eustace*, c. 1501,
Birmingham Museums & Art Gallery

of the imaginative composition. Burne-Jones describes the engraving as a 'drawing', too: 'the most beautiful drawing for an illustration I have ever seen'.[6] The work was pivotal in the development of Pre-Raphaelitism as well as changing contemporary illustration. Reid's brief mention of the 'little Düreresque town, with its pointed roofs and the fateful clock tower'[7] indicated one of the origins of the graphic compactness of the design in the work of the great German artist and engraver, Dürer, who was the inspiration for several Pre-Raphaelite compositions [204].[8]

Rossetti's Tennyson illustrations

When working on the Allingham volume, Rossetti was in one of his most creative phases, designing his contributions to an illustrated volume of Tennyson's poetry commissioned by the publisher Edward Moxon and embarking upon the Arthurian-themed murals for the newly built Oxford Union. His experiments in visual narrative in these projects were to have the greatest influence of any Pre-Raphaelite production. These ventures were not always well received. The reviews of the illustrated edition of the poems of Tennyson published by Moxon in 1857, for example, set a pattern of response to the individual members of the Pre-Raphaelite Brotherhood: Rossetti the obscure allegorizer, Millais the naturalist and Hunt somewhere in between. The critic and poet Richard Garnett (1835–1906), writing anonymously in the *Saturday Review*, responded to the illustrated volume in a long and interrogative essay. He would have preferred more contributions from Hunt:

> His Lady of Shalott is a fine weird figure of an elfin queen; and the expression of her face is not without power; but the web in which she is caught and from which she is vainly struggling to free herself is not the web of Tennyson's weaving....A painter may expatiate in symbolism as much as he pleases in his

was one of the first twentieth-century writers to express an interest in Pre-Raphaelite illustration, described the design as '*the* drawing…the drawing about which we have heard so much'.[5] It is interesting to see a multiplied, engraved illustration being designated as a 'drawing' so unequivocally, a designation that overlooks Rossetti's despair over the rendering of his original drawing by the engravers, whose skill has been interposed, as it were, upon the artist's delineation

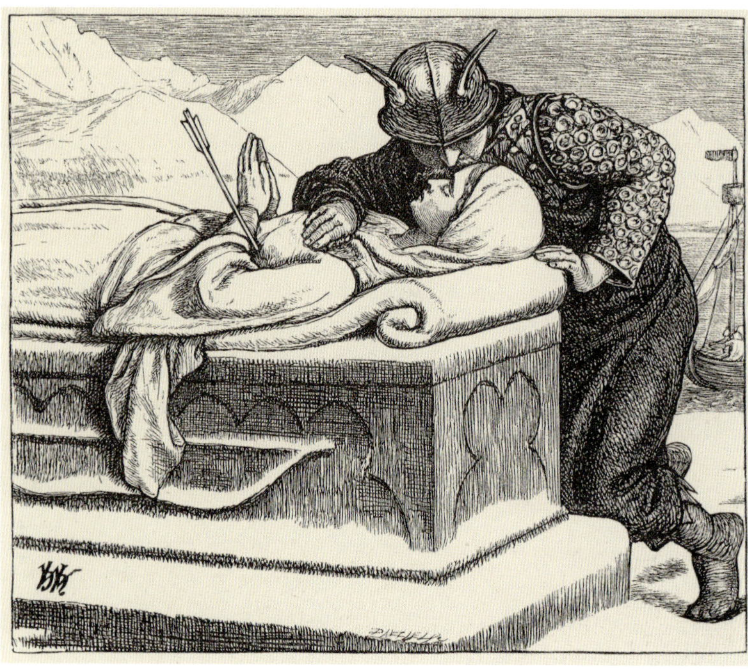

205 Dalziel Brothers after William Holman Hunt, *The Ballad of Oriana*, 1857, Birmingham Museums & Art Gallery

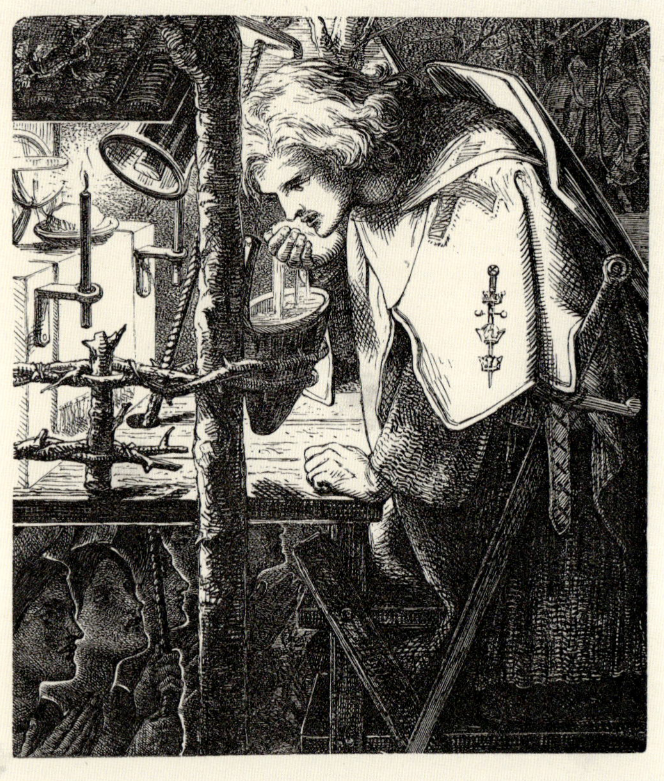

206 W. J. Linton after Dante Gabriel Rossetti, *Sir Galahad*, 1857, Birmingham Museums & Art Gallery

own pictures; but where he charges himself with interpreting the thoughts of the poet, he has no claim to such license….[He] has, moreover, caught the feeling of the 'recollections of the Arabian Nights' very thoroughly.…The noblest of Hunt's drawings is that which stands at the end of Tennyson's most perfect ballad, 'Oriana'. The 'pale, pale face so sweet and meek', of the maiden slain by her lover's own arrow, lies upturned on the bier – serene and pure in death as in life.[9]

Hunt's illustrations are a reminder of the outline style of the earliest phase of Pre-Raphaelitism. It was a mode he was to return to throughout his career.

Garnett found that 'there is always something to be studied and understood' in the works of Hunt and Millais.[10] Hunt's subjects were more diverse, too, representing several types of subject that were to interest him. In comparison with the relative straightforwardness of subjects such as 'Oriana' [205], Hunt's illustration for 'The Lady of Shalott' is

extraordinarily elaborate as well as original. The composition is based on circles and ovals in complex perspective, the female figure cutting across their intersections, her unloosened hair disrupting their organization. The balance between order and chaos is perfectly achieved. The published design represents a stage of development of the idea from the earlier 'stiff' pose (1850) [207] to the later design in which the hair and web are almost narrative characters (1857) [208]. The sense of passion unleashed after long imprisonment is vividly expressed.

Rossetti's designs caused particular puzzlement. There were fundamental objections to the imposition of Rossetti's

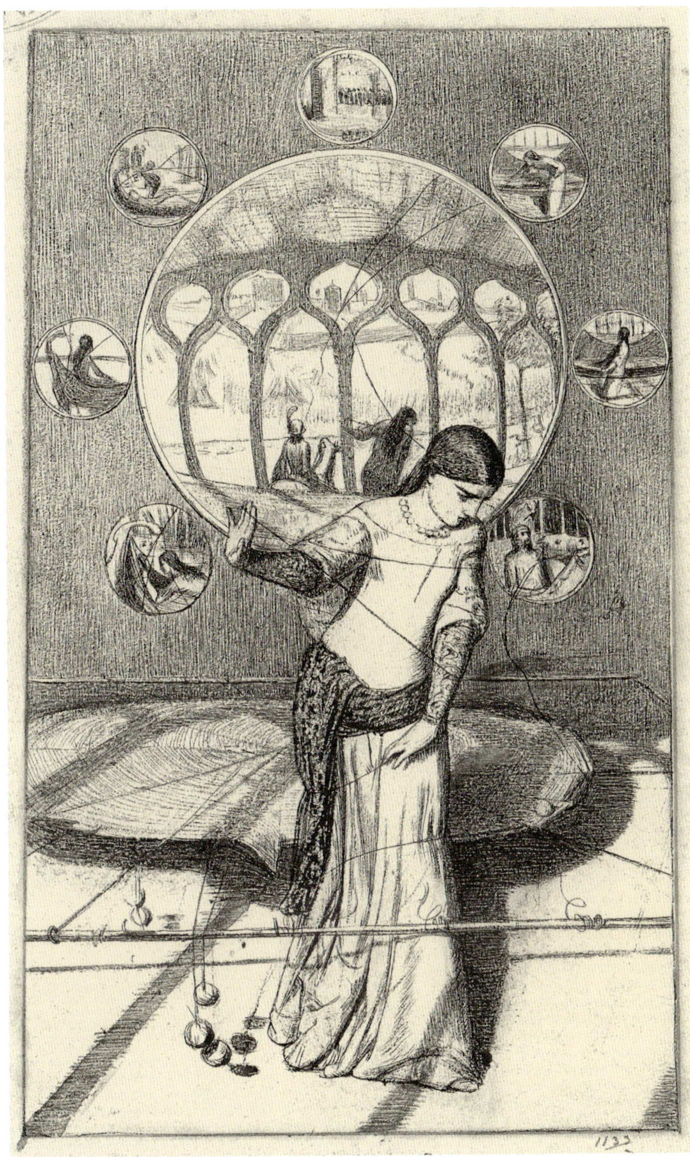

207 William Holman Hunt, *The Lady of Shalott*, 1850,
National Gallery of Victoria, Melbourne

pictorial imagination on Tennyson's poetic one. Garnett
picked up on the conflation between the worldly and
otherwordly that characterizes much of Rossetti's drawing
projects in his early career. Writing of the *Sir Galahad*
illustration [**206**], for example, he commented:

> The knight has alighted by the secret shrine in the
> forest, and is drinking holy water from a cup suspended
> before the taper-lit altar. The bell is swinging lustily; and
> below the table are four figures visible through the dark,
> solemnly pulling the rope. We presume them to be the
> angels; but if they are such, they might have discovered
> some less mechanical method of ringing the bell. There

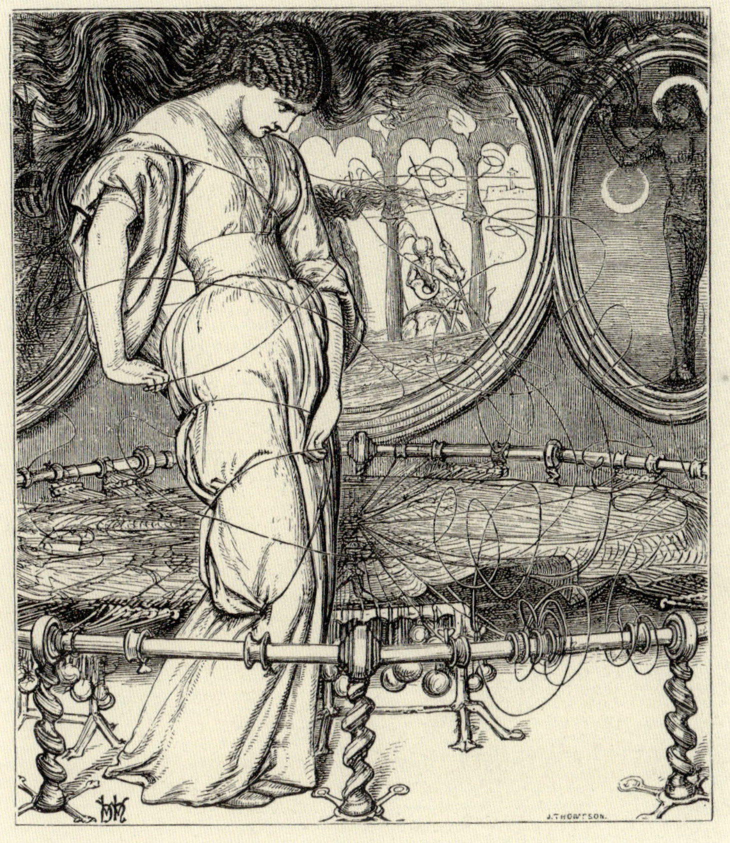

208 J. Thompson after William Holman Hunt, *The Lady of Shalott*,
1857, Birmingham Museums & Art Gallery

> is nothing in the drawing to mark the line between
> what is symbolic and what is real; and the result is an
> impression of absolute unreality.[11]

All of Rossetti's five illustrations are densely detailed,
crowded in composition and yet – even when describing
the ramparts high above a city – curiously airless.
They were designed carefully as graphic images and sit
well alongside type. Rossetti was always an instinctive
designer and idiosyncratic in his tastes, but was often
correct in his design decisions. He had already been
experimental in his use of medieval motifs in his
watercolour works; his densely populated and tightly
designed spaces full of brightly coloured objects and
strong patterns. In the Moxon Tennyson illustrations,
forced to abandon the differentiation between figures
and objects that colour affords, he made the most of
abrupt divisions of space and geometric patterning,
which help distinguish one surface from another but
militate against spatial depth.

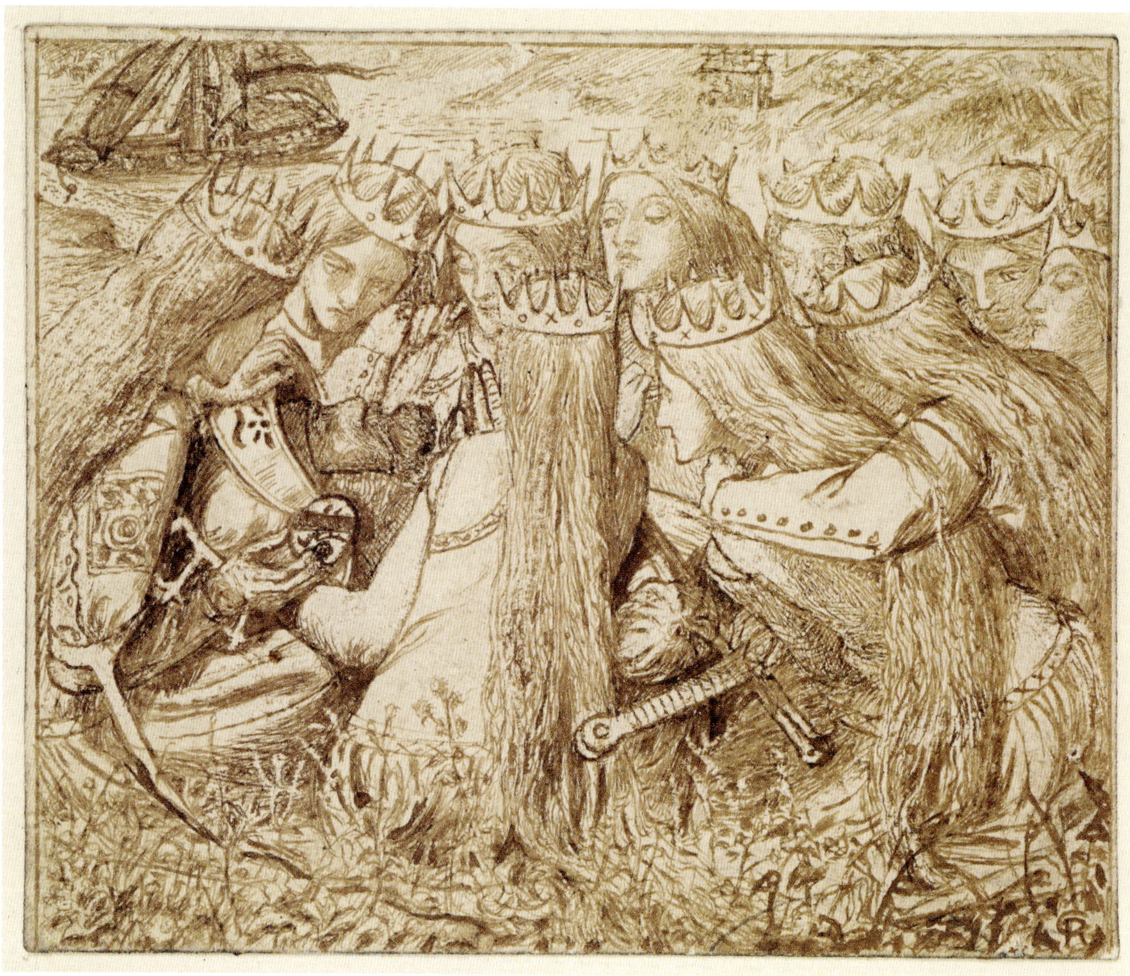

209 Dante Gabriel Rossetti, *King Arthur and the Weeping Queens*, c. 1856–57, Birmingham Museums & Art Gallery

Pattern is used effectively in all five illustrations: in the heraldic motifs embroidered on the robes of the weeping queens [209], for example, or the stars scattered on the cape of the angel who devours the ecstatic St Cecilia [212]. These patterns are particularly 'difficult' because they must fit into the other marks made to have a variety of other functions: to differentiate one surface from another, to indicate light or shadow, or to render the textures of different materials such as hair, fur, wood or metal. Rossetti has set both himself and the engraver a problem in handling these visual and technical challenges. He has set his viewer a visual puzzle, too: as a result of this dense patterning, the viewer is presented with ambiguous spaces that need close and careful examination. The designs for both *King Arthur and the Weeping Queens* [209] and *The Lady of Shalott* [210] are cases in point: where are the bodies of the King or the Lady? In the latter the

problem of 'finding the Lady' is made more acute by the flare of illumination from the candles around the pointed canopy of her bed, which creates a shadow across her face.[12]

Rossetti's illustration for the poem 'Mariana in the South' [211] is a reworking of Dürer's earliest gothic style in its treatment of drapery and the detail of the chamber, although the space is stretched in perspective . In print form, it takes on some of the elegant clarity of Aldus Manutius's illustrated edition of the Renaissance love allegory *Hypnerotomachia Poliphili* (1499, Birmingham Libraries & Archives) by Francesco Colonna, a copy of which was owned by Rossetti. The odd joining of two different engraved sources makes this illustration perhaps one of the strangest. Mariana's eroticized melancholy has an alarming religious expression and shocks by its juxtaposition of sacred and profane, spiritual and sensual: qualities shared with Rossetti's St Cecilia.

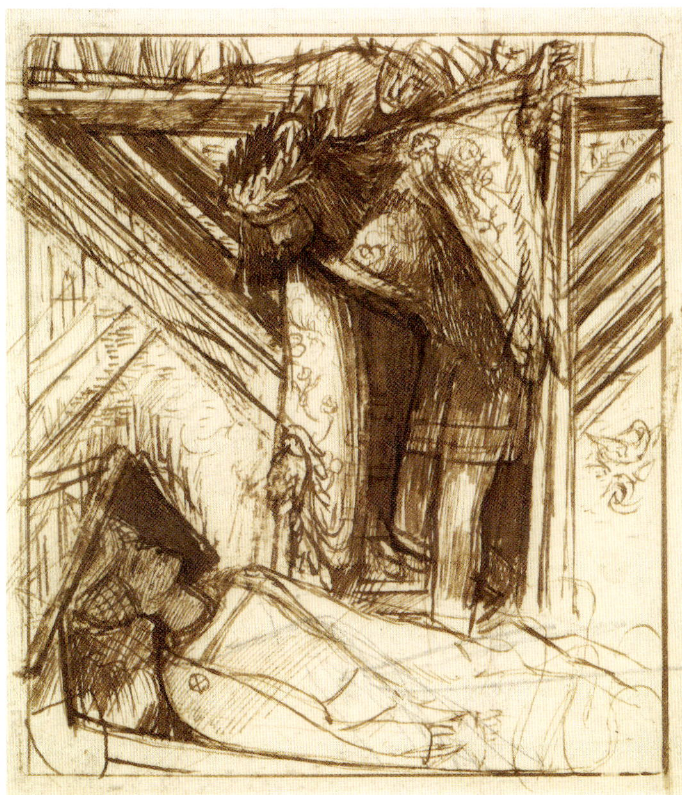

210 Dante Gabriel Rossetti, *Study for 'The Lady of Shalott'*,
c. 1856–57, Birmingham Museums & Art Gallery

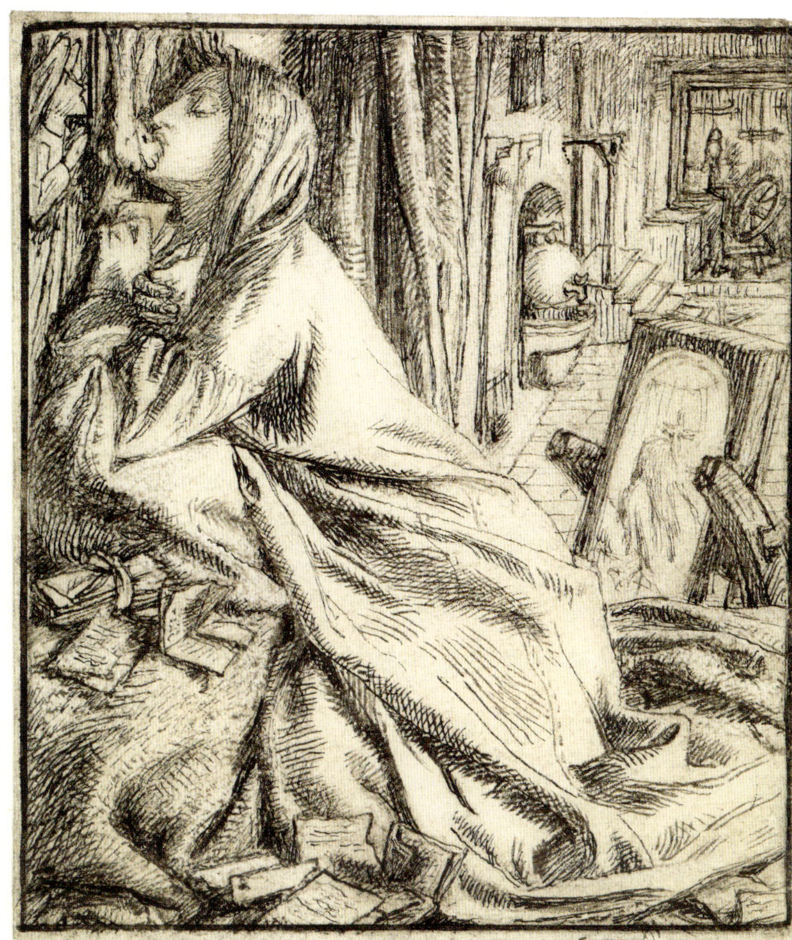

211 Dante Gabriel Rossetti, *Design for 'Mariana in the South'*,
c. 1856–57, Birmingham Museums & Art Gallery

Rossetti's design for the poem 'The Palace of Art',
in which he depicts St Cecilia [212], is a key example
of his method. The drawn space is extensive. It has been
delineated in a manner resembling Dürer in which
the details of distant landscapes – streets, buildings
and sea-going vessels – are outlined in uninflected black
lines. The central group of saint and angel is provocative,
while the banality of the apple-eating soldier, so close
to the viewer that his figure is cropped, acts as a foil to
the visionary nature of the saint's ecstasy. Reid, with a
novelist's sense of narrative, conjectures that the soldier

'might have been placed there to keep guard against
intruders till the lovers' meeting is accomplished'.[13] For
all its obscurity, it was a memorable design; two years
after its publication Garnett remembered this illustration
when reviewing Morris's Arthurian poems in *The Defence
of Guenevere* (1858) for the *Saturday Review*, and recalled
the problematic relationship of Rossetti's illustrations to
the poems:

Mr. Morris's poems bear exactly the same relation to
Tennyson's as Rossetti's illustrations of the laureate to
the latter's own conceptions. We observed in noticing
these designs that they illustrated anything in the
world rather than Tennyson, and have certainly seen no
reason to change our opinion. The more we view them,
the more penetrated we become with their wonderful
beauty (always excepting that remarkable angel in the

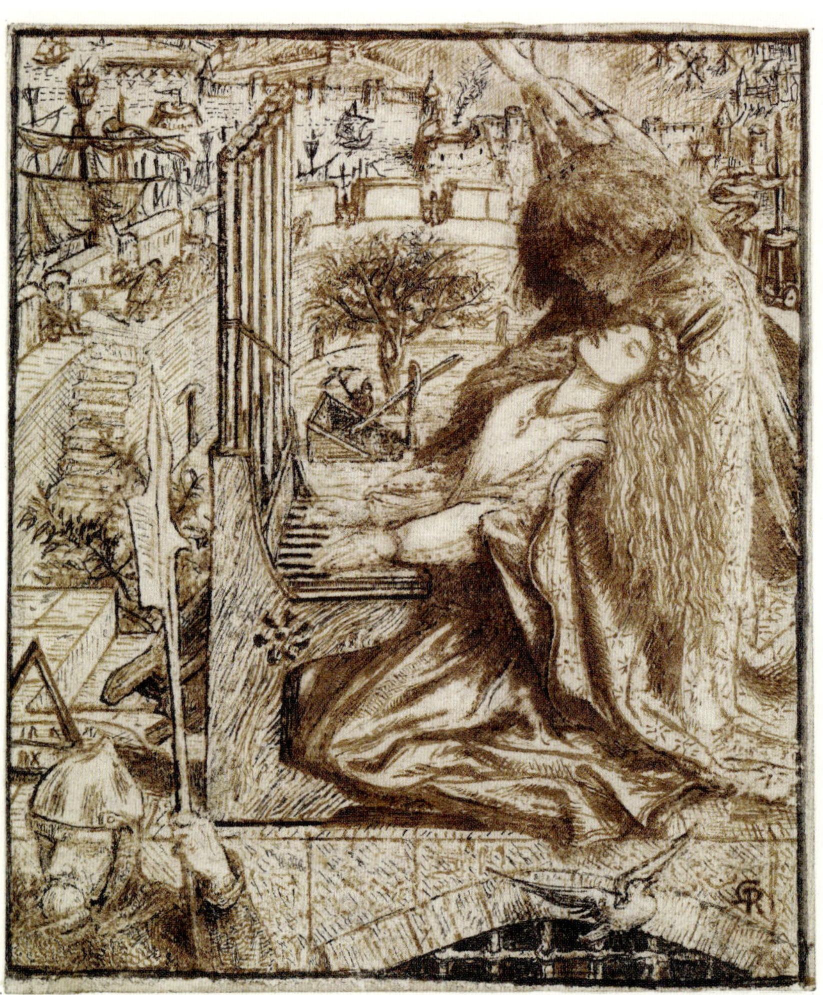

212 Dante Gabriel Rossetti, *Design for 'The Palace of Art' (St Cecilia)*, *c.* 1856–57, Birmingham Museums & Art Gallery

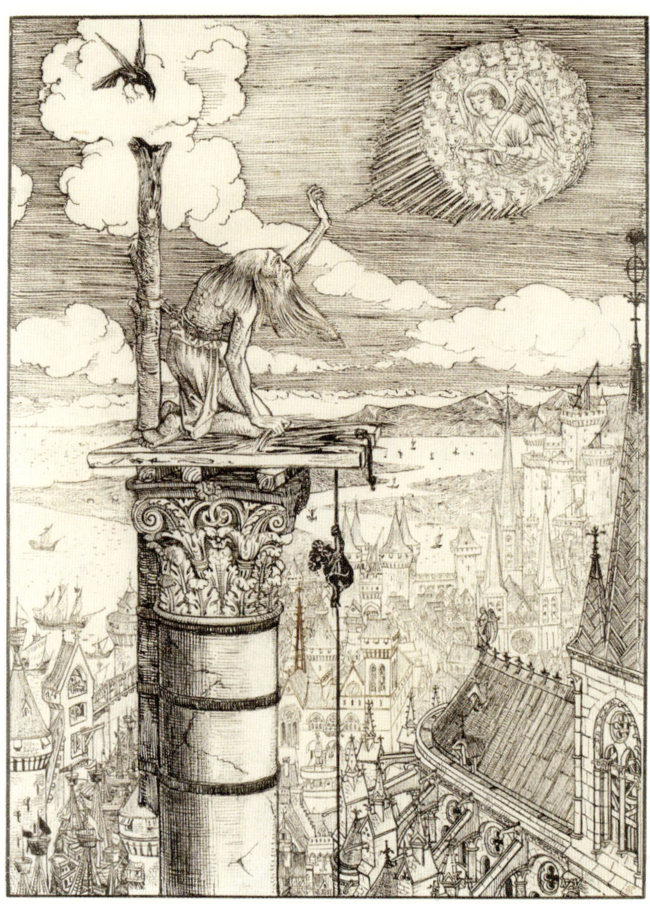

213 William Burges, *St Simeon Stylites*, 1860, Victoria and Albert Museum, London

Robinson Crusoe cap), but also the more impressed with their utter incompatibility with their text.[14] One of Tennyson's poems not tackled by the illustrators was 'St Simeon Stylites', an absence filled by the designer and architect William Burges (1827–81), then close to the Pre-Raphaelite circle. Burges was keen on poetic inspiration

for architecture. He told his students: 'paint the walls of your studios…illustrate your Tennyson' and he adorned his own copy of Tennyson's poems with illustrations and illuminations.[15] His vivid depiction of Simeon Stylites (1860 [**213**]) makes use of the Düreresque style more blatantly than Rossetti. The drawing depicts the emaciated saint kneeling on a Corinthian capital, a panoramic view of a medieval city stretching out below. Out of the clouds (which are based closely on Dürer's *Apocalyse* engravings) the saint is granted a vision before he dies. Beneath him the city gets on with its mundane business. The drawing unites the kind of architectural reconstructions of medieval towns so beloved of Pugin (taken up by Burges himself to illustrate projects in journals such as *The Builder*) with a more pictorial, Pre-Raphaelite mode of imagining the past. Burges developed this agenda, finding as one of his sources of inspiration the sketchbook of medieval draughtsman and architect Villard de Honnecourt.[16]

Millais's illustrations for Moxon and Dalziel

All of the Pre-Raphaelite contributions to the Moxon
Tennyson are striking, especially when set beside the
accomplished but unexceptionable drawings produced
by Mulready, Maclise and other well-established artists
whose work appears in the volume. Although the book
is now recognized as being of the highest importance
for the history of Victorian illustration, it was not a
commercial success, and some historians have expressed
doubts about the justification for its high reputation.
Geoffrey Wakeman, whose interest in illustration was
largely in the technical innovations made during the
nineteenth century, made a fundamental objection to
the Pre-Raphaelite designs: 'they are pictures rather than
illustrations, for the most part printed inside frames that
successfully divorce them from the text'.[17] Wakeman's
distinction is important because it notes a strong
pictorial characteristic of Pre-Raphaelite illustration that
distinguishes it from those of other artists. The earlier
tradition of illustration – seen in artists such as Turner –
was of the vignette, smaller than the plates for Moxon's
Tennyson, and of a shape more amorphous in design, the
picture appearing to develop out of the page. More often
than not a vignette would appear at the head of a poem or
at the end, observing an unwritten etiquette in what might
otherwise be the strained relationship between image and
text. The Pre-Raphaelite drawings for Moxon's Tennyson
disrupt the poetic text: their hard corners – so much a part
of a Pre-Raphaelite aesthetic – elbow aside the poems if we
contemplate their mysteries too long.

Millais's drawing for Allingham's *The Music Master*
has been overlooked in the general reception of the book,
which has tended to concentrate on Rossetti's *The Maids
of Elfen-mere*. To a large extent this was to be the fate of
Millais's work for the Moxon Tennyson, too. In his design
for Tennyson's poem 'St Agnes' Eve' [**214, 215**] Millais was

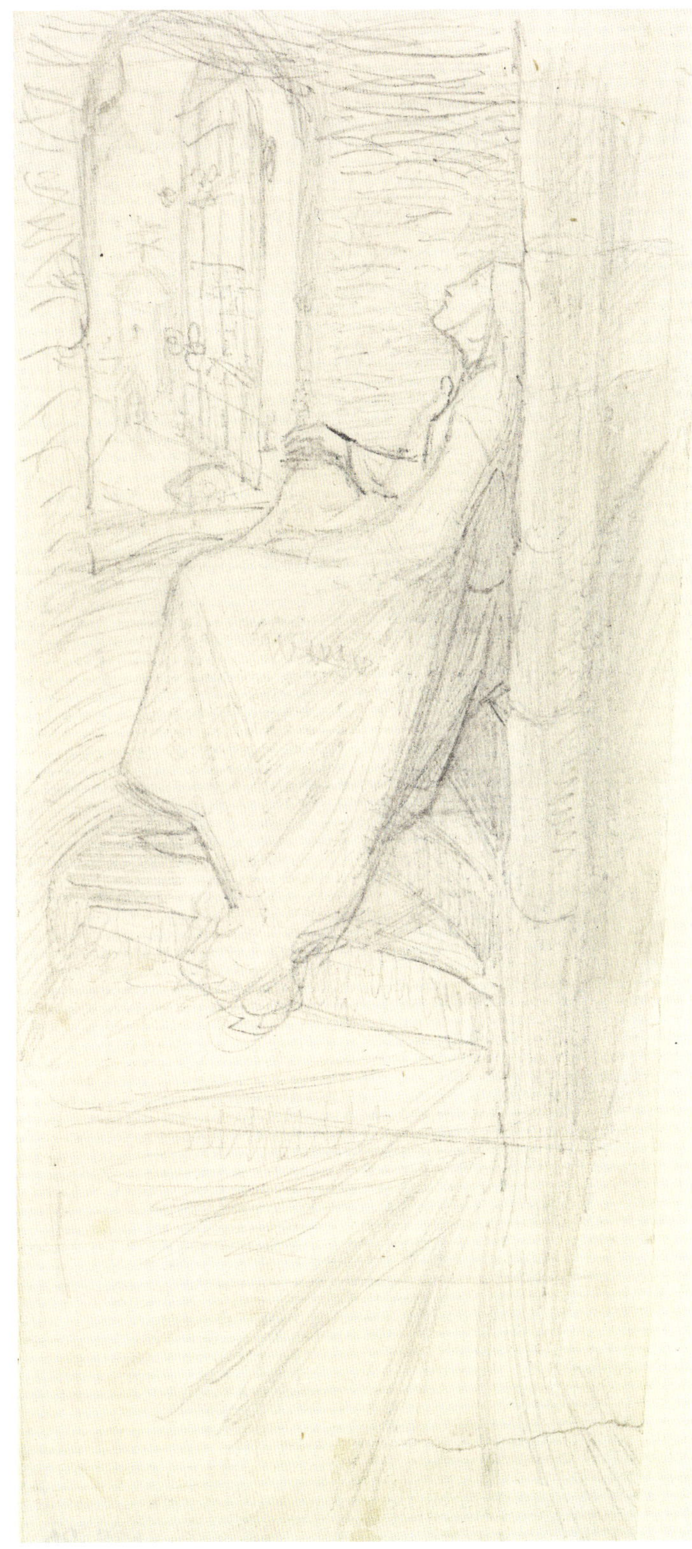

214 John Everett Millais, *Study for 'St Agnes' Eve'*, c. 1855–56,
Birmingham Museums & Art Gallery

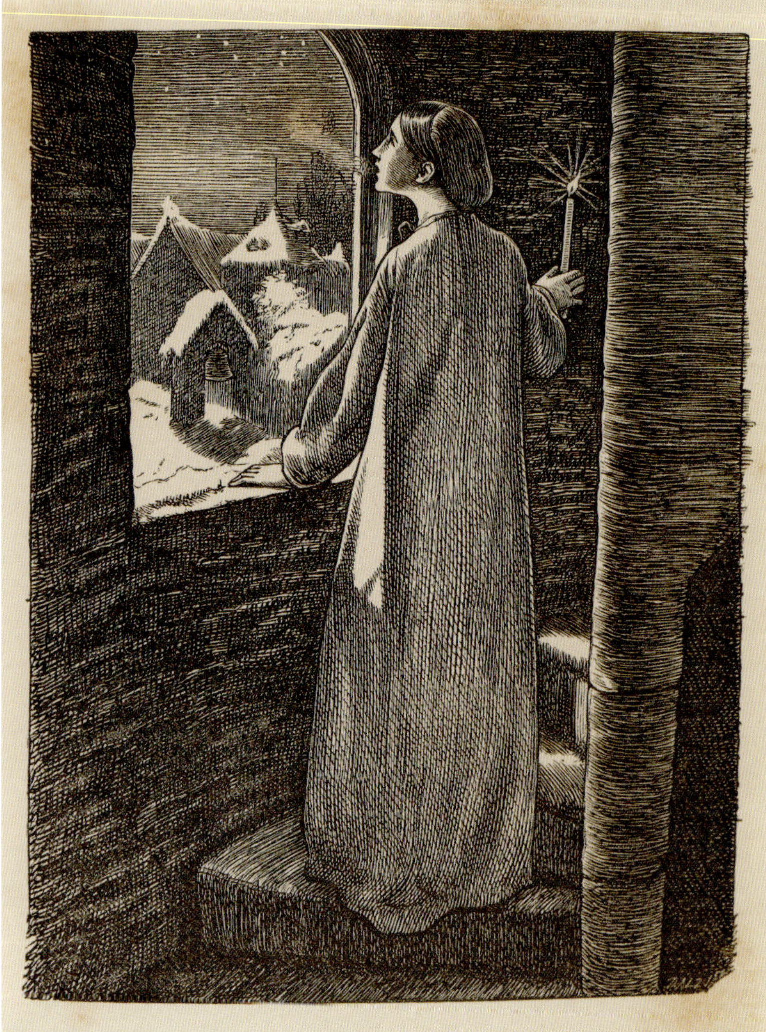

215 Dalziel Brothers after John Everett Millais, *St Agnes' Eve*, 1857, Birmingham Museums & Art Gallery

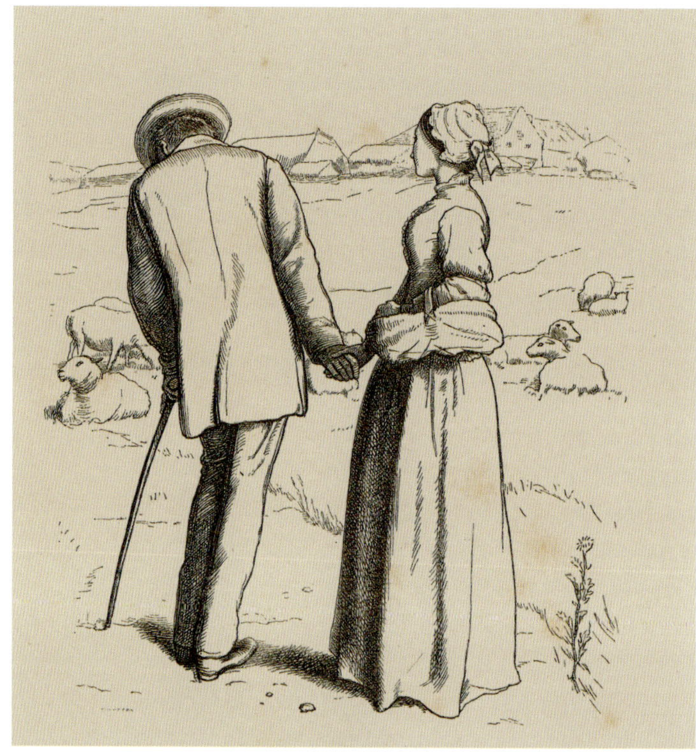

216 J. Thompson after John Everett Millais, *Edward Gray*, 1857, Birmingham Museums & Art Gallery

close to the telling sparseness of his painting *The Return of the Dove to the Ark* (1851, Ashmolean Museum, University of Oxford). The poignancy that is wrought from the depiction of the delicate tracery of breath against the winter's night sky has all of Tennyson's poetic imagery of breath and soul that opens the poem. Garnett was particularly lyrical in his critical response to the drawing:

> Pure and calm as the snow on the roof of the convent – hardly more earthly or substantial than her own breath, as it floats heavenward through the frosty air, where she earnestly yearns to be free to follow it – is the pale slight figure which gazes into the night, through the midnight window of the winding turret-stair. Dress, attitude, and landscape are all of the most perfect and natural simplicity that the intenseness of the expression is attained.[18]

Millais's work on the Moxon Tennyson showed his extraordinary range and the flexibility of his response to his sources. His illustrations demonstrate his abilities to select the most potent moment in a narrative and make emotionally charged drawings using only two figures. A good example is his design for the poem 'Edward Gray' [216, 217], although he was capable of extending the emotional effect into interrelated figures in group compositions such as that for 'Dora' [218].

Garnett described Millais's *Edward Gray* well, stressing the ordinariness of the scene while approving of its larger, more elevated quality:

> the face is, as it should be, turned away from the too curious enquiry of the whole world and not of Emma

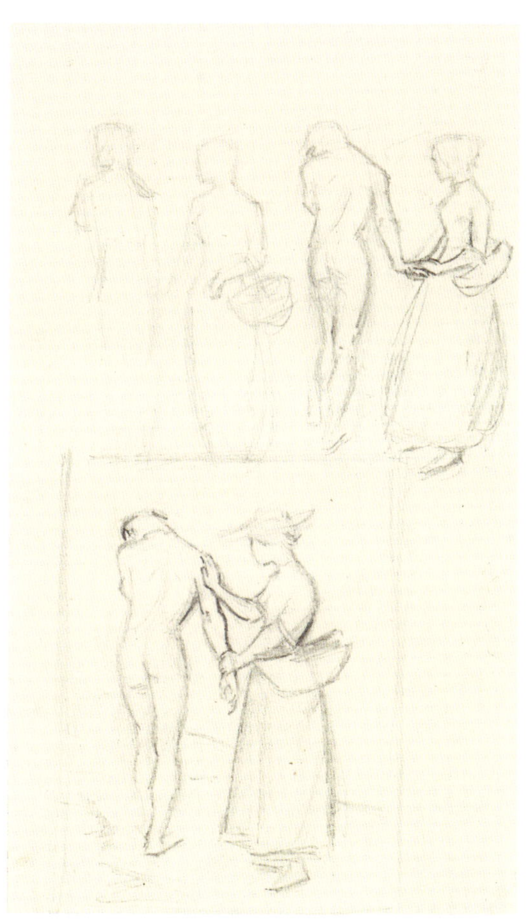

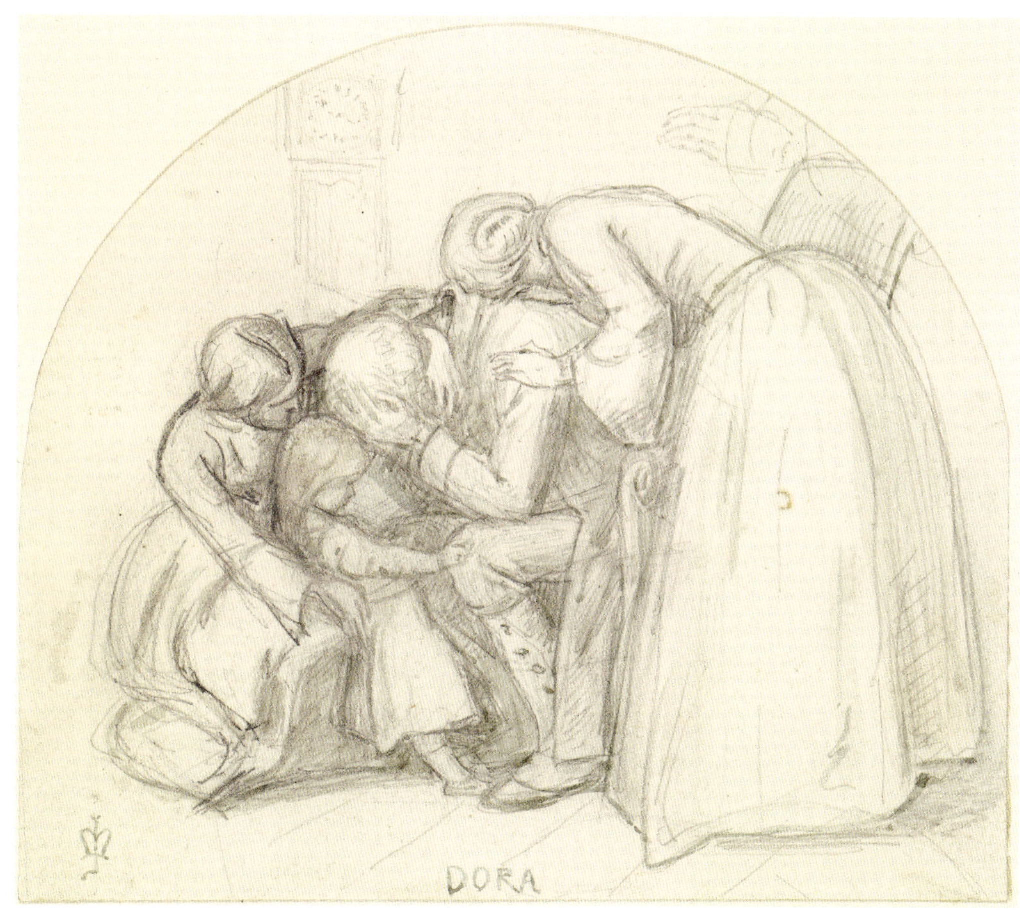

217 John Everett Millais, *Studies for 'Edward Gray'*, c. 1855–56, Birmingham Museums & Art Gallery

218 John Everett Millais, *Study for 'Dora'*, c. 1855–56, Birmingham Museums & Art Gallery

Moreland only. But the grasp of the hand, and the bowed figure of the young man leaning for support on his stick, express the convulsive passion of grief under which he is labouring, as truly and fully as the veiled face by the Pompeian fresco-painter represented the stern sorrow of Agamemnon.[19]

The reader of the poem was presented with a picture that deliberately removed the central image of grief – the face of the male figure – but revealed the depth of emotion in other compositional strategies.

If Rossetti's Moxon designs presented the reader with visual puzzles, the same might be said for Millais's *Parables of Our Lord*, begun in 1857 but not completed until 1863 [**219, 220**]. The delay was due to the demands Millais made on each design, which he conceived of not as 'ordinary illustrations', mere adjuncts to a text, but as 'separate

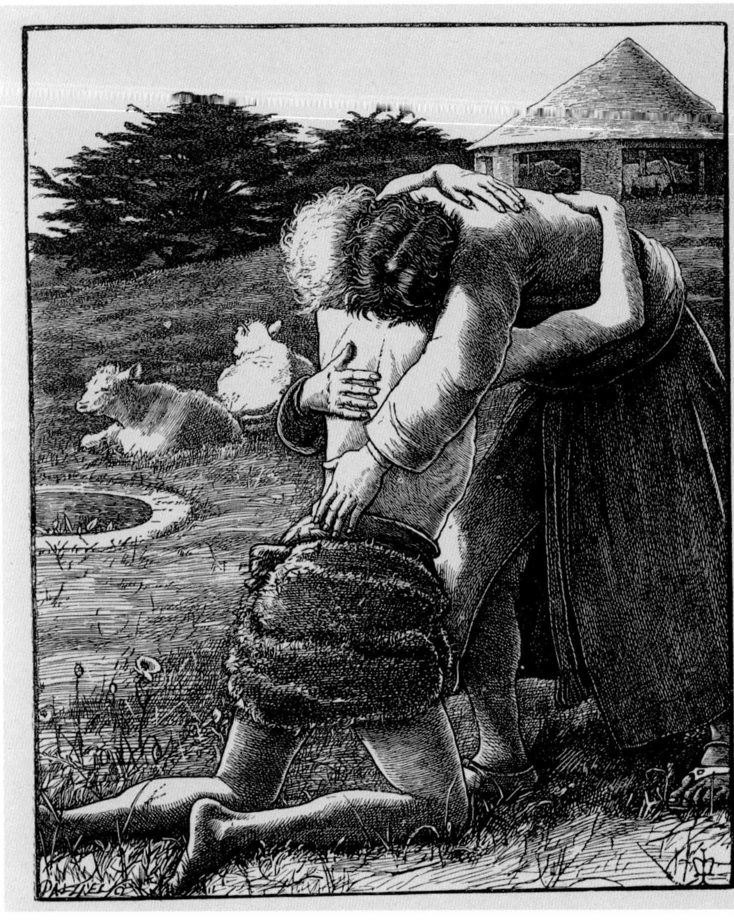

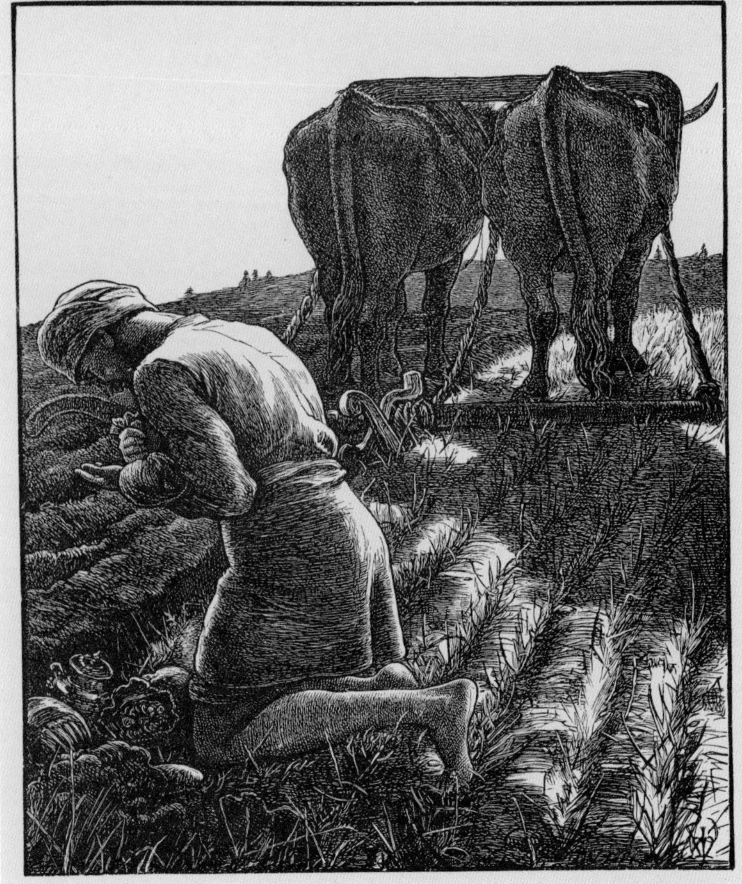

pictures', as he explained to the engravers, the Dalziels:
'I exert myself to the utmost to make them as complete
as possible.'[20] The artist was particularly exercised by the
composition of each image.

Millais's reading of these biblical stories is highly
individual. There is virtually nothing of the striving to place
the scenes in historical settings, no emulation of the Holy land
landscapes that were to preoccupy Hunt and which might
be thought of as a Pre-Raphaelite virtue. It is as if the scenes
were taking place in the present. The viewpoint is off-centre,
often disconcertingly so, making the central narrative point
obscure. The Victoria and Albert Museum has a juvenile
work by Millais illustrating the story of the Prodigal Son,
inscribed with the text: 'Father I have sinned against Heaven
and before thee. St Luke xv.18'. In this drawing demons and
angels fight above the head of the father and son, the demons
departing angrily, chased off by the angels. In the Dalziel
illustration [219] the story is told without any conventional
trappings of biblical painting, a feature of Millais's new-found
narrative approach. The calves sit fat and contented in their
field undisturbed by the emotional embrace of father and
son in the foreground; the cypresses loom on the horizon as
on the edge of an English estate park. Millais contrasts the
sun-filled background with the dark, shadowed figures in the
foreground.

In other plates, for example, *The Foolish Virgins*, the
entire drawing is obscured in an attempt to represent
failing light, rendering the composition difficult to read,
the precise outlines of figures and backgrounds lost. Was
this device part of Millais's concerted attempt to lose the
outline that had been so important to his earliest works?

219 Dalziel Brothers after John Everett Millais, *The Prodigal Son*, 1864,
   Birmingham Museums & Art Gallery
220 Dalziel Brothers after John Everett Millais, *The Hidden Treasure*,
   1864, Birmingham Museums & Art Gallery

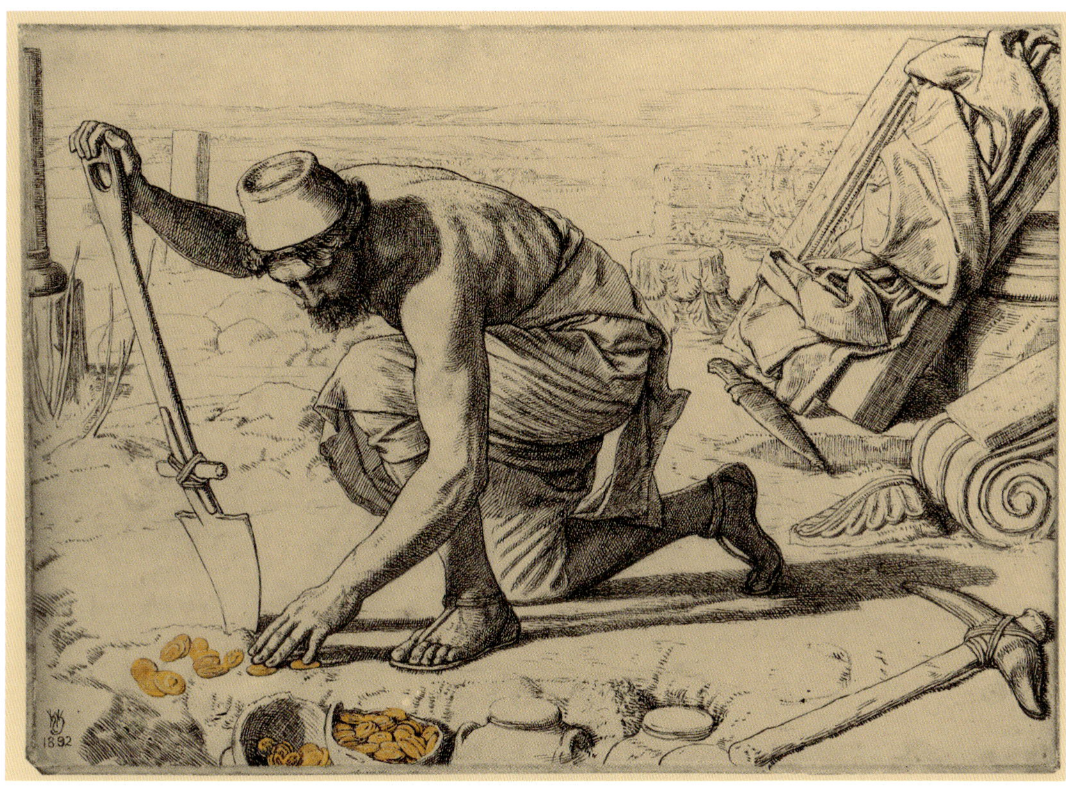

221 William Holman Hunt, *Old Buried Gold*, 1892, Courtauld Gallery, London

When published in book form the illustrations appeared before the text, each with a title printed underneath them. This arrangement suggests that the designs presented alternatives to the text and that they could be read apart from the biblical parables that they illustrated.

Dalziels' illustrated Bible project

Millais's method can be contrasted with that of Hunt. At the end of his career Hunt contributed designs for Edwin Arnold's epic poem on Christ, *The Light of the World* (edition published in 1893). His depiction of the verses for 'The Parables' (in Book IV of Arnold's work), 'The Hid Treasure', illustrates the lines 'Did some man find/Hid shekels in a field, – old buried gold/ Forgot of mouldering owner in the tomb –' [221]. It is a scene full of sunlight, the act of discovery brightly lit rather than shrouded in darkness; for Hunt, shadow only heightens the sense of illumination, it is not used to create mystery.[21] The sense of historical time and place is acute, too, from the implements that lie on the sand to the hat and sandals of the male figure. Perhaps the carved capital and the acanthus leaf suggest that some historical time has passed and that the finding of the precious hoard is possible now, in the present, as salvation is. Where Millais strove for a kind of revelatory obscurity in his description of the text, Hunt strove for clarity in order that the symbol could be read in full.

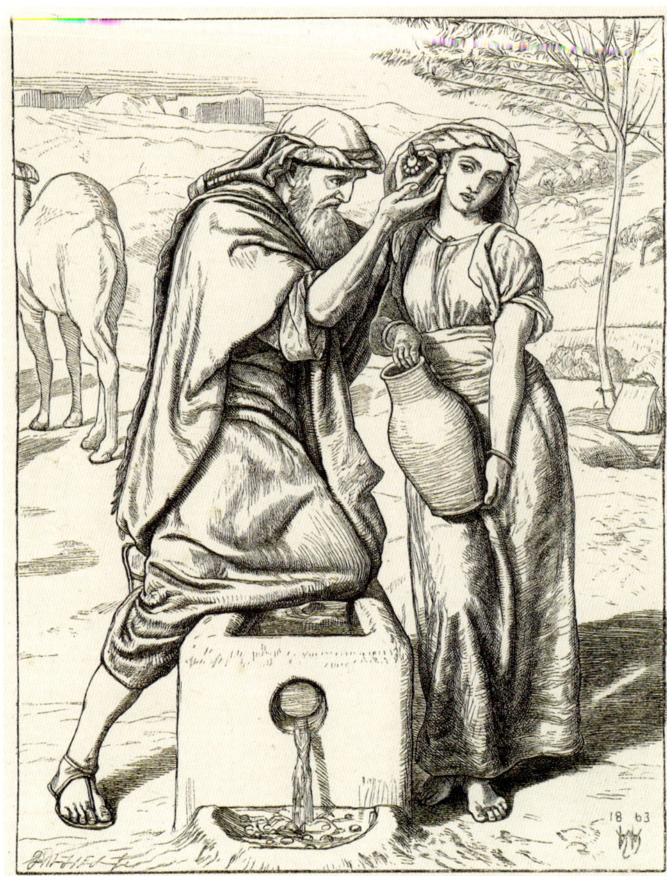

222 Dalziel Brothers after William Holman Hunt, *Eliezer and Rebekah at the Well*, 1863, published 1881, Birmingham Museums & Art Gallery

Clarity of line and composition continued to be a feature of his illustration work. Using the modified outline style he produced numerous fine illustrations including one, *Eliezer and Rebekah at the Well* (designed 1863) [**222**] for the Dalziel illustrated Bible. Hunt found the dramatic importance of a simple act – the gift of an earring to Rebekah, an episode in the story of Isaac. He contrasted the absorbed concentration of the man with the expression of modesty and pleasure of the young woman.[22]

The illustrated Bible project was much delayed and only a fragment of the planned work appeared first as *Dalziels' Bible Gallery* in 1881, followed by an expanded version, *Art Pictures from the Old Testament and Our Lord's Parables* in 1894 (incorporating Millais's *Parables* as well as several plates not published in the earlier volume). Both titles stress the 'art' aspect of the project, and, indeed, the abandonment of the full biblical text, while initially unplanned, subsequently became the symbol of the triumph of a pictorialist sensibility over textual meaning, a sign of contemporary challenges to the orthodoxy of religious belief and practice of the time. The status of the

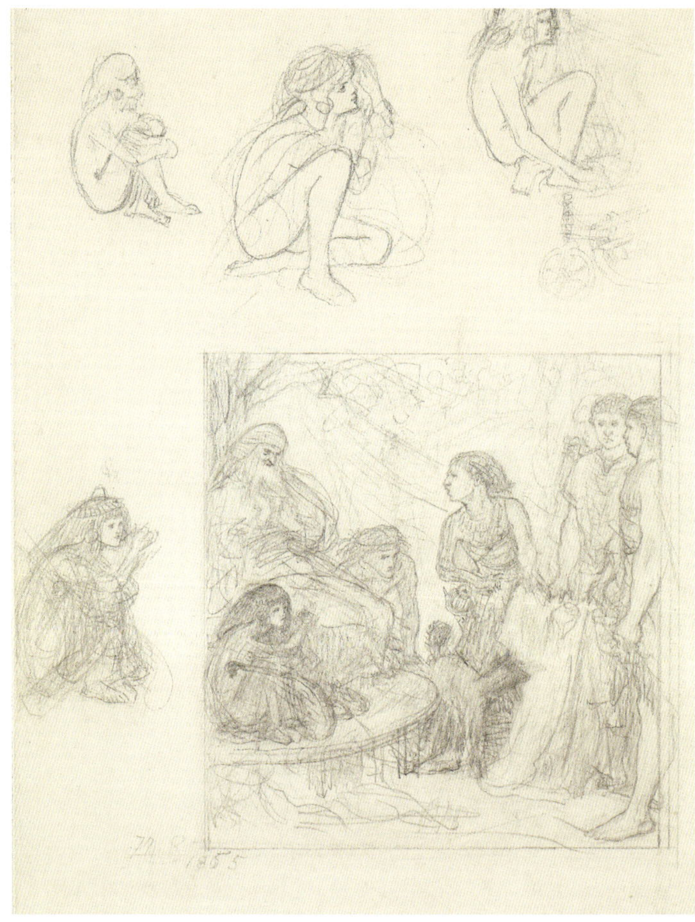

223 Ford Madox Brown, *Sheet of Studies for 'Joseph's Coat'*, 1865, Birmingham Museums & Art Gallery

illustrations is particularly interesting if we recall the relative paucity of religious painting at the Royal Academy, Hunt's works being the exception. Ford Madox Brown made three striking designs for the book: *Joseph's Coat* [**223, 224**], *The Death of Eglon* [**225**] and *Elijah and the Widow's Son*, all of which were subsequently translated into paintings. Brown's strenuous use of gesture, grimace, pattern and historical detail bring the viewer close to the emotional centre of the narratives. Burne-Jones, Poynter and Solomon made designs for the project, and those by Leighton are particularly strong and innovative.

Solomon was credited with by far the greatest number of images for the book; his best illustrations show as much a debt to Hunt and Millais as his earlier works did to Rossetti. For example, *Ruth, Naomi and the Child Obed* (1860) [**226**], while having some of the same atmosphere as Rossetti's *The Girlhood of Mary Virgin*, owes much to Millais's two-figure compositions, such as *The Black Brunswicker* [**161, 162**], in which deep personal and emotional dramas are worked out. In Solomon's drawing the grouping suggests mixed emotions and loyalties. Ruth's feelings for her mother-in-law (the mother of her former husband), and for her present husband and child, are clearly represented on her face, while Naomi is similarly moved; their closeness is more complex than first seems the case, and Solomon deals with the cross-currents of feeling with tenderness. The drawing predated the Dalziel commission and is slightly different from the engraved illustration.

Similarly, Solomon's original drawing and painting for *Hosannah!* were completed before the illustration on the same subject [**227**]. The focus is almost entirely on a young harpist in the temple, whose bowed head and closed eyes speak eloquently of his devotion. The viewer must scrutinize the head and face as the central subject, taking in the fanciful yet convincing historical accessories, the musical instrument and the costume, as part of the aesthetic assembly. There is virtually no 'subject', and *Hosannah!* is significant because it does not illustrate any particular passage in the Old Testament but is a more general evocation of religious devotion.

Burne-Jones's single contribution to the Dalziel Bible, the dark and sinister drawing for the parable of the boiling pot (Ezekiel 24:1–6) [**228**], is quite different in character to Solomon's. Although he disowned his first appearance in print – his frontispiece and title page for Archibald

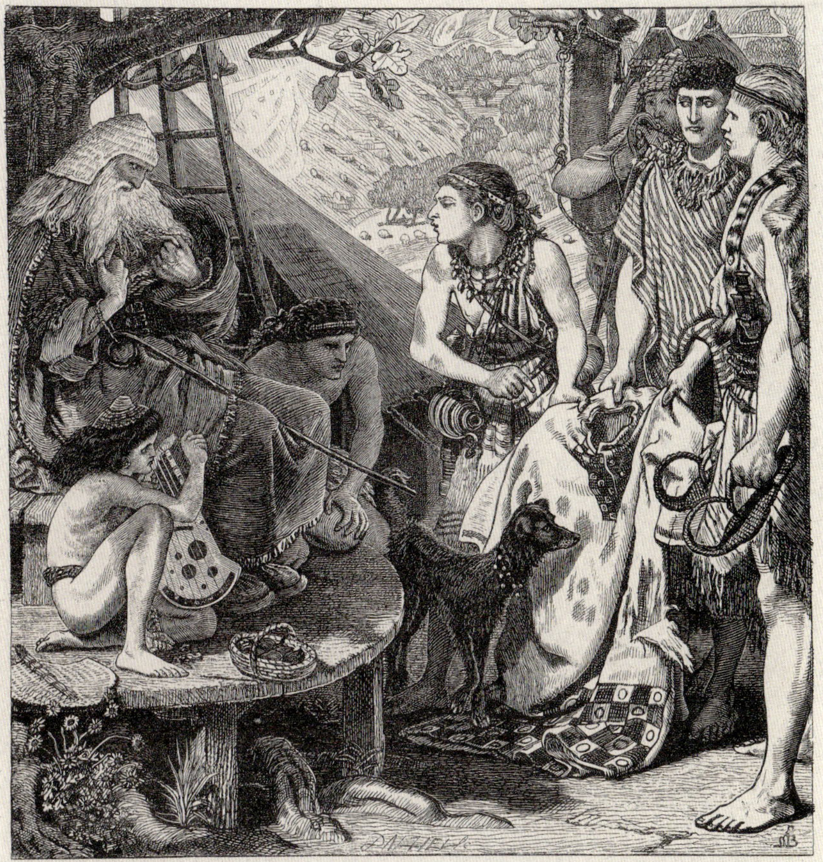

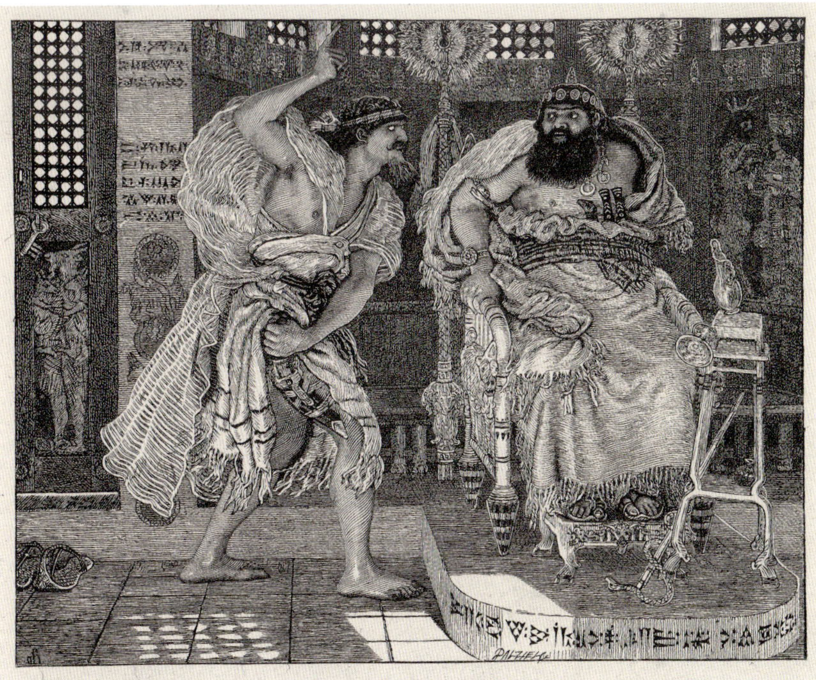

224 Dalziel Brothers after Ford Madox Brown, *Joseph's Coat*, published 1881, Birmingham Museums & Art Gallery

225 Dalziel Brothers after Ford Madox Brown, *The Death of Eglon*, published 1881, Birmingham Museums & Art Gallery

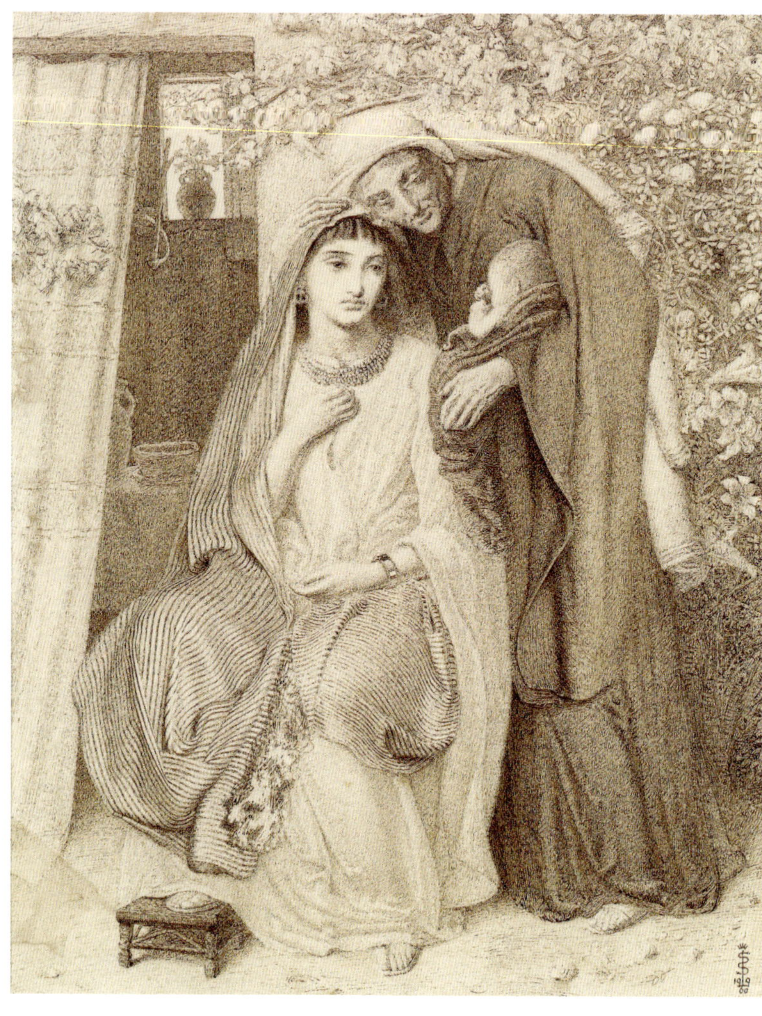

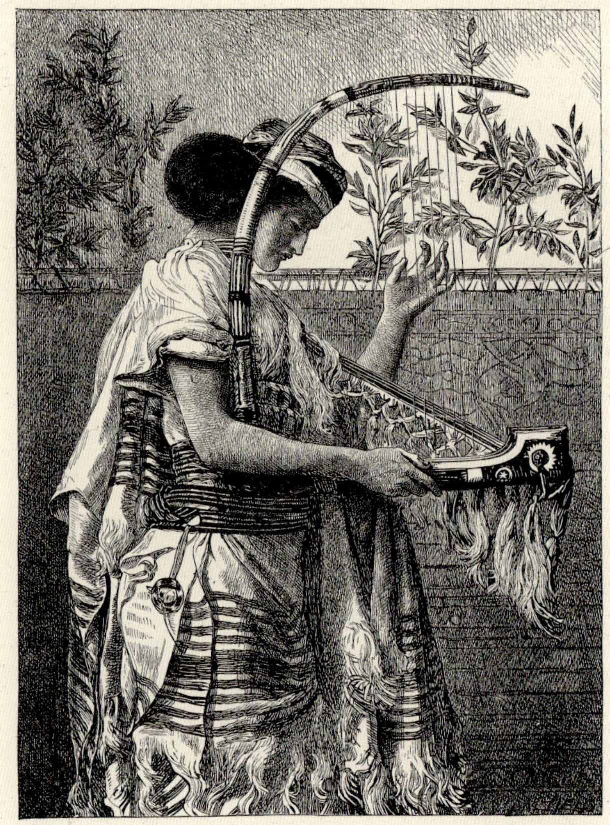

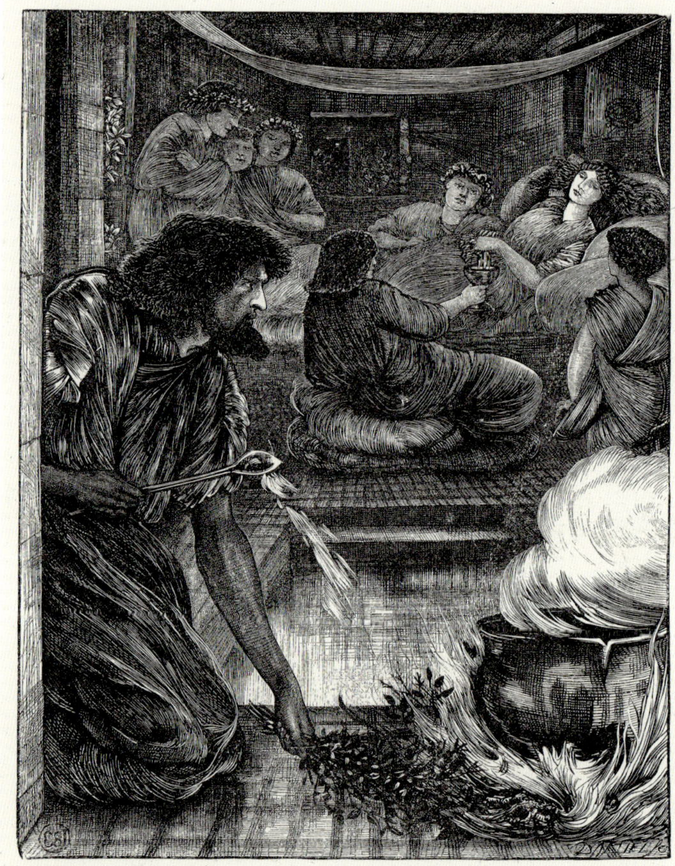

226 Simeon Solomon, *Ruth, Naomi and the Child Obed*, 1860, Birmingham Museums & Art Gallery

227 Dalziel Brothers after Simeon Solomon, *Hosannah!*, published 1881, Birmingham Museums & Art Gallery

228 Dalziel Brothers after Edward Burne-Jones, *Ezekiel and the Pot*, published 1881

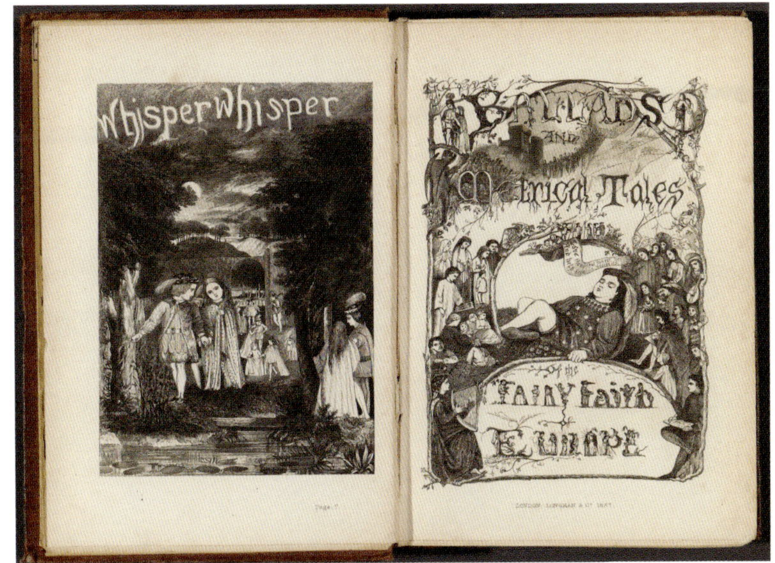

MacLaren's book of ballads and tales *The Fairy Family* (1857) [**229**] – the designs are nonetheless interesting in the history of illustration of the time. The contrast between the two projects is striking, however, *The Fairy Family* looking old-fashioned alongside the compositional intensity of *Ezekiel and the Boiling Pot*. Burne-Jones's skills as a narrator of stories was allied to his sense of surface design and can be seen in his work in other fields, such as decorated furniture and stained glass. It was in the rarefied pages of the private-press book – the Kelmscott Chaucer of 1895, for example – rather than in the haphazard pages of the commercial press that he demonstrated his skill as a decorator of the page.

Sandys and 'the tradition of Dürer'

Frederick Sandys also produced one design for the Dalziel Bible, *Jacob Hears the Voice of the Lord*, to illustrate the passage from Genesis 35:1. The design has tantalizing similarities to Hunt's much later drawing for *The Light of the World* [**154**] in combining a straightforward life drawing with an imaginative, poetic reading of the text. Here, the voice of God is represented by a light so blinding that Jacob is forced to shield himself from it. It was for his periodical illustrations, however, that Sandys became celebrated. The writer and printmaker Joseph Pennell (1857–1926) thought him 'in imaginative power, the greatest of all… in technique he is the legitimate successor of Dürer, in popularity he is a hopeless failure'. Later, in the same article, Pennell observed that

> In every one [of Sandys's designs] is seen the hand of the man able to carry on the tradition of Dürer, and yet bring it into line with modern methods.…All the spirit of early German art breathes through his drawings.[23]

Sometimes Sandys's references to Dürer are straightforward – the pose of his design for *If* (1866) [**230**], for example, which echoes the *Melencolia* of Dürer. At other times it is the feeling of the macabre, such as in the composition for

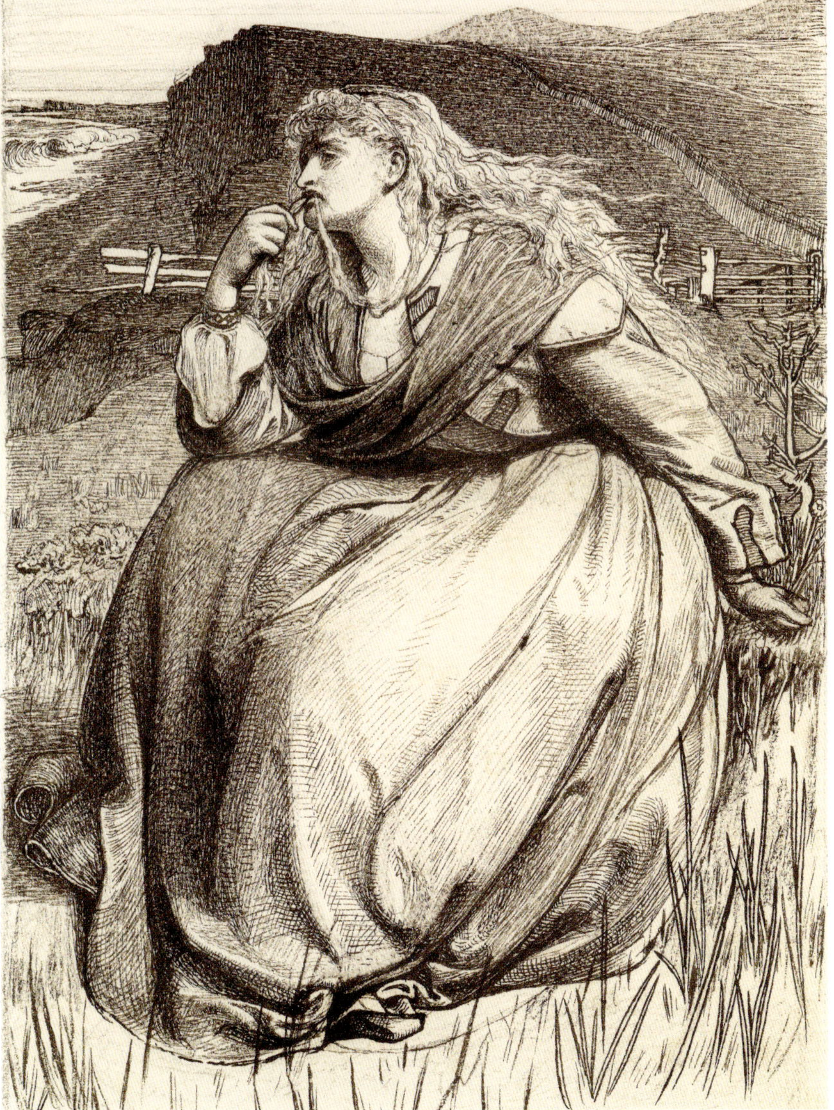

229 Edward Burne-Jones, *Title Page and Frontispiece to 'The Fairy Family'*, 1857, Birmingham Museums & Art Gallery

230 Frederick Sandys, *Design for 'If'*, 1866, Birmingham Museums & Art Gallery

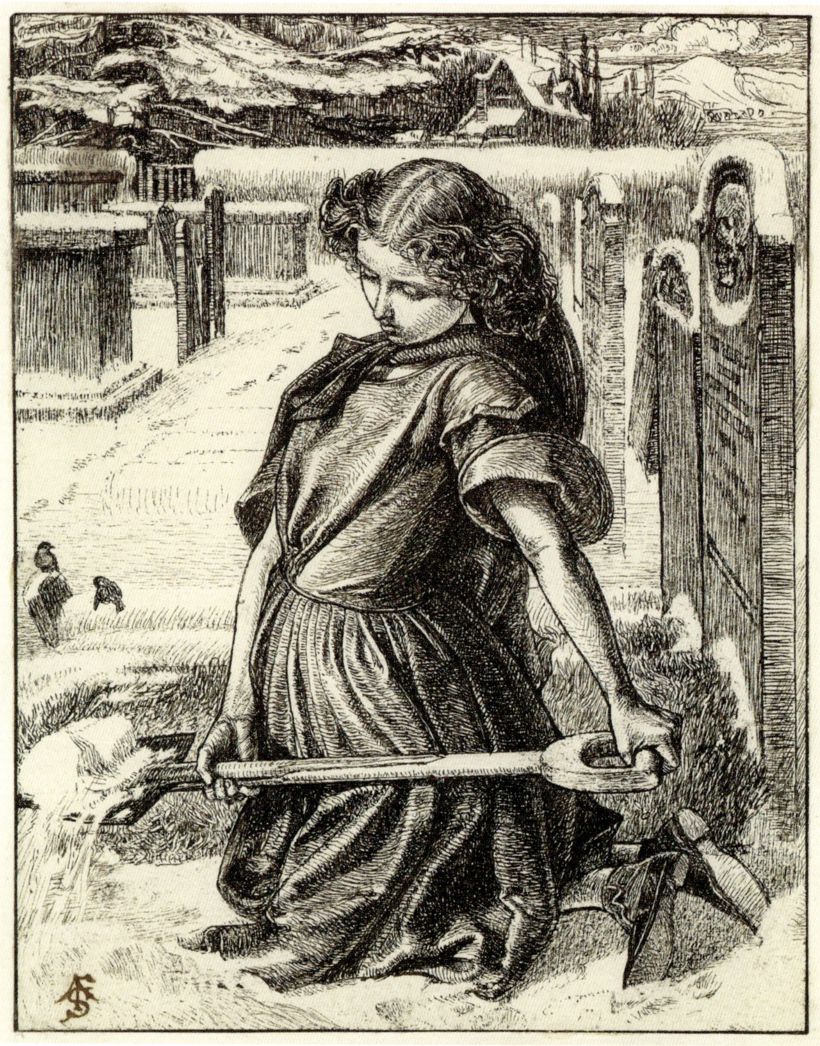

231 Frederick Sandys, *Design for 'The Little Mourner'*, 1862, Birmingham Museums & Art Gallery

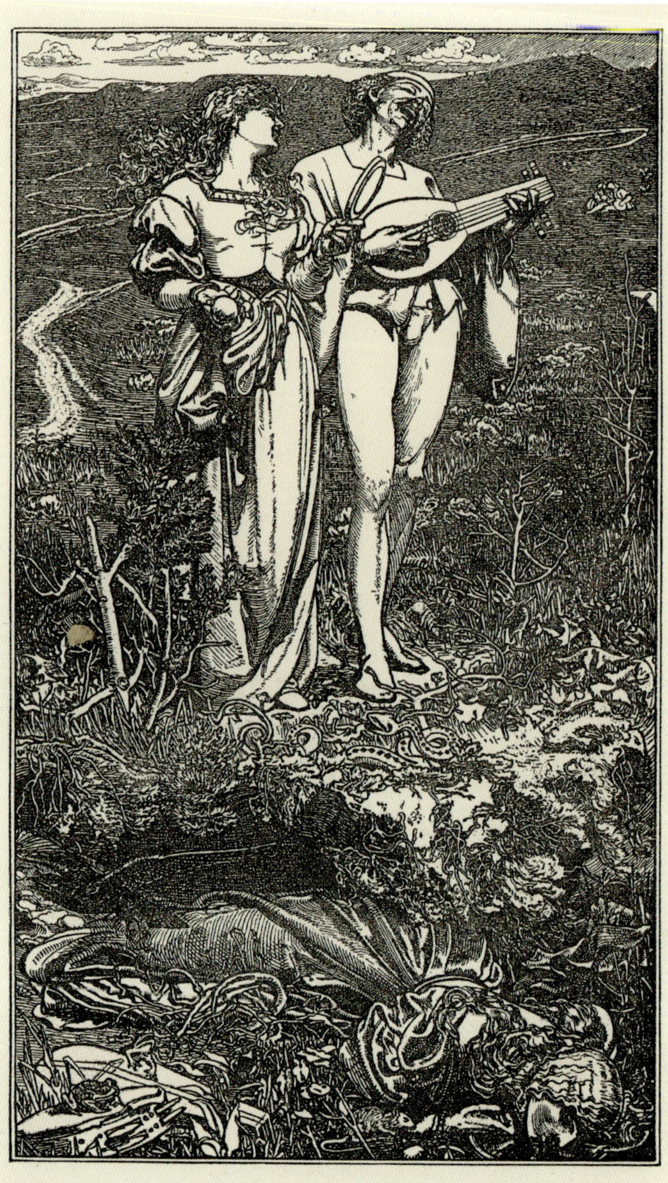

232 Frederick Sandys, *Amor Mundi*, 1865, published in the *Shilling Magazine*, Birmingham Libraries and Archives

The Little Mourner (1862) [231], that suggests the influence of Dürer and his contemporaries. Sometimes it is the more general stylistic features of Dürer's drawings that Sandys makes use of – the foreground undergrowth and the emphasis on folded fabric, for example, in *Amor Mundi* (1865) [232], designed to illustrate a poem by Christina Rossetti.

The impressive skill of Sandys's drawings for a wide variety of themes – from scenes of ancient history such as *Cleopatra Dissolving the Pearl* (1862) [233] to Düreresque subjects such as *The Old Chartist* [102] led to an almost cultish appreciation of his work, even if – as Pennell noted – his drawings were not popular when first published. Gleeson White's *English Illustration: The Sixties: 1855–70*, first published in 1897, had a full-page Swan Electric photogravure of Sandys's *Morgan Le Fay* (1863–64, Birmingham Museums & Art Gallery) as frontispiece, as a kind of paragon of graphic excellence. Elsewhere in his survey of illustration in the 1860s, White was highly complimentary about Sandys's work, observing of his impact on other artists:

in the hearts of artists. The general public may have forgotten its early volumes, but at no time since they were published have painters and pen-draughtsmen failed to prize them. During the 'seventies', no less than in the 'eighties' or 'nineties', men cut out the pages and kept them in their portfolios; so that today, in buying volumes of the magazine, a wise person is careful to see that the 'Sandys' are all there before completing the purchase.[24]

Illustration offered ways for the Pre-Raphaelites to make pictures for larger audiences. Despite the intervention of a commercial engraver, each artist developed new ways of presenting pictorial ideas and exploring new methods of composing pictures to allow them maximum graphic impact. All the members of the Brotherhood and many of their associates were involved in the art of illustration, making it one of the most concentrated and successful attacks on the status quo of British visual culture. After the 1860s the Pre-Raphaelite effect on illustration became so widespread that it was somewhat dissipated in power. It was only with the advent of the 'book beautiful', the founding of the Kelmscott Press and other small presses such as the Vale Press, and the experimental illustration of Charles Ricketts (1866–1931) and Laurence Housman, that the influence of Pre-Raphaelite illustration regained its initial impact; with Aubrey Beardsley (1872–98) it gained a new notoriety in the 1890s.

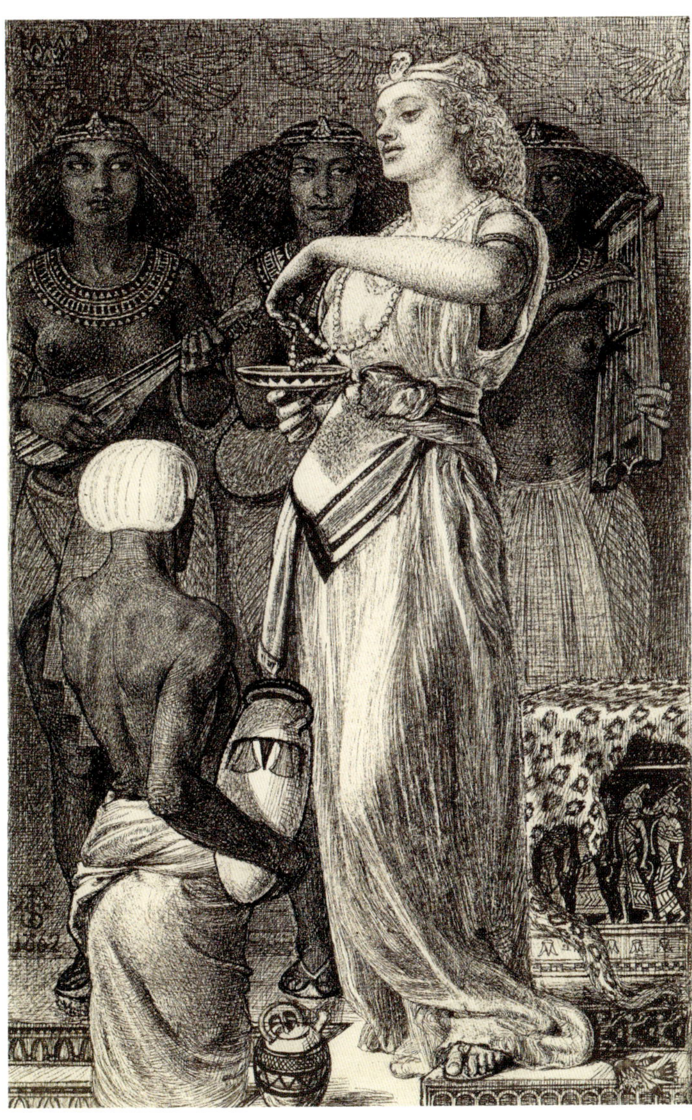

233 Frederick Sandys, *Design for 'Cleopatra Dissolving the Pearl'*, 1862, Birmingham Museums & Art Gallery

It is quite possible, although only thirteen of the thirty or so of illustrations by Frederick Sandys appeared in *Once a Week*, that these thirteen have been the most potent factor in giving the magazine its peculiar place

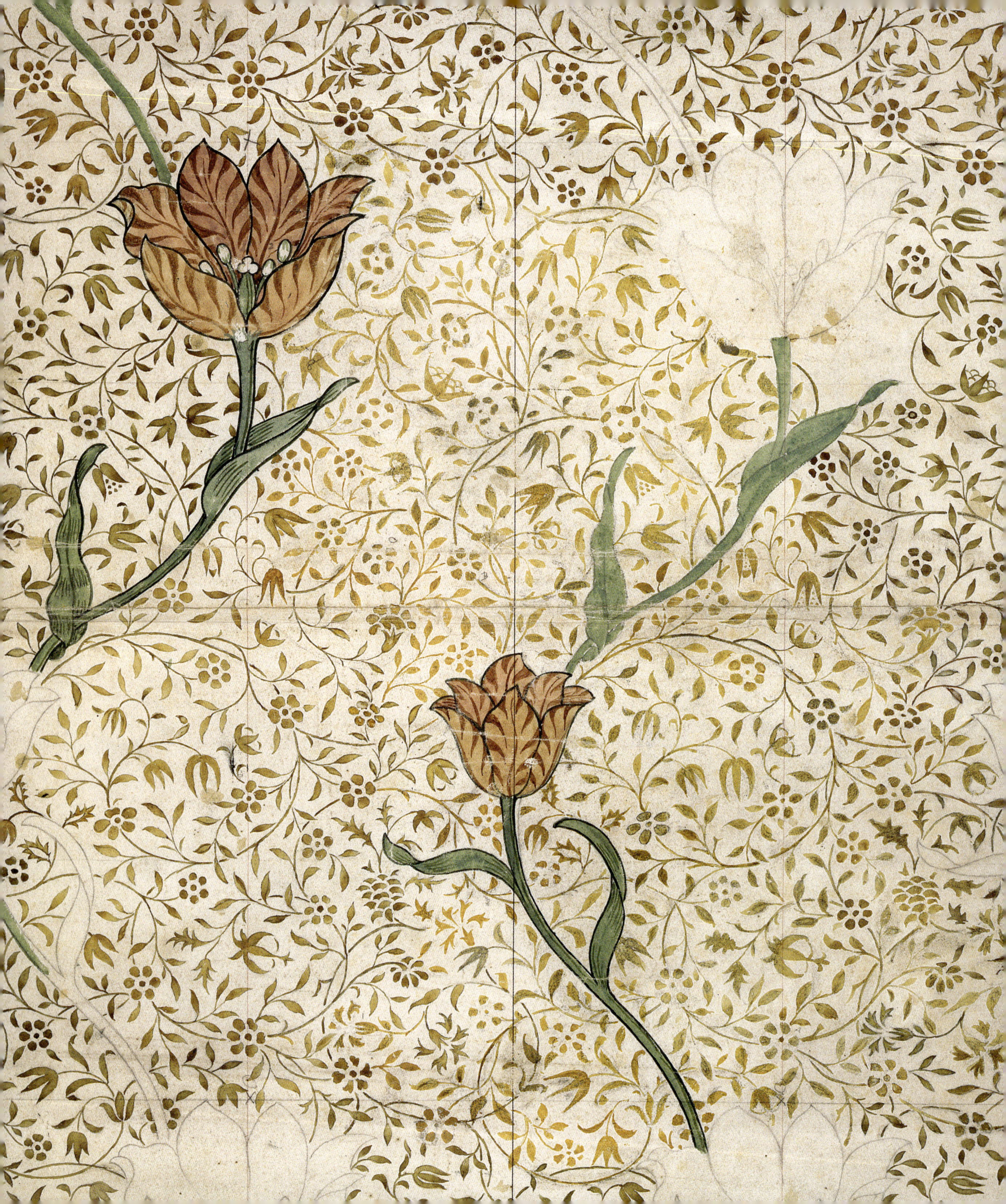

Chapter 7 *Working Drawings: Design and Pattern from the Pre-Raphaelites to the Arts and Crafts Movement*

In its first editorial article for the year 1848, the year of the formation of the Pre-Raphaelite Brotherhood, *The Art-Union* noted satisfactory progress in both the 'Fine' and 'Industrial' Arts and in their encouragement and development; it expressed great hopes for the Schools of Design, where drawing was the central subject, for inculcating a sense of the beautiful alongside practical instruction. Such ideas were part of the currency of debate around the methods of training designers and artists. William Dyce's report on continental Schools of Design noted the lack of separation between the disciplines at the point of training in France and Germany.[1] Despite calls for reform of the education system, the training of artists and designers remained quite separate – as they most often still are. Training was to find its most harmonious relationship in the practices of the artists and designers associated with the Arts and Crafts movement from the 1880s to the early decades of the twentieth century. Nonetheless, *The Art Journal* regularly included essays and reviews on both design and fine art in the mid-nineteenth century, and although the bulk of its pages were given over to artists, art exhibitions and academic and studio-based news stories, there was a sense of a new appreciation of craft and applied art. In many of these articles late-medieval and early-Renaissance workshop practices, with their integration of art and craft, artistry and artisanship, were held up as models for the present.

Following the Great Exhibition of 1851, the Schools of Design were heavily criticized and shown to be inadequate for training designers for industry. The entire programme of training was reviewed and new schools were founded under the supervision of a newly established Department of Practical Art in 1852. Elementary drawing classes were to be set up throughout the country, and regional Schools of Design were established in industrial centres such as Belfast, Birmingham, Manchester and the Potteries. These

234 William Morris, *Design for Wallpaper: 'Garden Tulip'*, 1885, Birmingham Museums & Art Gallery (detail)

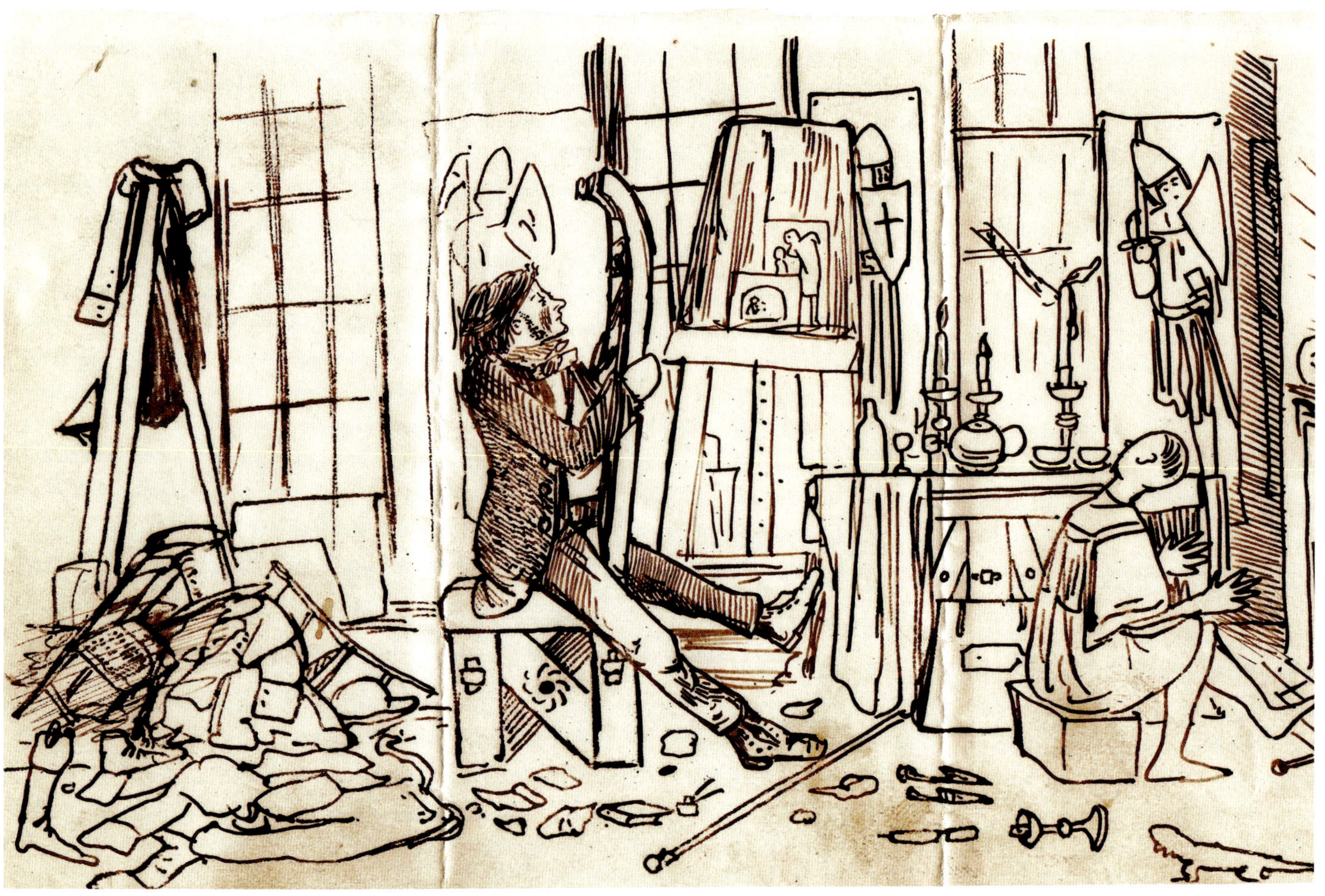

235 Edward Burne-Jones, *Self Portrait Caricature in Red Lion Square*, c. 1856, Mark Samuels Lasner Collection,
on loan to the University of Delaware Library

expanded the London-based schools of ornamental art
that already existed: separate schools for men at Somerset
House, with an elementary branch at Westminster, and
one for women at Gower Street, with one 'mixed school'
at Spitalfields.[2] These schools were to be important for the
development of the visual arts in Britain, not the least in the
recognition they gave to the role of women in design.

Ruskin's opinions on the complex relationship between
craftsmen, designers, architects and the societies that
produced them were more radical than those set out in
government reports. In his study of medieval architecture,
The Stones of Venice (1851–53), his criticism of contemporary
training in design was not simply of style or quality but of
the different natures of the societies that had developed in
medieval Venice and modern Britain. In a telling passage
he moved from the analysis of a historical building style,
the Gothic, to the criticism of the nexus of contemporary
commerce and manufacturing, where Ruskin explained
that in the new industrial practice of the division of labour

It is not, truly speaking, the labour that is divided;
but the men:– Divided into mere segments of men –
broken into small fragments and crumbs of life; so that
all the little piece of intelligence that is left in a man is
not enough to make a pin, or a nail, but exhausts itself
in making the point of a pin or the head of a nail.[3]

Ruskin explained that in Gothic architecture characteristics
such as 'savageness', 'naturalism' and 'grotesqueness',
among others, 'belonging to the building' also 'belong'
to the builder. He advised his readers not only to avoid
'unnecessary finish' in manufactured goods but never to
'encourage the manufacture of any article not absolutely
necessary, in the production of which *Invention* has no
share' and even never to 'encourage imitation or copying
of any kind'.[4] If the discerning consumer eschewed such
qualities, the industrial worker would cease to be a slave.
Free, he could express his creativity.

Ruskin's practical concern for artisans was demonstrated
in several educational schemes with a variety of social aims.

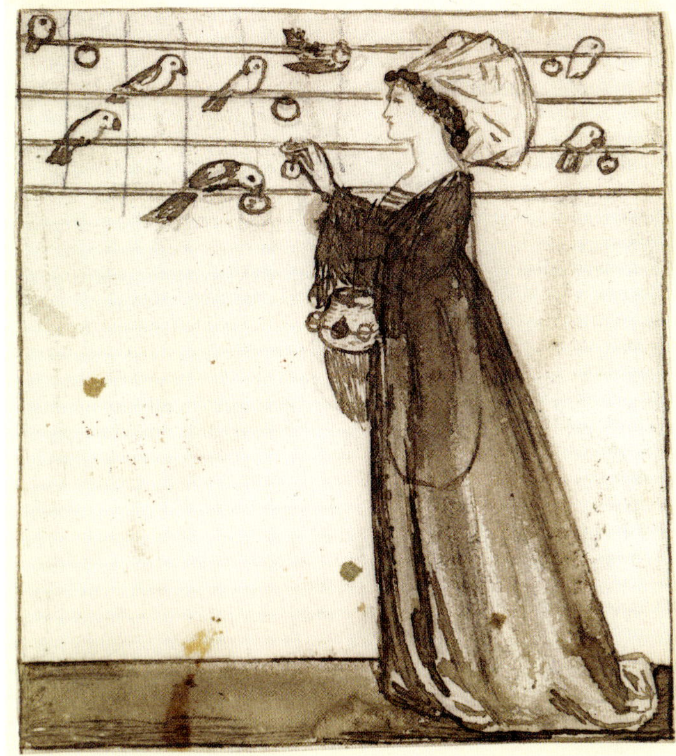

From his involvement as a teacher at the Working Men's College to the foundation of the Guild of Saint George, he advocated basic training in the arts, chiefly in drawing. In his *Fors Clavigera* pamphlets of the 1870s, Ruskin makes clear the ideals that the Guild would strive for. In redirecting the attention of artisans and craftsmen towards nature, Ruskin was inculcating an attitude to drawing for design that was akin to that practised by Gothic workmen: drawn from nature but expressive of their own talents and vision. Ruskin was not unique in his concerns with the training of workers, however. Thomas Seddon's enthusiasm for drawing and his understanding of the skills required to make drawings for design led him to form the North London School of Drawing and Modelling in Camden Town where artisans were taught basic drawing skills.[5]

To some extent, however, the practices of those Pre-Raphaelite artists designing for Morris, Marshall, Faulkner & Co. (and its later names and manifestations)[6] acted as a counterbalance to the kind of industrial-design training devised by Henry Cole, Richard Redgrave, Christopher Dresser (1834–1904) and others involved in the reform of the Schools of Design. The first active contribution of the Pre-Raphaelites to this design debate was the production of a type of decorative art that was applied to architectural schemes and furniture. Beginning with the enthusiastic decoration of painted furniture in the studio at Red Lion Square [235], this impulse to apply design to objects had evolved into ambitious pieces such as the 'Ladies and Animals' sideboard (1860), painted by Burne-Jones as a wedding present for his wife, Georgiana [236, 237]. In such designs the Pre-Raphaelites demonstrated a pictorialist sensibility less concerned with the function or structure of an object than with its decoration. They made drawings for works of design as if they were eventually to become easel pictures rather than panels for furniture. At this stage their contribution was concerned with art rather than craft, and

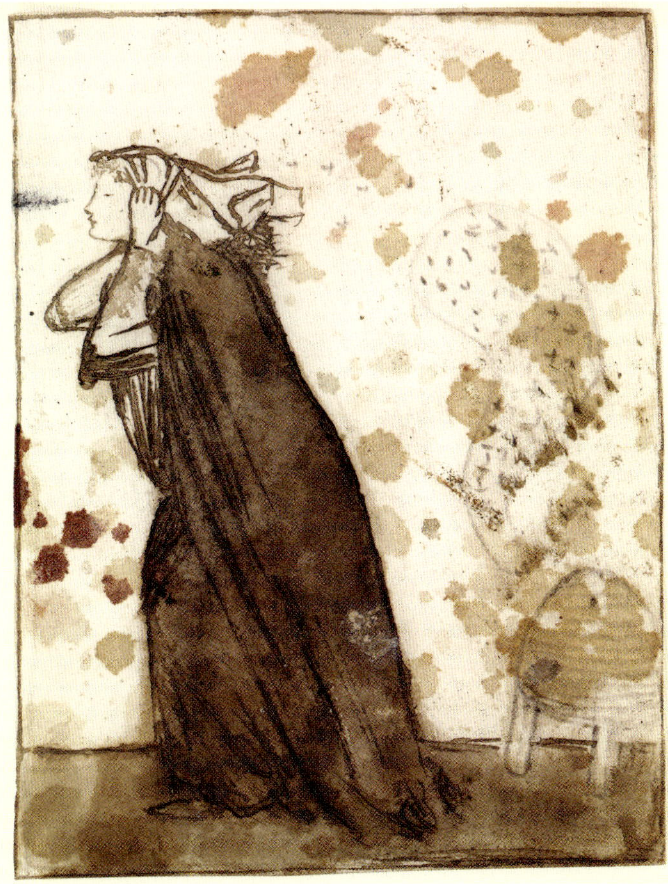

236 Edward Burne-Jones, *Design for the Ladies and Animals Sideboard: A Lady Feeding Parrots*, 1860, Birmingham Museums & Art
237 Edward Burne-Jones, *Design for the Ladies and Animals Sideboard: A Lady Pursued by a Swarm of Bees*, 1860, Birmingham Museums & Art Gallery

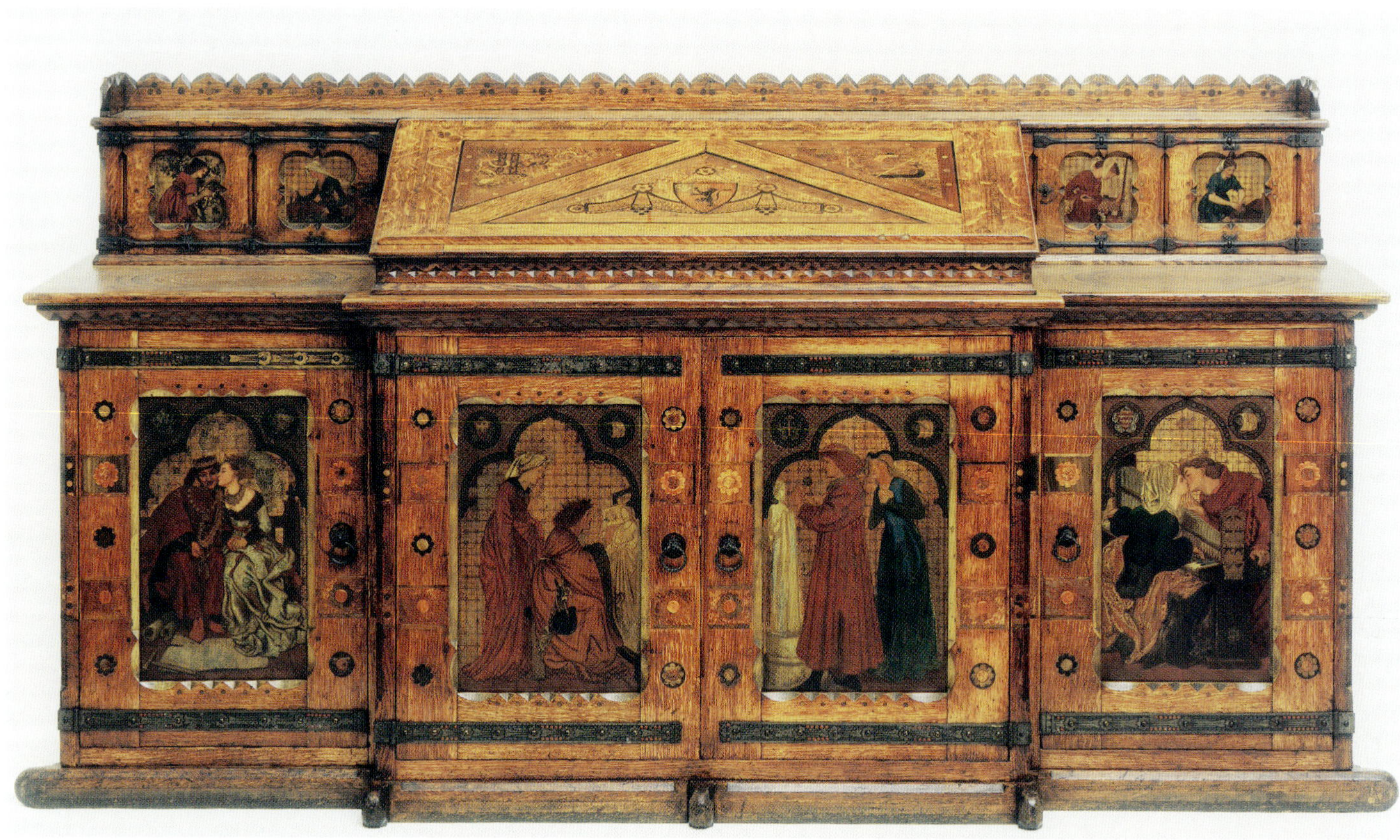

238 Morris, Marshall, Faulkner & Co., *King René's Honeymoon Cabinet*, 1861, Victoria and Albert Museum, London

scarcely at all with manufacturing processes. Later, through Morris's work and writings, craft became a vital issue in the discussion of the role of the arts in society.

The school of the medieval grotesque

The architect and designer John Pollard Seddon (1827–1906) commissioned the King René's Honeymoon Cabinet from Morris, Marshall, Faulkner & Co. in 1861 [238]. It depicted scenes of King René in the pursuit of various artistic activities (as well as, more generally, love). Brown's design, 'Architecture' [239], depicts the king being kissed by his wife as he contemplates architectural designs. As if to accentuate the pictorialist nature of the design and its ubiquity, Brown exhibited an easel painting of the subject in 1865, while all the images were reworked as stained-glass designs. Rossetti's design representing 'Music' [241, 242] became the basis of his frontispiece for *The Early Italian Poets*: *The Rose Garden* (1861), and Burne-Jones contributed a design representing 'Sculpture' [240]. In these designs fine-art practice breaks down traditional barriers of status between

fine art and design. In Michael Darby's opinion, the King René's Honeymoon Cabinet illustrates Seddon's 'passionate belief in the unity of the arts'.[7]

The Pre-Raphaelites had antiquarian interests that allied their decorative work with that of the Gothic revivalists, and there was an awareness of the importance of their design experiments within the Ecclesiological movement. Architect G. E. Street's paper 'On the Future of Art in England', delivered at the Anniversary Meeting of the Ecclesiological Society in June 1858, referred frequently to interior schemes by Rossetti and his circle as positive examples for architects and designers. Street noted the Pre-Raphaelite emulation of the 'northern art of the thirteenth century' and 'resistance to false and modern systems of thought and practice in art', as well as the Oxford Union murals.[8]

In his review of the International Exhibition of 1862, William Burges noted Rossetti's stained-glass designs for Morris, Marshall & Co. He defined the new pictorialism of Pre-Raphaelite furniture, regarding it as 'an overturn of the general ideas upon the dignity of painting in general,

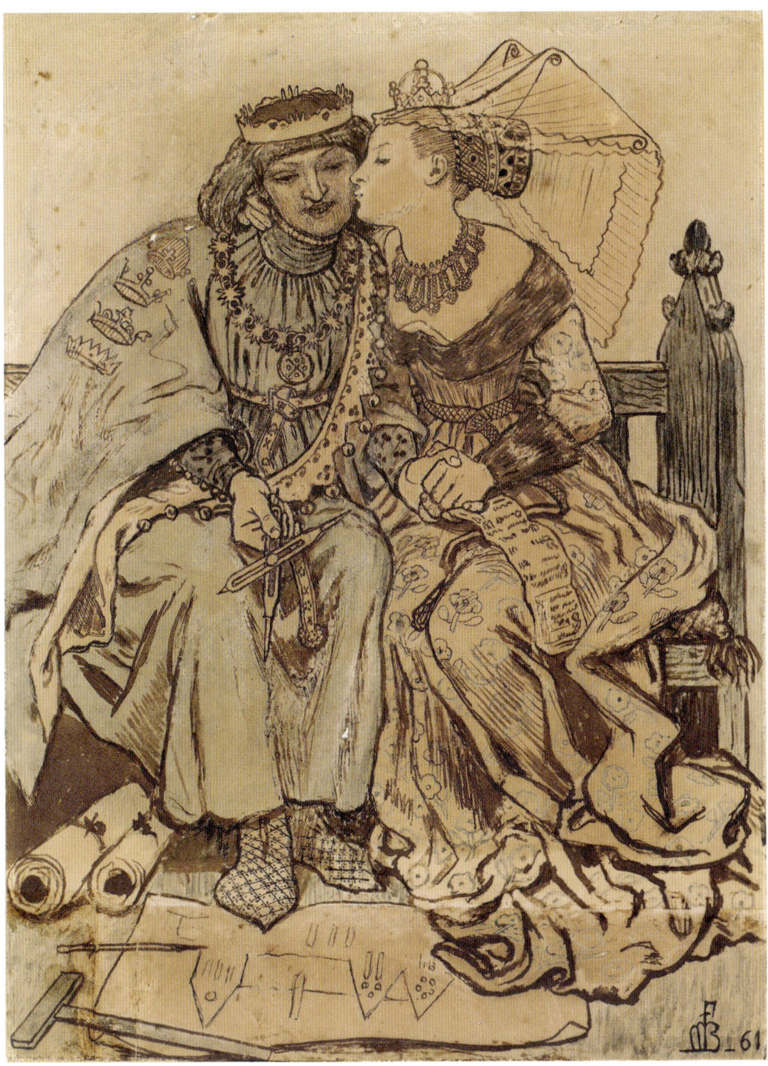

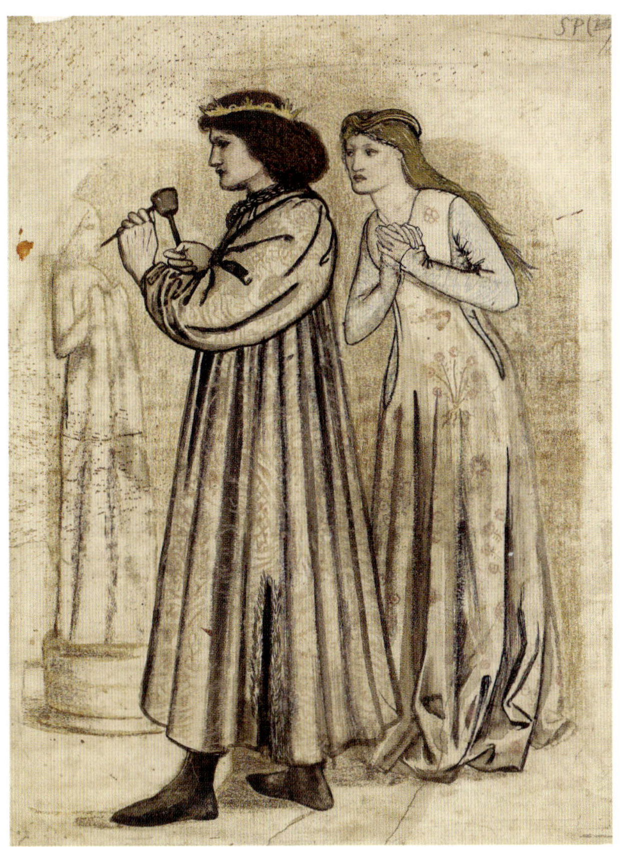

239 Ford Madox Brown, *Design for the King René's Honeymoon Cabinet: 'Architecture'*, 1861, Birmingham Museums & Art Gallery
240 Edward Burne-Jones, *Design for the King René's Honeymoon Cabinet: 'Sculpture'*, 1861, Birmingham Museums & Art Gallery

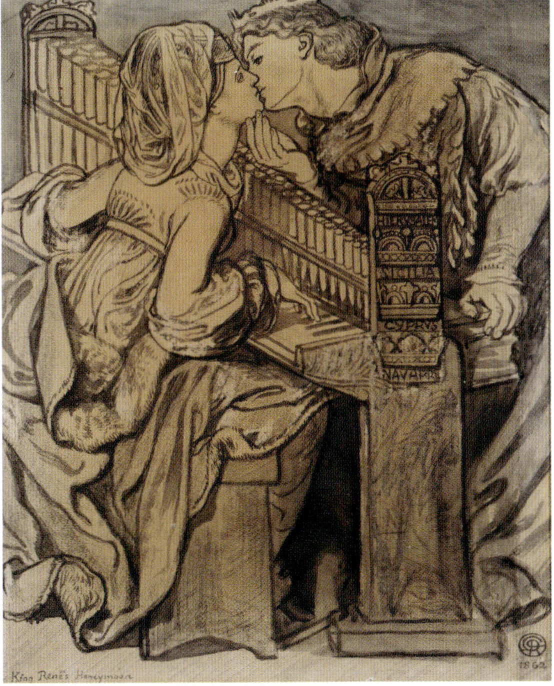

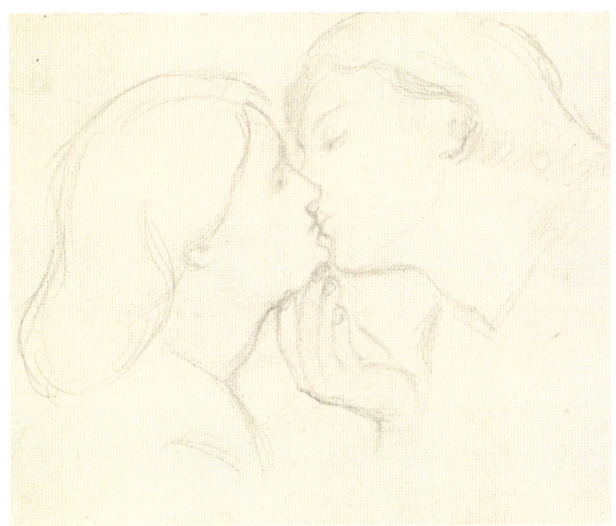

241 Dante Gabriel Rossetti, *Design for the King René's Honeymoon Cabinet: 'Music'*, 1861, The Williamson Art Gallery and Museum, Birkenhead, Wirral
242 Dante Gabriel Rossetti, *Study for the King René's Honeymoon Cabinet: 'Music'*, 1861, Birmingham Museums & Art Gallery

and of easel pictures in particular' and sensed an
Establishment plot against its direction:

> certain aimiable critics charitably advised the
> possessors of these heretical pieces of furniture, to
> frame the pictures and to burn the rest of the work; for
> it is but too evident, that if the best painters turn their
> attention to painting on walls of buildings and on
> panels of furniture, there will be but few easel pictures
> to send to the Exhibition of the Royal Academy.[9]

The production of painted furniture was one of the
most obvious ways in which artists could combine with
craftsmen to produce a 'designed article'. It is analogous to
the painted walls revived by Rossetti at the Oxford Union
(see Chapter 5). In this aesthetic, the decoration of the
wall, chair, table and cupboard can aspire to be as poetic
or dramatic – as full of narrative – as well as beautiful, as a
book or picture. The term 'grotesque' was used to describe
Pre-Raphaelite painted furniture and stained glass on its
first outing at the 1862 Exhibition. This grotesquerie was
linked to both drawing and an excess of imagination:

> Some painted and japanned furniture, exhibited
> by Messrs. Morris, Marshall, & Co., is simply
> preposterous. We believe that it is meant to be
> inexpensive; but some of the affixed prices scarcely bear
> out the assertion. We must totally decline to praise the
> design or execution of these specimens. The colouring
> in particular is crude and unpleasing, while the design
> is laboriously grotesque.…Much as we commend the
> introduction of painted ornamentation, we stipulate for
> good drawing and for agreeable colouration.[10]

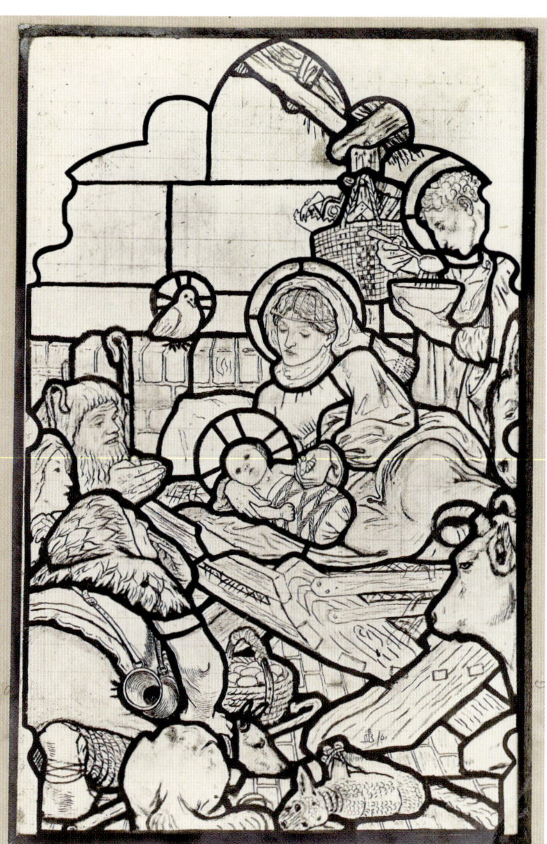

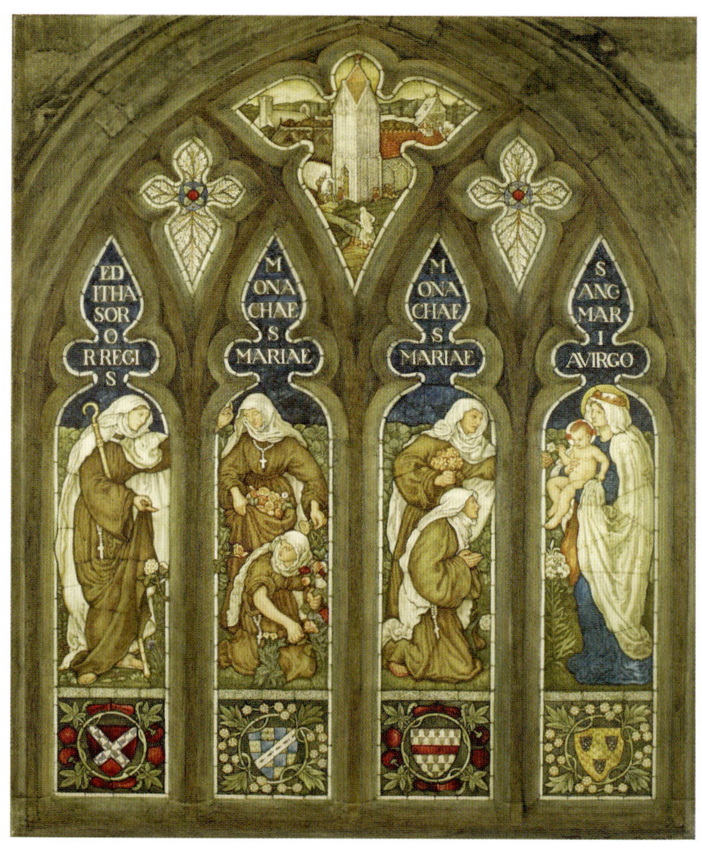

243 Ford Madox Brown, *Design for Stained Glass: 'The Nativity'*,
1861, photographed by Frederick Hollyer for Morris & Co.,
Birmingham Museums & Art Gallery

244 Thomas Matthews Rooke after Ford Madox Brown, *Design for
Stained Glass: 'St Editha and the Nuns of St Mary'*, 1908,
Birmingham Museums & Art Gallery

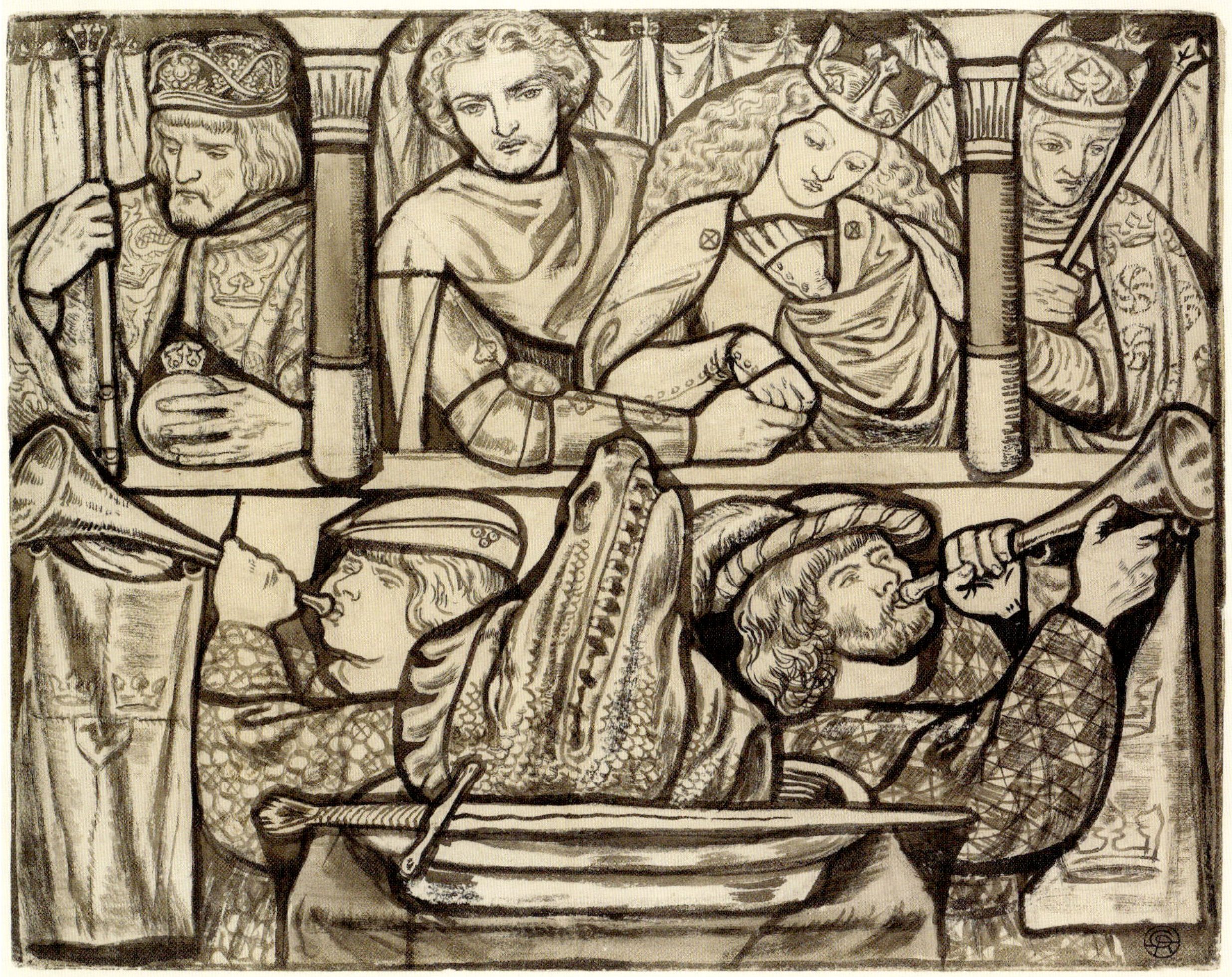

245 Dante Gabriel Rossetti, *Design for Stained Glass: 'The Wedding of St George and the Princess Sabra'*, 1861–62, Birmingham Museums & Art Gallery

246 William Morris, *Design for Stained Glass: 'The Ascension'*, 1861, Birmingham Museums & Art Gallery

Given that the Firm was staffed by artists it is unsurprising that the results took the form they did : pictures applied to surfaces. Both Brown and Rossetti's equally vivid imaginations produced bizarre drawings for stained glass in which all the characteristics of their paintings and graphic work were reproduced: awkward poses, distinctive points of view and off-centre compositions, repeated in lead and glass. The practice of stained-glass design challenged an artist's preconception of the function of drawing. Designing for glass was like drawing in light and pure colour; as Morris explained, the substantiality of paint had to be lost. Oil paint obliterates the underlying drawing but in stained glass the drawing is exposed as a leaded structure that defines the objects and the compositional framework. Morris himself was to observe the spirit of this drawing practice. He described the nature of glass painting and its qualities thus:

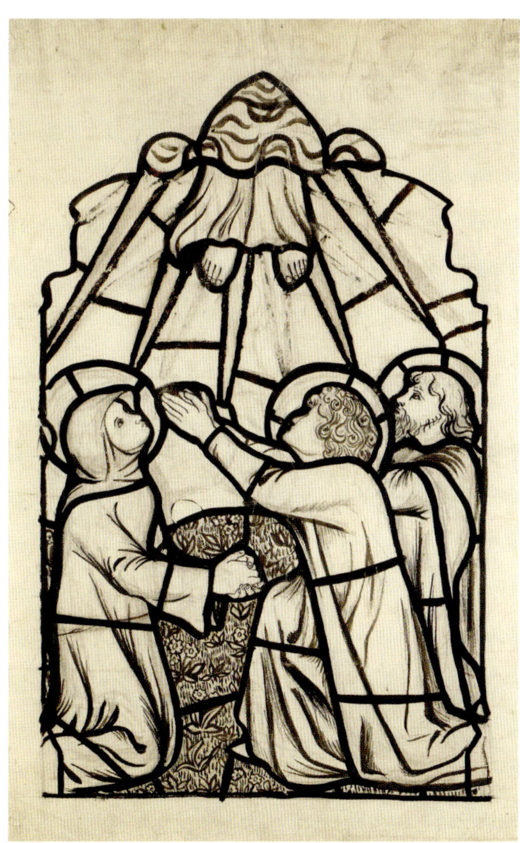

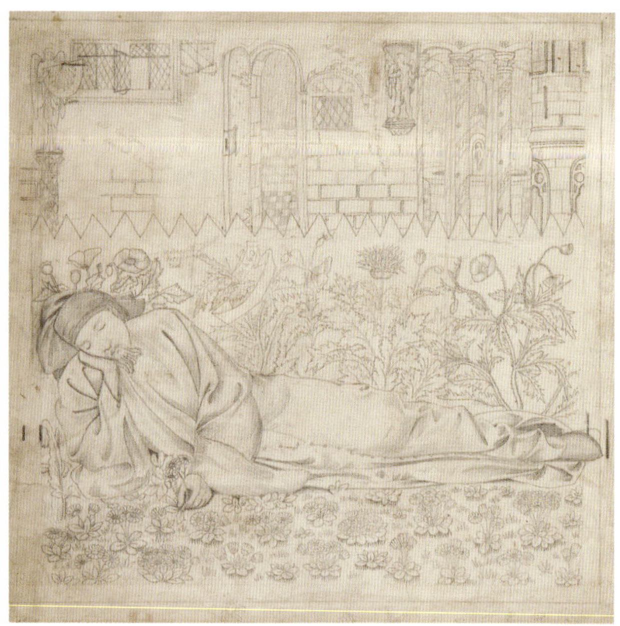

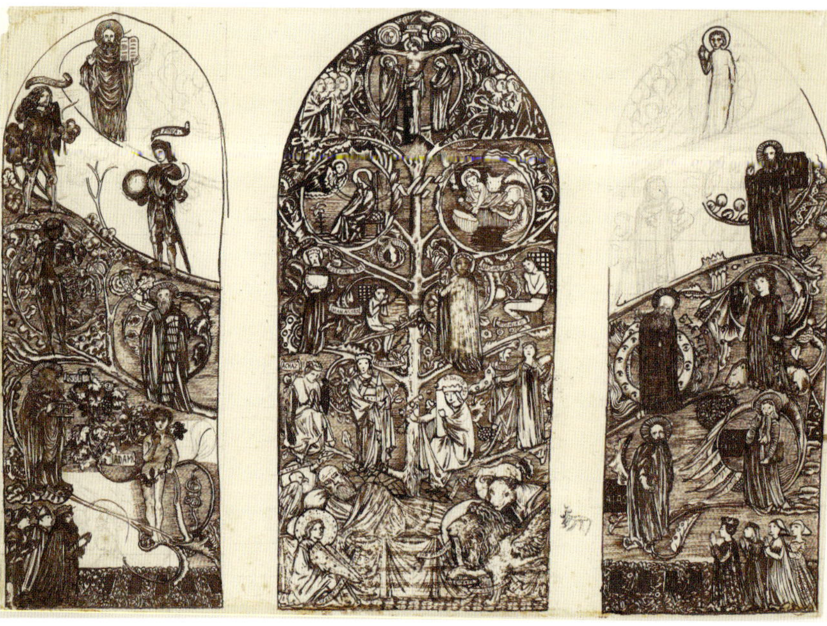

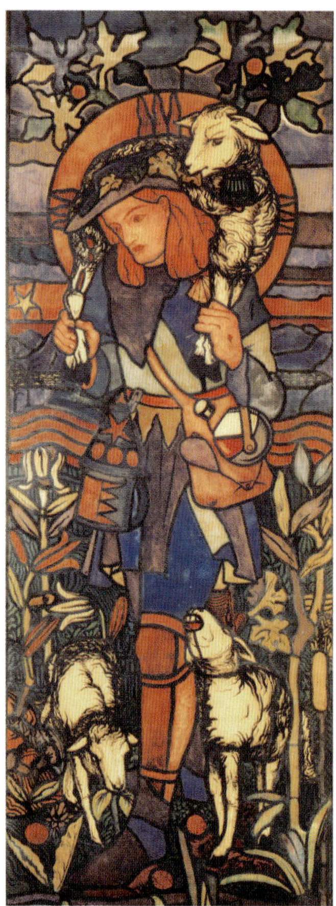

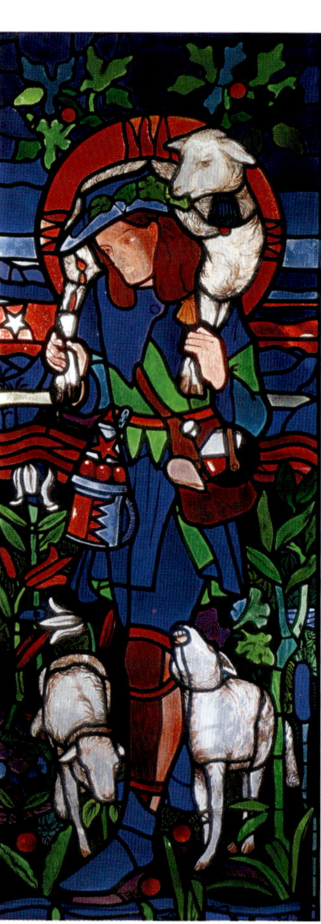

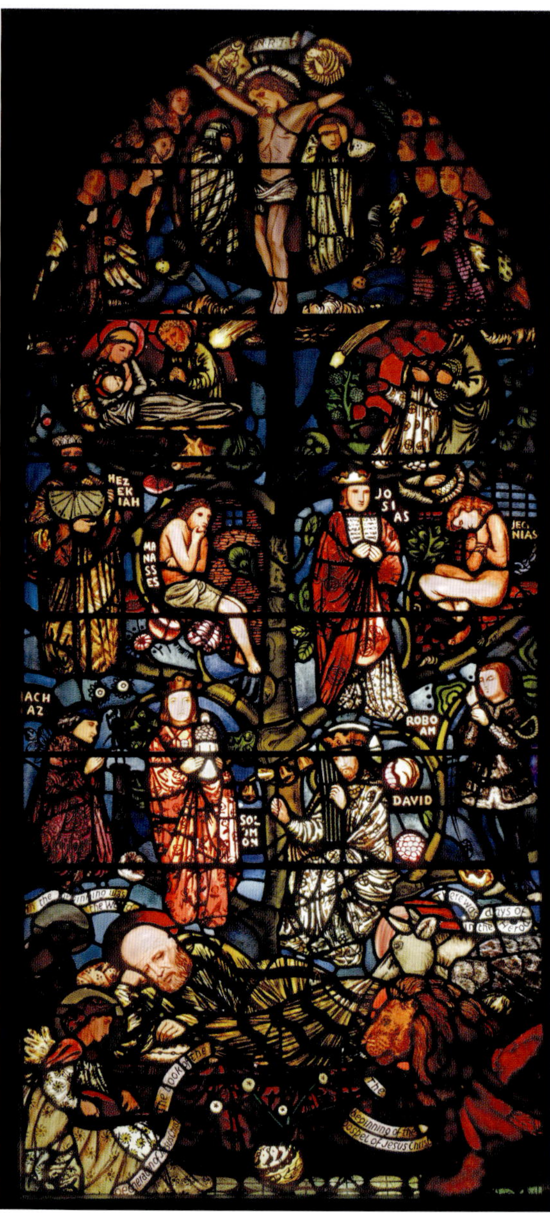

247 Edward Burne-Jones, *Design for Stained Glass: 'Chaucer Asleep'*, 1864, Birmingham Museums & Art Gallery

248 Edward Burne-Jones, *Design for Stained Glass: 'The Good Shepherd'*, 1857, Victoria and Albert Museum, London

249 James Powell & Sons, *The Good Shepherd*, 1861, Maidstone United Reformed Church, on loan to Birmingham Museums & Art Gallery

250 Edward Burne-Jones, *Design for Stained Glass: 'The Tree of Jesse'*, 1860–61, Birmingham Museums & Art Gallery

251 James Powell & Sons, *The Tree of Jesse*, 1861–62, Birmingham Museums & Art Gallery

In the first place, the drawing and composition have to
be much more simple, and yet more carefully studied,
than in paintings which have all the assistance of
shadow and reflected lights to disguise faults and assist
the groupings. In the next place, the light and shade
must be so managed that the strong outlines shall not
appear crude, nor the work within it thin; this implies
a certain conventionalism of treatment, and makes the
details of a figure so much more an affair of drawing
than of painting; because by drawing – that is, by filling
the outlines with other lines of proportionate strength –
the force of the predominant lines is less unnatural.[11]

It was a technique that particularly appealed to Burne-
Jones, whose design work was dominated by stained glass,
some of it among the finest and most original of the period.

From the mid-1850s onwards the Pre-Raphaelites and their
followers participated in a revival of stained-glass design,
producing numerous windows covering a wide variety
of subjects: biblical, dramatic and poetic literature, and
historical. The medium became a kind of alternative Royal
Academy exhibition. Ford Madox Brown was particularly
diverse in the commissions he produced, allowing his
imagination just as much freedom to compose pictures
for stained glass as for paint. Sometimes his commissions
directly reflect other projects, such as the panels illustrating
the story of Tristram and Isoude for the windows executed by
Morris, Marshall, Faulkner & Co. in 1862 for Harden Grange,
Yorkshire. It stands as a notable collaboration of the leading
Pre-Raphaelite artists, a symbol of cooperation within the
Arts and Crafts movement. Arthur Hughes designed *The
Birth of Tristram* [252], Rossetti the scene showing Tristram

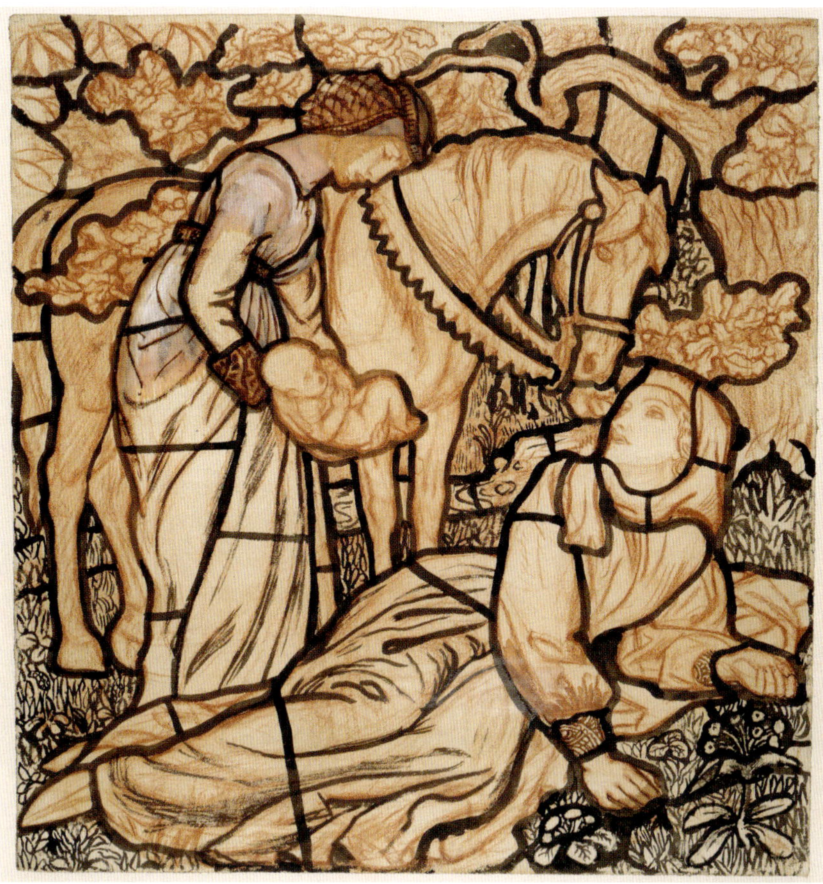

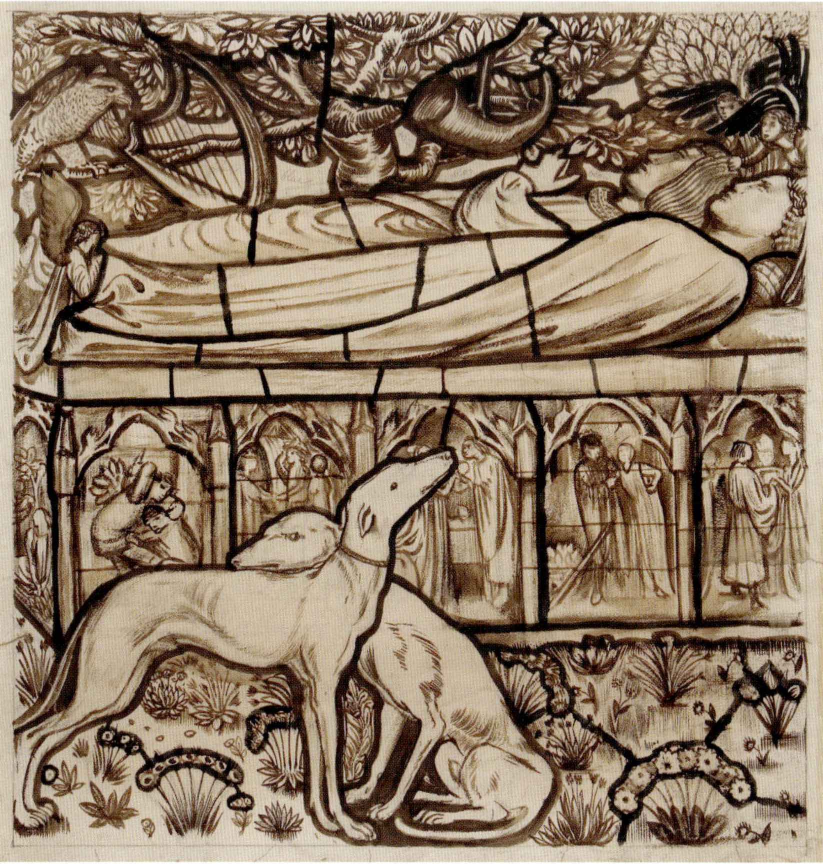

252 Arthur Hughes, *Design for Stained Glass: 'The Birth of Tristram'*, 1861,
Birmingham Museums & Art Gallery
253 Edward Burne-Jones, *Design for Stained Glass: 'The Tomb of Tristram
and Isoude'*, 1862, Birmingham Museums & Art Gallery

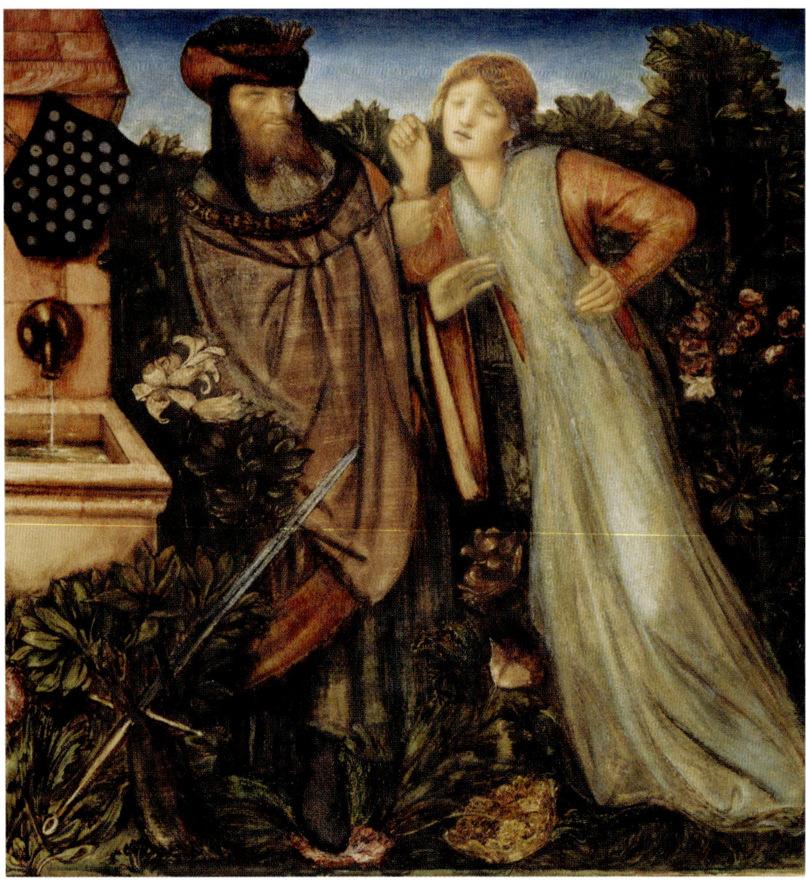

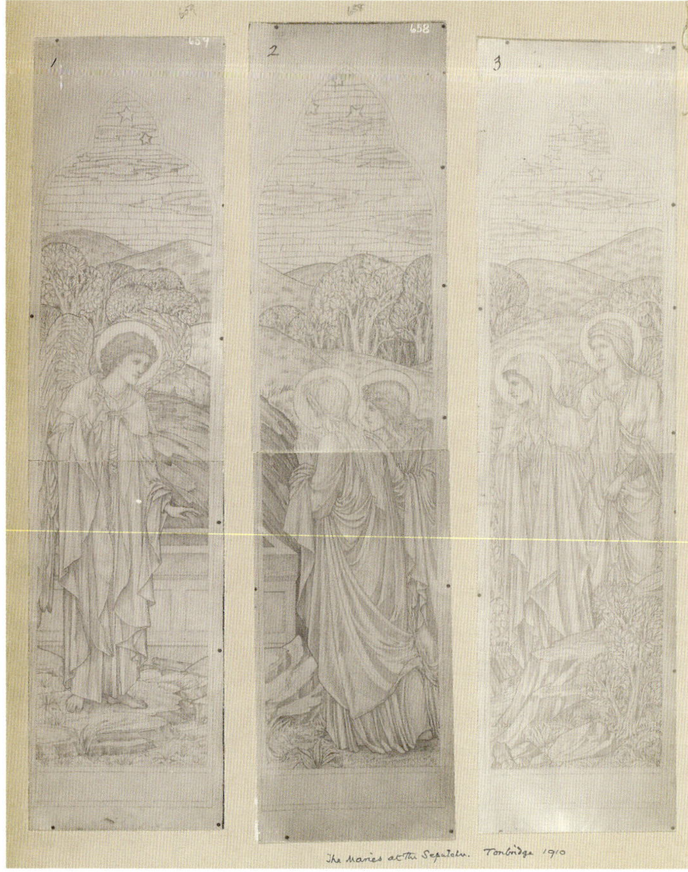

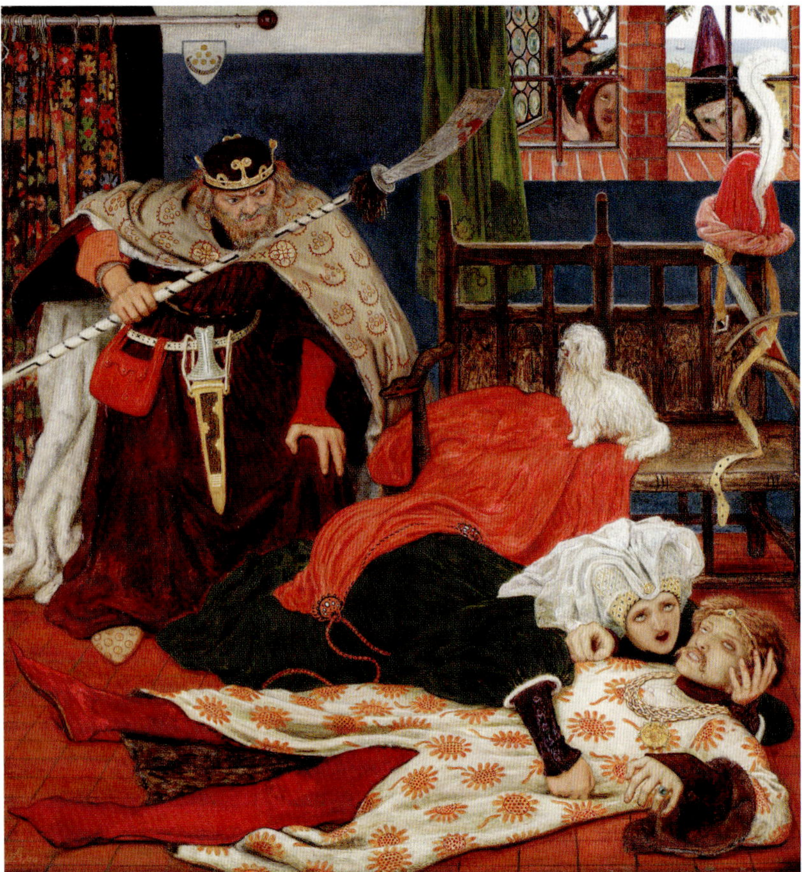

254 Edward Burne-Jones, *King Mark and la Belle Iseult*, 1862, Birmingham Museums & Art Gallery

255 Ford Madox Brown, *The Death of Tristram*, 1864, Birmingham Museums & Art Gallery

256 Henry Dearle, *Design for Stained Glass: The Three Maries at the Sepulchre*, 1910, photographed by Frederick Hollyer for Morris & Company, Birmingham Museums & Art Gallery

and La Belle Isoude drinking the love potion. Burne-Jones supplied four strong designs: *The Marriage of Tristram and Isoude*; *The Madness of Tristram*; *The Attempted Suicide of Isoude*; and *The Tomb of Tristram and Isoude* [253], the last showing the direct influence of Dürer. Prinsep, Brown and Morris each supplied one design. Despite this diversity, the entire scheme was harmonized by that strong black leading that functioned as a kind of drawn line, which both emphasized and simplified the compositions.

Designs such as these encouraged the growth of a new school of stained-glass art over the next half century, often of ambitious subject matter. The Birmingham School designs were particularly strong in experimenting with ambitious narratives, extending Arthurian and Dantesque imagery into the twentieth century, such as in the work of Florence Camm (1874–1960) [303, 304, 305]. Both Burne-Jones and Brown turned their images into paintings, further collapsing the difference between art and design [**254, 255**]. At a later stage in the history of Morris & Co., the design work was undertaken by John Henry Dearle (1860–1932), who became the chief designer for the company [**256**]. His drawing style imitated that of Burne-Jones in stained-glass window design, and Morris in textile design. His accuracy and technical prowess as a draughtsman were invaluable for the continuance of the company's work following Morris's death.

Drawing, design and society

As artist-designers, in what was to become known as the Arts and Crafts movement, the Pre-Raphaelites adopted a pragmatic approach to this new branch of their work. Rossetti's practices and techniques as a fine-art draughtsman needed only the merest modification for their application to design. His interests in medieval culture – in heraldic art, illumination and pattern – were accompanied by a sense of an entire world of the medieval, not only in its religious manifestations but also as a kind of poetic antiquarianism. John Pollard Seddon used his influence to obtain the commission for the reredos at Llandaff Cathedral for Rossetti on the basis of of Rossetti's early paintings. Rossetti's decorative impulse found expression in wall-painting, some furniture design and even jewelry. In this he was matched by Hunt, whose interest in the appearance of decorative and functional objects and furniture in paintings led to his designing various items, such as the lantern for *The Light of the World* [**154**], chairs and a lectern [**258**]. However, Hunt did not design for the Firm. In contemporary terms Rossetti might be seen as a stylist rather than a designer. His sense of pattern is evident

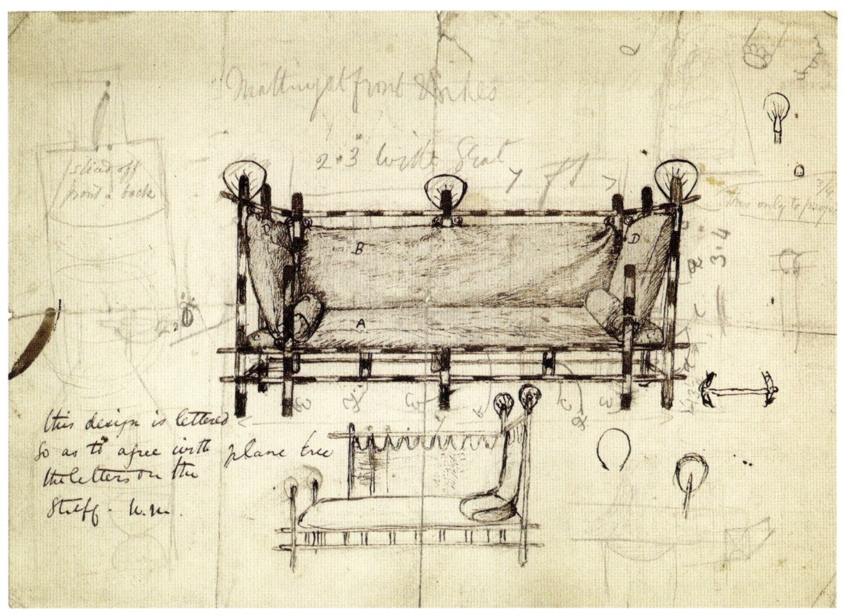

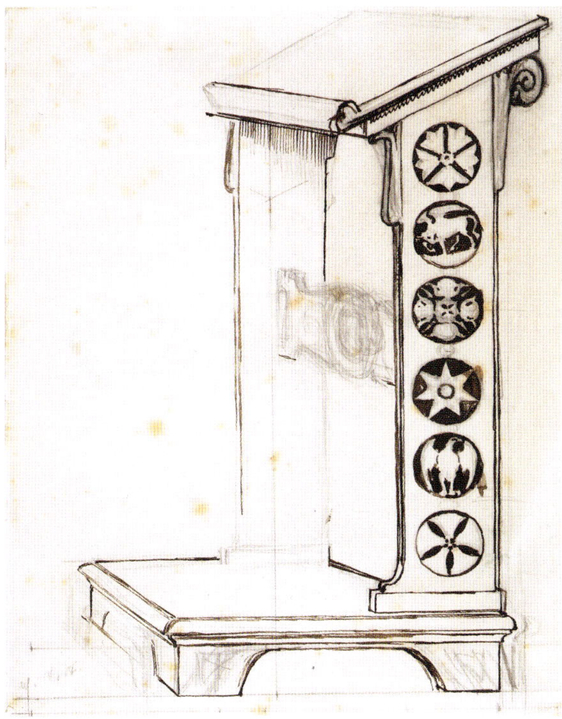

257 Dante Gabriel Rossetti, *Two Designs for a Sofa*, c. 1860, Birmingham Museums & Art Gallery
258 William Holman Hunt, *Design for a Lectern*, Cambridge, c. 1868, Victoria and Albert Museum, London

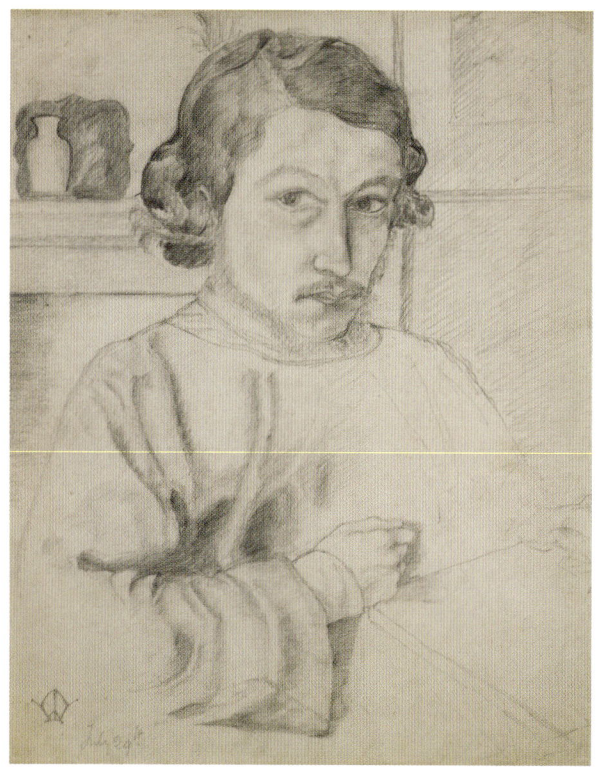

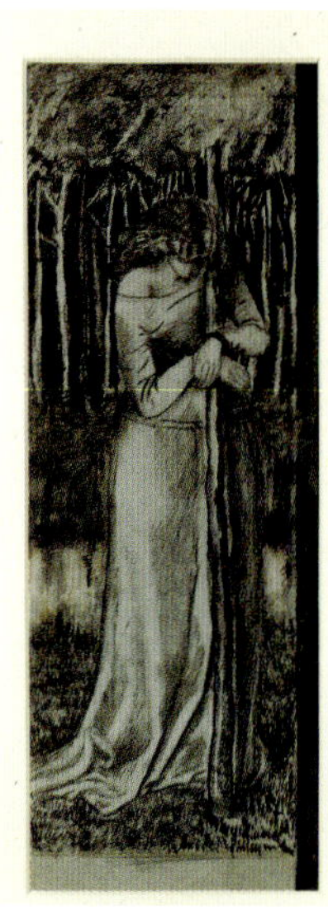

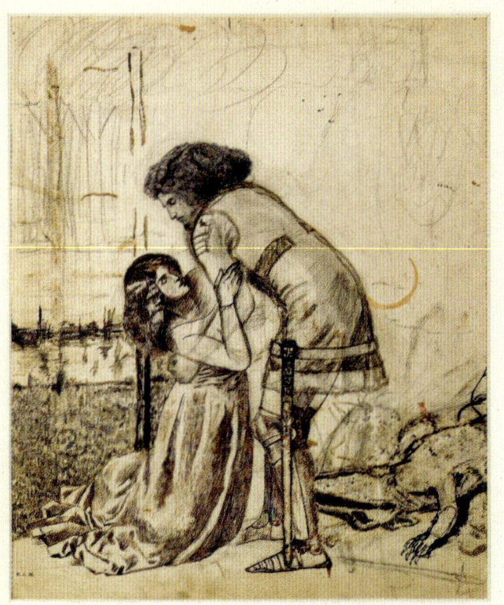

259 William Morris, *Self Portrait in a Smock*, 1856, Victoria and Albert Museum, London

260 William Morris, *Two Designs for the St George's Cabinet*, 1861, Victoria and Albert Museum, London

in his watercolour drawings in which he re-creates an experience of the medieval imagination. His rejection of the conventions that had grown up around pattern since the Renaissance was to have as profound an effect on design as the Brotherhood's rejection of the conventions of academic training had on painting.

Morris used the lecture platform to promote ideas about social reform in relation to class as well as design reform. In his lecture 'The Lesser Arts' in 1878 he outlined a history of design that stressed freedom of invention and the persistence of a craft-led practice of design, a kind of peasant art and architecture that

> clung fast to the life of the people, and still lived among the cottagers and yeomen in many parts of the country while the big houses were being built 'French and fine'.[12]

He steered a path between the insistence that 'designing cannot be taught at all in a school' and an acknowledgment of the recent but flourishing conditions in training in art and design. He encouraged a very simple academic programme of drawing and the history of art and design to back up technical training:

> all handicraftsmen should be taught to draw very carefully; as indeed all people should be taught

drawing who are not physically incapable of learning it: but the art of drawing so taught would not be the art of designing, but only a means toward *this* end, *general capability in dealing with the arts*....As to the kind of drawing that should be taught to men engaged in ornamental work, there is only *one best* way of teaching drawing, and that is teaching the scholar to draw the human figure: both because the lines of a man's body are much more subtle than anything else, and because you can more surely be found out and set right if you go wrong.[13]

For Morris, the invention of a new kind of pattern design, for which drawing was central, was an essential part of his practice. His own training had not been, to any significant extent, in drawing; his weaknesses in this department are easy to spot and they are chiefly to do with failures to observe proportion – of the hands, for example in his self-portrait (*c.* 1856) [259], or in his drawings of Princess Sabra for the St George's Cabinet (1861) [260]. His grasp of perspective is similarly challenged, although less vital in dealing with flat or decorative surfaces. The strangeness of the drawing style, the intensity of the subjects and the complexity of the groupings are certainly the ingredients of the medievalist grotesque noted by his contemporaries. It is

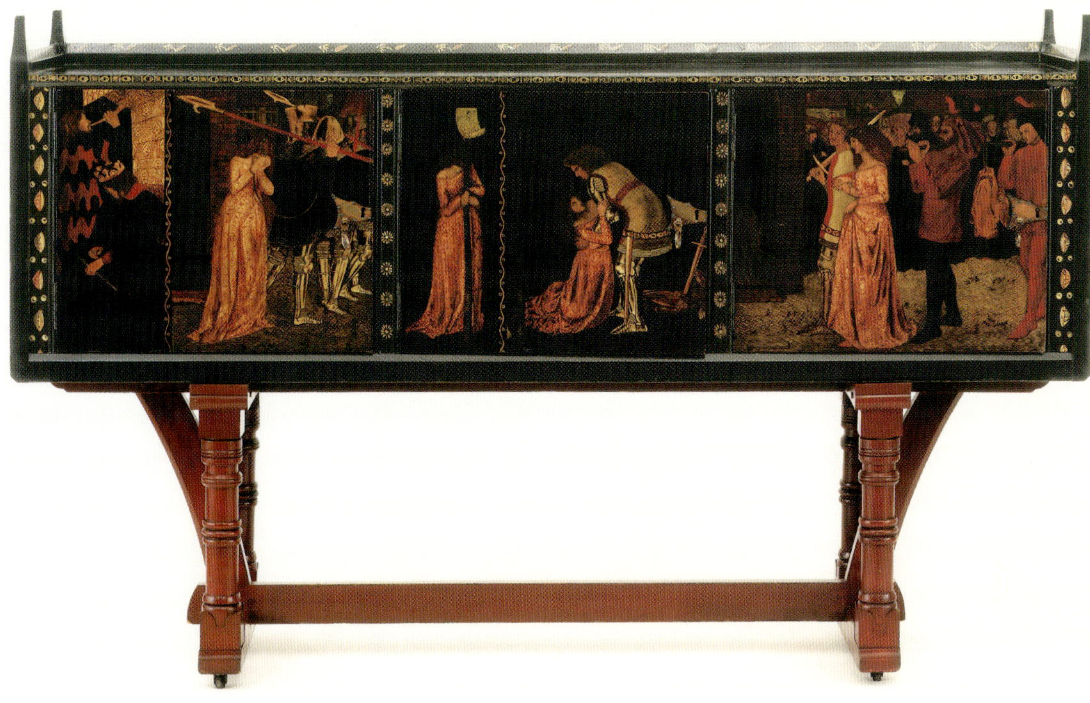

261 Morris & Co.,
St George's Cabinet, 1861,
Victoria and Albert
Museum, London

clear, too, that this is no affectation of awkwardness. These are the drawings of an almost untrained artist, yet one who was steeped in design history and who possessed a strong instinct for making things.

Morris's understanding of a concept of instinctive design is woven into the plot of *News from Nowhere*, begun in 1889 in response to a novel, *Looking Backward* (1888), by the American writer Edward Bellamy.[14] Morris's hero, William Guest, visits a country full of beauty and grace. He comes upon a house:

> a longish building with its gable ends turned away from the road, and long traceried windows coming rather low down set in the wall that faced us. It was very handsomely built of red brick with a lead roof; and high up above the windows there ran a frieze of figure subjects in baked clay, very well executed, and designed with a force and directness which I had never noticed in modern work before.[15]

This beauty was neither a copy of the art of the past, a kind of 'revivalist' art, nor the product of unwanted toil of an alienated worker class.

The artefacts of this future society are beautiful but, as Morris observed:

> a nineteenth-century club-haunter would have found them rough and lacking in finish; the crockery being

lead-glazed pot-ware, though beautifully ornamented; the only porcelain being here and there a piece of old oriental ware…[and the furniture lacked] the commercial 'finish' of the joiners and cabinet-makers of our time.[16]

Morris's mention of oriental ceramics here is telling. He expanded the repertoire of the Gothic revivalists into a greater acceptance of good design from other periods and cultures. In this he was anticipated by the designer Owen Jones (1809–74), whose *Grammar of Ornament* (1856) had set out, in the most splendid coloured plates, the vast range of decorative motifs, emblems and patterns, geometric and organic in inspiration, from around the world. The Great Exhibition and the contact it offered with international examples was, likewise, a huge influence in changing taste in pattern and applied design.

William De Morgan was particularly influenced by Middle Eastern decorative design. In his own words, De Morgan 'never became a Real Artist'; he was discouraged by his experience of the Academy, particularly of figure drawing. Influenced by his contemporaries Henry Holiday (1839–1927) and Simeon Solomon, he became interested in the wider concerns of Pre-Raphaelitism, including design. He was introduced to Morris in 1863.[17] De Morgan

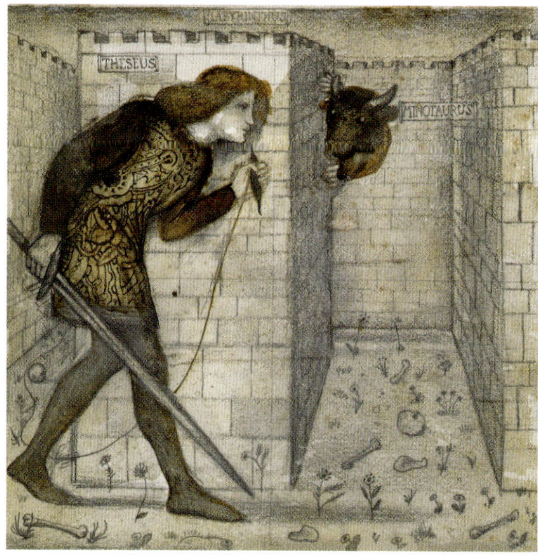

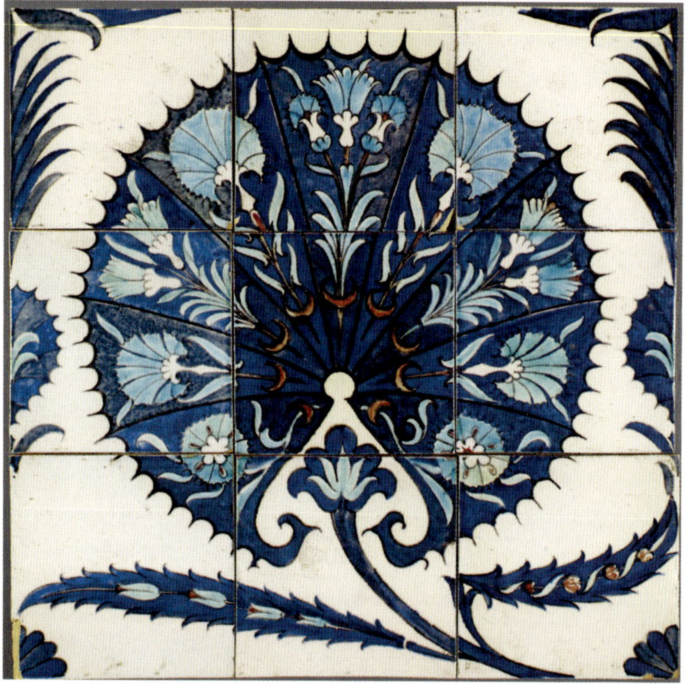

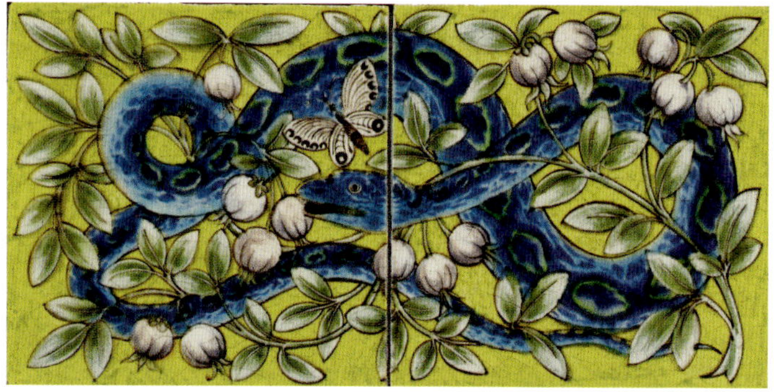

262 Edward Burne-Jones, *Design for a Tile: 'Theseus and the Minotaur'*, 1861, Birmingham Museums & Art Gallery

263 William De Morgan, *Tile Panel*, 1888–97, Birmingham Museums & Art Gallery

264 William De Morgan, *Tile Panel with Snake and Butterfly*, 1872–98, Birmingham Museums & Art Gallery (detail)

produced tile and stained-glass designs for the Firm, working in Morris's studio in the 1860s and experimenting with techniques in the production of ceramics.[18] His early flower and animal decorations, like those of Morris, owe much to a study of medieval herbals and illuminated manuscripts, as Martin Greenwood notes.[19] However, De Morgan is notable for making the shift from drawing directly from nature to producing flat, decorative designs for the embellishment of ceramics, both tiles and vessels. The nature of his surface patterns required him to develop a highly stylized line and a sense of abstraction derived from both the human figure and vegetation; significantly, De Morgan moved away from the pictorialist tendencies of Burne-Jones. For example, Burne-Jones's designs for *Theseus and the Minotaur* tile (1861) [262], while charming, reproduce a picture, whereas De Morgan's tile designs borrow from the flower and leaf patterns of Persian and Italian Renaissance ceramics [263, 264].

Nature and artifice

The role of plant drawing in the production of modern ornamental work can be traced back to Pugin's *Floriated Ornament* (1849) [268, 269]. In his introduction to the plates that form the main body of the work, Pugin anticipates the diverse practices, not only of Morris, but also of Christopher Dresser and Charles Annesley Voysey (1857–1941), who used flowers, leaves and other vegetation forms as the basis for ornamental motifs. Pugin reflected on the origins of his book:

> as by repeated copying the spirit of the original work is liable to be lost, so in decoration the constant reproduction of old patterns, without reference to the natural types for which they were composed, leads to debased forms and spiritless outline, and in the end to a mere caricature of a beautiful original. It is impossible to improve on the works of God; and the

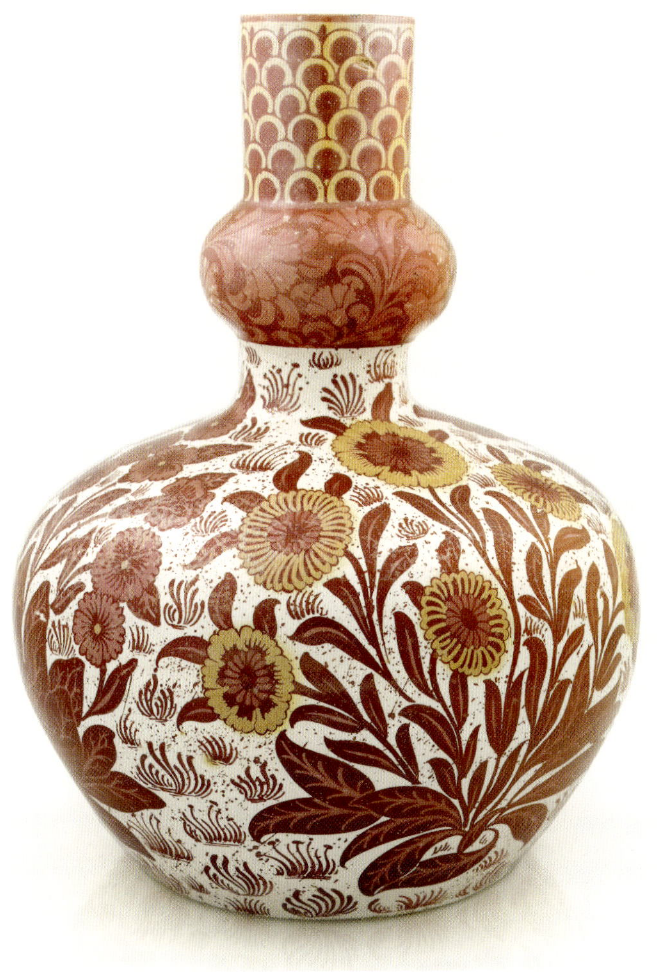

natural outlines of leaves, flowers, &c. must be more perfect and beautiful than any invention of man.[20] Pugin's examples are flat, stylized leaf and flower shapes, which could be adapted for stencilled decoration such as those he introduced into tile designs or ornamental wall-paintings. He stressed the need for 'adaptation' and 'disposition' of natural forms for their use in design. He believed that nature – rather than previously existing decorative schemes – was the '*fountain head* of beautiful design treated in the same spirit as the old, but new in form'.[21] In tempering the inspiration of the past with the primary experience of drawing on – or directly from – nature, Pugin was inspirational for his contemporaries working in surface pattern. While Morris and Crane were basically Puginian in advocating drawing directly from nature and modifying the spirit of old decorative design, they can also be seen as Ruskinian practitioners, deeply aware of issues of social class and the conditions of the workshop as much as the quality of the design.

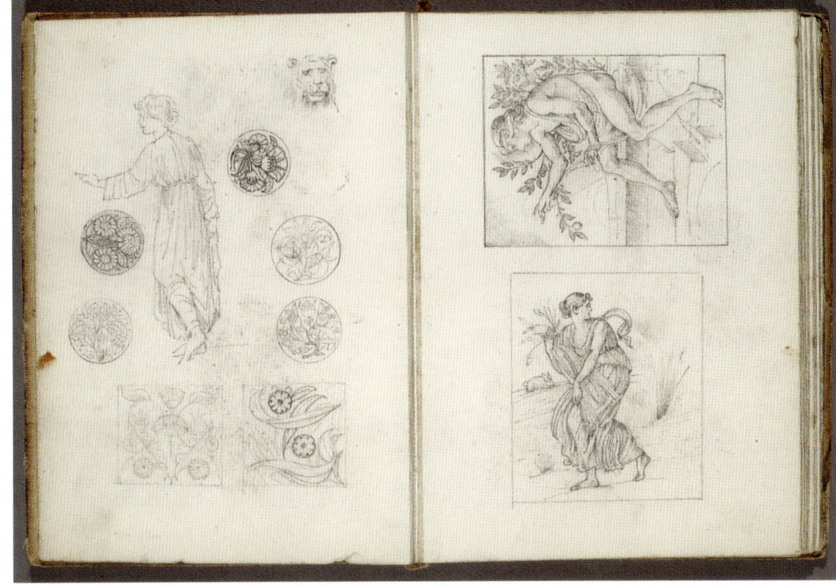

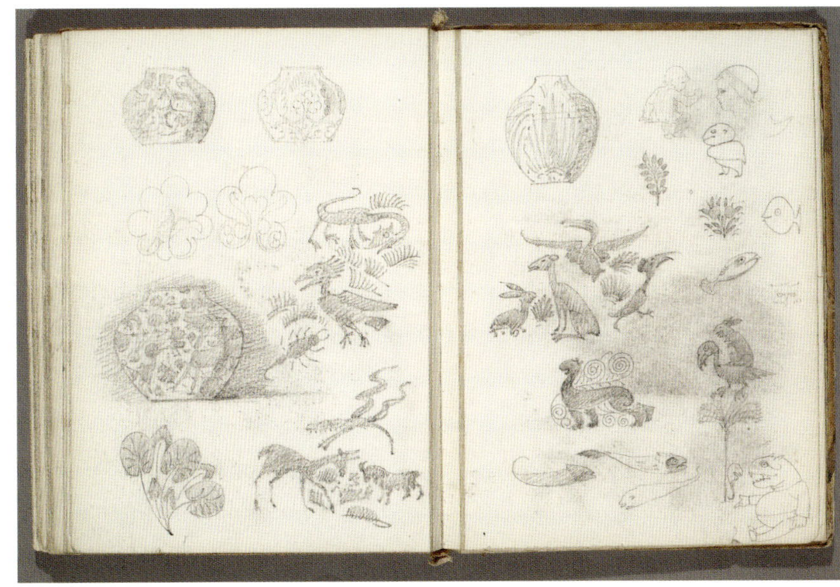

265 William De Morgan, *Bottle*, 1888–98, Birmingham Museums & Art Gallery

266, 267 William De Morgan, *Two Page-Openings from a Sketchbook*, undated, Birmingham Museums & Art Gallery

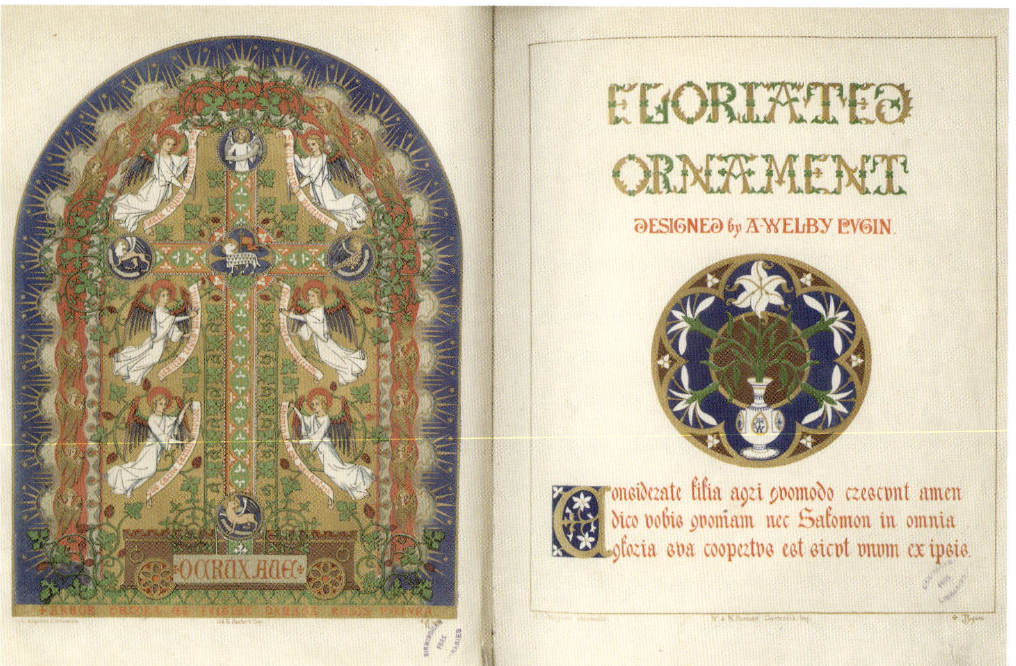
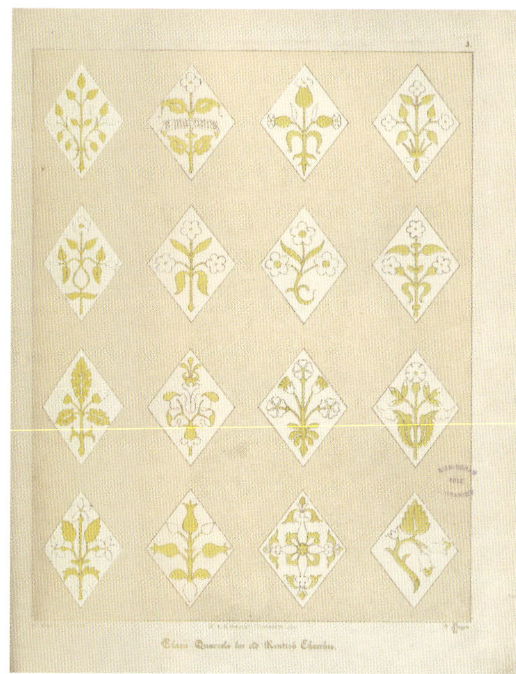

268, 269 Augustus Welby Northmore Pugin, *Frontispiece and Plate from 'Floriated Ornament'*, 1849, Birmingham Libraries & Archives

Christopher Dresser's *The Art of Decorative Design* (1862) was important in establishing a practice of deriving motifs and general design principles from nature. It was strikingly innovative and was quickly absorbed into the contemporary ethos of design in the mid-century, and elements of its design style find their way into the Aesthetic movement. This has some implication for drawing and the teaching of drawing being directed to the use of plant forms rather than the representation of them for their own sake. However, it refined and extended the use of a kind of 'scientific naturalism' to which Morris was opposed.[22]

Dresser's series of articles for *The Art Journal*, beginning in 1857, demonstrate a curious attitude to drawing because the emphasis in the illustrations is entirely diagrammatic [270]. They analyse the structure of the parts of the plant and flower and their function, much as a botanist would. In method, as well as tone, this approach was opposed to Ruskin's. Dresser described the flower as 'the most attractive part of the vegetable organism – hence it has gained the ornamentist's special attention'.[23] Such writings introduced the stylized botanical drawing that was the basis of Dresser's own industrial practice as a designer and which was advocated in his teaching for the Government Schools of Design. He used such diagrammatic work,

drawn in clear outline with watercolour washes added, for demonstration purposes in his teaching.

The application of natural forms through printed textiles and wallpaper was particularly important to the history of Arts and Crafts design because the Pre-Raphaelite pictorialist agenda was supplanted to a great extent by these more mechanical processes that required a different kind of graphic skill. Rarely dealing with the human body even as a schema, both wallpaper and textile designs demanded a degree of abstraction and an attention to nature. One of Morris's first designs, 'Daisy' (*c.* 1870) [275], appeared as a fabric design, a tile and as an applied design on walls and other surfaces. It became somewhat emblematic of Morris's design philosophy and appeared on the cover of the first number of *The Craftsman*, the journal of the American United Crafts group in 1901.[24] However, the simplicity of 'Daisy' was replaced in later fabrics and papers with a sophisticated graphic complexity that became Morris's most successful and characteristic contribution to the history of design [276, 277].

Perhaps the most extraordinary of the branches of design to encourage the revival of plant drawing was wallpaper. Arts and Crafts wallpaper patterns offered a way of reintroducing floral and vegetable motifs into the domestic setting and signalled a return to nature rather

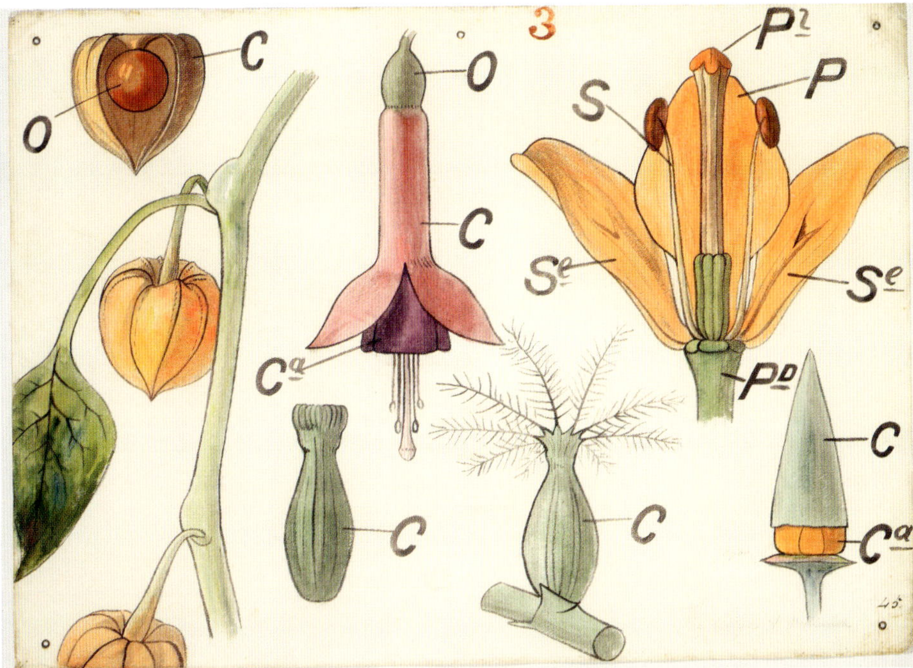

270 Christopher Dresser, *Demonstration Drawing*, c. 1855, Victoria and Albert Museum, London

than favouring artifice and illusion in pattern design. Plant drawing was a recurring theme in the writings and lectures of advanced designers, and alongside it came an emphasis on drawing from botanical specimens and an almost Ruskinian insistence on close observation. Walter Crane believed that 'a special development of applied design may almost be said to have come into existence with the modern use of wall papers'. He praised the 'beauty and character' of Morris's designs for surface pattern, adding that:

> since the revival of interest in art, the study of its history, and knowledge of style, a new impulse has been given, and patterns are constructed with more direct reference to their beauty, and interest as such, while strictly adapted to the methods of manufacture.[25]

In his contribution to *Arts and Crafts Essays* (1893) 'On Designing for the Art of Embroidery', the designer and illustrator Selwyn Image (1849–1930) advised embroidery designers to 'return again and again, and for evermore, to Nature', adding:

> Learn your business in the schools, but go out to Nature for your inspirations. See Nature through your own eyes, and be a persistent and curious observer of her infinite wonders. Yet to see Nature in herself is not everything, it is but half the matter; the other half is to know how to use her for the purposes of fine art, to know how to translate her into the language of art.[26]

The Gothic Revival architect J. D. Sedding (1838–91), who also designed wallpapers and metalwork, was more unorthodox in his advice:

> For the professional stylist, the confirmed conventionalist, an hour in his garden, a stroll in the embroidered meadows, a dip into an old herbal, a few carefully-drawn cribs from Curtis's *Botanical Magazine*, or even – for lack of something better – Sutton's last Illustrated Catalogue, is wholesome exercise, and will do more to revive the original instincts of a true designer than a month of sixpenny days at a stuffy museum. The old masters are dead, but 'the flowers', as Victor Hugo says, 'the flowers last always'.[27]

The emphasis in these various writings of Arts and Crafts designers is on nature as a source for a renewal of applied art. Through their design practices, Morris and his colleagues forged a link between the activity of reproducing nature faithfully and abstracting from it in order to produce good domestic design. Morris's desire to adorn walls with 'unmistakable suggestions of gardens and fields, and strange trees, boughs and tendrils' brought a Pre-Raphaelite ideal of nature into the domestic space, suitably stylized yet accurate, a balance between technology and art.[28]

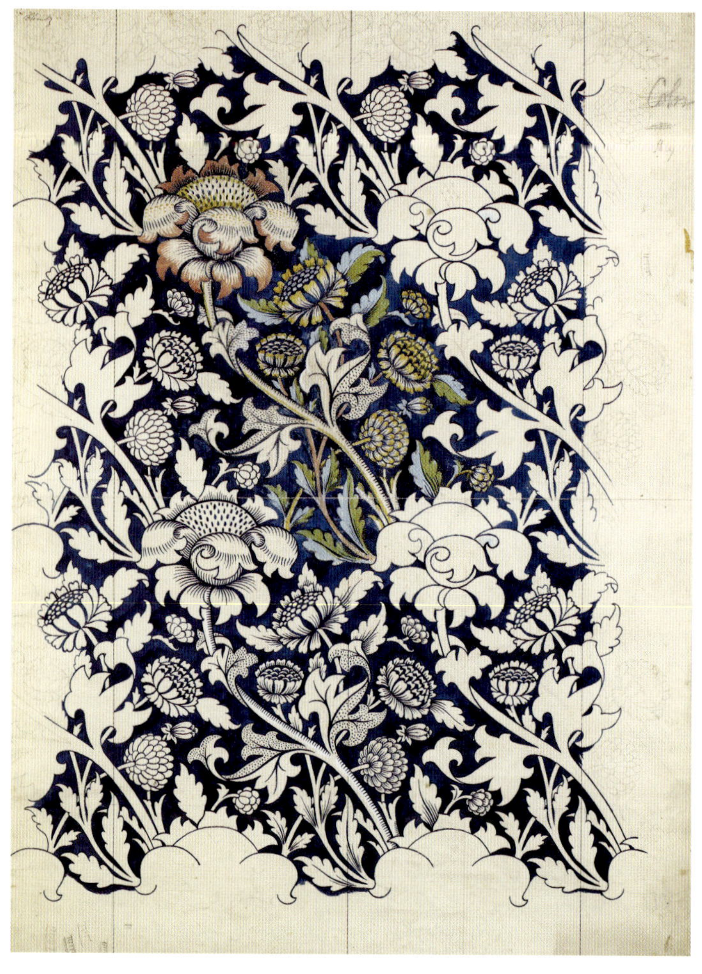

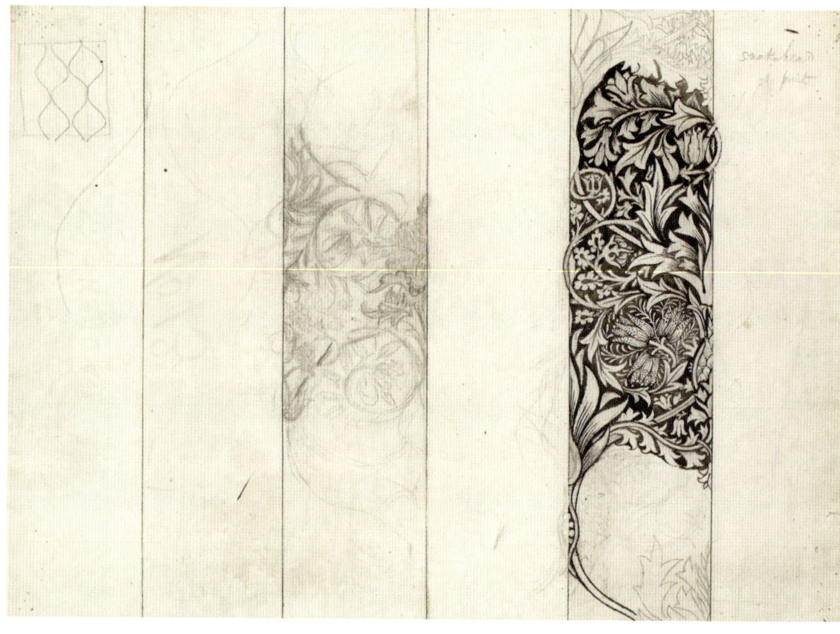

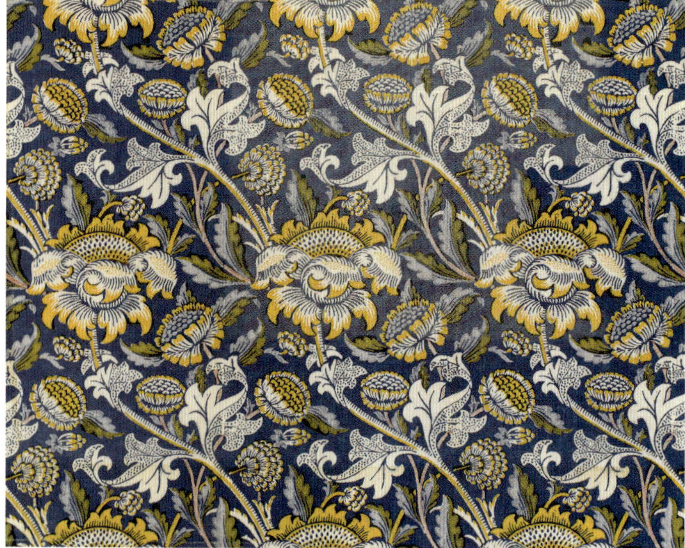

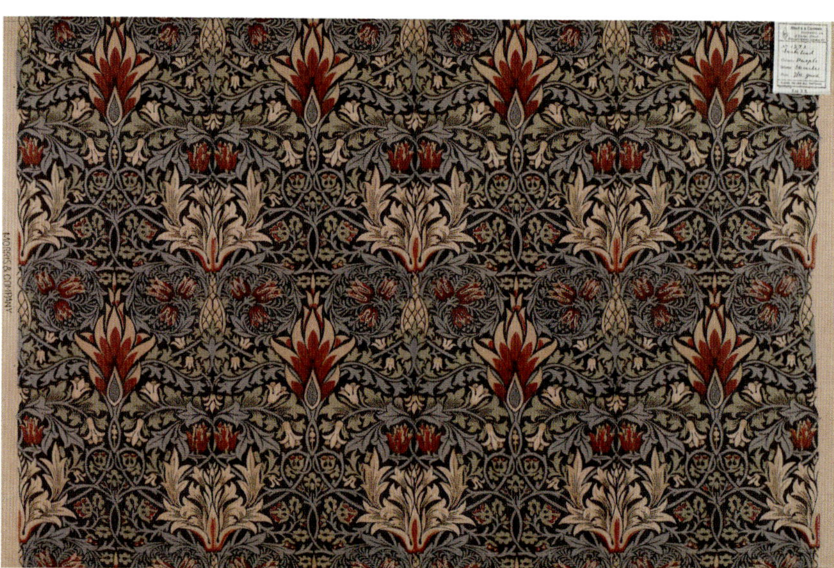

271 William Morris, *Design for a Printed Textile: 'Wey'*, 1882–83,
Birmingham Museums & Art Gallery

272 William Morris, *Printed Textile: 'Wey'*, 1883,
Birmingham Museums & Art Gallery

273 William Morris, *Design for a Printed Textile: 'Snakeshead'*, 1876,
Birmingham Museums & Art Gallery

274 William Morris, *Printed Textile: 'Snakeshead'*, 1876,
Birmingham Museums & Art Gallery

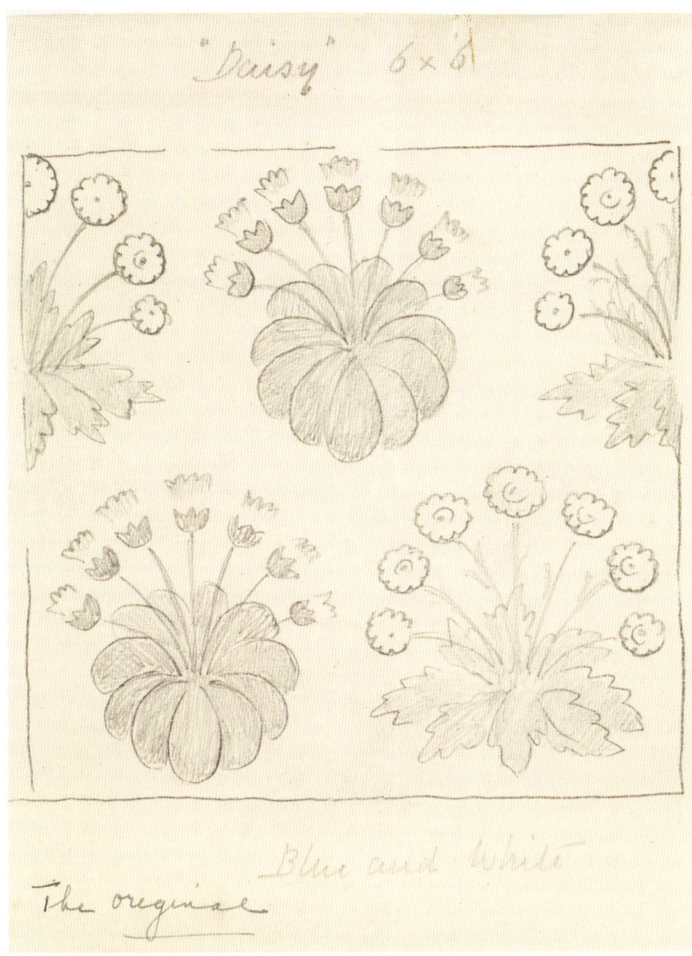

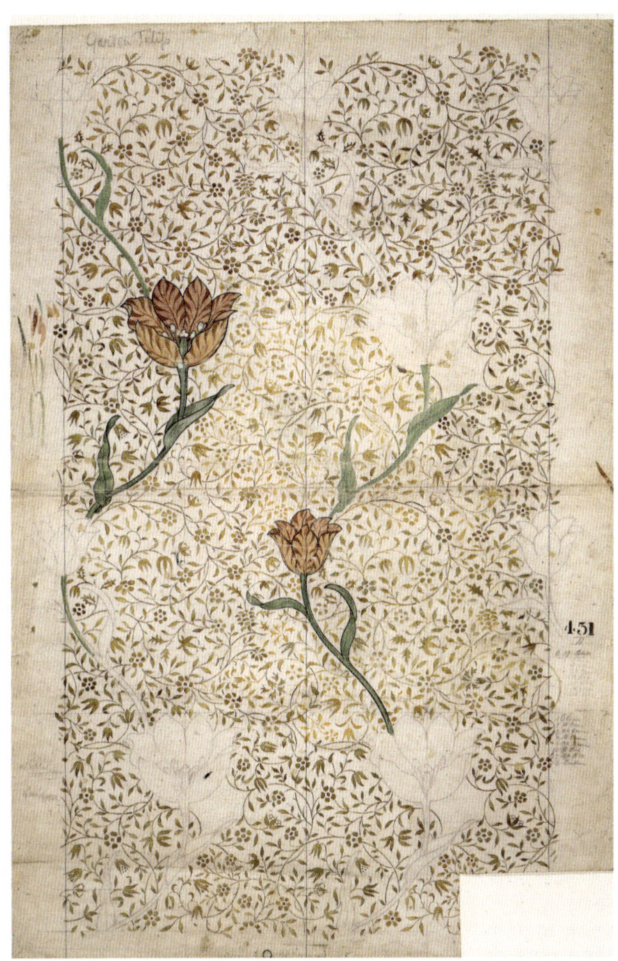

275 William Morris, *Design for a Tile: 'Daisy'*, *c.* 1870,
Birmingham Museums & Art Gallery
276 William Morris, *Design for a Wallpaper: 'Garden Tulip'*, 1885,
Birmingham Museums & Art Gallery

Morris developed the art he found in the illustrations of
medieval herbalists alongside the kind of flower drawing –
with its attention to 'truth to nature' – found in Ruskinian
Pre-Raphaelitism. In doing so he produced a highly stylized
plant drawing that could be accurate botanically while at
the same time fit into flat decorative schemes. This Arts
and Crafts agenda further transformed still life, plant and
flower drawing from a polite art of the upper-middle classes
into a practice that symbolized a new and radical form of
synthesizing art and design, and drawing, painting and
print. More importantly, it saw drawing as a central activity
in the training of the designer. It encouraged a creative
understanding of processes in the production of objects that
guided drawing and the study of design away from either
the Royal Academy or the Government Schools of Design.

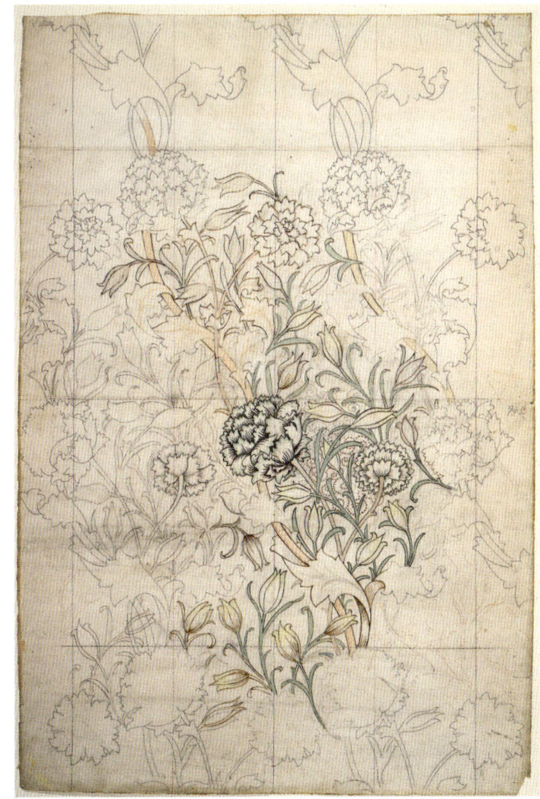

277 William Morris, *Design for a Wallpaper: 'Wild Tulip'*,
1884, Birmingham Museums & Art Gallery

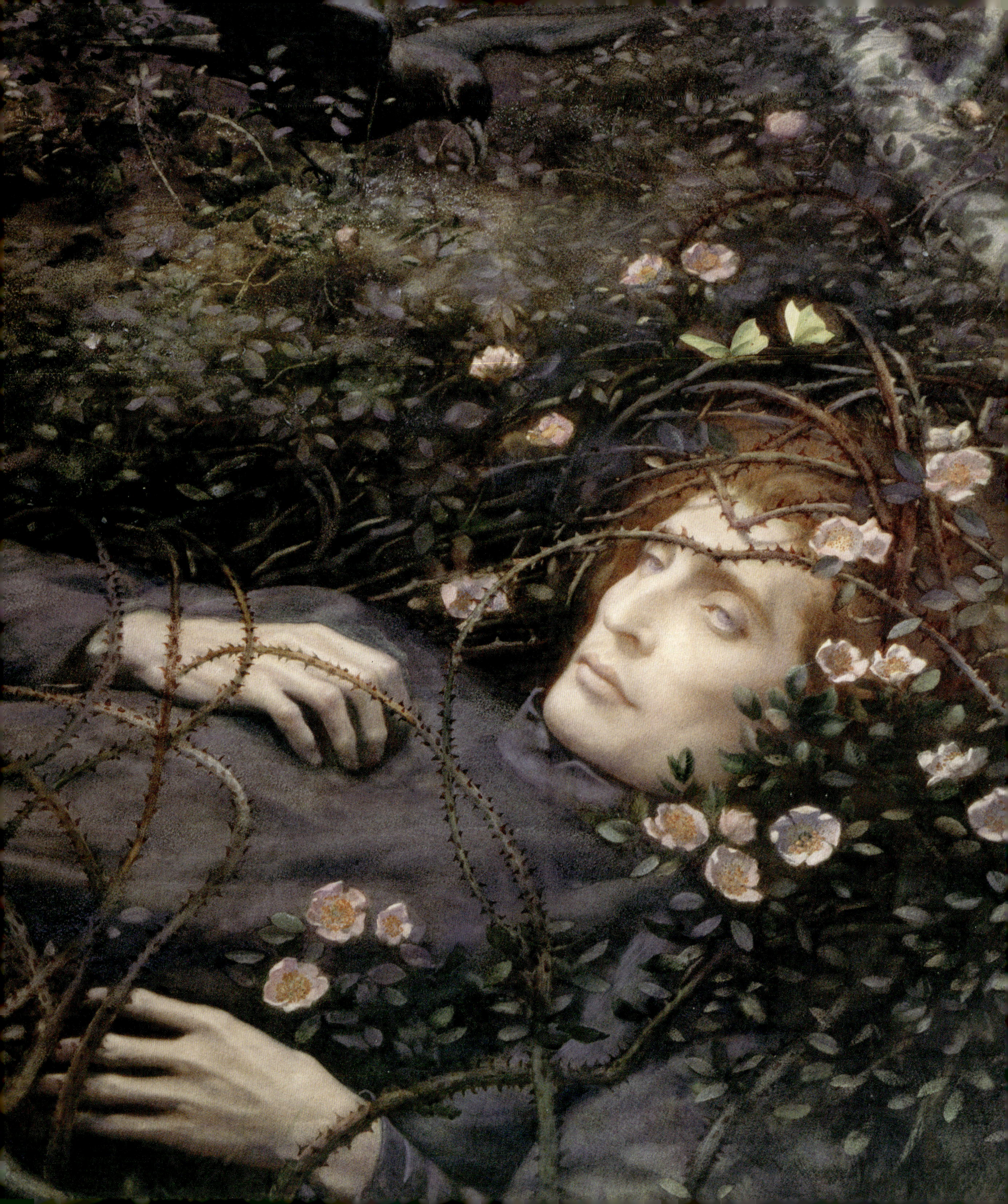

 The Aesthetics of Drawing from the 1860s to the 1890s: The Pre-Raphaelite Influence

Reappraisals of the role of drawing in the Renaissance and rediscoveries of overlooked or neglected artists were characteristics of the art and criticism of the 1860s and 1870s. To a great extent these critical positions can be seen as challenges to the canon, similar in nature to those launched by the Pre-Raphaelite Brotherhood earlier in the century. One of the formative contributions to this discourse was by Algernon Charles Swinburne, who published his 'Notes on the Designs of the Old Masters at Florence' in the *Fortnightly Review* in July 1868. The *Fortnightly* encouraged the kind of personal 'impression' contained in Swinburne's essay; in November of the following year, the same journal published Walter Pater's 'Notes on Leonardo da Vinci'.[1] Pater (1839–94) would seem to have borrowed the term 'note' from Swinburne along with others such as 'fragments' and 'studies', all of them implying informality and provisionality either in the object or in the point of view taken about it. They suggested a process of composition akin to drawing itself, allowing room for a personal interpretation of the work of art in complex, poetic or suggestive ways.

Swinburne mentions one of his enthusiasms, William Blake, when discussing Botticelli and Michelangelo in his *Fortnightly Review* essay. Blake's drawings, prints and poetry found a new audience following the publication of Alexander Gilchrist's *Life of Blake* in 1863, a work with which Rossetti was closely involved. Swinburne's *William Blake: A Critical Essay* (1868), now regarded as a formative work of Aesthetic movement theory, presented a Blake who was constitutionally both a rebel and an aesthete and whose very faith, as well as his tastes and artistic practices, were aesthetically driven. He was, too, a visionary, as Swinburne describes him:

> In the light of his especial faith all visible things were fused into the intense heat and sharpened into the keen outline of vision….To him the veil of outer things

278 Edward Robert Hughes, *'Oh, what's that in the hollow…?'*, 1893, Royal Watercolour Society (detail)

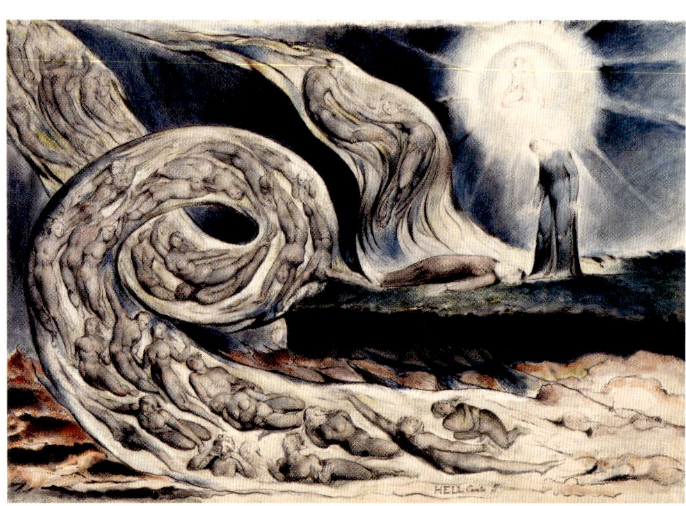

279 William Blake, *The Circle of the Lustful (The Whirlwind of Lovers)*, 1824–27, Birmingham Museums & Art Gallery

seemed always to tremble with some breath behind it: seemed at times to be rent in sunder with clamour and sudden lightning. All the void of the earth and air seemed to quiver with the passage of sentient wings and palpitate under the pressure of conscious feet.[2]

New criticism, old drawings

Having been regarded as part of the training of the artist but otherwise inferior to painting, drawing began to be considered the chief signifier of creativity. The new appreciation of Blake was part of that reassessment. Blake's visual expressions were experimental but tended towards the graphic in the form of drawings and engravings, and the images multiplied in his self-invented print processes. Swinburne's commentary on his work might be read alongside that of a new understanding of the art of drawing, in which it was seen as visionary and suggestive, and, rather than preparatory or provisional, central to the creative process. In his essay 'The School of Giorgione' (1877), Pater wrote of drawing as one of the 'essential pictorial

qualities' of visual art rather than a skill used to record the appearance of things. He stressed the sensual nature of what might otherwise be perceived as a preparatory stage in the production of a more complete pictorial expression, painting. For Pater, 'drawing' was not simply compositional; rather, it encoded the personality of the artist and permitted the visualization of abstractions:

> It is the *drawing* – the design projected from that peculiar pictorial temperament or constitution, in which, while it may possibly be ignorant of true anatomical proportions, all things whatever, all ideas however abstract or obscure, float up as visible scene or image….This *drawing*, then – the arabesque traced in the air by Tintoret's flying figures, by Titian's forest branches…these essential pictorial qualities must first of all delight the sense, delight it as directly and sensuously as a fragment of Venetian glass.[3]

Another aspect of the new appreciation of drawing needs to be remarked on here. The circulation of drawings in reproduction was a vogue of the latter decades of the nineteenth century, aided by the perfecting of the platinotype process by Frederick Hollyer (1838–1933). Simeon Solomon employed Hollyer to photograph drawings and paintings from the 1860s onwards and, as a result, his work continued to be circulated in photographic form after the disgrace following his arrest for homosexual activities in 1873 [280]. Even some of his preparatory and provisional images were issued, some of them remarkably frank about sexual desire and others obscurely allegorical. Appropriately framed photographs of drawings taken by Hollyer of works by Rossetti and Burne-Jones [281] became a part of the aspirational aesthetic interior for those unable to buy original drawings but keen to demonstrate their refined tastes.

Albums of photographs collected by Rossetti and Burne-Jones allowed both artists constant access to works otherwise restricted; photographs acted as a kind of

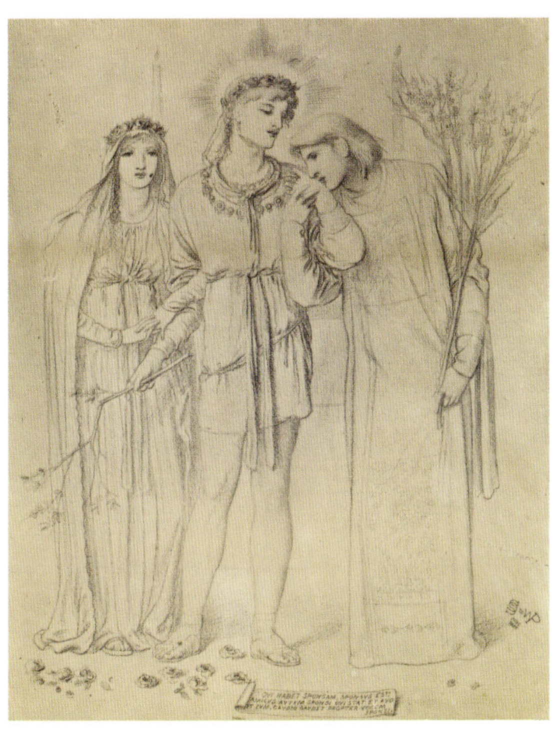

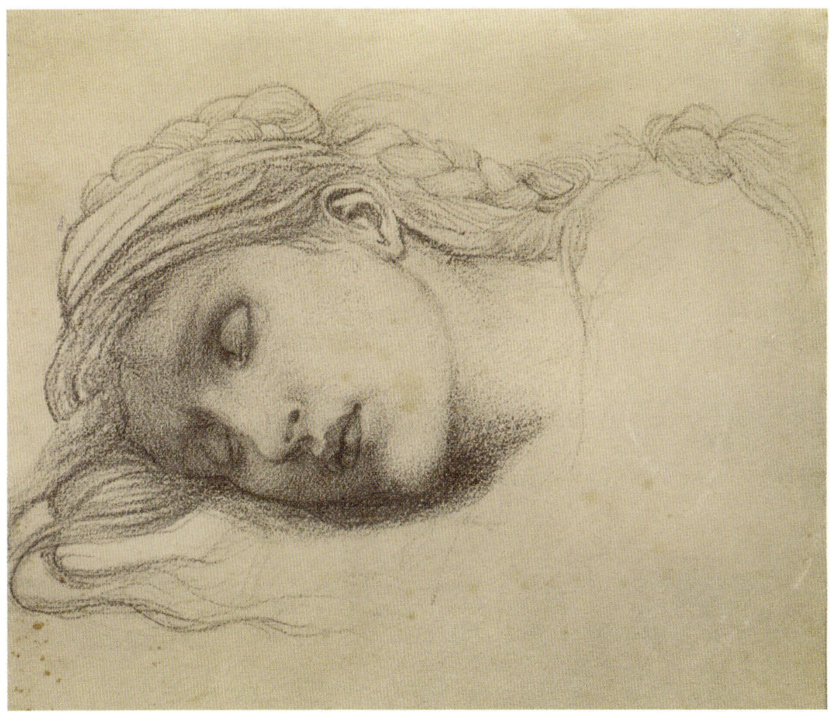

280 Frederick Hollyer after Simeon Solomon, *The Bride, the Bridegroom and the Friend of the Bridegroom,* after 1868, Birmingham Museums & Art Gallery

281 Frederick Hollyer after Edward Burne-Jones, *Study for 'The Garden Court': Sleeping Maiden,* c. 1883–85, Birmingham Museums & Art Gallery

personal collection akin to the cabinets of drawings and prints of an earlier age that encouraged deep and solitary contemplation. Burne-Jones used some of these photographed drawings – by Michelangelo, for example – in drawings, paintings and sketchbooks in the last decades of his life, using them to help create poses in works such as his Perseus cycle. Such a process was at the heart of an older academic endeavour – the copying of casts, the quotation of works by the Old Masters. Its revival in the activity of copying from photographs introduced a curious contradiction in later Pre-Raphaelite drawing practices – a seeming rejection of nature as the prime model and inspiration and a return to the power of art to produce

art. Such reflexivity became one of the key tendencies of Aestheticism but we can perceive its roots in the borrowings from Retzsch's outlines, medieval manuscript illustrations and Lasinio's engravings after Gozzoli that marked the early history of Pre-Raphaelite drawing.

Hollyer also photographed and sold choice specimens of Old Master drawings, reflecting a popular interest of the time, which had been shaped by the Grosvenor Gallery Winter Exhibitions of 1877–78 and 1878–79. In 1879, *The Athenaeum* could observe of the second of these events:

One thing must strike every student, and that is the amount of interest taken by visitors in the ancient drawings, although the adjoining room contains

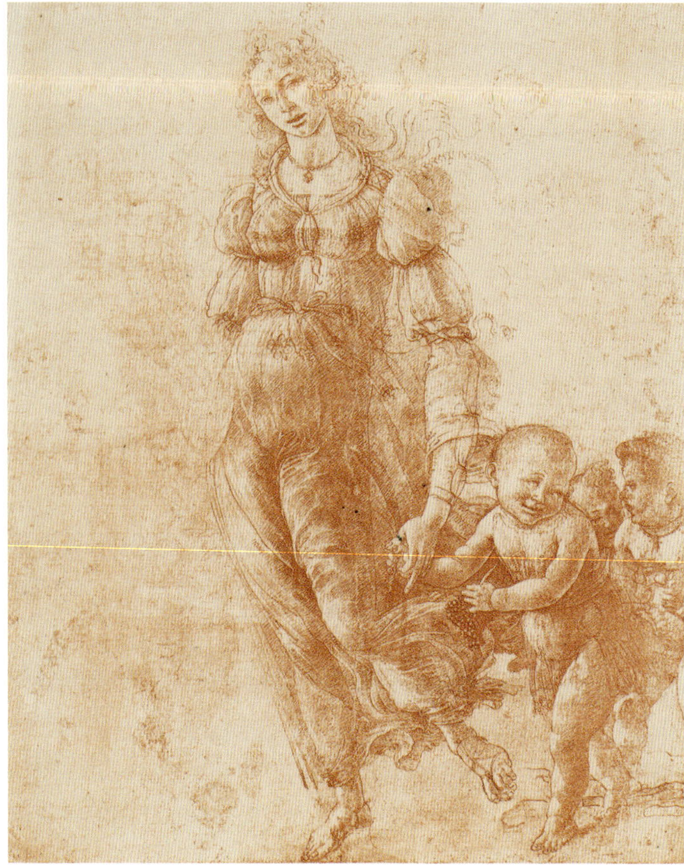

282 Sandro Botticelli, *Abundance*, c. 1475–82, reproduction published in the Grosvenor Gallery exhibition catalogue of 1877–78, private collection

the brilliant and apparently more attractive modern examples.

Elsewhere, the reviewer demonstrated a critical language in which drawing was discussed and qualities communicated to a general audience; for example, writing of a drawing of the Entombment of Christ:

> Less severely grand than the 'Hercules', it is more grandiose, more strictly and faithfully Mantegnesque; less dramatic, it is less spontaneous; more elaborate in thought and execution, it is more finished.[4]

Such thoughtful, discriminating criticism, if a little over-descriptive, became a feature of periodical art reviews in the last decades of the nineteenth century.

The catalogue for the first Grosvenor Gallery Exhibition of Old Master drawings was printed in large format with autotype illustrations after works by Mantegna, Leonardo, Michelangelo, Dürer and Botticelli. It had an introduction by J. Comyns Carr, the critic of *The Globe* and *The Pall Mall Gazette*, who had joined Sir Coutts Lindsay and Charles Hallé in setting up the Grosvenor Gallery in 1877. Carr had a peculiarly acute sensibility in regard to drawing. In his catalogue introduction he analysed its special quality:

> In one sense, indeed, a drawing by a great master may be said to make a stronger and more direct appeal to the imagination than the most highly-finished painting.…The material of a drawing is in itself so simple; there is so little in the mode of the execution with the silver point or with the pen, wherein one age can boast advantage over another, that our attention is carried at once to what is essential in the master's style. Expressed in such abstract language, this thought can scarcely escape us, nor can he himself escape the need of clear and precise definition.[5]

Moreover, Carr found that 'a collection of drawings appears altogether more modern than a gallery of paintings.'[6] He reproduced Botticelli's *Allegory of Abundance* (c. 1480–85, The British Museum) in autotype [282] as one of his illustrations. Here too we can see a shared interest that had developed between Pre-Raphaelitism and Aestheticism and which was, by the 1880s, forming popular taste. Swinburne, for example, considered Botticelli's drawings superior to his paintings: 'The dull and dry quality of his thin pallid colouring can here no longer impair the charm of his natural grace, the merit of his strenuous labour.'[7] The drawings, however faint, were evidence of Botticelli's creative imagination and skill and invited interpretation of their possible meanings. Indeed, the combination of incompleteness, technical excellence and obscurity produced a particular quality to these works:

> In all these [examples] is the same constant and noble effort to draw vigorously and perfectly, in many the same faint and almost painful grace, which give a distinct value and a curious charm to all the works of Botticelli.[8]

The relevance of Botticelli as a measure for contemporary achievement in drawing is also apparent. In his memoirs, Carr recalled Rossetti describing Burne-Jones as having 'oceans of imagination…and in this respect there has been

nobody like him since Botticelli'.[9] Carr himself thought that
it was Burne-Jones's delight

> as it was the delight of Botticelli, to be always
> exercising his invention on some theme of legendary
> beauty; and it was his gift, as indeed it was also
> Botticelli's, to be able to translate such themes into the
> appropriate language of art.[10]

Indeed, Burne-Jones became identified with some of the
graphic qualities of Botticelli as well as his favourite themes.
The reviewer for *The Athenaeum* described Burne-Jones's
contributions to the exhibition of drawings by modern
and contemporary artists at the Fine Art Society in the
winter of 1889–90 as 'charmingly graceful', adding that 'an
uncatalogued drawing on brown paper of the head of a saint
with a nimbus, by Mr. Burne-Jones, is in Botticelli's mood,
and almost worthy of that master'.[11]

The openness of Botticelli's imagery to interpretation
or speculation was clearly a fundamental part of this
appeal. Because the purpose and meanings of his allegories
and other subjects had been lost, there was scope for the
personal 'impression' to become a prime critical act and
for the critic to construct new narratives. Also – and this is
a quality shared with both Leonardo and Michelangelo –
Botticelli's drawings were seen as having a discrete beauty
of their own, produced by beautiful marks outlining poetic
concepts, yielding a complete aesthetic experience from
an incomplete work. The very incompleteness of drawing
supplanted more finished and permanent records of the
artist's imagination.

The mythological and allegorical subjects of Botticelli's
drawings and paintings were revivified in later Pre-

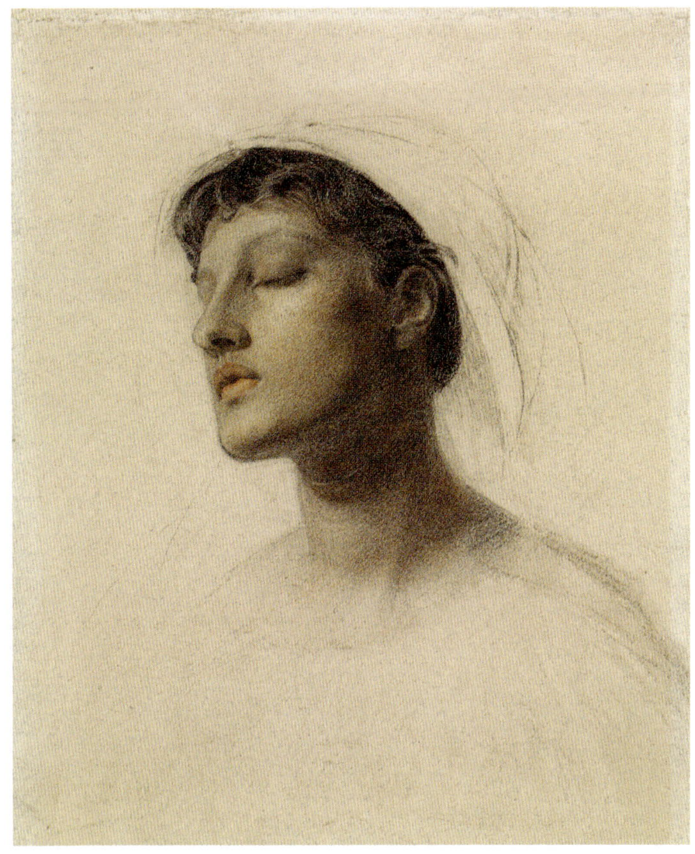

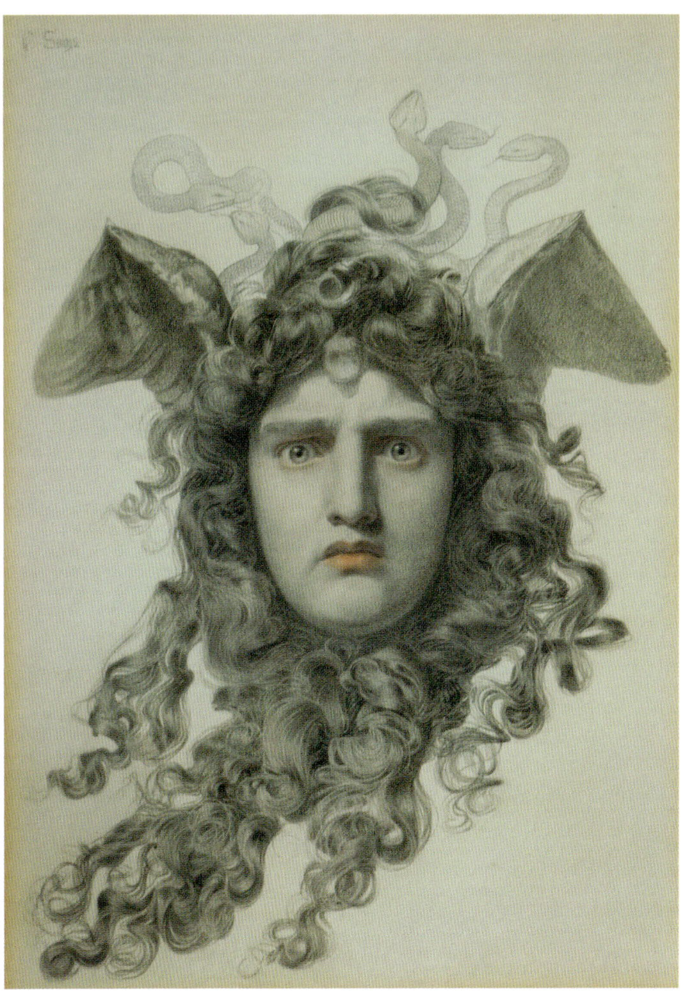

283 Frederick Sandys, *Study for 'The Waters of Lethe'*, 1870–74,
Birmingham Museums & Art Gallery
284 Frederick Sandys, *Medusa*, c. 1875,
Victoria and Albert Museum, London

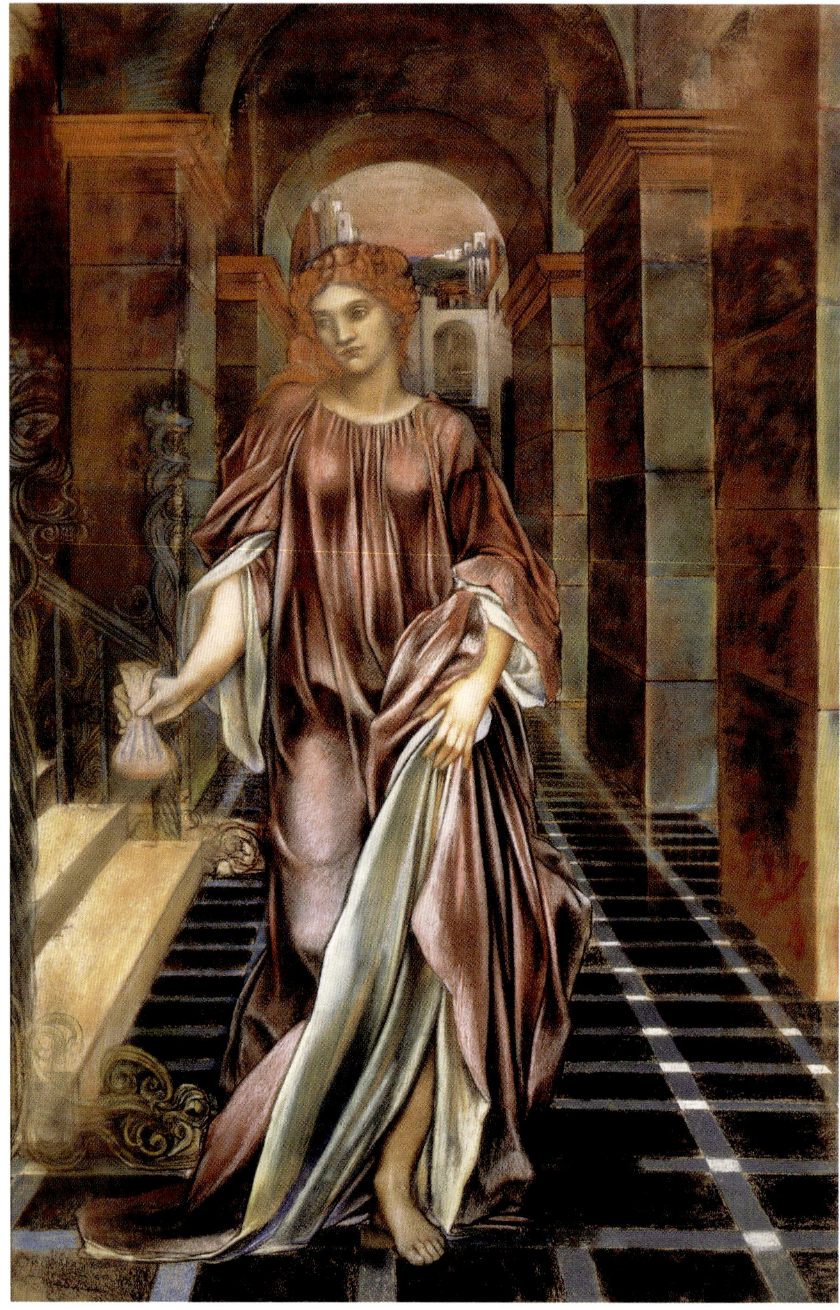

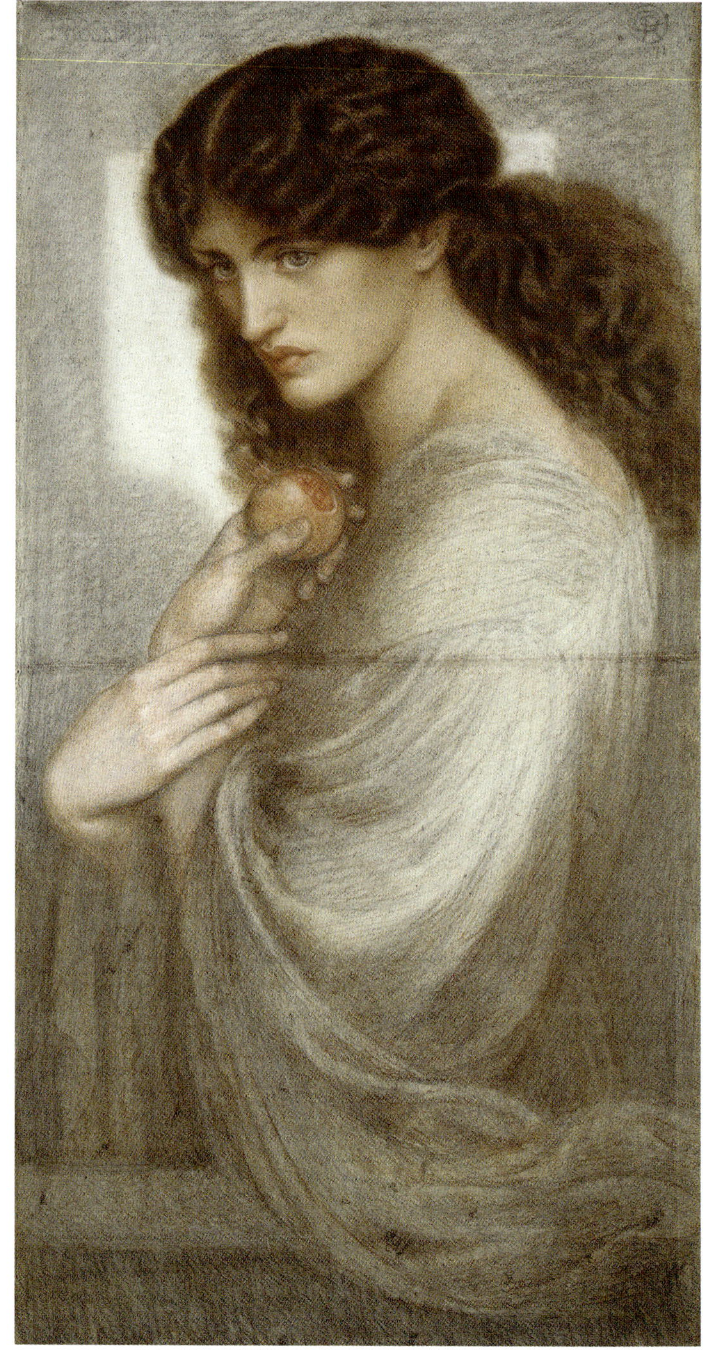

285 Evelyn De Morgan, *Medea*, c. 1889, National Trust,
Wightwick Manor and Gardens
286 Dante Gabriel Rossetti, *Proserpine*, 1871,
Ashmolean Museum, University of Oxford

Raphaelite works by Rossetti, Sandys, Burne-Jones, Solomon
and Evelyn De Morgan, all of whom used the human figure
to personify abstractions or embody myths. In his drawing
[283] for the painting *The Waters of Lethe* (1870–74, The
William Morris Gallery, Walthamstow), Sandys played with
an ambiguity between embodying the human longing for
forgetfulness of pain, and personifying the river Lethe that
brought oblivion to those passing through the underworld.
Both are represented in a woman's head with closed eyes.
Rossetti, Sandys and Solomon all attempted to depict the

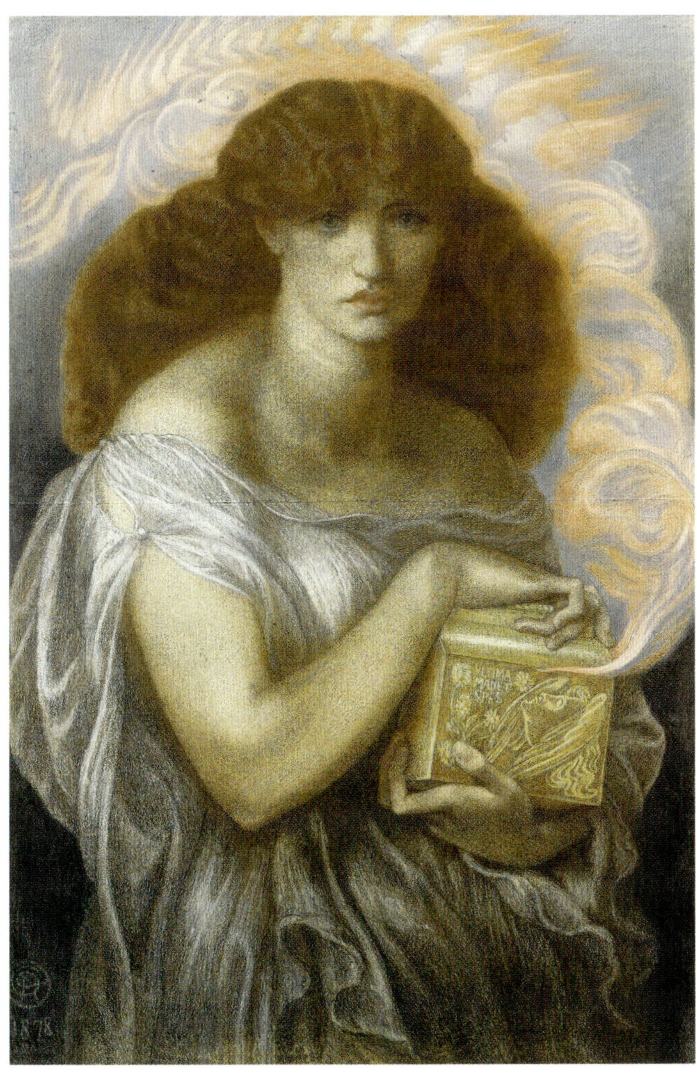

287 Dante Gabriel Rossetti, *Pandora*, 1878,
National Museums Liverpool (Lady Lever Art Gallery)

mythological figure who most evaded representation, Medusa. Sandys confronted her head-on in an attempt to come to terms with the horror of her stony stare (*c.* 1875) [284]. De Morgan reproduced the Botticelli type with its sweet expression and graceful figure in several guises such

as *Spring* (1869–70, The De Morgan Foundation) and as dramatic heroines such as Medea (1889) [285]. Rossetti was deeply influenced by Italian Renaissance art in this period, often of the most recondite type. Its impact on his work helped to produce some of his finest images representing mythological figures such as Astarte, Proserpine (1871) [286], Pandora (1878) [287] and Mnemosyne [114]. Rossetti's Mnemosyne was indistinguishable from his Astarte, his Pandora from his Proserpine, but rather than nuances of interpretation, it was their monumental beauty that helped make their visual impact. Their repetitive, obsessive quality remains one of their chief fascinations.

Drawing towards the fin de siècle

Rossetti is a recurring figure in the revival of drawing in the last years of the nineteenth century. After the memorial exhibition of his work at the Royal Academy in 1883, his drawings and watercolours emerged from the relative obscurity of his studio and the walls of private collections to become more widely known and appreciated. His pen drawing *Mary Magdalene at the Door of Simon the Pharisee* [175] became a key work in the continued interest in Pre-Raphaelite drawing. In 1896 Charles Ricketts reproduced it as the frontispiece of the first edition of the gift-book *The Pageant* for which he was art editor. The original drawing had gone missing in the previous decade and was known only through photographic copies, yet it had continued to exert an influence. Ricketts's own drawing, *Oedipus and the Sphinx* (1891) [288], for example, which was illustrated in the same publication, has clear echoes of Rossetti's composition in the leaning figure of Oedipus, the opposition of two figures and the explosive sense of a fatal dialogue just about to take place.

There is another curious instance of the impact of Rossetti's *Mary Magdalene* drawing. The figures in Burne-Jones's design for a window, *The Magdalene at Christ's Feet*

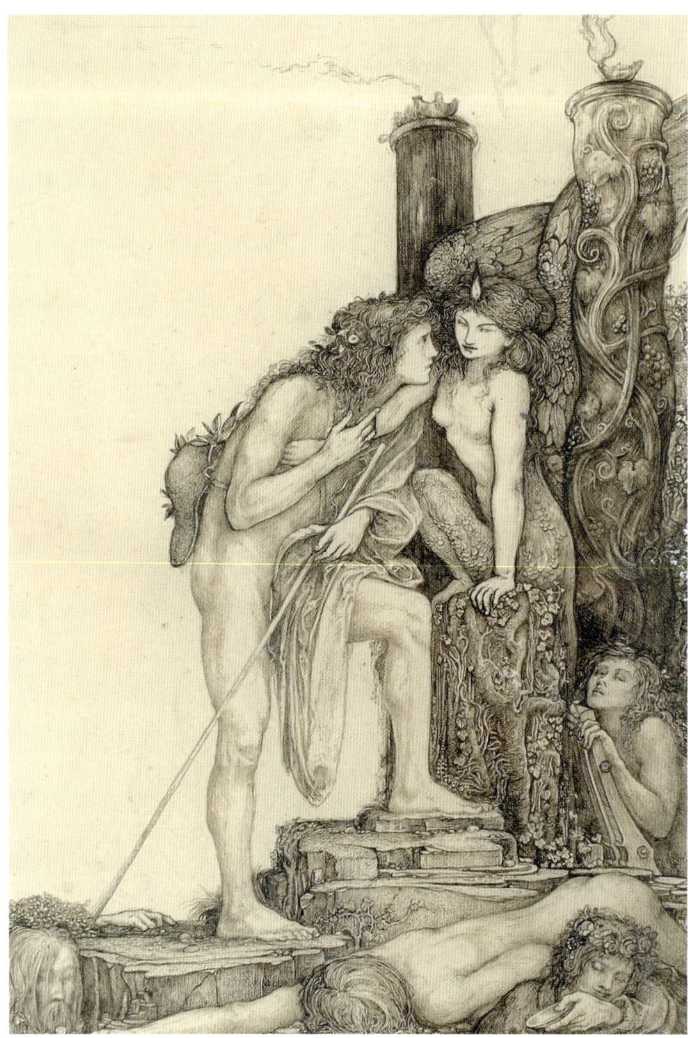

288 Charles Ricketts, *Oedipus and the Sphinx*, 1891, Tullie House Museum & Art Gallery

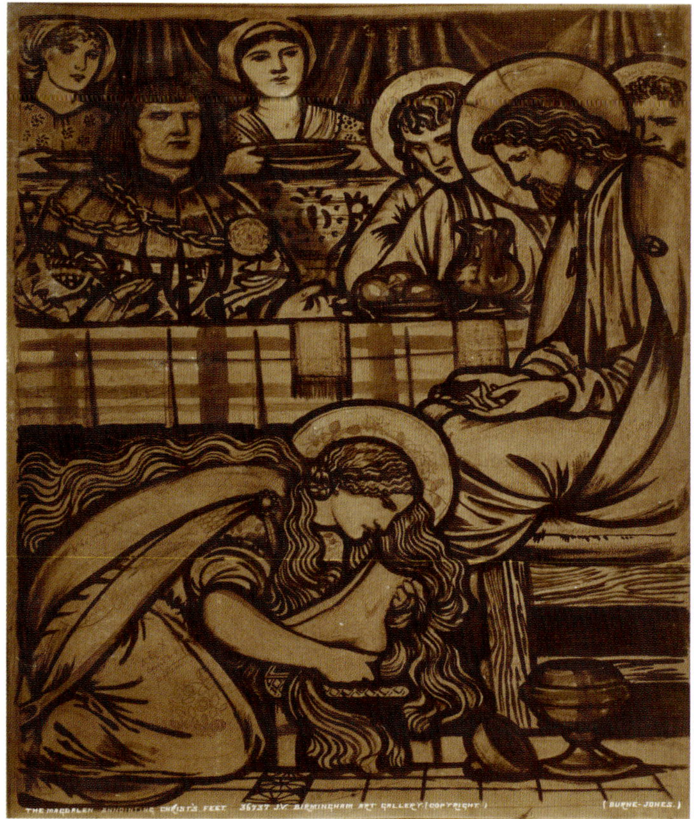

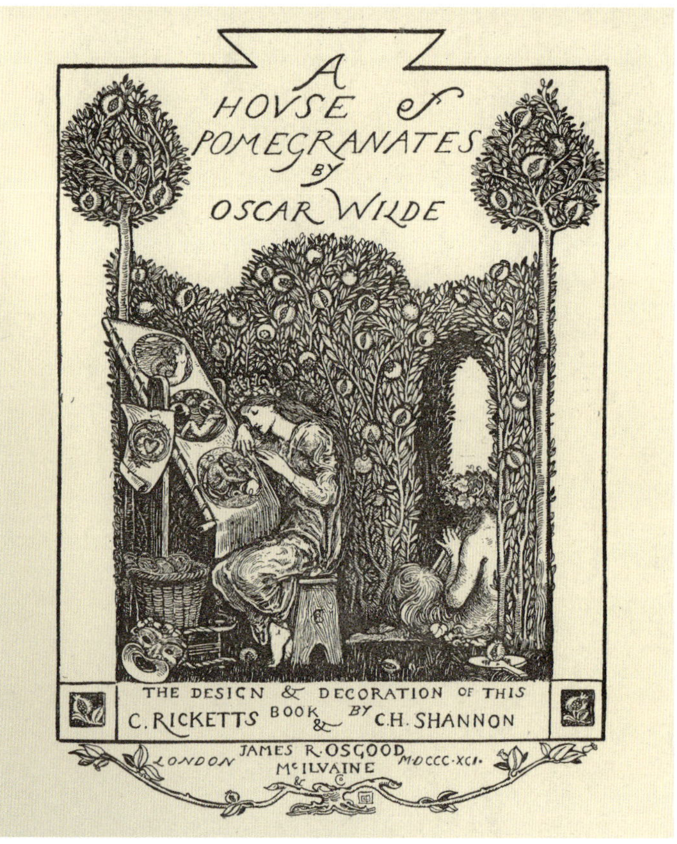

289 Edward Burne-Jones, *Design for Stained Glass: 'The Magdalen at Christ's Feet'*, 1863, photographed by Frederick Hollyer for Morris & Company, Birmingham Museums & Art Gallery

290 Charles Ricketts and Charles Shannon, *Title Page: 'A House of Pomegranates'*, 1891, Birmingham Libraries & Archives

(1863) [289] – the Magdalene with loosened hair, Christ's profile and an onlooker (perhaps Simon the Pharisee himself) – all closely resemble the memorable originals invented by Rossetti. It suggests either that Rossetti's figures made such an impression on Burne-Jones that he felt the need to replicate them, almost as if they were portraits of the biblical characters they represented, or that he was making a sequel to Rossetti's drawing, a 'what happened next', that involved the use of recognizable figures from the original.

The Pageant chose to celebrate Pre-Raphaelitism because, as Ricketts's biographer J. G. P. Delaney explained,

Ricketts and Shannon believed that the Arts and Crafts Movement in Britain was beginning to flounder in the hands of inferior artists who did not understand the great tradition established by the Pre-Raphaelites, so the first issue was devoted to these latter in the hope that this would have a beneficial influence on the movement.[12]

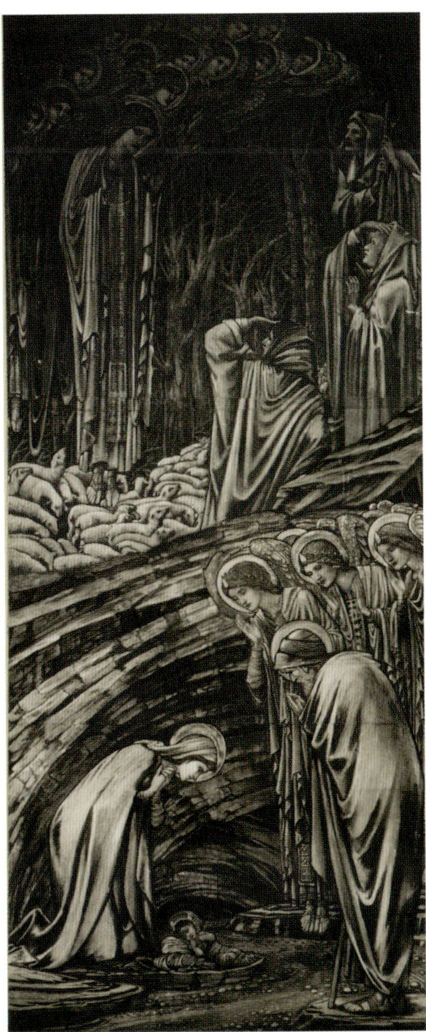

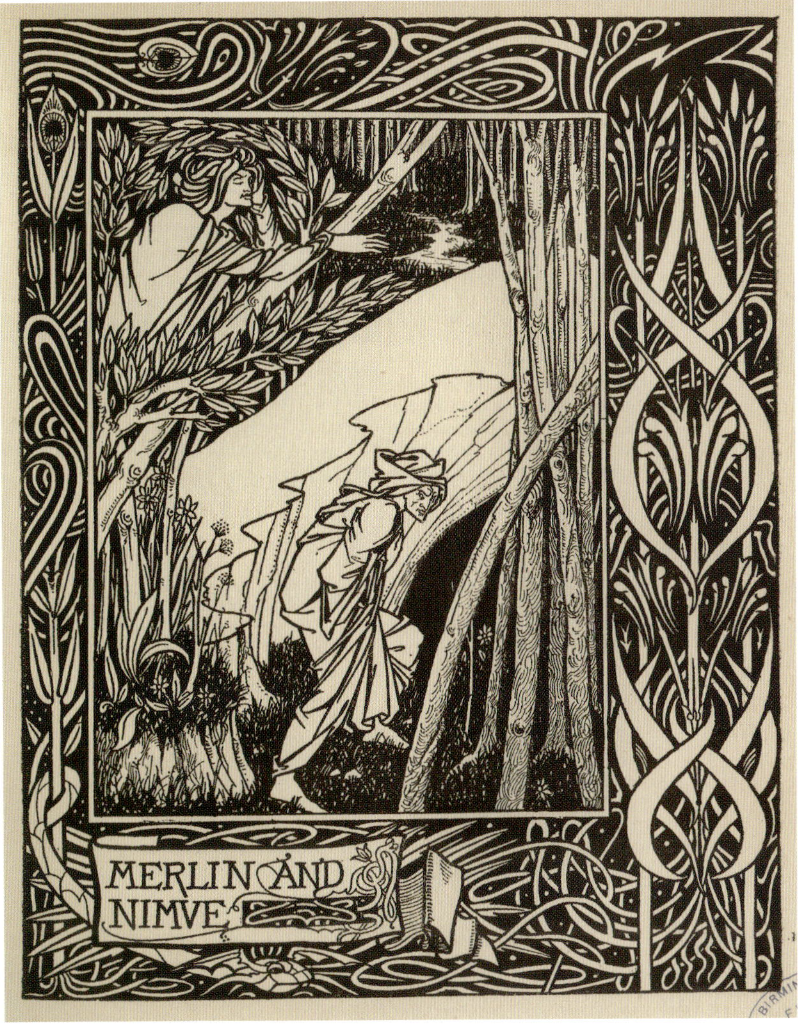

291 Edward Burne-Jones, *Design for Stained Glass: 'The Nativity'*, 1888, photographed by Frederick Hollyer for Morris & Company, Birmingham Museums & Art Gallery

292 Aubrey Beardsley, *Merlin and Nimuë*, c. 1893, Birmingham Libraries & Archives

Yet it is clear that it was not the drawings of Millais or Hunt that were the chief focus of this new enthusiasm. Perhaps they had become too accepted and their works too popular. There was a sense that public taste, even that of the well informed, was still catching up with Rossetti's experiments from the 1850s and 1860s. When Ricketts rediscovered *Mary Magdalene at the Door of Simon the Pharisee* in a furniture dealer's shop in 1896 he bought it for the collection he shared with Charles Shannon, a rare mixture of ancient, Renaissance and modern drawings and objets d'art.[13]

Ricketts's early drawings for various publications, such as *The Magazine of Art*, show the extent of Rossetti's influence on his imagination. His later designs for Oscar Wilde's *A House of Pomegranates* (1891) [**290**] and *The Sphinx* (1894), among other publications, while much simplified, have strong Rossettian elements: tangled hair, asymmetric

compositions, the use of decorative roundels. Indeed, the portrait painter John Singer Sargent (1856–1925) observed that 'Nothing that Ricketts ever did could have been done without Rossetti.'[14] In his pursuit of the excellence of Pre-Raphaelite illustration, Ricketts was rivalled by Aubrey Beardsley, whose use of the unbroken line – a continuation of the Pre-Raphaelite 'modified outline style' – is the very basis of his exploration of the possibilities of drawing.

In 1888, Beardsley left school in Brighton and came to work in London at an insurance office. He would have been able to see the Burne-Jones drawings at the New Gallery that year. Alongside notable paintings such as *The Rock of Doom* (1885–88), *The Tower of Brass* (1888) and *The Depths of the Sea* (1887), Burne-Jones exhibited what *The Athenaeum* described as

a number of beautiful drawings in chalk….Their

soundness and exquisite style are even greater than the pictures….Students of art and lovers of beauty should certainly examine [them] with attention.[15]

Perhaps more importantly, Beardsley could have seen a second exhibition, featuring designs by Burne-Jones for stained-glass windows for St Philip's Church, Birmingham (now Birmingham Cathedral). Fortunée De Lisle described the decorative scheme as 'probably the highest attainment of modern times in this branch of art'.[16] The most daring feature of these windows was the high degree of stylization both in composition and individual figures, drapery and accessories. The Nativity window [291] was of particular interest because it dramatized the subject in an arrestingly new asymmetric arrangement, the space divided by an overhanging rock that rises diagonally across the picture to form a cave-like space within which the Holy Family is depicted. This compositional device was borrowed by Beardsley for one of the illustrations for the *Morte D'Arthur*, his first major commission, published by Dent in two volumes in 1893–94. For the illustration *Merlin and Nimuë* [292], a subject Burne-Jones had previously treated in *The Tree of Forgiveness* (1882), Beardsley appropriated the overhanging rock, emphasizing its phallic thrust. It makes the highly stylized landscape sexually threatening.[17]

By the 1880s the public had been primed for a revival of interest in the drawings of the Old Masters and had gradually accepted the strangeness of Pre-Raphaelite compositional experiments and physical types. It was not ready, however, for a highly refined synthesis of Dürer, Botticelli, Michelangelo, Rossetti and Burne-Jones that was to emerge in the work of Beardsley in the last decade of the century. Beardsley presented that heady mixture of manner and motif, together with more unfamiliar pictorial elements, in his illustrative projects published from 1892 to his early death in 1898. He returned Pre-Raphaelitism to the world of controversy by 'making decadent' some

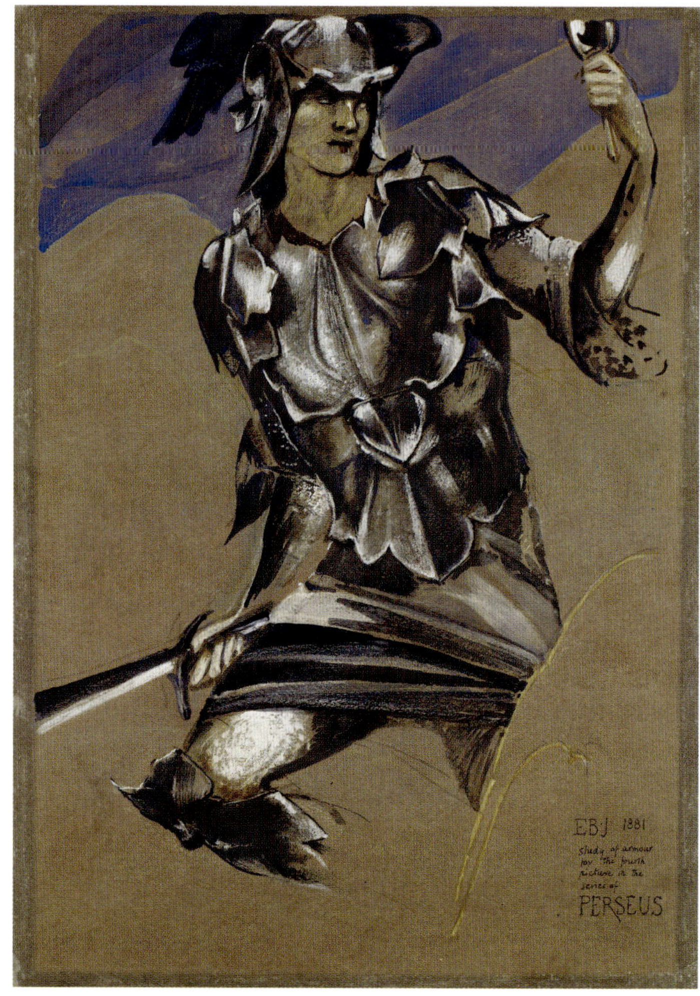

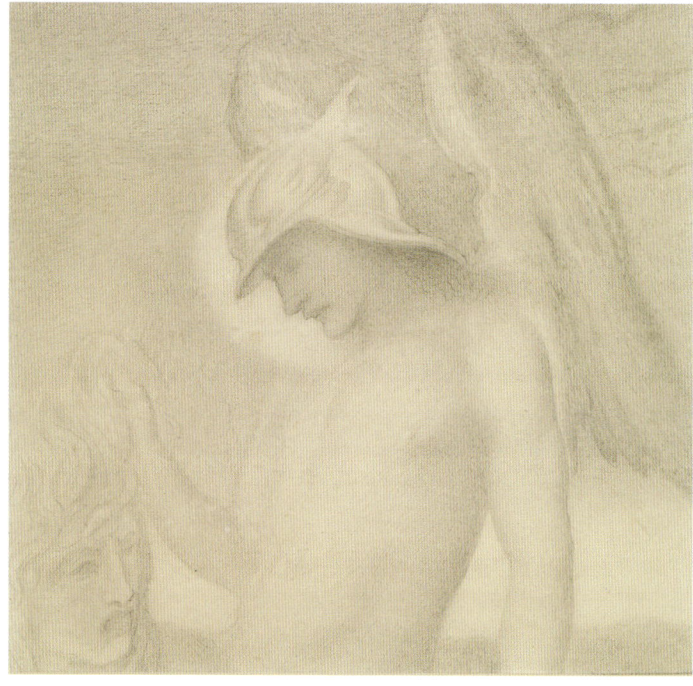

293 Edward Burne-Jones, *Study of the Figure of Perseus for 'The Finding of Medusa'*, 1881, Birmingham Museums & Art Gallery
294 Simeon Solomon, *Perseus With the Head of Medusa*, probably c. 1890s, Birmingham Museums & Art Gallery

of its themes and techniques. To some extent controversy
had never been far from the public reception of Pre-
Raphaelitism, and a connection between the second
generation of Pre-Raphaelites and sexual licence had
already been made in 1871 by the poet and novelist Robert
Buchanan in his notorious essay 'The Fleshly School of
Poetry', which specifically attacked Rossetti.[18] In 1892, just
before the widespread condemnation of Beardsley, Burne-
Jones was to be publicly admonished for unwholesomeness.

While acknowledging the beauty of Burne-Jones's work,
the critic Harry Quilter condemned it, using a language of
nationalistic fervour to make his point:

> I see clearly how fatal is their influence, how perverted
> their meaning, how vain their accomplishment. I see
> how little suited is this spirit of sick-sad dreams to the
> country I love, and the folks who have made England
> in the old time, and who are making it to-day. And
> as I look back over the great art of former times, I
> seek in vain for any painting or sculpture which has
> based its appeal, or found its beauty in a panegyric
> of the vanished years, in an endeavour to forget the
> circumstances, the obligations, and the meaning of the
> artist's own generation.[19]

He found the pictures 'unwholesome in themselves' and
defended his judgment in further analysis:

> They appear to me based upon a view of the passion
> and the power of love which is untrue and undesirable.
> The pictures are morbid, and not less so because the
> personages shown therein are apt to be epicure – though
> perhaps we may not rightly term the work *sensual*, it is
> so uniformly and intensely *sensuous*, that perhaps the
> baser intention had been less harmful in result.[20]

Quilter particularly disapproved of the characterization of
love in Burne-Jones's work:

> Not only loving but *love-sick* are all his characters
> – their love oppresses as a physical suffering – their

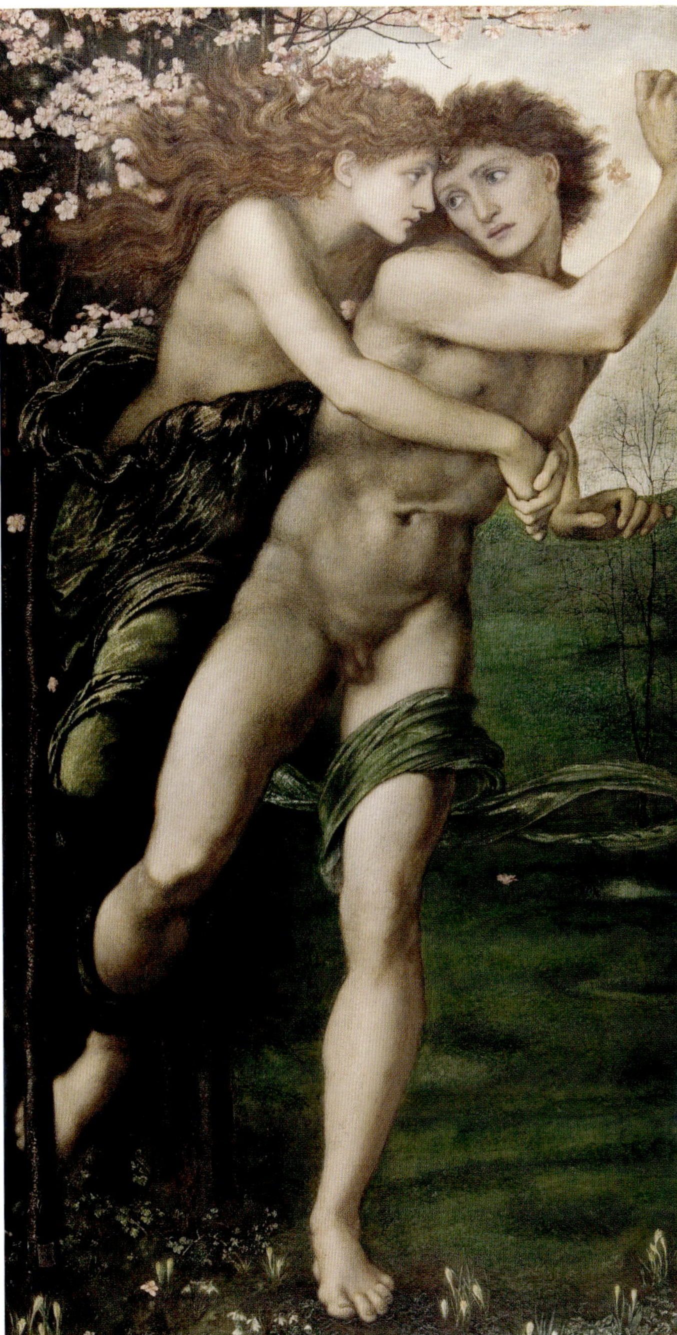

295 Edward Burne-Jones, *Phyllis and Demophöon*, 1870,
Birmingham Museums & Art Gallery

> heads and bodies droop beneath it….Something of
> the archaism of Botticelli and Mantegna clings to him
> still, and, to go no further than one of his peculiarities,
> he is apt to reduce both men and women to a type
> which, while partaking of the character of both, is a
> perfect representation of neither.[21]

Burne-Jones was clearly identified in the critical narratives
of the 1890s that objected to Aestheticism and saw recent
British art as decadent, even degenerate. In the process,
Pre-Raphaelitism became once more a battleground
some forty years after its inception. Quilter's objections

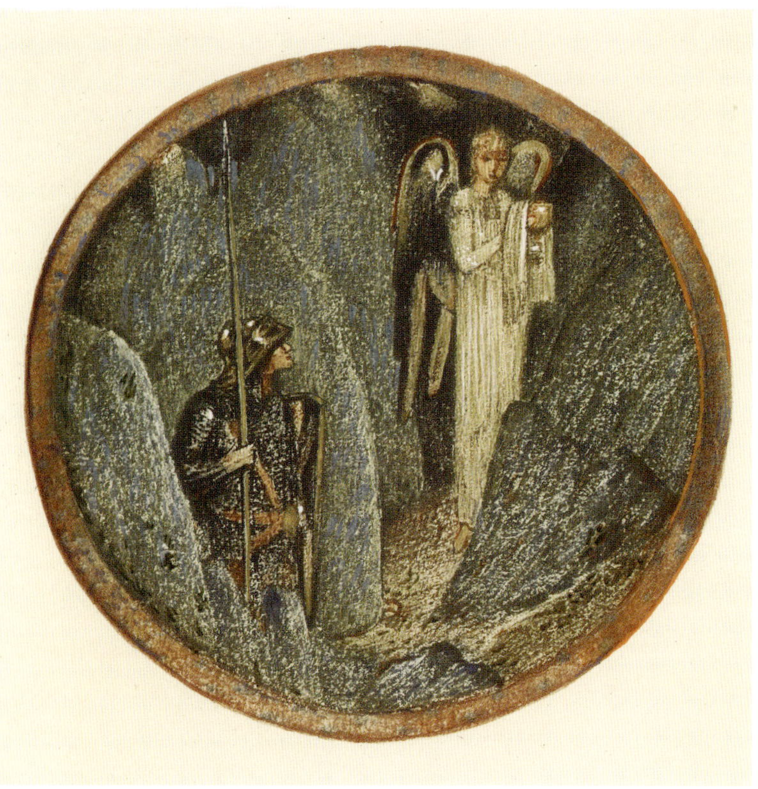

296 Edward Burne-Jones, *Honour's Prize*, printed 1905, Birmingham Museums & Art Gallery

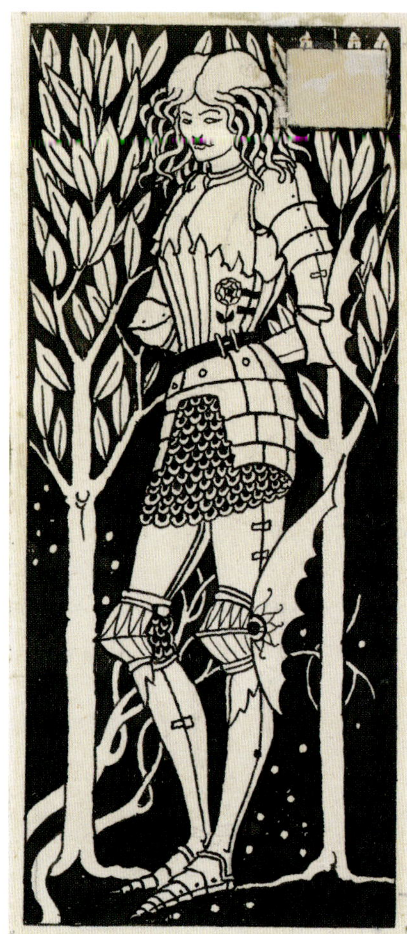

297 Aubrey Beardsley, *A Knight*, 1892, Victoria and Albert Museum, London

to the androgynous look of Burne-Jones's characters are similar to those raised against Simeon Solomon, still an unmentionable name since his public disgrace in the 1870s. Both artists had a strong tendency to feminize the masculine, even in the representation of heroic characters such as Perseus [294].

Indeed, the connection of Burne-Jones with both Rossetti and Solomon might have coloured Quilter's comments, which recall the complaints about the nudity of the male figure in Burne-Jones's *Phyllis and Demophöon* [295] at the annual exhibition of the Old Watercolour Society in 1870. Quilter revived the previous generation's objections to Pre-Raphaelitism, magnifying them to a moral outrage.

Quilter did have a basis for his observations on Burne-Jones's masculine types. Rather than being unambiguous images of masculine power, the male figure in Burne-Jones's work is often depicted as androgynous. This was a particular feature of his later compositions. H. de Burgh Daly writing in *Merry England* about the Perseus works exhibited at the New Gallery in 1888, noted the 'drawing more careful than learned…and the feminine character

which comes curiously and not pleasantly into subjects of action like the onslaught of Perseus on the dragon'.[22] Burne-Jones's sequence of drawings inspired by poetic names of flowers, the work published posthumously in 1905 as *The Flower Book*, offers a summary of the themes and motifs of the artist's career. In *Honour's Prize* [296], for example, an elegantly attenuated armoured knight pursues the Sanc Greal, held by an angel in a vision that floats above his head. The book is a kind of Symbolist botany, which reopened a discussion of the old names of flowers and revived interest in their amuletic qualities.

In many others of these images Burne-Jones depicts an armoured man wandering aimlessly through mazes and mists encountering a symbolic foe or being granted revelation. This is the characteristic of Burne-Jones borrowed most comprehensively by Beardsley, whose young knights, always slender and delicate – such as the one he designed as a chapter heading for the *Morte D'Arthur* (1894) [297] – seem preoccupied by their own ambiguities. Beardsley's knights and heroes – Perseus, Siegfried, Galahad – are depicted as languid and enfeebled. They

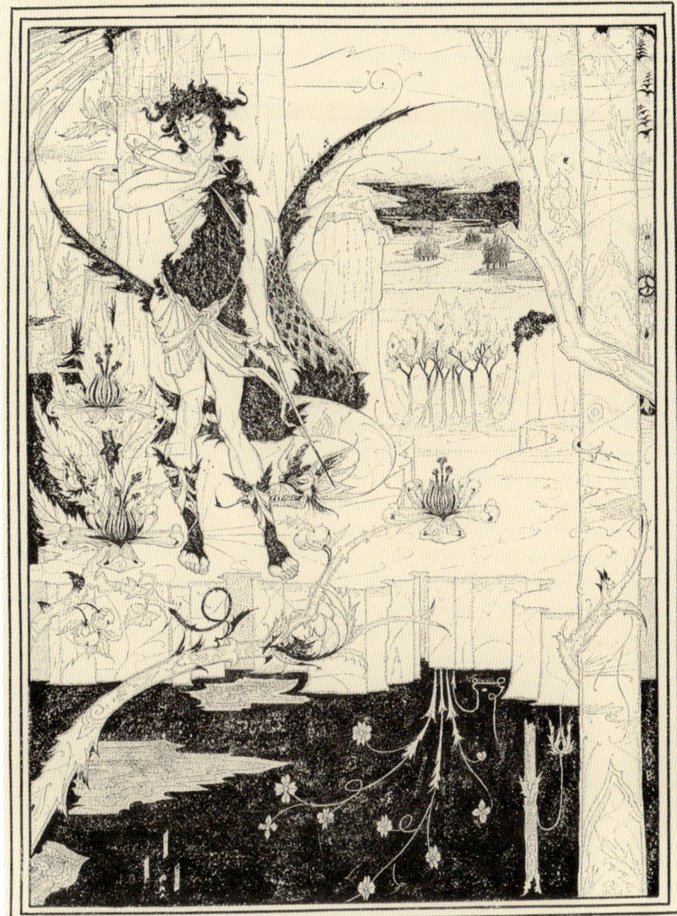

298 Aubrey Beardsley, *Siegfried*, 1892, photo-process print made for *The Studio* magazine, Victoria and Albert Museum, London

seem to be lost in a Symbolist forest of their own desires as if renouncing one quest – the search for the Grail – for another, the search for a sexual identity.

Beardsley's *Siegfried, Act II* [**298**], drawn in 1892, was published in *The Studio* in the following year. It contains not only the 'archaism of Botticelli and Mantegna' that Quilter found in Burne-Jones but other 'archaisms' too, particularly some derived from Dürer, such as the distant landscape. What was new in the drawing was the use to which these historical sources were put and what they amounted to. The fine lines described a puzzle rather than a solution; the invented bodies that had never seen the inside of a life room, the landscapes and the arbitrary divisions of space (the strip of drawing that forms the right-hand edge of the sheet, for example) were all in defiance of academic conventions. These graphic lines, marks and strategies celebrated the power of drawing to invent an imaginative space rather than copy nature. This was drawing as a constant surprise and revelation.

The female subject, too, became controversial in Beardsley's depictions. Self-absorbed, vain and cold, his

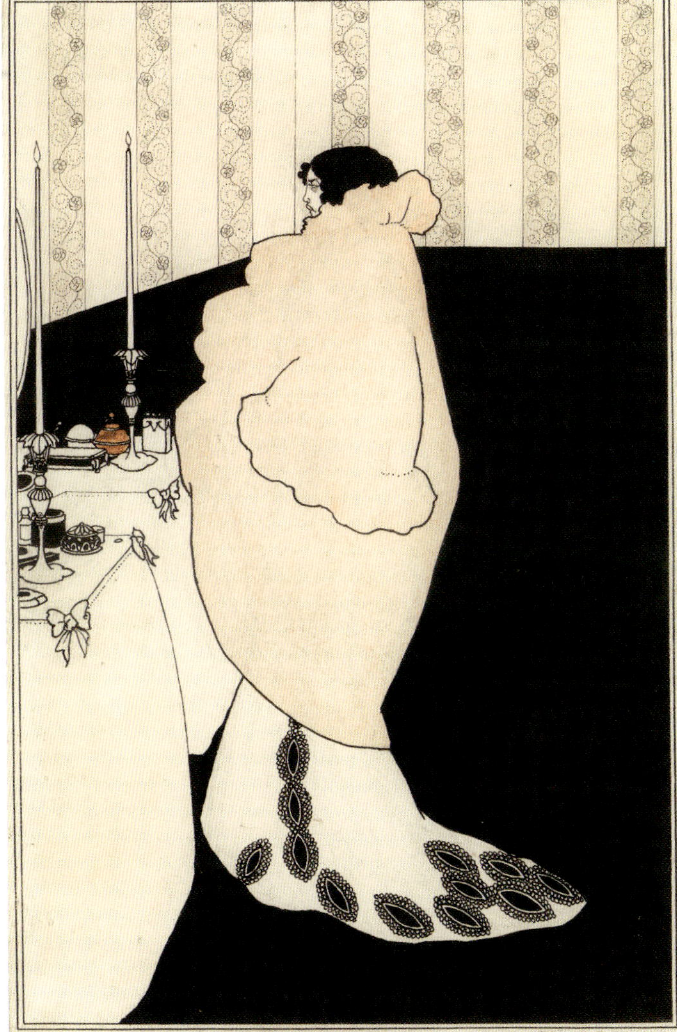

299 Aubrey Beardsley, *La Dame aux Camélias*, 1894, Tate

ideal was the female dandy, who, if not always actually cross-dressed, did so spiritually. She became the key motif of his later work. The 'Beardsley woman' was a construct of inked lines representing a thin, bold-faced female as confident as her male counterpart was confused. She was

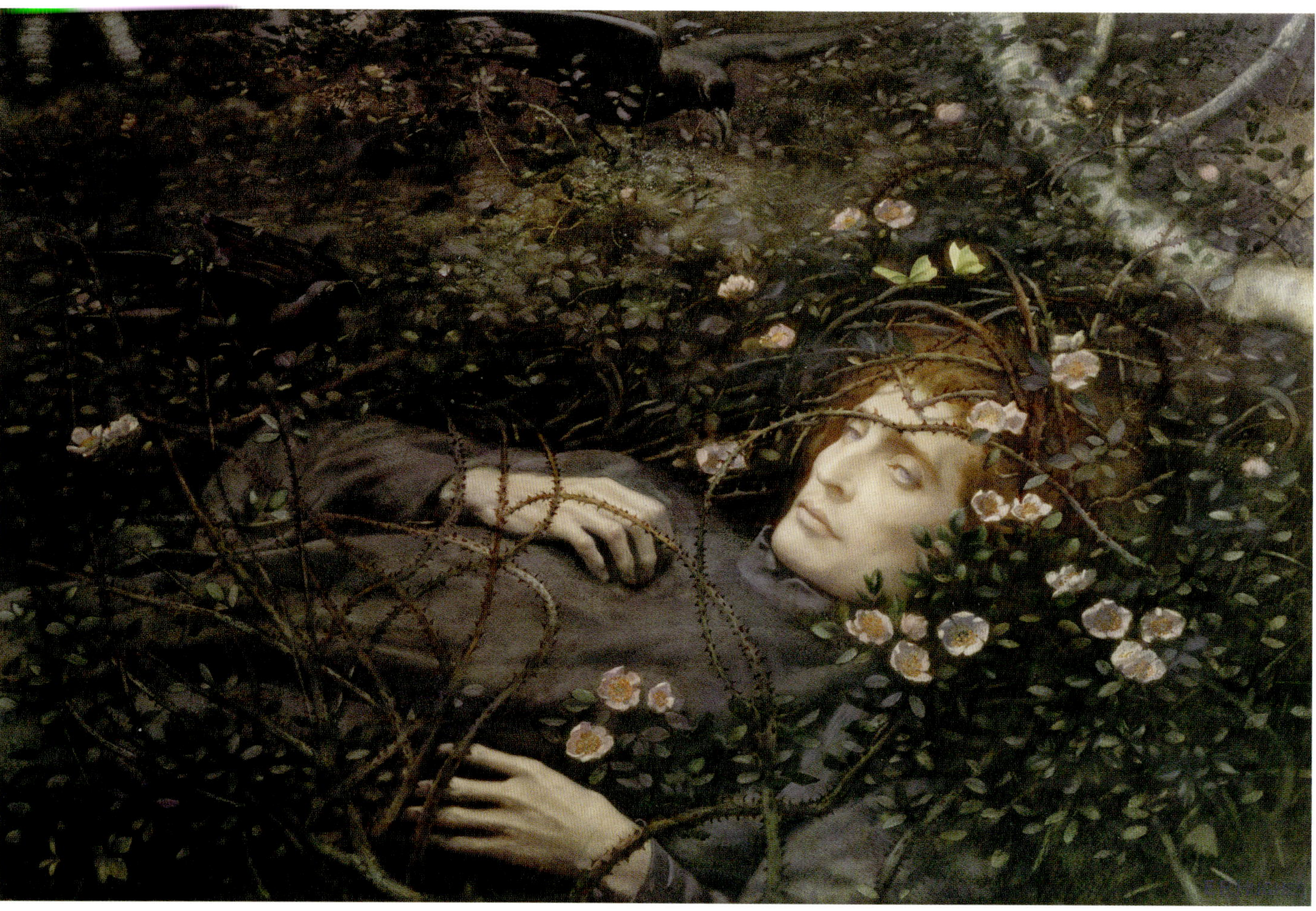

300 Edward Robert Hughes, *'Oh, what's that in the hollow...?'*, 1893, Royal Watercolour Society

nonetheless shocking – and she replaced the 'Rossetti woman' in advanced circles as the nineteenth century came to an end. Beardsley's *La Dame aux Camélias* (1894) [299] recalls Burne-Jones's *Le Chant d'Amour* as an image of sexual power reversed, a contemporary sexual anxiety dressed up in medieval clothes. Rossetti's coldly self-regarding beauties, such as Lilith, also come to mind. Yet Beardsley's adventurous use of line is what remains most characteristic. The graphic delineation of these complex ideas of sex and gender is too urgent to wait for paint but too significant to be preparatory – they need to be memorialized in the impermanence of drawing media.

Continuations and reflections

Despite the identification of Pre-Raphaelitism with 'decadence', several younger artists continued to pursue the themes of the Pre-Raphaelites of an earlier generation, reworking them in a highly polished hybrid style that suggests not Rossetti alone but also Brown, Hunt and Millais.[23] Edward Robert Hughes (1851–1914), the nephew of Arthur Hughes, who had close connections with the original Brotherhood, turned to themes favoured by them. His watercolour illustrating Christina Rossetti's poem 'Amor Mundi' (1893) [300], for example, took a daringly different viewpoint than Sandys's illustration published in 1865 [232]. Where Sandys featured the poet's idea of 'the valley track' and the 'downhill path' from which 'there's no turning back' and which ends in a hidden grave, Hughes concentrated entirely on the corpse, described by Christina Rossetti as the 'thin dead body which waits the eternal term'. The roses that threaten to obscure the corpse might be a reference to Burne-Jones's *Briar Rose* series, as John Christian suggests,[24] but just as easily they might refer to earlier 'truth-to-nature'

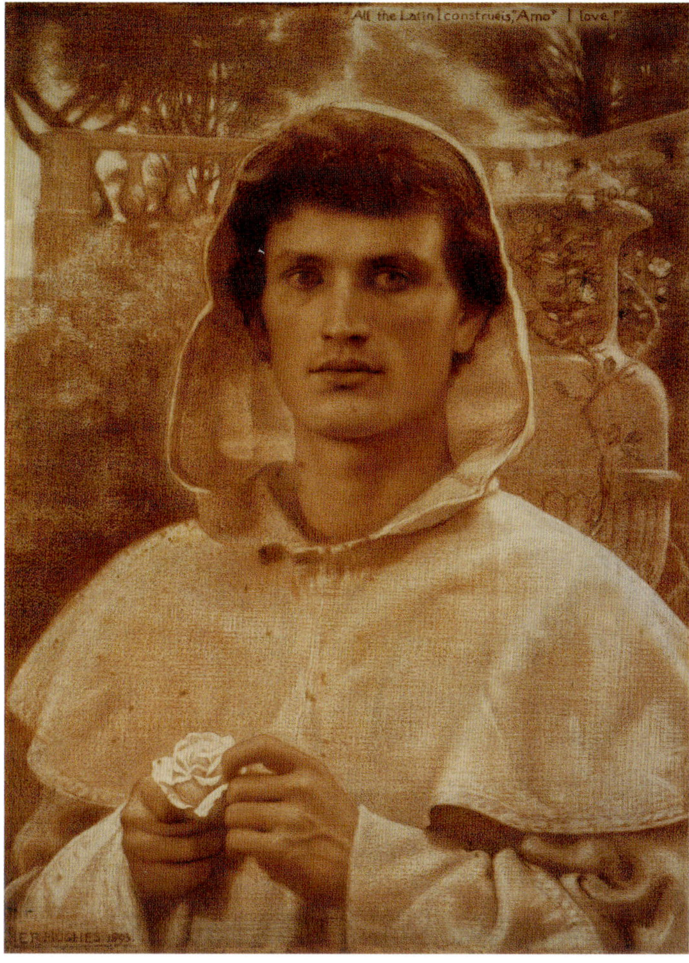

301 Edward Robert Hughes, *Study for a Picture ('Fra Lippo Lippi')*, 1893, The Williamson Art Gallery and Museum, Birkenhead, Wirral

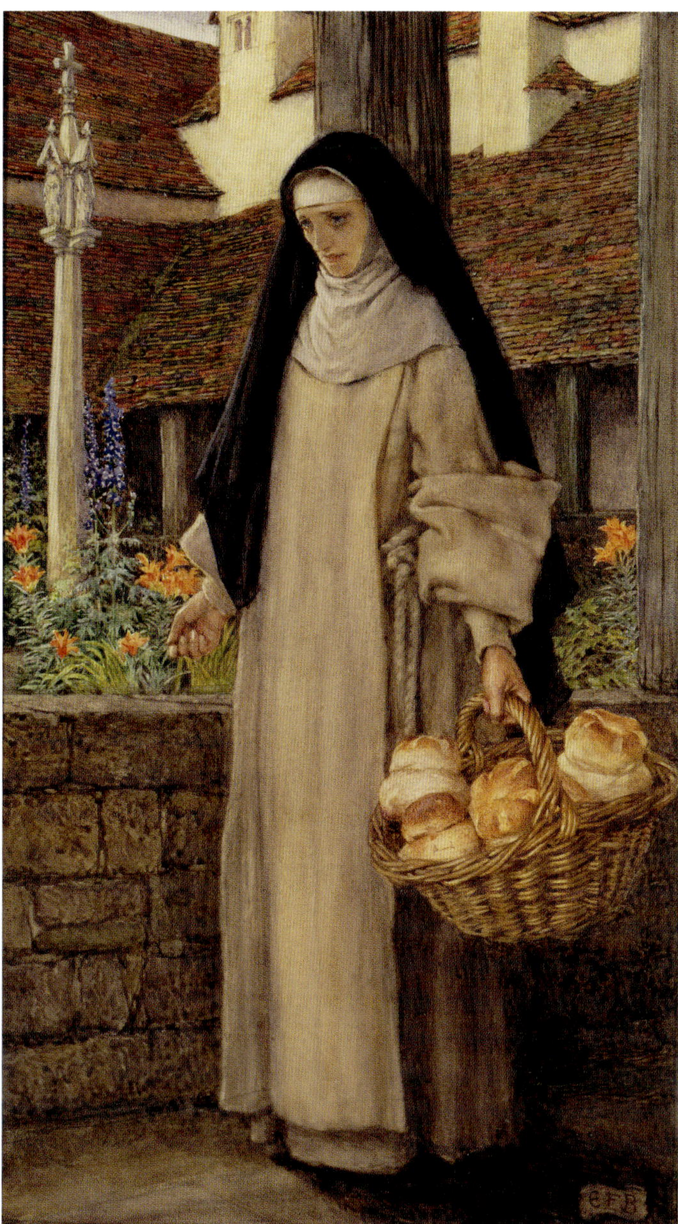

302 Eleanor Fortescue Brickdale, *Guinevere*, 1911, Birmingham Museums & Art Gallery

paintings such as Arthur Hughes's *The Long Engagement* [172] or even Millais's *Ophelia*, to which, indeed, this work might be a weird companion piece. A beautiful young woman is replaced in Hughes's watercolour by a beautiful young man, but both sink into the landscape, to be showered with the petals of dog roses.

Several other works of the last decades of the nineteenth century appear to be in dialogue with Pre-Raphaelite drawings from the generation before. E. R. Hughes's imaginary portrait of Fra Lippo Lippi (1893) [301], for example, depicts the painter-monk looking almost directly at the viewer. We are struck by the fresh beauty of the young man and his allure, undimmed by archaisms or affectations. Perhaps this is a part of Hughes's narrative interpretation of Browning's poem in which the artist-monk airs opposing approaches to making art. The inscription – 'All the Latin I construe is, "Amo" I love' –

suggests a more earthy subject, akin perhaps to Rossetti's *Bocca Baciata* (1859), celebrating physical beauty and the delights of love rather than more cerebral or aesthetic concerns. The young friar fondles the petals of a rose as he voices his philosophy. He lives in the world of the senses as much as in the realm of art, scarcely at all in the austere world of a monastic order. We can discern, too, the ghost of Solomon's homoerotic portrayals of Eros and Bacchus, their features taking on some of the allure of Rossetti's 'stunners', in Hughes's *Fra Lippo Lippi*.

Eleanor Fortescue Brickdale (1871–1945) had a successful career reviving Pre-Raphaelitism. Her work included several reimaginings of favourite Pre-Raphaelite themes such as *The Little Foot-Page* (1905, Walker Art Gallery), a subject

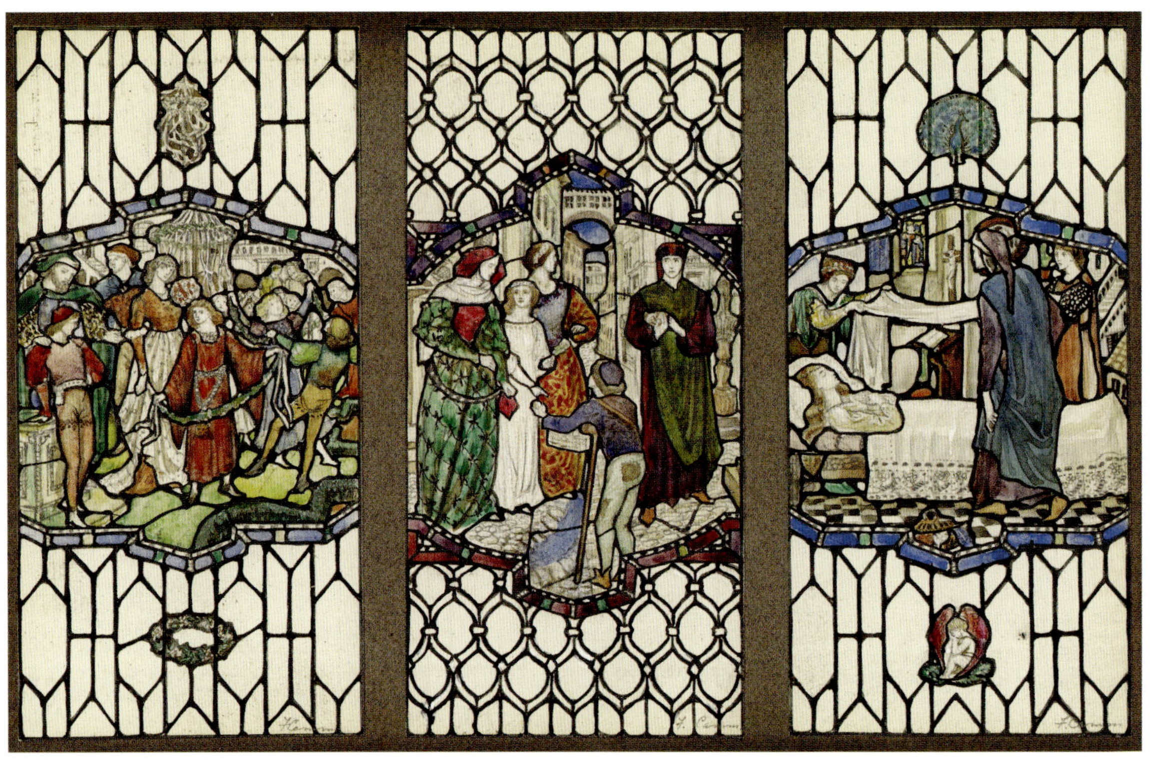

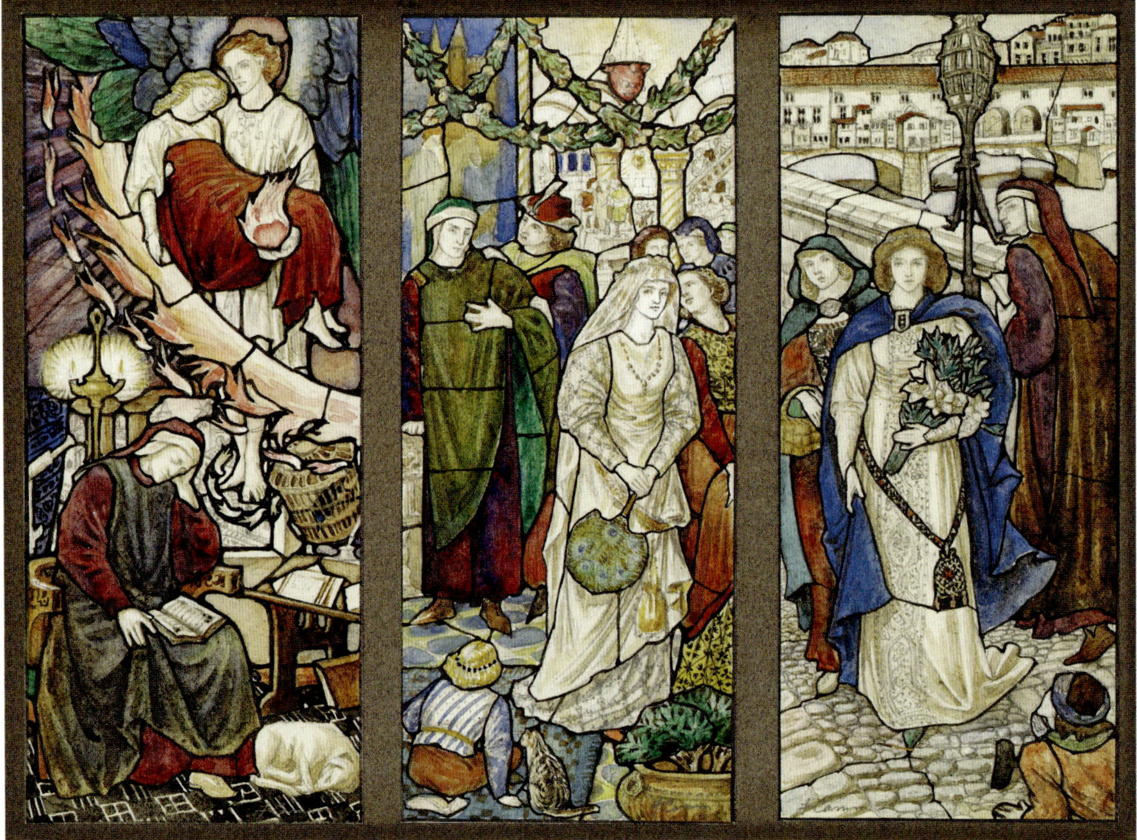

303, 304 Florence Camm, *Designs for Stained Glass: 'Dante and Beatrice'*, 1911, Birmingham Museums & Art Gallery

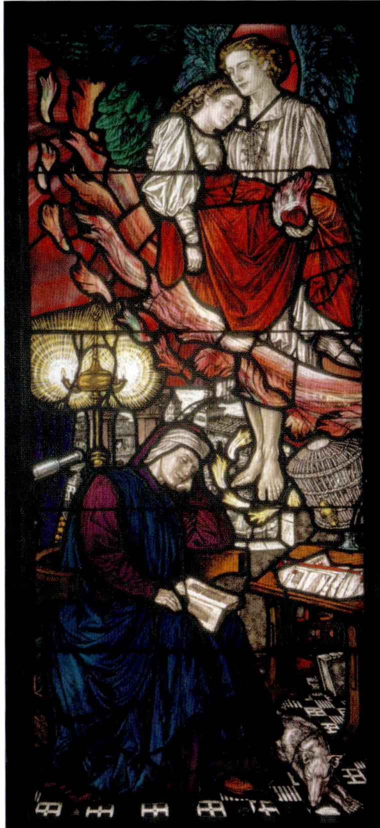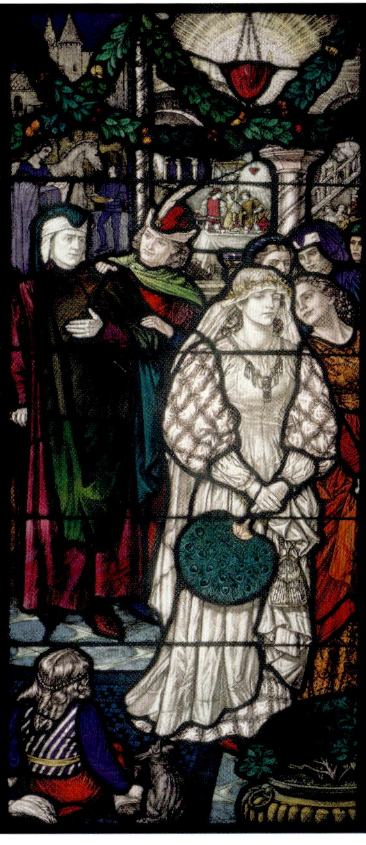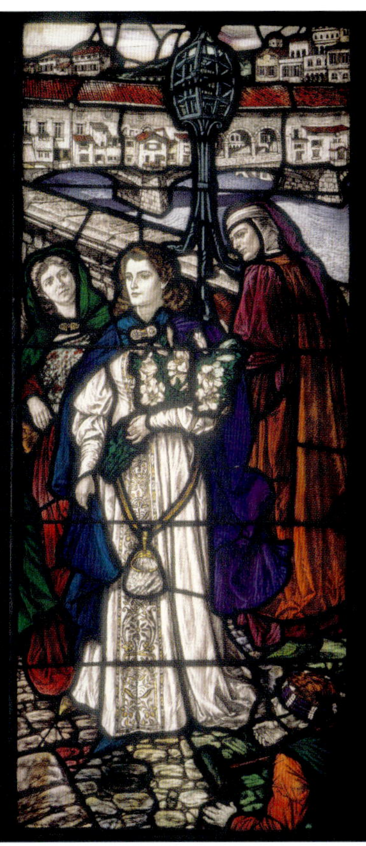

305 Camm & Company, *Dante and Beatrice*, 1911, Birmingham Museums & Art Gallery

exhibited by W. L. Windus at the Royal Academy in 1856. Her *Guinevere* (1910–11) [**302**] suggests a direct link with two works by Rossetti: *Sir Launcelot's Vision of the Sanc Greal* (1857) [**179, 180**] and that depicting the last meeting of two lovers, *Arthur's Tomb* (versions in 1854–55, private collection, and 1860, Tate). Brickdale might also have had in mind Morris's account of the meeting between Launcelot and the Queen in his *The Defence of Guenevere: and Other Poems* (1858). In Brickdale's version of this incident, the unfaithful Queen is depicted as guilt-ridden and haunted. She raises her arms in an ambiguous gesture of resignation or renunciation, but it has echoes of the gesture in Rossetti's design for the Oxford Union mural. The prosaic basket of bread only emphasizes the difference between the fatal woman of 'then' and the penitent nun of 'now'. The absence of Launcelot is an extraordinary withdrawal of the other side of the dialogue and the story.

These new versions of themes favoured by the Pre-Raphaelites selected a different narrative moment in the chosen stories or focused on familiar episodes from the viewpoint of a different character. Such is the case with the designs of Florence Camm, who was a successful stained-glass artist in the family workshop in Birmingham. Her drawings for several stained-glass schemes, including one series of six panels depicting the meetings and partings of Dante and Beatrice [**303, 304, 305**] and a set of four panels representing the Vision of the Holy Grail (1930, Birmingham Museums & Art Gallery), are striking in their use of Pre-Raphaelite imagery. Medieval graphic elements are presented in combination with strong geometric elements that anticipate Modernist design. In her designs for windows based on Dante's *Vita Nuova* (1911) [**303, 304**], Camm utilized the 'black line' method of stained-glass drawing recommended by Morris to make use of the idea of drawing with light, but she also introduced finer graphic elements into the etched surface of the glass. The results were sumptuous: a late flowering of Pre-Raphaelitism. Camm's drawings take Pre-Raphaelite graphic experimentation into a new century and are perhaps the last expression of an unbroken chain of influence from 1848 to the mid-1930s.

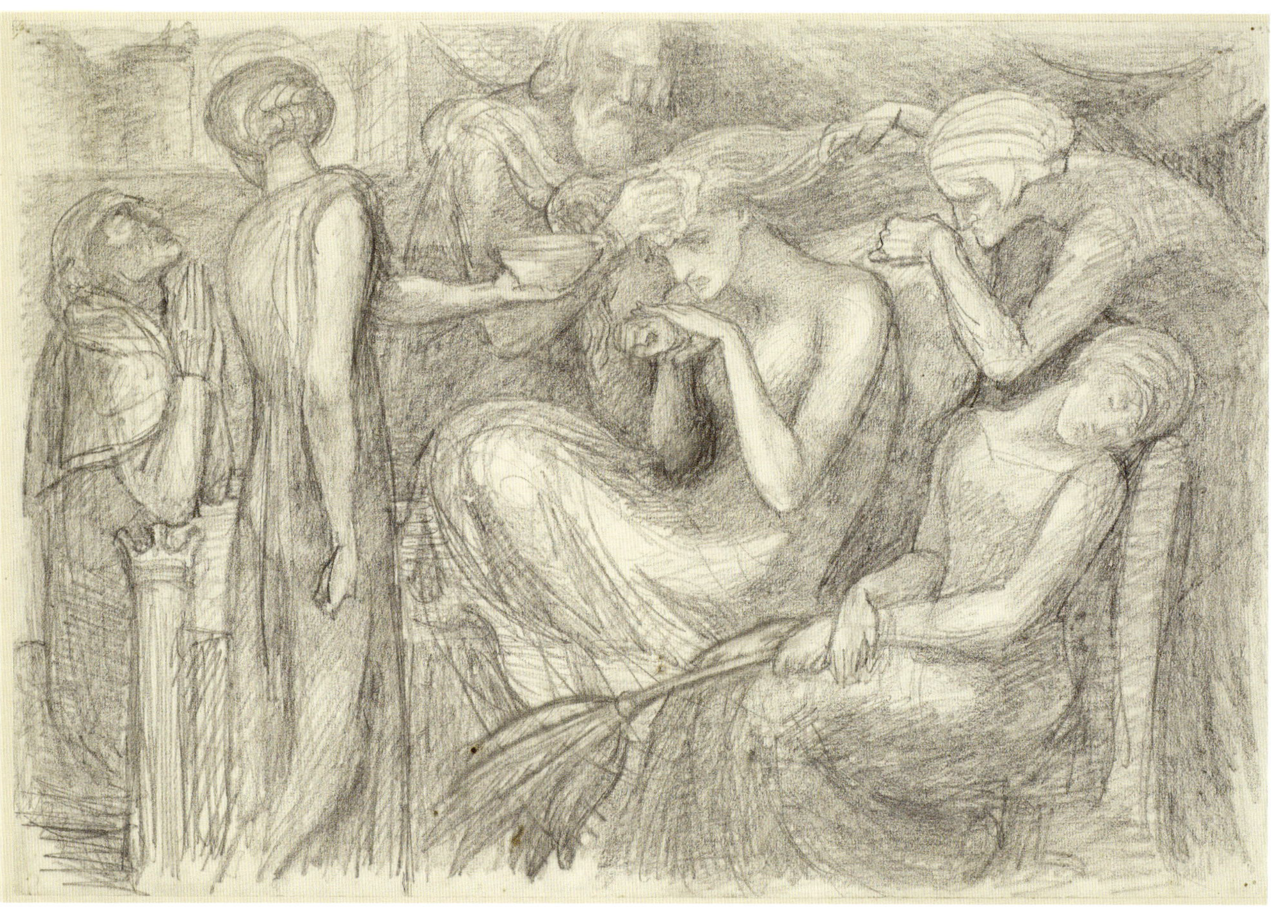

306 Dante Gabriel Rossetti, *The Death of Lady Macbeth, c.* 1875, Birminghams Museum & Art Gallery

Drawing conclusions

In his lecture 'The English Renaissance of Art' (1882), Oscar Wilde offered a history of contemporary Aestheticism that had its roots in Romanticism and Pre-Raphaelitism:

> If you ask nine-tenths of the British public what is the meaning of the word aesthetics, they will tell you it is the French for affectation or the German for a dado; and if you enquire about the Pre-Raphaelites you will hear something about an eccentric lot of young men to whom a sort of divine crookedness and holy awkwardness in drawing were the chief objects of art.

Wilde saw their contribution as forming 'a desire for a deeper spiritual value to be given to art as well as a more decorative value'.[25] It is striking that he chose drawing as the key aesthetic disturbance of the Pre-Raphaelites; the 'crookedness' and 'awkwardness' of their drawings and the emphasis on ornamentation and detail had been, as we have seen, a challenge to preconceptions about the propriety of representational forms and hierarchies of art more than a generation before. Wilde's acceptance of Pre-Raphaelitism as the originating factor of a renaissance in Britain took for granted the experimental nature of the work and its impact on the production of a school whose art would have a permanent value.

The dominance of Rossetti in this brief survey of the impact of the Pre-Raphaelites upon later Victorian drawing practices is attributable to his very ambiguity and 'incompleteness' as a technician: the potential of the drawn image for inviting interpretation, the expressive body replacing the 'correctly drawn' one, the idiosyncratic vision of a type of beauty – all of these played their part in the enduring appeal of his work. Certainly by the turn of the century Rossetti's reputation as the most inventive and stimulating draughtsman of his generation was secure, although often for strange reasons. In 1910, for example, T. Martin Wood began his study *Drawings of Rossetti* with the statement that

The intensely subjective nature of Rossetti's art is
what gives it fascination for its lovers; it belonged to
himself.…The last phase of his art was entirely one of
self-revelation.[26]

A stranger piece of evidence is used by Wood. In discussing
The Death of Lady Macbeth (*c.* 1875) [**306**], one of the least
characteristically Pre-Raphaelite of Rossetti's works, he
noted the 'bad drawing' of one of the figures, adding:

Those in sympathy with the nature of Rossetti's art do
not count this piece of bad drawing a disastrous flaw.
The rarity of genius makes them accept everything
gratefully; it disarms a caviling attitude. The fault in
their eyes even seems to add to the tense note struck as
a changed note in an over-sweet harmony.[27]

It is the very instability of Rossetti's technique that seems
to be the attraction for his admirers. We might consider it
emblematic of Pre-Raphaelite drawing, which is regarded
as unconventional and imaginative, even untutored
and primitive. It is also – despite the many revivalist
elements in technique and subject matter – of our time.
Despite the cluttered symbolism of late works such as *The
Question* (1875) [**307**], Rossetti is 'modern'. His interest in
the automatic – and, through Blake – in the concept of
'first thought/best thought' – makes him an inspiration
for artists working in the twenty-first century. Those who
consider the relationship between the image in nature,
the image in the imagination and the image on paper will
always find Rossetti fascinating.

The artist and writer W. Graham Robertson (1866–1948)
brought together aspects of the criticism of early Pre-
Raphaelite painting when he encountered Rossetti's art in
exhibition and recorded his initial puzzlement at Rossetti's
reputation, before 'the glamour fell upon me':

Any intelligent art student could out-paint Rossetti,
nearly any member of a life class could draw
better, and yet what they would produce would be

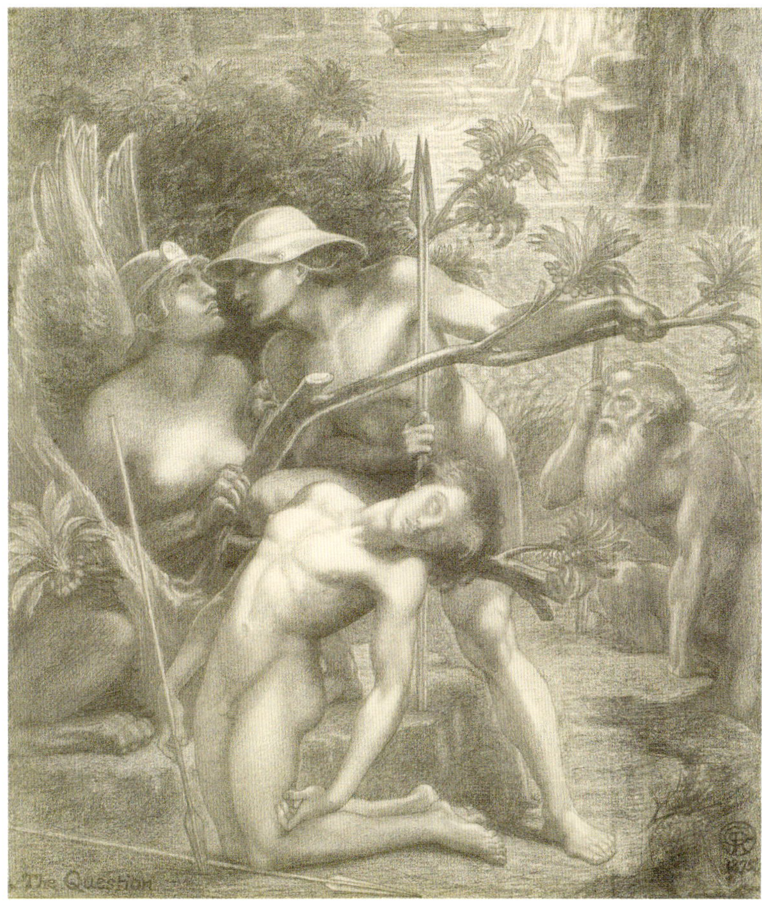

307 Dante Gabriel Rossetti, *The Question*, 1875,
Birmingham Museums & Art Gallery

of no import, while his slightest scribble is full of
suggestion.[28]

The slight scribble was perhaps the final modification of the
outline style and a liberation for the artist's imagination
through drawing. It was a recognition that excellence in
the life class was not the sole measure of talent, let alone of
genius, and that drawing might usurp the finish of painting
to produce suggestive works that invited interpretation and
the endless involvement of the viewer by capturing their
attention with the line, the mark, the blot and the scribble.

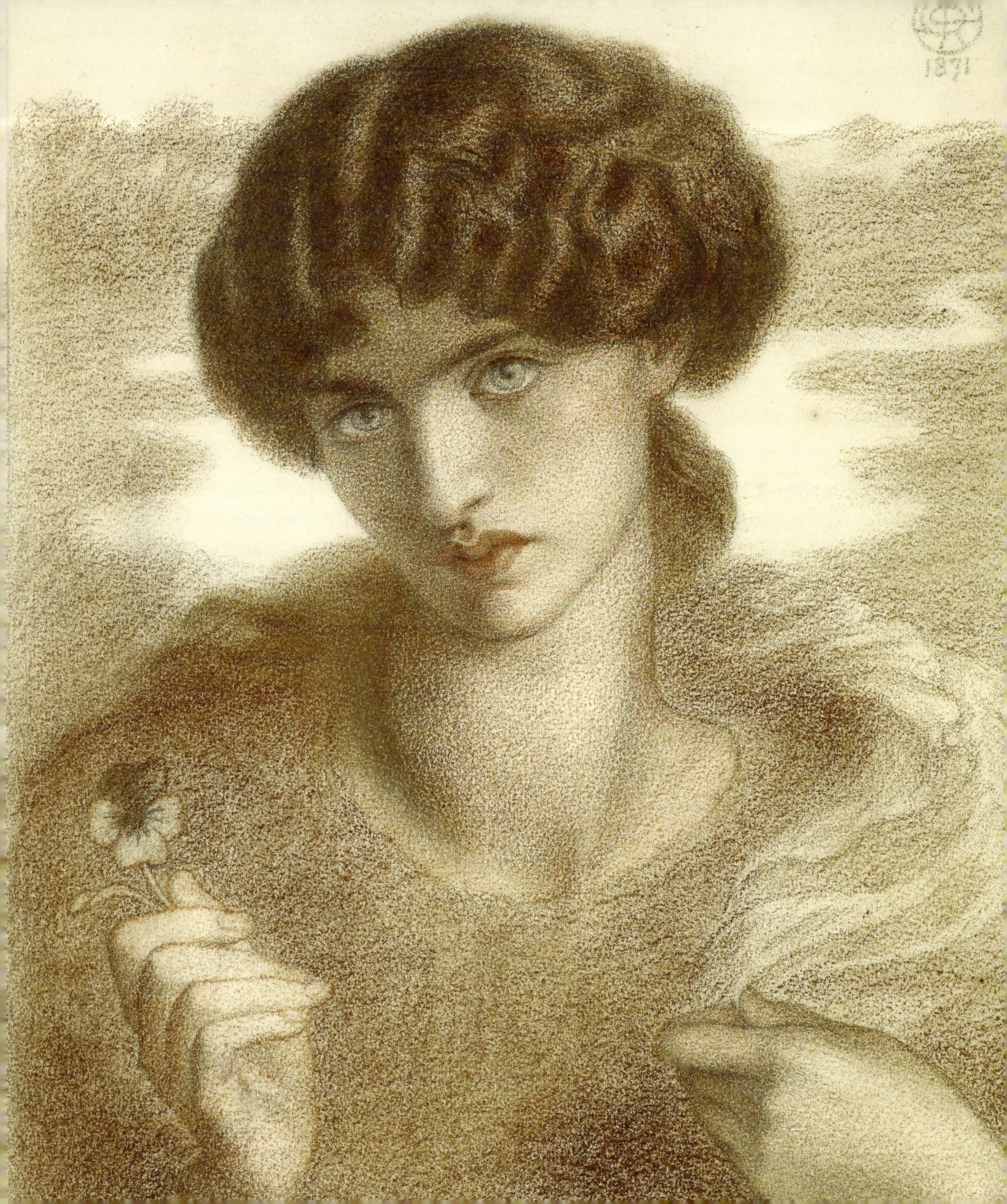

Notes

Drawings and Drawing: A Pre-Raphaelite Introduction

1 S. C. Malan, *Aphorisms on Drawing* (London: Longman, 1856), p. 9.
Malan's emphasis.
2 J. G. Millais, *The Life and Letters of Sir John Everett Millais* (London:
Methuen, 1899), vol. 1, pp. 44–45.
3 Ibid., p. 46.
4 The concept of unconscious expression was explored by Sigmund Freud
in the *Psychopathology of Everyday Life* (1901). The Surrealist poet André
Breton's ideas on 'psychic automatism' and on the artist as a 'recording
mechanism' are outlined in the *Manifeste du Surréalisme* (1924). The
most famous Surrealist automatist was André Masson (1896–1987). For an
outline of some of these connections between Freudian psychoanalysis,
Surrealism and drawing, see Roger Cardinal, 'André Masson and
automatic drawing', in Silvano Levy (ed.), *Surrealism: Surrealist Visuality*
(Keele: Keele University Press, 1995), pp. 79–94.
5 Anon., 'Manchester Art Treasures exhibition', *Quarterly Review*, no. 102
(1857), p. 200.
6 Millais, *Life and Letters*, vol. 1, pp. 56–57.
7 Anon., 'Pictures of the season', *Blackwood's Edinburgh Magazine*, no. 689
(1850), p. 82.
8 John Commander, *Pre-Raphaelite Drawings and Watercolours* (London:
Arts Council, 1953), p. 3.
9 Esther Wood, *Dante Rossetti and the Pre-Raphaelite Movement* (New
York: Charles Scribner, 1894), p. 25.
10 The entry is dated 5 March 1883. See [Beatrix Potter], *The Journal of Beatrix
Potter from 1881 to 1897*, ed. Leslie Linder (London: Warne, 1966), p. 31.

Chapter 1 *The Flat, the Antique and the Life: Academic Drawing and the Pre-Raphaelites*

1 Malcolm Warner, *The Drawings of John Everett Millais* (London: Arts
Council of Great Britain, 1979), p. 18.
2 Sir Joshua Reynolds, 'Discourse Two' (1770), in *The Literary Works of Sir
Joshua Reynolds* (London: Cadell, 1835), vol. 1, p. 324.
3 John Opie in Ralph Wornum (ed.), *Lectures on Painting by the Royal
Academicians* (London: George Bohn, 1848), p. 249. Opie's emphases.
4 See a discussion of this point raised by H. Cliff Morgan in his essay 'The
Schools of the Royal Academy', *British Journal of Educational Studies*, 21/1
(1973), pp. 88–103.
5 William Powell Frith, *My Autobiography and Reminiscences* (London:
Richard Bentley, 1888), vol. 1, pp. 35–36.
6 William Holman Hunt, *Pre-Raphaelitism and the Pre-Raphaelite
Brotherhood* (London: Macmillan, 1905), vol. 1, p. 35.
7 For Cotman's instruction methods, see Sydney D. Kitson, *The Life of John
Cotman* (London: Faber and Faber, 1937).
8 Letter 43.3, to his mother, Frances Mary Lavinia Rossetti, dated 15 August
1843. In [Dante Gabriel Rossetti], *The Correspondence of Dante Gabriel
Rossetti*, vol. 1: *The Formative Years, 1835–1862: Charlotte Street to Cheyne
Walk: 1835–1854*, ed. William E. Fredeman (Cambridge: D. S. Brewer,
2002), pp. 24–25.
9 *The Times* (9 June 1848), p. 9.
10 Ibid., p. 8.
11 Ann Rorimer, *Drawings by William Mulready* (London: Victoria and
Albert Museum, 1972), p. 11. Mulready's emphasis.
12 Ford Madox Hueffer, *Ford Madox Brown: A Record of his Life and Work*
(London: Longmans, Green, 1896), p. 12.
13 Ibid., pp. 14–15.
14 For a discussion of the impact of Brown's early training, see Tim Barringer,
'The effects of industry: Ford Madox Brown and artistic identities in
Victorian Britain', in Tessa Sidey (ed.), *Ford Madox Brown: The Unofficial
Pre-Raphaelite* (London: D. Giles, 2008), p. 25. Brown continued to draw
from the life, attending classes run by his friend Charles Lucy (1814–63) at
Tudor Lodge, Mornington Crescent and Dickinson Brothers' Academy in

308 Dante Gabriel Rossetti, *Water Willow*, 1871,
Birmingham Museums & Art Gallery (detail)

"

1847. My thanks to Laura MacCulloch for this information.

15 Wornum, 'Introduction', in Wornum (ed.), *Lectures on Painting by the Royal Academicians*, p. 35. Wornum's emphases.

16 Ibid.

17 *The Guardian* (15 May 1850), p. 346. For a study of the hopes and frustrations arising from the Westminster cartoons competitions, see T. S. R. Boase, 'The decoration of the new Palace of Westminster, 1841–1863', *The Journal of the Warburg and Courtauld Institutes*, 3/4 (1954), pp. 319–58.

18 [William Michael Rossetti and C. P. Cranch], *The Crayon*, no. 6 (1856), p. 180.

19 Ford Madox Brown, 'On the mechanism of a historical picture' part 1, *The Germ*, no. 2 (1850), p. 71.

20 Ibid.

21 Ibid.

22 William E. Fredeman (ed.), *The P. R. B. Journal: William Michael Rossetti's Diary of the Pre-Raphaelite Brotherhood 1849–53* (Oxford: Oxford University Press, 1975), Appendix 3, p. 108. Fredeman is a little ahistorical here because Samuel Smiles's successful *Self-Help* was not published until 1859.

23 See A. M. W. Stirling, *The Richmond Papers* (London: Heinemann, 1926), pp. 11–15.

24 For a history of the Hogarth Club and an assessment of its importance, see D. Cherry, 'The Hogarth Club: 1858–61', *Burlington Magazine*, no. 925 (1980), pp. 236–44.

25 Fredeman (ed.), *P. R. B. Journal*, Appendix 3, pp. 108–9.

26 Letter 48.10, to his brother, William Michael Rossetti, dated 20 August 1848. In [Rossetti], *Correspondence of Dante Gabriel Rossetti*, vol. 1, ed. Fredeman, p. 71.

27 Fredeman (ed.), *P. R. B. Journal*, p. 112.

28 See the discussion in Alastair Grieve's essay, 'Style and content in Pre-Raphaelite drawings 1848–50', in Leslie Parris (ed.), *Pre-Raphaelite Papers* (London: Tate Gallery, 1984), p. 24.

Chapter 2 *Direct and Heartfelt: Early Influences on Pre-Raphaelite Drawing*

1 Lord Lindsay, *Sketches of the History of Christian Art* (London: John Murray, 1847), 'Postscriptum', vol. 3, p. 419. Lindsay exhorted young artists to abandon convention: they should '[toss] to the winds the jargons of the schools' (ibid., p. 421).

2 For an account of Lasinio's career, see Donata Levi, 'Carlo Lasinio, curator, collector and dealer', *Burlington Magazine*, no. 1079 (1993), pp. 133–49.

3 [John Ruskin], 'Lord Lindsay on the history of Christian art', *Quarterly Review*, no. 161 (1847), p. 55. Ruskin's emphasis.

4 Hunt, *Pre-Raphaelitism*, vol. 1, p. 133.

5 Quoted in City Museum and Art Gallery Birmingham, *The Pre-Raphaelite Brotherhood, 1848–1862* (Birmingham: City Museum and Art Gallery, 1947) [exhibition catalogue], p. 4.

6 *The Times* (13 July 1854), p. 7.

7 Anon., 'Retzsch's outlines', *Fine Arts: The Mirror of Literature, Amusement and Instruction* (28 December 1833), p. 441.

8 Grieve, 'Style and content', p. 24.

9 [John Ruskin], *The Works of John Ruskin*, ed. E. T. Cook and A. Wedderburn (The Library Edition, London: George Allen, 1903–12), vol. 15, pp. 224–25. For a discussion of the wider issues Ruskin had with outline, see Jonah Siegel, *Desire and Excess: The Nineteenth-Century Culture of Art* (Princeton and Oxford: Princeton University Press, 2000), pp. 190–94.

10 Fredeman (ed.), *P. R. B. Journal*, Appendix 3, p. 110.

11 See Mary Bennett, 'An early drawing for *The Tempest* by John Everett Millais', *Burlington Magazine*, no. 977 (1984), pp. 503–5.

12 Anon., 'The Art-Union of London', *The Art-Union* (November 1842), p. 262. See the same publication, April 1843, for further references to the outline competitions which was won by Henry Selous (1803–90), who became the most successful imitator of Retzsch's style working in England.

13 Surtees, Virginia, *Dante Gabriel Rossetti: A Catalogue Raisonné* (Oxford: Oxford University Press, 1971), vol. 1, p. 12, cat. no. 42.

14 Mrs Anna Jameson, the writer on art and hagiography, published her study of representations of saints and martyrs, *Sacred and Legendary Art*, in 1848. It was an important study for antiquarians, collectors and amateurs. It is probable that Rossetti's inclusion of the statue of St Reparata was encouraged by Jameson's account of the saint and her relevance to the city of Florence.

15 See Judith Bronkhurst, *William Holman Hunt: A Catalogue Raisonné* (New Haven and London: Yale University Press, 2006), vol. 2, pp. 23–24, cat. no. D40. Bronkhurst doubts the Cyclographic connection assigned to it first by Edith Holman Hunt, the artist's wife, but points out that the drawing represents the first specific biblical text represented within the Brotherhood.

16 In his Introduction to *The New Life* in part 1 of *Dante and his Circle*, in *The Collected Works of Dante Gabriel Rossetti* (London: Ellis and Elvey, 1890), vol. 2, p. 1.

17 Clearly the subject had some importance for the young Millais because he executed a duplicate drawing now in the collection of the Royal Academy.

18 Hunt, *Pre-Raphaelitism*, vol. 1, p. 87.

Chapter 3 *Studying Nature Attentively: Ruskin and Pre-Raphaelitism*

1 Quoted in Birmingham, *Pre-Raphaelite Brotherhood*, p. 4.

2 See Ruskin's letters to the artist Anna Blunden (1830–1915), especially those for December 1857 in which he writes to her of the young ladies who might benefit from reading the book, in Virginia Surtees (ed.), *Sublime and Instructive: Letters from John Ruskin to Louisa Marchioness of Waterford, Anna Blunden and Ellen Heaton* (London: Michael Joseph, 1972), pp. 92–93.

3 Ruskin first put forward his advice to young artists in *Modern Painters*, vol. 1 (1843) (in *Works*, vol. 3, p. 423), where he takes issue with the lack of creativity in their training. He repeated it in his pamphlet *Pre-Raphaelitism* (in *Works*, vol. 12, p. 339).

4 *The Times* (13 May 1851), p. 8.

5 Ruskin, *Pre-Raphaelitism* (1851) (in *Works*, vol. 12, pp. 353–54).

6 Ruskin, *Praeterita* (1885–89) (in *Works*, vol. 35, p. 311).

7 Ruskin, *Notes on Prout and Hunt* (1880) (in *Works*, vol. 14, p. 384).

8 Ruskin, *Praeterita* (in *Works*, vol. 35, p. 79).

9 For a chronology of Ruskin's instruction and other early encounters with art, see Tim Hilton, *John Ruskin: The Early Years, 1819–59* (New Haven and London: Yale University Press, 1985).

10 Ruskin, *Praeterita* (in *Works*, vol. 35, pp. 308–9).

11 J. D. Harding, *Sketches at Home and Abroad* (London: Tilt, 1836), pp. 65–66.

12 Ruskin, *Modern Painters*, vol. 1 (in *Works*, vol. 3, pp. 248 and 251).

13 Ruskin, *The Elements of Drawing*, Letter 1 (1857) (in *Works*, vol. 15, p. 2).

14 Anon., 'The elements of drawing, with three letters to beginners', *The Athenaeum* (11 July 1857), p. 879.

15 Robert Hewison, *Ruskin and Oxford: The Art of Education* (Oxford: Clarendon Press, 1996).

16 William Bell Scott, *Autobiographical Notes*, ed. W. Minto (New York: Harper and Brothers, 1892), vol. 2, pp. 9–10.

17 Anon., 'Art matters', *New York Times* (14 April 1873), p. 4.

18 For discussion of American receptions of Ruskin and the Pre-Raphaelites, see Linda S. Ferber and William H. Gerdts, *The New Path: Ruskin and the American Pre-Raphaelites* (Brooklyn: Brooklyn Museum, 1985) and Theodore E. Stebbins and others, *The Last Ruskinians: Charles Eliot Norton, Herbert Moore, and their Circle* (Cambridge, Mass.: Harvard Art Museums, 2007).

19 Charles Eliot Norton, *Notes on Drawings by Mr Ruskin* (Cambridge, Mass.: John Wilson & Son, 1879), p. 3.

20 Anon., 'Bits of nature', *Fun* (16 May 1863), p. 90.

21 Ruskin, *Elements of Drawing*, Letter 2 (in *Works*, vol. 15, p. 94).

22 For a discussion of the initial impact of Ruskin on Brett, see Michael Hickox, 'John Brett and Ruskin', *Burlington Magazine*, no. 1121 (August 1996), pp. 521–25. Brett described the book as 'Letters' because each of the chapters of the book resembles correspondence with an individual reader and is signed by the author; it was a form later adopted in his long series of 'letters' on social issues, *Fors Clavigera*.

23 Coventry Patmore, 'A Pre-Raphaelite exhibition', *Saturday Review* (4 July 1857), pp. 11–13.

24 Millais thought Brett's *The Val D'Aosta* 'a wretched work like a photograph of some place in Switzerland'. The comment signals one of the stages of disaffection with Ruskin's critical choices within the Pre-Raphaelite Brotherhood. Quoted in Ruskin, *Academy Notes* (1855) (in *Works*, vol. 14, p. 22, note 2).

25 Ruskin, *Academy Notes* (1858) (in *Works*, vol. 14, p.154). For a discussion of the possible genesis of Brett's *The Hedger* in relation to Ruskin's writings, see Michael Hickox, 'John Brett and Ruskin', in Charles Brett and others, *John Brett: A Pre-Raphaelite in Cornwall* (Bristol: Sansom, 2006), pp. 29–43.

26 Ruskin, *Academy Notes* (1859) (in *Works*, vol. 14, p. 237).

27 Ibid., p. 236.

28 Allen Staley, *The Pre-Raphaelite Landscape* (2nd edn, New Haven and London: Yale University Press, 2001), p. 177.

29 The sequence of influence is obscure but some of Rosa Brett's watercolours in the Ruskinian mode appear to predate John Brett's well-known works.

30 Ruskin, *Elements of Drawing*, Letter 2 (in *Works*, vol. 15, p. 109).

31 Percy Bate, 'The late Frederick Sandys', *The Studio*, no. 139 (1904), p. 4.

32 From a letter to Louisa, Marchioness of Waterford, dated by Virginia Surtees as probably January 1860, in Surtees, *Sublime and Instructive*, pp. 35–36.

33 See J-A. George, 'Translating Tuscany: Francesca Alexander's *Roadside Songs* (1888)', *Forum for Modern Language Studies*, 39 (2003), pp. 227–38.

34 See Ruskin, *Works*, vol. 32, which contains *Roadside Songs of Tuscany* and other works by Alexander. In his Introduction to the volume, E. T. Cook outlines some of the background for the friendship of the American artist with Ruskin and his role in finding a publisher for her work. See also Jan Marsh and Pamela Gerrish Nunn, *Pre-Raphaelite Women Artists* (Manchester: Manchester City Art Gallery, 1997), pp. 138–39. For the identity of the model, see the discussion of Alexander's oil painting *Woman Sewing*, in Ferber and Gerdts, *The New Path*, pp. 228–30.

35 For a discussion of William Michael Rossetti's critical writings and their relation to Ruskin's, see Julie L'Enfant, *William Rossetti's Art Criticism: The Search for Truth in Victorian Art* (Lanham, Md.; Oxford: University Press of America, 1999). The quotations are from pp. 170–71.

Chapter 4 *Drawing the Circle: Portraits, Self-Portraits and Caricatures*

1 Anon., 'London exhibitions: conflict of the schools', *Blackwood's Edinburgh Magazine*, no. 526 (1859), p. 133.

2 Quoted in Hueffer, *Ford Madox Brown*, p. 165.

3 Elizabeth Helsinger, *Poetry and the Pre-Raphaelite Arts: Dante Gabriel Rossetti and William Morris* (New Haven and London: Yale University Press, 2008), p. 136. Helsinger deals with several aspects of the literary exploration of portraiture and its influence upon Rossetti in her Chapter 5.

4 Virginia Surtees (ed.), *The Diary of Ford Madox Brown* (New Haven and London: Yale University Press, 1981), 6 August 1855, p. 148.

5 F. G.Stephens, *Dante Gabriel Rossetti* (London: Seeley, 1894), p. 93.

6 Ibid., p. 10.

7 For a discussion of these Nazarener portraits, see Keith Andrews, *The Nazarenes* (Oxford: Clarendon Press, 1964).

8 For Murray's career and his relations with Ruskin, see David B. Elliott, *Charles Fairfax Murray: The Unknown Pre-Raphaelite* (Lewes, Sussex: Book Guild, 2000).

9 Indeed the work is thought by some scholars to be a late self-portrait by Ruskin. Certainly it has some of the characteristics of his acknowledged self-portraits. For a discussion of portraits of and self-portraits by Ruskin, see James S. Dearden, *John Ruskin: A Life in Pictures* (Sheffield: Sheffield Academic Press, 1999).

10 Betty Elzea, *Frederick Sandys 1829–1904: A Catalogue Raisonné* (Woodbridge, Suffolk: Antique Collectors' Club, 2001), p. 23.

11 For a discussion of the role of jewelry in artistic circles of the time, see Charlotte Gere and Geoffrey C. Munn, *Pre-Raphaelite to Arts and Crafts Jewellery* (Woodbridge: Antique Collectors' Club, 1999).

12 For Pre-Raphaelite connections with caricaturists and journalists, see, for example, Scott, *Autobiographical Notes*, vol. 1, p. 113. For other connections, see George Somes Layard, *The Life and Letters of Charles Samuel Keene* (London: Sampson Low, Marston & Company; New York: Macmillan, 1892) and Simon Houfe, *John Leech and the Victorian Scene* (Woodbridge: Antique Collectors Club, 1984). Millais's friendship with, and admiration for, Leech stimulated his own attempts at comic illustration, such as those in Birmingham, for example *Sleep at Any Price* (1850, Birmingham Museum and Art Gallery).

13 Martin Greenwood, *The Designs of William De Morgan* (Ilminster, Somerset: Dennis and Wiltshire, 1989), p.11. He also notes that Charles Dodgson ('Lewis Carroll') commissioned De Morgan to design a set of tiles illustrating his poem 'The Hunting of the Snark', which was published in 1876 with illustrations by Henry Holiday, an artist close to the Rossetti circle and the Firm.

14 Sidney Colvin, *Memories and Notes of Persons and Places* (London: Edward Arnold, 1921), p. 58.

15 See Philip Henderson, *Swinburne: The Portrait of a Poet* (London: Routledge and Kegan Paul, 1974), p. 57 and Rikky Rooksby, *A. C. Swinburne: A Poet's Life* (Aldershot: Scolar Press, 1997), pp. 119–20.

16 Colin Matthew, in Peter Funnell and Malcolm Warner, *Millais: Portraits* (London: National Portrait Gallery, 1999), pp. 148–49.

17 The title 'Unpainted masterpieces' has been used by Debra Mancoff to help describe the totality of Burne-Jones's many and varied drawing practices; see her essay 'Unpainted masterpieces: the drawings of Edward Burne-Jones', *Art Institute of Chicago Museum Studies*, no. 1 (2005) pp. 44–55.

Chapter 5 *Pre-Raphaelite Compositions: Drawing History, Drawing Modernity*

1 Quoted in the catalogue of Brown's exhibition in 1865 by Hueffer, *Ford Madox Brown*, p. 100.

2 Ibid.

3 Ruskin, 'The Art of England' (1884) (in *Works*, vol. 33, p. 271).

4 Paul Barlow, *Time Present and Time Past: The Art of John Everett Millais* (Aldershot: Ashgate, 2005), pp. 40–41.

5 Laurence Housman, 'Pre-Raphaelitism in art and poetry', in R. W. Macan (ed.), *Essays by Divers Hands*, new ser., no. 12 (London: Humphrey Milford; Oxford: Oxford University Press, 1933), p. 12.

6 Warner, *Drawings of John Everett Millais*, p. 8.

7 Leslie Parris in Tate Gallery, *The Pre-Raphaelites* (London: Tate Gallery, 1984), p. 174.

8 For a succinct account of this venture, see John Christian, *The Pre-Raphaelites in Oxford* (Oxford: Ashmolean Museum, 1974).

9 Patmore, 'A Pre-Raphaelite exhibition', p. 11.

10 Ibid.

11 Anon., 'Fine art gossip', *The Athenaeum* (11 July 1857), p. 886.

12 Harry Quilter, *Preferences in Art, Life and Literature* (London: Swan Sonnenschein, 1892), pp. 74–76.

13 James Orchard Halliwell (ed.), *The Thornton Romances: The Early English Metrical Romances of Perceval, Isumbras. Eglamour and Degrevant* (London: Camden Society, 1844). In his introduction to the volume Halliwell noted qualities that might have recommended the subject to Burne-Jones: 'The descriptive notices of early costume and architecture, are of peculiar interest; and it would perhaps be difficult to select a

romance of the kind of more merit', p. xxiii. The Kelmscott edition of the tale *Syr Degrevaunt* was published in 1898 with illustrations by Burne-Jones and borders by Morris.

14 Letter 57.12, to William Bell Scott, dated 7 February 1857. In [Rossetti], *Correspondence of Dante Gabriel Rossetti*, vol. 2, ed. Fredeman, p. 171. Rossetti's emphases.

15 For a discussion of this activity, see John Christian, 'The compulsive draughtsman', in Tessa Sidey and others, *The Hidden Burne-Jones* (London: D. Giles, 2007), pp. 7–27.

16 William Michael Rossetti, 'Dante Rossetti and Elizabeth Siddal with facsimiles of five unpublished drawings by Dante Rossetti in the collection of Mr Harold Hartley', *Burlington Magazine*, no. 3 (1903), p. 278.

17 See, for example, Jan Marsh, *Elizabeth Siddal: Pre-Raphaelite Artist, 1829–62* (Sheffield: Ruskin Gallery, 1991), pp. 18–19.

18 Ibid., p. 20.

19 Patmore, 'A Pre-Raphaelite exhibition', p. 12.

20 Rossetti, 'Dante Rossetti and Elizabeth Siddal', p. 277.

21 Virginia Surtees (ed.), *The Diaries of George Price Boyce* (Norwich: Real World, 1980), p. 17.

22 For this work in relation to Solomon's life and ideas, see Gayle M. Seymour, 'The life and work of Simeon Solomon, 1840–1905' (unpublished PhD dissertation, University of Santa Barbara, 1986).

23 For a history of the Dudley and its exhibits, see Dennis Lanigan, 'The Dudley Gallery: Watercolour Drawings Exhibitions, 1865–82', *The Journal of Pre-Raphaelite Studies*, no. 12 (2003), pp. 74–96.

24 Anon., 'The Dudley Gallery', *The Times* (11 February 1871), p. 4.

25 For a discussion of the painting in relation to Ford Madox Brown's painting of the balcony scene from *Romeo and Juliet* painted in the same year, see Angela Thirlwell, *William and Lucy: The Other Rossettis* (New Haven and London: Yale University Press, 2003).

26 R. St John Tyrwhitt, 'Pictures of the season', *Contemporary Review*, no. 8 (1868), p. 340.

27 Anon., 'The Dudley Gallery', *The Times* (13 February 1872), p. 4.

28 Anon., 'The General Exhibition of Water-colours', *The Times* (15 February 1869), p. 4. For an analysis of the importance of periodical reviews of the Dudley exhibitions in relation to Pre-Raphaelite influence, see Colin Cruise, 'Poetic, eccentric, Pre-Raphaelite: the critical reception of Simeon Solomon's work at the Dudley Gallery', in M. Giebelhausen and T. Barringer (eds), *Writing the Pre-Raphaelites: Text, Context, Subtext* (Aldershot: Ashgate, 2009), pp. 171–91.

29 Anon., 'Fine art General Water-colour Exhibition', *Illustrated London News* (12 February 1870), p. 181.

Chapter 6 *The Poetry of Illustration: Disseminating Pre-Raphaelite Drawing in the 1850s and 1860s*

1 In a letter to his brother dated 17 December 1844, the sixteen-year-old Rossetti recounted his purchases, made in France, of several prints and illustrated books. The Perrault *Contes des Fées* was described as 'full of the most exquisite cuts' but Rossetti noted that because they had been printed on very cheap paper 'the impressions are consequently ruined'. (See [Rossetti], *Correspondence of Dante Gabriel Rossetti*, vol. 1, ed. Fredeman, pp. 35–36.) The illustrators included Devéria and Nanteuil. Rossetti's comments are clearly those of an experienced collector of 'cuts', as popular wood engravings were known, although here he uses the term to include lithographs, which were popular in France.

2 See the writings of Forrest Reid (1875–1947), Gleeson White (1851–98) and Joseph Pennell (1857–1926) in which the illustrators of mid- to late-nineteenth-century Britain were treated as artists for the first time.

3 Ruskin, *The Cestus of Aglaia* (1865–66) (in *Works*, vol. 19, p. 101).

4 Anon., 'Art and poetry', *The Ecclesiologist*, no. 78 (June 1850), p. 47.

5 Forrest Reid, *Illustrators of the Eighteen-Sixties* (London: Faber, 1928), p. 35. Reid's emphasis.

6 For Rossetti's reaction to the engravers, see the account by Alicia Faxon, 'The medium is NOT the message: problems in the reproduction of Rossetti's art', *Victorian Periodicals Review*, no. 2 (1991), pp. 64–70 and Allan R. Life, 'The art of not "going halfway": Rossetti's illustration for the Maids of Elfen-mere', *Victorian Poetry*, nos 3/4 (1982), pp. 65–87. For Burne-Jones's description of *The Maids of Elfen-mere*, see Georgiana Burne-Jones, *Memorials of Edward Burne-Jones* (London: Macmillan, 1906), vol. 1, pp. 119–20.

7 Reid, *Illustrators of the Eighteen-Sixties*, p. 35.

8 For Dürer's influence on Burne-Jones's early work, see John Christian, 'Burne-Jones studies', *Burlington Magazine*, no. 839 (1973), pp. 92–99.

9 Richard Garnett, 'Tennyson', *Saturday Review* (27 June 1857), p. 602.

10 Ibid.

11 Ibid., p. 601.

12 The drawing is a clear influence on two major illustrators later in the century. Walter Crane provides a reminiscence of Rossetti's design in reverse for *The Sleeping Beauty* and Charles Ricketts imitates the composition for an illustration in a volume of poems by Lord De Tabley published in 1893.

13 Reid, *Illustrators of the Eighteen-Sixties*, p. 40.

14 Richard Garnett, Review of *The Defence of Guenevere and Other Poems*, *Literary Gazette* (6 March 1858), pp. 226–27.

15 See J. Mordaunt Crook and others, *The Strange Genius of William Burges* (Cardiff: National Museum of Wales, 1981), p. 148.

16 Burges reviewed the publication of Villard's sketchbook for *Building News* in 1859. Villard's influence on Burges's subsequent style can be seen in his architectural drawings and sketchbooks, for example, in the 1861 sketchbook now in the RIBA collection, London and a collection of architectural drawings dated around 1870 in the Victoria and Albert Museum. Particularly striking is the use of the pen and the method of inscription in Villard's manner.

17 Geoffrey Wakeman, *Victorian Book Illustration: The Technical Revolution* (Newton Abbot: David and Charles, 1973), p. 70.

18 Garnett, 'Tennyson', p. 602.

19 Ibid.

20 Quoted in Paul Goldman, *John Everett Millais: Illustrator and Narrator* (Aldershot: Lund Humphries, 2004), p. 10. The Dalziel brothers, George (1815–1902) and Edward (1817–1905), owned one of the most successful engraving companies in Victorian Britain. Their considerable fame and success was achieved through the employment of large numbers of experienced and accurate engravers to produce high-quality wood-engraved book illustration, although Rossetti was particularly critical of their skill and accuracy. For an account of their careers, see George and Edward Dalziel, *The Brothers Dalziel: A Record, 1840–1890* (London: Methuen, 1901; repr. 1978).

21 For an account of the drawing and its inclusion in the volume, see Bronkhurst, *William Holman Hunt*, vol. 2, cat. nos D408 and App.B33.

22 For the biblical story, see Genesis 24 (particularly v. 22); for a detailed account of Hunt's design and its commission, see Bronkhurst, *William Holman Hunt*, vol. 2, cat. nos D227 and App.B26.

23 Joseph Pennell, 'A golden decade in English art', *The Savoy*, no. 1 (1896), pp. 119 and 121.

24 Gleeson White, *English Illustration: The Sixties, 1855–70* (3rd edn, London: Constable, 1906), pp. 172–73.

Chapter 7 *Working Drawings: Design and Pattern from the Pre-Raphaelites to the Arts and Crafts Movement*

1 See Anon., 'Continental Schools of Design', *Chambers's Edinburgh Magazine* (16 May 1840), pp. 132–33; for later discussions of this subject, see Anon., 'Mr Redgrave's letter on the School of Design', *The Edinburgh Review*, no. 172 (1847), pp. 452–61, which comments on Richard Redgrave's letter on design education published in *The Builder*, December 1846.

For Redgrave's role in developing the new curriculum for the Schools of Design, see Anthony Burton, 'Richard Redgrave as art educator, museum official and design theorist', in Susan P. Casteras and Ronald Parkinson (eds), *Richard Redgrave 1804–1888* (New Haven and London: Yale University Press, 1988), pp. 48–70.

2 For a succinct report on the work of the new government department, see *The Times* (13 May 1852), p. 5.

3 Ruskin, *The Stones of Venice*, vol. 2 (1853) (in *Works*, vol. 9, p. 196).

4 Ibid. Ruskin's emphasis.

5 See Raymond Watkinson, *Pre-Raphaelite Art and Design* (London: Studio Vista, 1970), pp. 138–39.

6 The partners of 'the Firm', as it was known in the Pre-Raphaelite circle, were Morris, Burne-Jones, Rossetti, Brown, the architect Philip Webb, the engineer and surveyor Peter Paul Marshall (1830–1900) and the mathematician Charles Faulkner (1833–92). The original partnership was dissolved in 1875 and the new firm, Morris and Co., established under Morris's sole management. For a history of the company, see Pat Kirkham, 'The Firm: Morris & Company', in Diane Waggoner (ed.), *The Beauty of Life: William Morris and the Art of Design* (London: Thames and Hudson, 2003), pp. 32–63.

7 Michael Darby, *John Pollard Seddon* (London: Victoria and Albert Museum, 1983), p. 14.

8 The quotations are from G. E. Street's lecture 'On the future of art in England', as reprinted in *The Ecclesiologist*, no. 127 (1858), pp. 232–40.

9 William Burges, 'The late exhibition', *The Ecclesiologist*, no. 143 (1862), pp. 336–39.

10 Anon., 'The International Exhibition', *The Ecclesiologist*, no. 140 (1862), pp. 168–76.

11 Quoted in Raymond Watkinson, *William Morris as Designer* (London: Trefoil, 1990), p. 39.

12 William Morris, 'The lesser arts', in *Hopes and Fears for Art: Five Lectures Delivered in Birmingham, London and Nottingham, 1878–1881* (London: Ellis and White, 1882), p. 24.

13 Ibid., pp. 26–27.

14 See A. L. Morton's Introduction to William Morris, *Three Works* [*News from Nowhere, The Pilgrims of Hope, A Dream of John Ball*] (London: Lawrence and Wishart, 1973), pp. 24–32.

15 See Chapter 3 of *News from Nowhere* in ibid., p. 192.

16 See Chapter 16 of *News from Nowhere* in ibid., pp. 284–85.

17 Mark Hamilton, *Rare Spirit: A Life of William De Morgan, 1839–1917* (London: Constable, 1997), p. 23.

18 Ibid., p. 25. See also Greenwood, *Designs of William De Morgan*.

19 Greenwood, *Designs of William De Morgan*, p. 10.

20 A. W. N. Pugin, *Floriated Ornament: A Series of Thirty-one Designs* (London: Henry Bohn, 1849), unpaginated.

21 Ibid., Pugin's emphasis.

22 For an overview of Christopher Dresser's career, see Harry Lyons, *Christopher Dresser: The People's Designer 1834–1904* (Woodbridge, Suffolk: Antique Collectors' Club, 2005). For a discussion of Morris's opposition to 'scientific naturalism' in domestic interiors, see Ellen E. Frank, 'The domestication of nature: five houses in the Lake District', in U. C. Knoepflmacher and G. B. Tennyson (eds), *Nature and the Victorian Imagination* (Berkeley and Los Angeles: University of California Press, 1977), pp. 68–92.

23 Christopher Dresser, 'Botany, as adapted to the arts and art-manufacture', *Art Journal*, no. 38 (1858), p. 37.

24 For a discussion of Morris's influence on American arts and crafts, see Diane Waggoner (ed.), *The Beauty of Life: William Morris and the Art of Design* (London: Thames and Hudson, 2003).

25 Walter Crane, 'Of wallpapers', in William Morris and others, *Arts and Crafts Essays* (London: Rivington, Percival, 1893; repr. Bristol: Thoemmes Press, 1996), pp. 53–55. The collection of essays, which proved highly influential on design debates of the time, was published by the Arts and Crafts Exhibiting Society (founded in 1887) on the occasion of their fourth exhibition. Morris had been elected President of the Society in 1891 and provided the Preface to the volume.

26 Selwyn Image, 'On designing for the art of embroidery' in ibid., pp. 419–20.

27 J. D. Sedding, 'Design', in ibid., pp. 412–13.

28 For a discussion of the application of Morris's ideal of design from natural sources, see Frank, 'The domestication of nature', pp. 78–80.

Chapter 8 *The Aesthetics of Drawing from the 1860s to the 1890s: The Pre-Raphaelite Influence*

1 For discussion of the interconnections between the publication of these essays on Renaissance art, see Laurel Brake, 'The "wicked *Westminster*", the *Fortnightly*, and Walter Pater's *Renaissance*', in John O. Jordan and Robert L. Patten (eds), *Literature and the Marketplace: Nineteenth-Century British Publishing and Reading Practices* (Cambridge: Cambridge University Press, 1995), pp. 289–305.

2 A. C. Swinburne, *William Blake: A Critical Essay* (1868), quoted in Eric Warner and Graham Hough, *Strangeness and Beauty: An Anthology of Aesthetic Criticism* (Cambridge: Cambridge University Press, 1983), vol. 1, pp. 233–34.

3 Walter Pater, *The Renaissance: Studies in Art and Poetry* (4th edn, London: Macmillan, 1893); ed. Donald L. Hill (Berkeley and Los Angeles: University of California Press, 1980), pp. 103–4; Pater's emphases.

4 Anon., 'Grosvenor Gallery exhibition', *The Athenaeum* (4 January 1879), pp. 23–24.

5 J. Comyns Carr, *The Grosvenor Gallery Illustrated Catalogue: Winter Exhibition 1877–8* (London: Librairie de l'Art and Chatto and Windus, 1877), p. iv.

6 Ibid., p. vi.

7 A. C. Swinburne, *Essays and Studies* (London: Chatto and Windus, 1911), p. 326.

8 Ibid., p. 327.

9 J. Comyns Carr, *Some Eminent Victorians* (London: Duckworth, 1908), p. 67.

10 Ibid., p. 74.

11 Anon., 'Exhibition of studies in various mediums', *The Athenaeum* (16 November 1889), p. 680.

12 J. G. P. Delaney, *Charles Ricketts: A Biography* (Oxford: Oxford University Press, 1999), p. 100.

13 Ibid., pp. 115–16.

14 Quoted in ibid., p. 35.

15 Anon., 'The New Gallery', *The Athenaeum* (19 May 1888), p. 636.

16 Fortunée de Lisle, *Burne-Jones* (3rd edn, London: Methuen, 1907), p. 157.

17 For discussion of Beardsley's *Morte D'Arthur* project, see Stephen Calloway, *Aubrey Beardsley* (London: Victoria and Albert Museum, 1998). For the context for Beardsley's overt sexual motifs, see Linda Gertner Zatlin, *Aubrey Beardsley and Victorian Sexual Politics* (Oxford: Oxford University Press, 1990).

18 Robert Buchanan's essay, 'The fleshly school of poetry: Mr. D. G. Rossetti', was published in the *Contemporary Review*, no. 18 (1871).

19 Quilter, *Preferences in Art, Life, and Literature*, p. 76.

20 Ibid., p. 77.

21 Ibid., p. 208.

22 H. de Burgh Daly, 'Reviews and views', *Merry England*, no. 62 (1888), p. 134.

23 For a discussion of this period and its art, see John Christian (ed.), *The Last Romantics: The Romantic Tradition in British Art* (London: Lund Humphries with the Barbican Art Gallery, 1989).

24 Ibid., p. 95.

25 Oscar Wilde, 'The English renaissance of art', in *Essays and Lectures* (Methuen, 1908), pp. 179–80.

26 T. Martin Wood, *Drawings of Rossetti* (London: George Newnes; New York: Charles Scribner, 1910), p. 7.

27 Ibid., p. 13.

28 W. Graham Robertson, *Time Was* (London: Hamish Hamilton, 1931), p. 58.

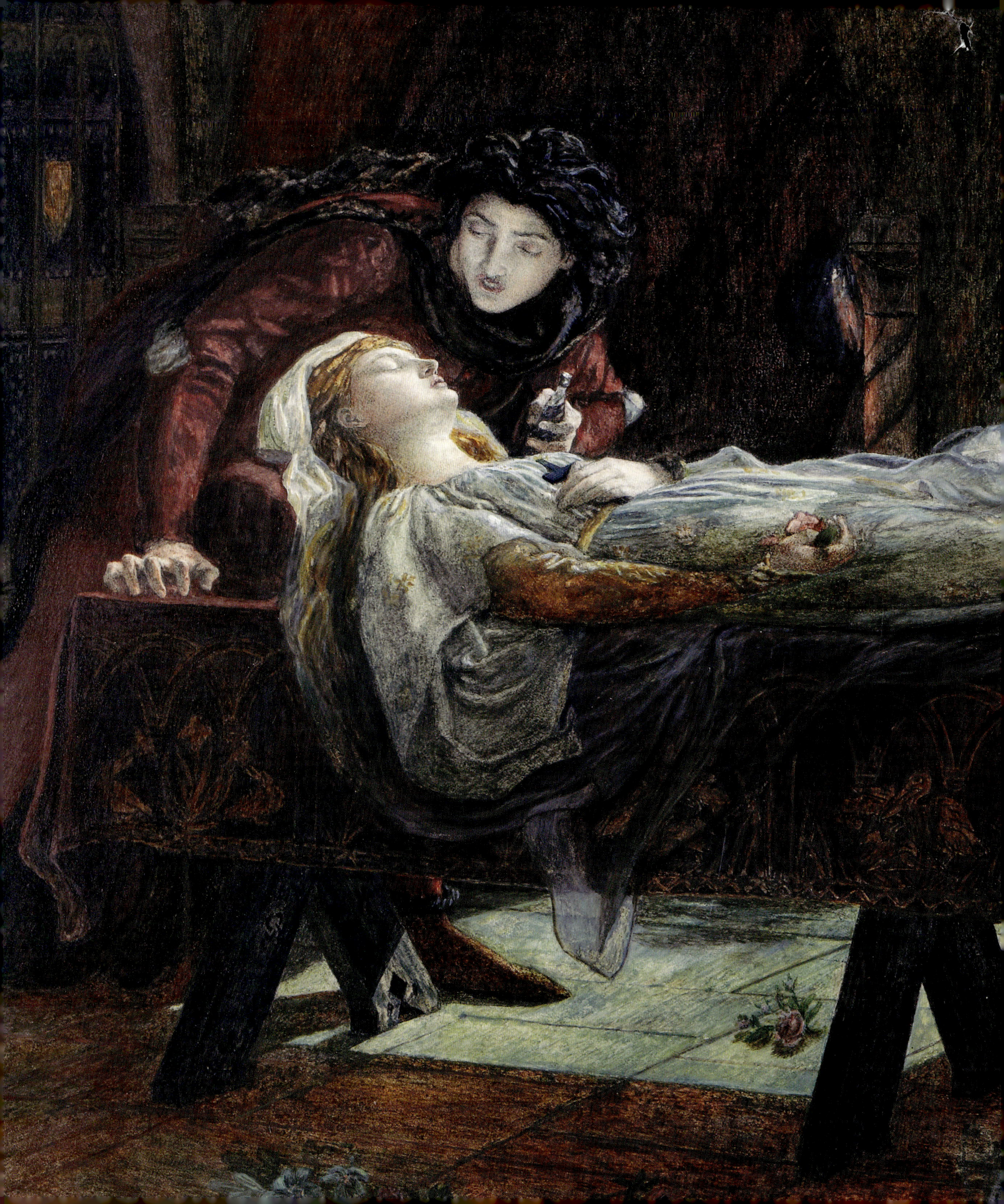

List of Works

Works are listed by artist, then chronologically.
Numbers in square brackets refer to the illustrations.
Measurements are given in millimetres, height before
width before depth.

Alexander, Francesca (1837–1917)
Rispetti, c. 1868–82 [103]
Pen and brown ink on paper: 380 × 275
Birmingham Museums & Art Gallery; purchased, 1969
(1969P1)

Roadside Songs of Tuscany, 1885 [not illustrated]
Bound volume, published by George Allen (Orpington,
Kent, 1885): 313 × 244 × 34
Birmingham Libraries & Archives
Exhibited in Birmingham only

Beardsley, Aubrey (1872–1898)
A Knight, 1892 [297]
Design for a chapter heading for Sir Thomas Malory's
Morte D'Arthur, published by J. M. Dent & Co. (London,
1893–94)
Pen and black ink on paper: 170 × 76
Victoria and Albert Museum, London

Siegfried, 1892–93 [298]
Photographic reproduction made for *The Studio* magazine:
220 × 155
Victoria and Albert Museum, London

Merlin and Nimuë, c. 1893 [292]
Process reproduction, 211 × 165 (image), printed in Sir
Thomas Malory, *Morte D'Arthur*, vol. 1, published by
J. M. Dent & Co. (London, 1893–94)
Two bound volumes: 246 × 204 × 50 (vol. 1), 246 × 204 × 55
(vol. 2)
Birmingham Libraries & Archives
Exhibited in Birmingham only

La Dame aux Camélias, 1894 [299]
Pen and ink, ink wash and watercolour on paper:
279 × 181
Tate; presented by Colonel James Lister Melvill at the
request of his brother, Harry Edward Melvill, 1931

Beerbohm, Max (1872–1956)
Dante Gabriel Rossetti in his Back Garden, c. 1904 [140]
Watercolour over pencil with pen and ink on paper:
201 × 313
Birmingham Museums & Art Gallery; purchased with
grant aid administered by the Victoria and Albert Museum,
1981 (1981P2)

Blake, William (1757–1827)
The Circle of the Lustful (The Whirlwind of Lovers), 1824–27
[279]
Pen and ink and watercolour over pencil with scratching-
out on paper: 370 × 523
Birmingham Museums & Art Gallery; presented by the
Trustees of the Public Picture Gallery Fund, with assistance
from the National Art Collections Fund and the Feeney
Trust, 1919 (1919P2)

Botticelli, Sandro (*c.* 1445–1510)
Abundance, c. 1475–82 [282]
Frontispiece to the Grosvenor Gallery *Illustrated Catalogue,
Winter Exhibition of Drawings by the Old Masters and
Water-Colour Drawings by Deceased Artists of the British
School*, 1877–78
Process reproduction: 195 × 154 (image)
Private collection
Exhibited in Birmingham only

Bowler, Henry (1824–1903)
Luccombe Chine, Isle of Wight, 1860 [93]
Watercolour on paper: 354 × 250
Victoria and Albert Museum, London

Arthur Hughes, 1858 [132]
Pencil on paper: 207 × 224 (uneven)
National Portrait Gallery, London; purchased, 1999
Exhibited in Birmingham only

Brett, John (1831–1902)
The Hedger, c. 1859 [92] [not exhibited]
Monochrome wash and bodycolour on paper: 250 × 185
Private collection

Gentian, 1862 [72, 91]
Watercolour on paper: 107 × 146
The Williamson Art Gallery and Museum, Birkenhead,
Wirral

February on the Isle of Wight, 1866 [94]
Watercolour and bodycolour with gum on paper: 460 × 354
Birmingham Museums & Art Gallery; presented by Herbert
Martin, 1919 (1919P70)

Brett, Rosa (1829–1882)
Farnhurst, 1853 [95]
Watercolour on paper: 280 × 310
Private collection

Study of Two Rabbits, undated [96]
Pencil on paper: 530 × 730
Private collection

Brickdale, Eleanor Fortescue (1871–1945)
Guinevere, 1911 [302]
Watercolour on paper: 445 × 265
Birmingham Museums & Art Gallery; presented by an
anonymous donor, 1911 (1911P67)

Brown, Ford Madox (1821–1893)
Study for 'Lear and Cordelia', 1843–44 [36]
Pen and iron gall ink over pencil on paper: 201 × 277
Birmingham Museums & Art Gallery; purchased and
presented by subscribers, 1906 (1906P754)

Study for 'The Seeds and Fruits of English Poetry', 1845 [33]
[not exhibited]
Chalk on paper: 340 × 503
Cecil Higgins Art Gallery, Bedford

Three Studies for 'The Spirit of Justice', 1845:
A Baron and his Advisor, 1845 [30]
Pen and brown ink over pencil on paper: 361 × 230
Birmingham Museums & Art Gallery; presented by Harold
Hartley, 1905 (1905P18)
Head of a Baron, 1845 [31]
Black chalk on paper: 283 × 175
Birmingham Museums & Art Gallery; purchased and
presented by subscribers, 1906 (1906P715)
Study for 'The Spirit of Justice', 1845 [32]
Pencil, watercolour and bodycolour on paper: 757 × 517
Manchester City Galleries
Exhibited in Birmingham only

Discobolus, 1845 [25]
Black chalk on paper: 435 × 254
Birmingham Museums & Art Gallery; purchased and
presented by subscribers, 1906 (1906P718)

Sheet of Nude Studies, 1845 [not illustrated]
Pencil on paper: 287 × 385
Birmingham Museums & Art Gallery; purchased and
presented by subscribers, 1906 (1906P671)

Study of a Male Nude Posed as a Sculptor, 1847 [22]
Chalk with grey wash on paper: 387 × 174
Birmingham Museums & Art Gallery; purchased and
presented by subscribers, 1906 (1906P709)

Study of a Male Nude Holding a Staff, 1847 [24] [not
exhibited]
Pencil on paper: 252 × 134
Birmingham Museums & Art Gallery; purchased and
presented by subscribers, 1906 (1906P672)

Three Studies for 'Chaucer at the Court of Edward III', 1845–51:
Compositional Study, 1845 [not illustrated]
Pencil with brown ink on paper: 330 × 240
Birmingham Museums & Art Gallery; purchased and
presented by subscribers, 1906 (1906P681)
Drapery Study for the Black Prince, 1848 [not illustrated]
Black chalk on paper with touches of white chalk on brown
toned paper: 206 × 165
Birmingham Museums & Art Gallery; purchased and
presented by subscribers, 1906 (1906P783)
Study for the Jester, 1847 [not illustrated]
Pencil on paper: 237 × 176
Birmingham Museums & Art Gallery; purchased and
presented by subscribers, 1906 (1906P778)

Chaucer at the Court of Edward III, 1847–51 [34]
Oil on canvas: 3720 × 2960
Art Gallery of New South Wales, Sydney
Exhibited in Sydney only

Self Portrait, 1850–53 [122] [not exhibited]
Black chalk on light brown paper: 250 × 230
National Museums Liverpool (Walker Art Gallery)

Study of Emma Hill for 'The Last of England', 1852 [106] [not
exhibited]
Black and white chalk on two sheets of paper: 161 × 177
Birmingham Museums & Art Gallery; purchased and
presented by subscribers, 1906 (1906P791)

Study for 'The Last of England', 1852 [152]
Pencil on paper, the image edged in brown ink: 408 × 365
Birmingham Museums & Art Gallery; purchased and
presented by subscribers, 1906 (1906P795)

The Last of England: 1852–55 [153]
Oil on panel, 825 × 750
Birmingham Museums & Art Gallery; purchased, 1891
(1891P24)
Exhibited in Birmingham only

Chaucer at the Court of Edward III, c. 1854 [35]
Watercolour with bodycolour on paper: 365 × 386
Birmingham Museums & Art Gallery; bequeathed by James
Richardson Holliday, 1927 (1927P356)

Design for Stained Glass: 'The Nativity', 1861, photographed by Frederick Hollyer for Morris & Co. [243] [not exhibited]
Photographic print mounted in bound volume: 278 × 175
Birmingham Museums & Art Gallery; presented anonymously, 1940 (1940P604.5)

Design for the King René's Honeymoon Cabinet: 'Architecture', 1861 [239]
Brush and brown ink with watercolour over pencil on brown paper: 444 × 318
Birmingham Museums & Art Gallery; bequeathed by James Richardson Holliday, 1927 (1927P351)

The Death of Sir Tristram, 1864 [255] [not exhibited]
Oil on canvas: 642 × 584
Birmingham Museums & Art Gallery; presented by the Trustees of the Public Picture Gallery Fund, 1916 (1916P26)

Compositional Study for 'Joseph's Coat' with Three Studies for the Figure of Jacob's Grand-daughter, 1865 [223]
Pencil on paper: 391 × 291
Birmingham Museums & Art Gallery; purchased and presented by subscribers, 1906 (1906P788)

Study for ' The Entombment', 1867 [not illustrated]
Pen and black ink on paper: 264 × 240
Birmingham Museums & Art Gallery; presented by the Trustees of the Public Picture Gallery Fund, 1916 (1916P27)

The Death of Eglon, Dalziel Brothers after Ford Madox Brown, published 1881 [225] [not illustrated]
Wood engraving by the Dalziel Brothers on India paper in bound volume: 152 × 188 (image); 430 × 360 × 43 (volume)
Birmingham Museums & Art Gallery; presented by Wilfred Phillips, 1920 (1920P713.1.53)

Joseph's Coat, Dalziel Brothers after Ford Madox Brown, published 1881 [224] [not illustrated]
Illustration for *Dalziels' Bible Gallery*, published by Routledge (London, 1881)
Wood engraving by the Dalziel Brothers on India paper in bound volume: 188 × 152 (image); 430 × 360 × 43 (volume)
Birmingham Museums & Art Gallery; presented by Wilfred Phillips, 1920 (1920P713.1.22)

Brown, Lucy Madox (1843–1894)
The Dancing Faun, 1869 [192] [not exhibited]
Black chalk on grey-green paper: 585 × 333
Private collection

The Tomb Scene from Romeo and Juliet, 1870 [193, 309]
Watercolour and bodycolour on paper: 610 × 810
National Trust, Wightwick Manor and Gardens

Burges, William (1827–1881)
St Simeon Stylites, 1861 [213]
Pen and ink on paper, 385 × 277
Victoria and Albert Museum

Burgess, Arthur (d. 1887)
Two Unused Designs after John Ruskin for 'Proserpina: Studies of Wayside Flowers', c. 1875:
Unidentified Botanical Specimen [85]
Pen and ink on uncut woodblock: 62 × 100 × 22
Birmingham Museums & Art Gallery; purchased, 1905 (1905P145)
Primula [86]
Pen and ink on uncut woodblock: 100 × 50 × 22
Birmingham Museums & Art Gallery; purchased, 1905 (1905P158)

Burne-Jones, Edward (1833–1898)
Self-Portrait Caricature in Red Lion Square, c. 1856 [235] [not exhibited]
Pen and ink on paper: 121 × 197
Mark Samuels Lasner Collection, on loan to the University of Delaware Library

Title Page and Frontispiece to 'The Fairy Family, 1857 [229]
Title Page and frontispiece by an unidentified engraver after Burne-Jones, printed in Archibald MacLaren, *The Fairy Family: A Series of Ballads and Metrical Tales Illustrating the Fairy Faith of Europe*, 1857, published by Longman, Brown, Green, Longmans & Roberts (London, 1857)
Bound volume: 197 × 140 × 30
Birmingham Museums & Art Gallery; bequeathed by James Richardson Holliday, 1927 (1927P1616)

Design for Stained Glass: 'The Good Shepherd', 1857 [248]
Ink and watercolour on paper: 1280 × 477
Victoria and Albert Museum, London

Going to the Battle, 1858 [8] [not exhibited]
Pen and ink and wash on vellum: 223 × 195
Fitzwilliam Museum, Cambridge; bequeathed by James
Richardson Holliday, 1927

The Good Shepherd, 1861 [249]
Stained, painted and leaded glass by James Powell & Sons:
1320 × 510
Maidstone United Reformed Church, on loan to
Birmingham Museums & Art Gallery

The Knight's Farewell, 1858 [182]
Pen and black ink on vellum: 176 × 242
Ashmolean Museum, University of Oxford; bequeathed by
John Bryson, 1977

Study for a Mural: 'The Wedding of Sir Degrevaunt', 1860
[181]
Pencil on blue paper, squared up for transfer: 289 × 288
Birmingham Museums & Art Gallery; bequeathed by James
Richardson Holliday, 1927 (1927P452)

Five Designs for the Ladies and Animals Sideboard, 1860:
A Lady Feeding Pigs [not illustrated]
Pen and brown wash over pencil on paper: 76 × 75
A Lady Feeding Parrots [236]
Pen and brown wash over pencil on paper: 92 × 84
A Lady Feeding Goldfish [not illustrated]
Pen and brown wash over pencil on paper: 79 × 68
A Lady Frightened by a Newt [not illustrated]
Pen and brown wash over pencil on paper: 110 × 85
A Lady Pursued by a Swarm of Bees [237]
Pen and brown wash over pencil on paper: 110 × 83
Birmingham Museums & Art Gallery; presented by W. M.
Keeley, 1971 (1971P272-276)

Design for Stained Glass: 'The Tree of Jesse', 1860–61 [250]
Pen and brown ink over pencil on cream-toned paper:
307 × 420
Birmingham Museums & Art Gallery; bequeathed by James
Richardson Holliday, 1927 (1927P437)

The Tree of Jesse, 1861–62 [251]
Stained, painted and leaded glass by James Powell & Sons,
2310 × 1000
Birmingham Museums & Art Gallery; presented by the
Friends of Birmingham Museum & Art Gallery, 1977
(1977M1)
Exhibited in Birmingham only

Design for a Tile: 'Theseus and the Minotaur', 1861 [262]
Pencil, brown wash and pen and ink on paper: 261 × 255
Birmingham Museums & Art Gallery; bequeathed by James
Richardson Holliday, 1927 (1927P594)

Design for the King René's Honeymoon Cabinet: 'Sculpture',
1861 [240]
Pen, indian ink and wash over coloured chalk and pencil on
paper: 550 × 342
Birmingham Museums & Art Gallery; purchased and
presented by subscribers, 1904 (1904P528)

Design for Stained Glass: 'The Annunciation', 1862 [9]
Brown wash, indian ink and watercolour over pencil on
paper: 788 × 786
Birmingham Museums & Art Gallery; bequeathed by James
Richardson Holliday, 1927 (1931P64)

Design for Stained Glass: The Tomb of Tristram and Iseult,
1862 [253] [not exhibited]
Black ink and brown wash over pencil on paper laid on
canvas: 641 × 642
Birmingham Museums & Art Gallery; presented by Charles
Fairfax Murray, 1912 (1912P37)

King Mark and La Belle Iseult, 1862 [254] [not exhibited]
Watercolour, bodycolour and gum on paper, 585 × 555
Birmingham Museums & Art Gallery; presented by Sir John
T. Middlemore, Bart., 1912 (1912P28)

Design for Embroidery: 'Chaucer's Legend of Good Women',
1863 [not illustrated]
Pencil on paper: 266 × 362
Birmingham Museums & Art Gallery; purchased and
presented by subscribers, 1904 (1904 P13)

Design for Stained Glass: 'The Building of the Ark', 1863 [not illustrated]
Brown ink and wash over pencil on paper, laid on canvas: 658 × 660
Birmingham Museums & Art Gallery; presented by Charles Fairfax Murray, 1901 (1901P9)

Design for Stained Glass: 'The Magdalen at Christ's Feet', 1863, photographed by Frederick Hollyer for Morris & Co. [289] [not exhibited]
Photographic print mounted in bound volume: 289 × 221
Birmingham Museums & Art Gallery; presented anonymously, 1940 (1940P604.5)

Design for Stained Glass: 'Chaucer Asleep', 1864 [247]
Pencil on toned paper: 460 × 462
Birmingham Museums & Art Gallery; purchased and presented by subscribers, 1903 (1904P517)

Three Studies for 'Le Chant d'Amour', c. 1865–1868:
Lover, c. 1865 [184]
Brown wash and white bodycolour on brown paper: 216 × 209
Birmingham Museums & Art Gallery; purchased and presented by subscribers, 1904 (1904P226)
Woman's Head, 1868 [185]
Red chalk on cream laid paper: 310 × 235
Aberystwyth University, School of Art Gallery and Museum; bequeathed by George Powell, 1882
Seraph, 1868 [186]
Red chalk on cream laid paper: 340 × 235
Aberystwyth University, School of Art Gallery and Museum; bequeathed by George Powell, 1882

The Petition to the King, 1865–67 [183]
Pencil and black chalk on paper: 352 × 604
The British Museum, London

Phyllis and Demophöon, 1870 [10, 197]
Bodycolour and watercolour with gold medium and gum on composite layers of paper laid on canvas: 915 × 458
Birmingham Museums & Art Gallery; presented by the John Feeney Charitable Trust, 1916 (1916P37)
Exhibited in Birmingham only

William Morris as an Ancient Poet, c. 1870–73 [147] [not exhibited]
Pencil on paper: 125 × 79
Birmingham Museums & Art Gallery; bequeathed by James Richardson Holliday, 1927 (1927P554)

The Sirens, c. 1878–80 [146] [not exhibited]
Pencil on cream-toned paper: 40 × 93
Birmingham Museums & Art Gallery; bequeathed by James Richardson Holliday, 1927 (1927P557)

The Boiling Pot, Dalziel Brothers after Edward Burne-Jones, published 1881 [228] [not illustrated]
Illustration for *Dalziels' Bible Gallery*, published by Routledge (London, 1881)
Wood engraving by the Dalziel Brothers on India paper in bound volume: 178 × 133 (image); 430 × 360 × 43 (volume)
Birmingham Museums & Art Gallery; presented by Wilfred Phillips, 1920 (1920P713.1.68)

Study of the Figure of Perseus for 'The Finding of Medusa', 1881 [293]
Watercolour, bodycolour, silver medium and chalk on grey-brown paper: 376 × 263
Birmingham Museums & Art Gallery; presented by an anonymous donor, 1898 (1898P46)

Design for Stained Glass: 'The Nativity', 1888, photographed by Frederick Hollyer for Morris & Co. [291] [not exhibited]
Photographic print mounted in bound volume: 328 × 133
Birmingham Museums & Art Gallery; presented anonymously, 1940 (1940P604.2)

Self Portrait Caricature: 'Unpainted Masterpieces', early 1890s [148]
Pen and ink over pencil on notepaper: 176 × 107
Birmingham Museums & Art Gallery; purchased, 1980 (1980P128)

Honour's Prize, undated [296]
Collotype print from *The Flower Book*, published by The Fine Art Society (London, 1905): 158 × 162 (image, circular)
Birmingham Museums & Art Gallery; purchased, 1953 (1953P5.32)

Burne-Jones, Philip (1861–1926)
Album of Caricatures, late 1870s:
Page from an Album of Caricatures [149]
Mr De Morgan and E. B–J. [150]
Bound volume: 315 × 270 × 28
Private collection
Exhibited in Birmingham only

Camm, Florence (1874–1960)
Designs for Stained Glass: ' Dante and Beatrice', 1911 [303–04]
Pen and ink and watercolour over pencil on paper, laid on card; upper lights: three sheets, each 152 × 75, laid on card 163 × 251; lower lights: three sheets, each 183 × 75, laid on card 192 × 254
Birmingham Museums & Art Gallery; transferred from Staffordshire County Museum, 1988 (1988M487)
Exhibited in Birmingham only

Dante and Beatrice, 1911 [305]
Stained, painted and leaded glass by Camm & Company; three panels, each 1490 × 620
Birmingham Museums & Art Gallery; transferred from Staffordshire County Museum, 1988 (1988M58.1-3)
Exhibited in Birmingham only

Claxton, Florence (fl. 1859–1889)
The Choice of Paris: An Idyll, 1860 [105]
Watercolour with gum heightened with gold paint on paper: 268 × 378
Victoria and Albert Museum, London

Collins, Charles Allston (1828–1873)
The Devout Childhood of St Elizabeth of Hungary, 1852 [71]
Pencil, pen and ink and wash on paper: 273 × 175
Tate; bequeathed by Mrs Louise d'Este Oliver, 1920

Collinson, James (1825–1881)
An Incident in the Life of St Elizabeth of Hungary, 1850 [70]
Pen and ink over traces of pencil within brown ink border on paper: 400 × 456
Birmingham Museums & Art Gallery; purchased through the Christina Feeney Bequest Fund, 1929 (1929P38)

Christ Blessing the Children (Ex ore infantium et lactantium perfecisti laudem), 1850 [197]
Illustration in *The Germ* (February 1850), facsimile edition (1901)
Etching in bound journal: 226 × 145
Birmingham Museums & Art Gallery; accessioned 1979 (1979P217.3)

Colonna, Francesco (1433?–1527), attrib.
Hypnerotomachia Poliphili, 1499 [not illustrated]
Bound volume published by Aldus Manutius (Venice, 1499), 318 × 215 × 45
Birmingham Libraries & Archives
Exhibited in Birmingham only

Antonio Allegri di Correggio (*fl.* 1494–1534)
Christ Presented to the People (Ecce Homo), c. 1525–30 [65] [not exhibited]
Oil on poplar: 997 × 800
The National Gallery, London; purchased, 1834

Henry Dearle (1860–1932)
Design for Stained Glass: The Three Maries at the Sepulchre, 1910, photographed by Frederick Hollyer for Morris & Co. [256] [not exhibited]
Three photographic prints mounted in bound volume: 294 × 72, 303 × 72 and 294 × 72
Birmingham Museums & Art Gallery; presented anonymously, 1940 (1940P604.2)

De Morgan, Evelyn (1855–1919)
Medea, c. 1889 [285]
Pastel on paper: 1350 × 840
National Trust, Wightwick Manor and Gardens

De Morgan, William (1839–1917)
Tile Panel with Snake and Butterfly, 1872–98 [264, detail]
Twelve tiles in earthenware with painted decoration over
a white slip, mounted as a panel, the central two tiles
depicting a butterfly and a snake entwined with foliage and
fruit: 630 × 825
Birmingham Museums & Art Gallery; presented by H.C.
Mossop, 1941 (1941M81.1, 1941M81.2) and purchased with the
aid of the Friends of Birmingham Museum and Art Gallery
and the MGC/V&A Purchase Grant Fund, 1981 (1981M73.1,
1981M73.2,1981M74, 1981M75, 1981M76, 1981M78, 1981M91.1,
1981M98, 1981M98.2, 1981M94)

Tile Panel, 1888–97 [263]
Nine tiles in earthenware with painted decoration over a
white slip, mounted as a panel: 151 × 152
Birmingham Museums & Art Gallery; presented by H.C.
Mossop, 1941 (1941M80)

Bottle, 1888–98 [265]
Earthenware decorated with lustres painted by Fred
Passenger over a white slip: 262 (height)
Birmingham Museums & Art Gallery; purchased with the
aid of the Friends of Birmingham Museum and Art Gallery
and the MGC/V&A Purchase Grant Fund, 1981 (1981M42)

Sketchbook, undated [266, 267]
Bound volume: 266 × 195 × 25
Birmingham Museums & Art Gallery; purchased with the
aid of the Friends of Birmingham Museum and Art Gallery
and the MGC/V&A Purchase Grant Fund, 1981 (1981M315)

Deverell, Walter Howell (1827–1854)
Study for 'The Banishment of Hamlet', 1847 [43] [not
exhibited]
Brush and grey ink with pen and black and brown inks and
white heightening over pencil on off-white paper: 251 × 250
Ashmolean Museum, University of Oxford; bequeathed by
John Bryson, 1977

Study for 'Twelfth Night', c. 1850 [42]
Pen and ink on paper: 216 × 292
Tate; purchased 1919

Dresser, Christopher (1834–1904)
Demonstration Drawing, c. 1855 [270] [not exhibited]
Watercolour and bodycolour on paper laid on canvas:
550 × 755
Victoria and Albert Museum, London

Dürer, Albrecht (1471–1528)
St Eustace, c. 1501 [204]
Engraving on paper: 358 × 262
Birmingham Museums & Art Gallery; presented by the
Trustees of the Public Picture Gallery Fund, 1905 (1905P167)

Dyce, William (1806–1864)
Study for 'The Vision of Sir Galahad and his Company', c.
1847 [28] [not exhibited]
Ink and black chalk touched with white on green paper,
235 × 306
Aberdeen Art Gallery & Museums Collections

Farrer, Thomas Charles (1839–1891)
Woman Sewing, 1854 [84] [not exhibited]
Pencil with white bodycolour on cream paper: 303 × 235
Princeton University Art Museum; Gift of Professor Charles
Ryskamp, in memory of Mr Gerard B. Lambert, Class of
1908

Flaxman, John (1755–1826)
*Compositions from the Hell, Purgatory and Paradise of
Dante Alighieri*, 1807:
Paradise: Beatrice and Dante, 1807 [44]
Engraving 134 × 189 (image) printed in *Compositions by
John Flaxman, Sculptor, R.A. from The Divine Poem of
Dante Alighieri*, published by Longman, Hurst, Rees and
Orme (London, 1807)
Bound volume: 285 × 363 × 31
Birmingham Libraries & Archives
Exhibited in Birmingham only
Purgatory: The Salutation, 1807 [203]
Engraving 138 × 192 (image) printed in *Compositions by John
Flaxman, Sculptor, R.A. from The Divine Poem of Dante
Alighieri*, published by Longman, Hurst, Rees and Orme

(London, 1807)
Bound volume: 285 × 363 × 31
Birmingham Libraries & Archives
Exhibited in Birmingham only

Dante's Purgatory, 1836 [not illustrated]
Bound volume, part of *Oeuvre de Flaxman: Recueil de ses
compositions gravées par Réveil*, published by Réveil and
Audot, 8 vols (Paris, 1836): 158 × 238 × 13
Birmingham Museums & Art Gallery; presented by the
Misses Wallis, 1920 (1920P472.7)

Dante's Paradise, 1836 [not illustrated]
Bound volume, part of *Oeuvre de Flaxman: Recueil de ses
compositions gravées par Réveil*, published by Réveil and
Audot, 8 vols (Paris, 1836): 158 × 238 × 12
Birmingham Museums & Art Gallery; presented by the
Misses Wallis, 1920 (1920P472.5)

Harding, James Duffield (1797 or 1798–1863)
A Hunt Scene in Windsor Forest, undated [79]
Black chalk and watercolour with white bodycolour on
paper: 176 × 246
Birmingham Museums & Art Gallery; bequeathed by J.
Leslie Wright, 1953 (1953P242)

Lessons on Trees, *c.* 1860 [not illustrated]
Bound volume, published by W. Kent & Co and Messrs
Windsor and Newton (London, *c.* 1860): 378 × 280 × 34
Birmingham Libraries & Archives
Exhibited in Birmingham only

Hollyer, Frederick (1838–1933)
The Bride, the Bridegroom and the Friend of the Bridegroom,
after 1868 [280]
Platinotype of a drawing by Simeon Solomon, dated 1868:
232 × 178
Birmingham Museums & Art Gallery; presented by Alan
Green, 1981 (1981P91)

Study for 'The Garden Court': Sleeping Maiden, *c.* 1883–85
[281]
Platinotype of a study by Edward Burne-Jones for *The
Garden Court* (*Briar Rose* series): 212 × 237
Birmingham Museums & Art Gallery; accessioned in 1970
(1970P140)

Hughes, Arthur (1842–1915)
William Michael Rossetti, 1854 [131]
Pen and ink on paper: 173 × 108
Private collection

Two Studies for 'The Long Engagement', *c.* 1858:
Pencil on paper: 254 × 172 [170]
Birmingham Museums & Art Gallery; presented by Charles
Alexander Munro, 1959 (1959P11)
Pencil heightened with white chalk on paper: 244 × 177 [171]
Birmingham Museums & Art Gallery; presented by John N.
Bunney and Miss S.E. Bunney, 1998 (1998P80)

The Long Engagement, 1859 [172]
Oil on canvas: 1070 × 533
Birmingham Museums & Art Gallery; presented by the
executors of Mr Edwin T. Griffiths, 1902 (1902P13)

Design for Stained Glass: 'The Birth of Tristram', 1861 [252]
Red chalk and ink wash over pencil with touches of
bodycolour on paper: 585 × 545
Birmingham Museums & Art Gallery; presented by Charles
Fairfax Murray, 1912 (1912P39)

Hughes, Edward Robert (1851–1914)
Study for a Picture ('Fra Lippo Lippi'), 1893 [301]
Red and brown chalk on paper: 677 × 480
The Williamson Art Gallery and Museum, Birkenhead,
Wirral

'Oh, what's that in the hollow, so pale, I quake to follow?'
'Oh, that's a thin, dead body, which waits the eternal term.'
1893 [278, 301]
Watercolour with gum and scratching-out on paper:
632 × 933
Royal Watercolour Society

Hunt, William Henry (1790–1864)
Bird's Nest, Apple Blossoms and Primroses, *c.* 1845–50 [76]
Watercolour, bodycolour and gum on paper: 226 × 301
Birmingham Museums & Art Gallery; presented by the
Trustees of the Public Picture Gallery Fund, 1905 (1905P166)

Hunt, William Holman (1827–1910)
Hyperion, 1847 [49]
Pen and black ink on paper: 114 × 258
Courtauld Gallery, London

One Step to the Death Bed, 1848 [48] [not exhibited]
Pen and brown and black ink: 187 × 279
Yale Center for British Art; Bequest of Richard L. Purdy

Daniel Praying, 1849 [59]
Pen and black and brown ink with pencil within ink border
on paper: 210 × 260 (image); 232 × 276 (sheet)
Private collection

The Lady of Shalott, 1850 [207] [not exhibited]
Black chalk and pen and ink on paper: 235 × 142
National Gallery of Victoria, Melbourne; Felton Bequest,
1921

My Beautiful Lady, 1850 [198]
Illustration in *The Germ* (January 1850), facsimile edition
(1901)
Etching in bound volume: 226 × 139
Birmingham Museums & Art Gallery; accessioned in 1979
(1979P217.2)

Study for 'Claudio and Isabella', 1850 [37, 310]
Pen and black ink with touches of brown ink, wash and
pencil: 318 × 191
Syndics of the Fitzwilliam Museum, Cambridge

Study for 'Valentine Rescuing Sylvia from Proteus', 1850 [47]
Pen and black ink and pencil on paper: 235 × 318 (image,
arched top); 276 × 365 (sheet)
The British Museum, London

Valentine Rescuing Sylvia from Proteus, 1850–51 [46] [not
exhibited]
Oil on canvas: 985 × 1333
Birmingham Museums & Art Gallery; purchased 1887
(1887P953)

John Everett Millais, 1853 [126]
Black, red and blue chalks, with traces of pencil, on grey
paper, laid on card: 327 × 248
National Portrait Gallery, London; presented by L. G.
Esmond Morse, 1937

Walter Howell Deverell, 1853 [129]
Black and red chalk with wash on paper: 355 × 260
Birmingham Museums & Art Gallery; presented by the
artist, 1907 (1907P134)

Dante Gabriel Rossetti, 1853 [121]
Coloured chalks on cream paper: 286 × 259
Manchester City Galleries
Exhibited in Birmingham only

Study for 'The Awakening Conscience', 1853 [155] [not
exhibited]
Pen and brown ink: 121 × 79 (to ink border)
The Pollitt Collection

Two Studies for 'The Finding of the Saviour in the Temple':
Compositional Study, c. 1854 [157]
Pencil on paper: 356 × 508
Birmingham Museums & Art Gallery; presented by the
Friends of Birmingham Museum and Art Gallery, 1985
(1985P65)
Study of the Heads of Mary and Jesus, 1858 [156]
Charcoal, black chalk and watercolour on paper: 264 × 370
National Museums Liverpool (Walker Art Gallery)

The Finding of the Saviour in the Temple, 1854–55, 1856–60 [158]
Oil on canvas: 857 × 1410
Birmingham Museums & Art Gallery; presented by J. T.
Middlemore, 1896 (1896P80)
Exhibited in Birmingham only

The Ballad of Oriana, 1857 [207] [not exhibited]
Illustration to *Poems by Alfred Tennyson D.C.L., Poet
Laureate*, published by Edward Moxon (London, 1857) [the
'Moxon Tennyson']
Wood engraving by the Dalziel Brothers in bound volume:
81 × 93 (image); 235 × 175 × 40 (volume)
Birmingham Museums & Art Gallery; transferred from
Birmingham Reference Library, 1963 (1978P203.10)

The Lady of Shalott, 1857 [208]
Illustration to *Poems by Alfred Tennyson D.C.L., Poet Laureate*, published by Edward Moxon (London, 1857) [the 'Moxon Tennyson']
Wood engraving by J. Thompson in bound volume: 94 × 81 (image); 235 × 175 × 40 (volume)
Birmingham Museums & Art Gallery; transferred from Birmingham Reference Library, 1963 (1978P203)

Sir Galahad, 1857 [206] [not exhibited]
Illustration to *Poems by Alfred Tennyson D.C.L., Poet Laureate*, published by Edward Moxon (London, 1857) [the 'Moxon Tennyson']
Wood engraving by W. J. Linton in bound volume: 94 × 80 (image); 235 × 175 × 40 (volume)
Birmingham Museums & Art Gallery; transferred from Birmingham Reference Library, 1963 (1978P203.43)

Life Study of a Seated Female Nude, Seen from Behind, 1858 [20] [not exhibited]
Pen and ink and wash heightened with white bodycolour on buff paper: 511 × 356
Birmingham Museums & Art Gallery; presented by the Friends of Birmingham Museum and Art Gallery, 1946 (1946P24)

Robert Braithwaite Martineau , 1860 [130]
Black, red, blue, ochre and white chalks on paper: 762 × 533
National Museums Liverpool (Walker Art Gallery)

Eliezer and Rebecca at the Well, 1863 [222]
Illustration for *Dalziels' Bible Gallery*, published by Routledge (London, 1881)
Wood engraving by the Dalziel Brothers on India paper in bound volume: 179 × 136 (image); 430 × 360 × 43 (volume)
Birmingham Museums & Art Gallery; presented by Wilfred Phillips (1920P713.2.15)

Design for a Lectern, Cambridge, c. 1868 [258]
Pen and ink over pencil: 229 × 184
Victoria and Albert Museum, London

Study of a Male Nude for 'May Morning on Magdalen Tower', 1888–89 [10] [not illustrated]
Pen and ink over pencil, red and white chalk on cardboard:

467 × 311
Birmingham Museums & Art Gallery; presented by the Friends of Birmingham Museums & Art Gallery, 1985 (1985P83)

The Hid Treasure (Old Buried Gold), 1892 [221] [not exhibited]
Pen and black ink with traces of pencil and some gold bodycolour: 257 × 355
Courtauld Gallery, London

First Study for 'The Light of the World', undated [154] [not exhibited]
Pen and brown ink on discoloured paper (an envelope): 125 × 72
Ashmolean Museum, University of Oxford; bequeathed by John Bryson, 1977

Lasinio, Giovanni Paolo (1789-1855)
The Drunkenness of Noah, 1832 [41]
Engraving after Giuseppe Rossi from a fresco by Benozzo Gozzoli, 170 × 334 (image), printed in *Pitture a Fresco del Campo Santo di Pisa*, published by Tipografia all'Insegna di Dante (Florence, 1832)
Bound volume: 493 × 332 × 27
Birmingham Libraries & Archives

Maclise, Daniel (1806–1870)
Study for 'The Spirit of Justice', c. 1848 [29]
Pencil on paper, squared for transfer: 248 × 160
The British Museum, London

Una and the Red Cross Knight, undated [not illustrated]
Pencil on paper: 241 × 181
The British Museum, London

Millais, John Everett (1829–1896)
The Pancrastinae, 1842 [14] [not exhibited]
Pencil and chalk on cream wove paper: 490 × 632
Royal Academy of Arts, London

Pope Gregory and the Slaves from Britannia, 1843 [58]
Pen and brown ink on paper: 203 × 305F
Courtauld Gallery, London

Andrea Ferara: The Armoury, 1844 [51]
Pen and brown ink on paper, 315 × 484
Birmingham Museums & Art Gallery; purchased, 1983
(1983P71)

The Marble Faun, c. 1844 [19]
Pencil on cream wove paper: 737 × 525
Royal Academy of Arts, London

Study of the Head of the Virgin Mary, after Correggio, 1837
[66] [not exhibited]
Pencil on paper: 290 × 238
Birmingham Museums & Art Gallery; presented by the
National Art Collections Fund, 1916

Study for 'Ferdinand Lured by Ariel', 1848 [53]
Pen and ink on paper: 284 × 20
National Museums Liverpool (Walker Art Gallery)

Ferdinand Lured by Ariel, 1848 [54] [not exhibited]
Oil on panel: 648 × 508
The Makins Collection

Study for 'Isabella': Head of a Boy, 1848 [3]
Pencil on paper, laid on card: 257 × 202
Birmingham Museums & Art Gallery; purchased and
presented by subscribers, 1906 (1906P653)

Study for 'Isabella': Two Heads, 1848 [4] [not exhibited]
Pencil on toned paper: 354 × 251
Birmingham Museums & Art Gallery; purchased and
presented by subscribers, 1906 (1906P651)

Lovers by a Rosebush ('My Beautiful Lady'), 1848 [39]
Pen and ink on paper: 254 × 165
Birmingham Museums & Art Gallery; purchased, 1920
(1920P12)

Garden Scene, 1849 [74]
Pen and black ink on paper: 280 × 205
Private collection
Exhibited in Birmingham only

*Study for 'Christ in the House of his Parents' ('The
Carpenter's Shop')*, c. 1849 [6] [not exhibited]
Pencil on paper: 190 × 337
Tate; bequeathed by H. F. Stephens, 1932

Christ in the House of his Parents ('The Carpenter's Shop'),
1849–50 [5] [not exhibited]
Oil on canvas: 864 × 1397
Tate; purchased with assistance from the Art Fund and
various subscribers, 1921

*Compositional Study, Possibly Related to 'The Eve of the
Deluge'*, 1850 [68] [not exhibited]
Pencil on paper: 206 × 123
Birmingham Museums & Art Gallery; purchased and
presented by subscribers, 1906 (1906P633)

Study for 'Mariana', 1850 [72]
Pen and ink on paper: 350 × 200
Victoria and Albert Museum, London

Study for ' St Agnes of Intercession', 1850 [199]
Pencil on tracing paper, laid on paper: 109 × 175
Birmingham Museums & Art Gallery; presented by
subscribers, 1906 (1906P625.1)

St Agnes of Intercession, 1850 [200]
Etching on paper: 117 × 188
Birmingham Museums & Art Gallery; presented by
subscribers, 1906 (1906P625.2)

Three Studies for 'A Huguenot':
Study for the Principal Figures, c. 1851 [159]
Pencil on paper: 153 × 82
Birmingham Museums & Art Gallery; purchased and
presented by subscribers, 1906 (1906 P621)
Study for the Principal Figures, c. 1851 [not illustrated]
Pen and ink over pencil on paper: 136 × 85
Birmingham Museums & Art Gallery; purchased and
presented by subscribers (1906 P622)
Finished Compositional Study, 1852 [160]
Pen and ink over pencil on paper: 192 × 99
Birmingham Museums & Art Gallery; purchased, 1920
(1920P11)

Study for 'The Order of Release, 1746', 1852 [163]
Pen and brown ink over pencil on paper: 120 × 82
Birmingham Museums & Art Gallery; purchased and
presented by subscribers (1906P624)

Two Studies for 'Ophelia', 1852:
Study of the Head of Elizabeth Siddal [p. 6, 63]
Pencil on paper: 232 × 307
Birmingham Museums & Art Gallery; purchased and
presented by subscribers, 1906 (1906P664)
Exhibited in Birmingham only

Finished Compositional Study [64]
Pen and ink on paper, 160 × 283 (arched top)
Plymouth City Museum & Art Gallery (Alfred A. de Pass
Collection)

Two Sets of Studies for 'The Proscribed Royalist, 1651', cut
from a single sheet, 1852 [164, 165]
Pencil on paper: 157 × 82; 155 × 137
Birmingham Museums & Art Gallery; purchased and
presented by subscribers, 1906 (1906P584, 1906P585)

The Proscribed Royalist, 1651, 1852–53 [166]
Oil on panel: 254 × 200
Birmingham Museums & Art Gallery; accepted by HM
Government in lieu of Inheritance Tax and allocated to
Birmingham Museums & Art Gallery, 2010 (2010.0128)

Frederic George Stephens, 1853 [127]
Pencil on paper: 216 × 152
National Portrait Gallery, London; presented by the sitter's
son, Holman Stephens, 1929

Natural Ornament (Effie Gray Ruskin) 1853 [145]
Pen and brown ink on paper: 185 × 233
Birmingham Museums & Art Gallery; purchased and
presented by subscribers, 1906 (1906P604)

Sheet of Studies Caricaturing the Post-Raphaelesque Style,
1853 [15] [not exhibited]
Pen and brown ink on paper: 188 × 234
Birmingham Museums & Art Gallery; purchased and
presented by subscribers, 1906 (1906P602)

Retribution, 1854 [151, 167]
Pen and brown ink on paper: 214 × 275
The British Museum, London

Three Studies for Illustrations to 'Poems by Alfred Tennyson
D.C.L., Poet Laureate', published by Edward Moxon
(London, 1857) [the 'Moxon Tennyson'], *c.* 1855–56:
Edward Gray [217]
Pencil on paper: 169 × 95
Birmingham Museums & Art Gallery; purchased and
presented by subscribers, 1906 (1906P630)
Dora [218]
Pencil and wash on paper: 135 × 153 (arched top)
Birmingham Museums & Art Gallery; purchased and
presented by subscribers, 1906 (1906P647)
St Agnes' Eve [214]
Pencil on paper: 168 × 73 (uneven)
Birmingham Museums & Art Gallery; presented by
subscribers, 1906 (1906P595)

Edward Gray, 1857 [216] [not exhibited]
Illustration to *Poems by Alfred Tennyson D.C.L., Poet*
Laureate, published by Edward Moxon (London, 1857) [the
'Moxon Tennyson']
Wood engraving by J. Thompson in bound volume, 89 × 83
(image), 235 × 175 × 40 (volume)
Birmingham Museums & Art Gallery; transferred from
Birmingham Reference Library, 1963 (1978P203.49)

St Agnes' Eve, 1857 [215] [not exhibited]
Illustration to *Poems by Alfred Tennyson D.C.L., Poet*
Laureate, published by Edward Moxon (London, 1857) [the
'Moxon Tennyson']
Wood engraving by the Dalziel Brothers in bound volume,
95 × 73 (image), 235 × 175 × 40 (volume)
Birmingham Museums & Art Gallery; transferred from
Birmingham Reference Library, 1963 (1978P203.44)

Finished Compositional Study for 'The Vale of Rest', 1858
[169]
Pen and ink and ink wash heightened with white
bodycolour on paper: 175 × 287
Birmingham Museums & Art Gallery; purchased and
presented by subscribers, 1906 (1906P650)

Recto and Verso of a Sheet of Studies Including Studies for 'The Black Brunswicker', c. 1859–60 [161, 162] [not exhibited]
Pencil on paper: 147 × 113
Birmingham Museums & Art Gallery; purchased and presented by subscribers, 1906 (1906P623)

'Was it Not a Lie?', 1860 [168]
Illustration to Anthony Trollope's *Framley Parsonage*, published in *Cornhill Magazine*
Wood engraving by the Dalziel Brothers on paper: 182 × 127
Birmingham Museums & Art Gallery; accessioned 1978 (1978 P618.2)

The Hidden Treasure, 1864 [220]
Illustration to *The Parables of Our Lord*, published by Routledge, Warne & Routledge (London, 1864); reprinted by the Society for the Promotion of Christian Knowledge (1885)
Wood engraving by the Dalziel Brothers on paper in bound volume: 140 × 108 (image)
Birmingham Museums & Art Gallery; presented by John Crowther, 1970 (1970P47.4)

The Prodigal Son, 1864 [219] [not exhibited]
Illustration to *The Parables of Our Lord*, published by Routledge, Warne & Routledge (London, 1864); reprinted by the Society for the Promotion of Christian Knowledge (1885)
Wood engraving on paper by the Dalziel Brothers in bound volume, 140 × 108 (image)
Birmingham Museums & Art Gallery; presented by John Crowther, 1970 (1970P47.16)

Moore, Albert (1841–1893)
Study of an Ash Trunk, 1857 [97]
Watercolour on paper: 303 × 229
Ashmolean Museum, University of Oxford; purchased, 1959

Morris, William (1834–1896)
Self Portrait in a Smock, 1856 [259] [not exhibited]
Pencil on paper: 286 × 222
Victoria and Albert Museum, London

Jane Burden, 1857 [115]
Pencil on paper: 104 × 76
The British Museum, London

Two Designs for the St George's Cabinet, 1861 [260]
The Princess Tied to the Stake
Pencil, pen and ink, and brush and ink, on blue paper: 447 × 158
St George Rescuing the Princess
Pencil, pen and ink, and brush and ink, on paper: 437 × 354
Victoria and Albert Museum, London

St George's Cabinet, Morris, Marshall, Faulkner & Co., 1861 [261] [not exhibited]
Painted and gilded mahogany, pine and oak, with copper mounts: 1110 × 1780 × 430
Victoria and Albert Museum, London

Design for Stained Glass: 'The Ascension', 1861 [246]
Brush and black ink with brown ink over pencil on paper: 940 × 593
Birmingham Museums & Art Gallery; purchased and presented by subscribers, 1903 (1904P534)

King René's Honeymoon Cabinet, Morris, Marshall, Faulkner & Co., 1861 [238] [not exhibited]
Oak, inlaid with various woods, with painted metalwork and painted panels: 1334 × 2520 × 870/
Victoria and Albert Museum, London

Design for a Tile: 'Daisy', c. 1870 [275]
Pencil on paper: 220 × 213
Birmingham Museums & Art Gallery; presented by Mrs Roma Jones, 1990 (1990P5)

Design for a Printed Textile: 'Snakeshead', 1876 [273]
Pencil and black wash on Whatman paper: 507 × 679
Birmingham Museums & Art Gallery; purchased with the aid of the Friends of Birmingham Museum and Art Gallery, 1941 (1941P397)

Printed Textile 'Snakeshead', 1876 [274]
Dyed and block-printed cotton: 663 × 975
Birmingham Museums & Art Gallery; purchased with the aid of the Friends of Birmingham Museum and Art Gallery, 1941 (1941M398)

Design for a Printed Textile: 'Wey', 1882–83 [271]
Pencil and watercolour heightened with white bodycolour
on paper: 985 × 670
Birmingham Museums & Art Gallery; purchased with the
aid of the Friends of Birmingham Museum and Art Gallery,
1941 (1941P395)

Printed Textile 'Wey', 1883 [272]
Block-printed cotton, 576 × 996
Birmingham Museums & Art Gallery; purchased with the
aid of the Friends of Birmingham Museum and Art Gallery,
1941 (1941M396)

Design for a Wallpaper: 'Wild Tulip', 1884 [277]
Watercolour over pencil and crayon on paper: 997 × 645
(visible area)
Birmingham Museums & Art Gallery; purchased with the
aid of the Friends of Birmingham Museum and Art Gallery,
1941 (1941P397)

Design for a Wallpaper: 'Garden Tulip', 1885 [234, 276]
Watercolour over pencil on paper, squared up for transfer:
997 × 648 (visible area)
Birmingham Museums & Art Gallery; purchased with the
aid of the Friends of Birmingham Museum and Art Gallery,
1941 (1941P412)

The 'Kelmscott Chaucer', 1896 [not illustrated]
Bound volume: 87 woodcut illustrations by Edward Burne-
Jones with text on Perch paper, bound in full-white, tooled
pigskin: 435 × 300 × 87
Birmingham Museums & Art Gallery; presented by Colonel
Harold Wilkinson, 1934 (1934P675)
Exhibited in Birmingham only

Two 'Window Books', c. 1900–10 [243, 256, 289, 291]
Bound volumes containing photographs by Frederick
Hollyer of stained glass designs, for consultation by clients
of Morris & Co.: 385 × 323 and 381 × 323
Birmingham Museums & Art Gallery; presented
anonymously, 1940 (1940P604.2, 1904P604.5)

Mulready, William (1786–1863)
Life Study of a Seated Female Nude, Seen from Behind, 1853 [21]
Black and red chalk on paper, 363 × 297
Victoria and Albert Museum

Seated Male Nude, mid-1850s [16]
Red and black chalk on wove paper: 530 × 436
Royal Academy of Arts, London

Murray, Charles Fairfax (1849–1919)
Self Portrait Aged Seventeen, 1866 [134]
Pencil and chalks on brown paper: 470 × 380
Private collection

Edward Burne-Jones, c. 1869 [136]
Pencil and brown wash on paper: 328 × 217
The Whitworth Art Gallery, The University of Manchester

William Morris, 1870 [135]
Pencil and brown wash on paper: 356 × 255
The Whitworth Art Gallery, The University of Manchester

John Ruskin, 1875 [137]
Watercolour and bodycolour on paper: 476 × 311
Tate; purchased as part of the Oppé Collection with
assistance from the National Lottery through the Heritage
Lottery Fund, 1996

Opie, John (1761–1807)
Lectures on Painting Delivered at the Royal Academy of Arts,
printed 1809 [not illustrated]
Bound volume, published by Longman, Hurst, Rees and
Orme (London, 1809): 260 × 216 × 25
Birmingham Libraries & Archives
Exhibited in Birmingham only

Overbeck, Johann Friedrich (1789–1869)
Cartoon for 'Religion Glorified by the Fine Arts', c. 1840 [26]
[not exhibited]
Pencil and chalk on three pieces of cream paper: 1420 × 1180
The Royal Collection

Madonna and Child, 1842 [27]
Pencil and grey wash on paper: 230 × 232 (diameter)
The British Museum, London

Prout, Samuel (1783–1852)
The Altstadt, Prague, undated [80]
Pencil on grey paper: 411 × 265
Birmingham Museums & Art Gallery; presented by the
Trustees of the Public Picture Gallery Fund, 1905 (1905P7)

Sketches at Home and Abroad, after 1844 [not illustrated]
Bound volume, published by J. Rimmel and Son and
Hullmandel & Walton, Lithographers (London, undated
[after 1844]): 388 × 290 × 23
Birmingham Libraries & Archives
Exhibited in Birmingham only

Pugin, Augustus Welby Northmore (1812–1852)
*Design for the Frontispiece of the Second Volume of
'Examples of Gothic Architecture'* (1836), 1834 [58]
Pen with red and black ink on paper: 276 × 231
Victoria and Albert Museum

*Frontispiece and Plate from 'Floriated Ornament: A Series of
Thirty-One Designs'*, 1849 [268, 269]
Plates chomolithographed by H. C. Maguire from designs
by Pugin, printed by M. & N. Hanhart and published by
Henry G. Bohn (London, 1849)
Bound volume: 335 × 261 × 23
Birmingham Libraries & Archives
Exhibited in Birmingham only

Retzsch, Moritz (1779–1857)
The Tempest, Act 1, Scene 2, 1841 [52]
Engraving, 181 × 233 (image), printed in Moritz Retzsch,
Retzsch's Outlines to Shakespeare, eight vols bound together,
published by Ernst Fleischer (Leipzig and London, [1828-46])
Bound volume: 247 × 337 × 49
Birmingham Libraries & Archives
Exhibited in Birmingham only

Faust in his Study, 1816 [57]
Steel engraving by J. Brain, 90 × 102 (image), printed
in *Goethe's Faust in Two Parts*, trans. Anna Swanwick,
published by George Bell and Sons (London, 1879)
Bound volume: 240 × 180 × 40
Birmingham Libraries & Archives
Exhibited in Birmingham only

Reynolds, Joshua (1723–1792)
*The Works of Sir Joshua Reynolds, Knight; Late President of
the Royal Academy*, 1801 [not illustrated]
Bound volume, first of a set of three volumes, published by
T. Cadell and W. Davies (London, 1801): 217 × 137 × 29
Birmingham Libraries & Archives
Exhibited in Birmingham only

Ricketts, Charles (1866–1931)
Oedipus and the Sphinx, 1891 [288]
Pen and ink on paper: 236 × 155
Tullie House Museum and Art Gallery, Carlisle

John Leicester Warren Lord de Tabley, *Poems Dramatic and
Lyrical*, 1893 [not illustrated]
Published by Elkin Matthews and John Lane (London,
1893) and Macmillan and Company (New York, 1893):
19.7 × 13.7 × 32
Birmingham Libraries & Archives
Exhibited in Birmingham only

Ricketts, Charles (1866–1931) and **Charles Haslewood
Shannon (1863–1937)**
Title Page to Oscar Wilde's 'A House of Pomegranates', 1891 [290]
Bound volume, published by James R. Osgood, McIlvaine &
Co. (London, 1891): 216 × 172 × 25 (volume)
Birmingham Libraries & Archives
Exhibited in Birmingham only

Rooke, Thomas Matthews (1842–1942)
*Design for Stained Glass: 'St Editha and the Nuns of St
Mary'*, after Ford Madox Brown, 1908 [244]
Watercolour with bodycolour on paper, laid on board:
930 × 760
Birmingham Museums & Art Gallery; presented by the
University of Birmingham, 1959 (1959P41)

Rossetti, Dante Gabriel (1828–1882)
Christina Rossetti, 1847 [116] [not exhibited]
Pencil on paper: 110 × 840
Victoria and Albert Museum, London; presented by Mrs
Moeller, 1928

Self Portrait, 1847 [119] [not exhibited]
Pencil touched with white on paper: 197 × 178
National Portrait Gallery, London; purchased 1891

Study for 'The Raven: Angel Footfalls', 1847 [60]
Pen and brown ink with brown and grey wash on paper:
222 × 175
Birmingham Museums & Art Gallery; purchased and
presented by subscribers, 1903 (1904P268)

Genevieve, 1848 [38]
Pencil and pen and ink on paper: 277 × 147
Syndics of the Fitzwilliam Museum, Cambridge

Faust: Margaret in the Church , 1848 [61]
Pen and brown ink on paper, 178 × 121
Tate; presented by E. Percival Allam, 1948

The Girlhood of Mary Virgin, 1848–49 [73] [not exhibited]
Oil on canvas: 832 × 654
Tate; bequeathed by Lady Jekyll, 1937

*Dante Drawing an Angel on the First Anniversary of the
Death of Beatrice*, 1849 [40, 56]
Pen and brown ink on paper: 400 × 320
Birmingham Museums & Art Gallery; purchased and
presented by subscribers, 1903 (1904P485)
Exhibited in Birmingham only

Study for 'Ecce Ancilla Domini!', 1849 [62]
Pencil on pale blue paper: 177 × 98
Birmingham Museums & Art Gallery; purchased and
presented by subscribers, 1903 (1904P290)

A Parable of Love (Love's Mirror), c. 1849–50 [107] [not
exhibited]
Pen and black ink over pencil with ink wash on paper:
195 × 175
Birmingham Museums & Art Gallery; purchased an
presented by subscribers, 1903 (1904P491)

Rossovestita, 1850 [11]
Watercolour and pen and ink over pencil on paper, laid on
card: 260 × 156
Birmingham Museums & Art Gallery; purchased and
presented by subscribers, 1903 (1904P452)

Thomas Woolner, 1850 [133]
Pen and ink with ink wash on laid paper: 169 × 109
Birmingham Museums & Art Gallery; purchased and
presented by subscribers, 1903 (1904P368)

'Of course!': Caricature of William Holman Hunt, early 1850s
[17]
Pen and brown ink with ink wash on laid notepaper,
180 × 111
Birmingham Museums & Art Gallery; purchased and
presented by subscribers, 1903 (1904P436)

'Slosh!': Caricature of John Everett Millais, early 1850s [18]
Pen and brown ink with ink wash on laid notepaper:
179 × 111
Birmingham Museums & Art Gallery; purchased and
presented by subscribers, 1903 (1904P437)

*Study of Elizabeth Siddal for 'The Return of Tibullus to
Delia'*, 1851 [67] [not exhibited]
Pencil on cream toned paper: 200 × 182
Birmingham Museums & Art Gallery; purchased and
presented by subscribers, 1903 (1904P302)

Thomas Woolner, 1852 [125]
Pencil on paper: 155 × 146 (hexagonal)
National Portrait Gallery; purchased, 1953

*Beatrice Meeting Dante at a Marriage Feast, Denies him her
Salutation*, 1852 [12]
Watercolour and bodycolour on paper, 349 × 425
Art Gallery of New South Wales, Sydney
Exhibited in Sydney only

Study of a Male Nude for 'Giotto Painting the Portrait of Dante', c. 1852 [23]
Black chalk on paper: 690 × 492
Birmingham Museums & Art Gallery; purchased and presented by subscribers, 1903 (1904P375, verso)

William Holman Hunt, 1853 [128]
Pencil and grey wash with scratching-out on paper: 274 × 206
Birmingham Museums & Art Gallery; purchased and presented by subscribers, 1903 (1904P392)

Rossetti Sitting to Elizabeth Siddal, 1853 [109]
Pen and ink shaded with the finger, on notepaper: 129 × 175
Birmingham Museums & Art Gallery; purchased and presented by subscribers, 1903 (1904P480)
Exhibited in Birmingham only

Study for 'Found', c. 1853 [174]
Pen and black ink over pencil on paper: 393 × 381
Birmingham Museums & Art Gallery; purchased and presented by subscribers, 1903 (1904P232)

The Maids of Elfen-Mere, 1854 [201] [not exhibited]
Pen and ink on paper: 127 × 83
Yale Center for British Art; Paul Mellon Fund

The Maids of Elfen-Mere, c. 1854–55 [202]
Illustration to William Allingham's *The Music Master: A Love Story, with Two Series of Day and Night Songs*, published by Routledge (London, 1855)
Wood engraving by the Dalziel Brothers on paper: 126 × 76 (image)
Birmingham Museums & Art Gallery; presented by Harold Hartley, 1924 (1924P278)

Study of Elizabeth Siddal, 1855 [110]
Pencil on paper: 320 × 166
Birmingham Museums & Art Gallery; purchased and presented by subscribers, 1903 (1904P260)

Ford Madox Brown in Profile, c. 1856–57 [124]
Pen and ink with ink wash on laid paper: 110 × 80
Birmingham Museums & Art Gallery; purchased and presented by subscribers, 1903 (1904P435)

Three Studies for Illustrations to 'Poems by Alfred Tennyson D.C.L., Poet Laureate' published by Edward Moxon (London, 1857) [the 'Moxon Tennyson'], c. 1856–57:
Design for 'The Palace of Art': St Cecilia [212]
Pen and brown ink with black ink on paper: 99 × 82
Design for 'Mariana in the South' [211]
Pen and black ink on paper: 100 × 84
Study for 'The Lady of Shalott' [210]
Pen and brown ink over pencil on paper: 106 × 90
Birmingham Museums & Art Gallery; purchased and presented by subscribers, 1903 (1904P235, 1904P237, 1904P279)

Three Studies for the Oxford Union Murals, 1857:
The Sleeping Launcelot [179]
Pen and brown ink over pencil with touches of red chalk on paper: 252 × 320
Guenevere in the Apple Tree [180]
Pen and brown ink over pencil on paper: 256 × 359
The Angel of the Holy Grail [not illustrated]
Pen and brown ink on paper: 181 × 105
Birmingham Museums & Art Gallery; purchased and presented by subscribers, 1903 (1904P272, 1904P274)

Sir Launcelot in the Queen's Chamber, 1857 [7] [not exhibited]
Pen and black and brown ink on paper: 262 × 354
Birmingham Museums & Art Gallery; purchased and presented by subscribers, 1903 (1904P404)

Sheet of Studies of Jane and William Morris and a Child (possibly Arthur Foord Hughes), 1857 [113] [not exhibited]
Pen and brown ink over pencil on paper: 256 × 300
Birmingham Museums & Art Gallery; presented by Emily Hughes, 1934 (1934P689)

The Tune of the Seven Towers, 1857 [178] [not exhibited]
Watercolour on paper: 314 × 365
Tate; purchased with assistance from Sir Arthur Du Cros
Bart. and Sir Otto Beit KCMG through the Art Fund, 1916

King Arthur and the Weeping Queens, c. 1856–57 [209]
[not exhibited]
Pen and brown ink on paper: 82 × 92
Birmingham Museums & Art Gallery; purchased and
presented by subscribers, 1903 (1904P236)

*Two Studies for 'Mary Magdalene at the Door of Simon the
Pharisee'*, c. 1858
Study of a Female and Male Figure [176]
Pencil, pen and brown ink on pale grey laid paper: 268 × 145
Study for the Composition [177]
Pen and brown ink with ink wash over pencil on paper:
235 × 184
Birmingham Museums & Art Gallery; purchased and
presented by subscribers, 1903 (1904P458, 1904P276)

Mary Magdalene at the Door of Simon the Pharisee, 1858–59
[175] [not exhibited]
Pen and ink on paper laid on fine linen on a stretcher:
508 × 457
Fitzwilliam Museum, Cambridge; Ricketts and Shannon
Collection

Mary Magdalene at the Door of Simon the Pharisee, 1859
[not illustrated, but see 175]
Half-tone reproduction: 167 × 147
Published in *The Pageant* by Messrs Henry and Company,
London, 1896: volume dimensions 263 × 201 × 23
Birmingham Libraries & Archives

How They Met Themselves, 1860 [108] [not exhibited]
Pen and ink and wash on paper: 270 × 213
Fitzwilliam Museum, Cambridge; bequeathed by J.R.
Holliday, 1927

Two Designs for a Sofa, c. 1860 [257]
Pen and brown ink over pencil on paper: 253 × 352
Birmingham Museums & Art Gallery; purchased and
presented by subscribers, 1903 (1904P471)

Algernon Charles Swinburne, 1861 [138] [not exhibited]
Watercolour and bodycolour over pencil with black and
coloured chalks, white bodycolour and scratching-out on
paper: 182 × 158
Fitzwilliam Museum, Cambridge; presented by Charles
Fairfax Murray, 1909

Design for the King René's Honeymoon Cabinet: 'Music', 1861
[241] [not exhibited]
Ink and wash on paper: 432 × 337
The Williamson Art Gallery and Museum, Birkenhead,
Wirral
Design for the King René's Honeymoon Cabinet: 'Music', 1861
[242]
Pencil on paper: 113 × 134
Birmingham Museums & Art Gallery; purchased and
presented by subscribers, 1903 (1904P320)

Self Portrait, 1861 [120]
Pencil on paper: 285 × 232
Birmingham Museums & Art Gallery; purchased and
presented by subscribers, 1903 (1904P479)

Two Designs for Stained Glass: The Story of St George, 1861–
62:
St George Slaying the Dragon, 1861–62 [not illustrated]
Black pen and ink and wash with scratching-out and
touches of white on paper: 495 × 625
Birmingham Museums & Art Gallery; purchased and
presented by subscribers, 1903 (1904P243)
The Wedding of St George and the Princess Sabra, 1861–62
[245] [not exhibited]
Ink on paper, 493 × 621
Birmingham Museums & Art Gallery; purchased and
presented by subscribers, 1903 (1904P245)

Christina Rossetti in a Tantrum, 1862 [117]
Pen and ink on paper: 221 × 178
National Trust, Wightwick Manor and Gardens

Algernon Charles Swinburne, 1860 [139] [not exhibited]
Pencil on paper: 356 × 330
Mark Samuels Lasner Collection, on loan to the University of
Delaware Library

Two Pairs of Designs for Pocket Watches, c. 1863 [not
illustrated]
Pen and brown ink on blueish paper: 111 × 61
Pen and black ink on buff paper: 152 × 68
Birmingham Museums & Art Gallery; purchased and
presented by subscribers (1904P322, 1904P323)

The Meeting of Beatrice and Dante in Paradise, 1864 [45] [not
exhibited]
Watercolour on paper, 257 × 304
Manchester City Galleries

Ford Madox Brown, 1867 [123]
Pencil on paper: 205 × 160 (visible area)
Private collection

Fanny Cornforth, 1868 [111]
Red chalk on paper: 495 × 345 (visible area)
Birmingham Museums & Art Gallery; purchased and
presented by subscribers, 1903 (1904 P486)

Jane Morris, 1871 [112] [not exhibited]
Pen and brown ink on laid notepaper: 226 × 180
Birmingham Museums & Art Gallery; purchased and
presented by subscribers, 1903 (1904P394)

Proserpine, 1871 [286] [not exhibited]
Black and coloured chalks on greyish paper: 970 × 460
Ashmolean Museum, University of Oxford; bequeathed by
Miss May Morris, 1939

Water Willow, 1871 [308]
Coloured chalks on pale green paper: 339 × 273
Birmingham Museums & Art Gallery; purchased and
presented by subscribers, 1903 (1904P391)

The Death of Lady Macbeth, 1875 [306] [not exhibited]
Pencil on paper, 353 × 508
Birmingham Museums & Art Gallery; purchased and
presented by subscribers, 1903 (1904P346)

The Question, 1875 [307] [not exhibited]
Pencil on paper: 480 × 415
Birmingham Museums & Art Gallery; purchased and
presented by subscribers, 1903 (1904P239)

Study of Jane Morris for 'Mnemosyne', 1876 [114]
Pastel on paper: 560 × 455
Private collection

Pandora, 1878 [287] [not exhibited]
Coloured chalks on paper: 1008 × 667
National Museums Liverpool (Lady Lever Art Gallery)

Ruskin, John (1819–1900)
The Ambulatory, Chartres Cathedral, 1840 [80]
Pencil and blue wash with white bodycolour on grey paper:
365 × 260
Birmingham Museums & Art Gallery; presented by the
Association of Friends of Birmingham Museum and Art
Gallery, 1937 (1937P379)

An Italian Village, 1845 [78]
Pencil, pen and ink and wash with white bodycolour on
paper: 295 × 225
Birmingham Museums & Art Gallery; purchased and
presented by subscribers, 1906 (1907P148)

View from San Miniato al Monte, Florence, 1845 [81]
Pen and brown wash over pencil on paper: 334 × 484
Birmingham Museums & Art Gallery; presented
anonymously, 1907 (1907P140)

Cascade de la Folie, Chamonix, 1849 [82]
Pen and ink, watercolour and bodycolour on paper: 461 × 373
Birmingham Museums & Art Gallery; purchased through
the Public Picture Gallery Fund, 1905 (1905P2)

Eight Studies of a Primrose, probably 1870s [87]
Pencil, pen and ink, watercolour and bodycolour on blue
paper: 195 × 150
Birmingham Museums & Art Gallery; presented
anonymously, 1904 (1907P144)

Elements of Drawing, 1857 [not illustrated]
Bound volume, published by Smith Elder & Co. (London, 1857): 193 × 13 × 23
Private collection

Study of Ivy, 1872 or later [75]
Watercolour with touches of bodycolour over pencil on paper: 455 × 347
The British Museum; purchased, 1979

Christina Rossetti, 1877 [118] [not exhibited]
Pastel on paper: 832 × 654
Present whereabouts unknown

Plate from 'Proserpina: Studies of Wayside Flowers': Contorta Purpurea (Purple Wreath-wort), c. 1877 [88]
From a bound volume published by George Allen (Orpington, 1875–86)
Engraving by George Allen: 178 × 105 (to border); 330 × 254 (sheet)
Birmingham Museums & Art Gallery; accessioned in 1978 (1978 P519.7)

Two Plates from 'The Laws of Fésole', c. 1877:
The Two Shields [90]
From a bound volume published by George Allen (Orpington, 1877–79)
Engraving by George Allen: 145 × 91 (to border); 332 × 257 (sheet)
Birmingham Museums & Art Gallery; accessioned in 1978 (1978P520.1)
Decorative Plumage I: Peacock [89]
From a bound volume published by George Allen (Orpington, 1877–79)
Engraving by George Allen: 153 × 100 (to border); 332 × 257 (sheet)
Birmingham Museums & Art Gallery; accessioned in 1978 (1978P520.2)

Sandys, Frederick (1829–1904)
A Nightmare, 1857 [141, p. 9]
Zincotype on paper: 334 × 487 (image, arched top); 507 × 630 (sheet)
Birmingham Museums & Art Gallery; presented by Miss Halkett, 1931 (1931P213)

Study of Wild Arum, Grass and a Tree Stump, 1858 [98] [not exhibited]
Black chalk touched with white on grey-brown paper: 210 × 348
Birmingham Museums & Art Gallery; purchased and presented by subscribers, 1906 (1906P807)

Study of Wild Arum and Grass at the Foot of a Tree, 1858 [99]
Pencil on light brown paper: 185 × 155
Birmingham Museums & Art Gallery; purchased and presented by subscribers, 1906 (1906P811)

Study of Ivy on a Tree Stump, 1858 [100]
Pencil and watercolour on paper: 170 × 85
Birmingham Museums & Art Gallery; purchased and presented by subscribers, 1906 (1906P869)

Study of Ivy on an Old Wall, 1858 [101]
Pencil touched with white chalk on pale grey paper, 360 × 257
Birmingham Museums & Art Gallery; purchased and presented by subscribers, 1906 (1906P809)

The Old Chartist, 1862 [102]
Wood engraving by Joseph Swain, published in *Once A Week*, 1862: 106 × 128
Aberystwyth University, School of Art Gallery and Museum; purchased 1924

Design for 'Cleopatra Dissolving the Pearl', 1862 [196, 233]
Pen and black ink on paper, 184 × 115
Birmingham Museums & Art Gallery; purchased and presented by subscribers, 1906 (1906P832)

Design for 'The Little Mourner', 1862 [231]
Pen and black ink on paper: 139 × 108
Birmingham Museums & Art Gallery; purchased and presented by subscribers, 1906 (1906P834)

The Little Mourner, 1862 [not illustrated]
Wood engraving by the Dalziel Brothers: 164 × 130
Birmingham Museums & Art Gallery; purchased and presented by subscribers, 1906 (1906P835)

Amor Mundi, 1865 [232]
Reproduction of a wood engraving by Joseph Swain, 170 × 99 (image), originally published in *The Shilling*; from Mary Sandys (ed.), *Reproductions of Woodcuts by F. Sandys, 1860-1866*, published by Carl Hentschel (London, 1910)
Bound volume: 255 × 195 × 19
Birmingham Libraries & Archives
Exhibited in Birmingham only

Design for 'If', 1866 [230]
Pen and black ink on paper: 183 × 136
Birmingham Museums & Art Gallery; purchased and presented by subscribers, 1906 (1906P844)

Study for 'The Waters of Lethe', 1870–74 [283]
Red and black chalk on light grey-green paper: 223 × 175
Birmingham Museums & Art Gallery; purchased and presented by subscribers, 1906 (1906P856)

Portrait of a Lady (Mary Emma Jones), c. 1873 [143]
Coloured chalks on buff paper: 555 × 490
Birmingham Museums & Art Gallery; purchased and presented by subscribers, 1903 (1904P499)

Mrs Charles Augustus Howell, c. 1873–74 [144] [not exhibited]
Coloured chalks on dark buff paper: 695 × 911
Birmingham Museums & Art Gallery; presented anonymously, 1925 (1925P97)

Medusa, c. 1875 [284]
Black and red chalks on greenish paper: 727 × 546
Victoria and Albert Museum

Charles Augustus Howell, 1882 [142] [not exhibited]
Coloured chalks on pale blue paper: 910 × 650
Ashmolean Museum, University of Oxford; presented by John Bryson, 1942

Siddal, Elizabeth (1829–1862)
The Haunted Wood, c. 1856 [188]
Bodycolour on paper: 120 × 112
National Trust, Wightwick Manor and Gardens

Clerk Saunders, 1857 [187]
Watercolour with bodycolour and coloured chalks on paper, laid on stretcher: 284 × 181
Syndics of the Fitzwilliam Museum, Cambridge

Solomon, Simeon (1840–1905)
Faust and Marguerite, c. 1856 [189]
Pen and ink and pencil on paper: 254 × 202
Tate; bequeathed by Alfred M. H. Solomon and the estate of Marguerite I. R. Solomon, 1993

The Death of Sir Galahad While Taking a Portion of the Holy Grail Administered by Joseph of Arimathea, c. 1857–59 [191]
Pen and ink over pencil on paper: 185 × 166
Birmingham Museums & Art Gallery; presented by Mr A. E. Anderson, 1922 (1922P19)

Babylon Hath Been a Golden Cup, 1859 [190]
Pen with black and brown ink over traces of pencil on paper: 266 × 283
Birmingham Museums & Art Gallery; purchased (Alfred Leadbeater Bequest Fund), 1925 (1925P452)

Ruth, Naomi and the Child Obed, 1860 [226]
Pen and brown ink over pencil on paper: 292 × 229
Birmingham Museums & Art Gallery; presented by the Trustees of the Public Picture Gallery Fund, 1911 (1911P63)

Hosannah!, c. 1862 [227]
Illustration for *Dalziels' Bible Gallery*, published by Routledge (London, 1881)
Wood engraving by the Dalziel Brothers on India paper in bound volume: 165 × 120 (image); 430 × 360 × 43 (volume)
Birmingham Museums & Art Gallery; presented by Wilfred Phillips, 1920 (1920P713.1.67)

A Saint of the Eastern Church, 1867–68 [194] [not exhibited]
Watercolour, bodycolour and gum on paper: 452 × 328
Birmingham, Museums & Art Gallery; presented by the Misses Bunce, 1900 (1900P1)

Dawn, 1871 [195]
Watercolour and bodycolour on paper: 353 × 507
Birmingham Museums & Art Gallery; presented by the Trustees of the Public Picture Gallery Fund, 1909 (1909P57)

Perseus with the Head of Medusa, probably *c.* 1890s [294]
Pencil on paper: 272 × 287
Birmingham Museums & Art Gallery; presented by Cecil F.
Crofton, 1908 (1908 P310)

A Pre-Raphaelite Studio Fantasy, undated [16] [not exhibited]
Pen and ink on paper: 180 × 220
Private collection

Stanhope, John Roddam Spencer (1829–1908)
Study for 'Thoughts of the Past, c. 1859 [173]
Pen and ink on paper: 610 × 318
Tate; presented by Mrs Evelyn de Morgan, 1917

Stephens, Frederick George (1828–1907)
Dethe and the Riotours, 1852 [50]
Pen and black ink on off-white paper: 295 × 446
Ashmolean Museum, University of Oxford; bequeathed by
John Bryson, 1977

Turner, Joseph Mallord William (1775–1851)
The Falls of the Rhine at Schaffhausen, 1831–32 [83]
Pencil, pen and ink, watercolour and bodycolour on paper:
309 × 457
Birmingham Museums & Art Gallery; purchased 1891
(1891P31)
Exhibited in Birmingham only

Blenheim Palace and Park, 1833 [not illustrated]
Watercolour with gum and scratching-out on paper:
298 × 469
Birmingham Museums & Art Gallery; presented by Sir
Edward Parkes, 1920 (1920 P1)

*The Klemenskapelle with Burg Rheinstein and Burg
Reichenstein*, 1844 [not illustrated]
Pencil and watercolour on paper: 172 × 235
Birmingham Museums & Art Gallery; presented by the
Friends of Birmingham Museum and Art Gallery, 1945
(1945P56)

Samuel Rogers, *Italy: A Poem*, 1830 [not illustrated]
Bound volume published by Cadell & Moxon (London,
1830): 203 × 138 × 31
Private collection

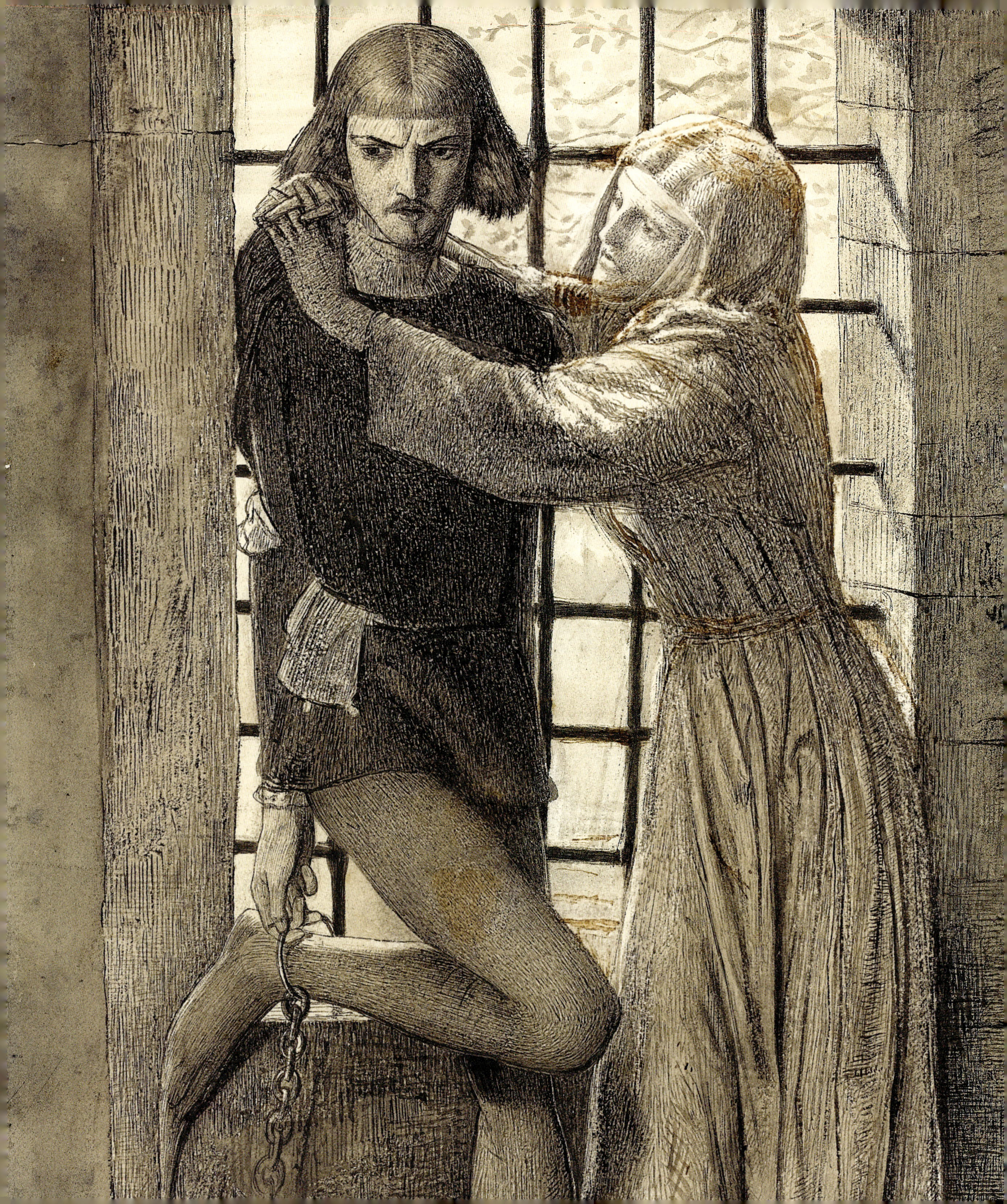

Bibliography

Andrews, Keith, *The Nazarenes* (Oxford: Clarendon Press, 1964)

Anon., 'Art and poetry', *The Ecclesiologist*, no. 78 (June 1850), p. 47

Anon., 'Art matters', *New York Times* (14 April 1873), p. 4

Anon., 'The Art-Union of London', *The Art-Union* (November 1842), p. 262

Anon., 'Bits of nature', *Fun* (16 May 1863), p. 90

Anon., 'Continental Schools of Design', *Chambers's Edinburgh Magazine* (16 May 1840), pp. 132–33

Anon., 'The Dudley Gallery', *The Times* (11 February 1871), p. 4

Anon., 'The Dudley Gallery', *The Times* (13 February 1872), p. 4

Anon., 'The elements of drawing, with three letters to beginners', *The Athenaeum* (11 July 1857), pp. 879–81

Anon., 'Exhibition of studies in various mediums', *The Athenaeum* (16 November 1889), p. 680

Anon., 'Fine art General Water-colour Exhibition', *Illustrated London News* (12 February 1870), p. 181

Anon., 'Fine art gossip', *The Athenaeum* (11 July 1857), p. 886

Anon., 'The General Exhibition of Water-colours', *The Times* (15 February 1869), p. 4

Anon., 'Grosvenor Gallery exhibition', *The Athenaeum* (4 January 1879), pp. 23–25

Anon., *The Guardian* (15 May 1850), pp. 345–46

Anon., 'The International Exhibition', *The Ecclesiologist*, no. 140 (1862), pp. 168–76

Anon., 'London exhibitions: conflict of the schools', *Blackwood's Edinburgh Magazine*, no. 526 (1859), pp. 127–42

Anon., 'Manchester Art Treasures exhibition', *Quarterly Review*, no. 102 (1857), pp.165–203

Anon., 'Mr Redgrave's letter on the School of Design', *The Edinburgh Review*, no. 172 (1847), pp. 452–61

Anon., 'The Mulready exhibition', *The Times* (9 June 1848), p. 8

Anon., 'The New Gallery', *The Athenaeum* (19 May 1888), pp. 635–36

Anon., 'Pictures of the season', *Blackwood's Edinburgh Magazine*, no. 689 (1850), pp. 77–83

Anon., 'Retzsch's outlines', *Fine Arts: The Mirror of Literature, Amusement and Instruction* (28 December 1833), pp. 441–42

Ashwin, Clive (ed.), *Art Education: Documents and Policies, 1768–1975* (London: Society for Research into Higher Education, 1975)

Banham, Joanna, and Jennifer Harris, *William Morris and the Middle Ages: A Collection of Essays* (Manchester: Whitworth Art Gallery, 1984)

Barlow, Paul, *Time Present and Time Past: The Art of John Everett Millais* (Aldershot: Ashgate, 2005)

Barringer, Tim, 'The effects of industry: Ford Madox Brown and artistic identities in Victorian Britain', in Tessa Sidey (ed.), *Ford Madox Brown: The Unofficial Pre-Raphaelite* (London: D. Giles, 2008), pp. 16–31

Bate, Percy, *The English Pre-Raphaelite Painters: Their Associates and Successors* (London: George Bell, 1901)

Bate, Percy, 'The late Frederick Sandys', *The Studio*, no. 139 (1904), pp. 3–17

Bennett, Mary, 'An early drawing for *The Tempest* by John Everett Millais', *Burlington Magazine*, no. 977 (1984), pp. 503–5

Bennett, Mary, *PRB Millais PRA* (Liverpool: Walker Art Gallery; London: Royal Academy, 1967) [exhibition catalogue]

Bermingham, Ann, *Learning to Draw: Studies in the Cultural History of a Polite and Useful Art* (New Haven and London: Yale University Press, 2000)

Birmingham, City Museum and Art Gallery, *The Pre-Raphaelite Brotherhood, 1848–1862* (Birmingham: City Museum and Art Gallery, 1947) [exhibition catalogue]

Boase, T. S. R., 'The decoration of the new Palace of Westminster, 1841–1863', *The Journal of the Warburg and Courtauld Institutes*, 3/4 (1954), pp. 319–58

Boe, Alf, *From Gothic Revival to Functional Form: A Study in Victorian Theories of Design* (Oslo: Oslo University Press; Oxford: Basil Blackwell, 1957)

310 William Holman Hunt, *Study for 'Claudio and Isabella'*, 1850, Fitzwilliam Museum, Cambridge (detail)

Brake, Laurel, 'The "wicked *Westminster*", the *Fortnightly*, and Walter Pater's *Renaissance*', in John O. Jordan and Robert L. Patten (eds) *Literature and the Marketplace: Nineteenth-Century British Publishing and Reading Practices* (Cambridge: Cambridge University Press, 1995), pp. 289–305

Brett, Charles, Michael Hickox and Christiana Payne, *John Brett: A Pre-Raphaelite in Cornwall* (Bristol: Sansom, 2006)

Brett, David, 'Drawing and the ideology of industrialization', *Design Issues*, 3/2 (1986), pp. 59–72

Bronkhurst, Judith, *William Holman Hunt: A Catalogue Raisonné*, 2 vols (New Haven and London: Yale University Press, 2006)

Brown, Ford Madox, 'On the mechanism of a historical picture' part 1, *The Germ*, no. 2 (1850), pp. 70–73

Burges, William, 'The late exhibition', *The Ecclesiologist*, no. 143 (1862), pp. 336–39

Burne-Jones, Georgiana, *Memorials of Edward Burne-Jones*, 2 vols (London: Macmillan, 1906)

Burton, Anthony, 'Richard Redgrave as art educator, museum official and design theorist', in Susan P. Casteras and Ronald Parkinson (eds), *Richard Redgrave 1804–1888* (New Haven and London: Yale University Press, 1988), pp. 48–70

Calloway, Stephen, *Aubrey Beardsley* (London: Victoria and Albert Museum, 1998)

Carr, J. Comyns, *The Grosvenor Gallery Illustrated Catalogue: Winter Exhibition 1877–8* (London: Librairie de l'Art and Chatto and Windus, 1877)

Carr, J. Comyns, *Some Eminent Victorians* (London: Duckworth, 1908)

Casteras, Susan P., *Pocket Cathedrals: Pre-Raphaelite Illustration* (New Haven: Yale Center for British Art, 1991)

Casteras, Susan P., and Ronald Parkinson (eds), *Richard Redgrave 1804–1888* (New Haven and London: Yale University Press, 1988)

Casteras, Susan P., and Linda H. Peterson, *A Struggle for Fame: Victorian Women Artists and Authors* (New Haven: Yale Center for British Art, 1994)

Cherry, D., 'The Hogarth Club: 1858–61', *Burlington Magazine*, no. 925 (1980), pp. 236–44

Christian, John, 'Burne-Jones studies', *Burlington Magazine*, no. 839 (1973), pp. 92–99

Christian, John, 'The compulsive draughtsman', in Tessa Sidey and others, *The Hidden Burne-Jones* (London: D. Giles, 2007), pp. 7–27

Christian, John, *The Pre-Raphaelites in Oxford* (Oxford: Ashmolean Museum, 1974)

Christian, John (ed.), *The Last Romantics: The Romantic Tradition in British Art* (London: Lund Humphries with the Barbican Art Gallery, 1989)

Clegg, Jeanne, and others, *John Ruskin* (London: Arts Council, 1983)

Codell, Julie F., 'Painting Keats: Pre-Raphaelite artists between social transgressions and painterly conventions', *Victorian Poetry*, 33 (1995), pp. 341–70

Colvin, Sidney, *Memories and Notes of Persons and Places* (London: Edward Arnold, 1921)

Commander, John, *Pre-Raphaelite Drawings and Watercolours* (London: Arts Council, 1953)

Contreras, Jorge L., 'James Collinson, the Campo Santo, and the birth of the Pre-Raphaelite Brotherhood', *The Journal of Pre-Raphaelite Studies*, new ser., no. 15 (2006), pp. 5–18

Crook, J. Mordaunt, and others, *The Strange Genius of William Burges* (Cardiff: National Museum of Wales, 1981)

Cruise, Colin, 'Poetic, eccentric, Pre-Raphaelite: the critical reception of Simeon Solomon's work at the Dudley Gallery', in M. Giebelhausen and T. Barringer (eds), *Writing the Pre-Raphaelites: Text, Context, Subtext* (Aldershot: Ashgate, 2009), pp. 171–91

Cruise, Colin, 'Sick-sad dreams: Burne-Jones and Medievalism', in Catherine Marshall and Stefano-Maria Evangelista (eds), *Yearbook of English Studies*, 40 (2010), pp. 121–40

Cruise, Colin, '"Sincerity and earnestness": Rossetti's first exhibitions 1849–53', *Burlington Magazine*, no. 1210 (2004), pp. 4–12

Cruise, Colin, and others, *Love Revealed: Simeon Solomon and the Pre-Raphaelites* (London: Merrell, 2005)

Curtis, Gerard, *Visual Words: Art and the Material Book in Victorian England* (Aldershot: Ashgate, 2002)

Daly, H. de Burgh, 'Reviews and views', *Merry England*, no. 62 (1888), pp. 130–36

Dalziel, George and Edward, *The Brothers Dalziel: A Record, 1840–1890* (London: Methuen, 1901; repr. 1978)

Darby, Michael, *John Pollard Seddon* (London: Victoria and Albert Museum, 1983)

Day, Lewis F., 'A disciple of William Morris', Art Journal (March 1905), pp. 84–85

Dearden, James S., *John Ruskin: A Life in Pictures* (Sheffield: Sheffield Academic Press, 1999)

Delaney, J. G. P., *Charles Ricketts: A Biography* (Oxford: Oxford University Press, 1999)

Dresser, Christopher, 'Botany, as adapted to the arts and art-manufacture', *Art Journal*, no. 38 (1858), pp. 37–39

Elliott, David B., *Charles Fairfax Murray: The Unknown Pre-Raphaelite* (Lewes, Sussex: Book Guild, 2000)

Elzea, Betty, *Frederick Sandys 1829–1904: A Catalogue Raisonné* (Woodbridge, Suffolk: Antique Collectors' Club, 2001)

Elzea, Rowland (ed.), *The Correspondence between Samuel Bancroft, Jr. and Charles Fairfax Murray 1892–1916* (Wilmington, Del.: Delaware Art Museum, 1980)

Engen, Rodney, *Pre-Raphaelite Prints* (London: Lund Humphries, 1995)

Esposito, Donato, 'Dalziel's Bible Gallery (1881): Assyria and the biblical illustration in nineteenth-century Britain', in Stephen Holloway (ed.), *Orientalism, Assyriology and the Bible* (Sheffield: Sheffield Phoenix Press, 2006), pp. 267–96

Faxon, Alicia, 'The medium is NOT the message: problems in the reproduction of Rossetti's art', *Victorian Periodicals Review*, no. 2 (1991), pp. 64–70

Ferber, Linda S., and William H. Gerdts, *The New Path: Ruskin and the American Pre-Raphaelites* (Brooklyn: Brooklyn Museum, 1985)

Frank, Ellen E., 'The domestication of nature: five houses in the Lake District', in U. C. Knoepflmacher and G. B. Tennyson (eds), *Nature and the Victorian Imagination* (Berkeley and Los Angeles: University of California Press, 1977), pp. 68–92

Fredeman, William E. (ed.), *The P. R. B. Journal: William Michael Rossetti's Diary of the Pre-Raphaelite Brotherhood 1849–53* (Oxford: Oxford University Press, 1975)

Fredeman, William E., 'Pre-Raphaelites in caricature: "The Choice of Paris: An Idyll" by Florence Claxton', *Burlington Magazine*, no. 693 (1960), pp. 523–29

Frith, William Powell, *My Autobiography and Reminiscences*, 2 vols (London: Richard Bentley, 1888)

Funnell, Peter, and Malcolm Warner, *Millais: Portraits* (London: National Portrait Gallery, 1999)

Garnett, Richard, Review of *The Defence of Guenevere and Other Poems*, *Literary Gazette* (6 March 1858), pp. 226–27

Garnett, Richard, 'Tennyson', *Saturday Review* (27 June 1857), pp. 601–2

George, J-A., 'Translating Tuscany: Francesca Alexander's *Roadside Songs* (1888)', *Forum for Modern Language Studies*, 39 (2003), pp. 227–38

Gere, Charlotte, and Geoffrey C. Munn, *Pre-Raphaelite to Arts and Crafts Jewellery* (Woodbridge: Antique Collectors' Club, 1999)

Gere, John, *Pre-Raphaelite Drawings in the British Museum* (London: British Museum Press, 1994)

Giebelhausen, M., *Painting the Bible: Representation and Belief in Mid-Victorian Britain* (Aldershot: Ashgate, 2006)

Giebelhausen, M., and T. Barringer, *Writing the Pre-Raphaelites: Text, Context, Subtext* (Aldershot: Ashgate, 2009)

Goldman, Paul, *Beyond Decoration: The Illustrations of John Everett Millais* (New Castle, Del.: Oak Knoll Press, 2006)

Goldman, Paul, *John Everett Millais: Illustrator and Narrator* (Aldershot: Lund Humphries, 2004)

Gray, Nicolette, *Rossetti, Dante and Ourselves* (London: Faber and Faber, 1947)

Greenstead, Mary (ed.), *An Anthology of the Arts and Crafts Movement* (Aldershot: Lund Humphries, 2005)

Greenwood, Martin, *The Designs of William De Morgan* (Ilminster, Somerset: Dennis and Wiltshire, 1989)

Grieve, Alastair, 'A notice on illustrations to Charles Kingsley's "The Saint's Tragedy" by three Pre-Raphaelite artists', *Burlington Magazine*, no. 794 (1969), pp. 290–93

Grieve, Alastair, 'The Pre-Raphaelite Brotherhood and the Anglican High Church', *Burlington Magazine*, no. 794 (1969), pp. 294–97

Grieve, Alastair, 'Style and content in Pre-Raphaelite drawings 1848–50', in Leslie Parris (ed.), *Pre-Raphaelite Papers* (London: Tate Gallery, 1984), pp. 23–43

Halliwell, James Orchard (ed.), *The Thornton Romances: The Early English Metrical Romances of Perceval, Isumbras. Eglamour and Degrevant* (London: Camden Society, 1844)

Hamilton, Mark, *Rare Spirit: A Life of William De Morgan, 1839–1917* (London: Constable, 1997)

Hamlyn, Robin, and Michael Philllips, *William Blake* (London: Tate Publishing, 2000)

Harding, J. D., *Sketches at Home and Abroad* (London: Tilt, 1836)

Haslam, Ray, 'According to the requirements of his scholars: Ruskin, drawing and art education', in Robert Hewison (ed.), *Ruskin's Artists: Studies in the Victorian Visual Economy* (Aldershot: Ashgate, 2000), pp. 147–65

Helsinger, Elizabeth, *Poetry and the Pre-Raphaelite Arts: Dante Gabriel Rossetti and William Morris* (New Haven and London: Yale University Press, 2008)

Henderson, Philip, *Swinburne: The Portrait of a Poet* (London: Routledge and Kegan Paul, 1974)

Hewison, Robert, *John Ruskin: The Argument of the Eye* (Princeton, NJ: Princeton University Press, 1976)

Hewison, Robert, *Ruskin and Oxford: The Art of Education* (Oxford: Clarendon Press, 1996)

Hickox, Michael, 'John Brett and Ruskin', *Burlington Magazine*, no. 1121 (August 1996), pp. 521–25

Hilton, Tim, *John Ruskin: The Early Years, 1819–59* (New Haven and London: Yale University Press, 1985)

Houfe, Simon, *Fin de siècle: The Illustrators of the Nineties* (London: Barrie and Jenkins, 1992)

Houfe, Simon, *John Leech and the Victorian Scene* (Woodbridge: Antique Collectors Club, 1984)

Housman, Laurence, 'Pre-Raphaelitism in art and poetry', in R. W. Macan (ed.), *Essays by Divers Hands*, new ser., no. 12 (London: Humphrey Milford; Oxford: Oxford University Press, 1933), pp. 1–29

Hueffer, Ford Madox, *Ford Madox Brown: A Record of his Life and Work* (London: Longmans, Green, 1896)

Hunt, John Dixon, *The Wider Sea: A Life of John Ruskin* (London: Dent, 1982)

Hunt, William Holman, *Pre-Raphaelitism and the Pre-Raphaelite Brotherhood*, 2 vols (London: Macmillan, 1905)

Jameson, Anna, *Sacred and Legendary Art*, 2 vols (London: Longman, Brown, Green and Longmans, 1848)

Jeffrey, Rebecca A., 'A rediscovered study for Walter H. Deverell's lost painting *The Banishment of Hamlet*', *Burlington Magazine*, no. 974 (984), pp. 282–84

Kirkham, Pat, 'The Firm: Morris & Company', in Diane Waggoner (ed.), *The Beauty of Life: William Morris and the Art of Design* (London: Thames and Hudson, 2003), pp. 32–63

Lambert, Susan, *Reading Drawings: An Introduction to Looking at Drawings* (London: Trefoil Press, 1984)

Landow, George P., 'Ruskin, Holman Hunt and going to nature for oneself', in Robert E. Rhodes and Del Ivan Janik (eds), *Studies in Ruskin: Essays in Honor of Van Akin Burd* (Athens, Ohio: Ohio University Press, 1982), pp. 60–84

Landow, George P., 'William Holman Hunt's letters to Thomas Seddon', *Bulletin of the John Rylands University Library of Manchester*, 66/1 (1983), pp. 139–72

Lanigan, Dennis, *A Dream of the Past: Pre-Raphaelite and Aesthetic Movement Drawings from the Lanigan Collection* (Toronto: University of Toronto Art Centre, 2000)

Lanigan, Dennis, 'The Dudley Gallery: Watercolour Drawings Exhibitions, 1865–82', *The Journal of Pre-Raphaelite Studies*, no. 12 (2003), pp. 74–96

Layard, George Somes, *The Life and Letters of Charles Samuel Keene* (London: Sampson Low, Marston & Company; New York: Macmillan, 1892)

L'Enfant, Julie, *William Rossetti's Art Criticism: The Search for Truth in Victorian Art* (Lanham, Md.; Oxford: University Press of America, 1999)

Levi, Donata, 'Carlo Lasinio, curator, collector and dealer', *Burlington Magazine*, no. 1079 (1993), pp. 133–49

Levy, Silvano (ed.), *Surrealism: Surrealist Visuality* (Keele: Keele University Press, 1995)

Life, Allan R., 'The art of not "going halfway": Rossetti's illustration for the Maids of Elfen-mere', *Victorian Poetry*, nos 3/4 (1982), pp. 65–87

Lindsay, Lord, *Sketches of the History of Christian Art*, 3 vols (London: John Murray, 1847)

Lisle, Fortunée de, *Burne-Jones* (3rd edn, London: Methuen, 1907)

Loizeaux, Elizabeth Bergmann, *Yeats and the Visual Arts* (Syracuse, NY: Syracuse University Press, 2003)

Lucas, E. V., *The Colvins and their Friends* (London: Methuen, 1928)

Lyons, Harry, *Christopher Dresser: The People's Designer 1834–1904* (Woodbridge, Suffolk: Antique Collectors' Club, 2005)

MacCarthy, Fiona, *William Morris: A Life for Our Time* (London: Faber, 1994)

Malan, S. C., *Aphorisms on Drawing* (London: Longman, 1856)

Mancoff, Debra, 'Unpainted masterpieces: the drawings of Edward Burne-Jones', *Art Institute of Chicago Museum Studies*, no. 1 (2005) pp. 44–55

Marsh, Jan, *Elizabeth Siddal: Pre-Raphaelite Artist, 1829–62* (Sheffield: Ruskin Gallery, 1991)

Marsh, Jan, *Insights: The Pre-Raphaelite Circle* (London: National Portrait Gallery, 2005)

Marsh, Jan, and Pamela Gerrish Nunn, *Pre-Raphaelite Women Artists* (Manchester: Manchester City Art Gallery, 1997)

Millais, J. G., *The Life and Letters of Sir John Everett Millais*, 2 vols (London: Methuen, 1899)

Morgan, H. Cliff, 'The Schools of the Royal Academy', *British Journal of Educational Studies*, 21/1 (1973), pp. 88–103

Morris, William, *The Hollow Land, and Other Contributions to the Oxford and Cambridge Magazine* (London: Longmans, Green, 1903; repr. 1996)

Morris, William, *Hopes and Fears for Art: Five Lectures Delivered in Birmingham, London and Nottingham, 1878–1881* (London: Ellis and White, 1882)

[Morris, William], *The Letters of William Morris*, ed. Philip Henderson, (London: Longmans, Green, 1950)

Morris, William, *Three Works* [*News from Nowhere, The Pilgrims of Hope, A Dream of John Ball*] (London: Lawrence and Wishart, 1973)

Morris, William, and others, *Arts and Crafts Essays* (London: Rivington, Percival, 1893; repr. Bristol: Thoemmes Press, 1996)

Norton, Charles Eliot, *Notes on Drawings by Mr Ruskin* (Cambridge, Mass.: John Wilson & Son, 1879)

O'Gorman, Francis, 'Ruskin and particularity: *Fors Clavigera* and the 1870s', *Philological Quarterly*, 79/1 (2000), pp. 119–56

Ormond, Richard, *Daniel Maclise 1806–70* (London: National Portrait Gallery, 1972)

Osborne, Victoria, 'A British Symbolist in Pre-Raphaelite circles: Edward Robert Hughes RWS, 1851–1914' (unpublished MPhil dissertation, University of Birmingham, 2010)

Østermark-Johansen, Lene, *Sweetness and Strength: The Reception of Michelangelo in Late Victorian England* (Aldershot: Ashgate, 1998)

Parris, Leslie (ed.), *Pre-Raphaelite Papers* (London: Tate Gallery, 1984)

Pater, Walter, *The Renaissance: Studies in Art and Poetry* (4th edn, London: Macmillan, 1893); ed. Donald L. Hill (Berkeley and Los Angeles: University of California Press, 1980)

Patmore, Coventry, 'A Pre-Raphaelite exhibition', *Saturday Review* (4 July 1857), pp. 11–12

Pennell, Joseph, 'A golden decade in English art', *The Savoy*, no. 1 (1896), pp. 112–24

Penny, Nicholas, *Ruskin's Drawings* (Oxford: Phaidon, 1989)

Petherbridge, Deanna, *The Primacy of Drawing: An Artist's View* (London: South Bank Centre, 1991)

Popham, A. E., *A Handbook to the Drawings and Water-colours in the Department of Prints and Drawings* (London: British Museum, 1939)

[Potter, Beatrix], *The Journal of Beatrix Potter from 1881 to 1897*, ed. Leslie Linder (London: Warne, 1966)

Preston, Kerrison, *Blake and Rossetti* (London: Alexander Moring, 1944)

Prettejohn, Elizabeth, *The Art of the Pre-Raphaelites* (London: Tate Publishing, 2007)

Pugin, A. W. N., *Floriated Ornament: A Series of Thirty-one Designs* (London: Henry Bohn, 1849)

Quilter, Harry, *Preferences in Art, Life and Literature* (London: Swan Sonnenschein, 1892)

Reade, Brian, *Aubrey Beardsley* (New York: Viking Press; London: Studio Vista, 1967)

Reid, Forrest, *Illustrators of the Eighteen-Sixties* (London: Faber, 1928)

Reynolds, Sir Joshua, *The Literary Works of Sir Joshua Reynolds*, 2 vols (London: Cadell, 1835)

Rix, Brenda, 'Prints: spreading the word', in Katharine Lochnan and Carol Jacobi, *Holman Hunt and the Pre-Raphaelite Vision* (Toronto: Art Gallery of Ontario, 2008), pp. 171–88

Roberts, Leonard, *Arthur Hughes: His Life and Works* (Woodbridge, Suffolk: Antique Collectors' Club, 1997)

Robertson, W. Graham, *Time Was* (London: Hamish Hamilton, 1931)

Rooksby, Rikky, *A. C. Swinburne: A Poet's Life* (Aldershot: Scolar Press, 1997)

Rorimer, Ann, *Drawings by William Mulready* (London: Victoria and Albert Museum, 1972)

Rose, Andrea, *Birmingham Museums and Art Gallery: Pre-Raphaelite Drawings: Dante Gabriel Rossetti* (Chicago and London: University of Chicago Press, 1977)

Rose, Andrea, *Pre-Raphaelite Portraits* (Oxford: Oxford Illustrated Press, 1981)

Rosenfeld, Jason, and Alison Smith, *Millais* (London: Tate Gallery, 2007)

Rossetti, Dante Gabriel, *The Collected Works of Dante Gabriel Rossetti*, 2 vols (London: Ellis and Elvey, 1890)

[Rossetti, Dante Gabriel], *The Correspondence of Dante Gabriel Rossetti*, ed. William E. Fredeman and others, 6 vols (Cambridge: D. S. Brewer, 2002)

Rossetti, William Michael, 'Dante Rossetti and Elizabeth Siddal with facsimiles of five unpublished drawings by Dante Rossetti in the collection of Mr Harold Hartley', *Burlington Magazine*, no. 3 (1903), pp. 273–95

Rossetti, William Michael, *Some Reminiscences*, 2 vols (New York: Charles Scribner, 1906)

[Rossetti, William Michael, and C. P. Cranch], *The Crayon*, no. 6 (June 1856), pp. 179–84

[Ruskin, John], 'Lord Lindsay on the history of Christian art', *Quarterly Review*, no. 161 (1847), pp. 1–57

[Ruskin, John], 'The Pre-Raffaellites', *The Times* (13 May 1851), p. 8

[Ruskin, John], *The Works of John Ruskin*, ed. E. T. Cook and A. Wedderburn, 39 vols (The Library Edition, London: George Allen, 1903–12)

Schoenherr, Douglas, 'The cartoon book and Morris & Co's sale of Burne-Jones's cartoons in 1901–1904', Journal of Stained Glass, no. 29 (2005), pp. 82–135

Scott, William Bell, *Autobiographical Notes*, ed. W. Minto, 2 vols (New York: Harper and Brothers, 1892)

Seymour, Gayle M., 'The life and work of Simeon Solomon, 1840–1905' (unpublished PhD dissertation, University of Santa Barbara, 1986)

Sidey, Tessa, and others, *Ford Madox Brown: The Unofficial Pre-Raphaelite* (London: D. Giles, 2008)

Sidey, Tessa, and others, *Hidden Burne-Jones* (London: D. Giles, 2007)

Siegel, Jonah, *Desire and Excess: The Nineteenth-Century Culture of Art* (Princeton and Oxford: Princeton University Press, 2000)

Smith, Jonathan, *Charles Darwin and Victorian Visual Culture* (Cambridge: Cambridge University Press, 2006)

Spens, Michael (ed.), *High Art and Low Life: 'The Studio' and the Fin-de-siècle* (London: Studio International, 1993)

Spielmann, M. H., 'Francesca Alexander and *The Roadside Songs of Tuscany*', *Magazine of Art*, no. 18 (1895), pp. 295–99

Staley, Allen, *The Pre-Raphaelite Landscape* (2nd edn, New Haven and London: Yale University Press, 2001)

Staley, Allen, and Christopher Newall, *Pre-Raphaelite Vision: Truth to Nature* (London: Tate Publishing, 2004)

Staley, Allen, and others, *The Post-Pre-Raphaelite Print: Etching, Illustration, Reproductive Engraving and Photography in England in and around the 1860s* (New York: Columbia University, 1995)

Stebbins, Theodore E., and others, *The Last Ruskinians: Charles Eliot Norton, Herbert Moore, and their Circle* (Cambridge, Mass.: Harvard Art Museums, 2007)

Stephens, F. G., *Dante Gabriel Rossetti* (London: Seeley, 1894)

Stirling, A. M. W., *The Richmond Papers* (London: Heinemann, 1926)

Street, G. E. 'On the future of art in England', *The Ecclesiologist*, no. 127 (1858), pp. 232–40

Sumner, Ann, *John Brett: A Pre-Raphaelite on the Shores of Wales* (Cardiff: National Museum and Gallery, 2001)

Sumner, Ann, *Ruskin and the English Watercolour: From Turner to the Pre-Raphaelites* (Manchester: Whitworth Art Gallery, 1989)

Suriano, Gregory, *The Pre-Raphaelite Illustrators* (New Castle, Del.: Oak Knoll Press, and London: British Library, 2000)

Surtees, Virginia, *Dante Gabriel Rossetti: A Catalogue Raisonné*, 2 vols (Oxford: Oxford University Press, 1971)

Surtees, Virginia (ed.), *The Diaries of George Price Boyce* (Norwich: Real World, 1980)

Surtees, Virginia (ed.), *The Diary of Ford Madox Brown* (New Haven and London: Yale University Press, 1981)

Surtees, Virginia (ed.), *Sublime and Instructive: Letters from John Ruskin to Louisa Marchioness of Waterford, Anna Blunden and Ellen Heaton* (London: Michael Joseph, 1972)

Swinburne, A. C., *Essays and Studies* (London: Chatto and Windus, 1911)

Tate Gallery, *The Pre-Raphaelites* (London: Tate Gallery, 1984)

Thirlwell, Angela, *Into the Frame: The Four Loves of Ford Madox Brown* (London: Chatto and Windus, 2010)

Thirlwell, Angela, *William and Lucy: The Other Rossettis* (New Haven and London: Yale University Press, 2003)

Treuherz, Julian, 'The Pre-Raphaelites and medieval illuminated manuscripts', in Leslie Parris (ed.), *Pre-Raphaelite Papers* (London: Tate Gallery, 1984), pp. 153–69

Tyrwhitt, R. St John, 'Pictures of the season', *Contemporary Review*, no. 8 (1868), pp. 339–48

Waagen, G. F., 'To the Editor of the Times', *The Times* (13 July 1854), p. 7

Waggoner, Diane (ed.), *The Beauty of Life: William Morris and the Art of Design* (London: Thames and Hudson, 2003)

Wakeman, Geoffrey, *Victorian Book Illustration: The Technical Revolution* (Newton Abbot: David and Charles, 1973)

Walton, Paul, *The Drawings of John Ruskin* (Oxford: Clarendon Press, 1972)

Warner, Eric, and Graham Hough, *Strangeness and Beauty: An Anthology of Aesthetic Criticism*, 2 vols (Cambridge: Cambridge University Press, 1983)

Warner, Malcolm, *The Drawings of John Everett Millais* (London: Arts Council of Great Britain, 1979)

Watkinson, Raymond, *Pre-Raphaelite Art and Design* (London: Studio Vista, 1970)

Watkinson, Raymond, *William Morris as Designer* (London: Trefoil, 1990)

White, Gleeson, *English Illustration: The Sixties, 1855–70* (3rd edn, London: Constable, 1906)

Wickham, Annette, 'Leighton and the "Kensington Life Academy"', Leighton Drawings database, http://www.rbkc.gov.uk/lordleightonsdrawings/ldeessays/essay3.asp

Wilcox, Scott, and Christopher Newall, *Victorian Landscape Watercolours* (New Haven: Yale Center for British Art, 1992)

Wilde, Oscar, 'The English renaissance of art', in *Essays and Lectures* (Methuen, 1908)

Wildman, Stephen, and John Christian, *Edward Burne-Jones: Victorian Artist-Dreamer* (New York: Metropolitan Museum of Art, 1998)

Wildman, Stephen, and others, *Waking Dreams: The Art of the Pre-Raphaelites from the Delaware Art Museum* (Alexandria, Va.: Art Services International, 2004)

Willsdon, Clare, *Mural Painting in Britain 1840–1940: Image and Meaning* (Oxford: Oxford University Press, 2000)

Witt, John, *William Henry Hunt (1790–1864): Life and Work with a Catalogue* (London: Barrie and Jenkins, 1982)

Wood, T. Martin, *Drawings of Rossetti* (London: George Newnes; New York: Charles Scribner, 1910)

Wornum, Ralph (ed.), *Lectures on Painting by the Royal Academicians* (London: George Bohn, 1848)

Zatlin, Linda Gertner, *Aubrey Beardsley and Victorian Sexual Politics* (Oxford: Oxford University Press, 1990)

Picture Credits

Aberdeen Art Gallery & Museums Collections
28
Aberystwyth University, School of Art Gallery and Museum
102, 185, 186
Art Gallery of New South Wales, Sydney
12, 34
Ashmolean Museum, University of Oxford
43, 50, 97, 142, 154, 182, 286
Trustees, Cecil Higgins Art Gallery, Bedford, England
33
© The Samuel Courtauld Trust, The Courtauld Gallery, London
49, 55, 221
Reproduced with the permission of Birmingham Libraries & Archives
41, 44, 52, 57, 203, 232, 268, 269, 290, 292
© Birmingham Museums & Art Gallery
1, 3, 4, 7, 9, 10, 11, 15, 17, 18, 20, 22, 23, 24, 25, 30, 31, 35, 36, 39, 40, 46, 51, 56, 60, 62, 63, 66, 67, 68, 70, 76, 77, 78, 79, 80, 81, 82, 83, 85, 86, 87, 88, 89, 90, 94, 98, 99, 100, 101, 103, 106, 107, 109, 110, 111, 112, 113, 120, 124, 125, 128, 129, 133, 140, 141, 143, 144, 145, 146, 147, 148, 152, 153, 157, 158, 159, 160, 161, 162, 163, 164, 165, 166, 168, 169, 170, 171, 172, 174, 176, 177, 179, 180, 181, 184, 190, 191, 194, 195, 196, 197, 198, 199, 200, 202, 204, 205, 206, 208, 209, 210, 211, 212, 214, 215, 216, 217, 218, 219, 220, 222, 223, 224, 225, 226, 227, 228, 229, 230, 231, 233, 234, 236, 237, 239, 240, 241, 242, 243, 244, 245, 246, 247, 251, 252, 253, 254, 255, 256, 257, 262, 263, 264, 265, 266, 267, 271, 272, 273, 274, 275, 276, 277, 279, 280, 281, 283, 289, 291, 293, 294, 295, 296, 302, 303, 304, 305, 306, 307
©The Trustees of the British Museum
27, 29, 47, 75, 115, 151, 167, 183
©Fitzwilliam Museum, Cambridge
8, 37, 38, 108, 138, 175, 187, 309
Mark Samuels Lasner Collection, on loan to the University of Delaware Library
139, 235
Maidstone United Reformed Church/©Birmingham Museums & Art Gallery
249
© The Makins Collection/The Bridgeman Art Library
54
© Manchester City Galleries
32, 45, 121
© National Museums Liverpool
2, 53, 122, 130, 156, 287
© The National Gallery, London
65
National Gallery of Victoria, Melbourne
207
© National Portrait Gallery, London
119, 125, 126, 127, 132
© NTPL/John Hammond/Wightwick Manor (National Trust)
285
© NTPL/Paul Highnam/Wightwick Manor (National Trust)
188, 193, 308
© NTPL/Derrick E. Witty/Wightwick Manor (National Trust)
117
Plymouth City Museum & Art Gallery
64
Princeton University Art Museum/Bruce M. White
84
Private collection
16, 59, 95, 96, 131, 134, 192
Private collection/Art Gallery of New South Wales, Sydney
118
Private collection/©Birmingham Museums & Art Gallery
123, 149, 150, 282
Private collection/The Bridgeman Art Library
92

© Private collection c/o Christie's Images Ltd., 2010
114
Private collection/Tate Photography, 2010
74
Royal Academy of Arts, London
13, 14, 19
The Royal Collection © 2010 Her Majesty Queen Elizabeth II
26
Royal Watercolour Society
278, 300
© Tate, London, 2010
5, 6, 42, 61, 71, 73, 137, 173, 178, 179, 299
Tullie House Museum & Art Gallery
288
© V&A Images/Victoria and Albert Museum, London
21, 58, 69, 93, 104, 105, 116, 213, 238, 248, 258, 259, 260, 261, 270, 287, 297, 298
The Whitworth Art Gallery, The University of Manchester
135, 136
The Williamson Art Gallery and Museum, Birkenhead, Wirral
72, 91, 301
The Pollitt Collection/Witt Library, The Courtauld Institute of Art, London
155
Yale Center for British Art
48, 201

Lenders to the Exhibition

Thanks are due to the anonymous private lenders and the following institutions for generously allowing their works to be shown in the exhibition.

Numbers given refer to the illustrations.

Aberystwyth University, School of Art Gallery and Museum 102, 185, 186
Art Gallery of New South Wales, Sydney 12, 34
Ashmolean Museum, University of Oxford 50, 97, 182
Birmingham Libraries & Archives 3, 9, 11, 17, 18, 22, 23, 30, 31, 35, 36, 39, 51, 56, 60, 62, 63, 70, 76, 77, 78, 79, 80, 81, 82, 83, 85, 86, 87, 88, 89, 90, 94, 99, 100, 101, 103, 109, 110, 111, 120, 124, 128, 129, 133, 140, 141, 143, 145, 148, 152, 153, 157, 158, 159, 160, 163, 164, 165, 166, 168, 169, 170, 171, 172, 174, 176, 177, 179, 181, 184, 190, 191, 195, 196, 197, 198, 199, 200, 202, 204, 208, 210, 211, 212, 214, 217, 218, 220, 222, 223, 226, 227, 229, 230, 231, 233, 236, 237, 239, 240, 242, 243, 244, 246, 247, 250, 251, 252, 256, 257, 262, 263, 264, 265, 266, 267, 271, 272, 273, 274, 275, 276, 277, 279, 280, 281, 283, 289, 291, 293, 294, 296, 302, 303, 304, 307
The British Museum, London 27, 29, 47, 75, 115, 167, 183
The Courtauld Gallery, London 49, 55
Fitzwilliam Museum, Cambridge 37, 38, 187
Maidstone United Reformed Church 249
Manchester City Galleries 32, 121
National Museums Liverpool (Walker Art Gallery) 53, 130, 156
National Portrait Gallery, London 125, 126, 127, 132
National Trust, Wightwick Manor and Gardens 117, 188, 193, 285
Plymouth City Museum & Art Gallery 64
Private collections 59, 74, 95, 96, 114, 123, 131, 134, 149, 150, 282
Royal Academy of Arts, London 14, 19
The Royal Watercolour Society 300
Tate 42, 61, 71, 137, 173, 189, 299
Victoria and Albert Museum, London 58, 69, 93, 105, 213, 248, 258, 260, 284, 297, 298
The Whitworth Art Gallery, The University of Manchester 135, 136
The Williamson Art Gallery and Museum, Birkenhead, Wirral 91, 301

Author's Acknowledgments

My research into Pre-Raphaelite drawing and its contexts was facilitated by two fellowships, a Residential Fellowship at the Yale Center for British Art, and the University of Delaware Library/Delaware Art Museum Fellowship in Pre-Raphaelite Studies. I am grateful to Amy Meyers, Scott Wilcox, Elizabeth Fairman, Gillian Forrester and Kraig Binkowski at the Yale Center for British Art, and to Susan Brynteson, Tim Murray and L. Rebecca Johnson Melvin at the University of Delaware Library and Danielle Rice and Margaretta Frederick at Delaware Art Museum for all their help. Special thanks go to Mark Samuels Lasner for his generosity in allowing me access to his collection of books, drawings, manuscripts and ephemera on loan to the University of Delaware Library.

I should like to thank Rita McLean, Head of Birmingham Museums, and to join her in acknowledging the staff of Birmingham Museums & Art Gallery, who organised the major loan exhibition *The Poetry of Drawing: Pre-Raphaelite Designs, Studies and Watercolours*, which this book accompanies. I am particularly grateful to Victoria Osborne, organizing curator for the exhibition, who contributed so much to the project throughout. My thanks are due, too, to Andy Horn, Varshali Patel, Hollie Smith-Charles, Toby Watley, Tessa Sidey, Jane Thompson-Webb and the collections care team, especially Gill Casson, Claire Daly, Haydn Roberts and Veronika Vlkova Antoniou; to Adrian Phillips, Colin Edmonds and the technical team; to David Rowan, Luke Unsworth and David Bailey, who photographed the majority of the works in this book; and to Tom Heaven, Carmel Girling, Jason Lewis, David Powell and Katherine Bradley who have supported the exhibition project in various ways. I also join Rita McLean in thanking the staff at the exhibition's partner venue, The Art Gallery of New South Wales, Sydney, and in acknowledging the work of our publisher, Thames & Hudson, in producing this handsome accompanying book. Particular thanks go to Julian Honer, Jacky Klein, Flora Spiegel, Susanna Friedman, Amy Visram, the book's copy-editor Monica Kendall, and its designer Thomas Gravemaker.

I am grateful for the assistance provided by Harriet Drummond and Rosie Henniker-Major at Christie's and by Simon Toll at Sotheby's. My colleagues at the University of Aberystwyth, Robert Meyrick and Neil Holland, have been generous in their support throughout the project, and I would like also to express my appreciation to Peter Francis and Patsy Williams of St Deiniol's Library, Hawarden, Flintshire, for their help in the course of my research. In addition, my thanks go to Chris Hay, Robert Ebbutt and the staff of Birmingham Libraries and Archives for allowing me access to material in their collections. Staff in the Print Rooms of the British Museum, Tate, and the Victoria and Albert Museum were patient in attending to my requests to view works, as were the staff at numerous museums and galleries in answering queries and facilitating loan requests.

The following people helped in a variety of ways and made my work much easier: Tim Barringer, Charles Brett, Scott Buckle, Nicholas Callow, David Elliott, Donato Esposito, Jane Fletcher, Alan Hackwood, Charlotte Gere, Laura MacCulloch, Catherine Maxwell, Christopher Newall, Christiana Payne, Elizabeth Prettejohn, Liz Pye, Simon Reynolds, Mary Rutterford, Alison Smith, Paul Spencer-Longhurst, Angela Thirlwell, Julian Treuherz, Annette Wickham, Simon Wilson and Amelia Yeates.

This research could not have been completed without the previous publication of substantial books in the field of Pre-Raphaelite studies such as the catalogues raisonnés of Rossetti's works by Virginia Surtees and of Holman Hunt's by Judith Bronkhurst, as well as essential exhibition catalogues devoted to Millais by both Mary Bennett and Malcolm Warner, and to Burne-Jones by Stephen Wildman.

Finally, I should like to add my thanks to those of Rita McLean in her Director's Foreword and acknowledge the debt of gratitude owed to the funders of this book and of the exhibition, The City of Birmingham Museums & Art Gallery Development Trust, The Limoges Trust, The Paul Mellon Centre for Studies in British Art and The William A. Cadbury Trust, and to the public and private lenders who have permitted access to their collections and have kindly lent works and allowed them to be reproduced in this book. This project would not have been possible without their generosity.

Colin Cruise

Index